lonely planet

PORTUGAL

Joana Taborda, Bruno Carvalho, Daniel James Clarke, Sandra Henriques, Marlene Marques, Maria Sena

CONTENTS

Plan Your Trip

The Guide

Elevador de Santa Justa (p66), Lisbon

Toolkit

Storybook

Quinta do Bomfim (p323), Douro Valley

PORTUGAL

THE JOURNEY BEGINS HERE

Portugal lives for the simple pleasures. It doesn't take much to find happiness here: a glass of wine at the end of a work day, a summer barbecue with friends or the eternal pursuit of sunset – the perks of living on the west coast.

When I'm away from home, it's the sea I yearn for. Sometimes I glimpse it from a distance. Other times I fully immerse myself into it, with a swim along the coast, a plate of fresh barnacles or a full-on seafood feast. I like walking across the dunes of Vila Nova de Milfontes when the houses fade away, and all you see is scrubland and the Atlantic. But Portugal isn't just about the beaches. There's a blossoming arts scene in its cities and villages, unforgettable trails through mountains and the coast and, above all, friendly folks who will gladly share a table with you.

My favourite experience is watching the night fall near the Alqueva lake. I take my tripod with me and wait patiently for a shot of the clear starry skies above me.

Joana Taborda

@cityodes

Born and raised in Lisbon, Joana enjoys hopping on a train to little-known towns and drinking the local craft beer wherever she gets off. To escape winter, she spends her time between the capital and the semitropical island of Madeira.

WHO GOES WHERE

Our writers and experts choose the places which, for them, define Portugal.

Nothing quite captures the essence of Porto like walking from Ribeira to Foz do Douro. When the morning fog lifts, Ribeira awakens, still misty, revealing its tall ochre buildings. From there, the city's architecture reveals itself in layers, from mysterious crumbling palaces to tiny fishers' neighbourhoods, ending in lavish historical mansions and gardens and the crashing waves of the Atlantic.

Bruno Carvalho & Maria Sena

@amasscook

Maria and Bruno live in Porto. They are writers, guides and authors of the food blog Amass. Cook.

From the magnificent panorama of Silves' Moorish castle surrounded by sweet-scented orange groves to the Beira's hilltop Monsanto, where myths and boulders define the slumbering streets, Portugal's hinterlands promise an intimate and enchanting way to meet the country. Whether you're being offered a glass of *vinho*, serenaded with a story, or invited to help yourself to the freshest of oranges, hospitality runs in the nation's blood, especially in these rural corners.

Daniel James Clarke

@danflyingsolo

Daniel is a British-born writer and photographer who made the Algarve, and later Lisbon, home.

I'm stumped for words whenever someone asks me what's my favourite part of Lisbon. In the 20-plus years I've lived here, I've seen the good, the bad, and the ugly. But, if pressed to choose, I have a soft spot for the neighbourhood of Madragoa because of the perfect blend of old and new, locals and tourists, Instagrammable cafes and traditional *tascas* (cheap, family-owned restaurants).

Sandra Henriques

@sandra.henrqes.writer

Published author, travel blogger at tripper.pt, and horror writer, Sandra grew up in the Azores Islands and has been based in Lisbon since 1997.

Every year I travel after the best waves around the planet, but I always come back thinking that Portugal offers some of the most incredible surf spots. Of all the lands by the sea, Nazaré is the one that attracts me the most. By far, I dare to surf 'the biggest waves in the world', but the connection to the sea and the fresh fish on the table are always good reasons to return to this lovely fishing village.

Marlene Marques

@marleneonthemove

Marlene is a surfer and journalist.

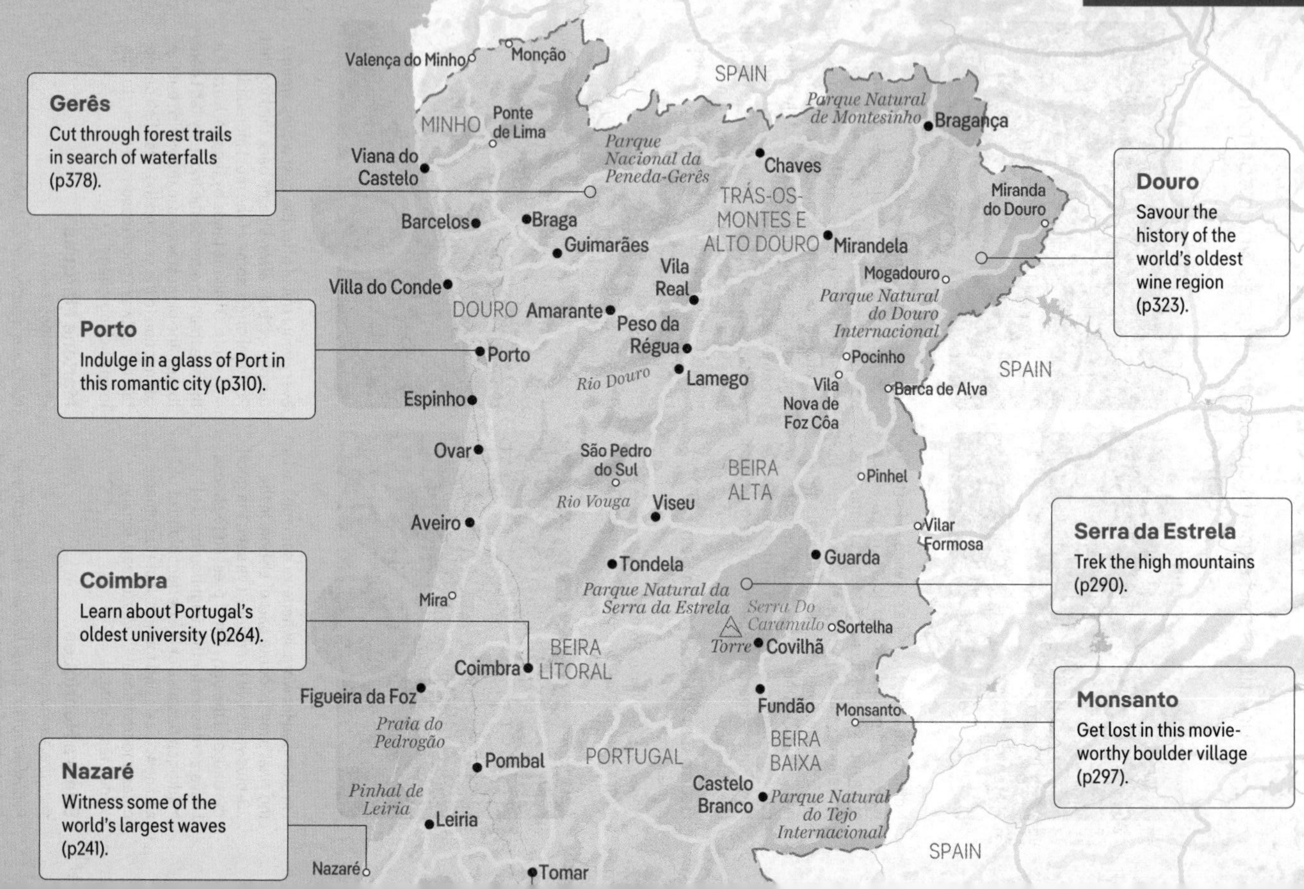

Gerês
Cut through forest trails in search of waterfalls (p378).

Porto
Indulge in a glass of Port in this romantic city (p310).

Coimbra
Learn about Portugal's oldest university (p264).

Nazaré
Witness some of the world's largest waves (p241).

Douro
Savour the history of the world's oldest wine region (p323).

Serra da Estrela
Trek the high mountains (p290).

Monsanto
Get lost in this movie-worthy boulder village (p297).

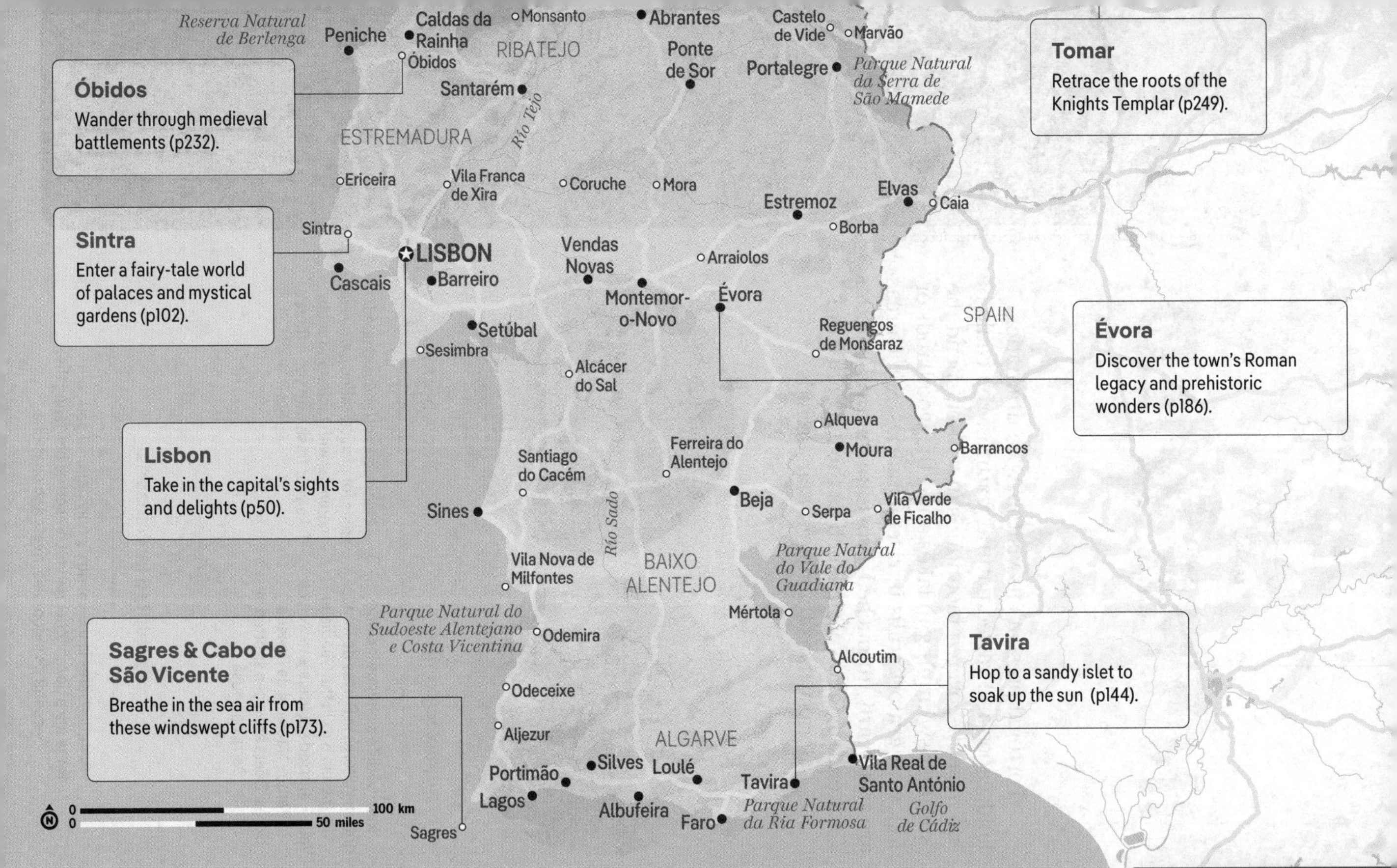

Óbidos
Wander through medieval battlements (p232).

Sintra
Enter a fairy-tale world of palaces and mystical gardens (p102).

Lisbon
Take in the capital's sights and delights (p50).

Sagres & Cabo de São Vicente
Breathe in the sea air from these windswept cliffs (p173).

Tomar
Retrace the roots of the Knights Templar (p249).

Évora
Discover the town's Roman legacy and prehistoric wonders (p186).

Tavira
Hop to a sandy islet to soak up the sun (p144).

Reserva Natural de Berlenga
Peniche
Caldas da Rainha
Óbidos
Monsanto
RIBATEJO
Santarém
Abrantes
Ponte de Sor
Castelo de Vide
Marvão
Portalegre
Parque Natural da Serra de São Mamede
ESTREMADURA
Rio Tejo
Ericeira
Vila Franca de Xira
Coruche
Mora
Estremoz
Elvas
Caia
Borba
Sintra
LISBON
Cascais
Barreiro
Vendas Novas
Arraiolos
Montemor-o-Novo
Évora
Setúbal
Sesimbra
Reguengos de Monsaraz
SPAIN
Alcácer do Sal
Alqueva
Moura
Barrancos
Ferreira do Alentejo
Santiago do Cacém
Beja
Serpa
Vila Verde de Ficalho
Sines
Rio Sado
Vila Nova de Milfontes
BAIXO ALENTEJO
Parque Natural do Vale do Guadiana
Parque Natural do Sudoeste Alentejano e Costa Vicentina
Odemira
Mértola
Alcoutim
Odeceixe
Aljezur
ALGARVE
Portimão
Silves
Loulé
Tavira
Vila Real de Santo António
Lagos
Albufeira
Faro
Parque Natural da Ria Formosa
Golfo de Cádiz
Sagres
0 100 km
0 50 miles

IN THE WILD

Portugal presents its visitors with dramatic landscapes and varied natural features. You could be up in snow-covered mountains in winter, spend the summer swimming in lakes amid the woodlands or follow migratory trails in river estuaries. Some areas are still nearly untouched, providing natural habitats for endangered species such as the lynx and rare flora such as the naked-man orchids.

Animal sightings

Rare wildlife sightings include griffon vultures in Portas de Rodão, the Iberian lynx in the Guadiana Valley, and red squirrels and wolves in Parque Nacional da Peneda-Gerês. Deers are often spotted in Serra da Lousã.

Picnic break

Many parks offer designated areas for picnics called *parque de merendas* with tables and seats. Take your trash with you if there's no bin.

Protected landscapes

Peneda-Gerês is the country's only national park, but there are a dozen other natural preserves bordering the country's mountains, rivers and coastline.

Cascata do Arado (p378), Parque Nacional da Peneda-Gerês

BEST WILDLIFE EXPERIENCES

Catch the flamingos' annual migration or spot dolphins throughout the year with a boat ride along the ❶ **Península de Tróia**. (p127)

Get your adrenaline fix at ❷ **Serra da Estrela**, a mountain with a diverse terrain fit for skiing, rock climbing and paragliding. (p290)

Venture beyond the ❸ **Parque Natural da Ria Formosa** in the Algarve to spot dolphins on a marine biologist-led boat tour. (p137)

Listen to cascading waterfalls and discover remote villages while looking out for the wild horses roaming through ❹ **Parque Nacional da Peneda-Gerês**. (p377)

Take in the constellations with a stargazing session in ❺**Alqueva**, Portugal's most recent starlight tourism destination. (p196)

Bacalhau do Porto

REEL CATCH

The Portuguese have always turned to the sea for a portion of its fare. The codfish that is ubiquitous hails from Norway, sure, but many other treats are caught right off the coast, from barnacles clinging to the rocky cliffs of Berlenga island to the shoals of golden bream on the Algarve coast. Freshly grilled or baked, there's no shortage of recipes here.

Codfish

There are 365 ways of cooking *bacalhau*. It's a process of patience that requires pre-soaking the salted cod for at least 24 hours and changing the waters regularly.

Cast a line

You can acquire a recreational fishing licence via the ICNF (icnf.pt). Children under 16 can fish without a permit, as long as they're with someone who holds one.

BEST SEAFOOD EXPERIENCES

Cast a line or join a fishing tour at ❶ **Barragem de Santa Clara**. (p219)

Visit a fish market and sample the traditional seafood stew in a copper pan known as a *cataplana* in the ❷ **Algarve**. (p129)

Taste the fish drying on the beaches of ❸ **Nazaré** and visit its museum to learn about this ancient tradition. (p241)

Watch sardines being tucked into tins by hand in a canning factory in ❹ **Matosinhos**. (p317)

Dig into a plate of *choco frito* (fried cuttlefish) at one of the restaurants in ❺ **Setúbal**. (p123)

SWEET BAKE-OFF

The *pastel de nata* may take the spotlight, but the Portuguese's sweet tooth goes way beyond this world-famous custard tart. Pretty much every town has perfected their own pastry, and in some places, that's reason enough to visit. At Christmas, it's a real feast with families filling the table with an array of regional desserts, from doughnut-like *filhoses* to a fruit-infused slice of *bolo rei*.

Spice it up

During the Age of Exploration, the Portuguese gained access to many spices like cinnamon, a sprinkle of which is still added to local desserts.

Pastelarias

Step inside these traditional pastry shops and you'll be spoilt for choice with sweets. Choose whatever takes your fancy or ask for the local speciality.

Resourceful nuns and monks

The scholastic life within the church gave birth to many heavenly sweet delights, often known as *doces conventuais* (traditional convent puddings). Egg whites were used to starch clothes, while the yolks ended up in a cake mix.

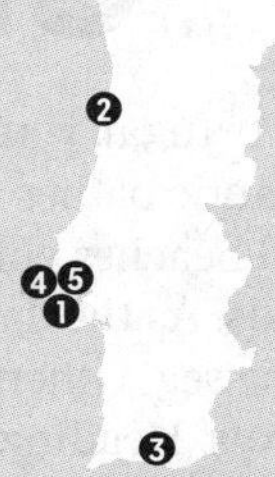

BEST PASTRY EXPERIENCES

Try the original recipe of the *pastel de nata* freshly baked at ❶ **Pastéis de Belém.** (p78)

Play chef at ❷ **Oficina do Doce** to make and learn more about the history of *ovos moles*, sweet egg yolk treats from the convents of Aveiro. (p278)

Enjoy *Doce Fino do Algarve,* colourful marzipan dough sweets crafted in various shapes (often fruits) that make the most of the ❸ **Algarve's** almond trees. (p147)

After a hike through Sintra stop at ❹ **Casa Piriquita** for a *travesseiro*, a pillow-shaped pastry. (p103)

Get into the Christmas spirit with the sweets from ❺ **Confeitaria Nacional** in Lisbon. (p66)

MAKE A SPLASH

In Portugal, you're never too far from the coast. The Atlantic bathes half of the country's borders, where wild beaches entwine with calm coves and secluded islands. As the days start heating up, locals crave a dip in the sea. Others hold on till winter to surf the giant waves. Heading inland, rivers and reservoirs invite you to swim or sail under the stars. Expect crowds and heavy traffic in August, especially down south.

Beach season

The season officially begins on the 15 June and ends 15 September. While the lifeguard might be on duty, that doesn't mean the sun is always out.

Sweet memories

In summer, you'll spot vendors carrying coolers filled with *bolas de Berlim*, a doughnut-like sweet stuffed with a delicious eggy custard.

Accessible beaches

Portugal has over 200 accessible bathing areas, featuring reserved parking, walkways and adapted toilets. Some spots may come with amphibious wheelchairs allowing easier water access.

Ribeira d'Ilhas (p120), Ericeira

BEST WATER EXPERIENCES

Paddle along the 1 **Alqueva lake** on an evening canoe tour while gazing at the stars, or relax in the warm waters of the surrounding river beaches. (p197)

Swim at serene barrier islands or paddle a kayak through the lagoons of the 2 **Parque Natural da Ria Formosa**, a stunning nature reserve along the southeast of the Algarve. (p137)

Put your surfing skills to the test with a class at one of the surfing schools in 3 **Peniche** on the west coast. (p239)

Experience canyoning amid the waterfalls of 4 **Serra da Estrela**, an adventure-filled ride combining hiking, swimming and abseiling. (p290)

Go windsurfing and embrace the strong Atlantic winds off the northern beaches of 5 **Costa Verde**. (p362)

MEMORABLE TRAILS

Whether you're yearning for a view of the mountains or can't get enough of that ocean breeze, there's a trail in Portugal for you. In a few hours, you could be walking or cycling along riverside paths overlooking historical landmarks. A few more days on the road and you may wind up in a quiet patch of sand along the coast, a remote medieval village or a well-known pilgrimage site.

Hunting season

The hunting season runs from mid-August to late February. When hiking, wear bright colours and veer off areas with red-and-white signs saying 'Zona de Caça'.

Responsible hiking

Always stick to the signposted trails, respect the wildlife and don't pick plants, especially if you're around protected reserves.

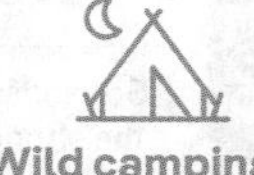

Wild camping

Wild camping is prohibited in protected areas. Look for official camping sites *(parques de campismo)*, many in coastal zones. Motorhome owners should find *áreas de serviço para autocaravanas* for overnight stays.

Passadiços do Paiva (p281)

BEST TRAIL EXPERIENCES

Take on the west coast for wild surfing spots and dune-backed beaches along the ❶ **Rota Vicentina**, a network of hiking and cycling trails stretching from the Alentejo to the Algarve. (p213)

Follow a craggy coastline trail with caves ripe for kayak adventures at the ❷ **Percurso dos Sete Vales Suspensos**. (p157)

Venture through the valleys of the ❸ **Arouca Geopark**, following the wooden walkways of Passadiços do Paiva or stepping out into one of the world's longest pedestrian suspension bridges. (p282)

Explore the remote villages on the country's northeastern borders by following the trails of the ❹ **Rota da Terra Fria**. (p339)

Cycle along the ❺ **Ecovia de Porto de Mós** and discover some of Portugal's largest caves. (p247)

Mural by Bordalo II, Lisbon

STREET ART

Portugal has a long history of decorating cities and streets with colourful tiles and creative cobblestone patterns. More recently, buildings, walls and other urban spaces have become canvases for national and international artists. Old neighbourhoods have transformed into open-air galleries, underground stations have been injected with colour, and even small villages have bold murals, thanks to emerging street art festivals in places like Covilhã.

Underground art

From the B&W caricatures at the airport to the stained-glass features of Olaias, Lisbon's underground stations are a work of art.

Hall of Fame

Portugal's most famous street artists include Vhils, renowned for carved mural portraits, and Bordalo II, who repurposes trash into giant animal sculptures.

BEST STREET ART EXPERIENCES

Visit ❶ **Covilhã** during the annual WOOL urban art festival to see freshly painted murals. (p295)

Check out the latest urban art talents at the ❷ **Underdogs Gallery** in Lisbon's Marvila neighbourhood. (p80)

See stunning tile-covered facades adorning churches and the train station in ❸ **Porto.** (p310)

Catch ❹ **Festival MURO** in July to see a Lisbon neighbourhood revamped with new murals. (p84)

Admire the sea creatures depicted in the cobblestones near ❺ **Parque das Nações** in Lisbon. (p80)

FABULOUS FESTIVITIES

No matter the month, the Portuguese always seem to find an excuse to party – whether it's throwing sardines on the grill in honour of a patron saint, a rowdy street parade to celebrate graduation or dressing up to recreate a medieval tale. Things kick off in the summer with music festivals inviting international acts and small towns hosting their own shindigs. Pick your season and join the action.

Música pimba

Pimba is the traditional soundtrack to festivities. It gets people of all ages dancing – the cheeky innuendo lost on the youngest of revellers.

Seasonal celebrations

The grape harvest is in full swing in autumn. Harvest programs *(vindimas)* are held across the country's wine regions, including the Douro, the Alentejo and Palmela.

Music festivals

Summer brings an array of music festivals, with NOS Alive and Super Bock Super Rock being the most anticipated. Check the calendar and you might just catch your favourite band on the road.

BEST FESTIVE EXPERIENCES

Step back to the Middle Ages at the ❶ **Feira Medieval de Silves**. (p151)

Celebrate at ❷ **Queima das Fitas**, when serenades and parades take over the streets of Coimbra in honour of graduation. (p264)

Look out for the *caretos* with their fringed suits and devilish-looking masks parading during the ❸ **Carnaval de Podence**. (p338)

Hit the streets of Porto during ❹ **Festas de São João** to witness the city's biggest party. (p310)

Sample delicious chocolate treats at the ❺ **Festival Internacional de Chocolate** in Óbidos. (p41)

THE WINELANDS

Wine has been a cherished drink around these parts ever since the Romans. Some of the world's oldest vineyards are here, growing anywhere from steep terraces to flatlands and sandy soils. The Douro Valley and the Alentejo may claim most of the shelves, but they're only one part of the 14 wine regions out there. Whether it's a sweet glass of Port, a crisp green wine or a bold red, you're bound to find something to suit your taste buds.

Wine stats

The Portuguese are among the biggest wine drinkers in Europe. In 2020 the country consumed 51.9L per capita, ranking above Italy and France.

Wine quality

Vinho de mesa (table wine) is often the cheapest option on the menu. Meanwhile, the *vinho regional* and the DOC are produced under stricter regulations.

Reasonable deals

While vintage ports can run for hundreds of euros, most Portuguese wine is pocket-friendly, with decent bottles costing less than a fiver at the supermarket.

Douro wine region (p323)

BEST WINE EXPERIENCES

Stop for a wine tasting amid the steep terraces of the ❶ **Douro Valley**, arriving through the winding roads or hopping on the historic MiraDouro train. (p323)

Head to the ❷ **Vinho Verde** region for a first-hand taste of *vinho verde* (green wine). (p366)

Tour the Port wine cellars scattered across ❸ **Vila Nova de Gaia** to find your favourite vintage. (p316)

Sip the Algarve's lesser-known regional wines under the shade of an ancient olive tree in ❹ **Morgado do Quintão**. (p153)

See the traditional Roman winemaking methods of *vinho de talha* around ❺ **Vidigueira**. Come in November to taste the season's new wine. (p201)

ARTISAN SOUL

Handmade crafts are an essential part of Portuguese culture. Here you can find artisans hand-weaving blankets on century-old looms, potters spinning ceramic vases on a wheel, and embroidery artists stitching patterns to traditional clothes. While interest in these skills had waned, lately, there's been a resurgence of it, with young creatives returning to their roots and bringing their own style to the craft.

Tiles

Azulejos (hand-painted tiles) arrived in Europe through the Moors. King Manuel I took a shine to them on a visit to Spain in 1498, spurring the Portuguese tradition, still prominent in cities like Lisbon and Porto.

Cork

Beyond bottle stoppers, cork has become a resourceful material for artists in the Alentejo who craft anything from wallets to bags, and even bikinis.

Craft fairs

You can meet local artisans at monthly craft fairs known as *feiras de artesanato*. Towns like Barcelos and Vila de Conde put on a good display, but you can also find handmade crafts in smaller urban flea markets.

Olaria Patalim (p202), São Pedro do Corval,

BEST CRAFT EXPERIENCES

Admire the intricate paintings turned tapestries at the ❶ **Museu das Tapeçarias de Portalegre**. (p208)

Watch potters in action or spin the wheel yourself at the workshops around ❷ **São Pedro do Corval**, Portugal's largest ceramic hub. (p201)

Surround yourself with forest silence while learning new crafts at ❸ **Cerdeira**, a recovered schist village now a creative retreat. (p272)

Discover the origins of the colourful ceramic cockerel that has become a symbol of Portugal in the northern town of ❹ **Barcelos** before packing it as a souvenir. (p358)

See the infamous fruit-shaped bowls of Bordalo Pinheiro, an iconic feature of Portuguese homes, at the local factory in ❺ **Caldas da Rainha**. (p239)

Azenhas do Mar (p107)

ICONIC VILLAGES

Sitting atop a cliff, hugging the coast or strategically positioned within medieval walls, Portugal's villages feel lost in time. Those looking for a quiet respite away from the big cities will find it here, in tiny cottages by the sea or in stone-built villages lost amid the mountains. Some places are so magical that they've become the background for fantasy sagas. Keep your camera handy and go stage your own adventure.

Village trails

If you're keen to hop between villages, check out routes like the Historical Villages (aldeiashistoricasdeportugal.com) or the Schist Villages (aldeiasdoxisto.pt).

Fantasy setting

Scenes from *House of the Dragon*, the *Game of Thrones* prequel, were shot in the screen-worthy villages of Penha Garcia and Monsanto.

BEST VILLAGE EXPERIENCES

Take in the dramatic cluster of whitewashed houses clinging to a cliff at coastal ❶ **Azenhas do Mar**. (p107)

Meander the medieval streets of ❷ **Monsaraz** and head to the nearby observatory for a stargazing session. (p200)

Venture to ❸ **Piódão** to see its enchanting rows of schist houses. (p296)

Marvel at ❹ **Monsanto**, where houses are wedged between and under mammoth boulders. (p297)

Explore the templar village of ❺ **Dornes** set along the margins of the Rio Zêzere. (p256)

TIME TRAVELLING

While Portugal as a nation was only founded in 1143, its cultural identity has been forged over thousands of years. Travelling through the country today, you'll encounter numerous traces of its past, from megalithic settlements to Roman villas and Renaissance palaces. Its colonial heritage and religious persecutions remain a touchy subject for some, but efforts have been made to tell this other side of the story.

Age of Exploration

The Age of Exploration is still a glorified topic, but locals are slowly turning a page to acknowledge the country's colonial role.

Great Earthquake

In 1755 Lisbon was struck by a massive earthquake that forever changed the city's foundations and shook the minds of thinkers during the Age of Enlightenment.

A peaceful revolution

The 25th of April marks the day of the Carnation Revolution, when, in 1974, Portugal cut ties with the Estado Novo dictatorship that haunted the country for nearly 50 years.

BEST HISTORY EXPERIENCES

Learn prehistoric crafts and discover the paths of Neolithic people with ❶ **Ebora Megalithica** at megalithic sites in the outskirts of Évora. (p190)

Admire well-preserved Roman mosaics, filled with mythological and geometric motifs, at the ❷ **Ruínas de Conímbriga**. (p270)

Uncover Portugal's Arabic roots in a former Islamic neighbourhood at the museum village of ❸ **Mértola**. (p220)

Pass through the lavish halls of Sintra's ❹ **Palácio da Pena**, with tiled facades, fresco ceilings and mountain views. (p104)

Visit the ❺ **Castelo de Tomar** to follow the Knights Templars' route through Portugal. (p249)

REGIONS & CITIES

Find the places that tick all your boxes.

The Minho

VERDANT LANDSCAPES AND DEEP TRADITIONS

Head to medieval Guimarães to discover Portugal's birthplace or step inside Braga's nearly 1000-year-old cathedral. In Citânia de Briteiros, you'll encounter a Celtic settlement, while Viana do Castelo marvels visitors with its hilltop sanctuary. The refreshing *vinho verde* hails from here, produced in vineyards scattered between mountains and river valleys.

p347

Porto, the Douro & Trás-os-Montes

HISTORY AND WINE CULTURE

Porto captivates with its artistic vibe and riverside setting. You can taste the world's best Ports just across its margins in Vila Nova de Gaia, and continue your tasting journey in the Douro wineries. Winding roads lead you to stone villages and the prehistoric rock art of Vila Nova de Foz Côa.

p305

The Beiras

COAST, COUNTRYSIDE, CITIES AND SUMMITS

Home to Portugal's oldest university, Coimbra is perhaps the most visited place in the Beiras. But there's much more to this region than its lively student city. From the lush highlands of the Serra da Estrela, to the sprawling beaches on the coast and the cinematic schist villages of Lousã, you'll enjoy every detour.

p259

Estremadura & Ribatejo

MEDIEVAL HISTORY, NATURE AND RELIGION

Templar towns and castles dot this region sandwiched between the Rio Tejo and the Atlantic with Tomar and Óbidos leading the way. The history of this region dates far longer, with dinosaur prints found amid its mountains. On the coast, giant waves attract surfers to Nazaré, while inland pilgrims trek to Fátima.

p227

Lisbon

CITY OF HILLS AND GOLDEN LIGHT

Portugal's capital is booming and it shows no signs of stopping. The warm climate, the welcoming people and the delicious food has made Lisbon a prime spot for nomads over the last decade. Long-time residents fight to keep it authentic, while embracing the city's modern side too.

p50

Lisbon Coast

OCEAN VIEWS AND HERITAGE SITES

Enchanting beaches and seaside villages lie north and south of the capital, with Guincho and Ericeira drawing surfers in particular. The area of wooded hills around Sintra offers some dreamy palaces, while fish-loving Setúbal is the gateway to the secluded coves of the Parque Natural da Arrábida and the offshore Península de Tróia.

p97

Estremadura & Ribatejo p227

Lisbon p50

Lisbon Coast p97

The Alentejo p181

The Algarve p129

The Alentejo

RURAL HEARTLAND AND ANCIENT CULTURE

It's all about slowing down in the Alentejo. You can spend days on end sampling the region's wineries, gazing at the stars or hiking the wild coastline. History unfolds in every corner, whether it's Unesco-listed Évora, the medieval castles in Monsaraz and Marvão, or the traditional workshops dedicated to handmade crafts.

p181

The Algarve

A SUN-KISSED COASTAL PLAYGROUIND

Every summer, locals and tourists flock to the Algarve for a much-awaited beach holiday. The choice is vast, with party towns like Portimão, surf-worthy waves in Sagres or quieter shores near Tavira. Award-winning golf courses, fresh seafood and historic inland villages also add to the appeal of this region.

p129

ITINERARIES

Portugal Highlights

Allow: 10 days **Distance:** 1000km

This grand journey takes you to the country's most iconic sites. From the capital, you'll depart towards the fairy-tale village of Sintra then venture south to explore the Algarve coast. You'll have time to visit Portugal's oldest university and sample a glass of Port straight from the cellars.

Palácio Nacional de Sintra (p102)

SERGII FIGURNYI/SHUTTERSTOCK ©

1 LISBON 1 DAY

Start in **Lisbon** (p50), spending a few days exploring the city's enchanting neighbourhoods. Choose between historic sites or modern art hubs, but don't miss a chance to sample a *pastel de nata* (custard tart). As the sun sets, head to the riverside or brave the hills to capture the pink-hue skies from one of the city's numerous viewpoints.

1-hour train from Rossio station

2 SINTRA 1 DAY

Get up early and catch the train from Rossio station to **Sintra** (p102), where royal palaces and mystical gardens await. You can reach some attractions on foot, but you'll need to catch a ride to reach the castle and **Palácio da Pena** perched on a hill.

3-hour drive

Detour: *A day here can feel rushed; stay a little longer and pair your visit with a wine tasting in Colares (p108) or a trip down the coast.*

3 LAGOS 2 DAYS

Return to Lisbon on the train and then drive off to **Lagos** (p167) in the Algarve. After visiting the historic centre, spend some time unwinding on the beach. The next day take a boat trip or rent a kayak to reach the rocky formations of **Ponta da Piedade**. Alternatively, head even further to reach the picturesque coves near **Algar de Benagil**.

2¾-hour drive

ANNA_PUSTYNNIKOVA/SHUTTERSTOCK ©

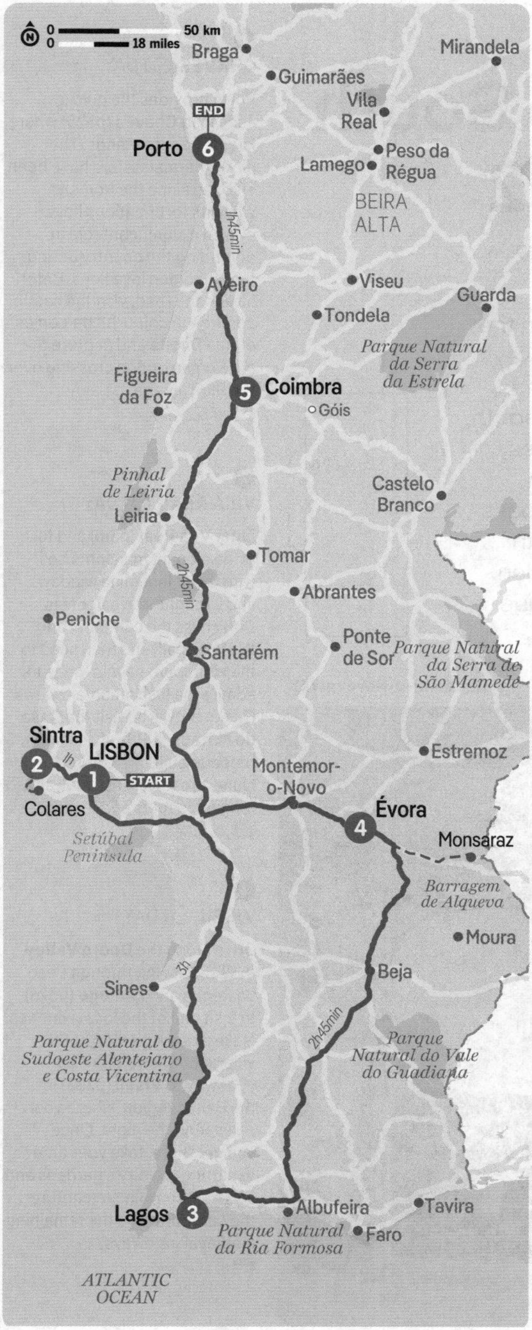

4

ÉVORA 1 DAY

Step back in time with a visit to **Évora** (p186). Within its medieval walls are striking architectural landmarks, from the cinematic columns of the Templo Romano to the pointy spires of the Gothic cathedral. The town square was once the site of some gruesome episodes courtesy of the Inquisition.

Detour: *Marvel at the views from the village of Monsaraz (p200), then take a dip in the nearby Alqueva lake.*

2¾-hour drive

5

COIMBRA 1 DAY

Students in black capes wander the streets of **Coimbra** (p264), home to the country's oldest university. Explore the grounds, visit the city's churches or get lost in the old cobbled town, listening to the sound of fado in the streets. An evening stroll along the river leads you to a footbridge named after one of Portugal's historic couples.

1¾-hour drive

1¾-hourtrain from Coimbra-B to Porto Campanhã

6

PORTO 2 DAYS

Colourful buildings line the riverside of **Porto** (p310). From here, the city rises on a hill, with historic sites dotted throughout. Step inside the local market and check out one of the world's prettiest bookshops, before climbing up **Torre dos Clérigos** for panoramic views. Cross the bridge towards **Vila Nova de Gaia** to tour the Port wine cellars.

GUBIN YURY/SHUTTERSTOCK ©

ITINERARIES

North to South on the N2

Allow: 8 days **Distance:** 739km

The N2 is Portugal's equivalent to Route 66 in the US. Away from the highways, you'll stick to the old roads travelling from north to south, starting in historic Chaves and ending by the sea in Faro. In between, you'll pass through valleys filled with vineyards, discover hidden schist villages and conquer numerous castles.

Montemor-o-Novo (p194)

LUISPINAPHOTOGRAPHY/SHUTTERSTOCK ©

1 CHAVES 1 DAY

Porto provides the quickest access to **Chaves** (p325) where kilometre zero stands. The city's thermal waters have been enjoyed since the Romans, while its fortifications have played a significant role in defending the country during the Napoleon invasions. Before hitting the road, visit the castle, admire the colourful balconies of Rua Direita and capture the old Roman bridge crossing over the Rio Tâmega.

1¼-hour drive

2 VILA REAL 1 DAY

Enter **Vila Real** (p318) and take in the elegant manor houses with their Manueline windows and wrought-iron balconies. Don't miss the cathedral and the town hall, and then head to the Miradouro da Vila Velha to admire the lush mountain views. On the outskirts, visit the **Casa de Mateus** (p318), an iconic baroque building featured on the Mateus rosé bottles; book ahead for guided tours and tastings.

2-hour drive

3 VISEU 1 DAY

Drive along the **Douro Valley** (p323), passing through Peso da Régua and **Lamego** (p326) to visit one of the local wineries. Make a quick pit stop at the village of Castro Daire on your way to **Viseu** (p283) in the Beiras region, where you can spend the night. Once you get there, take your time exploring the city's gardens and squares, stopping to capture the cathedral and the remaining medieval gateways.

1½-hour drive

4

SERRA DA LOUSÃ 2 DAYS

From Viseu, the road takes you through the **Serra da Lousã** (p271), where picturesque schist villages hide among the hills. But before you get there, you'll have to cross Santa Comba Dão, the birthplace of former dictator António de Oliveira Salazar. From here, drive a short section of the IP3 to continue towards Góis, where the stone cottages stand out alongside its river beach.

***Detour:** Go off track to visit the creative village of Cerdeira (p272), where artists share their crafts.*

3-hour drive

5

MONTEMOR-O-NOVO 1 DAY

Bid farewell to the hilltop villages and cross over to the Alentejo (p181). In between, stop at Abrantes to visit the town's castle overlooking the Rio Tejo. From here, the landscape changes dramatically, giving room to golden fields with their lonesome cork trees. When you reach **Montemor-o-Novo** (p194), you can visit ancient castle ruins and treat yourself to a traditional Alentejo meal.

***Detour:** If you fancy a swim, stop off at Parque Ecológico do Gameiro for a dip at a serene river beach.*

3¼-hour drive

6

FARO 2 DAYS

Continue into the countryside, passing through Viana do Alentejo and **Castro Verde** (p225) before entering the sinuous roads along Serra do Caldeirão, a sign that you've reached the Algarve. **São Brás de Alportel** (p143) is the first town, and then it's just a few kilometres down to **Faro** (p134). Walk in the historic centre then drive or ferry to the beach.

ITINERARIES

Coastal Wonders

Allow: 5 days **Distance:** 700km

If you're all about chasing the sea, this is the route for you. Whether you want to test your surf skills, kayak through caves or simply rest your feet in the sand, there's a spot for you on this trip covering Portugal's southwest coast.

Nazaré (p241)

ALEKSEY SNEZHINSKIJ/SHUTTERSTOCK ©

1

ERICEIRA 1 DAY

It's easy to reach **Ericeira** (p117) from Sintra or Lisbon. While many head here for the beach, the town itself is worth exploring with its whitewashed houses trimmed in blue and top-notch seafood restaurants. But this is surfers territory, too, with a well-preserved coastline and iconic breaks making it a World Surfing Reserve.

1¼-hour drive

2

NAZARÉ 1 DAY

The big wave action happens in **Nazaré** (p241) at Praia do Norte, where surfers have broken records riding waves up to 30m high. Safe to say that it's just for the experts, but you can watch it all standing at Sítio da Nazaré (reached via a funicular). Downtown is the Praia da Vila da Nazaré, where you can see fish hanging out to dry.

Detour: *Take a break in Peniche (p239), before setting off to the Berlengas archipelago (p239) on a ferry, a prime spot for snorkelling and diving.*

3-hour drive

WERA FEDO/SHUTTERSTOCK ©

0 50 km
0 19 miles
Parque Natural da Serra da Estrela
Coimbra
Figueira da Foz
Pinhal de Leiria
Leiria
Nazaré
2
Tomar
Berlengas Archipelago
Parque Natural das Serras de Aire e Candeeiros
Abrantes
Peniche
1h15min
Santarém
Ponte de Sor
Ericeira
1
START
Estremoz
3hr
LISBON
Montemor-o-Novo
Évora
Setúbal Peninsula
Parque Natural da Arrábida
Sesimbra
Reserva Natural das Lagoas de Santo André e da Sancha
Beja
Sines
Vila Nova de Milfontes
3
Parque Natural do Vale do Guadiana
Parque Natural do Sudoeste Alentejano e Costa Vicentina
1h45min
1h30min
Tavira
5
Lagos
Albufeira
Faro
END
Sagres
4
Parque Natural da Ria Formosa

3

VILA NOVA DE MILFONTES

1 DAY

Stop at the coastal town of **Vila Nova de Milfontes** (p211) in the middle of the beautiful Parque Natural do Sudoeste Alentejano e Costa Vicentina. Here you can tuck into some super-fresh seafood and enjoy a lazy day at one of the pristine beaches. There are surf schools and stand-up paddle rentals if you feel like getting active too.

Detour: *On your way down the coast, swing by Sesimbra for fun coasteering amid the Arrábida hills.*

1¾-hour drive

2-hour bus from the centre of Milfontes

4

SAGRES

1 DAY

Stick to the coast until you hit laid-back **Sagres** (p173), the most southwestern point in Portugal. Visit its dramatically situated fort, surf good waves and contemplate the endless clifftop views, catching the magical sunset from nearby Cabo de São Vicente.

1½-hour drive

5

TAVIRA

1 DAY

Spend your last day in peaceful **Tavira** (p144), one of the Algarve's prettiest towns. Discover the ruins of a hilltop castle, an old Roman bridge and a smattering of Gothic and Renaissance churches. Then take the ferry out to the car-free **Ilha de Tavira** (p146) to enjoy white-sand beaches. Faro is the closest airport to fly-out.

ITINERARIES

Porto & the North

Allow: 7 days **Distance:** 507km

Starting in Porto, you'll set off to explore the highlights of the North. From medieval cities that gave birth to the nation, to prehistoric archaeological sites and waterfalls surrounded by forest paths, there's a lot to take in.

1

PORTO 2 DAYS

Playing rival with the capital, **Porto** (p310) has a lot in its favour. Its creative vibe is contagious, with museums like Serralves showcasing regular contemporary art exhibitions and iconic buildings like the Leixões cruise terminal and Casa da Música attracting architecture fans. Combine that with Port wine tastings, riverside walks and a prestigious cuisine, and the competition is fierce.

1¼-hour drive

2

DOURO VALLEY 1 DAY

Zigzag your way through the **Douro Valley** (p323) following the N222. Stop in Peso da Régua and visit the Museu do Douro to learn more about this famous wine region. The road continues to **Pinhão** (p323), where you can catch a river cruise or unwind at one of the local estates. In **Vila Nova de Foz Côa** (p340), tap into your inner archaeologist as you discover prehistoric cave paintings.

1¼-hour drive

3

BRAGANÇA 1 DAY

Step into the heart of Trás-os-Montes with a visit to **Bragança** (p334). The castle, the medieval citadel and the Romanesque Domus Municipalis are among the city's most iconic buildings. There are also museums featuring regional artefacts like the Iberian masks worn during the colourful carnival festivities.

***Detour:** Iberian wolves and deer roam free in the nearby Parque Natural de Montesinho (p339).*

2-hour drive

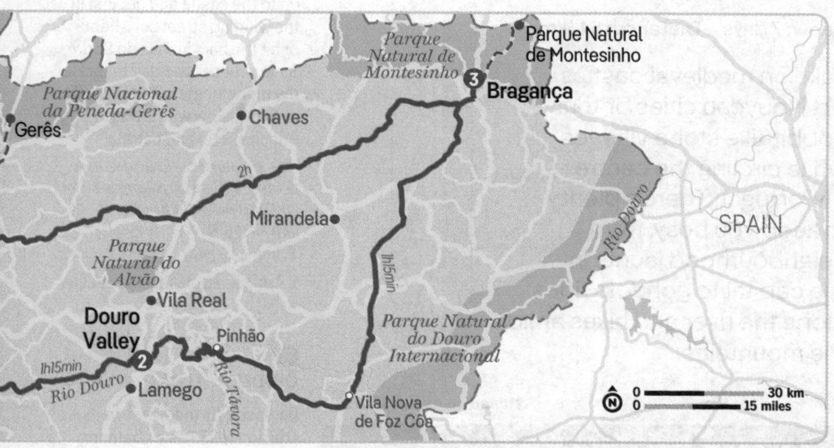

4

GUIMARÃES 1 DAY

Guimarães (p369) was the first capital of Portugal. The medieval lanes have been well preserved, as has the castle where Afonso Henriques, the nation's first king, is said to have been born. But beyond the monuments, there are also museums and lively squares lined with terrace cafes and colourful houses.

30-minute drive

5

BRAGA 1 DAY

In **Braga** (p352), you'll find a sea of churches. Portugal's oldest cathedral is here, along with the imposing baroque Santuário do Bom Jesus do Monte on the city's outskirts. Climb the 580 steps to the top, or take the water-run funicular.

***Detour:** Take a side-jaunt to Gerês (p377) for a hike in the wild and visit impressive shrines.*

45-minute drive

1-hour, 45-minute bus from Braga bus terminal

6

VIANA DO CASTELO 1 DAY

Head to the coast and settle in at **Viana do Castelo** (p360). Take in the spectacular view from the mountaintop site of Santuário do Monte de Santa Luzia and wander through the town's medieval square. With a little more time, you can also squeeze in a beach day along the **Costa Verde** (p362).

ITINERARIES

Lisbon & the Midlands

Allow: 7 days **Distance:** 546km

Take on medieval castles, Art Nouveau cities or tour hobbit-like stone villages while circling the centre of Portugal. There's plenty to keep you busy, from neighbourhood jaunts in the capital to gondola rides along the river and hikes amid the mountains.

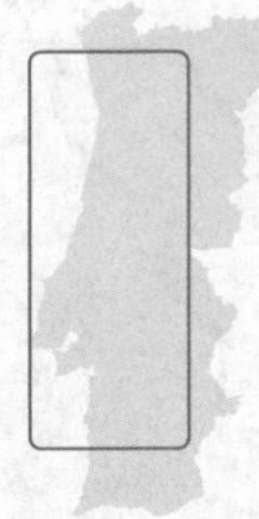

Museu de Aveiro (p275)

SAIKO3P/SHUTTERSTOCK ©

1

LISBON ⏱2 DAYS

Enjoy a brief stay in **Lisbon** (p50), touring the city's downtown and visiting the ruins of its earthquake-ravished convent. In the evening, head up to the castle and get lost in the winding streets of Alfama or hit the bars in Cais do Sodré. Save your second day to tackle the monuments in **Belém** (p75) or take it slow with a walk along Príncipe Real and Estrela.

Detour: *If you have a few days to spare, explore the palaces in Sintra (p102) or relax at the beaches of Cascais (p109).*

1¼-hour drive

1¾-hour bus from Campo Grande station

2

ÓBIDOS ⏱1 DAY

Enclosed by medieval walls, **Óbidos** (p232) is a charming town where bookshops take over every corner and sour cherry liqueur is poured in a chocolate cup. While Rua Direita gets all the traction, especially during festive seasons, it's worth venturing outside the main street and climbing up the battlements to fully experience the wonders of this Portuguese village.

1¼-hour drive

3

FIGUEIRA DA FOZ ⏱1 DAY

Continue driving north until you reach **Figueira da Foz** (p271). Take a walk along the seaside promenade and grab an ice cream, before dipping your toes in the water at Praia de Buarcos. From here to Aveiro, you'll pass along the Costa de Prata (Silver Coast) stacked with even more beaches.

50-minute drive

2-hour train

4

AVEIRO 1 DAY

Riverside **Aveiro** (p275) stands out with its streets lined with Art Nouveau buildings. Take a trip in a *moliceiro*, a gondola-style boat that was once used to collect algae, or head down the coast to admire the stripped-houses of Costa Nova. Back on dry land, taste the *ovos moles* from one of the city's *pastelarias* or try making it yourself at Oficina Doce.

Detour: *Take the opportunity to explore the scenic walkways of the Passadiços do Paiva, or follow the 516 Arouca, one of the world's longest suspension bridges.*

2-hour drive

5

PIÓDÃO 1 DAY

Like a miniature village, **Piódão** (p296) emerges around the curve with its schist houses cascading down the valley. Nearby, look out for the dramatic Fraga da Pena waterfall or dive into the river beach of Foz d'Égua.

Detour: *Squeeze in a trip to Serra da Estrela (p290) for a ski session in winter, or enjoy a hike amid the woodlands throughout the year.*

2-hour drive

6

TOMAR 1 DAY

Templar flags hang around the streets of **Tomar** (p249). Once the headquarters of the Knights Templar, the Convento de Cristo is the main attraction with its striking mix of Gothic and Renaissance elements. The town is also home to a medieval synagogue, forest trails and a quirky match museum.

Detour: *Continue your Templar route in Dornes (p256), where a defensive tower sits amid an enchanting peninsula facing the Rio Zêzere.*

WHEN TO GO

Whenever you're free. Portugal is more than those summer beach days – every season brings a unique experience.

The sun is quintessential to the Portuguese lifestyle. The second it warms up, locals are eager for a swim, hitting beaches up and down the coast. Summers are long and hot, with sunny days arriving as early as May and, if you're lucky, continuing all the way through November. Beach time aside, this is the season of street parties, with people dining on fresh fish and dancing until the wee hours.

Autumn brings the scent of roasted chestnuts while wineries in the Douro and Alentejo prepare for the grape harvest. Winter shows the first signs of snow in the Serra da Estrela. Spring is the time to sample cherries and enjoy the blossoming almond trees.

Want a Bargain?

If you're on a budget, consider travelling outside of summer. In Lisbon and the Algarve, you can expect to pay the highest premium for rooms from mid-July to the end of August, with slightly lower prices from June to mid-July and in September. Between November and April, prices are substantially less (as much as 50%).

I LIVE HERE

CITRUS COOL

Laima and Fábio, a couple based in Azeitão, share their gardening and motorhome travel journey at @uma_casa_verde

'The best time to visit Portugal is between September to May. It's an off-peak season for many campsites to stay with our motorhome. The air feels fresher and cooler, fields are green again, and nothing beats a warm, blue-sky day in December in Alentejo. Winter is also the season of some of our favourite fruits – oranges and tangerines. They are the most delicious between January and May.'

Marchas populares (p74), Lisbon

LEFT: DASYTNIK/SHUTTERSTOCK © RIGHT: HOMYDESIGN/SHUTTERSTOCK ©

NORTADA

During summer, the west coast is often hit by a flux of northerly winds, known as the Nortada. It blows stronger in places like Guincho and Sagres, making them prime spots for activities such as windsurfing.

Weather through the year

JANUARY	FEBRUARY	MARCH	APRIL	MAY	JUNE
Ave. daytime max: **15°C**	Ave. daytime max: **16°C**	Ave. daytime max: **18°C**	Ave. daytime max: **20°C**	Ave. daytime max: **22°C**	Ave. daytime max: **25°C**
Days of rainfall: 10	Days of rainfall: 8	Days of rainfall: 6	Days of rainfall: 7	Days of rainfall: 5	Days of rainfall: 2

DIP IN THE OCEAN

Near the capital, the seawater temperature is around 20°C in summer and 15°C in winter. Even on the hottest days, the water can be deceivingly brisk. Expect cooler temperatures in the north and slightly warmer in the south.

The Big Carnivals & Parades

Portugal's **Carnaval** features much merrymaking in the pre-Lenten celebrations. Loulé (p139) has the best parades, but Torres Vedras, Sesimbra and Ovar all throw a respectable bash. **February or March**

Braga (p352) honours its religious roots during **Semana Santa** (Holy Week), when thousands of visitors come to join the church processions.. **March–mid-April**

University students in Coimbra (p264) celebrate graduation with a bang by throwing an eight-day-long street party for **Queima das Fitas**. **May**

The Minho's most spectacular festival, **Romaria de Nossa Senhora d'Agoni**a, in Viana do Castelo (p360) includes fireworks and lively parades with people dressed in folk costumes, and others sporting giant-paper-mache heads. **August**

I LIVE HERE

WAVES

Portuguese Carolina and German-born Paul are avid surfers who run the surf hostel @surfeatsleeplisbon

'We see surfing as a form of therapy. Even if the time is short, we take every opportunity to get in the water. Autumn and spring are ideal for advanced surfers. The weather is warm, but the North Atlantic sends over bigger swells, giving excellent surfing conditions with light offshore winds. For beginners, the months between June and August are the best, as the waves tend to be smaller.'

Peniche (p239)

Local & Quirkier Festivals

For a few days only a floating bridge emerges between Alcoutim (p150) and the town of San Lucar in Spain to recreate an old smuggler's route for the **Festival do Contrabando**. **March**

The world-renowned two-week **Fantasporto** international festival in Porto (p310) celebrates fantasy, horror and just plain weird films. **April**

Festas de São João (p310) is a favourite up north, where Porto, Braga and Vila do Conde throw elaborate processions, music and feasting, while folks go around whacking each other with plastic hammers. **June**

Santa Casa Alfama (p74) celebrates Lisbon's fado roots with live concerts across its historic neighbourhood, be it the Fado museum or the rooftop of the cruise terminal. **September**

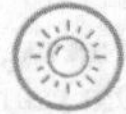

BLISTERING SUN

The Algarve may be considered one of the sunniest spots in Portugal, but the highest record temperatures have been registered in the Alentejo, where it can hit up to 40°C in some places.

JULY
Ave. daytime max: **28°C**
Days of rainfall: 0

AUGUST
Ave. daytime max: **28°C**
Days of rainfall: 1

SEPTEMBER
Ave. daytime max: **26°C**
Days of rainfall: 3

OCTOBER
Ave. daytime max: **23°C**
Days of rainfall: 8

NOVEMBER
Ave. daytime max: **18°C**
Days of rainfall: 9

DECEMBER
Ave. daytime max: **15°C**
Days of rainfall: 10

Arco da Rua Augusta (p62), Lisbon

GET PREPARED FOR PORTUGAL

Useful things to load in your bag, your ears and your brain.

Clothes

Layers With an average of 300 days of sunshine each year, Portugal is renowned for its warm climate. However, it does rain and even snows up in the mountains. Many houses are poorly insulated, so it gets quite cold inside. Really, you need to experience winter here to really understand it. In the evenings, it can get windy, so always carry an extra layer just in case.

Comfy shoes Unless you're going to a special ceremony, leave your fancy heels or shiny Oxfords at home. Instead, bring some flat shoes that you feel comfortable exploring in or even hiking boots if you plan on hitting the trails.

Hat Even in winter, that sun is intense – and, on a fresh, windy day, deceptive.

Manners

Portuguese is not the same as Spanish. Even if they don't call you out, some people may get offended if you confuse the two.

There is no need to rush here. Go with the flow, enjoying a sit-down meal at a restaurant or lingering at a kiosk with a coffee.

More than the weather, small talk here often goes **straight to football**.

READ

The Book of Disquiet (Fernando Pessoa; 1982) Unedited fragments of text published posthumously.

A Short Book on the Great Earthquake (Rui Tavares; 2020) A journey through the events that shook Lisbon on 1 November 1755.

Journey to Portugal (José Saramago; 1990) Tales of cultural discovery while travelling across Portugal.

Bode Inspiratório (Escape Goat; 2020) Serial novel written by 46 Portuguese authors during the Covid-19 pandemic.

Words

Olá (oh-lah) is how you say 'hello' in Portugal.

Bom dia (boñ dee-uh) literally translates as 'good day', but can also be used to say 'good morning'. If it's later in the day, you can use *boa tarde* (boh-uh taar-de) for 'good afternoon', and *boa noite* (boh-uh noy-te) for 'good evening'.

Tudo bem (too-doo bayñ) is a short way of saying 'how are you?' and can also act as a reply if you want to say 'everything is good'.

Se faz favor (suh fash fuh-vor) is the most common way to say 'please'; you can also use it to call the waiter's attention at a restaurant.

De nada (deh nah-dah) is the equivalent of 'you're welcome'.

Cafézinho is a cute term for 'coffee'. The Portuguese like to add the suffix 'inho' to many words to express affection or sometimes even sarcasm.

Desculpe (desh-kool-pe) is mostly used to apologise, as in 'sorry', but it can also stand for 'excuse me' when you want to approach someone for directions.

Socorro (soo-koh-roo) is what you should shout if you need to cry for help.

Saying thank you. If you identify as a man, you should say *obrigado* (oo-bree-gah doo), while if you identify as a woman you should say *obrigada* (oo-bree-gah dah). Many words have female and male versions in Portuguese, but this one is probably the first one you'll use. Gender-neutral versions are slowly being introduced by adding an 'e' at the end like so: *obrigade*.

WATCH

Os Verdes Anos (Paulo Rocha; 1963) A picture of the capital in the 1960s; part of the Cinema Novo movement.

Lisbon Story (Wim Wenders; 1994) Drama-musical shot in Lisbon, featuring former Madredeus' lead singer Teresa Salgueiro.

Vitalina Varela (Pedro Costa; 2019) Drama feature following a Cape Verdean immigrant on her arrival to Portugal.

Variações (João Maia; 2019) Biographical film about Portuguese singer and gay icon António Variações.

LISTEN

O Monstro Precisa de Amigos (Ornatos Violeta; 1999) Final release of the alt rock band led by Manel Cruz, which occasionally makes a comeback.

Excuse Me (Salvador Sobral; 2016) Debut album of the jazz and soul singer who won the Eurovision Song Contest in 2017.

Mariza Canta Amália (Mariza; 2020) Fado singer Mariza pays tribute to the genre's diva with an album featuring her best songs.

Encore (Capicua; 2021) Porto-based rapper celebrates the stage with this EP compiling her live acts before the Covid-19 lockdown hit.

MARCELO TRAD/SHUTTERSTOCK ©

Arroz de pato **(rice with duck and chorizo)**

THE FOOD SCENE

Freshly baked sweets, a coast full of seafood delicacies and lively wine festivals will fill your culinary tour of Portugal.

The best way to break the ice with a Portuguese is to talk about food. Folks are proud of their cuisine, and they'll happily guide you to their favourite *tasca* (tavern) or *pastelaria* (pastry and cake shop). Between themselves, they discuss their best codfish recipes (there are more than 300) and where to get the best pastry in town.

Whether you're ordering seafood or meat, it's all about simple flavours here, letting the main ingredient shine through. Sometimes that means sliding a piece of pork into a bun. Other times it's getting the freshest fish and slapping it onto the grill. Add a glass of local wine and you have the foundation of Portuguese cuisine. But there's also room for innovation here, with the country upgrading its traditional markets with gourmet food stalls and local chefs leading its rising Michelin-star restaurants.

A meal is always best enjoyed with family or friends, and ordering a round of *petiscos* – think tapas, only slightly bigger – to pick at and share is the ideal way to experience the diversity of Portuguese cuisine.

Portuguese Home Staples

If you're lucky enough to be invited to somebody's home for a traditional meal, you can expect the staple basket of bread and a bottle of wine laid out on the table. Before the main meal, your hosts will likely offer you a selection of Portuguese cheeses and sausages to nibble on.

A look inside the pantry and you'll find various cooking essentials: olive oil, used

Best Portuguese Dishes

AÇORDA
Bread soup typical from the Alentejo.

ARROZ DE PATO
Oven-baked rice dish with duck and chunks of chorizo.

FRANCESINHA
Multi-layered meat sandwich covered in melted cheese and a rich sauce.

BACALHAU À BRÁS
Codfish with potato sticks, scrambled eggs, olives and parsley.

to sautée garlic and onion at the start of most recipes and soak seafood dishes like *bacalhau* (codfish) and *polvo* (octopus); parsley and coriander, used interchangeably for fish and meat recipes; bay leaf, reserved for garnishing meat dishes; eggs and spices like cinnamon, which are integral for regional desserts such as *farófias* (poached meringues) or *arroz doce* (rice pudding).

Of course, you can't forget the canned fish. Beyond tuna, the Portuguese have mastered other tinned fish combos like spicy sardines or squid in tomato sauce. If you have all these ingredients, you're halfway there to prepare a Portuguese meal yourself.

Vegetarians & Vegans

Portugal isn't the easiest country to be a vegetarian. Even the cheese isn't always meat-free. Until a few years ago, you were stuck with soup, salad or omelette. Luckily, things are beginning to change. While you'll still struggle to order veggie-friendly dishes in the traditional *tascas*, other restaurants are adapting their menus and adding at least one vegetarian option. Some might even go out of their way to cook you something on the spot like vegetable rice or pasta. Vegans have it harder, as many pastries are egg-based. Choices significantly increase in the big cities where chefs are taking traditional recipes and reinventing them as greener alternatives, replacing clams with mushrooms to make *cogumelos à bulhão pato* or ditching codfish for leek in the *alho à francês*. Burger houses and Indian restaurants easily cater for vegetarians and vegans too.

Though only 10% of Portuguese are vegetarians, there's a growing movement to reduce meat consumption, especially among young people. Odds are the number will keep increasing, and so will the menu options.

MAURO RODRIGUES/SHUTTERSTOCK ©

Grilled *polvo* (octopus)

MAGDALENA PALUCHOWSKA/SHUTTERSTOCK ©

FOOD & WINE FESTIVALS

Essência do Vinho *(essenciadovinhoporto.com; dates vary)* A wine festival in Porto.

Festival Internacional de Chocolate *(festivalchocolate.cm-obidos.pt; Apr)* Chocolate lovers descend on the pretty medieval town of Óbidos.

Santos Populares *(culturanarua.pt/programacao/festas-de-lisboa; Jun)* Lisbon's lively street party is your chance to feast on chargrilled sardines and mackerel.

Feira do Alvarinho *(feiradoalvarinho.cm-moncao.pt; Jul)* Monção in the Minho pays tribute to Alvarinho white wine.

Festival do Marisco *(festivaldomarisco.com; Aug)* Seafood festival paired with live music acts hosted in Olhão.

Feira da Castanha *(facebook.com/feira.castanha.marvao; 2nd weekend of Nov)* Taste roasted chestnuts and sample wine at this festival held inside Marvão's medieval walls.

Festival Internacional de Chocolate

POLVO À LAGAREIRO
Octopus soaked in olive oil.

LEITÃO DÀ BAIRRADA
Suckling pig dish typical in central Portugal.

CATAPLANA
Seafood stew cooked in a special pan, famous in the Algarve.

CARNE DE PORCO À ALENTEJANA
Surf and turf dish, with pork and clams.

Local Specialities

Favourite Petiscos

Salada de polvo – octopus salad
Chouriço assado – flamed-grilled chorizo
Tábua de queijos e enchidos – sausage and cheese board
Amêijoas à bulhão pato – clams with garlic sauce
Peixinhos da horta – fried green beans
Pica-pau – beef loin strips

Snacks & Street Food

Tremoços – lupin beans
Bifana – pork sandwich
Prego – beef sandwich
Pão com chouriço – chorizo bread
Salgados – savoury treats

Sweet Treats

Pastel de nata – custard tart, ideally served warm and dusted with cinnamon
Travesseiro – flaky pillow-shaped pastry filled with almond-and-egg-yolk custard; find them in Sintra
Ovos moles – Aveiro is famous for its eggy, sugary pastries

Portuguese sweets

Bola de Berlim – sweet doughnut filled with eggy custard usually eaten on the beach
Torta de Azeitão – sponge-cake roll stuffed with a sweet-egg yolk paste
Pão de Ló – fluffy cake that is often gooey in the centre

Dare to Try

Tripe –people from Porto aren't called *tripeiros* (tripe-eaters) for nothing; try the tasty *tripas à moda do Porto,* made of tripe, beans and sausage
Arroz de cabidela – rice soaked in chicken's blood may sound foul, but it's a bloody good delicacy; the pork variant is called *arroz de sarrabulho*
Morcela – sausage made with pig's blood and perhaps rice and pork
Caracóis – these are smaller and less fancy than *escargot* (snails)

MEALS OF A LIFETIME

Euskalduna Studio (p313) Ring the bell to access this intimate Michelin-star restaurant located in Porto.

Tasca do Celso (p213) Enjoy a delicious seafood feast at this rustic-chic spot on the Alentejo coast in Vila Nova de Milfontes.

Vila Joya (p142) Treat yourself at this two-Michelin-star restaurant 9km west of Albufeira overlooking the sea or sample more affordable treats in the beach bar.

THE YEAR IN FOOD

SPRING

In late spring and early summer, you'll see signs advertising *caracóis* (snails). These little delicacies are cooked in olive oil, garlic and herbs and are quite tasty. They go nicely with a cold beer.

SUMMER

Head to the market for bountiful fruits and vegetables: plump tomatoes, figs, *nésperas* (loquats) and other delights. Sardines, much loved along the coast, are available from May through October.

AUTUMN

In September the Alentejo and the Douro Valley begin their grape harvest; it's a festive time to visit, and some wineries allow visitors to take part. It's also the season of pomegranates and chestnuts.

WINTER

Portuguese enjoy hearty meals such as *cozido à portuguesa*, a dish of mixed roast meats, potatoes, cabbage and carrots, alongside rich soups like *canja* (chicken soup) or *caldo verde* (potato kale soup).

PORTUMEN/SHUTTERSTOCK ©

Vines in the Douro (p323)

HOW TO... Visit the Wine Regions

Portugal's vineyards are scattered across the country, planted in sandy soils by the coast, in sprawling plains amid the countryside or on steep terraces overlooking a river. It's this last scene that comes to mind when you mention places like the Douro Valley, one of the oldest demarcated wine regions in the world and the birthplace of the beloved Port wine. But that is just one of the dozen regions occupying this fruitful land. You could travel the whole country searching for the best vintage or stick to one area, touring the grounds to find your favourite cellar or winery. Many of these estates offer tastings and guided visits, and some even host Michelin-star restaurants with carefully curated food-and-wine pairings. Below is a step-by-step list of how to plan your trip to the Portuguese winelands.

Pick a Season

While you can visit the vineyards pretty much year-round, some experiences are only available at certain times of the year. Plan to arrive in late August or September to harvest the grapes and participate in the traditional barefoot stomping that still takes place at some wineries.

Choose Your Region

Some of the most popular regions include the Douro and the Alentejo, but there is much more to discover – from the refreshing *vinho verde* (young wine) hailing from the Minho to the sweet Moscatel produced in Setúbal, on the outskirts of Lisbon. For a complete overview of the Portuguese wine regions, check out Wines of Portugal (winesofportugal.com).

Select a Winery

Once you decide on a region, you can start searching for wineries. Wine Tourism Portugal (winetourismportugal.com) provides a list of these and information about wine experiences across Portugal. Bookings are highly recommended, especially to visit Port wine cellars and famous estates. Note: if you're considering participating in the harvest, you should start contacting wineries at least a month in advance.

Sample the Wine

It's finally time to sit back and drink that glass of Portuguese wine. Take small sips, and if you really enjoy it, you can always take a bottle or five home.

CRUSHING IT

Bring a pair of old clothes, and wash your feet and legs before hopping in the tank (some wineries may provide boots). Once inside, raise your knees as high as you can and gently press the grapes with your feet. This is a slow process and requires patience, so take your time. There's usually some music in the background to get you in the stomping mood. Your experience should last about 30 minutes, but the grapes will remain there for a couple more days to be trodden by the workers and the following guests.

Rota Vicentina

THE OUTDOORS

Grab a board and ride the waves or stick to dry land to follow the numerous trails crossing Portugal's coastline and valleys.

Portugal has a coastline of nearly 1000km. Surfers make the most of it, hitting the beaches off season to catch the biggest swells. The oceanfront cliffs have also become a magnet for hikers and cyclists eager to explore routes such as the Rota Vicentina with its endless stretch of wild beaches. Beyond the shores, Portugal's trails take you through vineyards, across rocky mountains and along riverbanks. The country's rivers offer water sports, including diving, canyoning and kayaking.

Surfing

People have been riding waves in Portugal since 1926, making it one of Europe's first surfing spots. Big waves are common here, especially around Nazaré, where world records have been broken, but there are swells of all sizes, suitable for surfers of any level. Across the coast, you'll find 30 to 40 major reefs with remarkable consistency. Numerous surf schools in the Algarve and along the west coast offer classes and all-inclusive packages, often featuring accommodation.

The best waves in the south generally occur in winter. Further north, spring and autumn tend to be the best seasons. Waves at these times range from 2m to 4.5m high. Summer is ideal for beginners, with waves ranging from 1m to 1.5m. Despite the crowds, it's fairly easy to head off and find your own stretch.

Outdoor Sports

HORSE RIDING
Ride along old smuggler routes past vulture colonies near the Spanish border in Marvão. (p203)

ROCK CLIMBING
Explore the granite peaks of Parque Nacional da Peneda-Gerês. (p377)

COASTEERING
Progress between the tides of a rocky shore by swimming, climbing and jumping into the water from the Algarve cliffs. (p172)

FAMILY ADVENTURES

Look for dolphins (p137) – and learn about them from an onboard marine biologist – as you ply the waters off Ria Formosa on a boat trip departing from Faro.

Kayak with your kids (p272) down the idyllic Rio Mondego from Penacova to Coimbra.

Catch the narrow-gauge train (p146) to the lovely beach of Praia do Barril in Tavira.

Cycle or stroll along the coastal route (pp115) from the charming town of Cascais to the untouched sands at Guincho.

Ride the chop (p239) on board the speedy Viamar boat crossing from Peniche to the Berlengas archipelago.

Pedal a rail bike (p204) down abandoned train tracks with Rail Bike Marvão, taking in the serenity of nature and the breathtaking views.

Cycling

Whether it's a leisurely cycle along the beach or an intense workout in the forest, there is a trail for you. In the north, Rio Lima features a handful of short greenways (ranging from 5km to 16km), while the 49km Ecopista do Dão follows a repurposed train track from Viseu through villages and vineyards. Down south, the ambitious Ecovia do Litoral is a long-distance route across the Algarve that connects Cabo de São Vicente at Portugal's southwestern tip to Vila Real de Santo António near the Spanish border.

BEST SPOTS

For the best outdoor spots and routes, see map on p46.

Cyclists in Vila Real de Santo Antonia (p149)

Bike paths are also becoming common in cities, along with bike- and scooter-sharing schemes. Along the coast, trails have popped up in venues such as the Estremadura's Pinhal de Leiria and the Lisbon coast between Cascais and Praia do Guincho. You can ride on your own or have expert cyclists lead on a guided tour.

Walking & Hiking

Celebrating 10 years in 2022, the Rota Vicentina has become a big draws for hikers. The route connecting the Alentejo and the Algarve features two long-distance trails: one along the west coast (226km) and the other inland (263km). The Via Algarviana takes you through the southern coast, starting in Alcoutim and ending in Cabo de São Vicente. Those looking to explore historical villages can follow the GR22, a walking tour of about 600km. Shorter trails are on the outskirts of Lisbon around Sintra or Arrábida.

A system of coloured blazes marks trails. White and red are used for long routes (GR, *grandes rotas*), while yellow and red represent smaller trails (PR, *pequenas rotas*). Beat the heat by visiting in spring or autumn. Tourist offices can provide maps, but mobile apps like Walkbox and AllTrails may offer additional guidance.

DIVING
Go diving in the Berlengas archipelago off the coast of Peniche. (p239)

PARAGLIDING
Head inland to the prime launch site in Linhares in the Serra da Estrela. (p293)

CAVING
Explore a cave or two in the Parque Natural das Serras de Aire e Candeeiros. (p247)

WINDSURFING
Praia do Cabedelo near Viana do Castelo is a world-championship windsurfing site. (p363)

ACTION AREAS

Where to find Portugal's best outdoor activities.

Surfing

1. Matosinhos (p317)
2. Figueira da Foz (p271)
3. Nazaré (p243)
4. Peniche (p239)
5. Ericeira (p120)
6. Praia do Guincho (p115)
7. Carcavelos (p116)
8. Sagres (p175)

Cycling

1. Ecovia do Rio Lima (p365)
2. Ecopista do Dão (p287)
3. Ciclovia do Guincho (p115)
4. Ecopista de Évora (p189)
5. Ecovia do Litoral (p179)

Hiking
1 Passadiços do Paiva (p281)
2 GR22 (p297)
3 Rota Vicentina (p45)
4 Rota da Terra Fria (p339)
5 Percurso dos Sete Vales Suspensos (p164)
Natural Parks
1 PN de Montesinho (p339)
2 PN da Peneda-Gerês (p377)
3 PN do Alvão (p323)
4 PN do Douro Internacional (p344)
5 PN da Serra da Estrela (p290)
6 PN da Arrábida (p125)
7 PN do Vale do Guadiana (p222)
8 PN do Sudoeste Alentejano e Costa Vicentina (p177)
9 PN da Ria Formosa (p140)
Diving
1 Berlengas Archipelago (p239)
2 Sagres (p175)
3 Portimão (p162)
4 Lagos (p169)
Atlantic Ocean
Peniche
Óbidos
das Serras de Aire e Candeeiros
Santarém
Rio Tejo
Ponte de Sor
de Vide
Marvão
Portalegre
Parque Natural da Serra de São Mamede
Ericeira
Vila Franca de Xira
Coruche
Mora
Estremoz
Elvas
Caia
Borba
Sintra
LISBON
Barreiro
Cascais
Montemor-o-Novo
Arraiolos
Vendas Novas
Évora
Setúbal
Sesimbra
Reguengos de Monsaraz
Alcácer do Sal
Alqueva
Moura
Barrancos
Ferreira do Alentejo
Santiago do Cacém
Beja
Vila Verde de Ficalho
Sines
Rio Sado
Rio Guadiana
Serpa
Vila Nova de Milfontes
Parque Natural do Vale do Guadiana
Mértola
Odemira
Parque Natural do Sudoeste Alentejano e Costa Vicentina
Odeceixe
Alcoutim
Aljezur
Silves
Vila Real de Santo António
Portimão
Albufeira
Loulé
Tavira
Lagos
Sagres
Faro
Parque Natural da Ria Formosa
Golfo de Cádiz
0 100 km
0 50 miles

PORTUGAL

THE GUIDE

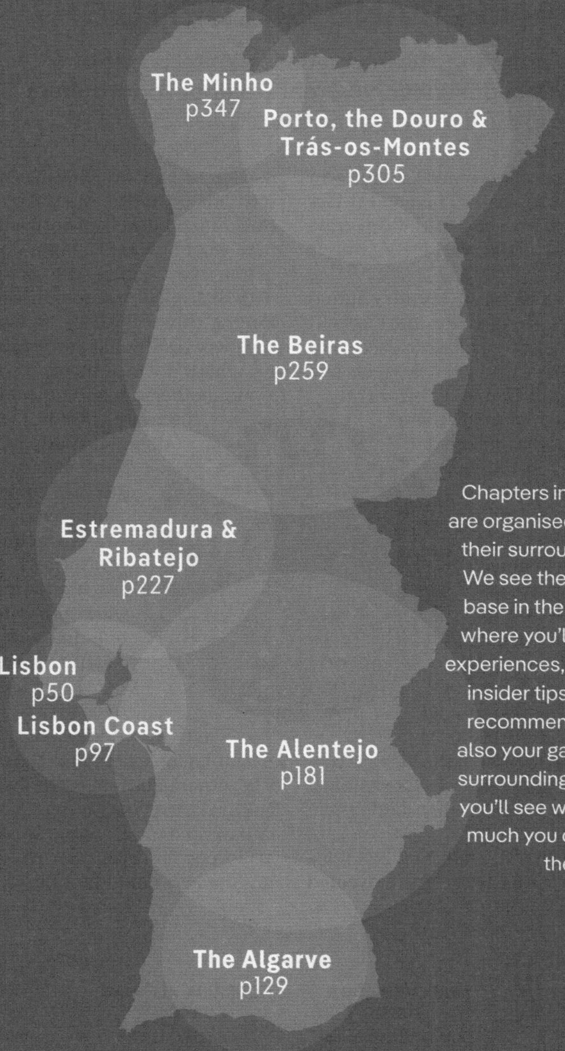

Chapters in this section are organised by hubs and their surrounding areas. We see the hub as your base in the destination, where you'll find unique experiences, local insights, insider tips and expert recommendations. It's also your gateway to the surrounding area, where you'll see what and how much you can do from there.

Ponta da Piedade (p167), Lagos

MBVI/SHUTTERSTOCK ©

LISBON

CITY OF HILLS AND GOLDEN LIGHT

Effortlessly charming, the Portuguese capital is one of Europe's hottest destinations. Great weather, food, culture and safety top the list of reasons to visit.

In 2016, Lisbon experienced a surge in the number of tourists. The capital city of Portugal became one of the top travel destinations in the world. Its fame is still on the rise.

The old city charm of laundry hanging to dry on balconies, the effortless but worldly cuisine, the unique glazed tiles covering buildings in clustered streets and that unique light bouncing off terracotta rooftops had been there for decades, so what changed then? More low-cost flights to Lisbon and several awards and inclusion in 'best of' lists explain part of what seemed like an overnight success. It felt too fast for many *lisboetas* (people who live in Lisbon), who fear unsustainable mass tourism. The higher demand for picturesque, refurbished houses for short-term rental in the historic centre stripped neighbourhoods like Alfama, Mouraria and Graça of what made them unique: the locals.

On the other hand, as Lisbon has done many times in the past, the city reinvented itself in neighbourhoods like Marvila, Santos, Cais do Sodré, Madragoa and Alcântara. Small pockets of authenticity subsist here where there is a lower concentration of tourist attractions, and newer businesses (which openly cater to the well-travelled foreign clientele) thrive in harmony with the more traditional and established ones. As a matter of fact, they often recommend one another. And after the tourist crowds discovered Lisbon, along came the digital nomads and the expats.

Tourism is seen as a threat and an opportunity, a short-lived workaround for an economic crisis and the best product such a historical city as Lisbon has to offer (and one that will never cease to attract more visitors).

Warm and welcoming, diverse and artistic, Lisbon is a city for all kinds of travellers: the frugal backpackers and the luxury tourists with unique tastes, the foodies and the cultural travellers, the past-seeking history buffs and the avant-garde contemporary art lovers, the solo urban explorers and the multigenerational families.

THE MAIN AREAS

BAIRRO ALTO & CAIS DO SODRÉ
Nightlife and live music. p56

BAIXA-CHIADO & ROSSIO
Downtown: sprawling squares and historic shops. p62

MOURARIA, ALFAMA & GRAÇA
The historic centre. p68

BELÉM
Grand palaces and Manueline architecture. p75

THE DAILY PHOTOO/SHUTTERSTOCK ©

Pink Street (p58)

PARQUE DAS NAÇÕES & MARVILA
Contemporary architecture and street art. **p80**

MARQUÊS DE POMBAL & AVENIDAS NOVAS
Urban parks and art museums. **p85**

SANTOS, MADRAGOA & ALCÂNTARA
Industrial vibes and local life. **p90**

Find Your Way

The historic centre can feel like a maze, and hills can discourage even intrepid of explorers, but that also means stumbling upon memorable views. Lisbon feels small and easy to cover, but there are more sights and stops than you'd realise at first glance.

FROM THE AIRPORT

Aeroporto Humberto Delgado is about a half-hour drive from the city centre. If you're travelling with a large group or heavy luggage, hail a cab or a rideshare service (the pickup spot is outside Departures). If travelling solo, opt for the Metro (Red Line) or bus.

WALK

Walking is a great way to take in the atmosphere of the city. Mind the slippery cobblestones when it rains and reserve plenty of energy for steep hills (the view from the top makes the climb worth it).

TAXI & RIDESHARES

Taxi and ride-share companies don't always see eye to eye, and locals use the latter more than the former. The convenience of a fixed route and payment options usually trumps the colourful experience of a taxi ride. Choose your favourite, but for longer distances only.

PUBLIC TRANSPORT

Hop on the old trams for scenic rides through the historic neighbourhoods but avoid rush hour. Opt for the urban trains (Cais do Sodré and Santa Apolónia) to get to Lisbon's east and west edges in less time and avoid traffic. In the heart of the city, the Metro is a comfortable and quick way to get around.

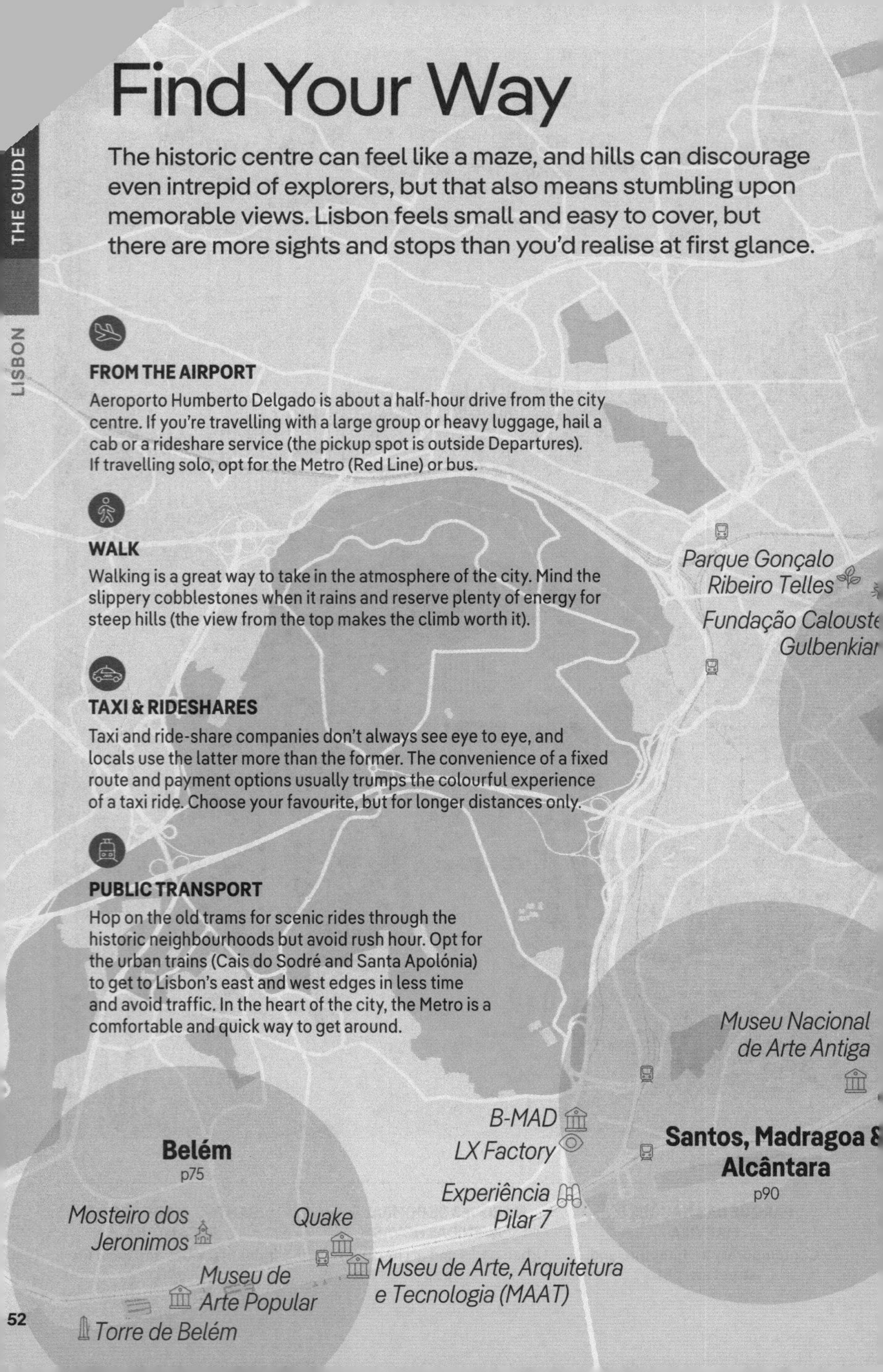

Parque Gonçalo Ribeiro Telles

Fundação Calouste Gulbenkian

Museu Nacional de Arte Antiga

B-MAD

LX Factory

Experiência Pilar 7

Santos, Madragoa & Alcântara
p90

Belém
p75

Mosteiro dos Jeronimos

Quake

Museu de Arte Popular

Museu de Arte, Arquitetura e Tecnologia (MAAT)

Torre de Belém

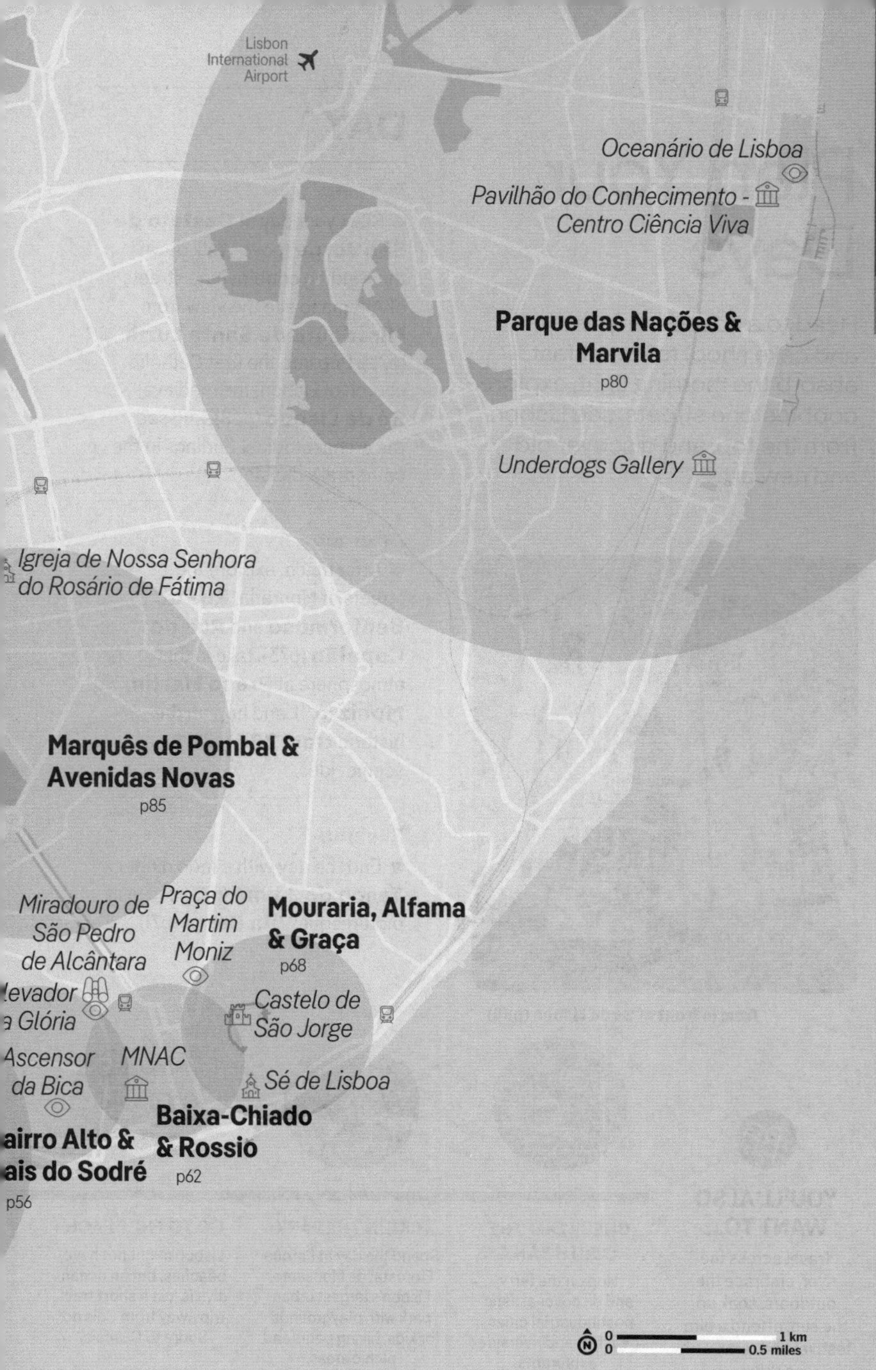

Lisbon International Airport

Oceanário de Lisboa

Pavilhão do Conhecimento - Centro Ciência Viva

Parque das Nações & Marvila
p80

Underdogs Gallery

Igreja de Nossa Senhora do Rosário de Fátima

Marquês de Pombal & Avenidas Novas
p85

Miradouro de São Pedro de Alcântara

Praça do Martim Moniz

Mouraria, Alfama & Graça
p68

Elevador da Glória

Castelo de São Jorge

Ascensor da Bica

MNAC

Sé de Lisboa

Baixa-Chiado & Rossio
p62

Bairro Alto & Cais do Sodré
p56

0 1 km
0 0.5 miles

Plan Your Days

Head to a *pastelaria* (pastry and cake shop) for breakfast, absorb the morning light, explore cobblestone streets, see Lisbon from the top, and discover old and new art.

MARKUS MAINKA/SHUTTERSTOCK ©

Tram in front of Sé de Lisboa (p68)

DAY 1

Morning

● Start your day at **Castelo de São Jorge** (p69). Walk down the winding cobblestone streets of Alfama to see the view from **Miradouro de Santa Luzia** (p73). Pop into the first Catholic church of Lisbon, the medieval **Sé de Lisboa** (p68), and see the archaeological findings in the cathedral's cloisters.

Afternoon

● After lunch, explore the streets of Mouraria, **Rua do Benformoso** and **Rua do Capelão** (p73), take in the atmosphere at **Praça Martim Moniz** (p71), and hop on the historic **tram 28E** (p72) for a scenic ride.

Evening

● End the day with a fado dinner at **Tasco do Jaime** (p73) and visit picturesque **Vila Berta** (p71).

YOU'LL ALSO WANT TO...

Travel across the river, embrace the outdoors, soak up the sun, attend a film festival and relax with a drink.

CHECK OUT THE SOUTH BANK

Hop on the ferry and discover artistic postindustrial cities, beaches and riverside restaurants.

HIKE IN THE PARK

Spend the day at Parque Florestal de Monsanto, Lisbon's largest urban park with playgrounds for kids, hiking paths and picnic areas.

GO TO THE BEACH

Lisbon might not have beaches, but an ocean dive is just a short train trip away from Cais do Sodré to Cascais.

DAY 2

Morning

- Learn about the city's roots at the **Lisbon Story Centre** (p64) in Praça do Comércio, and check out the **Centro Interpretativo da História do Bacalhau** (p64) next door. Take in the view from the top of **Arco da Rua Augusta** (p62).

Afternoon

- Take tram 15E from Praça do Comércio to grab lunch by the river and admire the Manueline architecture of the **Torre de Belém** (p76) and **Mosteiro dos Jerónimos** (p76). Stop at **Pastéis de Belém** (p78) for a classic *pastel de nata* (custard tart).

Evening

- Finish the day visiting the temporary exhibitions at **MAAT** (p76), the Museu de Arte, Arquitetura e Tecnologia, and have dinner with a view at the **MAAT Café & Kitchen** (p79).

DAY 3

Morning

- Admire contemporary architecture at Parque das Nações from the top of the **cable car** (p82) or visit the family favourite **Oceanário do Lisboa** (p82).

Afternoon

- After lunch, walk or cycle from Oriente to Marvila along the river. Stop by **Underdogs Gallery** (p80) to discover up-and-coming contemporary artists or head to a cultural event at **Fábrica Braço de Prata** (p82).

Evening

- End your day spending time browsing the shops at **The Triangle** (p61) and stay for dinner. After hours, head for drinks to Cais do Sodré's **Pink Street** (p58) or Alcântara's **Docas** (p95).

ATTEND A FILM FESTIVAL
From horror movies to independent flicks and documentaries, Lisbon hosts plenty of film festivals.

SEE THE SUN SET
Find your spot in Cais das Colunas or Avenida Ribeira das Naus to watch the sun slowly setting beyond the Ponte 25 de Abril.

LOUNGE AT AN ESPLANADA
Sometimes you want to just sit at a cafe's *esplanada* (open-air terrace), drinking coffee and people-watching.

GO TO A FOOTBALL MATCH
A Benfica vs Sporting football match is always an event, even if you don't follow any of the teams.

BAIRRO ALTO & CAIS DO SODRÉ

NIGHTLIFE AND LIVE MUSIC

In the 1980s and 1990s, *Caishodré* (locals pronounce Cais do Sodré as a one-word mashup) was where many people went for cheap booze and getting lost in the crowd until dawn. Bairro Alto was more select, with bouncers at some bars, strict opening hours and, overall, more orderly, glass-in-hand patrons.

While Cais do Sodré has cleaned up its act, *lisboetas* still have plenty of 'remember when' tales to tell. Bairro Alto – residential neighbourhood by day and barhopping destination by night – has lost some classic bars and made way for new ones but still caters to a mixed crowd of locals and tourists looking for cheap beer and cocktails. There is no other place in Lisbon where you can experience the city's nightlife at its rawest.

TOP TIP

Bairro Alto and Cais do Sodré are best explored on foot, although walking up and down the hills can pose a challenge on rainy days, as the uneven cobblestones of the streets become hard to navigate. Hop on Ascensor da Bica or Elevador da Glória to reduce distances and tackle the hills.

Ascensor da Bica

Ascensor da Bica

THE OTHER POPULAR LIFT

It's technically a funicular, but everyone calls it a lift – or Ascensor da Bica, the official name above the station's entrance. In action since 1892, Bica connects Rua de São Paulo (Cais do Sodré) to Rua do Loreto (Bairro Alto) until 9pm, but it's primarily used as a tourist attraction, rather than by locals. In fact, it's one of the most-photographed public transportations in the city because of the steep street that gives the lift its name, perhaps rivalled only by tram 28E (p72).

Elevador da Glória

SEE STREET ART

Since 1882 this mustard-yellow lift has been helping *lisboetas* shortcut the steep climb, connecting Praça dos Restauradores to Bairro Alto in less than five minutes. These days, it's mostly a tourist attraction but also still sparingly used as public transit. On the right side going up, notice the street art murals. In 1987, Portuguese rock band Rádio Macau recorded 'O Elevador da Glória', an upbeat tune that uses the lift and the ride as a metaphor for their fast rise from nobodies to fame.

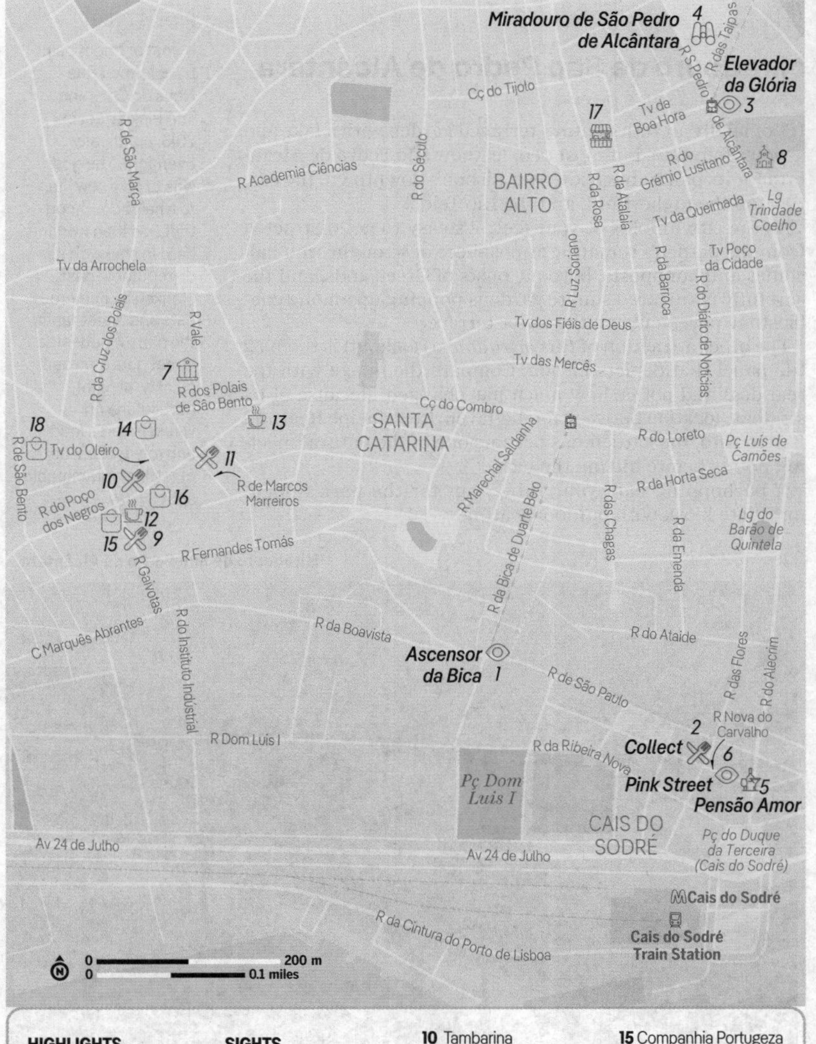

HIGHLIGHTS
1 Ascensor da Bica
2 Collect
3 Elevador da Glória
4 Miradouro de São Pedro de Alcântara
5 Pensão Amor
6 Pink Street

SIGHTS
7 Atelier-Museu Júlio Pomar
8 Igreja de São Roqu

EATING
9 Dear Breakfast
10 Tambarina
11 Zapata

DRINKING
12 Hello, Kristof
13 The Mill

SHOPPING
14 Apaixonarte
15 Companhia Portugeza do Chá
16 Mercearia Poço dos Negros
17 MOBA
18 Palavra de Viajante

Miradouro de São Pedro de Alcântara

VIEW OVER LISBON'S DOWNTOWN

It's officially an 18th-century terraced garden with a lake and a water fountain, but most people know São Pedro de Alcântara for its panoramic view over Lisbon's downtown, the castle atop the highest hill, and the Rio Tejo.

As the city unfolds at your feet, it's easy to get distracted from the garden's romantic atmosphere of wrought-iron balconies and lampposts, baroque busts of Greek gods, and the carefully manicured square gardens popping up among cobblestone pavements on the lower terrace.

The other attraction of this *miradouro* (lookout) is the 1952 tile panel that depicts Lisbon. Compare the image with the real deal and notice how much has changed. Because of its strategic location between foodie-favourite Príncipe Real and Bairro Alto, the garden has become one of the natural meeting points before hitting the bars.

If barhopping isn't your thing, opt for the park's open-until-late kiosk with outdoor seating.

PINK STREET

A coat of bright paint transformed Rua Nova do Carvalho into Pink Street in 2013, practically overnight. The goal was to give new life to a neighbourhood that was then working hard to shake off its disreputable past. Flanked by numerous bars and restaurants, the narrow pedestrian street gets crowded quickly at night, particularly on weekends. It's loud and rowdy then, but a quiet, Instagrammable spot by day.

Miradouro de São Pedro de Alcântara

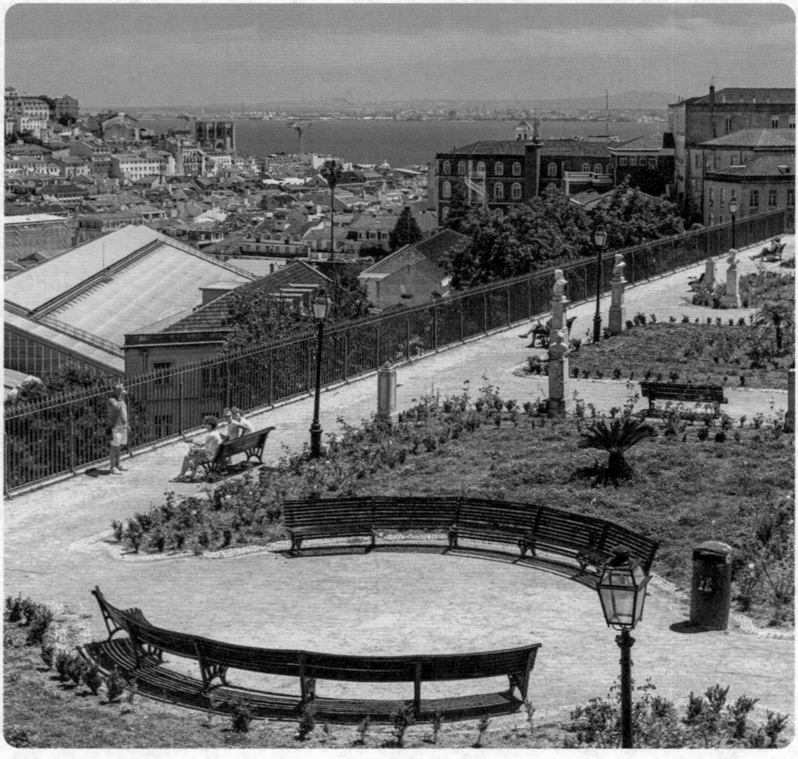

TOP: HORACIO VILLALOBOS/GETTY IMAGES © BOTTOM RIGHT: RYTIS BERNOTAS/SHUTTERSTOCK ©

Pensão Amor

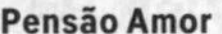

Pensão Amor

NOD TO A BOHEMIAN PAST

Pensão Amor doesn't sugar-coat it: it's a bar at an old, cheap, five-floor pension that was previously used as a brothel in Cais do Sodré, and it's decorated as such. It pays tribute to the neighbourhood's past as the first stop for sailors looking for a good night on the town after months at sea. In business for over a decade, it's one of Pink Street's top attractions and most famous bars. Come for the signature cocktails named very suggestively; stay for the fun of exploring the different rooms or catching one of the live events (anything from a concert to a burlesque show).

Collect

FOOD, RADIO AND RECORDS

Collect is a family-owned business run by Mariana Barosa (DJ Mary B) and João Maria Girão (DJ João Maria), who have worked in the music industry for nearly 30 years, and Bernardo Girão, who works in the food industry. The business started as a pop-up, appointment-only showroom selling records in the neighbourhood of Santos and, in mid-2019, took over a former restaurant in Cais do Sodré to become one of the newest cocktail bars. The ground floor is the bar and a burger joint. The 1st floor is the secondhand record store and the HQ of the house's online radio station, also named Collect, which hosts frequent live DJ sets. It's one of Lisbon's newest afternoon-to-evening hangout spots.

THE LEGACY OF FRÁGIL

At 126 Rua da Atalaia, a bar revolutionised Lisbon's nightlife in 1982, when Bairro Alto was the only partying destination in the city. Eight years earlier, Portugal had risen from a nearly 50-year conservative dictatorship, a tight regime that had set the country back decades regarding culture, women's rights and the LGBTIQ+ community. At Frágil, everyone was welcome. Well, almost everyone because the bouncers (both women) still had a say in who was allowed in. Regulars included prominent authors and journalists, poets and musicians, filmmakers and students. And although this iconic bar closed three decades later (there's an Irish pub at that location now), its social impact lives on.

Praça Luís de Camões

MORE IN BAIRRO ALTO & CAIS DO SODRÉ

Visit Bairro Alto by Day

WHEN BARS GO TO SLEEP

Bairro Alto is a quiet, low-key residential neighbourhood in the morning, and loud and dismissive after sunset. It's not photogenic, and a lot of its appeal comes from the tiny bars, but at a little over 500 years of age, this historic quarter doesn't have to prove its worth.

As you walk into the heart of the neighbourhood, through **Rua do Grémio Lusitano**, across the street from the baroque **Igreja de São Roque**, the quiet sinks in. Weekend mornings are always busier, with bar owners cleaning up spilt drinks, broken glasses and assorted litter. The sound of scrubbing and splashing water bounces off the graffitied

WHERE TO GO OUT IN BAIRRO ALTO & CAIS DO SODRÉ

Galeria Zé dos Bois
Known by locals as ZDB, this art centre in the heart of Bairro Alto hosts regular concerts at 10pm Wednesday to Sunday.

Musicbox
A hybrid concert hall and dance venue known for alternative music.

Titanic Sur Mer
Owned by Portuguese musician Manuel João Vieira, this is an eclectic music venue by the river.

walls and up to closed windows and drawn curtains – short-term rentals, most likely.

Cross the narrow alleyways back and forth as many times as you like, rubbing shoulders with elderly shoppers on their way to the supermarket (while keeping tabs on the neighbours), noticing the windows with clothes hanging out to dry (rare these days, as locals have moved away to quieter and cheaper locations). Or do a quick survey and walk down one of the main streets: **Rua da Rosa** to Ascensor da Bica, or **Rua das Gáveas** to **Praça Luís de Camões**.

On Travessa da Boa Hora, check **MOBA** (Mercado dos Ofícios do Bairro Alto), at the neighbourhood's former produce market, now home to the workshops of several local craft professionals.

Explore The Triangle

AN UNOFFICIAL NEIGHBOURHOOD

The cluster of these three streets – Poço dos Negros, Poiais de São Bento and São Bento – forms a perfect triangle on Lisbon's map and a microcosm. A no-neighbourhood that is, nevertheless, a community, wedged between Bairro Alto and Santos.

Ask a *lisboeta* where one neighbourhood ends and the other begins, and you won't get the same answer. It could be because of an old grudge, some age-old rivalry between quarters, but it's most likely because boundaries in this city tend to blur. At The Triangle, no one cares about borders. People focus on supporting local businesses, where the clientele is a mix of locals, expats and digital nomads.

Here, on the route of tram 28E, you'll find speciality stores such as **Apaixonarte** (a shop and gallery for art produced by Portugal-based artists), **Companhia Portugeza do Chá** (a tea store that produces its own blends, including the city-inspired Lisbon Breakfast), **Mercearia Poço dos Negros** (a grocery store selling artisanal Portuguese products) and **Palavra de Viajante** (an independent bookshop of travel-related non-fiction and fiction books).

Newer cafes **The Mill** and **Hello, Kristof** share the street with established restaurants **Zapata** (Portuguese cuisine) and **Tambarina** (food from Cabo Verde). Off to the side streets, the museum-gallery **Atelier-Museu Júlio Pomar** (Rua do Vale) feeds the soul, and the cafe **Dear Breakfast** (Rua Gaivotas) feeds the need for out-of-hours breakfasts.

THE CAOS DO SODRÉ DOCUMENTARY

In 2022 Portuguese actress and musician Carolina Torres launched her debut feature film *Caos do Sodré* on YouTube (in Portuguese, without subtitles). During the 1½-hour documentary, Torres interviews musicians, bar owners, music journalists and regular customers who share a history with the bohemian Cais do Sodré of the past. The tales, some humorous, some dramatic, include a fact-checked true story featuring Martin Luther King's on-the-lam assassin.

Primas
LGBT-friendly bar in the heart of Bairro Alto. Drinks are cheap, food is simple andthe football table is not just for decoration.

Páginas Tantas
A former favourite of journalists, it's the place to go in Bairro Alto for post-dinner drinks and live jazz music.

Incógnito
Drink beer and simple cocktails as you dance the night away to 1980s and '90s alternative rock in The Triangle.

BAIXA-CHIADO & ROSSIO

DOWNTOWN: SPRAWLING SQUARES & HISTORIC SHOPS

The neighbourhoods of Baixa-Chiado and Rossio are the first part of Lisbon most travellers truly see. The spacious squares with black-and-white patterns of *calçada portuguesa* are one of the city's calling cards. Another is the golden light bouncing off the Rio Tejo in the last few hours of the day, practically all year long, as the sun sets behind the Ponte 25 de Abril.

Marked by the Great Earthquake of 1755 that wiped out most of Lisbon's downtown, the city's riverside Baixa is a testament to Marquês de Pombal's visionary plans to rebuild and replan – hence these perfectly laid-out streets and squares.

Rossio still has the mark of old posh socialite soirées, nights at the theatre, and day trips to the countryside of Sintra.

TOP TIP

The 'drug dealers' in Rua Augusta are Lisbon's oldest scam. Portugal decriminalised the use of illicit drugs in 2001, but it isn't the same as legalising them, so don't expect an Amsterdam-like experience. Scammers target tourists on the busiest streets of Baixa, selling fake drugs.

Arco da Rua Augusta

Arco da Rua Augusta

VIEW DIFFERENT LAYERS OF LISBON

Head up to the *miradouro* (lookout) at Arco da Rua Augusta and take in the city that unfolds at your feet. Facing the street of the same name, see the chaotic-but-orderly Chiado on your left and, on the right, the Alfama with the castle perched on top and the buildings beneath it cascading downhill. The carefully planned puzzle piece that is post-1755-earthquake Baixa fits neatly between the two. Turn around to admire the geometric patterns of Praça do Comércio and the marble steps and columns of Cais das Colunas leading to the river.

Ascensor do Lavra

LISBON'S OLDEST BUT MOST OVERLOOKED FUNICULAR

While visitors flock to Rua da Bica and Calçada da Glória for the picture-perfect memory of Lisbon's iconic mustard-yellow lifts, Lavra gets a fraction of the attention as travellers use it mainly as the public transit shortcut from Baixa to Jardim do Torel. Yet it's the oldest in the city and the first street funicular in the world, operating since 1884. The trip lasts less than two minutes, but it beats tackling the steep 188m of Calçada do Lavra on foot.

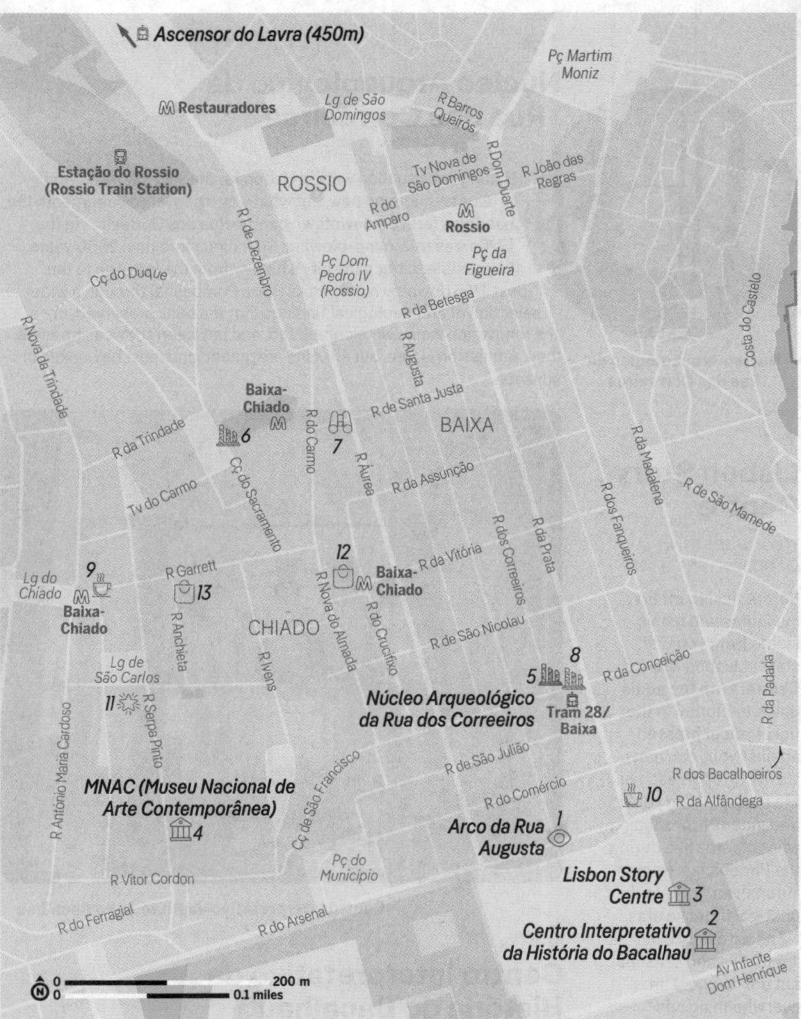

HIGHLIGHTS
1 Arco da Rua Augusta
2 Centro Interpretativo da História do Bacalhau
3 Lisbon Story Centre
4 MNAC (Museu Nacional de Arte Contemporânea)
5 Núcleo Arqueológico da Rua dos Correeiros

SIGHTS
6 Convento do Carmo & Museu Arqueológico
7 Elevador de Santa Justa
8 Galerias Romanas

DRINKING
9 A Brasileira
10 Martinho da Arcada

ENTERTAINMENT
11 Teatro Nacional de São Carlos

SHOPPING
12 Armazéns do Chiado
13 Livraria Bertrand

Núcleo Arqueológico da Rua dos Correeiros

2500 YEARS OF LISBON

Halting construction work in Lisbon for the sake of preserving artefacts is nothing new, but what was discovered underneath the headquarters of a downtown bank in Rua dos Correeiros in the 1990s was truly mind-blowing. Spanning more than 2000 years, it's possible to trace the city's history from the Iron Age to the post-1755 downtown (known as Baixa Pombalina) through a wide selection of archaeological findings that the bank preserved, once the renovation works were completed, and has been showcasing since then. Admission is free, but all visits are guided and must be booked in advance.

Núcleo Arqueológico da Rua dos Correeiros

Lisbon Story Centre

TO UNDERSTAND LISBON, START HERE

Before ticking off art museums and iconic sights from your list, start at Lisbon Story Centre. With the audio guide (included in the ticket price) pressed against your ear, move slowly through each of the rooms where you'll find videos reproducing what life was like during the Phoenician, Roman, Moorish and pre- and post-earthquake eras.

The experience here is immersive and sensorial, but don't expect an overwhelming info dumping.

Even in the room replicating the sensations of the 1755 earthquake and tsunami, the special effects are just a light vibration under your seat and a swinging (well-secured) chandelier above your head.

Centro Interpretativo da História do Bacalhau

Centro Interpretativo da História do Bacalhau

ALL ABOUT SALTED COD

Portugal's obsession with *bacalhau* (salted cod) isn't a mystery, but one of the newest attractions in Lisbon's downtown exists to answer all the questions. It's filled, from bottom to top, with several depictions of *bacalhaus* in all shapes and forms. The interactive experience establishes the economic roots of *bacalhau* fishing, focuses on testimonials of former fishers, and even addresses the role of this 'typical' dish in the dictatorship's propaganda. Visitors, one at a time, can also safely experience the loneliness of being in a tiny boat in the middle of the vast ocean. The visit ends around a virtual table, and the culinary experience can go on with lunch or dinner at next door Terra Nova, the centre's restaurant.

MNAC

CONTEMPORARY PORTUGUESE ART MUSEUM

This small museum in Chiado is often overlooked in lieu of its bigger sibling, the Museu Nacional de Arte Antiga. But for those who appreciate local art and how it sheds light on the society of a certain period, MNAC (Museu Nacional de Arte Contemporânea) must not be left off your itinerary. It showcases works of notable Portuguese artists from the mid-19th century to today, but don't expect to find an extensive collection. One hour is enough time to visit the whole museum. The collection includes Columbano Bordalo Pinheiro's *O Grupo do Leão,* depicting several 19th-century intellectuals and artists at their usual hangout, Rossio restaurant Leão d'Ouro, including his brother, cartoonist Rafael Bordalo Pinheiro. Modernist Almada Negreiros' *Varina* and Paula Rego's *Self-Portrait in Red* are other highlights.

CHIADO

Baixa-Chiado has endured great tragedy but also stands for renovation and reinvention, especially following the Great Earthquake of 1755.

But up a gentle slope, in Chiado, you'll feel a bit of that old pre-earthquake Lisbon, with narrower streets and smaller squares *(largos)*. The buildings, albeit housing modern companies and shops now, have kept their Art Nouveau facades and the few decor details that remained after the ravaging 1988 fire.

MNAC

HEMIS/ALAMY STOCK PHOTO ©

FOR PAULA REGO FANS

In Cascais' Museum Quarter, Casa das Histórias (p113), set in a building designed by Eduardo Souto de Moura as per the artist's request, showcases dozens of paintings spanning her 60-year career.

BEST PASTELARIAS

Confeitaria Nacional
In business at the same Praça da Figueira location since 1829; it's known for the Christmas cakes *bolo rainha* and *bolo rei*.

Pastelaria Benard
Next door to A Brasileira, Benard started in 1868 as a tea house; today it has the best croissants downtown.

Pastelaria Alcôa
The place on Rua Garrett to taste-test all the *doces conventuais* (egg-and-sugar-based sweets created by Portuguese nuns).

MOUNIR TAHA/SHUTTERSTOCK ©

Rua do Carmo

MORE IN BAIXA-CHIADO & ROSSIO

Go Shopping in Baixa-Chiado

THE SHOPPING HUB

Shopping centres come and go, but three streets remain the classic shopping hub of Baixa-Chiado: Rua Augusta, Rua do Carmo and Rua Garrett.

Rua Augusta, the main pedestrian street connecting Rossio to Praça do Comércio, is busy with overpriced restaurants (stay away from laminated menus advertising non-Portuguese dishes like paella), street performers and mass-produced souvenir shops. But it's also where you'll find clothes shops with most of the international brands you'd see at a large department store.

Rua do Carmo, with a few surviving facades after the 1988 fire, is where you'll find artisans (although not many and not a lot of variety) spread between impressive piece of **urban art of Bordalo II** next to **Elevador de Santa Justa** and the shopping centre **Armazéns do Chiado**.

Rua Garrett remains as it's always been: luxury brands, boutiques, *pastelarias*, and the oldest bookshop in the world still in business, **Livraria Bertrand**, with occasional buskers.

Imagine Lisbon Before the Earthquake

WHY LISBON'S DOWNTOWN LOOKS 'NEW'

The 1755 cataclysm was not just an earthquake. It was a quake followed by a fire that quickly spread and a tsunami on one of

WHERE TO SHOP LOCAL IN BAIXA-CHIADO & ROSSIO

Chapelaria Azevedo Rua
The oldest hat-maker in Portugal, in business since 1886 at the same address in Rossio.

Luvaria Ulisses
A store selling custom-made gloves on Rua do Carmo. Its tiny space can only welcome one client at a time.

Casa Pereira da Conceição
Go for the decor and architecture; stay for the scent of freshly ground coffee. For connoisseurs and first-timers.

the most important dates for Catholics: 1 November, All Saints Day. The tragedy and chaos that ensued on the holy day led Voltaire and other Illuminists to question God's existence and will. It was a ripple effect that reverberated throughout Europe.

In Lisbon, though, the urgent task at hand was to rebuild. The project was led by Marquês de Pombal, prime minister to Dom José I, a man so ambitious that he didn't hesitate to immortalise himself in a grand statue (in the middle of the roundabout at the top of Avenida da Liberdade) and with a carved bust at the feet of the king's equestrian statue in **Praça do Comércio**.

Convento do Carmo is the best-known attraction connected to the earthquake, and there's nothing quite as impressive as looking down that hallowed aisle of Gothic arches.

In 1771, while rebuilding, workers unearthed a series of arched structures identified as Roman. Visiting the **Galerias Romanas** at Rua da Conceição is only possible twice a year (April and September), and tickets fly as soon as reservations open.

BEST GINJINHA BARS

A Ginjinha
This *ginjinha* (cherry liqueur) spot in Rossio is, for many, the first and only stop to have a shot of the sour cherry liqeur.

Ginjinha Rubi
Artisanal *ginjinha* made with cherries from Óbidos. Admire the tile panel while enjoying your drink.

Ginjinha Sem Rival
The usual place for the ritual pre- or post-theatre shot of *ginjinha*.

Discover Pessoa's Baixa-Chiado

TRACING THE MODERNIST AUTHOR'S LIFE

Poet, translator, writer and one of the founders of Portuguese modernism, Fernando Pessoa was not only born and raised in Lisbon (except for a 10-year stint in South Africa when young), he lived and worked in Baixa-Chiado for most of his adult life. Some of the cafes and bars of the neighbourhood were his favourite hangouts to write, drink and discuss literature. In his work, Lisbon sometimes leaps off the page, and other times it's a subtle reference, but the city is always there.

The bronze statue outside cafe **A Brasileira** in Chiado is probably Pessoa's most well-known depiction, but it's also the most misinterpreted. A bit antisocial, as he preferred to focus on his writing and multiple writer personalities, Pessoa's lifted hand is actually waving people off, not inviting them to sit.

Just down the street from Largo do Chiado, there's another statue across the square from **Teatro Nacional de São Carlos**, in front of the house where the writer was born on the auspicious day of 13 June (Lisbon and St Anthony Day). The family had moved there on account of his father's job as an opera critic.

Another of the writer's favourite spots was **Martinho da Arcada**, a cafe where he was a regular along with fellow modernist author and painter Almada Negreiros.

At **71 Rua da Prata** (1st floor) Pessoa wrote the Portuguese slogan for Coca-Cola in 1928 (look for the green door next to a souvenir shop). At **42 Rua da Assunção** (2nd floor), he met Ofelia Queirós in 1919, the love of his life and with whom he exchanged dozens of letters (later compiled in the book *Cartas de Amor*).

Conserveira de Lisboa
Tinned fish (sardines, mackerel or tuna) are among Lisbon's most authentic souvenirs. Find the usual and the more exotic.

Hospital das Bonecas
Established in 1830, this doll hospital is also a toy store with a museum upstairs.

Manteigaria Silva
This family-owned grocery store is a top place to buy *bacalhau* (salted cod); it also sells local charcuterie and wine.

MOURARIA, ALFAMA & GRAÇA

THE HISTORIC CENTRE

Alfama, Mouraria and Graça are Lisbon's traditional neighbourhoods, known for sweeping views of the city and the cluster of narrow streets and colourful houses cascading downhill towards the Rio Tejo. Getting lost in the streets is the way to get the city's historic centre under your skin and feel Lisbon's true essence of laundry hanging to dry, neighbours gossiping but also checking in on each other, of elderly women selling *ginjinha* by the glass from their doorsteps.

Alfama, the oldest neighbourhood, has seen many versions of Lisbon over the centuries and parts of it survived the 1755 earthquake, so it's one of the few places you can find medieval houses. Mouraria, built as a ghetto in 1147 for the Moors as a 'gesture of good faith' from Dom Afonso Henriques, has never truly outgrown its outsider trait; fado, then a marginal music genre, was born here. Graça is the newest of the three, with its tile facades and once-enclosed villas, where most of the buildings were made in the 19th century to accommodate the growing population of factory workers who moved to Lisbon from other parts of Portugal.

TOP TIP

The picturesque historic neighbourhoods are a jumble of narrow streets, interior courtyards and steep hills. Walking around alone at night can feel unsafe in the empty and poorly lit streets. In the daytime, walking or using trams and buses are the best ways to get around.

Sé de Lisboa

Sé de Lisboa

LISBON'S OLDEST CATHOLIC CHURCH

The boxy, castle-looking stone building doesn't go unnoticed on the side of the street leading up to Alfama's *miradouros*, and if you wait for the right moment, it's the perfect backdrop for a photo of tram 28E descending – a classic Lisbon image. Inside, check out the high ceilings and stained-glass windows of the medieval church first, but then make your way to the cloisters where you can witness an ongoing live archaeological excavation. The unearthed layers reveal aspects of Lisbon's Roman and Islamic past.

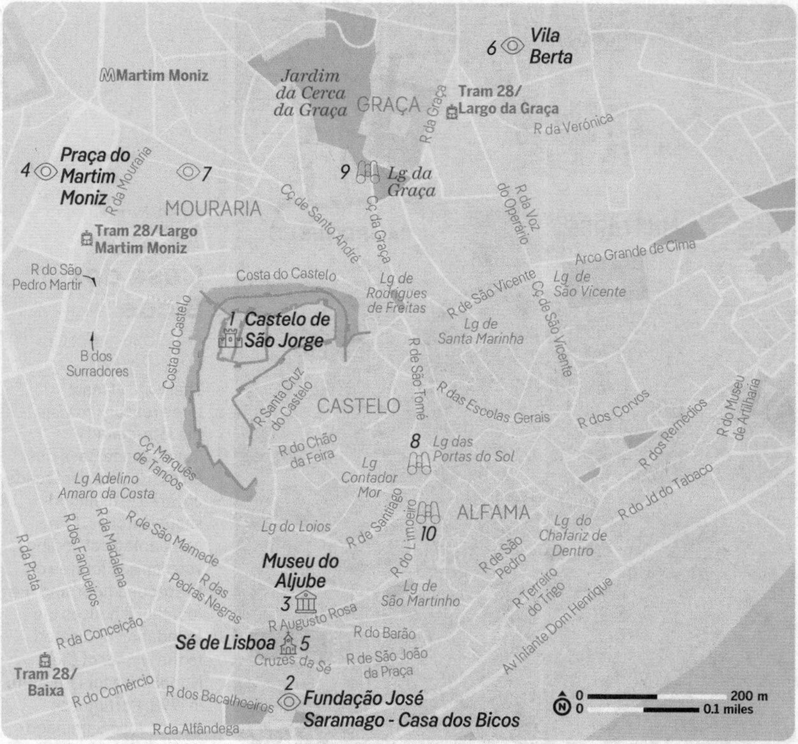

HIGHLIGHTS
1 Castelo de São Jorge
2 Fundação José Saramago – Casa dos Bicos
3 Museu do Aljube
4 Praça do Martim Moniz
5 Sé de Lisboa
6 Vila Berta

SIGHTS
7 Largo da Severa
8 Largo das Portas do Sol
9 Miradouro da Graça
10 Miradouro de Santa Luzia

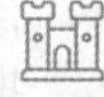

Castelo de São Jorge

HILLTOP SEMI-AUTHENTIC MEDIEVAL FORTRESS

The castle walls embrace the highest of Lisbon's seven hills, overlooking terracotta rooftops, the shimmering river, and the red iron bridge connecting both sides of the Tejo. Some brave the uphill climb just for that sight; others want the experience of travelling back in time to when the country's first king took the castle from the Moors. That historical and seen-as-heroic feat would fit the conservative dictatorship's rhetoric of national pride, leading to a restoration of the castle in the 1940s. It might not be as authentic as you might expect, but it's still, at least partly, a 900-year-old medieval fortress.

Castelo de São Jorge

TOP LEFT: HORACIO VILLALOBOS/GETTY IMAGES) © BOTTOM RIGHT: MAMA_MIA/SHUTTERSTOCK ©

Museu do Aljube

Museu do Aljube

PORTUGAL'S YOUNG DEMOCRACY MUSEUM

Four of the six floors of this museum tell the story of one of the darkest periods of Portugal's recent history: the conservative dictatorship, known as the Estado Novo, and the fight for democracy that culminated with the peaceful military coup on the morning of 25 April 1974. Set inside the former political prison, where the opponents to the regime were jailed and tortured, the Museu do Aljube gives a punch-in-the-gut account of the nearly five decades of the totalitarian regime and the colonial agenda that supported it through personal testimonies, documents, and photos of those who perished at the hands of PIDE, the political police. Other floors include information about the building, archaeological findings and a shop.

Casa dos Bicos

THE JOSÉ SARAMAGO FOUNDATION

There are at least three reasons to visit the 16th-century Renaissance Casa dos Bicos: its peculiar facade covered in diamond-shaped stones, the archaeological findings you can see for free on the ground floor, and the fact that it houses the foundation dedicated to the winner of the Nobel Prize for Literature in 1998, Portuguese author José Saramago (1922–2010). The 1st floor, for ticket holders only, has a complete repository of the writer's career that includes photos, calendars and notebooks, manuscripts, books translated into different languages and, of course, the Nobel medal he won.

Campo das Cebolas

Praça Martim Moniz

THE HEART OF MOURARIA

Praça Martim Moniz marks the bustling heart of multicultural Mouraria, surrounded by rooftop bars, Asian food courts and shops selling spices in bulk. It's the quarter's top place for people-watching (sometimes a cricket match ensues, or skateboarders slide by), listening to the variety of languages spoken, and taking in the view of the hilltop castle. To the west of the square, notice the often-overlooked remains of the 14th-century city wall.

Mercado de Fusão, a series of stands selling street food, brought life to Praça Martim Moniz from 2012 to 2019. Recently, however, Mouraria locals have started to reclaim their square as a neighbourhood park meant for residents, not just for weekend passers-by. New projects are currently under way and expected to be completed in a couple of years.

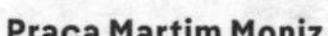

Praça Martim Moniz

VILA BERTA

Although most see A short walk from Largo da Graça, Vila Berta is a picturesque and quiet side street, with cute, same-style houses, with tiles and wrought iron balconies. But in the early 20th century, at the peak of industrialisation in Lisbon and the consequent population increase, this small cluster of houses was one of the many factory workers' neighbourhoods that proliferated in the city. Named vilas, they were a quarter within a quarter, sometimes no more than a gated block of houses around a courtyard. Renovated in 2016, Vila Berta is also one of Graça's popular places for the annual street celebrations in honour of the *santos populares* (popular saints).

WHERE TO EAT ASIAN FOOD

Local student Alexis Viegas recommends the top affordable Asian food spots in Martim Moniz.

Japanese snacks
Mercado Oriental is one of the best spots to buy Japanese snacks that you won't find in any other Lisbon supermarket. And at reasonable prices, too.

Street food
If you want to experience authentic Asian street food in Lisbon, head to the top floor of Amanhecer, on the west side of Praça Martim Moniz. I recommend Korean chicken at K-Bob and any noodles at Noodle Delight.

Bubble tea
SOHO LISBOA is a good spot for bubble tea, but The Milk'Tea Story is better. My suggestion is to try Milk Tea with matcha and tapioca.

ROSSHELEN/SHUTTERSTOCK ©

MORE IN MOURARIA, ALFAMA & GRAÇA

Classic Yellow Trams & Viewpoints

TRAMS AND MIRADOUROS

Yellow trams are ubiquitous in Lisbon's historic centre. The **28E** is the most popular, but locals also use them as public transit. To minimise your impact, try hopping on the 28E outside of rush hour. If your time to travel around is tight, look for alternatives – same experience, but slightly different routes. Tram **12E** travels to and from Martim Moniz, via Alfama's viewpoints and the Sé, while tram **25E** connects Praça da Figueira to Campo de Ourique (Prazeres), via Cais do Sodré and Santos.

As for *miradouros* in Mouraria, Alfama and Graça, they are a dime a dozen – and that's just accounting for the four official ones. From windy **Miradouro da Senhora do Monte**, between Graça and Mouraria, you can see Praça Martim Moniz, bits of downtown, and the winding street of Calçada do Monte that will take you down to the heart of Mouraria.

WHERE TO EAT IN MOURARIA, ALFAMA & GRAÇA

Ramiro
Upscale, chef-recommended restaurant for seafood and fresh fish near Intendente. €€€

Zé da Mouraria
No-reservation Portuguese traditional eatery in the heart of Mouraria. Lunch only. €€

Tasca Zé dos Cornos
No-reservations, family-owned canteen-style restaurant in Mouraria. Famous for grilled spare ribs with bean rice. €

Miradouro das Portas do Sol in Alfama is all about drinks in the sun at the outdoor cafe looking over the Rio Tejo, and, less than five minutes down the street, **Miradouro da Santa Luzia** renders the view romantic with its tile panels and pergola. **Miradouro da Graça** is the city's terrace to watch Lisbon wind down as the sun sets.

Explore a Typical Mouraria Street

MULTICULTURALISM AND FADO

Mouraria (Moorish Quarter) has been known as such since King Dom Afonso Henriques took over Lisbon in 1147 and forced the Muslim community to relocate here (then a ghetto outside the city walls) until the 15th century, when they were expelled unless they agreed to convert to Christianity. Since then, migrant communities have found their bearings here. People of 56 different nationalities have settled here over the years.

Few places have managed to avoid the advancements of gentrification in Mouraria, and **Rua do Benformoso** is one of them. This street connecting Martim Moniz to Largo do Intendente is flanked by Bangladeshi and Indian cheap eateries, barbershops, travel agencies, halal butchers, and Chinese restaurants and shops. The neighbourhood's multicultural heart lives and thrives here. Stroll down the street on a busy morning or post-lunch and absorb all the scents, all the languages, and all the life. This, in a nutshell, is Mouraria, and it's just a slight detour away from busier main street **Rua da Palma**.

On the other hand, you'll be able to tell **Rua do Capelão** is the street of fado – a tiny alleyway across Centro Comercial Martim Moniz – because of the sculpture of a Portuguese guitar at its entrance. The street winds up towards the small square **Largo da Severa**, a name also linked to the fado's mythos. Maria Severa Onofriana, the first *fadista* (fado singer), died on this street. But Rua do Capelão was also the birthplace of another *fadista*, Fernando Mauricio, known as the King of Fado in Mouraria.

Sitting on the park benches and enjoying the silence is one way to experience Mouraria. The other is to listen to the crossed conversations of passers-by. Across the square is **Casa da Severa** (you can't miss it, it's the white house in the middle), where Maria Severa Onofriana lived.

QUEER-FRIENDLY BARS IN GRAÇA

JOANA CÉSAR ©

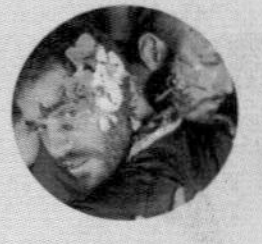

João Caçador and Lila Fadista from Fado Bicha recommend queer-friendly bars in the Graça neighbourhood. *@fadobicha*

Damas
A restaurant, a club and a concert venue very dear to the queer and trans community.

VALSA
A bar-restaurant owned by two Brazilian women, with strong ties to the Brazilian community. It feels like all the emerging art that's happening in Lisbon happens here first.

Tasco do Jaime
A very old and traditional *casa de fados*. It's not exactly open to the queer community, but in the summers, everything happens at their esplanade, so it kind of feels like all rules are off the table. You can sit on the wall near the terrace, listen to fado and still be part of the experience.

O Velho Eurico
Portuguese restaurant with a contemporary touch that maintains the classic taberna (simple restaurant) vibe. €€

Agulha no Palheiro
To *petiscar* (snack) or to eat a full meal, head to this quiet, away-from-the-tourist-crowds small restaurant in Alfama. €€

Cantinho do Aziz
Serves award-winning homemade-style Mozambican food created by chef Jeny Sulemange. €€

WHAT TO DO IN ALFAMA

Sofia Lopes Machaqueiro grew up in Alfama and now lives here with her husband and two children. *@sofialopesmachaqueiro*

What to visit
The Feira da Ladra market on Saturday mornings, the Mosteiro de São Vicente de Fora and the family-friendly park Jardim Botto Machado.

Where to eat
A Lareira, for lunch, and Maçã Verde, for dinner. Both serve traditional Portuguese cuisine with fixed daily menus *(prato do dia).* Maria Limão and Focaccia in Giro for brunch, and Davvero (Campo das Cebolas) for ice cream.

Where to drink
L'Ape Italian Lounge, a bar with outdoor seating near Miradouro da Senhora do Monte. It's perfect for early evening drinks and light eating. It hosts contemporary art exhibitions.

Party at Santos Populares

CELEBRATIONS TO HONOUR PATRON SAINTS

It's without much doubt Lisbon's most famed street celebration: *santos populares*. In honour of St Anthony (and St Vincent), Lisbon's historic neighbourhoods fill up with a beer-holding sardine-eating crowd, dancing the night away to a particular Portuguese music genre known as *música pimba* (imagine flashy dancers, high-pitched singers and tunes that mix pop with a folksy beat).

That's the daily (or rather, nightly) top activity during the month of June, peaking on the 13th, a holiday in Lisbon. The feast spreads across the city, but it's stronger in Alfama, Graça and Mouraria.

In addition to the religious portion of the celebrations, which includes the Catholic marriage of a small pre-selected group of low-income Lisbon couples, Baixa's Avenida da Liberdade becomes the stage for a parade of *marchas populares* – neighbourhood-based groups of singing and dancing locals competing for the award of best *marcha* of the year. And the competition is fierce!

Attend an Alfama Festival

FADO MUSIC AND FILMS

The **Cinalfama Lisbon International Film Festival** screens films three times a year, some on the streets of Alfama and some at a neighbourhood cultural association called Grupo Sportivo Adicense, one of the few remaining community-focused nonprofits in the area. Focusing on independent films from all over the world, all genres are welcome at Cinalfama. The festival's primary goal is to create new cinema fans and attract audiences to Alfama, breaking the language barrier (as all films are subtitled in English).

For more than a decade, the **Santa Casa Alfama** music festival has celebrated fado in September. Performers include both newcomers or seasoned *fadistas*, and the stage is Alfama itself as each show takes place in a different part of the neighbourhood, whether it's the Museu do Fado or a surprising outdoor location like the rooftop of the cruise port, a church or someone's window.

WHERE TO SHOP IN MOURARIA, ALFAMA & GRAÇA

Popat Store
The place to go in Lisbon for spices in bulk and Indian snacks.

Centro Comercial Martim Moniz
Street-shop style: three floors of cheap off-brand clothes and knick-knacks.

XVIII Azulejo e Faiança
Handmade, artisanal ceramic tiles produced according to 18th-century style and techniques.

BELÉM

GRAND PALACES AND MANUELINE ARCHITECTURE

Belém by the sea, at the mouth of the Tejo where the river and ocean mix, was once the port from where the Portuguese navigators set sail. It's forever linked to that part of the country's history, the so-called 'Age of Discoveries' or, to be more precise, the age of sea explorations. The prosperous finds of those days made Portugal one of the wealthiest countries in Europe, with profits used to build grand monuments such as the Mosteiro dos Jerónimos, to leave lasting symbols of the greatness of the country.

For the monarchy and the aristocrats of the 18th century, this was their countryside, an affluent riverside land where they would spend the summers. Today, the palaces have been turned into museums, the gardens into public botanical parks, and the manors into embassies, but it still retains an atmosphere of grandeur.

Busy during the day, in the evening Belém becomes quiet, even though it has one of Lisbon's biggest cultural centres.

TOP TIP

The quickest and traffic-free way to get in and out of Belém is by train. It departs about every half-hour from the Cais do Sodré train station, and the trip takes less than 10 minutes. The train station in Belém is within walking distance of most of the attractions.

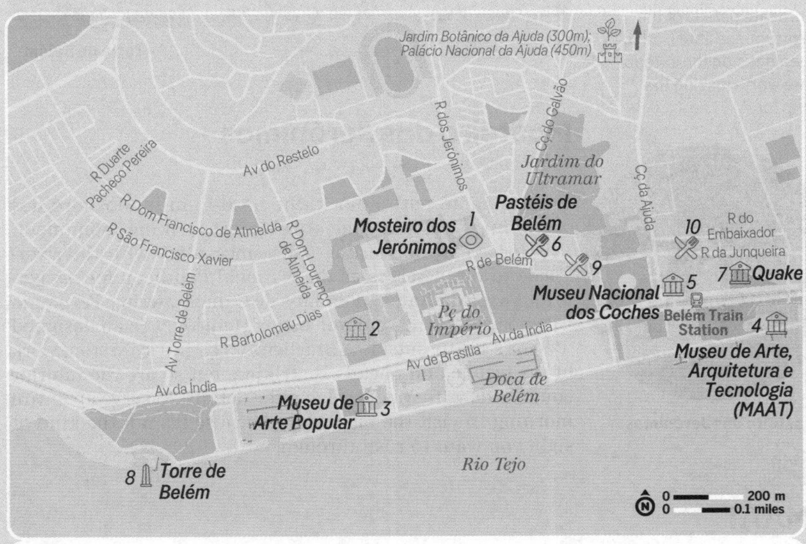

HIGHLIGHTS
1 Mosteiro dos Jerónimos
2 Museu Coleção Berardo
3 Museu de Arte Popular
4 Museu de Arte, Arquitetura e Tecnologia (MAAT)
5 Museu Nacional dos Coches
6 Pastéis de Belém
7 Quake
8 Torre de Belém

EATING
9 Manteigaria
10 Rui dos Pregos

Torre de Belém

MANUELINE-STYLE DEFENCE TOWER

A Unesco World Heritage Site since 1983, the tower used to be Lisbon's gateway, marking the location from where the Portuguese explorers set sail during the so-called 'Age of Discoveries'. A small wooden bridge connects the shore to this monument, one of Belém's most popular attractions. You can visit inside if you must tick it off a bucket list, but its true beauty can be seen from the outside. The intricate details of the Portuguese Late Gothic aesthetic on the exterior are worth making the trip for.

Torre de Belém

Mosteiro dos Jerónimos

THE MASSIVE MANUELINE MONASTERY

Occupying an entire block, the hard-to-miss Mosteiro dos Jerónimos is Manueline style's most striking monument. A Unesco World Heritage Site since 1983, with the riverside tower, it serves as the National Pantheon for navigator Vasco da Gama, poet Luís de Camões, writer Fernando Pessoa (p67) and sculptor Lagoa Henriques (who designed Pessoa's statue outside A Brasileira). The intricate stonework of the facade and portals is striking, but so are the interior courtyards with Mudéjar lace-like details. Reserve an entire morning to visit the monastery because it's not the kind of sight you want to rush through.

Mosteiro dos Jerónimos

MAAT

ART AND A SPECTACULAR VIEW

Shaped like a wave and covered in white, light-reflecting tiles, the MAAT (Museu de Arte, Arquitetura e Tecnologia) building practically blends in with the riverbank. Focusing on the connection between art, architecture and technology, the museum hosts several exhibitions throughout the year, shedding light on the works of contemporary artists who prompt debate on current events. Grada Kilomba's *The Boat* (2021) is the kind of work shown at MAAT, a thought-provoking piece on the slave trade (in which Portugal played a crucial but not-yet-addressed role), the 'Discoveries' and colonialism. Before or after visiting the current exhibitions, check the free-access roof for a different view of Belém and the river. Tickets include entrance to other exhibitions at next door Central Eléctrica.

Museu Nacional dos Coches

Museu Nacional dos Coches

ROYAL CARRIAGES AND COACHES

When in 2015 this museum transitioned from neighbouring Picadeiro Real to the contemporary building designed by Paulo Mendes da Rocha, opinions diverged. Love it or hate it, visitors now have a 360-degree view of the coaches and carriages used by the Portuguese Royal Family, the most notable being the one in which the last King of Portugal was assassinated (bullet holes included). The collection spans three centuries of ceremonial and day-to-day vehicles.

Museu de Arte Popular

PORTUGUESE FOLK ART MUSEUM

In 1940 it was one of the pavilions for the Portugal World Exhibition. In 1948 it was officially Museu do Povo (Museum of the People). Then, most likely due to its roots as a propaganda museum for the Estado Novo dictatorship, it closed permanently for decades until 2016. That year's soft opening was an attempt to reclaim Portuguese arts and crafts as a cultural trait, not a political agenda. The permanent collection includes folk art, traditional clothes and tools from mid-20th century rural Portugal, and frescoes depicting the country's core values and honourable work (as imposed by the dictatorship then).

Museu de Arte Popular

Quake

THE 1755 GREAT EARTHQUAKE EXPERIENCE

It was only a matter of time until Lisbon's most impactful tragedy had its own attraction. Although the Great Earthquake and its impacts are discussed at length in many of the city's sights, Quake has come to (quite literally) shake things up. Identified by the coloured RFID wristband provided at reception, each group is led through a series of rooms with interactive exhibitions on quakes until the big one everyone is there for: the 1755 Great Earthquake simulator. There's a stationary pew at the back of the replicated church for those who might need it. Book your tickets in advance and get there 10 minutes before your allotted time.

MANUELINE ARCHITECTURE

The Portuguese Late Gothic was called Manueline after Dom Manuel I, who ruled from 1495 to 1521. Self-centred and believing he was the embodiment of God on Earth, the king was at the forefront of the busiest period of Portugal's maritime expansion (later known as the Age of Discoveries). Since most of the other parts of Lisbon were wiped out during the earthquake, in Belém you'll find the greatest examples of this style's heavily ornate monuments: Torre de Belém and Mosteiro dos Jerónimos. Portugal was a wealthy country then, hence the over-the-top buildings and decor details influenced by the style of Eastern architecture the Portuguese navigators encountered.

MIN C. CHIU/SHUTTERSTOCK ©

Pastéis de Belém

MORE IN BELÉM

Taste Test Pastel de Nata

WHICH CUSTARD TART IS BETTER?

For years, the rival to **Pastéis de Belém**'s custard tarts was every other cafe in Lisbon (and the country). And that wasn't much of a competition. But then, Manteigaria came along in 2014, taunting everyone's sweet tooth with a more buttery, flaky pastry that divided the *pastel de nata* fans.

Of course, the recipes are different (one of them is centuries old and a well-kept secret), and neither tries to take the other's place. The queues at Pastéis de Belém, though, can test your patience (despite the speedy but courteous service).

Those who want to put it to rest and try one tart from each place simultaneously can now since **Manteigaria** (Rua de Belém) opened a shop less than five minutes down the street from Pastéis de Belém.

WHERE TO EAT PASTRIES IN BELÉM

Pastelaria Careca
According to *lisboetas*, the best croissants in town. Typically closes in August for the summer holidays. €

Pastelaria Versailles
One of Lisbon's classic *pastelarias* is now in Belém. What's the best pastry here? All of them. €

Arcádia
Porto-based pastry shop known for its chocolates and macarons. €

Visit Ajuda

LISBON'S LAST ROYAL PALACE

Walk up Calçada da Ajuda from the corner of the Versailles cafe or hop on tram 18E if you don't feel like tackling the steep hill to visit the never-finished **Palácio Nacional da Ajuda**, thanks to a lack of funding caused by the Royal Family running away to Brazil after the French invasions. The neo-classical palace was the last official royal residence in Lisbon; built in the early 19th century, it served as the royal residence from the 1860s until the end of the monarchy in 1910.

The palace may have had a convoluted past but wandering through its floors now is quite the experience for fans of decorative arts: frescoes, tapestries, velvet drapes, silk-covered walls and crystal chandeliers. The substantial art collection inludes Portugal's only El Greco painting, which hangs in the chaptel.

The interior courtyard of the palace no longer leads to doors and windows without rooms – the back of the building was closed and is now the home of the royal jewels, the **Museu do Tesouro Real**.

Whether the new museum looks great or is a strange new addition to the 19th-century building is still debatable. Three levels of dark, velvet-covered walls display gems and accessories in glass cases, which you access through thick gold-coloured doors resembling the ones of a vault.

After you've taken it all in, make your way downhill to **Jardim Botânico da Ajuda**, about a five-minute walk from the palace. An Italian botanist designed the garden per the Portuguese king's request, who wanted it to be a place of research and learning for his children. It's a tranquil, Renaissance-style two-terraced garden with an unobstructed view of Belém and the river.

WHAT TO DO IN BELÉM

Luli Monteleone, blogger and social media specialist, shares her tips. *@lulimoneleone*

Secluded park
Parque Moinhos de Santana is a peaceful little park with windmills away from the crowds.

Visit a museum
Museu Nacional dos Coches has a one-of-a-kind collection of coaches, which is unique in the world. Or see contemporary art at Museu Coleção Berardo.

Eat at a local restaurant
Rui dos Pregos is where you eat good food at an affordable price. It's great for just grabbing a beer.

Same view, different angle
The *jacarandás* in bloom on Avenida da Torre de Belém. There's also a quiet park at the top of that avenue. You can see the tower and a little bit of the ocean.

WHERE TO EAT WITH A VIEW IN BELÉM

Portugália
A Lisbon classic, this restaurant serves meat- and seafood-based meals in a privileged location. €€

Darwin's Café
Champalimaud Foundation's contemporary cuisine restaurant. Reservations needed. €€€

MAAT Café & Kitchen
The official restaurant and bar at MAAT (p76) is open until late, except on weekends. €€

PARQUE DAS NAÇÕES & MARVILA

CONTEMPORARY ARCHITECTURE AND STREET ART

For some *lisboetas*, the city's east side doesn't feel like part of Lisbon. That's partly because most locals still see Parque das Nações as Expo 98, the world exhibition of almost three decades ago. Older generations remember it as a piece of industrial property with no purpose – until it was rehabilitated into an urban park.

The same goes for Marvila, on the edge of town, between Parque das Nações and the Santa Apolónia train station. A place of warehouses and factories within the confines of the city – until the hipsters discovered it and embraced the potential gem it could become. With contemporary architecture and urban art, emerging artists and new businesses, it's not the pretty postcard-perfect Lisbon, but worth the exploration.

TOP TIP

Parque das Nações (or Oriente) is served by a public transit hub that includes trains, Metro and buses (including some from and to international destinations). Marvila is more isolated in terms of public transport, but it's on the route of frequent buses connecting the east side to the city centre.

ELEPHOTOS/SHUTTERSTOCK ©

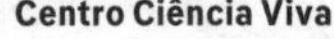
Centro Ciência Viva

Underdogs Gallery

VHILS' ART GALLERY IN MARVILA

Alexandre Farto, known by his artistic alias Vhils, is a renowned Portuguese urban artist. Farto's business persona co-owns Underdogs Gallery, an art gallery that took over one of the old warehouses in Marvila at Rua Fernando Palha, a short walk from Fábrica Braço de Prata (p82). In addition to solo and group exhibitions, mostly from artists who would probably never find a space at a more conventional gallery, the area also includes a shop for merchandise, art books, limited-edition collectables and art supplies.

Centro Ciência Viva

SCIENCE AND LEARNING FUN

Next door to the oceanarium, children can learn science in a fun way through games and immersive experiences at the Pavilhão do Conhecimento. Although most monitored rooms have activities in Portuguese only, in the Explora room, language is not a barrier. Initially designed for the San Francisco Exploratorium, this permanent exhibition has 40 interactive areas for kids (and grown-ups) to experiment on their own. Yes, touching the displays is allowed and encouraged. And staff come to the rescue in case you need assistance.

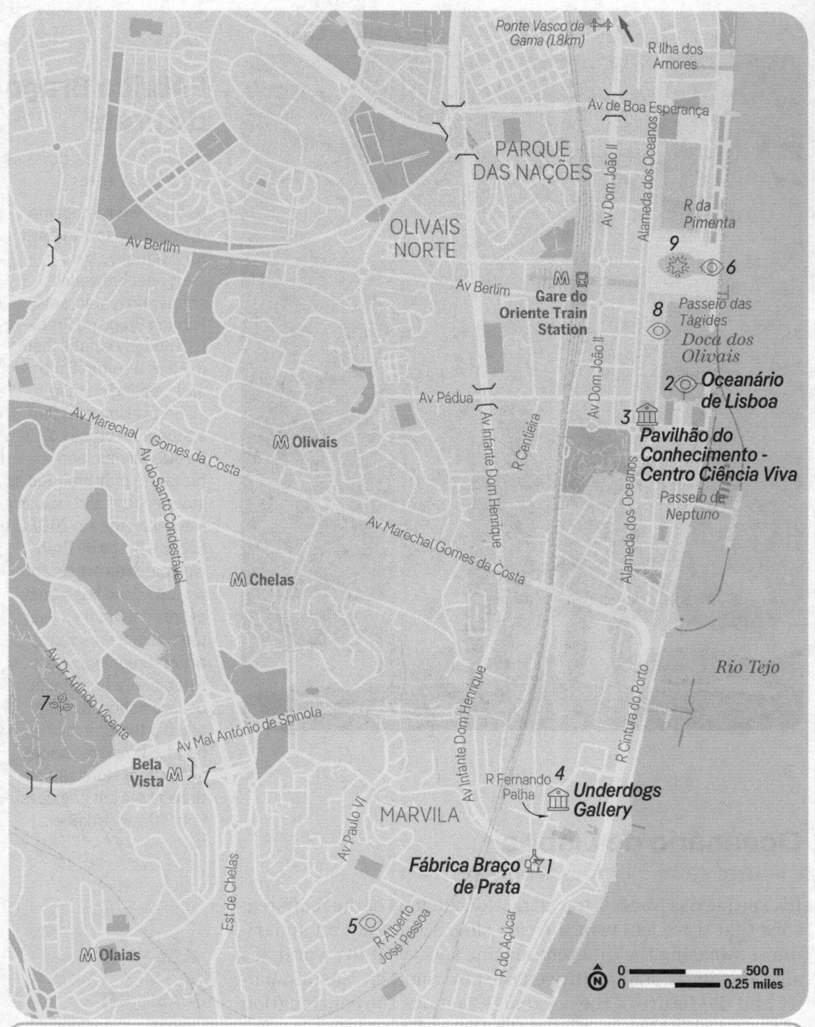

HIGHLIGHTS
1 Fábrica Braço de Prata
2 Oceanário de Lisboa
3 Pavilhão do Conhecimento – Centro Ciência Viva
4 Underdogs Gallery

SIGHTS
5 Azinhaga dos Alfinetes
6 Lago das Tágides
7 Parque da Bela Vista
8 Pavilhão de Portugal

ENTERTAINMENT
9 Altice Arena

Oceanário de Lisboa

MARTIN THOMAS PHOTOGRAPHY/ALAMY STOCK PHOTO ©

Oceanário de Lisboa

EUROPE'S SECOND-LARGEST AQUARIUM

It's Parque das Nações' top attraction and one of the main reasons that travellers visit the east side. More than an aquarium showcasing the different marine species of the world, it's also an educational facility on the environment, sustainability and the future of the oceans. In fact, it's the continuation of the mission that started at the World Expo 1998.

The main tank is at the centre of everything, as you go from one recreated natural habitat to the next, and by far the place that attracts the most crowds. Waiting for the right moment to snap that shark selfie might prove a difficult task as gleeful families approach the glass and obscure the view. The trick? Try beating the crowds to one of the benches on the side wings – the view of the tank is smaller but take those fleeting minutes of solitude to wait for the fish to swim around.

Expect to spend some time in queues during high season, although they move fast. Buying skip-the-line tickets online in advance is always the best time-saving option, particularly when travelling with small children.

Fábrica Braço de Prata

NEW MARVILA'S OLDEST CULTURAL HUB

Before Marvila became the new hot spot in town for alternative bars, craft beer breweries, shops and restaurants, Fábrica Braço de Prata had already established itself as a cultural hub and meeting point in Lisbon, taking over the abandoned offices of an old war munition factory. Firmly branded as independent and inclusive since it opened in 2007, Fábrica Braço de Prata welcomes all artists and art forms and has a busy events calendar all year long. Come for a show, a film screening, an art exhibition, a book launch or a workshop; browse and flip through the hundreds of used books at the bookstore; grab a drink at the bar or extend your stay with dinner.

CABLE CAR

Get the combined ticket to Oceanário that includes a round trip on the nearby cable car. From the *teleférico* you can see the Ponte Vasco da Gama stretching wide over the Rio Tejo. Use it to cut the cross-park trip short between Oceanário and Torre Vasco da Gama.

Oriente train station

ORIENTE STATION, ARCHITECT SANTIAGO CALATRAVA. GTW/SHUTTERSTOCK ©

MORE IN PARQUE DAS NAÇÕES & MARVILA

Contemporary Architecture Tour

A SELF-GUIDED TOUR OF THE HIGHLIGHTS

For contemporary architecture and urban art enthusiasts, Parque das Nações is an open-air museum. Following the ocean theme of World Expo 1998, most of the pieces and buildings in the urban park pay tribute to the Portuguese navigators (hence the profusion of the name Vasco da Gama everywhere), life at sea and mythical marine creatures.

In a little under 1½ hours, you can walk around the park to see the highlights, starting at Santiago Calatrava's **Oriente train station** – the iron and glass structure mimics a forest of trees, or maybe underwater plants (it's open to interpretation). Then, across the street, instead of entering Vasco da Gama shopping centre, walk around the right side of the building and turn right at Alameda dos Oceanos towards the oceanarium. Here you'll see three Portuguese creations: Carrilho da Graça's award-winning **Pavilhão do Conhecimento** (known as Centro Ciência Viva now), Siza Vieira's

WORLD EXPO 1998

For four months in 1998, all roads in Portugal led to the newly renovated Parque das Nações (previously a 1940s hydro port that had become an industrial wasteland used as storage). The theme was 'The Oceans: A Heritage for the Future', and 143 countries showcased their best exhibits at the individual pavilions that stretched across the urban park. People travelled from far and didn't mind queueing for hours in the sun for a chance to attend the event that was the talk of the town at that time.

WHERE TO GRAB A BEER IN MARVILA

Fábrica da Musa
Come for the beer with pun-riddled names, the live music, the food or the beer garden.

Dois Corvos
An institution in Marvila, a trip to the neighbourhood isn't complete without stopping for a Dois Corvos' Regular.

Lince
Taproom and brewery share the same space at one of the first craft beer companies born in Marvila.

award-winning **Pavilhão de Portugal** (with its distinctive gravity-defying sail-shaped roof) and artist Pedro Proença's **Monstros Marinhos** made in *calçada portuguesa* (Portuguese pavement) outside Oceanário.

Two more unmissable spots are next to each other, which you can reach by walking back to Alameda dos Oceanos or taking the scenic route near the river: Regino Cruz's UFO- or turtle-shaped events venue **Altice Arena** and sculptor João Cutileiro's **Lago das Tágides**, a riverside water feature with marble statues of the mythological muses bathing. The final stop is one of the largest bridges in the world, **Ponte Vasco da Gama**.

MARVILA'S RENAISSANCE

Lower house prices and plenty of empty warehouses waiting to be repurposed turned Marvila into one of Lisbon's most coveted neighbourhoods after the city's historic centre lost part of the battle to gentrification. Known for its industrial look, street art and the Art Nouveau building featured in the film *Night Train to Lisbon*, Marvila has often been compared to New York's Brooklyn. The recent riverside building complexes will probably attract a different crowd to this once almost-forgotten quarter, made relevant again in the early 2000s by local businesses such as the Dois Corvos Craft Brewery or cultural centre Fábrica Braço de Prata (p82). As real estate prices begin to surge here, it's too soon to tell if Marvila will lose its underground edge.

See Street Art in Marvila

PERMANENT DISPLAY OF URBAN ART

Most pieces of street art fade over time, are covered by a fresh coat of thick white paint or are taken over by someone who doesn't understand the urban artists' code of conduct. But there is one spot in Marvila where art is on permanent display: the **Azinhaga dos Alfinetes** neighbourhood.

The blocks of apartments hosted 2017's edition of **Festival MURO** (Lisbon's street art festival), and 15 buildings were used as blank canvases by artists that included Lisbon's The Caver, Brazilian Eduardo Kobra, and Portuguese artist Kruella D'Enfer, born in Tondela. Find it a five-minute walk from Marvila train station or a 10-minute walk from 728 bus stop at Rua do Açúcar.

Relax or Dance at Parque da Bela Vista

MARVILA'S URBAN PARK

A neighbourhood park for exercising, relaxing or family picnics most of the year, Parque da Bela Vista is also one of Lisbon's top open-air venues for summer festivals. Well-known **Rock in Rio Lisboa** takes over Bela Vista every two years (the next edition is in 2024) for two weekends of a star-studded line-up. But since 2022 there's a new kid in town. **MEO Kalorama** would like to become Lisbon's last summer festival of the year, closing the events season in the first week of September with an eclectic line-up ranging from electronic music to indie rock.

WHERE TO GRAB A BEER IN PARQUE DAS NAÇÕES

Esplanando
Laid-back cafe that turned the Portuguese people's penchant for lounging at an esplanada into a verb (and an attitude).

Já Te Disse
No-frills, cheap, open-until-late cafe and bar with outside seating across the street from the marina.

Fábrica Oitava Colina
Craft beer brewery and taproom with a rooftop bar, a short drive from the marina. Serves light food and snacks.

MARQUÊS DE POMBAL & AVENIDAS NOVAS

URBAN PARKS AND ART MUSEUMS

At the end of the 19th century, as the Lisbon population increased during industrialisation, the city expanded to the north of the Marquês de Pombal statue. The new neighbourhood was called Avenidas Novas (new avenues) because of its planned streets and building blocks, with squares and green areas for optimal neighbourhood life.

Mobility is good here, and you're never far from restaurants, shops and supermarkets – most within a 10-minute walk from one another. This part of the city never feels rushed or crowded. And if it does, the nearest park or quiet street is never far away.

Between this flat, easy-to-navigate area and Baixa sits the Marquês de Pombal roundabout, truly marking the heart of the city.

TOP TIP

This area is served by three Metro lines (main stops are São Sebastião, Saldanha, Campo Pequeno, Entrecampos and Campo Grande), suburban and long-distance trains, and frequent buses. Mostly flat and with wide avenues, it's easy to explore on foot.

Igreja de Nossa Senhora do Rosário de Fátima

Igreja de Nossa Senhora do Rosário de Fátima

1930S MODERNIST-STYLE CHURCH

A little of modernist Almada Negreiros' art can be found all over Lisbon, but one of the most surprising and lesser-known places is this church, designed by Pardal Monteiro, near the Calouste Gulbenkian Foundation. Built in the 1930s, this Catholic temple features the artist's stained-glass windows and mosaics. Enjoy the calming atmosphere surrounded by the works of some of the most accomplished artists of the same period, including Barata Feyo's *Christ on the Cross*. The church is open to all visitors for free but be mindful of ongoing religious services.

Parque Gonçalo Ribeiro Telles

EYESORE TURNED GREEN HAVEN

Praça de Espanha has had many incarnations, but after decades of being a place of heavy traffic and a public transit hub, it's now Lisbon's newest park. This green haven is named after Gonçalo Ribeiro Telles, who designed the nearby gardens at Gulbenkian Foundation and sadly passed away before he could see this one come to life. The only thing that remains from this area's previous life is the São Bento Arch – still a centrepiece of the roundabout-turned-garden but finally within reach of passers-by.

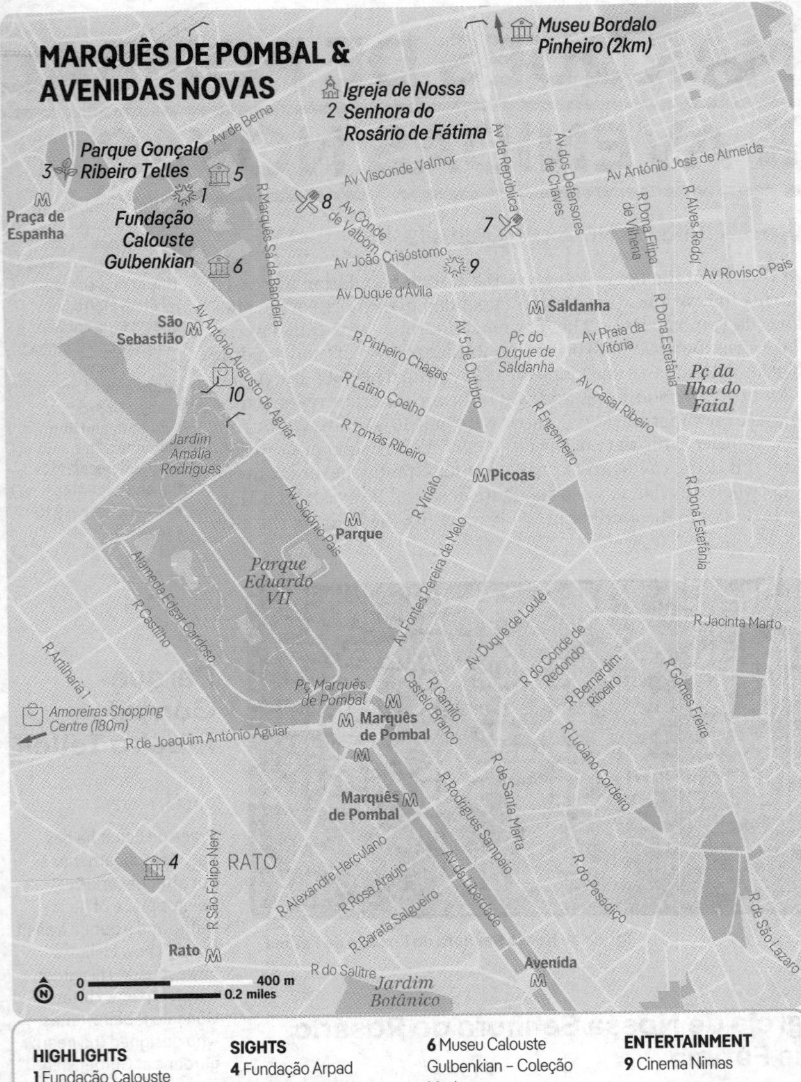

HIGHLIGHTS
1 Fundação Calouste Gulbenkian
2 Igreja de Nossa Senhora do Rosário de Fátima
3 Parque Gonçalo Ribeiro Telles

SIGHTS
4 Fundação Arpad Szenes-Vieira da Silva
5 Museu Calouste Gulbenkian – Coleção do Fundador
6 Museu Calouste Gulbenkian – Coleção Moderna

EATING
7 Choupana Caffé
8 Laurentina

ENTERTAINMENT
9 Cinema Nimas

SHOPPING
10 El Corte Inglés

Cafe, Gulbenkian Gardens

TOP RIGHT: GULBENKIAN, ARCHITECTS RUY JERVIS D'ATHOUGUIA, PEDRO CID AND ALBERTO PESSOA STOCKPHOTOSART/SHUTTERSTOCK © BOTTOM LEFT: SERGIO NOGUEIRA/ALAMY STOCK PHOTO ©

Museu Bordalo Pinheiro

THE FATHER OF PORTUGUESE COMICS

Rafael Bordalo Pinheiro is a lot more than the 19th-century Realist artist who designed vegetable-inspired tableware – although his cabbage-looking dishes and salad bowls are perhaps his most popular creations, alongside his Zé Povinho (a caricature of the Portuguese of that time, poor and resigned to their fate). He was also a cartoonist, a journalist, an illustrator and a ceramist. Visit the two-floor museum at Campo Grande to discover his early life as a satirist.

Ceramic plate by Rafael Bordalo Pinhaeiro

Fundação Calouste Gulbenkian

CULTURAL HUB AND URBAN PARK

Known for its mid-century-style gardens and buildings, the Calouste Gulbenkian Foundation is a cultural hub that *lisboetas* hold dear. Both of its museums, the **Foundation Museum** and the **Modern Art Museum**, have Portugal's most extensive and most important art collection, comprising pieces that Armenian-born Calouste Gulbenkian gathered in his lifetime. His goal, which remains the foundation's mission, was to support culture and the arts and provide easy-to-access education opportunities through scholarships and projects like the vans-turned-mobile-libraries that brought free books to isolated villages in Portugal, every two weeks, from the late 1950s to the early 1990s.

The surrounding Gulbenkian Gardens offer a cool summer breeze and a surprisingly cosy atmosphere in the colder weather, frequented mainly by families and students on their breaks from class at nearby universities and high schools. Used to humans, the park's waddling ducks will sometimes pester people for a few breadcrumbs (although feeding them is forbidden), but they mostly keep to themselves.

In addition to concerts and other events at the auditorium indoors, the outdoor amphitheatre is reserved for the recurrent, month-long live music event **Jazz em Agosto** in the summer. When no shows are scheduled the rest of the year, park users take over the stone seats to read, work or simply relax.

BEST INDIE BOOKSHOPS

Under the Cover
A curated selection of national and international magazines lines the walls of this small bookshop, right across the street from Gulbenkian.

Photo Book Corner
In 2020 this shop specialising in selling photography books online moved to the tiny space next door to Under the Cover.

Livraria Miosótis
This child- and pet-friendly bookshop near Arco do Cego sells new and used books from independent publishers, in several languages.

ALESSANDRO AVONDO/ALAMY STOCK PHOTO ©

Amoreiras 360 Panoramic View

MORE IN MARQUÊS DE POMBAL & AVENIDAS NOVAS

Head Out for Dinner & a Movie

FILMS FOR EVERYONE, POPCORN OPTIONAL

Two cinemas are within a short walking distance from one another in the Avenidas Novas neighbourhood. And, despite the geographical proximity, they cater to very different audiences. Dinner and a movie is the most local-feeling experience you can have here. All foreign films in Portugal are subtitled, not dubbed. Kids' movies are released with both options.

Cinema Nimas, owned by Portuguese film producer Paulo Branco, is a Lisbon institution. Focusing more on curated cycles dedicated to a specific director or a genre, this one-room theatre at Avenida 5 de Outubro is the place to go for the classics you haven't seen on the big screen yet or in a long time. Car-free **Avenida Duque d' Ávila** nearby has plenty of affordable Portuguese chain restaurants to choose

WHERE TO STAY NEAR AVENIDAS NOVAS

White Hotel Lisboa
Central boutique bed and breakfast with rooftop pool at Avenida da República. **€€€**

Evolution Lisboa
Brightly coloured design hotel in Saldanha with late check-out options available. **€€€**

Jupiter Lisboa
Four-star hotel near Campo Pequeno with 24/7 room service and babysitting services upon request. **€€€**

from, but if you want something more traditional, head to **Laurentina** (it specialises in *bacalhau*) at Avenida Conde Valbom.

The **El Corte Inglés** department store near Gulbenkian offers an all-in-one solution: rooftop terrace and chef-owned Portuguese restaurants on the top floor (including José Avillez's **Tasca Chic** and **Jacaré**, Henrique Sá Pessoa's **Balcão**, and Chef Kiko's **O Poke**), high-end shopping (everything from clothes and accessories to kitchen appliances and linens) and the largest selection of international films in the neighbourhood.

If you're in town in October, **Culturgest** in Campo Pequeno hosts **DocLisboa**, Lisbon's independent documentary film festival.

Explore Amoreiras

DETOUR OFF MARQUÊS DE POMBAL

Reserve one morning of your stay for a visit to **Amoreiras**. This upscale residential neighbourhood is less than a 20-minute walk (1.2km) up the street from **Parque Eduardo VII**, the carefully manicured mid-century park most famous for being the venue of recurring yearly events like the Lisbon Book Fair.

Start with the urban art wall near the shopping centre, known simply as **Muro das Amoreiras** since the 1990s. The 750-sq-metre wall – once a well-known spot for illegal spraying – welcomed the first commissioned pieces in 2017 (an event called Graffiti in Amoreiras). The wall is repainted white from time to time to welcome new works. After you've appreciated the local street artists, head to **Amoreiras 360 Panoramic View**, the paid viewpoint on the shopping centre's terrace from where you can see the whole of Lisbon.

A short 10-minute walk from the shopping centre is the **Fundação Arpad Szenes-Vieira da Silva** near Jardim das Amoreiras. Located at the old Lisbon silk factory, this small museum is dedicated to the life and art of Lisbon-born Vieira da Silva, Hungarian Arpad Szenes and their close friends.

A PERFECT DAY IN AVENIDAS NOVAS

Rafaela Mota Lemos, a content strategist and musician, shares how to make the best of her neighbourhood. *@rafaelamotalemos*

Where to hang out
Choupana Caffé has the best croissants in Lisbon and it's perfect for breakfast. Even though it's a noisy and busy cafe, it's also a great place for freelancers because the internet is fast. The gardens at Gulbenkian are also impeccable for a stroll while listening to a podcast.

Where to eat
We have great restaurants and cultural spaces within walking distance from one another, and I value that accessibility. Some recommended places to eat are Ararat (Armenian), UDON (Thai), Rubro (Spanish tapas) and the classic Galeto (Portuguese) – it's where *lisboetas* often go to celebrate important accomplishments.

Lumen Hotel
This hotel near Marquês de Pombal offers a daily immersive light-show experience in the garden. €€€

EPIC SANA Marquês
Five-star luxury hotel with rooftop pool near Parque Eduardo VII. €€€

WOT Lisbon Patio
Affordable hostel with private or family rooms and a spacious courtyard outside the kitchen/lounge area. €

SANTOS, MADRAGOA & ALCÂNTARA

INDUSTRIAL VIBES AND LOCAL LIFE

These three neighbourhoods have little in common except their geographical proximity and the fact that they belong to the same parish, Estrela. But there is beauty in their oddness.

Alcântara, markedly industrial and business-oriented, has a riverside quiet space for walking or cycling. And has managed to use what could be seen as the lesser appeal of rust and iron for its advantage, turning a bridge and an old factory into tourist attractions.

Santos, once known as the design district, swings between nightlife hot spot and deserted quarter without much to see, except people-watching and experiencing local life.

And, finally, Madragoa, the old quarter that doesn't show up on the map – founded in the 17th century by fishmongers who moved from Ovar near Aveiro (later known as *varinas*) and freed enslaved Africans – is one of the most underrated neighbourhoods in Lisbon.

TOP TIP

Several buses and trams serve this part of the city, but the quickest way to navigate is by taking the suburban train to Cascais from Cais do Sodré, particularly if you're going to Alcântara, the furthest from the city centre. Santos and Madragoa are best explored on foot.

Ler Devagar

LX Factory

INDUSTRIAL-STYLE BUSINESS CENTRE

This complex at the former fabrics and threads factory has been going strong since 2008. Mind the uneven cobblestones and the occasional traffic as you stroll through the industrial-looking, slightly run-down buildings housing restaurants, cafes, alternative shops, tattoo parlours, art stores and galleries, and, of course, one of the world's most beautiful bookshops, **Ler Devagar**. With the bridge over your head, rush hours are always noisier because of the traffic above, but it just takes a few minutes of getting used to.

HIGHLIGHTS
1 A Flor da Selva
2 B-MAD
3 Experiência Pilar 7
4 LX Factory
5 Museu da Marioneta
6 Museu Nacional de Arte Antiga

SIGHTS
7 Doca **de** Alcântara

DRINKING & NIGHTLIFE
8 Descarado
9 Doca de Santo
10 Dock's Club
11 Tinta nos Nervos

ENTERTAINMENT
12 A Barraca

SHOPPING
13 Ler Devagar

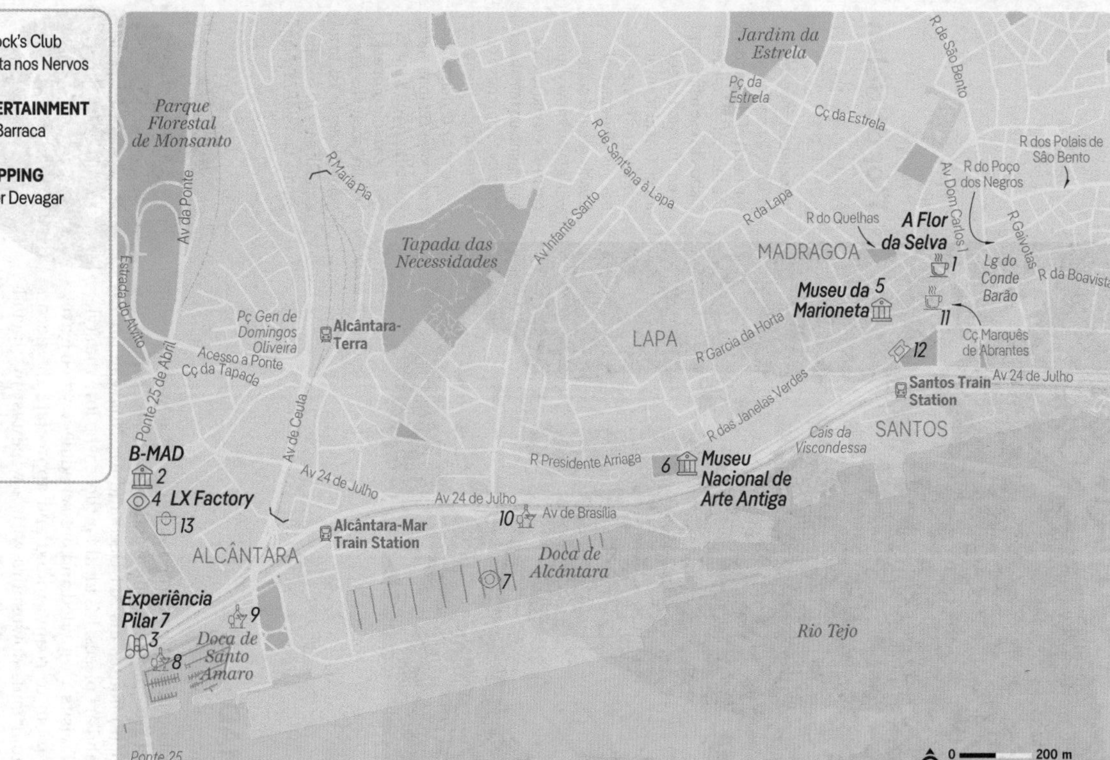

B-MAD

TOP LEFT: ILJA GENERALOV/SHUTTERSTOCK © BOTTOM RIGHT: HORACIO VILLALOBOS/GETTY IMAGES ©

Flor da Selva

FAMILY-OWNED COFFEE ROASTERS

In business since the 1950s, Flor da Selva, in the heart of Madragoa, is the last coffee roaster in Lisbon to use a firewood oven. You won't need a sign to find them at Travessa do Pasteleiro because the smell of freshly ground coffee will let you know you're close when you're only mid-climb up the street. Stop by to purchase one of their classic blends or, if you're a connoisseur, to order your custom-made favourite. If you want to see the whole process, enquire about the weekly guided tours or ask to take a sneak peek to see the production side of things.

B-MAD

ART DECO MUSEUM

Art collector and investor Joe Berardo's newest museum project (the previous one was Museu Coleção Berardo, in Belém) houses his Art Deco and Art Nouveau furniture and art pieces. It's ideal for those who love the style, but all visits are guided and pre-scheduled, which leaves little room to roam around and appreciate the decor. The tour ends downstairs with a wine tasting (included in the ticket price but optional), provided by Berardo's Setúbal-based wine estate Bacalhôa. Expect a sales pitch as you sip your samples in the interior courtyard and your guide explains the nuances of each one of the three wines (white, red and Moscatel).

Experiência Pilar 7

PONTE 25 DE ABRIL

There was a time when most travellers who visited Alcântara were either on their way back from Belém and did a quick pit stop at LX Factory, or were heading to the bars at the docks. Then a viewpoint opened at the top of the bridge's seventh pillar, Pilar 7, and the neighbourhood had a new attraction worth a visit. While engineering enthusiasts will appreciate the interactive exhibition on the history of the Ponte 25 de Abril, most rush through it on their way to the top to view Lisbon's industrial quarter, the river and Belém.

TOP RIGHT: AMNAT30/SHUTTERSTOCK © BOTTOM LEFT: MITRELIS/SHUTTERSTOCK ©

Pilar 7

Museu da Marioneta

THE ART OF PUPPETRY

Compact and cosy, the puppet museum at Convento das Bernardas is one of the lisboeta families' favourite places. Great to keep kids entertained for an hour on a rainy morning or scorching summer afternoon. The collection is relatively small but diverse and includes Asian and African masks, Punch & Judy and Sicilian puppets, theatre props, and typical Portuguese-made marionettes like the 18th-century Bonecos de Santo Aleixo. Museu da Marioneta also pays tribute to local artists and puppet companies with permanent exhibitions of their life work.

Museu da Marioneta

Museu Nacional de Arte Antiga

LISBON'S FIRST ART MUSEUM

With a collection of nearly 40,000 pieces, MNAA has been in the same building, Palácio Alvor, since it opened in 1884. The three floors of primarily Portuguese paintings, ceramics, jewellery and sculptures demand the visitor's full attention. One can rush through the 'top' artworks in one hour – the *Painéis de São Vicente* (under restoration until mid-2023) and Hieronymus Bosch's *Temptations of Saint Anthony*, to name a couple – but a thorough walk through all the rooms can easily take up an entire morning. Known for finding new ways to showcase its collection, the museum's latest installment is the nine-video series *In Our Care* released on MNAA's Facebook page, where museum keepers talk about their favourite masterpieces.

THE SPIRIT OF MADRAGOA

João Medeiros choreographed 2022's winning *marcha popular* 'Para Sempre Madragoa' (Forever Madragoa). He tells us what's to love about Madragoa. *@marchadamadragoa @__joao_medeiros__*

Unlike the other historic quarters of Lisbon, and despite the tourism boom, Madragoa is still a small neighbourhood where everybody knows each other. At the end of the day, people gather at the cafes while the kids play in the street. I like to see tourists in my neighbourhood, the cultural exchange and the different points of view. That's the spirit immortalised in the theme of the *marcha*: how Madragoa marks you forever and you always carry it in your heart.

Mila

MORE IN SANTOS, MADRAGOA & ALCÂNTARA

Strolling Rua da Esperança

THE SPIRIT OF MADRAGOA IN ONE STREET

Can the spirit of a neighbourhood that is so tough to pinpoint on a smartphone map be encapsulated in just one street? Folks who live in Madragoa seem to think so, and they'll probably point you in the direction of **Rua da Esperança**.

It makes no difference where in the street you start your stroll because it's the sensory experience that matters, but for clarity, consider the bottom of the street, between the water fountain (right) and the tiny park (left), as your starting point. On your way up, you'll notice how Madragoa embraces the new businesses as well as the more classical and well-established ones (and this is the neighbourly environment that permeates the whole quarter).

There's Instagrammable cafe and healthy food spot **Fauna e Flora**, independent bookshop **Tinta nos Nervos**, and secondhand clothes shop **Reuse**. But typical spots such as **Museu da Marioneta** (p93), a puppet museum, traditional

WHERE TO HAVE BRUNCH IN SANTOS, MADRAGOA & ALCÂNTARA

Fauna e Flora
Picture-perfect, no-filter-needed, healthy food cafe on Rua da Esperança with vegan and vegetarian options. €€

Dede's
Australian-owned cafe, a 10-minute walk from Museu da Marioneta, serves speciality coffee and all-day brunch. €€

Mila
At this cafe in Santos, you can transition from all-day breakfast and brunch to evening cocktails. €

restaurants like **O Tachadas** and **O Caldo Verde**, and small groceries and convenience stores owned by migrants also line the street. And all of that is Madragoa.

Have a Drink at Docas

ALCÂNTARA'S CLASSIC NIGHTLIFE SPOT

Like most of Lisbon, **Doca de Alcântara** (known to locals as just Docas) has reinvented itself over the years, attracting different styles of customers. **Descarado** for drinks and live DJ sets, **Dock's Club** for dancing (whatever your style, there's room for you on the dance floor) and **Doca de Santo** for a late dinner are still on the list of many locals' recommendations list.

There is nothing wrong with heading to the places locals know best, but you can also browse this riverside pier until you find something that piques your interest. Drinks at sunset from anywhere in Docas is never a bad deal.

Mingle with the Residents

THE NEIGHBOURHOOD'S CULTURAL HUBS

Lisbon's old quarters are full of small neighbourhood associations called *coletividades*. Here members meet for coffee, drinks or a game of cards, or, when the time comes, to rehearse the next *marcha popular,* the colourful and musical groups that parade down Avenida da Liberdade in mid-June for the popular saints' celebrations, *santos populares* (p74).

Once a cultural and educational hub for the neighbourhood's residents, some of these clubs have disappeared as gentrification and high rents have taken over the historic centre, making it impossible for the *coletividades* to survive. But it's different in Madragoa, and **Esperança Atlético Clube** has kept its doors open not only for members but for anyone who wants to hang out.

As the headquarters of the winning 2022 *marcha popular* (the last win for Madragoa had been almost 30 years before, with Alfama taking the first prize practically every year since), you can also learn more about that piece of local history. The language might be a barrier, but there are always ways to communicate.

Independent theatre **A Barraca** in Santos is the other cultural beacon in the neighbourhood. The bar on the top floor frequently hosts live music concerts and poetry readings.

MOCAMBO

There are no visible signs that reveal the 16th-century name of Madragoa: *mocambo* (the word for small village in Umbundu, one of the languages spoken in Angola). Formerly enslaved Africans were allowed to live here, have a house (but probably not own one) and engage in activities that marked their cultural identity. Lisbon's history is frequently whitewashed, but recent projects like Goethe Institut's ReMapping Memories and the African-Portuguese community have worked to bring these historical facts to life for a more accurate portrayal of Portugal's capital city.

WHERE TO EAT DINNER IN SANTOS, MADRAGOA & ALCÂNTARA

1300 Taberna
One of the oldest restaurants at LX Factory. Traditional Portuguese food with a contemporary approach. €€€

Varina da Madragoa
Traditional restaurant in the heart of Madragoa known for its *bacalhau à Brás* (salted cod mixed with egg and chips). €€

Borogodó
This Brazilian-Portuguese fusion cafe-restaurant is excellent for laid-back dinners at LX Factory. €€

LETHICIA COELHO/SHUTTERSTOCK ©

Palácio da Pena (p104)

LISBON COAST

OCEAN VIEWS AND HERITAGE SITES

Sprawling beaches, excellent surfing conditions, picture-perfect towns, and unique art and architecture: Lisbon Coast is full of surprises.

The region we decided to call Lisbon Coast doesn't technically exist as political, perfectly designed boundaries on a map. However, each city and town on this stretch of roughly 120km of rugged rocks – bathed (ferociously, in some months) by the Atlantic Ocean and within easy reach from Portugal's capital city – have enough in common to be lumped together into one area.

Cascais and Ericeira went from small fishing villages to burgeoning resort towns for aristocrats and royals in the 18th and 19th centuries. Sintra has always been the land of romantic palaces and dramatic landscapes, where every building seems over the top, and yet the town is tranquil, too. Setúbal, industrial at its core, has a country lifestyle quality which, surprisingly, doesn't clash with its status as the capital city of the district of the same name.

Over the years, each of these destinations turned to the sea for sustenance, even before Portugal was officially a country. And while their area of business might have changed from fishing to tourism, in the early 2000s, the ocean is the constant.

Lisbon Coast is manicured romantic gardens and protected natural parks, pristine tranquil beaches and surfing hot spots, extravagant palaces and simple whitewashed houses, dramatic coastal views and cobblestone streets to lose yourself in. It's ideal for a day trip or a weekend escape, for urban explorers and outdoors enthusiasts, for solo travellers and large families.

NVPHOTO/SHUTTERSTOCK ©

THE MAIN AREAS

Ericeira, p117

Whitewashed houses with vibrant blue trimmings line the streets of the historic centre. A coveted surfing destination, it's also home to a growing expat community.

Sintra, p102

Romantic and mysterious, this Unesco World Heritage town has been inspiring artists for centuries. Lavish palaces, and their legends, hide among its evergreen hills.

Cascais, p109

Formerly a fishing village, this now posh town is home to easy-to-reach beaches, a well-known surf spot and surprising street art.

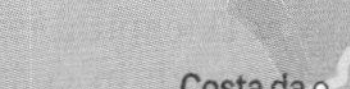

CAR

Driving is the easiest way to get around, and you can choose between fast trips on motorways (with tolls) or scenic drives by the sea or through the mountains. Parking might be difficult in historical centres.

BUS

Mafrense operates the urban buses to and from Ericeira (via Mafra). They depart from Campo Grande in Lisbon (near the Metro station). In Sintra and Cascais, frequent city buses connect several points of interest.

TRAIN

Sintra, Cascais and Setúbal are within easy reach by train from Lisbon. They're served by different lines so keep in mind that you won't be able to travel by train between them. There is no railway connecting Lisbon to Ericeira.

0 — 10 km
0 — 5 miles

Find Your Way

Considering the number of things to see, the winding roads that connect them, and the wealth of local heritage, allow at least a couple of days to visit all four destinations on the Lisbon Coast.

Setúbal, p123

Embraced by the ocean and the mountain, this southern post-industrial city has become a vibrant cultural travel destination in recent years.

Plan Your Time

Approach Lisbon Coast as a series of day trips but expect (and embrace) surprises and the unexpected. Sintra, Cascais, Ericeira and Setúbal aren't destinations to see in a hurry.

TRABANTOS/SHUTTERSTOCK ©

Quinta da Regaleira (p105)

If You Only Have One Day

- Catch an early train to **Sintra** (p102) and, from the town's train station, hop on the bus to head straight to **Palácio da Pena** (p104) and **Castelo dos Mouros** (p104). Both sites can take up a whole morning to visit thoroughly.

- Walk to the historical centre (approximately 1km downhill) and grab a snack or a coffee and a *travesseiro* at **Casa Piriquita** (p103). Spend the afternoon exploring the mystical **Quinta da Regaleira** (p105) and the **Palácio Biester** (p105) next door. Head back to the train station on foot for one last look at the Unesco World Heritage town.

Seasonal highlights

Spring, autumn and winter are balmy and welcoming for outdoor activities. Summer's long hot days call for time at the beach, sunrise to sunset. Sintra and Ericeira can be pretty unpredictable weather-wise.

FEBRUARY

Carnaval (Mardi Gras) is celebrated nationwide. For traditional celebrations, head to Sesimbra, near Setúbal.

MAY

Setúbal welcomes another edition of its International Music Festival. Temperatures rise, as does the need to spend time outdoors.

JUNE

On 29 June, Sintra celebrates one of the three *santos populares*, São Pedro (St Peter).

STOCKPHOTOSART/SHUTTERSTOCK ©, CÂMARA MUNICIPAL OF SETUBAL ©, MAURO RODRIGUES/SHUTTERSTOCK©

Weekend Getaway

- Spend the first day in **Cascais** (p109), slowly taking in the historical centre, the **street art murals** (p113) and the works of Paula Rego at **Casa das Histórias** (p112). Take in the atmosphere and, in the afternoon, visit **Boca do Inferno** (p112) or head to the dramatic seascapes of **Praia do Guincho** (p115).

- Next morning, drive on the scenic road N247 to **Ericeira** (p117). If you have time for detours, take a lunch break in **Azenhas do Mar** (p107). At your final destination, set off on a **walking tour of Ericeira** (p119) to take in the small coastal town.

Three Days to Explore the Coast

- On day one, take the train from Lisbon to **Setúbal** (p123) and explore the city centre, stopping for lunch at **Casa Santiago** (p123). Hop on the ferry to **Tróia** (p127) for a swim or to spend the night.

- Next day, head to Cais do Sodré in Lisbon to take the train to **Cascais** (p109) and explore the historical centre. Grab lunch at **Mercado da Vila** (p111) and then catch bus 403 to **Sintra** (p102). Hop off at **Cabo da Roca** (p108) if you have the time.

- Reserve day three for **Ericeira** (p117). Take a dip at **Praia dos Pescadores** (p117) then walk along the coast to see some historic convents and epic ocean views.

JULY
Ericeira welcomes another yearly edition of the Portuguese Surf Film Festival. Cascais hosts music festival EDP Cool Jazz.

AUGUST
Peak of beach season, school holidays and local festivities. The best time for refreshing dips. Cascais celebrates Festas do Mar.

SEPTEMBER
Back-to-school season. Expect more traffic, but less crowded sights. Setúbal celebrates local poet Bocage on 15 September.

NOVEMBER
The month for the Lisbon & Sintra Film Festival and the beginning of the surf season.

SINTRA

Mysterious and picturesque, Sintra is one of the top day-trip destinations for those visiting the Portuguese capital. This mountain-nestled town and Unesco World Heritage Site compels visitors to stay for longer than a few hours.

Famous for its microclimate, the weather here is unpredictable and often misty, but that just adds to Sintra's beauty. Plus, it explains why most of the majestic romantic palaces and the top-of-the-hill Moorish castle are shrouded in urban legends and ghost stories.

Portuguese Romantic-era writers Almeida Garrett, Alexandre Herculano and Eça de Queirós were inspired by Sintra and travelled there frequently in the 19th century. Others, including poet Lord Byron and composer Richard Strauss, were also influenced by the atmosphere and let it permeate their art. Staying at Lawrence's, a hotel that still exists today, Byron would immortalise the village in his 1812 poem 'Childe Harold's Pilgrimage'.

TOP TIP

If you're not pressed for time, hop on one of the public buses near the train station. Bus 434 covers the historic centre, Palácio da Pena and Castelo dos Mouros. Bus 435 serves the palaces of Quinta da Regaleira and nearby Biester, and Seteais.

MYTHS & LEGENDS OF SINTRA

Visit the tourism board's **Sintra Mitos & Lendas** (sintramitoselendas.pt) interactive centre near Palácio Nacional de Sintra to learn more about the region's centuries-old myths and legends. A series of touch displays, holograms and sensory experiences guide visitors through 17 information points, mixing fiction with historical facts.

An Impressive First Impression

A UNESCO WORLD HERITAGE EXPERIENCE

Catch one of the morning trains from Lisbon's Rossio station to get to Sintra. For most of the trip, the view is not that appealing – sprayed walls, stations showing significant signs of wear and tear, and the backs of apartment buildings. But, as the train starts to pull away from Portela de Sintra (the penultimate stop), you'll notice the red-and-yellow Palácio da Pena and the stone walls of Castelo dos Mouros (p104) – unless the hills of Sintra are hidden in the mist.

When you arrive, turn left towards **Volta do Duche**, the winding road (notice the **Moorish water fountain** on your left as you walk up) that takes you to the heart of the town: **Palácio Nacional de Sintra** (also known as Palácio da Vila). Take in the view from the palace steps: colourful, elaborate buildings, the forested hills behind them, and the castle on top.

Behind those buildings, there are narrow, steep staircases and streets lined with restaurants, cafes and shops. Either immerse yourself in the crowds or bypass them as you make your way to the road behind (the one that takes you up the hill and by some of the palaces).

Whether you're continuing your uphill exploration or not,

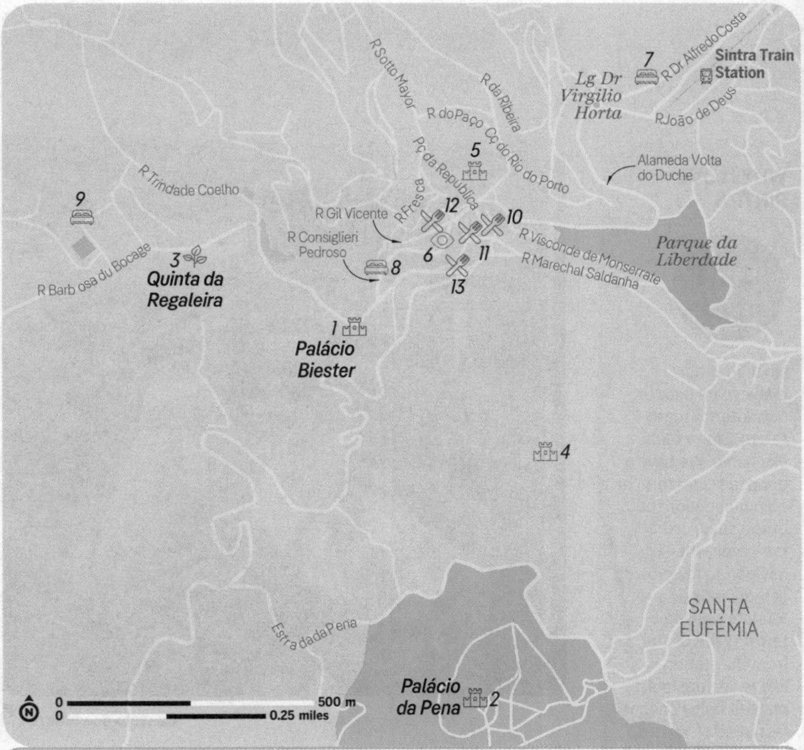

HIGHLIGHTS	SIGHTS	SLEEPING	EATING
1 Palácio Biester	**4** Castelo dos Mouros	**7** Chalet Saudade	**10** Casa Piriquita
2 Palácio da Pena	**5** Palácio Nacional de Sintra	**8** Lawrence's Hotel	**11** Piriquita II
3 Quinta da Regaleira	**6** Sintra Mitos & Lendas	**9** Tivoli Palácio de Seteais	**12** Romaria de Baco
			13 Tascantiga

stop by **Casa Piriquita** for a *travesseiro* (a cream-filled, sugar-covered pastry made with eggs and almonds).

Whatever time you think you have to stroll around town, it will never feel like enough, but expect to spend the day. Better yet, stay the night.

WHERE TO EAT IN SINTRA

Tascantiga
Snacks and finger food in a laid-back environment with an outdoor terrace in the historical centre. €€

Romaria de Baco
Traditional Portuguese restaurant, with a couple of vegetarian options, near Palácio Nacional de Sintra. €€

Piriquita II
The second location in Sintra of Casa Piriquita. Serves the same *travesseiros*, but it's often less crowded. €€

WHY I LOVE SINTRA

No matter how many years pass or how intermittently I return, Sintra feels like home. We have a bond, a secret form of communication that puts a smile on my face even when I'm navigating the crowds of mesmerised tourists walking towards the centre from the station – I like to see the look on their faces on that last bend of Volta do Duche when they see the palace, the hills and the colourful houses. Time stands still. And we are all in awe while we catch our breath.

Sandra Henriques

KRIVINIS/SHUTTERSTOCK ©

Castelo dos Mouros

Sintra's Most Famous Attractions

SEE THE CLASSICS

Rising from a thickly wooded peak and often enshrouded in swirling mist, **Palácio da Pena** is Sintra's crown jewel. Here you can easily lose track of time, admiring the gardens, the colourful architecture and each intriguing decor detail. There's a lot to take in.

Castelo dos Mouros, the 10th-century fortress, might be less visually appealing than its next-door neighbour, but don't underestimate it. Take time to explore the walls, see the views and imagine what medieval life was like here.

Walking back along the steep road that winds down the hill is part of the experience, but it can be a longer trip than

WHERE TO STAY IN SINTRA

Lawrence's Hotel
This romantic 18th-century hotel has hosted some famous guests, the most notable being Lord Byron. **€€€**

Chalet Saudade
Near Sintra train station, this three-star guesthouse is a charming traditional building surrounded by gardens. **€€**

Tivoli Palácio de Seteais
An 18th-century romantic luxury hotel just steps from Quinta da Regaleira. **€€€**

the 15 minutes you might anticipate. The walk should be done safely, before nighttime, in favourable weather (particularly if you're not used to hiking) and always taking care of traffic.

Travel to Palácio da Pena by bus and then, if you can, walk to Castelo dos Mouros. There's no magic formula to visit them thoroughly, but allow one hour to visit each site, plus another 15 minutes for travelling from one to the next. Tickets to Pena must be booked in advance.

Visit the Mystic Palaces

THE STUFF OF FOLK TALES

Within 10 minutes' walk of the historical centre, two palaces share a property wall: **Quinta da Regaleira** and **Palácio Biester**.

Regaleira needs little in the way of introduction. Compared to Dante's seven circles of hell, its legendary initiation well is everyone's first stop. Descend at your own risk, for they say the estate owner performed black magic rituals down there. Looking at it from the top makes our heads spin, so perhaps not everyone needs to experience it further. For those who prefer not to awaken any evil spirits inadvertently, there are plenty of outdoor features to explore. After all, Quinta da Regaleira is the creation of Luigi Manini, an Italian architect and set designer. Maybe not every square inch of the property has a hidden Masonic meaning or secret messages behind it.

Next door, after being left abandoned for years, Biester opened for the first time in early 2022, fully restored. Also known as the House of Witches (maybe because of its pointy black roofs; or maybe not), it was the family home of Frederico and Amélia. Legend has it that they lost their only daughter, and the couple died shortly after. Despite these skin-crawling facts, the info sheets in the rooms only mention the romantic architecture and decor.

After touring the palace, follow the steep path to the viewpoint and end your visit at the teahouse next to the greenhouses.

SINTRA IN POP CULTURE

SINtra (Escorpião Azul, 2018), a Portuguese graphic novel written by Tiago Cruz and illustrated by Inês Garcia, takes on the town's lore to create a scary tale around a mother and three daughters who turn out to be not what they seemed. The abandoned house featured in the book is real (and was built by Regaleira's former owner), the story is fictional, and the creatures are inspired by local fauna.

The 1999 horror movie *The Ninth Gate* was primarily filmed in Sintra. Many parts of the town are easily recognisable from the film, including a couple of rooms of the Palácio Biester (then a semi-abandoned property).

GETTING AROUND

The easiest way to reach Sintra is taking the 40-minute train trip from Lisbon's Rossio station. The town's centre is best explored on foot, but hop on a bus at the station for the hilltop sights. To explore the beaches and the coast, it's best to drive.

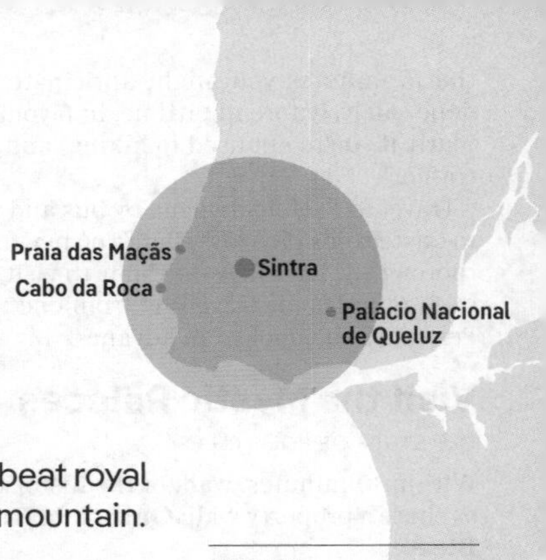

Praia das Maçãs
Sintra
Cabo da Roca
Palácio Nacional de Queluz

Beyond Sintra

North Atlantic's dramatic coast, an offbeat royal palace and the slow-paced life of the mountain.

The area surrounding Sintra is often relegated to the bottom of priorities for many travellers, who believe they have already seen all of the majestic palaces and romantic landscapes on offer. Well, they're missing out. Palácio Nacional de Queluz, a former royal palace semi-hidden behind apartment blocks in one of Sintra's suburbs, and Cabo da Roca, the westernmost edge of Portugal's mainland, with its lighthouse permanently exposed to the never-temperate North Atlantic, both have striking architecture and unpredictable but charming weather worth experiencing. But planning, patience and willpower to visit these offbeat places will be required.

TOP TIP

Travelling beyond Sintra by public transport is possible but can be sluggish out of rush hour and outside of the high season. If possible, hire a car. Ridesharing is usually more reliable during peak tourism season, but it's the luck of the draw.

Cabo da Roca (p108)

SIMON DANNHAUER/SHUTTERSTOCK ©

Praia das Maçãs

Hit the Beaches

SUN, SURF, SAND – AND WIND

Typically windy and chilly, the beaches around Sintra are best enjoyed by surfers more than folks looking for a relaxed day in the sun. Even so, a couple of them are worth the trip, even if you visit outside of beach season or don't care for a swim.

Golden-sand **Praia das Maçãs** is a local favourite, particularly with families in the summer and to have Sunday lunch at one of the restaurants with ocean views. **Azenhas do Mar**, roughly 2km further north from Maçãs, is probably the most photogenic of the two, with its clifftop houses and scenic views. The beach here, at the bottom of the cliff, is quite small, but there's also a natural saltwater pool right next to it to cool off in. A relatively easy 1.8km walking path connects Praia das Maçãs to Azenhas do Mar; it takes roughly 20 minutes to reach the village on foot.

You can get to Praia das Maçãs by car from Sintra in around 20 minutes (the easiest and fastest option) or by bus 441 (from Portela de Sintra, next to Centro Cultural Olga Cadaval). The same bus also connects Maçãs and Azenhas do Mar. From the end of March to the end of October, opt for the scenic 45-minute ride on the electric tram.

BEST SEASIDE RESTAURANTS BEYOND SINTRA

Água e Sal
Fish dishes are the speciality at this Azenhas do Mar restaurant, best enjoyed with a glass of young house wine on tap. Book ahead to grab one of the outdoor tables. €€€

Restaurante Azenhas do Mar
This restaurant perched above the saltwater pool has plenty of seafood dishes and local wines. Kids' menu available. €€

Neptuno
This wood-panelled restaurant at Praia das Maçãs is a local classic, best known for its simply seasoned catch-of-the-day dishes. €€

WHERE TO STAY NEAR SINTRA

Pousada Palácio de Queluz
Expect high ceilings and a royal feeling at this historical hotel across the street from Palácio Nacional de Queluz. **€€€**

Penha Longa Resort
Luxury hotel with eight restaurants and a golf course, a 15-minute drive from Sintra. **€€€**

O Moinho da Roca
Windmill turned guesthouse with breakfast included, a five-minute drive from Cabo da Roca. **€**

Visit Palácio Nacional de Queluz

A LUXURIOUS ROYAL RESIDENCE

The azure-and-white **Palácio Nacional de Queluz** is the official house of three generations of Portuguese royalty.

Upon entry, two grand ballroom-style lounges, with floor-to-ceiling mirrors and dramatic chandeliers, but no furniture, set the tone for what you are about to encounter. The information sheet on each room is in Portuguese only, so make sure you grab an audio guide when purchasing your ticket.

As expected from an 18th-century palace, all that glitters is gold, and each square inch of wall is covered in frescoes and gold-plated wood moulds. There are two rooms, though, that are worth more of your attention: the **Ambassadors Room** (notice the ceiling fresco in the centre, portraying the royal family at a concert) and the **Picnic Room** (each detail points to the room's purpose, including the honeycomb shapes in the ceiling).

After you've tallied up all the decor idiosyncrasies of the palace, a tiled corridor depicting mythological scenes and the seasons leads you to the gardens – planned and designed like a romantic private park, with manicured hedges, lakes and marble statues.

It takes 20 minutes by train from Sintra and a 10-minute walk from the Queluz-Belas station, via the Felício Loureiro park, to reach the palace.

COLARES WINE REGION

In the Colares wine region, the sandy soils and proximity to the Atlantic combine to produce robust, bitter reds from a local grape called Ramisco. It might not be a wine for all palates (expect a coarse aftertaste and dry mouth), but the once-niche production has recently grown in popularity. Chef Gordon Ramsay's visit in 2021 for his show *Uncharted* may have given it a push, or simply shed a light on a wine familiar to Colares locals.

Check out Cabo da Roca

EUROPE'S WESTERNMOST POINT

Wild and wonderful **Cabo da Roca** (Rock Cape) is a sheer 150m cliff, facing the roaring sea, 18km west of Sintra. It's mainland Europe's westernmost point and a terrific sunset spot. It doesn't matter in which season you visit – the famous Sintra microclimate is almost always intense here. Prepare for a cold breeze that can quickly turn into a fierce wind.

Once you arrive skip the lighthouse (although it makes for a great photo op, it's usually where everyone heads first; check before your trip to see if it's open to visitors) and head straight to the cross that marks the spot: you have officially reached the westernmost point of mainland Europe. There will likely be crowds, but wait for them to clear and enjoy the view, salt in the hair and all. Weather permitting, of course.

The best way to reach Cabo da Roca is to take bus 403 from the Sintra train station (the one that says Cascais; not all buses go via Cabo da Roca, so check with the driver when boarding). The journey takes around 40 minutes along a winding road with close to a dozen stops – but it's not even a nuisance once you take in the mountain and sea views and the charming villages with colourfully painted bus stops.

GARDEN ROUTE

The European Historic Gardens Route includes the Palácio Nacional de Queluz, the parks of Monserrate and Pena in Sintra andthe gardens of the Gulbenkian Foundation in Lisbon.

GETTING AROUND

Hiring a car is the best way of getting around Greater Sintra. Buses are available but are scarce and sometimes follow irregular schedules outside rush hour.

CASCAIS

A fishing village turned town in the 14th century by royal decree, Cascais would grow and, six centuries later, attract the Portuguese and foreign aristocratic elites who flocked to this seaside place for the summer, following the example set by the Portuguese royal family. Part of that mixed past explains the contrasts: seaside manors (some turned into hotels), family-owned traditional restaurants, urban art murals, and carefully curated galleries and museums.

At the end of the Cascais Line, the proximity to Lisbon by train makes it one of the top beach destinations in the summer, with a patch of sand for every taste. With that popularity comes crowded beaches, but for most visitors, it's worth the hassle. Perfect waves for surfers, laid-back urban beaches, monuments and Roman ruins, sprawling parks and natural wonders to entertain the kids, picturesque lighthouses and grand mansions for the image-perfect memory all await.

TOP TIP

If you have the time, get off the train in Monte Estoril, the last-but-one stop, and head to the coastal walking path. It's roughly a 15-minute walk (1.3km) to Cascais alongside beaches, bars and cafes, and picture-worthy manors.

Explore Cascais' Historic Centre

TAKE IN ALL THE CONTRASTS

The Cascais experience starts at the trip from Cais do Sodré, especially if you're lucky to get one of the window seats on the left side of the train carriage: from Belém onwards, you'll get river and sea views for most of the journey.

From Cascais train station, it's less than a five-minute walk to **Santini** on Avenida Valbom. Cascais' artisanal ice cream shop, established in 1949 by an Italian immigrant, is a classic stop unless it's too early in the day for a double scoop in a waffle cone (it doesn't open before 2pm).

A short walk from here, notice the wavy B&W pattern of the *calçada portuguesa* (cobblestone pavement) on your left. You're at the heart of the historic centre, with its narrow winding streets, small shops and diverse selection of restaurants. Follow the scent of spices to **Rua Frederico Arouca** if you're feeling like Indian food, or head to Rua da Misericórdia for a drink with a view at the **House of Wonders** rooftop bar.

ROMAN RUINS

Blink and you might miss the Roman ruins in Cascais' historical centre. At Rua Marques Leal Pancada, near Museu da Vila, a glass structure encloses the remains of a 1st-century tank, most likely linked to the fishing industry. The remains of a Roman villa can also be visited in Freiria, a village about 20 minutes by car from Cascais.

WHERE TO STAY IN CASCAIS

Villa Cascais
A four-star boutique hotel in a 19th-century restored manor, with views of Cascais bay. **€€€**

Pestana Cidadela Cascais
Luxury hotel in the Cidadela Art District, near art galleries, cafes and restaurants. **€€€**

Cascais Boutique Hostel
Affordable five-room accommodation with two shared bathrooms near the Museum Quarter. **€**

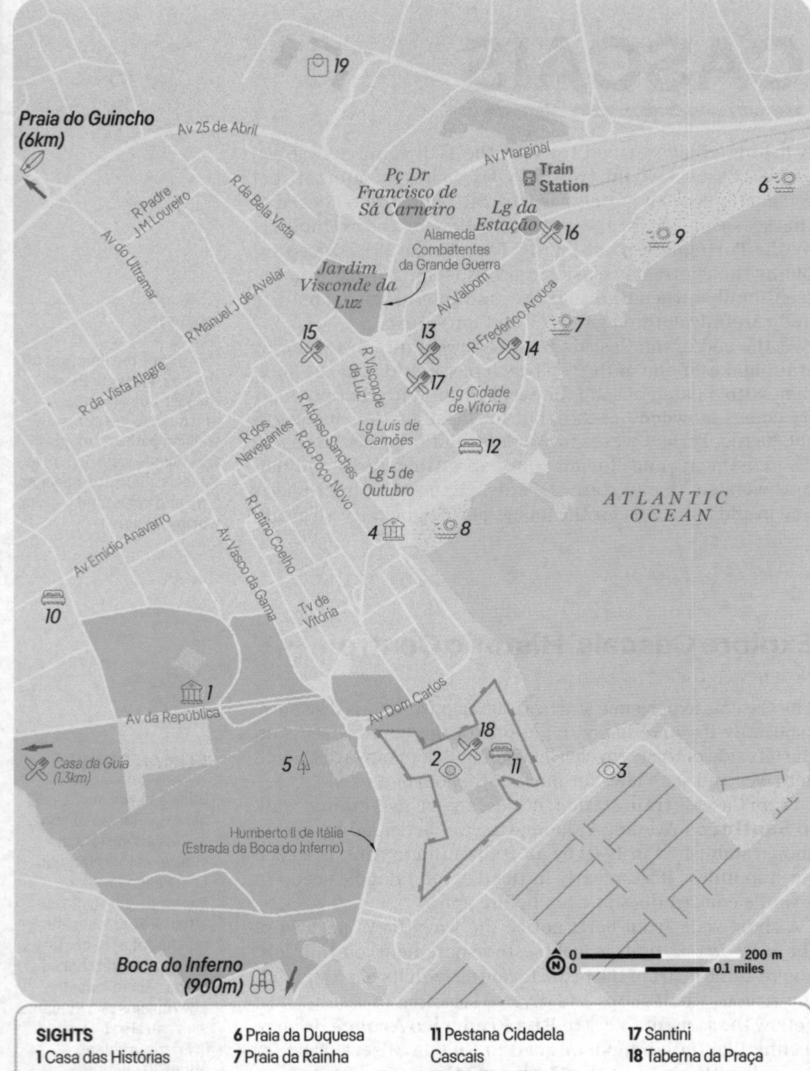

SIGHTS
1 Casa das Histórias Paula Rego
2 Cidadela Art District
3 Marina de Cascais
4 Museu da Vila
5 Parque Marechal Carmona
6 Praia da Duquesa
7 Praia da Rainha
8 Praia da Ribeira
9 Praia da Ribeira de Cascais

SLEEPING
10 Cascais Boutique Hostel
11 Pestana Cidadela Cascais
12 Villa Cascais

EATING
13 Cantinho do Avillez
14 House of Wonders
15 Moules & Gin
16 Roots Cafe
17 Santini
18 Taberna da Praça

SHOPPING
19 Mercado da Vila

GIANCARLO LIGUORI/SHUTTERSTOCK ©

Central Cascais

SEASIDE MANORS

In the 19th century, wealthy Portuguese families began to choose Cascais as their summer destination, which meant an increased need for proper homes for the season. Most of the seaside manors along the shore between Cascais and Estoril were designed by architect Raul Lino. **Visit Cascais** (visitcascais.com), the local tourism office, developed a self-guided 5km walking tour through Lino's houses; the Rota Raul Lino is available to download online.

Walk down **Rua das Flores** until you see the ocean. Two possible paths unfold: the one on the left takes you to one of three beaches: **Praia da Rainha**, **Praia da Ribeira de Cascais** and **Praia da Duquesa**; the one on the right takes you to the not-very-big patch of sand known as **Praia da Ribeira**. Which is the best option is down to luck, influenced by many factors including the day of the week and the season (weekends, national holidays and summers are always busier).

At Praça 5 de Outubro, visit **Museu da Vila** to learn more about the town's history or continue along Passeio de Dom Luis I, walking by the ocean. Passeio de Dona Maria Pia takes you straight to the **Marina de Cascais**, but before that, take a left to visit **Cidadela Art District**. Owned and renovated by Grupo Pestana, the former fortress is now a quiet quarter with an artistic vibe and a clean-looking style. At the complex, you'll find art galleries, restaurants and cafes, and two independent bookshops. **Déjà Lu** is a not-for-profit bookshop that sells secondhand books and donates 100% of its profits to local organisations who work with people with Down syndrome). **INDIE, not a bookshop** is, in fact, a bookshop,

WHERE TO EAT IN CASCAIS

Moules & Gin
The name says it all: they serve mussels (*moules*, in French) and gin. Five minutes' walk from the train station. **€€**

Casa da Guia
An iconic house and food court in Cascais, with several restaurants and cafes near the road to Guincho. **€€**

Mercado da Vila
The town's market food court features several local chef-owned restaurants; near the bus terminal. **€€**

BEST DESTINATION FOR GOLF

Along with Estoril and Sintra, Cascais is part of the **Lisbon Golf Coast**, recognised twice as the best golf destination in Europe. Before the awards, though, golf had been a pretext to visit for decades. Oitavos Dunes and Quinta da Marinha are the two golf courses in Cascais.

ALEXANDRE ROTENBERG/SHUTTERSTOCK ©

Casa das Histórias

despite the name, and it's the place where you'll probably find that book that you didn't know you were looking for until you walked in.

If you take a rain check on the marina and continue along Avenida Dom Carlos I to your left, **Boca do Inferno** is a 20-minute walk away (1.6km). It's Cascais' most famous natural attraction, but the pounding waves people expect to see as advertised are dependent on the ideal weather conditions, most common in the winters when the sea is rougher. But the view is worth it all year long.

Discover the Art of Paula Rego

UMISSABLE MUSEUM QUARTER SPOT

The first attraction is the building that houses the art of Portuguese-born, London-based Paula Rego. The terracotta-coloured pyramids are hard to miss – designed by Portuguese architect Eduardo Souto de Moura.

Most of the works on display (the exhibitions rotate every six months) were donated by the artist herself; others are

WHERE TO EAT IN CASCAIS

Roots Cafe & Pizzeria
This restaurant near Cascais train station serves snacks and healthy dishes, with vegetarian options. €

Cantinho do Avillez
The fourth restaurant of Cascais-born chef José Avillez serves travel-influenced Portuguese cuisine. €€€

Taberna da Praça
Laid-back atmosphere, Portuguese *petiscos* (tapas) and wine by the glass in the Cidadela Art District. €€

part of private collections. Whatever the theme of the ongoing showcase, the goal is to take visitors on a journey through the artist's work (and life, by osmosis) – a career spanning close to 60 years, from the early 1960s until her passing at the age of 87, in 2022.

Like Rego herself, her art is unapologetically feminist, and pro-women's and abortion rights, and most of her pieces are raw, leaving you with a punch-in-the-gut sensation. At **Casa das Histórias** – literally House of Stories – the feel is more of an art gallery than an overly explanatory museum, with plenty of space to get close to each piece and attempt a personal interpretation. A secondary wing of the museum is reserved for the work of other artists whose lives somehow crossed paths with Paula Rego's, personally or professionally.

If you need a breather from some of Rego's pieces after the tour, take a stroll through **Parque Marechal Carmona**, a gated park across the street from the museum, with a lake and a few hiking paths.

Find Street Art in an Unlikely Place

CASCAIS' SURPRISING URBAN ART SCENE

Street art may not be the first thing that comes to mind when you think of Cascais. But for a few years, somewhat regularly, the local government, in partnership with Mistaker maker (a platform for artistic intervention), organised an event to promote and showcase street art called MURALIZA (a play on the words wall, *muro*, and moralise, *moralisa*), which ran consistently until 2017.

Although the event hasn't happened since then, the pieces by Portuguese artists remain scattered around town, mostly intact. You can easily find some of those works in the historic centre, not too far from the train station.

At **Travessa dos Navegantes**, you'll see a remarkable piece depicting some Cascais classic locations painted by Exes, although it's covered by ivy and rundown since its creation in 2014. Across the street, there's a smaller and newer piece (2022) depicting the typical *azulejos* (blue-and-white tiles), mismatched, like a genuinely Portuguese facade, made by Cascais local artist Add Fuel.

Also check out the mural of the old fisherman by Youth One at **Travessa Visconde da Luz**; *Conta-me Histórias* by Mário Belém (partly taken over by random tags) and an older piece by Add Fuel (2015), both at **Rua Nova da Alfarrobeira**; and *Magma* by Arraiano at **Avenida Valbom**.

RESPONSIBLE TOURISM AT QUINTA DO PISÃO

The **Quinta do Pisão** natural park, about 10km from Cascais, focuses on sustainability and activities in nature. Visitors can explore the park's different habitats on foot, on one of the bicycles available for hire, or on a donkey or horse with a guide. Every two years (the last one happened in May 2022), they host **LandArt Cascais**, a curated event with outdoor exhibitions where art and nature mix.

GETTING AROUND

Trains to Cascais depart frequently throughout the day from Cais do Sodré. In the historic centre, exploring on foot is the best option.

For remoter destinations, you can rely on a modern and regular network of public buses if you need an alternative to hiring a car.

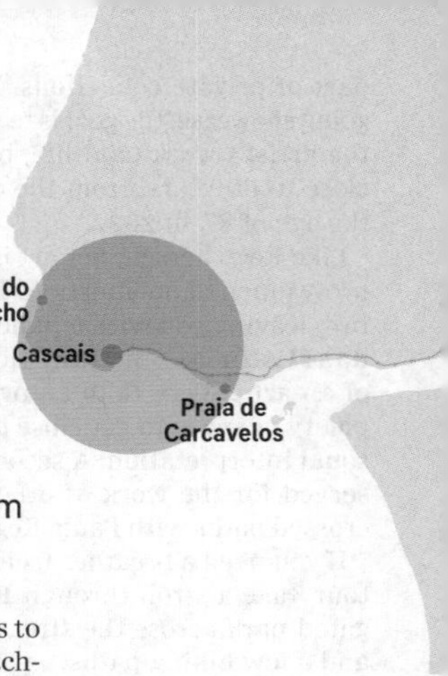

Praia do Guincho
Cascais
Praia de Carcavelos

Beyond Cascais

Explore the beaches a short train trip away from Cascais, surf or relax with a seaside drink.

The ocean takes centre stage when it comes to most things to do near Cascais. After all, it's the reason why the area stretching west and east from town is called the Portuguese Riviera.

At a short distance by train, it's possible to explore a different beach every day (or one in the morning and another in the afternoon), some of which are just a stone's throw from the station. Pack light, put on your flip-flops, throw your towel over your shoulder, and you're good to go. There are also plenty of seaside restaurants and cafes, in case it's not beach weather.

And then there's Guincho. Frequently windy and a little on the cooler side in the summer, it's the ideal location for windsurfing and kitesurfing.

TOP TIP

Get to Guincho from Cascais by car (15 minutes). To get to the Linha de Cascais beaches, take the train.

Praia do Guincho

ANDREONEGIN/SHUTTERSTOCK ©

Surfing lessons, Praia do Guinchos

Surfing at Praia do Guincho

THE SPOT FOR EXPERIENCED SURFERS

You won't often hear anyone around you mentioning **Praia do Guincho** and going to the beach in the same sentence unless the ocean there is surprisingly calm that day. The scenery is stunningly dramatic: the rough sea, the wavy dunes and the Mediterranean vegetation peeking through the sand, the hills of Sintra in the backdrop. No wonder they used this setting in one of the opening scenes of the 1969 James Bond movie *On Her Majesty's Secret Service*. Thankfully Guincho is safe from development, since it's sheltered in Sintra's natural park.

Without many options to seek shelter, enjoying a relaxing day when the wind throws sand in your face is hard. The workaround? Make the best of your time and book a lesson at a local **surf school** or grab a drink with a view at the nearby **Bar do Guincho** – the usual meeting point for surfers. Experienced surfers who are itching to ride the waves can always count on some one-on-one local recommendations. As for regular championships and events, check the Cascais City Council (cascais.pt) website for upcoming competitions.

BIKE RENTALS IN CASCAIS

Look for the MobiCascais kiosk at the train station, where you can rent an electrical or traditional biCas (the name the local city council gave to their shared bicycles) or an electric scooter. Exploring the city centre on two wheels might not be the most comfortable experience for less-experienced cyclists, so check out the 10km seaside lane to Guincho instead.

WHERE TO STAY NEAR CASCAIS

Hotel Inglaterra Estoril
A four-star hotel walking distance from Estoril train station, once the favourite of WWII spies. **€€€**

Hotel Praia Mar
Affordable four-star hotel in Carcavelos 10 minutes' walking distance from the beach. **€**

Palácio Estoril Golf & Wellness Hotel
Five-star hotel with on-site restaurant, five minutes from the Estoril Casino. **€€€**

ESTORIL, HOME OF SPIES

A safe and sunny haven for royalty, Estoril was also used as a refuge for escapees from WWII in the 1940s. But that meant that spies and double agents would follow. And they did. It's believed that Ian Fleming, perhaps the most famous secret agent of them all, wrote his first James Bond novel, *Casino Royale*, in Estoril.

NIKOLPETR/SHUTTERSTOCK ©

Praia de Carcavelos

Discover the Cascais Line's Beaches

A BEACH FOR EVERY TASTE

Of all the beaches along the railway line that connects Lisbon to Cascais, **Praia de Carcavelos** is perhaps the most famous, which also makes it one of the most crowded in the summer. Come the cold weather, though, it's a marvellous place for a relaxing seaside walk. The 30-minute train trip plus the 15-minute walk (1.2km) to get here are worth it just for the view – from the beach or one of the many cafes and restaurants.

If you prefer something even closer to the train station, **Praia da Azarujinha** is an easy five-minute walk from the São João do Estoril stop. It's smaller and not as photogenic as others, but you can hop off the train and it's right there.

Praia de São Pedro, a five-minute walk from São Pedro do Estoril station, is ideal for beachgoers who like to spend the day in one location: seaside cafes and restaurants, perfect sand and crystal-clear waters, and a promenade.

At **Praia do Tamariz**, five minutes' walk from Estoril train station, a great experience and good service come with a price. Literally. For those who want a quiet day at this small beach, book a beach bed for the day (€19 to €23) at the private area run by **Reverse Pool & Beach Lounge**.

GETTING AROUND

It's easy to get around the greater Cascais area by train (to reach towns to the west) and city bus (for sights further east). If you're pressed for time, opt for hiring a car, hailing a cab, or using a rideshare app.

ERICEIRA

Presumably named after *ouriço* (the Portuguese word for sea urchin), Ericeira has a history that can be traced back to the Phoenicians.

In 1910, during the Republican revolution and after the murder of Portugal's last king and his heir apparent, the remaining members of the royal family fled to Brazil (then a Portuguese colony) from the Praia dos Pescadores beach.

In the 1800s, the small coastal town became the royal's favourite summer destination for therapeutical baths (high iodine concentrations being the reason), and other aristocratic families followed. Its source of income would soon shift from fishing to seasonal tourism in the 1950s, and it has remained pretty much the same since then. Later, the excellent conditions for surfing would take over as one of Ericeira's main attractions.

Despite all the coming and going of the summer crowds, Ericeira has remained genuine, a small town where the connection to the ocean is an overarching identity trait.

TOP TIP

Ericeira is best explored on foot. If you're driving, finding parking in the centre is hard, especially on weekends. It's best to park near supermarkets or house blocks along N116 off the town centre, within walking distance.

Get to Know Ericeira's Town Centre

THE QUIET SEASIDE LIFE

If you're heading to Ericeira just for the day, arrive as early as possible in the morning. As you wander into the cluster of narrow cobblestoned streets and white-and-blue houses, the smell of the ocean rises in the air and you'll meet a mix of locals and surfers. If it's summer, sun-seeking beachgoers probably won't get here until after lunch.

Make your way down to your first stop, the small square **Praça da República**, known locally as Jogo da Bola. This is the spot to engage in people-watching while sitting on one of the benches, surrounded by **pastelarias** (pastry and cake shops) and local businesses (not open before 10am). For breakfast or a pre-walk pastry (check if they have the local *ouriço*) and coffee, head to **Pão da Vila** by the square.

Before heading to the beach, make a pit stop at **Casa de Cultura da Ericeira**. Even if none of the ongoing exhibitions strikes your fancy, or if this local cultural centre is closed when you visit, the Art Nouveau facade is worth a look.

Continue down that street (Rua Mendes Leal) to **Praia dos Pescadores**, Ericeira's most central and sheltered beach. If you have the time, go down for a swim (if it's beach season) or for a seaside stroll (if the Atlantic Ocean isn't too rough).

SURF-FOCUSED FILM FESTIVAL

For over a decade, Ericeira has hosted the Portuguese **Surf Film Festival** in the summer. Most screenings happen indoors at Casa da Cultura da Ericeira, but Praia dos Pescadores is the chosen location for a section of the festival called Special Beach Sessions, which showcases classic or out-of-competition films outdoors.

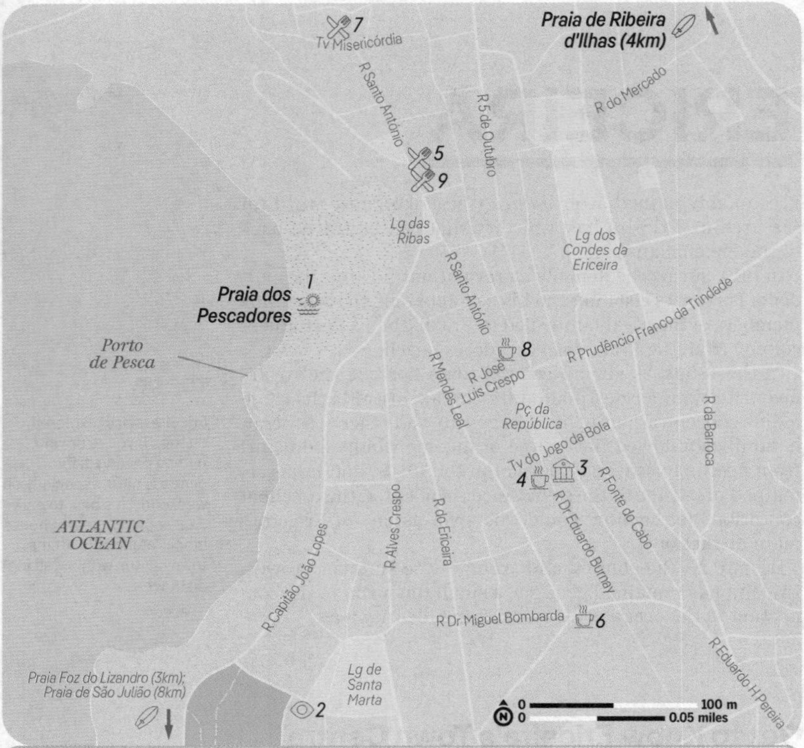

HIGHLIGHTS
1 Praia dos Pescadores

SIGHTS
2 Casa de Cultura da Ericeira
3 Centro de Interpretação da Reserva Mundial de Surf

EATING
4 Café Salvador
5 Casa da Fernanda
6 Casa Gama
7 GiG Green is Good
8 Pão da Vila
9 Tasquinha do Joy

WHERE TO EAT IN ERICEIRA

Tasquinha do Joy
Laid-back restaurant with daily specials and a view to Praia dos Pescadores. Food is simple and portions are generous. €€

Estrela do Mar
A 10-minute drive from Ericeira, in Ribamar, locals swear by the shellfish soup that makes the trip worthwhile. €€

GiG Green is Good
This healthy food restaurant, with vegan and vegetarian options, serves a fixed-price lunch menu and all-day brunch. €€

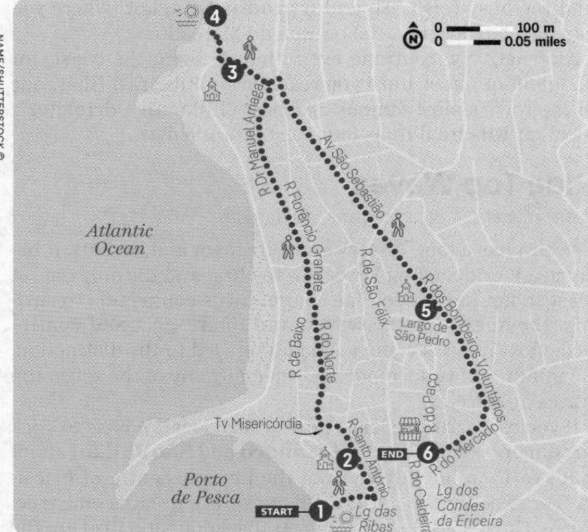

NAME/SHUTTERSTOCK ©

Historic Chapels & Sea Views Walking Tour

Start your walk at the 1 **Praia dos Pescadores** where you can take in the view of the fishing port or spare a few moments to contemplate the Atlantic on one of the pavement benches. To the right of the beach, you can see the 2 **Capela da Boa Viagem**, the tiny chapel that marks the spot from where the surviving members of the royal family were exiled to Brazil in 1910. If it's open, check out the temple's interior, entirely covered in *azulejos*, except for the terracotta floor.

About a 10-minute walk north via the picture-worthy streets Rua do Norte and Rua Dr Manuel Arriaga, you can see a similar 17th-century interior decor at 3 **Capela de São Sebastião**. The peculiar hexagonal chapel overlooks the 4 **Praia de São Sebastião**, a spot for surfing and bodysurfing. While its sandy shore practically disappears at high tide, make time to walk down the *calçada portuguesa* staircase to the viewpoint.

On your way back to town via Rua do Carmo, stop at the 17th-century 5 **Igreja de São Pedro**, Ericeira's main church,

BEST FOR THE LOCAL PASTRY OURIÇOS

Café Salvador
The first stop to try an *ouriço* (a small, compact cake made with sugar, eggs and almonds) should be at Jogo da Bola in Ericeira's historic centre.

Casa da Fernanda
Across the street from Praia dos Pescadores, this is the place for a coffee and a couple of *ouriços* with a view.

Casa Gama
The oldest *pastelaria* in Ericeira. The *ouriço* was born at this family-owned bakery and cafe in the early 20th century.

WHERE TO STAY IN ERICEIRA

Selina Boavista Ericeira & Surf School
Pet-friendly hostel with private and shared rooms, five minutes from Praia dos Pescadores. €€

Ericeira Surf House
A 10-minute drive from the town centre, this weekly-rent B&B also offers surf lessons. €€

Reserva FLH Hotels Ericeira
Two-star boutique hotel in the heart of the historic centre, a stone's throw from Praia dos Pescadores. €

THINGS TO KNOW ABOUT ERICEIRA

Portuguese author **Catarina Raminhos** shares tips on what to do in her hometown. *@catarinaraminhos*

Seaside walking
You can cross Ericeira end-to-end alongside the beach for kilometres. There are many cafes and bars with sea views, where parents can relax while the kids play nearby.

Going local
The rhythm here is all about slow living, and the sense of community is strong. Many digital nomads chose to live here, too, so it's quite common to hear and speak English.

Eating well
You'll never have a bad meal in Ericeira. Besides fresh fish and seafood restaurants, there are also places with vegetarian and vegan options. One of my recommendations is pizzeria Souldough.

and the busy fresh fish and 6 **produce market** (where you can also buy local crafts) on Rua do Mercado.

Alternatively, continue even further along the coast, for about 30 minutes, until you reach Praia Ribeira d'Ilhas, one of the town's most famous beaches. Chill with a drink (or a meal) at Ribeira d'Ilhas Surf Restaurant & Bar.

Ride Top Waves

EUROPE'S FIRST WORLD SURFING RESERVE

Ericeira has a long history as a surf town and, in 2011, it became a World Surfing Reserve – the first and the only one, at least so far, in Europe. The community's connection to surfing, the quality of the waves, and the respect and continued effort in preserving local habitats led to the distinction. Be mindful of your impact as you enjoy any of the seven top waves at Ericeira.

If you're starting to learn how to surf, locals advise to stick to calmer beaches **Foz do Lizandro** and **São Julião,** about a 10- to 15-minute drive from the historic centre of Ericeira. For experienced surfers, this town is a dream come true. Coxos, Crazy Left, Pedras Brancas, Backdoor and Reef are the names of some of the most famous waves.

And then there's **Ribeira d'Ilhas**. Consistent waves and picture-perfect views make this beach one of the most famous in Ericeira and frequently the chosen stage for big national and international surfing events.

For surf enthusiasts who prefer to stay on firm land and watch others skilfully ride the North Atlantic waves, head to **Centro de Interpretação da Reserva Mundial de Surf** at Jogo da Bola to learn about the different kinds of waves, the local biosphere and the history of Ericeira's surfer community.

GETTING AROUND

Buses operated by Mafrense depart Campo Grande Metro station in Lisbon to Ericeira approximately every hour. Routes 207 or 209, where stops are marked as A8 or A21 (two motorways), are the fastest. From the bus terminal in Ericeira (Parque Intermodal da Ericeira), it's a 15-minute downhill walk (1.5km) to the historic centre. Alternatively, you can hop on the shuttle bus (which runs every 15 or 30 minutes, depending on the time of day).

If you're driving and are not pressed for time, choose the scenic route on EN247 over the motorways.

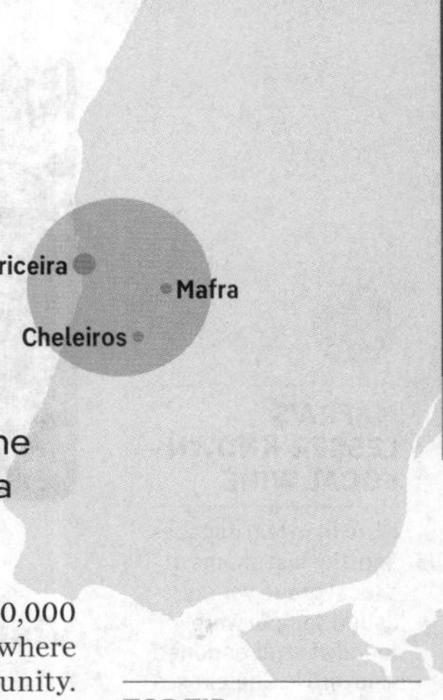

Ericeira
Mafra
Cheleiros

Beyond Ericeira

It's not all surf and sand in Ericeira. Beyond the coastal town, there's a baroque palace with a famous library to explore.

Although it's larger than Ericeira, with approximately 90,000 people living in the area, Mafra has a rural atmosphere, where nature and heritage are essential values for the community. Strike up a conversation with any local and they'll tell you how they value that quality of life. That ambience of *vila saloia* (small countryside town) is ever-present.

Mafra has endured a couple of dramatic episodes: the French invasions in 1807 (when Napoleon's troops took over the palace) and the exile of the Portuguese royal family to Brazil (following the Republican revolution of 1910, which ended the monarchy). In literature, Mafra and its convent were immortalised by José Saramago in his 1982 historical novel *Baltasar and Blimunda*.

TOP TIP

Drive or hail a taxi to get to Mafra from Ericeira. Rideshare options are sometimes available but are unreliable.

Palácio Nacional de Mafra (p122)

MAFRA'S LESSER-KNOWN LOCAL WINE

More than two decades ago, the last strains of a local grape variety called Jampal were found at an abandoned vineyard in Cheleiros, a small village 15 minutes from Mafra. Today the local winery Manzwines produces the only wine in the world that is 100% Jampal. Dona Fátima is their award-winning bestseller white wine.

DIEGO GRANDI/SHUTTERSTOCK ©

Library, Palácio Nacional de Mafra

Visit Palácio Nacional de Mafra

THE PALACE WHERE ROYALS SUMMERED

A Unesco World Heritage Site since 2019, **Palácio Nacional de Mafra** is the country's largest monument. It's also one of the reasons tourists flock to the town of Mafra, a 10-minute drive from Ericeira.

After purchasing tickets, most people skip the church and head straight to the staircase to the palace. But, if you're not in a hurry, head out to see the **Basílica** first. It won't take more than 30 minutes to see it properly. Notice the Italian Carrara marble statues as you walk towards the entrance. In addition to the typically baroque white and red marble interiors and pastel-colour frescoes, the six organs here are the main attraction.

Return to the palace and make your way through grand salons, private chambers and long corridors. The rooms are sparsely furnished, but you can still imagine what 18th-century royal life was like from the few pieces available at their summer residence. Besides, in most areas, it's the ceiling frescoes that demand your attention. And when it comes to attention-grabbing features, the hunting lounge is very much on theme. As the set route means you can't avoid walking through it, avert your eyes if you don't wish to see the typical items that would be displayed in such a room.

The final room, and the one everyone wants to get to as soon as possible, is the library, one of the most important libraries in 17th-century Europe. Although you're not allowed beyond the velvet rope, you can see its long, book-filled corridors from the entrance.

GETTING AROUND

Mafrense buses serve all of Ericeira and the surrounding area, but routes and schedules can be confusing for people who don't travel by bus in the area frequently. A better option is to hire a car and sightsee at your own pace.

SETÚBAL

Considered a city within the urban area of Greater Lisbon, Setúbal is, geographically, already a part of Alentejo in the Portuguese south. It's the birthplace of 18th-century Portuguese poet Bocage and world-famous football coach José Mourinho (self-titled 'the special one' at some point in his two-decade-long career). Both have streets and squares named after them.

Nestled between the Arrábida hills and the Atlantic Ocean, this small seaside city (roughly 125,000 people live here) overcomes the lack of unmissable monuments with picturesque facades, narrow car-free streets, gardens, and squares with wavy patterns of *calçada portuguesa*.

It's worth a day trip from Lisbon, but it has enough charm to convince visitors to stay overnight. Beaches, urban gardens and Arrábida's natural park are less than a 10-minute drive from Setúbal's historical centre.

TOP TIP

If you're staying downtown or in the historic centre of Lisbon, it's quicker to catch the ferry to Barreiro from Terreiro do Paço and then the train from Barreiro (the station is to the left of the ferry) to Setúbal.

Explore Setúbal's City Centre

POSTINDUSTRIAL CHARM

Just seconds after you step off the train into **Praça do Quebedo**, the charm of the historic centre begins to unfold, but it will still feel a bit rough around the edges. Take a left to Rua de Santa Maria and then a sharp right to Largo do Corpo Santo; here, at this tiny square, you can visit the **Sé de Setúbal** and, if it's open, **Casa do Corpo Santo – Museu do Barroco**.

Walk down Travessa de Santa Maria and turn left until you reach Largo da Misericórdia. This square, with benches around a central tree and cafes, is an excellent spot for a drink and to take in the city. But, if time is of the essence, continue along either one of the streets to the heart of Setúbal: **Praça de Bocage**. Admire the design of the square's ground, the statue of the poet it was named after, and, if it's open, visit the 18th-century **Igreja de São Julião**.

FISHY HISTORY

Once a fishing village, 19th-century Setúbal became the home of several tinned fish factories, including one of the largest in Portugal. The last plant closed permanently in 1985.

WHERE TO EAT IN SETÚBAL

Casa Santiago
This centrally located restaurant is famous for Setúbal's signature dish *choco frito* (deep-fried cuttlefish). €€

Sem Horas
Close to Setúbal's main street Avenida Luísa Todi, specialising in sandwiches and *petiscos* (tapas). €€

O Miguel
Grilled fish is the speciality at this family-owned restaurant by the bay and near the Setúbal fresh fish market. €€

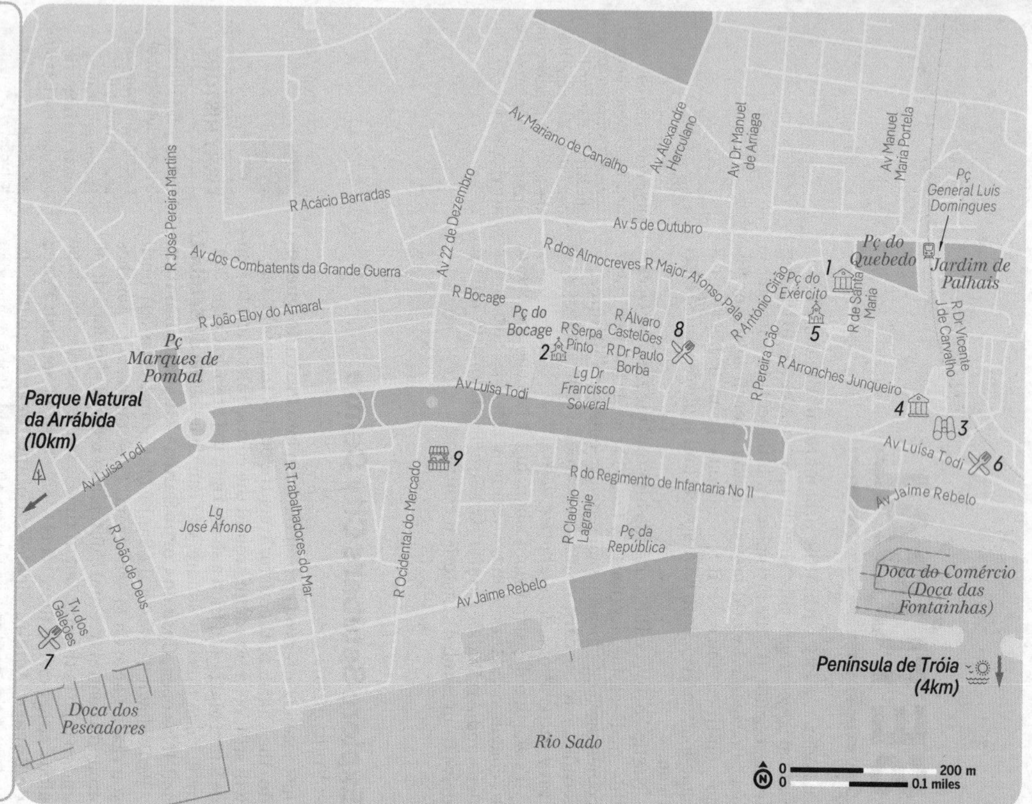

SIGHTS
1 Casa do Corpo Santo – Museu do Barroco
2 Igreja de São Julião
3 Miradouro de São Sebastião
4 Museu do Trabalho Michel Giacometti
5 Sé de Setúbal

EATING
6 Casa Santiago
7 O Miguel
8 Sem Horas

SHOPPING
9 Mercado do Livramento

Praça de Bocage (p123)

PARQUE NATURAL DA ARRÁBIDA

The natural park and protected area surrounding the city of Setúbal is home to rare local species of orchids and the chosen nesting location for the Bonelli's eagle. In addition to these protected species, Arrábida is also known for its secluded, pristine beaches, **Praia do Portinho da Arrábida** being one of the most famous among locals and tourists.

Next, cross busy Avenida Luísa Todi and head towards **Mercado do Livramento**. Setúbal's fresh fish market (closes at 4pm) is one of the most beautiful markets you can set eyes on, with rows of fish stands and panels of blue-and-white *azulejos*.

Alongside the avenue, on the opposite side of the market and towards the sardines roundabout, walk for 10 minutes to **Museu do Trabalho Michel Giacometti**. Visit the museum or take in the view from nearby **Miradouro de São Sebastião** – better yet, do both.

GETTING AROUND

The best public transit option to reach Setúbal is by train. Take Fertagus (also known as the bridge train) at Lisbon's Entrecampos and switch trains and lines in Pinhal Novo. Get off at Praça do Quebedo instead of Setúbal – this is the station closest to the city's historical centre.

Ericeira
Mafra
Cheleiros

Beyond Setúbal

Ocean water dips, dolphin spotting and beach-lounging afternoons are a short trip away from Setúbal.

The sandbank known as Península de Tróia, officially part of Grândola, is 25km long and 1.5km wide – and, in some parts, even less than that. With the Atlantic Ocean on the west side and the Rio Sado on the east, it was only natural it would become a beach and tourist resort. Long before that, the Romans settled here (until the 6th century CE) and dedicated themselves to fishing and making *garum* (a fish-based salty condiment).

The beach resorts (for paying guests only) appeared in the final couple of decades of the 20th century. The marina, other hotels and restaurants, the casino and the ferry ports followed soon after.

TOP TIP

The ticket on the passenger-only ferry is free from Tróia to Setúbal. Trips are fairly regular in all seasons.

Península de Tróia

LIFECOLLECTIONPHOTOGRAPHY/SHUTTERSTOCK ©

STUART BLACK/ALAMY STOCK PHOTO ©

Praia d a Comporta

RESPONSIBLE DOLPHIN WATCHING

One of Europe's three known resident bottlenose dolphin communities lives in the Rio Sado and frequently travels between Setúbal and Tróia. When going on a tour to watch dolphins, remember that there's always a chance you won't see any – they are wild animals, after all. Most companies obey a strict code of conduct when it comes to observing these creatures, and brief tour-goers before sailing off.

Spend the Day on the Tróia Peninsula

SETÚBAL'S FAMOUS BEACH RESORT

The sandy **Península de Tróia**, a short 15-minute ferry ride from downtown Setúbal, doesn't try to be something else, so expect the expected: a tourist resort with expensive seaside hotels, a casino and a marina full of private yachts and boat tours advertising dolphin-watching expeditions.

In the summer, the beaches closest to the marina and the ferry stop are always the busiest, as car-free beachgoers rarely plan to stay for more than a couple of hours. The view of the bay and the hills of Parque Natural da Arrábida is the payoff for the lack of peace and quiet.

For more secluded sandy shores by the ocean, walk until **Praia Tróia Mar** (10 minutes), **Praia da Questa** (20 minutes) or **Praia da Costa da Galé** (about a half-hour away). And if you get to Tróia by car (for that you have to take the other ferry from Setúbal, which arrives at the southern port), you can explore beaches further south in **Comporta**. Or, to see something different, drive 10 minutes to Tróia's **Roman ruins** (with optional guided tours in July and August).

Golfing is one more reason to visit. The award-winning **Tróia Golf** course is a short 10-minute drive from the marina.

GETTING AROUND

The best way to get around the greater Setúbal area is combining a hired car with public transit. If you're planning to explore Tróia only on foot, park the car near the Setúbal terminal and catch the passenger-only catamaran to the sandy peninsula (return ticket is free). For travellers wanting to know more of Tróia and the Setúbal mountain area of Arrábida, driving is the best option. The ferry to Tróia for cars and passengers departs every hour from the Setúbal terminal.

CAIO PEDERNEIRAS/SHUTTERSTOCK ©

Praia do Camilo (p167)

THE MAIN AREAS

FARO
Regional capital flanked by protected islands. **p134**

TAVIRA
Enchanting historic streets perfect for strolling. **p144**

SILVES
Picturesque inland Moorish castle town. **p151**

THE ALGARVE

A SUN-KISSED COASTAL PLAYGROUND

Portugal's southernmost region serves up bountiful beaches and fresh-from-the-boat seafood. Inland are historic towns, whitewashed villages and mountain trails.

In the 1960s, tourism discovered the Algarve. Sleepy fishing villages suddenly became the refuge of wealthy international visitors, and the secret spread quickly.

With over 300 days of annual sunshine and some of Europe's most spectacular cliff-backed sandy bays, it's unsurprising that a tourism boom followed. Alongside the arriving planes of passengers, there came a vast shift and rapid growth in the region's economy. It's hard to imagine those fishers could have foreseen their next generations taking cave-seeking travellers, rather than nets, out on their boats.

Long before tourism, this corner of Portugal had seen its fair share of arrivals: Phoenicians, Carthaginians, Romans, Visigoths, North African Moors and, later, the Christian Reconquista. Five centuries of Moorish influence left a significant legacy, from the region's name (Al-Gharb) to whitewashed architecture. In the 15th century, it was here that Prince Henry the Navigator led the seafaring start of what would become known as the Age of Discovery and the beginning of Portugal's vast colonial empire.

Nowadays, the Algarve still promises a sun-kissed escape for surfers, beachgoers and late-night revellers, yet it has also become a destination for those who aren't beelining for the beach. Eco-conscious resorts, solar-powered sightseeing boats, a spotlight on regional wines, and renewed interest in rural tourism on hinterland trails have helped elevate it to a year-round destination, with a few 'secrets' still waiting to be explored.

TLF IMAGES/SHUTTERSTOCK ©

PORTIMÃO
Sardine city with a party beach. **p158**

LAGOS
Water sports, rock formations and nightlife. **p167**

SAGRES & CABO DE SÃO VICENTE
Windswept cliffs and wild beaches. **p173**

Portimão, p158

The region's second city is renowned for its sardine history, Praia da Rocha's vast sandy beach, shipwreck diving and the surrounding, cave-heavy coastline.

Sagres & Cabo de São Vicente, p173

Beach breaks beckon surfers to Sagres, and Europe's most southwesterly point captivates. Beyond, you'll find the unspoilt shores and trails of the Costa Vicentina.

Silves, p151

Sail back in time up the Rio Arade to this steep, ochre-hued town, crowned with a Moorish castle and surrounded by vineyards and orange groves.

Lagos, p167

Craggy cove beaches, endless water sports and cinematic rock formations are topped off with seafood, cocktails and clubbing – Lagos has the lot!

Find Your Way

The Algarve could be crossed east to west in under two hours. However, the winding roads to hidden beaches and hilltop villages, and detours to coastal towns, don't just invite you to slow down, they compel you to do so.

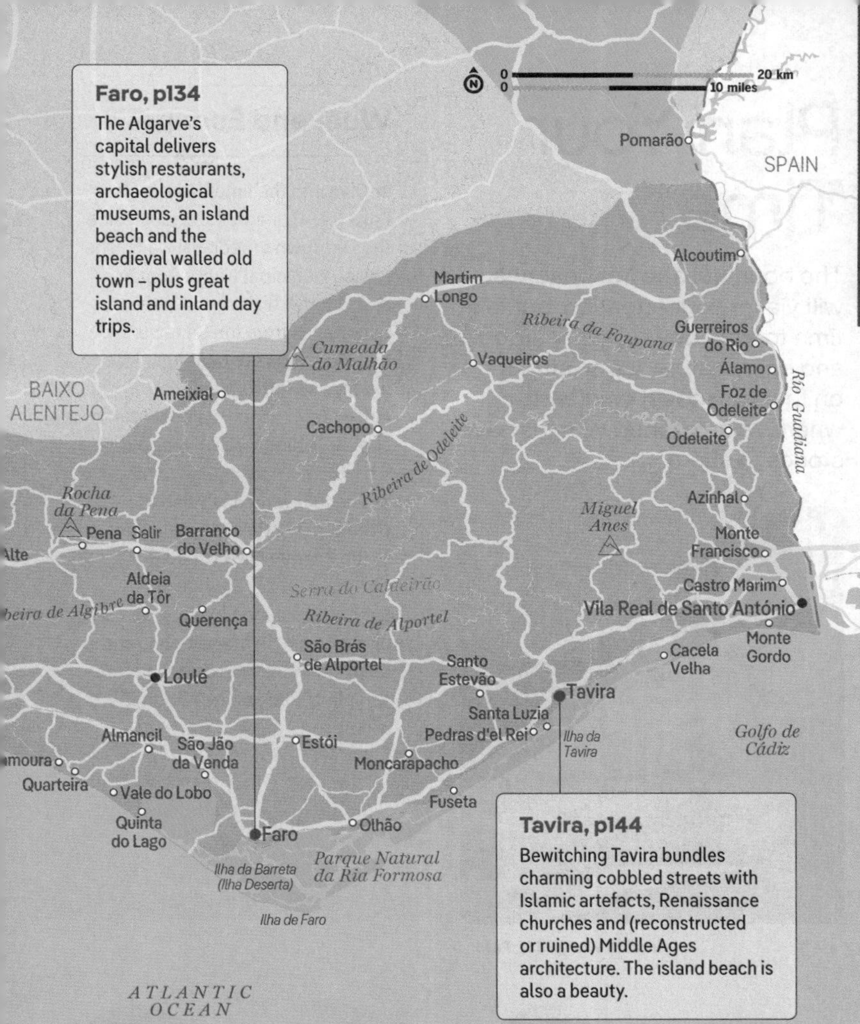

Faro, p134

The Algarve's capital delivers stylish restaurants, archaeological museums, an island beach and the medieval walled old town – plus great island and inland day trips.

Tavira, p144

Bewitching Tavira bundles charming cobbled streets with Islamic artefacts, Renaissance churches and (reconstructed or ruined) Middle Ages architecture. The island beach is also a beauty.

CAR

With four wheels, you'll be free to dictate your schedule. Secluded bays, countryside *quintas* (vineyards) and hard-to-reach hiking trails become easily accessible. Toll roads are (slightly) faster. Taxis (and apps such as Bolt and Uber in cities) provide an alternative for occasional remote visits.

BUS

Vamus Algarve provides a decent (if sometimes delayed) integrated bus service across the Algarve, complemented by local municipality buses in the main cities. Buses give better access to beaches and smaller villages than trains, though schedules are often commuter-focused, requiring some forward planning.

TRAIN

The Algarve's ageing trains trundle along at a sightseeing pace between Lagos in the west, to Faro, and then to Vila Real de Santo António in the east. While most stations are conveniently located, others (Albufeira, in particular) are too far from their destinations to walk.

Plan Your Time

The bountiful array of beaches will vie for your attention, but take time to slow down over seafood and enjoy nature-laden strolls on the west coast or inland, where whitewashed villages have stories to share.

DANIEL JAMES CLARKE ©

Arco da Vila (p136), Faro

Weekend Escape

- Dive into the timeless streets of **Faro** (p134) ona walking tour inside the Old Town's medieval walls. The Museu Municipal tracks Roman and Moorish history, while the panoramas from the Sé tower will help you find your bearings. After lunch, visit the Roman ruins of **Milreu** (p142) or take a boat tour to spot **dolphins** (p141) in the wild.

- The following day, head to **Olhão** (p139), the main gateway to the **Parque Natural da Ria Formosa** (p140). Lounge on the barrier island beaches, go birdwatching in the salt pans and enjoy local seafood dishes before sampling some of the regional wines.

Seasonal highlights

Soaring temperatures and crowds define summer. Spring and autumn bring better deals, great hiking and quieter beaches. Winter (usually) offers some of Europe's best weather and bargains at near-empty resorts.

FEBRUARY

Cooler days call for a colourful carnival, and Loulé hosts one of the biggest (sometimes in March, depending on Lent).

APRIL

Wildflowers and orange trees have blossomed for pretty hikes, and Easter celebrations generally mark the end of the low season.

JUNE

Huge parties such as Carvoeiro's Black and White Night celebrate summer's arrival. Official beach season begins.

MAURO RODRIGUES/SHUTTERSTOCK ©, SUN SHOCK/SHUTTERSTOCK ©, PRZEMYSLAW BUNKOWSKI/SHUTTERSTOCK ©

A Week on the Coast

- After two days around Faro, turn east to pretty **Tavira** (p144) and explore its warren of storied streets. Take a ferry to **Ilha de Tavira** (p146) before savouring an octopus meal in **Santa Luzia** (p146).

- Next, head west. Hike the cinematic clifftop **Percurso dos Sete Vales Suspensos** (p157) and kayak into sea caves. Detour slightly inland to visit the magnificently restored Moorish castle in **Silves** (p151) before devouring sardines in **Portimão** (p158). Later marvel at the dramatic **Ponta da Piedade** (p167) headland in Lagos.

- Heading to the west coast, relax or surf in seafaring **Sagres** (p173) before hopping between the untamed beaches of the **Costa Vicentina** (p177).

Diving Deeper

- With an additional week, make a loop inland to the mountain trails and hinterlands before returning south along the eastern border. Start in the Serra de Monchique for hiking and panoramas at **Fóia** (p155), the Algarve's highest peak, before being pampered in the thermal spa town of **Caldas de Monchique** (p155).

- The whitewashed rural villages, waterfalls and birdwatching of the **Serra do Caldeirão** (p157) await, while the historic inland city of **Loulé** (p139) is the place for traditional crafts. Continuing to the **Rio Guadiana** (p148), you can (loosely) follow it south to the ocean, stopping at salt pans and a castle before easily looping back to Faro.

JULY
International festivals such as Afro Nation in Portimão, Loulé Jazz Festival and Lagoa's Candlelight Markets.

AUGUST
Sample local flavours at Olhão Seafood Festival and Portimão's Sardine Festival, or step back in time at Silves' Medieval Fair.

OCTOBER
Make a beeline to nature reserves for migratory birdwatching, and follow the Rota do Petisco to sample small regional plates.

NOVEMBER
Prices and crowds shrink as waves grow for experienced surfers in Sagres. Some businesses in resort towns shut for winter.

FARO

Faro has witnessed – and lost – a lot. Plundered of treasures by the Earl of Essex in 1597, it was also devastated by two earthquakes in the 18th century. This, and a fast-following tsunami, heavily damaged the city, although Lagos fared much worse, meaning the title of regional capital was transferred to Faro. Luckily, there are remains of heritage and history – something for which we can thank previous residents.

It flourished as the Roman port of Ossónoba after Phoenician and Carthaginian stints, and still has remains of open-air mosaicked villas. Later, the Moorish made Faro home, leaving Islamic ceramics and artefacts that now adorn the city's museums. In 1249, Alfonso III retook the city, making it the last major Moorish stronghold to be recaptured.

For many, Faro is a fleeting plane-window glimpse before heading to nearby resorts. If you stay a while, however, you'll find a laid-back yet lived-in base with great island and inland day trips.

TOP TIP

Faro Airport is less than a 15-minute drive to the centre. Próximo public buses regularly connect the airport, city centre and beach. The 'Aerobus' by Vamus directly links the airport with the main western coastal towns a handful of times per day, with reduced services from November to April.

BEST ALGARVE GOLF COURSES

Quinto do Lago
Just outside Faro, the three courses at this luxury resort combine world-class facilities with lake views.

Monte Rei
Designed by the legendary Jack Nicklaus, this award-winning course surrounded by serene countryside is an hour east of Faro.

Vale do Lobo
With two 18-hole championship courses and impeccable views across the Atlantic, this club is worth the 30-minute drive from Faro.

Tour the Town

BEYOND THE OLD CITY WALLS

From the Palacete Belmarço, turn right towards the **Igreja de São Francisco** (Sunday opening is only for mass), with its white facade hiding an impressive interior – a medley of gold gilding and blue and white *azulejos* (hand-painted tiles) narrating the life of St Francis. Heading back towards the centre, the small **Museu Regional do Algarve** (open weekdays) doesn't take long to visit but does provide a brief insight into the region's rural life with reconstructions of 19th-century homes and stores.

At the 16th-century **Igreja de São Pedro**, take a short pause to look inside the tri-nave church and admire the baroque altarpiece before continuing to Faro's most captivating (and creepy) church, **Igreja de Nossa Senhora do Carmo**. Stepping inside the late-baroque twin-towered church (closed Sunday), you'll be bowled over by the heavily gilded interior, crafted by master sculptor Manuel Martins in 1736. The biggest draw for many intrigued visitors is the Capela dos Ossos, dating from the 19th century. It's constructed from over 1000 skulls and bones of exhumed Carmelite monks – the walls will ghoulishly stare back at you.

Another architectural city highlight is **Teatro Lethes**, a 17th-century building that once housed a Jesuit college before falling into private hands and being reborn as a small and splendid theatre – it's worth checking if performances are scheduled during your visit.

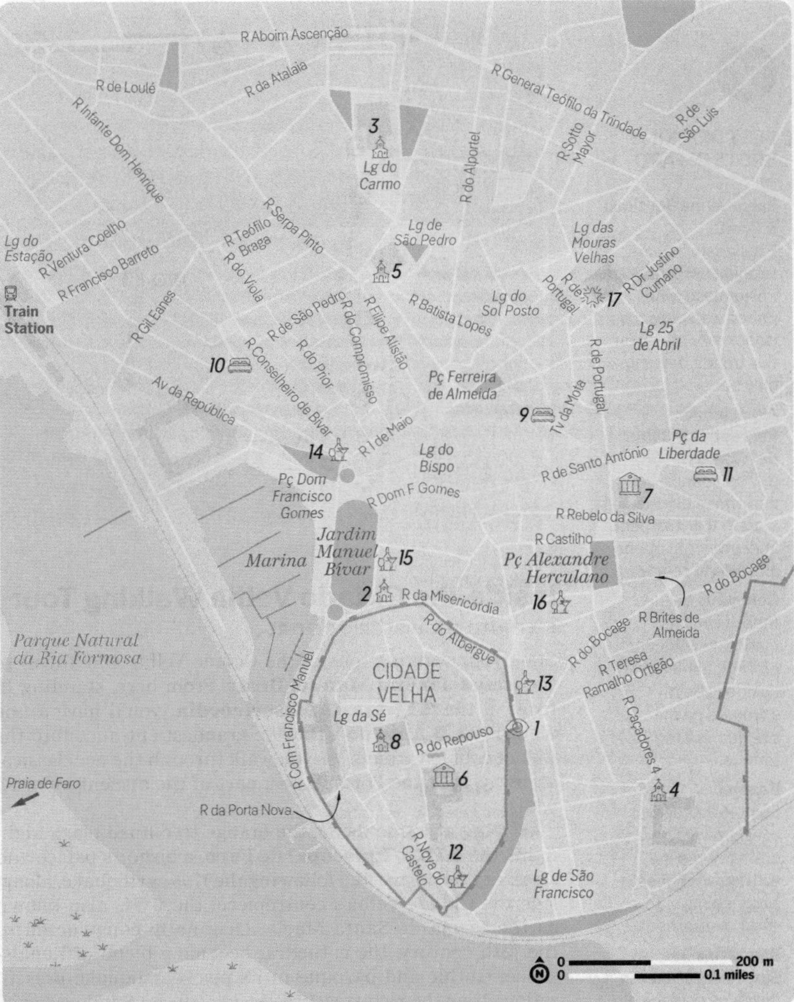

SIGHTS
1 Arco do Repouso
2 Igreja da Misericórdia
3 Igreja de Nossa Senhora do Carmo & Capela dos Ossos
4 Igreja de São Francisco
5 Igreja de São Pedro
6 Museu Municipal
7 Museu Regional do Algarve
8 Sé

SLEEPING
9 3HB Faro
10 Casa da Madalena Backpackers
11 Lemon Tree Stay

DRINKING & NIGHTLIFE
12 Associação Recreativa e Cultural de Músicos
13 Bago Wine Bar
14 Boheme
15 Columbus Bar
16 Epicur Wine Boutique & Food

ENTERTAINMENT
17 Teatro Lethes

BEST DRINKING SPOTS IN FARO

Epicur Wine Boutique & Food
Passionate owners suggest personalised Portuguese wine paired with *petiscos* (snack-size plates) in this trendy, evening-only bar.

Associação Recreativa e Cultural de Músicos
DJs and bands perform under the stars in this laid-back and late-night open-air cultural courtyard.

Columbus Bar
Steps from the marina, mixologists craft global-inspired cocktails best savoured on the *calçada*-coated terrace.

Boheme
Sample Portugal's ever-growing craft-beer scene with knowledgeable suggestions at this small central spot.

Bago Wine Bar
Sip regional wines in the shadow of the old walls while admiring the grand Palacete Belmarço.

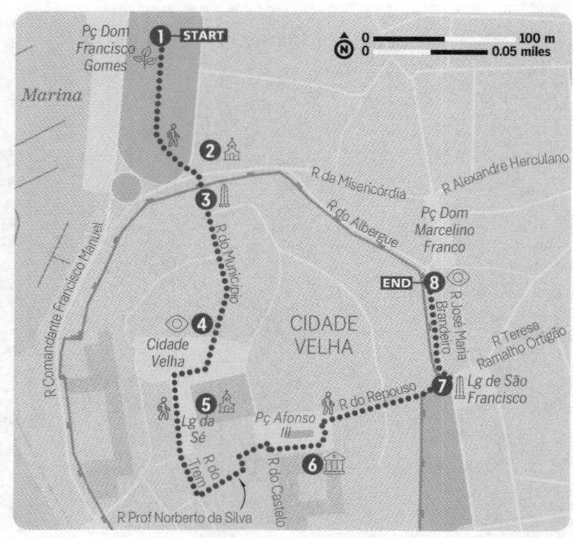

Inside the Cidade Velha Walking Tour

STEP INTO THE HISTORIC CENTRE

Start your walking tour of the Cidade Velha (Old Town) in the leafy **1 Jardim Manuel Bivar**. From here, standing in front of the **2 Igreja da Misericórdia**, you'll have a fine view of the **3 Arco da Vila**, the grandest entrance into the web of cobbled streets. As you walk through the neoclassical archway, spot the Porta Árabe, part of the ancient Moorish walls.

Arriving at Largo da Sé, the orange tree-lined plaza highlights the **4 Paço Episcopal de Faro**, a bishop's palace and seminary reconstructed following the 1755 earthquake, alongside the Cidade Velha's centrepiece, the **5 Sé**, also known as the Igreja de Santa Maria. Originally constructed in the 13th century, the cathedral became a blend of Renaissance, Gothic and baroque in its post-earthquake presentation. Tour the rich treasures inside (closed Sundays), such as the highly ornate gilded altarpiece, before climbing the tower for excellent panoramas of the Parque Natural da Ria Formosa.

WHERE TO STAY IN FARO

Casa da Madalena Backpackers
This renovated, small, central hostel offers bunks, breakfast, a terrace and a homey vibe. €

Lemon Tree Stay
Contemporary rooms (some with terraces), a communal kitchen and a peaceful courtyard. €€

3HB Faro
Modern and luxurious. You'll be spoilt with a spa, two restaurants and a rooftop pool. €€€

Allow at least an hour in the **6 Museu Municipal** (closed Monday), housed in and around the cloisters of the Convento de Nossa Senhora da Assunção. Be guided through the city's history by Islamic artefacts, religious paintings and Roman archaeological finds – the well-preserved Mosaic of Oceanus is particularly remarkable. Pass through the walls at **7 Arco do Repouso** to see their oldest section to your right, while the whimsical **8 Palacete Belmarço** will be to your left.

An Active Island Beach Day

TANNING OR TRAILS

Faro's main beach, **Praia de Faro**, on the road-linked Ilha de Faro, provides all the wave-lapped golden sands, water sports and beach cafes you'll need for a day in the sun. For a more active beach day, pack your trainers and follow the trails for a few hours before settling in for a sandy sunset. Starting close to the large car park before the bridge, the Ludo Trail follows the lagoon system of the Parque Natural da Ria Formosa, from salt pans and marshes to forest.

Along the way, there's plenty of potential birdlife to spot, including the colourful long-beaked Eurasian hoopoe, flamingos and, on lucky occasions, the very rare purple gallinule. To turn the route into a circular coastal loop, cross the Quinta do Lago Bridge over the marshes back to the beach. From here, it's a little over 3km along the island's shoreline back to Praia de Faro, allowing for swimming stops and endless Atlantic Ocean views.

Boat Trips Beyond the Barrier Islands

DOLPHINS IN THE WILD

Countless boat trips tour the **Parque Natural da Ria Formosa** from Faro's marina; however, you'll have to go beyond the barrier islands for the best chance at spotting dolphins. The chances of sightings year-round are high, although the species (such as common, striped and bottlenose) you'll witness may vary depending on the season. On even luckier sailings, whales and orcas may also make an appearance. Ocean Vibes, a marine-biologist-led tour company, offers trips alongside its wildlife research, promising a responsible and conservation-focused experience.

ALGARVE WINES

Jorge Santos and Pedro Rodrigo founded Faro's Epicur Wine Boutique & Food to share their local wine knowledge. Here are Jorge's quick Algarve *vinhos* tips.

In Portugal, the wines from the Algarve aren't well known. Because of the region's heat, the grapes get really sweet and, being near the ocean, you also get a slightly salty flavour. That's a mix you don't often find in Portugal. There are four subregions, and while Tavira is flat, you'll find more mountains in Lagoa and Portimão, so the grape is a little bit sweeter due to the hotter altitude.

MORE ISLAND ESCAPES

Parque Natural da Ria Formosa is a complex 60km-long system of barrier islands, wetlands, marshes, dunes and salt pans stretching from just west of Faro to slightly beyond Cacela Velha.

GETTING AROUND

Faro's centre is flat and walkable. A reliable city bus network, operated by Próximo, is available, with services usually starting from the modern, open-air station next to the intercity terminal. Line 16 connects the city with the airport, followed by Praia de Faro, and takes around 20 minutes. If you're visiting Faro for the day, the intercity bus and train stations are central, and a spacious free car park (Largo de São Francisco) is near the old town walls.

Beyond Faro

Faro is the perfect base for island escapades, trips to popular beach resorts and explorations of the interior's less-visited towns.

Long before lavish modern mansions sprang up in these parts, the Romans had set the tone. In Estói and Vilamoura, ruins of opulent ancient villas are presented in open-air museums, while the small bridge near the 12th-century Castle of Paderne also hails from this period. Inland, the city of Loulé blends numerous architectural styles with cultured creativity, allowing insight into the region's varied handicrafts.

Along the coast, the Parque Natural da Ria Formosa dominates. A vast system of salt pans, lagoons and wetlands form a protected refuge for wildlife, while beachgoers seek seclusion on the barrier islands. Further west, Albufeira provides the party alongside a spirited old town and golden craggy coves.

TOP TIP

The cheapest way to access the islands of Parque Natural da Ria Formosa is by public ferry from Olhão.

Mercardo Municipal, Loulé

The City of Carnival, Markets & Historic Cultures

ARCHITECTURE AND ARTEFACTS IN LOULÉ

Loulé, 40 minutes inland from Faro by (slow) bus, has a diverse array of architectural treasures. The **Banhos Islâmicos de Loulé** (closed Monday) opened to the public in early 2022 and are the only (known) example of Islamic baths in Portugal. Nearby, the heavily restored remains of Loulé Castle (closed Sunday), once part of the greater city walls, house the **Museu Municipal**, displaying Roman and Islamic artefacts in cabinets and under a glass floor. The **Antigo Convento do Espírito Santo** (closed Sunday and Monday) is also worth a visit for the neoclassical cloisters and the contemporary art museum housed in the space, while the impressive Art Nouveau **Mercardo Municipal** rounds off an architectural tour. Loulé also hosts the Algarve's largest carnival celebration, usually in February or March, depending on Lent.

THE CHURCH WORTH A DETOUR

One of the Algarve's best examples of *azulejos* (traditional hand-painted tiles) is found in the small town of Almancil. The 18th-century **Igreja de Sao Lourenco de Almancil** (with small admission charge) is something of a masterpiece, although you wouldn't know it from the exterior. With its walls and ceiling coated in blue and white tiles depicting São Lourenço's life, you can follow the detailed stories spilling in every direction. A 20-minute drive from Faro, it's a small detour worth making en route to Loulé. It's closed on Sunday and over lunch.

Hands-On Crafts in Loulé

GET TO KNOW CREATIVE TRADITIONS

Loulé and its surrounds have a long and proud history of handicrafts, with its first trade fair taking place in 1291. As you stroll the streets, you'll find a small network of six **workshops** (mainly closed on weekends) dedicated to traditional techniques. Palm weaving, copper smithing, a clay studio and textile works are highlighted in their respective spaces. As part of the **Loulé Criativo** (loulecriativo.pt) programme, you can participate in artistic practices, with workshops and courses hosted throughout the year. Classes cover anything from tile painting to stitching, and can be booked online. For local artisanal products, pop into the **Project TASA** store – its work focuses on keeping traditional Algarvian arts alive.

Seafood, Storks & Statues

GATEWAY TO THE RIA FORMOSA

Arriving in **Olhão** from Faro (a scenic, 10-minute train journey), you'll quickly get the feeling of being in a living and working city. Mainly visited as a gateway to the central islands of Parque Natural da Ria Formosa, there isn't a whole lot to see in the city itself. Spotting stork nests above buildings and following the **Caminho das Lendas**, a short walk just back from the waterfront showcasing a handful of local myths and legends in

THE ALGARVE'S INTERIOR

Continue inland from Loulé to spot eagles in the Serra do Caldeirão (p157) and explore the quintessential rural Algarvian villages of Querença and Alte.

WAYS TO TOUR THE RIA FORMOSA

MarioSUP
Kayak and SUP tours to Ilha da Armona from Olhão provide an active option.

Ocean Vibes
Departing Faro, this three-hour boat tour to the main islands is led by a marine biologist.

From Here Faro
Enjoy a silent (and sustainable) trip on these solar-powered boats to learn about the park's birdlife.

BEST TRADITIONAL SEAFOOD DISHES

Xerém de conquilhas
This Moorish-influenced corn-flour dish is similar to porridge and made with shellfish, though the cockle version from Olhão is the most celebrated.

Cataplana
Perhaps the most iconic Algarve recipes, this clam-shaped, usually copper pot (which gives the dish its name) is sealed full of seafood and then steamed to make a delicious fish stew.

Sardinhas assadas
Salt-seasoned sardines are grilled over charcoal to create a simple but beloved dish, especially during celebrations.

Arroz de lingueirão
You'll find a vast variety of *arroz de marisco* (seafood rice stews) across the region, and this traditional version, using razor clams, is one of the tastiest.

Ilha da Armona

open-air statue format, provides some entertainment while waiting for the ferry.

On the waterfront, home to the Algarve's largest fishing port, seafood rules supreme, whether eating it freshly grilled or watching the early morning action at the **Mercados de Olhão** (closed Sunday). For a few days in August, it's even more lively when the **Festival do Marisco** brings plenty of chances to sample local seafood specialities.

Spot Flamingos in the Salinas

SALT PAN CYCLING OR STROLLS

Surrounding Olhão, *salinas* (salt pans) and marshland provide some of the nearest wildlife and bird spotting opportunities in **Parque Natural da Ria Formosa**. While the trails are walkable, hiring a bicycle near the ferry pier will maximise your time. Heading west of the city, you'll first pass through the **Salinas de Olhão**, potentially spotting a spectrum of colours, depending on the salt concentration. Keep your eyes peeled for flamingos, ducks and curlews, with sightings at their highest from October until March. Beyond, at the **Salinas do Grelha**, you can float in a salt-dense lake (book ahead).

WHERE TO STAY IN THE RIA FORMOSA

Stork Hostel
This neat hostel with dorms, privates and relaxing terraces is close to Olhão's ferries. €

Orbitur Ilha de Armona
These small, cabin-style lodgings offer the chance to stay on Ilha de Armona. €€

Houseboats
Barco Casa rents a few permanently anchored ecological houseboats close to Ilha da Culatra. €€€

An Island-Hopping Escape

INTO THE NATURAL PARK

Boarding the ferry at the Cais de Embarque de Olhão and sailing off towards the outer barrier islands, as gulls dance above and sand bars glide by, promises the start of a perfect Algarve beach day. With a total change of pace from the tourist resorts, and vastly different scenery from the cliff-backed beaches further west, these isles are car-free paradisiacal escapes.

Ilha da Armona welcomes you with a small beach and a handful of restaurants. To access the vast swathes of sand, follow the pavement through the village (keep an eye out for Mediterranean chameleons) until you reach the boardwalk. Just beyond the beach bar, the lapping waves await. The village has a cabin-style camp if you wish to spend the night.

Ilha da Culatra and **Ilha do Farol** are slightly deceptive names, as they are actually part of the one island, so you could hop between them with the same ferry or even on a long leisurely walk. Like Armona, the best beaches are on the Atlantic side, though those around the piers facing the lagoon have more tranquil waters. Both tiny villages have some dining options, and Praia do Farol has a seasonal kayak and SUP rental shop.

To visit **Ilha Deserta** (also known as Ilha da Barretta), which is uninhabited apart from a single daytime-only restaurant, you'll need to take the ferry from Faro rather than Olhão.

Wetlands, Wildlife & Water Sports

SIGHTINGS ABOVE AND BELOW

Protected by the outer barrier islands, the calm waters of the Ria Formosa's lagoons are not only a haven for wildlife but also for water sports. While the usual suspects, such as jet skis, operate in boat-permitted waters, low-impact options are the best way to discover the shallower protected wetlands. Typical wildlife found in the park include the endangered seahorses hiding in the seagrasses, the Mediterranean chameleon, European polecats and otters. Winged sightings include storks, spoonbills and the purple swamphen – the park's symbol. Hundreds of other temporary flying residents can be sighted during the spring and autumn migrations.

Kayak and SUP tours and rentals allow for one of the most intimate ways to explore, with the chance to get up close to oyster nurseries and shellfish farms. To better understand the park's migratory and native birdlife, walking tours led by local experts along the wetlands are informative. Boats also offer sightings, although picking a solar-operated vessel to reduce engine noise is essential. To witness dolphins in the

COASTAL SUSTAINABILITY

Alfredo Rodrigues, a marine biologist, researcher and founder of *@oceanvibesalgarve* dolphin-watching tours, shares how to sustainably enjoy the coast.

When choosing a tour, a little research can make a big environmental difference. Consider responsible operators using local guides or biologists, electric or solar boats for shorter trips, and avoid swimming with seahorses, as almost 90% of their population has been lost in the Ria Formosa. If you can, try to visit in autumn as the wildlife is better – dolphins can be spotted year-round beyond the Ria Formosa – and with fewer boats, the pressure on the environment is reduced. Finding tours with a related research project means you'll support both tourism and environmental studies.

WHERE TO EAT LUNCH IN THE RIA FORMOSA

Cais Aqui
A friendly cafe near the Ilha do Farol ferry, serving affordable snacks, salads and wraps. €

Lanacosta
Sand-surrounded terrace for seafood, snacks and drinks on Ilha da Armona's far side. €€

Estaminé
Ilha Deserta's only restaurant is a solar-powered, seafood-focused, sea-view splendour. €€€

wild, you'll (usually) need to go beyond the islands. While rare sightings can happen in the inner lagoons, they are seen year-round in the ocean beyond. If you're fortunate, whales sometimes make an appearance during their migratory period (usually late February until May and October and November).

Roman Ruins & Palace Gardens

REMNANTS OF A PRESTIGIOUS PAST

To delve deeper into the region's Roman history, head north of Faro to the Roman ruins of **Milreu**, a 20-minute journey by car or bus. This large and luxurious villa was inhabited from the 1st to the 11th century CE by high-society families, and there are plenty of well-preserved details. The intact fish mosaics, temple and central pool are particularly interesting. There's a small visitors centre, but as a mainly open-air site, some of the marble sculptures and other artefacts have been relocated into the city's museum. Continuing the regal theme, the pink rococo-style **Palácio de Estoi**, since converted into a *pousada* (upscale inn), is a 15-minute walk away. Non-guests can wander the public areas, including a few well-heeled rooms and down the grand tile-coated staircase to the French-inspired gardens.

MORE BEACHES WEST OF FADO

Beyond the island beaches of the natural park, there are countless other spots to lay out your towel.

Praia da Falésia
A peaceful spot on this beach, backed by orange-hued cliffs and nearly 6km in length, is only a short walk away.

Praia de São Rafael
Fantastic kayak and SUP tours to the caves leave from this rugged beach. To the west, craggy cliff trails will take you to even more stunning bays.

Praia da Galé
This accessible beach is most scenic on the eastern end, where you'll find a couple of ocean-facing restaurants.

The Refined Resort with Ancient Ruins

ROMAN RUINS AND MARINA MEALS

Vilamoura, 35 minutes from Faro by car, is an upscale resort focused around a yacht-heavy marina. While luxury villas line the roads en route, the Roman ruins of **Cerro da Vila** (closed weekends) were the original opulent residency. Just behind the restaurants on the marina's north, a small archaeological site guides you through the villa ruins, mosaics and the remnants of a bathing complex. The attached museum goes beyond the Roman period, with artefacts and discoveries spanning the Bronze age to the Moorish rule. If the beach is calling, walk to the eastern end of **Praia da Falésia**, where a beach club serving Thai food offers a coastal alternative to the marina restaurants.

Old Town Meets Party Town

TRADITION AND TOURISM HOT SPOT

If one place has shifted most from small fishing village to mass tourism, it's **Albufeira**. With a reputation for wild parties on its late-night strip, it's one of the best destinations in the Algarve for revelry. Still, those looking for a more peaceful trip might find some solace in the cobblestone streets of the

WHERE TO EAT AROUND ALBUFEIRA

O Catraio
Wallet-friendly local dishes are done well on a small pedestrian street in Albufeira's old town. €€

A Sardinha
Fresh fish of all kinds, against the backdrop of rocky Praia dos Arrifes' crystal-clear waters. €€

Vila Joya
With two Michelin stars, chef Dieter Koschina serves up an incredible daily menu. Reservations essential. €€€

SOPOTNICKI/SHUTTERSTOCK ©

Vilamoura

old town, where a few pretty churches and a tiny sacred-art museum offer a little heritage. Also worth a visit is the small **Museu Municipal de Arqueologia** (closed Monday), with mosaics, vases and other locally excavated items spanning the prehistoric, Roman and Islamic periods.

Cork & Countryside

INTO THE SERENE INTERIOR

Slip away to the cork-coated lands of **São Brás de Alportel**, a 30-minute drive north of Faro. The town's surrounds are rich with olives, figs and carobs, and some of the local cork producers, such as the **Eco-Cork Factory**, run tours. In town, the **Museu do Traje** is housed in an old cork tycoon's mansion. Its main feature is an ever-changing display of local costumes from the 19th and 20th centuries, alongside exhibits on the town's history, agriculture and the cork industry. It's also worth popping in to see local handicrafts in **Casa do Artesão** (closed weekends), and to admire the neoclassical marble altarpiece in **Igreja Matriz de São Brás de Alportel** (if it's open).

BEST PAMPERING IN THE ALGARVE

Algarve Spa Week, usually running for seven days in March and October, sees some of the region's premium spas offer up to 50% discounts. Other top spa options:

7 Seven Spa
The Algarve's largest spa (inside Vilamoura's Hilton) has everything, from Turkish baths and a zen garden to thermal pools and facials.

VILA VITA Parc Resort
Enjoy holistic and signature treatments using botanical extracts and essential oils in this five-star Porches hotel.

Bela Vista Hotel & Spa
Praia da Rocha's boutique spa offers premium local-inspired products (think almonds and oranges) in a serene setting.

GETTING AROUND

The main destinations (Estói, Loulé, Olhão, Vilamoura and Albufeira) are well served from Faro by Vamus buses. Olhão's train station is relatively central, and the ride provides better views of the Ria Formosa than the bus route. Ferry tickets to the islands are purchased from the wooden hut near Olhão's pier around 30 minutes before each departure – queue for the correct window for the island you wish to visit. Cycling is also popular in the Faro vicinity, as it's relatively flat, with bike rentals readily available. If driving, it's always advisable to choose car parks just outside the old centres to avoid congested narrow and one-way roads.

TAVIRA

As one of the first Phoenician settlements in Portugal, with preceding Bronze Age roots, Tavira isn't just one of the Algarve's prettiest towns but also one of the oldest.

The storied streets have seen Romans and Moors, both of which have left cultural marks visible in the town's architecture and museums. Later, during the Age of Discovery, Tavira flourished as expeditions departed to North Africa, and maritime trade grew. Nowadays, the only boats you'll see are those of fishers and ferries to the scenic and sandy Ilha da Tavira.

By the 16th century, Tavira had grown to be the Algarve's most populated city, and you can still spot opulent Renaissance reminders of these years. Earthquakes, a plague and, more recently, the dying bluefin tuna fishing industry reduced Tavira to a shell of its previous grandeur, at least until tourism discovered the town's narrow whitewashed streets, countless churches, hospitable restaurants and paradisiacal island beaches.

TOP TIP

With regular ferries from the city centre (the last return trip varies by season), a campground and a handful of fair-priced bars and restaurants, camping on Ilha de Tavira is an attractive summer alternative to a city stay for island lovers.

ALGARVIAN CRAFTS

Tavira's collection of independent stores provides an excellent opportunity to shop for local handicrafts. **Casa das Portas** is a fine spot to pick up ceramics and other artisanal creations, while **Casa Matias** stocks a wide range of woven baskets. Embroidery and decorative lace are two traditional crafts to keep an eye out for, as are traditional copper *cataplana* (seafood stew) cooking pots. Cork products are common, with anything from shoes to handbags being crafted from this sustainable and renewable material.

Along & Across the Gilão

ROMAN BRIDGE RIVERSIDE WALK

Starting from the **Mercado da Ribeira**, a recovered 19th-century market, stroll along the riverbank, passing through the leafy **Jardim do Coreto** and **Praca da República**, before crossing the Rio Gilão on the **Ponte Velha**. It is believed this seven-arched bridge was constructed by the Romans as part of an integral trade route, though the current appearance dates from the 17th century. Across the river, small artisan shops and inviting restaurants line the streets, with the **Jardim da Alagoa**, backed by the **Igreja de Nossa Senhora da Ajuda ou de São Paulo**, a charming spot to dine.

A few minutes away is **Igreja do Carmo**, another of Tavira's 37 churches. Inside, highly artistic baroque and rococo decor makes this one of the most impressive, though sadly it is often closed.

Stroll the Salt Pans

MEMORIES OF A FISHING PAST

Following the Rio Gilão from the city centre to the coast, the white **Salinas of Tavira** stretch out in both directions. The 2km road to the west of the river will bring you to **Cais das Quatro Águas**, where you can easily continue by ferry to Ilha de Tavira (p146). On the east bank, paths pass the ruins of the **Forte do Rato** before ending at a tiny museum

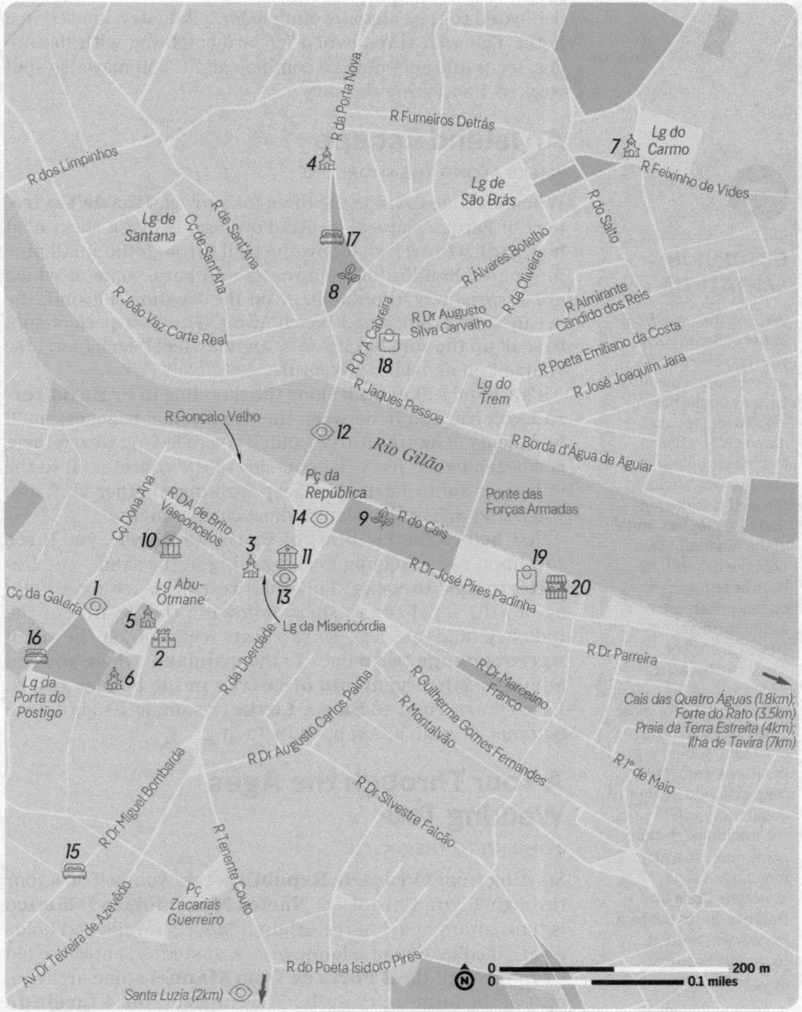

SIGHTS
1 Camera Obscura
2 Castelo
3 Igreja da Misericórdia
4 Igreja de Nossa Senhora da Ajuda ou de São Paulo
5 Igreja de Santa Maria do Castelo
6 Igreja de Santiago
7 Igreja do Carmo
8 Jardim da Alagoa
9 Jardim do Coreto
10 Museu Municipal de Tavira
11 Núcleo Museológico Islâmico
12 Ponte Velha
13 Porta de Dom Manuel
14 Praça da República

SLEEPING
15 HI Tavira – Pousada de Juventude
16 Pousada Convento Tavira
17 São Paulo Boutique Hotel

SHOPPING
18 Casa das Portas
19 Casa Matias
20 Mercado da Ribeira

dedicated to the collapsed tuna fishing industry, housed in a hotel. The area is renowned for birdwatching, with flamingos, terns and spoonbills a common sight. You may also spot workers harvesting the salt.

An Island Escape

WALKS ALONG THE SHORELINE

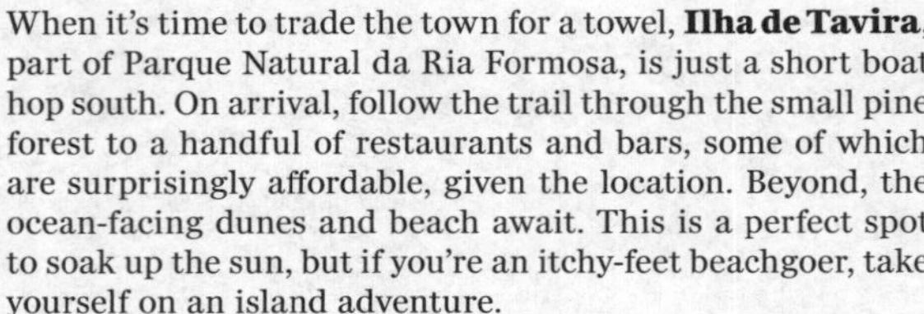

When it's time to trade the town for a towel, **Ilha de Tavira**, part of Parque Natural da Ria Formosa, is just a short boat hop south. On arrival, follow the trail through the small pine forest to a handful of restaurants and bars, some of which are surprisingly affordable, given the location. Beyond, the ocean-facing dunes and beach await. This is a perfect spot to soak up the sun, but if you're an itchy-feet beachgoer, take yourself on an island adventure.

It's around a 2km walk along the shoreline to **Praia da Terra Estreita**, and in between the two marked beaches, you'll find plenty of footprint-free sand. If you're feeling weary, there is a beach bar or ferry (lagoon-side of the concession) to the village of Santa Luzia, but keep walking another 2km and you'll find one of the island's most curious sights.

Just before the facilities of **Praia do Barril**, you'll see row upon row of ageing anchors lying in the sand – the **Cemitério das âncoras**. This final resting place pays homage to the local tuna fishers following the decline of the industry (and species). To rest your feet, hop on the small **narrow-gauge train** back to the mainland, where you can admire a **2000-year-old olive tree** in the holiday resort. Lastly, turn right to **Santa Luzia** to sample its signature octopus, or grab a taxi back to Tavira.

OCTOPUS IN SANTA LUZIA

Walking the waterfront street of Santa Luzia, you'll quickly notice the restaurant menus have a common theme – *polvo* (octopus). It's so entrenched in this fishing village's identity that it holds the (self-designated) title of 'Octopus Capital of the Algarve'. Since 1927, the fishers here have been focused on this prized catch, as the surrounding shores are full of small crustaceans, which attract the octopuses. The original pots (called *alcatruz*) used for trapping the creatures were made from clay, and though some fishers still use the traditional design, many now use a more modern but similar structure. **Casa do Polvo** is one of the best restaurants around to sample the local delicacy.

A Tour Through the Ages Walking Tour

CLIMBING TO THE CASTLE

Starting from **1 Praça da Republica**, take yourself on a tour through Tavira's history. **2 Núcleo Museológico Islâmico** is built around part of the original Moorish walls and holds a varied collection of Islamic pieces. Just after, enter the old town through the **3 Porta de Dom Manuel** stone archway, part of the former city walls. On your right, the **4 Igreja da Misericórdia** has impressive panels of tiles. Further on, the **5 Museu Municipal de Tavira** is a palace turned gallery.

WHERE TO STAY IN TAVIRA

HI Tavira – Pousada de Juventude
Housed in a central, century-old building, with reliable bunks and privates and a simple breakfast. €

Pousada Convento Tavira
This imposing, reconstructed 16th-century convent makes for a grand base with a pool and cloisters. €€€

São Paulo Boutique Hotel
A handful of boutique suites in a renovated historic house with a small saltwater pool. €€€

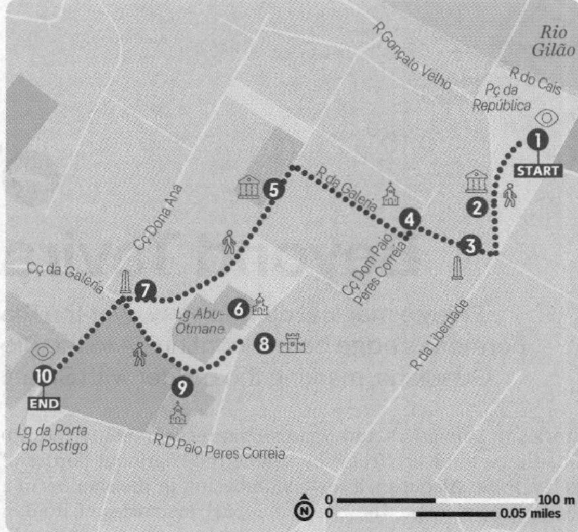

Heading up, the **6 Igreja de Santa Maria do Castelo**, a 13th-century Gothic cathedral reconstructed post-1755 with an Italian design, is located where the mosque would once have been. The old water tower nearby houses the **7 Camera Obscura**.

Turning towards the ruined **8 Castelo**, enter the botanic gardens and climb the ramparts. Phoenicians and Moors occupied this site, but most of what remains are from the 17th century. Peer through the fence to see some medieval archaeological digs, including a Phoenician wall, next door. Continue to **9 Igreja de Santiago** before admiring the **10 Pousada Convento Tavira**, a grand 16th-century convent, since reconstructed and converted into a luxury hotel.

BEST REGIONAL SWEET TREATS

Doce fino do Algarve
These small, colourful marzipan dough delicacies are styled in various shapes (often fruits or animals) and make the most of the Algarve's almond trees.

Dom Rodrigo
Wrapped in foil, these sticky sweet egg and cinnamon treats have been a staple since the 18th century.

Queijo de figo
Figs and almonds (usually with brandy) create this dense cheese-wheel-shaped cake.

Morgado
Dome-shaped and coated in white fondant, the insides of the *morgadinho* are bursting with an egg and almond paste.

GETTING AROUND

Tavira's centre is compact, walkable and relatively flat, except for the area leading to the castle. Affordable ferries to Ilha de Tavira regularly depart from the centre (from just beyond the Mercado da Ribeira) in beach season, as well as from Cais das Quatro Águas, a 30-minute walk through the *salinas*. Water taxis are more expensive but flexible. The bus station is riverside, while the train station is a short walk from the river and historic centre. Vamus bus 105 links Tavira to Santa Luzia, but not on evenings or weekends. There is plenty of parking by the Mercado Municipal, especially in the afternoon after the market has closed.

Beyond Tavira

Enjoy a magical clifftop view over the Ria Formosa's edge before continuing to the Rio Guadiana, marking the border with Spain.

Stories of smugglers and Spanish aggression define the Rio Guadiana, a far cry from the serene international border of today. From Alcoutim, a town slumbering in the shadow of a 14th-century castle, the river runs past memories of Roman settlements, Moorish fortress ruins and salt pans before spilling into the ocean just beyond Vila Real de Santo António, a city stamped with Marquês de Pombal's signature grid-style design. Archaeological findings have shown life alongside the river since the Iron Age, with the Alans, Visigoths, Phoenicians and Greeks all known to have been here. While the major conflict of the Portuguese Restoration War left its marks, the Algarve's far-eastern corners now offer tranquil, crowd-free trails.

TOP TIP

When driving towards Alcoutim, turn off towards the river after Odeleite – it will take a little longer, but it's a more handsome drive.

Cacela Velha

STUDIO F22 RICARDO ROCHA/SHUTTERSTOCK ©

Watch the Fishers of Fuseta

SWIRLING LOW-TIDE BEACH

For one of the finest beaches on the lagoon side of the barrier islands, head to **Praia da Fuseta Ria**, a 20-minute train journey from Tavira, getting off at Fuseta-A station. This well-equipped beach has river bars sitting alongside colourful fishing boats, a beach cafe, plus SUP, kayak and kitesurfing rentals. The lagoon's tranquil waters provide a calm swim, though there is a ferry to the outer island for those who crave the ocean. The real magic comes at low tide when licensed fishers hand dig for clams in the river bed and the usually water-enveloped old **Fuseta Lifeboat Station** becomes accessible on foot.

A Whitewashed Clifftop Village

A DIVINE CHURCH VIEW

Some Algarve views are unforgettable, and the swirling of cyans and white sands at the Parque Natural da Ria Formosa's eastern edge, when seen from above, are precisely that. **Cacela Velha** is a little over 10 minutes from Tavira by car, and the tiny white and blue village perched on a cliff is well worth a detour. There's a 17th-century fort, a cemetery, a couple of cafes and an ancient well, but it's the views over the lagoon from outside the **Igreja de Nossa Senhora da Assunção** that really dazzle. Stairs lead down to the waters and, at low tide, you can walk through the shallows to the beach – just be sure to return before levels rise.

Salinas & Castle Strolls

TRAILS, WILDLIFE AND FORTIFICATIONS

Start your trip to the Algarve's eastern edges at **Vila Real de Santo António**, a 25-minute drive or train from Tavira. Wander around the pedestrian centre and grab a coffee on Praça Marquês de Pombal, before heading towards the **Reserva Natural do Sapal de Castro Marim e Vila Real de Santo António**.

Trails pass through this protected swathe of marshes and salt pans, with seasonal wildlife sightings including flamingos, chameleons and storks. There's a natural spa, **Água-mãe** (closed in winter), offering mineral-rich mud treatments and bathing sessions, and a small interpretation centre (closed weekends) providing park information.

Towering above the *salinas* are the imposing walls of 13th-century **Castelo de Castro Marim**. After the steep climb to

BEST BEACHES NEAR TAVIRA

Praia do Homem Nu
Translated as 'naked man', this is unsurprisingly an official nudist beach slightly west of Praia do Barril.

Praia de Cacela Velha
Spectacular from above, the swirling blue hues of this beach are also magical when walked over at low tide.

Praia de Santo António
At the Algarve's eastern edge, this flat, accessible, forest-backed beach has trails to escape the sun.

Praia Fluvial do Pego Fundo
An inland river beach near Alcoutim with calm waters, verdant surrounds and a beach bar.

WHERE TO STAY NEAR TAVIRA

Camping Ria Formosa
Facilities for caravans and tents in the resort town of Cabanas, with pools and playgrounds. **€**

Pedras d'el Rei
Large tourist resort close to Praia do Barril, with small villa-style accommodation. Dog-friendly. **€€**

Monte Rei Golf & Country Club
Luxurious and vast two-course golf resort enveloped by countryside 15 minutes from the beach. **€€€**

get inside the fortifications, you'll find a small and informative museum, the walls of the old castle, and a quaint church, with fine views over the river and nearby **Forte de São Sebastião**.

The Blue Dragon Rover

WALKS ALONG THE RIVER

Providing a pit stop between Castro Marim and Alcoutim, small **Odeleite** has a church, windmills and a few restaurants overlooking the **Barragem de Odeleite**. While this reservoir doesn't seem special from land, the 'Blue Dragon' nickname hails from the dragon shape visible from an aerial view. There's a raised *praia fluvial* (river beach) here, and peaceful walks around the Odeleite Dam. To visit the nearby low-wall Roman ruins, detour off the main road and follow the river route to Alocutim – you'll spot them to your left after around 20 minutes.

HIKE OR SAIL THE GUADIANA

Spanning the southeastern border with Spain, the Rio Guadiana has seen plenty of stories, smuggling and drama over the years. Nowadays, it makes for one of the Algarve's more tranquil destinations. For walkers or cyclists, the 65km **Grande Rota do Guadiana** follows the river downstream, from Alcoutim to Vila Real de Santo António. With impressive river vistas over Spain, a small museum and even smaller Roman ruins, it's a trail of serenity rather than big-ticket sights. A quicker day-trip alternative is to take a Guadiana river cruise from Vila Real de Santo António. Some trips stop halfway at Foz de Odeleite, while others continue for a visit in Alcoutim before returning.

Smugglers, a Zip Line & Storied Borders

THE FINAL FRONTIERS

Sitting along the river across from Spain, and a short journey to the regional Alentejo border, **Alcoutim**, a 50-minute drive from Tavira, has something of a final frontier feel about it. In days gone by, smuggling was rife across the river, and each March the **Festival do Contrabando** pays homage to the illegal activities of the past. A floating footbridge is erected between Alcoutim and **Sanlúcar de Guadiana**, the village's Spanish counterpart, accompanied by cultural entertainment and traditional crafts while 'tax officers' roam the streets.

For the rest of the year, crossings can be made by ferry or on a rented kayak. Alternatively, the **Limite Zero zip line** provides one of the world's more unique border crossings, hurtling you across from Spain at 70km/h, crossing a time zone en route.

Although Alcoutim's history is storied, little remains of its former defence walls, and you can walk the main highlights in around an hour. Follow the steep streets to the 14th-century **Castelo de Alcoutim**, where you'll be rewarded with the village's best views. There's an **archaeological museum** inside, which houses the medieval castle-wall ruins, local artefacts and a fascinating exhibition of Islamic board games. Beyond that, there are a few churches, a river beach and terraced bars to pause a while.

GETTING AROUND

Trains from Tavira to Fuseta-A and Vila Real de Santo António are a good choice. The bus to VRSA also passes near Cacela Velha, but the bus stop is on the main road, a 30-minute walk from the village. Inland from the Guadiana, heading towards Alcoutim, a car is essential.

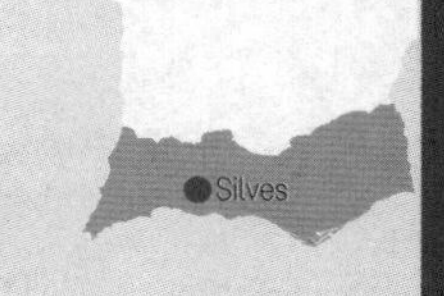

SILVES

Shrouded by fragrant orange groves, aged vineyards, hills and hardy olive trees, Silves' sandstone castle surveys its scenic surroundings from high above. The Rio Arade meanders through; once traversed by Phoenicians and Carthaginians as an important trade route, it's now tracked by migratory birds.

Defined by its Moorish history, Silves – or Xelb, as it was known then – was a wealthy cultural powerhouse, serving as the capital of Al-Gharb. The Moors built the castle (since heavily restored) over what was likely a Roman fort, and left numerous traces of Islamic art and stories from the Almohad period, displayed in the town museums and the out-of-town Casa da Cultura Islâmica e Mediterrânica. Shifting hands between the Moors and Christians twice, the town finally fell to King Afonso III, and the mosque was converted into the cathedral. Slowly, Silves transitioned to serenity as the town's status ebbed – until travellers heeded its laid-back invitation once again.

TOP TIP

Spring is an enchanting time to wander the dusty streets around Silves' surrounding orchards, thanks to the sweet scent of blossoms. February usually brings the almond tree's whites and pinks, while orange groves follow in March.

Step Back in Time in Silves

THE ALGARVE'S ANCIENT CAPITAL

Starting from the river, at the **Ponte Velha de Silves**, set off on a walking tour of the town. The 76m-long, five-arch bridge is often referred to as the 'Roman Bridge', though its construction dates from the 14th century. Follow the narrow, pedestrian streets to the **Praça do Município**, a tree-shaded square with a fountain, perfect for a coffee stop. At the **Centro de Interpretação de Património Islâmico** (closed weekends), which also doubles as the tourist office, you can learn a little about the land, water and poetry of the Moorish culture. Across the square, the imposing red sandstone **Portas da Cidade** is the sole surviving door to the upper part of the city.

Just beyond, the **Museu Municipal de Arqueologia** offers a more in-depth look at the city's history, from the Paleolithic age to the 17th century. Constructed around an impressive Moorish cistern, there are further archaeological finds with a focus on the Almohad period of the 12th and 13th centuries.

Continue climbing to **Sé** (closed weekends), a grand Gothic cathedral that has subsequently been restored and sits on the site of an old mosque. Finally, crowning the town, the russet-coloured and heavily restored sandstone Moorish **Castelo de Silves** (combined ticket with the archaeological museum) stands before you. Inside, you can walk the walls for sublime countryside views, climb down to the

A MEDIEVAL SPECTACLE

For around 10 days in August, the streets of Silves are transported back in time as one of the Algarve's best events, the **Feira Medieval**, takes over the town. Costumed performers reenact ancient Moorish and Christian traditions, processions move through the historic streets, and medieval tournaments drum up a crowd while veiled dancers juggle fire.

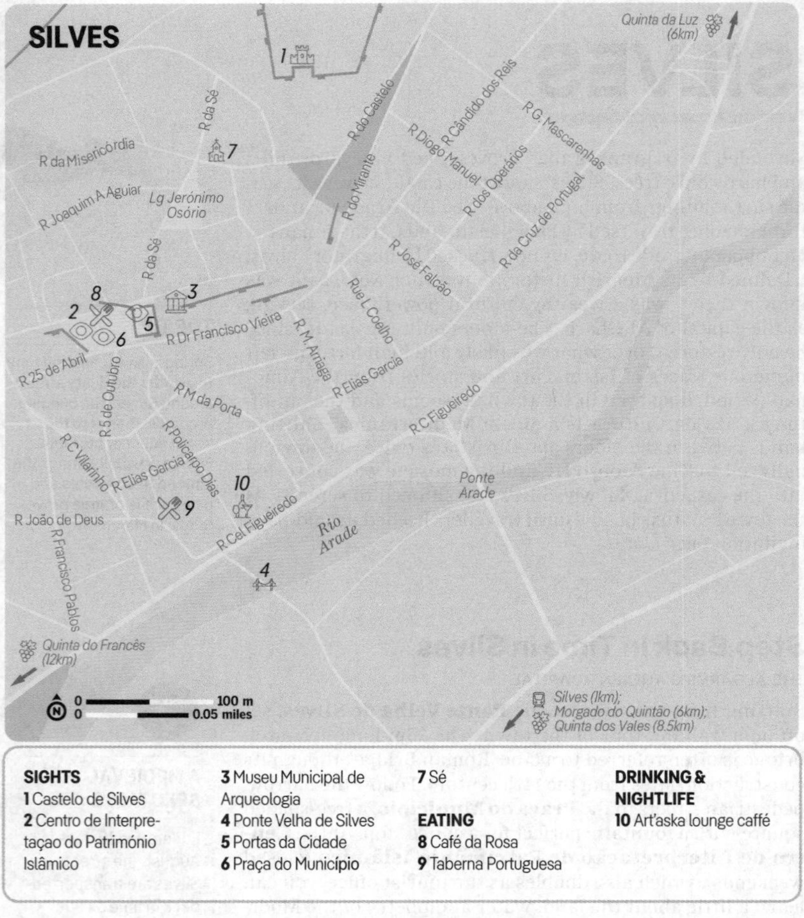

SILVES

SIGHTS
1 Castelo de Silves
2 Centro de Interpretaçao do Património Islâmico
3 Museu Municipal de Arqueologia
4 Ponte Velha de Silves
5 Portas da Cidade
6 Praça do Município
7 Sé

EATING
8 Café da Rosa
9 Taberna Portuguesa

DRINKING & NIGHTLIFE
10 Art'aska lounge caffé

12th-century cistern, and stroll among the excavated ruins of Almohad dwellings.

Sip the Decadent Wine of Silves

VISIT THE VINEYARDS

Of the Algarve's four DOC sub-wine-regions, it's Lagoa and Portimão's hillier surroundings that bring a distinguishable charac-

WHERE TO EAT & DRINK IN SILVES

Café da Rosa
Blue-tiled cafe serving great pastries, best enjoyed on the shaded fountain-side terrace. €

Art'aska lounge caffé
This fun spot (think chairs on the ceiling) has craft beers, local wines and small plates. €

Taberna Portuguesa
Traditional dishes in a brick-vaulted dining room (or outside), with a decent set-price lunch menu. €€

JUERGEN WACKENHUT/SHUTTERSTOCK ©

Boats on the Rio Arade

ter, and the municipality of Silves straddles both. At **Morgado do Quintão**, founded by the Count of Silves at the start of the 19th century, join a weekday wine-pairing lunch under the shade of a 2000-year-old olive tree. Enveloped by vines, this laid-back, communal affair matches the estate's wines with a three-course menu – you can also join the harvest here in October. With an attractive art-gallery-style garden, **Quinta dos Vales** offers an exceptional but pricer experience, guiding you through the winemaking process before you blend, bottle, label and cork your personalised *vinho*. Family-run **Quinta do Francês** is another spectacular spot for a winery and cellar tour, followed by a personalised tasting.

Sailing Along the Rio Arade

TRACKING THE ANCIENT TRADE ROUTE

The **Rio Arade** has long been an important trade route. From the Phoenicians to the Moors, ships stacked with goods have traversed these waters, where the tides dictate the schedule. While most group boat trips start in Portimão or Ferragudo, visiting Silves briefly, some local boat operators (such as SilvesTours) offer private departures from here.

Following the natural flow, you'll be whisked along development-free river banks, returning before reaching the sea. Peaceful countryside views, birds overhead and the wildlife-laden wetlands await those who follow this long-lost trade route.

WHY I LOVE SILVES

When I was six, a wrinkled hand passed me an orange straight from the tree in one of Silves' many orchards, and somehow I've managed to treasure that orange ever since. Nearly 30 years on, that orange may be as wrinkled as the hand that gifted it to me, but the grin from that holiday returns every time I spot Silves' magnificent castle from across the river, sip a coffee under the trees outside Café da Rosa, or roam the dusty, sweet-scented trails beyond the town. Silves is timeless, and its stories and charm ooze from every building and smile. Slow down, order a bottle of local wine – and of course, savour the local oranges.

Daniel James Clarke

GETTING AROUND

Silves' centre is compact yet steep, so comfortable shoes are advisable. Avoid driving on the narrow streets by using the large, free car park next to the municipal pools. A car (and designated driver) is essential to visit many vineyards, although a couple of the closest are within walking distance. The train station is a 25-minute walk south from the centre, including a short stretch on the main road.

Beyond Silves

Continue inland from Silves to admire panoramic vistas from the lofty peaks of the Algarve and explore whitewashed hilltop towns.

Almond and orange groves, cork-coated hinterlands, revitalised vineyards and historic watermills – the Algarve's interior is less developed, less visited and longs to be explored on foot. From 902m Mt Fóia, the Algarve's highest peak, the Serra de Monchique sprawls outwards, with the glistening ocean providing the perfect backdrop to the panorama. Hiking trails pass waterfalls, mountain villagers brewing fiery local liquor and the almost theme-park-like Caldas de Monchique thermal springs. Beloved by Romans and more recent royalty, this woodland-shrouded spot has welcomed sulphur-scented spa seekers for centuries. To the east, eagles keep an eye over the Serra do Caldeirão, where whitewashed hill towns of *fontes* (streams) and an often-forgotten Bronze Age dolmen hide.

TOP TIP

Check the fire-risk warnings and grab trail maps and information from Monchique's tourism office before heading out hiking.

Caldas de Monchique

PRISMA BY DUKAS PRESSEAGENTUR GMBH/ALAMY STOCK PHOTO ©

Hike the Algarve's Highest Peak

PANORAMIC VISTAS AND WATERFALL TRAILS

On the **Serra de Monchique**, starting at the top isn't a bad idea. **Fóia**, the highest point (902m), is a 45-minute drive inland from Silves, and from here you can enjoy magnificent vistas across the Algarve and the Atlantic Ocean. It's the starting point for one of the many trails in the mountain range – the **Trilho da Fóia**. The 7km circular trail descends deep into agricultural terraces, through lavender-infused scrub, and passes small streams in the cork-strewn countryside before climbing back up to Fóia on the north slope. An alternative (and longer) loop, which visits the impressive **Cascata do Barbelote**, also begins nearby.

The Mountain Village of Medronho

SLOW-PACED STRONG LIQUOR

A 20-minute drive west of Fóia, **Marmelete** is an easy-to-miss, inconspicuous village on the road from Monchique to Aljezur – but there is something brewing in these mountains. Dotting the local landscape, the red fruits of the *medronho* tree are instantly recognisable and, courtesy of Marmelete's residents, they are distilled into *aguardente* (firewater). At **Casa do Medonho** (closed weekends), you can learn more about the fruit-to-firewater process. If you schedule a visit in advance, you'll also have the chance to visit the licensed distilleries around town and potentially participate in the production process. It's a personal experience, providing an intimate look into this village's mountain life.

Revive in the Thermal Springs

MOUNTAIN SPA TREATMENTS IN CALDAS DE MONCHIQUE

Thermal waters flow through the mountains of Monchique, renowned for their healing powers and high alkaline (9.5pH) levels. From the Romans to royalty, the valley village of **Caldas de Monchique** has been pampering and soothing for centuries, and retains a whimsical ambience. A shaded walk through the **Parque Fonte dos Amores** is the perfect way to cleanse the mind, following trickling streams and spotting locals filling up bottles from the source. For the body, book into the **Villa Termal Caldas de Monchique Spa** for a revitalising mud wrap, water ritual and dip in the thermal pools.

BEST INLAND ADRENALINE KICKS

In recent years, the **Autódromo Internacional do Algarve** has found its place on the world stage, thanks to the presence of Formula 1 races. The track isn't just reserved for elite drivers, with enthusiasts also able to take it on. The racing school experience places you behind the wheel of a revved-up supercar for a couple of laps with professional supervision. There is also a go-kart track for more family-friendly fun. Jeep safaris and off-road quad tours in the lower mountains and cork-forested backcountry offer another four-wheel escapade.

TO THE COSTA VICENTINA

Drive 15 minutes west and spot the medieval castle of Aljezur (p179) before continuing to paradisiacal Praia da Amoreira.

WHERE TO EAT AROUND MONCHIQUE

Cafetaria O Planalto da Fóia
Once you've hiked to Fóia, this reliable cafe provides coffee, cakes and snacks to refuel. **€**

Foz do Banho
Verdant views near Caldas de Monchique with good-value traditional *pratos do dia* (daily specials). **€€**

Café Vintage Tapas & Wine
Retro decor, quality wines and tasty but small plates in the heart of Monchique town. **€€**

Armação de Pêra

FRANGO À GUIA

Chicken piri-piri, one of the Algarve's most famous dishes, provides a hot-sauce story steeped in history. During the Age of Discovery, fiery chillies were brought back from the Americas and grown in the Portuguese colonies of Cabo Verde and Mozambique, where it's said the sauce was invented. Later, as many Portuguese returned from these colonies in the 1970s, the chillies were infused with more European ingredients, such as garlic, olive oil and lemon. The best place to try it is the Algarvian town of **Guia**, celebrated as the 'Chicken Capital'. **Restaurante Ramires**, with a fast-paced *frango* (chicken) service across three floors, is regarded as the creator of the combination. Order it *com* (with) or *sem* (without) piri-piri sauce.

Silves' Sliver of Coast

A DOSE OF GOLDEN SANDS

Stretching towards the coast, the municipality of Silves has its own sliver of beaches, concentrated around **Armação de Pêra**, a 20-minute drive southeast. The coastal town is fronted by the expansive **Praia de Armação de Pêra**, which is backed by high-rise apartment blocks and a few historic buildings, though it has all the facilities and water-sport rentals you'd need. Further east, behind **Praia Grande de Pêra**, sits **Lagoa dos Salgados**. The boardwalk around this lagoon provides informative signs highlighting the birdlife you may spot. En route back to Silves, you'll pass through

WHERE TO EAT AROUND THE SERRA DO CALDEIRÃO

Germano biciArte café
Pause for great coffee and snacks in Alte's cafe-meets-bike-repair shop. €

Cafe D Rosa
Coffee and sandwiches – perfect for refuelling between trails – on Querença's pretty church square. €

Janela da Serra
Settle in for quality small-plate snacks on the terrace of this popular cycling pit stop in Salir. €€

Alcantarilha, where the **Igreja Matriz de Alcantarilha** is worth a pause to visit the chilling chapel of bones.

Quintessential Villages Around the Serra do Caldeirão

WHITEWASHED HILLTOP STOPS

Slowly rising towards the border with Alentejo, the **Serra do Caldeirão** mountains peak in **Pelados** at 589m. Hiking trails cross the scrub and cork-tree-coated hills, renowned for their birdlife. You can spot birds of prey such as goshawks and the short-toed eagles – and perhaps even the endangered Bonelli's eagle. The circular **Rocha de Pena** trail is an excellent introduction to the range.

More than anything, the *serra* is a place to slow down, and spending a day hopping between the mountain villages will introduce you to a different Algarve. **Alte**, a 30-minute drive from Silves, is perhaps the Algarve's quintessential rural village. Whitewashed streets lead to *fontes* (streams) alongside former wells and mills, with a *praia fluvial* (river beach) in which to cool off. The **Queda do Vigário** waterfall, a short walk from the village, promises a refreshing dip in spring, though there can be little water in the summer.

Continue to **Salir**, a village born from a 12th-century Moorish castle (ruins of the walls remain). Lastly, call at well-restored **Querença**, an adorable village focused around the plaza of **Igreja Matriz de Querença**. At the **Polo Museológico da Água** (closed weekends), find aged equipment from the surrounding waterways and collect maps for the local trails.

More Caves & Bays

HIKES AND BEACHES

From the beaches of Silves municipality, head west to hike one of the Algarve's most dramatic and beautiful trails, the **Percurso dos Sete Vales Suspensos**, and kayak inside **Benagil Cave**, or drive east towards the coves and beaches of **Albufeira** (p142).

POTTERY FROM PORCHES

Clay has been an integral part of Algarvian history for millennia, but with the arrival of the Romans and later the Moors, it became an art form. Evident in the *azulejos* (hand-painted tiles) adorning countless walls, and in the Islamic pottery garnishing the displays in Faro's museums, it's a tradition that lives on today. In homes across the region, you'll spot colourful clay bowls, plates, jugs and wall art, and the small town of Porches is where you'll find some of the Algarve's best modern producers. At renowned Porches Pottery, you can witness the artisans working and shop their signature designs, while nearby Olaria Pequena offers slightly more contemporary pieces.

GETTING AROUND

With a car, the many trails and viewpoints of the Serra de Monchique are within a 45-minute drive of Silves. Monchique (the town and springs) can be accessed by bus, although you'll need to transfer through Portimão. To visit the beaches without a car, you'll need to change bus at Lagoa's main terminal to connect to Armação de Pêra or any of the more dramatic beaches nearby. For Alte and the Serra do Caldeirão, limited bus connections via SB Messines make a day trip near impossible without a car.

PORTIMÃO

It's fair to say Portimão isn't a tourism-focused destination. Most visitors are beachgoers and revellers who quickly pass through the region's second city to reach Praia da Rocha's swathe of golden sand, following in the long-gone footsteps of the usual suspects – Phoenicians, Greeks and Carthaginians. The Romans later named it Portos Magnus before it fell into Moorish and Christian hands. Sadly, remnants of bygone times are limited to discoveries such as the megalithic tombs of Alcalar, the Roman ruins of Abicada and a small museum artefact collection.

The 19th century saw Portimão's fishing and canning industries boom, leading to a rapid city expansion. While those industries have also near disappeared, the simple sardine is still honoured in a festival every August. Today Portimão is still very much a port city, but the edges have been somewhat polished, and visitors will find themselves mingling with modern Algarvian life.

TOP TIP

Check ahead for events so you can book tickets to join the party or steer clear until a quieter date.

Discover the City of Sardines

ALONG THE WATERFRONT

Medieval Portimão has long faded away, apart from some small hidden stretches of the wall, making a walking tour of the city about more modern features. Dive straight into the sardine history that has defined the city at the **Museu de Portimão**. This extremely modern museum is housed in a renovated 19th-century fish-canning factory, with plenty of original features, such as the extended row of sinks still visible. A short video (with English subtitles) introduces the factory's operation when sardines and mackerel were abundant. Then you can walk through the canning procedure, with artistic human-size statues 'performing' the various steps of the process alongside original equipment. Displays on archaeological finds in the surrounding area, plus an underwater submarine-themed room focused on the city's waters, are also here.

Leaving the museum, wander along the **Ribeirinha** waterfront, the true soul of the city, where the catch would be offloaded, notifying workers to flock to the factory. Nowadays, the scent of freshly grilled sardines floats through the air at the northern end. It's a perfect spot for a local lunch. Away from the estuary, **Igreja de Nossa Senhora da Conceição**, a 15th-century Gothic-style church that saw substantial

PORTIMÃO FESTIVALS

Portimão – and Praia da Rocha in particular – have become a magnet for impressive international festivals during the summer months when revellers dance on the sand until the early hours.

AMNAT30/SHUTTERSTOCK ©

Museu de Portimão

reworking following the 1755 earthquake, is worth a peek, as is the **Igreja do Antigo Colégio da Companhia de Jesus** (closed weekends), a Jesuit college that opened in 1707.

Sandy (or Dancing) Feet

BEACH BARS AND CLIFFTOP CLUBS

Just south of Portimão, vast **Praia da Rocha** is flanked by ochre-hued cliffs and high-rise apartments. From the sands far below, you'll forget about the city, thanks to the ample space even in the busiest months. Bars, cafes and water sports provide everything you need for a beach day.

For a more snazzy shoreline experience, head to **NoSoloÁgua**, a trendy beach club with a pool, cabanas and an inflatable waterpark on the ocean in front. By night – or when huge international festivals take over the beach in

BEST RESTAURANTS IN PORTIMÃO

Dona Barca
Get an affordable grilled-sardines fix, just back from the river. €

Tapa Latina
Central and cosy *petiscos* (snack-size plates), with a few outside tables. An excellent spot for a light lunch. €

Fogo de Chão Portimão
This Brazilian *rodizio* restaurant, with all-you-can-eat meats, is a great choice before a night out in Praia da Rocha. €€

A Casa da Rocha
Seafood-heavy menu with daily specials and dazzling clifftop views over Praia dos Três Castelos. €€

WHERE TO PARTY IN PORTIMÃO

NoSoloÁgua Portimão
This beach club and bar delivers good beats and cocktails around the pool or terrace.

On The Rocks
A late-night bar for live music and clifftop views over Praia da Rocha.

The Loft
Portimão's gay late-night weekend-party venue. The owners also operate the Garage Bar, open weeknights.

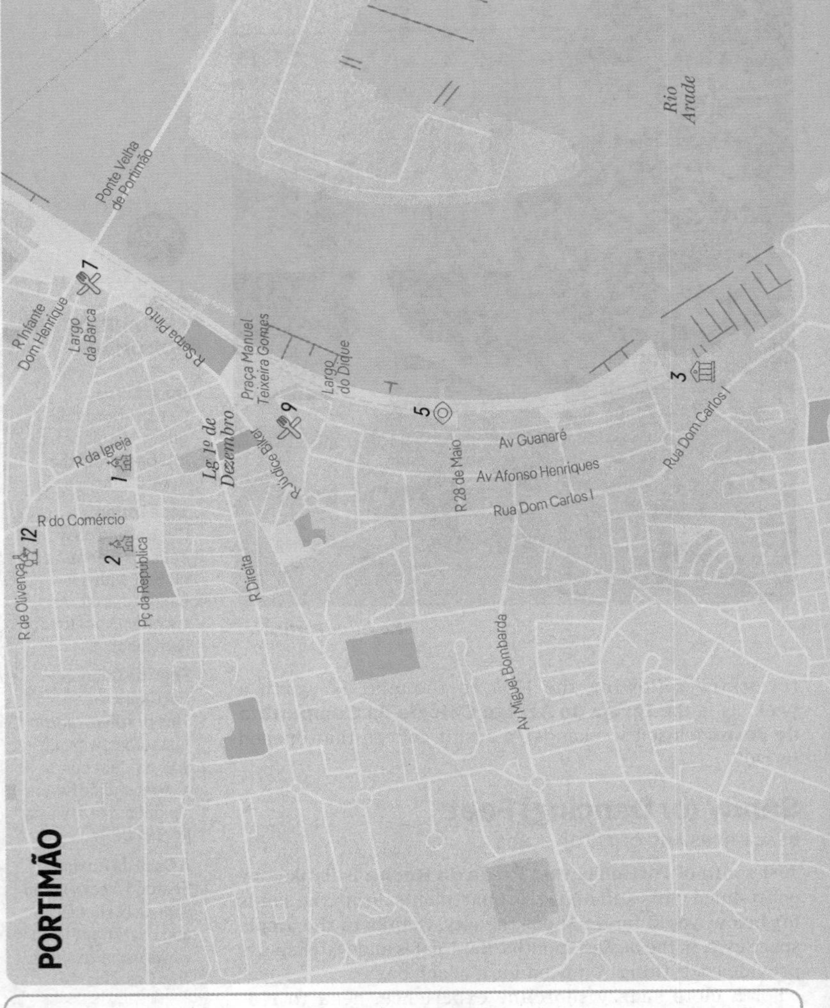

SIGHTS
1 Igreja de Nossa Senhora da Conceição
2 Igreja do Antigo Colégio da Companhia de Jesus
3 Museu de Portimão
4 Praia da Rocha
5 Ribeirinha

EATING
6 A Casa da Rocha
7 Dona Barca
8 Fogo de Chão Portimão
9 Tapa Latina

DRINKING & NIGHTLIFE
10 NoSoloÁgua Portimão
11 On The Rocks
12 The Loft

summer – the vibe shifts, with the strip of bars and clubs on the clifftop partying until the early hours.

Dive Sunken Shipwrecks

A DIVER'S UNDERWATER PLAYGROUND

In 2012 the first of four warships was purposefully sunk off Portimão's coast, marking the beginning of the **Ocean Revival Project**. This intriguing artificial reef brings together vessels from the same Portuguese Navy fleet, repurposing them as a divers' adventure playground while creating new environments for marine life to thrive. Wreck divers will

Praia da Rocha (p159)

DIVING IN PORTIMÃO

Arlindo Serrao, an experienced wreck diver from Portimão and founder of *@portugaldive*, shares why he loves the city's coastline.

The Algarve offers diverse underwater scenarios, such as reefs, swim-throughs, wrecks and caves. Offshore from Portimão, you can experience complex dives or enjoy open-water courses with various fish species, attractive underwater flora and the beautiful seabed, then relax at the beach afterwards. The Ocean Revival Project is incredible, with four navy ships lying underwater – I love to swim through the engine rooms and imagine how it was when the ship was sailing and protecting our coast. Don't expect to be underwater with dozens of others, because Portugal is a relatively new diving destination.

relish the opportunity to explore the interiors of the ships, which range from 44m to 102m in length.

Operators such as Portugal Dive, or PORTISUB, the local dive association, are the starting point for arranging your underwater visit. To learn more about the project, visit the **Museu de Portimão**, where you can 'experience' the park in a submerged submarine-styled room.

GETTING AROUND

Portimão is easily explored on foot, as the main centre is reasonably compact. It's around a 30-minute walk to Praia da Rocha. Alternatively, the 33 Citybus runs until early evening. The old part of the city has a confusing and complex one-way road system, so opt for one of the many car parks around the edge.

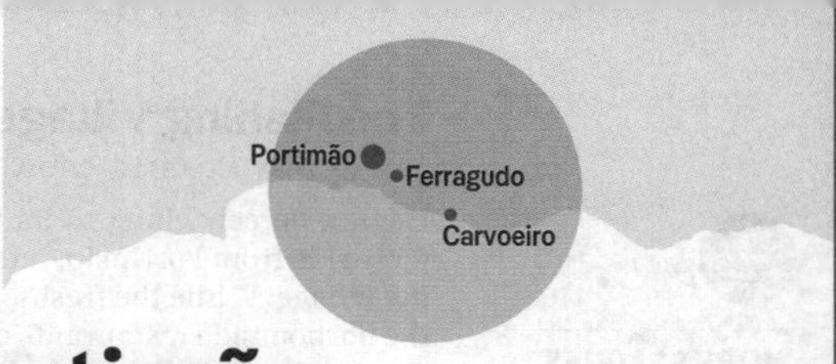

Portimão
Ferragudo
Carvoeiro

Beyond Portimão

Small fishing villages turned holiday towns, epic caves and some of the country's best coast-hugging cliff trails straddle Portimão.

East of Portimão, across the wildlife-heavy Rio Arade estuary, tiny fishing villages have grown outwards, and thankfully not upwards, into family-friendly holiday-villa-style resorts. In the quay of Ferragudo, where the fishing industry started flourishing in the 14th century, you can still witness fishers fixing their nets and unloading their catch to be grilled fresh on the restaurant terraces.

Beyond, the cliffs climb and fall along the craggy coastline, creating perhaps the region's most memorable hiking trail, complete with cinematic clifftop panoramas, wave-lapped bays and caves ripe for kayak adventures. To the west, the boardwalks around the Ria de Alvor promise a serene birdwatching stroll, with sandpiper, stilt, tern and (mostly seasonal) flamingo sightings.

TOP TIP

The marked (and unofficial) trails spanning the nearby cliffs are spectacular, but with no barriers, be wary of erosion warnings.

Ferragudo (p164)

The Fishing Village of Ferragudo

SEAFOOD BY A CASTLE-CROWNED BEACH

Having fiercely clung to its traditions, **Ferragudo**, a short ferry ride from Portimão, retains some of the feeling of a fishing village. While the fresh-off-the-boat seafood dished up at the harbourside restaurants comes with a premium price tag, there's something timeless about the setting. Small colourful boats bob in the background while fishers unload their catch and scrub their decks – the perfect sideshow to lunch. After dining, wander the backstreets adorned with magenta bougainvillea and trailing plants before resting on Ferragudo's largest golden-sand bay, **Praia Grande**, in the shadow of the impressive, privately owned (and thus closed) Castelo de São João do Arade.

MORE BEACHES NEAR PORTIMÃO

Praia de Boião
Secluded, yet sometimes busy due to the impressive skylit cave next door (be aware of potential cliff and cave erosion).

Praia dos Careanos
Stairs lead down to this copper-cliff-framed treat. Praia do Vau next door is an accessible beach.

Praia de Nossa Senhora da Rocha
Two side-by-side beaches, separated by a scenic cliff topped with a chapel jutting into the ocean.

Carvoeiro's Craggy Coastline

BOARDWALK ROCK FORMATIONS

It didn't take long for **Carvoeiro**, a 30-minute bus ride from Portimão, to rise from a simple fishing village to the Algarve's holiday poster child – and you'll quickly see why. One of the region's most attractive and laid-back resorts, it makes for an enjoyable half-day visit. While the main beach is relatively small, the cluster of houses and reliable restaurants rising up the hillsides on either side make it particularly photogenic. Follow the **clifftop boardwalk** for cerulean panoramas before arriving at **Algar Seco**, a series of rock formations and caves you can explore on foot before enjoying a drink among them at **Boneca Bar**. From here, you could follow the cliffs to Vale de Centeanes, the start (or end) point of the Percurso dos Sete Vales Suspensos.

UP THE RIO ARADE

The Rio Arade winds its way through Silves before converging with the ocean between Ferragudo and Portimão. From both, you can take boat tours to Silves, historic capital of the Algarve.

A Cinematic Clifftop Trail

RAMBLE CLIFFS, COVES AND BEACHES

Nothing captures the cinematic essence of the central Algarve coast better than the **Percurso dos Sete Vales Suspensos**. This 6km linear trail tracks dramatic cliffs into sand-filled valleys. While steep and stony in parts, the route is of moderate difficulty. Rather than rushing, pack a picnic and swimsuit and make it a full day of cove-hopping and rock-arch admiring. Stretching from **Vale de Centeanes** to **Praia da Marinha**, it can be covered in either direction. Start early (golden hour provides the best photos) at **Praia da Marinha**, a scenic,

WHERE TO STAY BEYOND PORTIMÃO

CasaTuia
Inland, these glamping tents with Balinese-inspired touches provide a tranquil alternative to a coastal sleep. **€€**

O Castelo Guest House
Renovated rooms in a yellow castle-esque building with views or balconies overlooking Carvoeiro's beach. **€€**

Casa Rei das Praias
Upscale sea-view rooms and suites close to Ferragudo's beaches, with a spa and two pools. **€€€**

FEDERICA GRASSI/GETTY IMAGES ©

Praia da Marinha

cliff-hugged bay of grottoes that quickly gets busy – it's perfect for a pre-trail paddle. The cliff trail passes a few fenced sinkholes offering peeks into the caves below, before arriving at the most famous one, Benagil Cave. Here you could hire a kayak to visit the grotto before moving on to quieter bays. At **Praia do Carvalho**, excellent for a picnic stop, descend stairs through a cave tunnel onto the golden sands. Back on the trail, the **Farol de Alfanzina** lighthouse, surrounded by wooded terrain, will begin to loom in the distance, marking the start of the final stretch to **Vale de Centeanes**, where a well-deserved beach bar awaits.

To avoid hunting for parking, and the need to retrace your steps, make use of the bus connections via Lagoa.

Kayak into the Algarve's Sea Cave

CROWD-HEAVY SKYLIGHT GROTTO

While there are countless sea caves along the Algarve's coast, none have captured the attention quite like **Benagil**. While some might say it's become a tourist trap, there's no denying the grotto, illuminated by a natural skylight and only accessible by water, is extraordinary. However, it's best to

BEST COASTAL TOURS NEAR PORTIMÃO

Zip&Trip
Hunt out alternative, less-crowded caves and secret bays around Alvor on this adventurous snorkelling tour.

Wildwatch
Marine-biologist-led dolphin-spotting tours departing from Ferragudo.

Algarve SUN BOAT Trips
Explore the coastline and caves on these solar-powered boat tours departing from Portimão Marina.

Algarve Freedom Kayaks
Skip the boats altogether and take a kayak tour from Ferragudo to Carvoeiro, stopping at caves and beaches only accessible by sea.

WHERE TO DRINK WITH A VIEW BEYOND PORTIMÃO

Club Nau
From lunch until late, this beachfront restaurant-cum-bar in Ferragudo is lively, sometimes with live music. €€

Caniço
The views and elevator-in-the-cliff access are the stars here. Great for an Alvor beachside beverage. €€

Quinta dos Santos
Enjoy quality dishes, vineyard views and the estate's own wines and craft beers near Lagoa. €€€

ANGELINA DIMITROVA/SHUTTERSTOCK ©

Passadiços de Alvo

UP IN THE AIR

Some would say that the migratory birds of the Algarve get the best views when passing through. Luckily, those of us without wings can also appreciate the cinematic coastline and scenic mountains from above. **Portimão Aerodrome** (located near Alvor) is the place to get your kicks, with the highest tandem parachute jumps promising over a minute of free fall from 15,000ft (4500m) before slowing down to relish the dazzling cerulean-hued ocean vistas. Scenic flights along the dramatic cave-littered coast offer a slower perspective. For a less adrenaline-fuelled way to take to the skies, join **Algarve Balloons** on a small group or private hot-air-balloon flight over the western Algarve hinterlands.

manage your expectations – even at sunrise, it's becoming hard to find the cave's beach footprint-free. While tours from near and far offer excursions into the cave, new regulations don't allow passengers to disembark from boats, so if you want to set foot on the sands, consider an alternative to a tour.

The best starting point is **Praia de Benagil** (though parking can be a hassle), where you'll find kayak and SUP rentals, allowing you to make the short journey yourself. Due to the strong currents and constant boats, swimming into the cave is not advisable.

Boardwalks & Birdwatching

BEACH-BACKED WETLANDS

Heading west from Portimão, the town of **Alvor** is just a 10-minute drive away and is home to the **Passadiços de Alvor**, one of the largest boardwalk trails in the Algarve. Skirting the dunes and **Ria de Alvor Nature Reserve**, the estuary's wetlands are a haven for birdlife year-round, although July and August see a dip in numbers. Black-winged stilts, greater flamingos and Caspian terns can all be spotted, depending on the season.

GETTING AROUND

On weekdays, Citybus 14 runs from Portimão to Alvor, with some stops close to other beaches en route. Ferragudo is a short hop by bus, train or seasonal ferry from the Museu de Portimão or the marina. To the east, Vamus buses connect Portimão with Carvoeiro and Praia da Marinha for the Percurso dos Sete Vales Suspensos. From May until October, the EVA Cliffs Line offers a daily pass, allowing you to easily hop between some of the most popular beaches. Driving the coastal roads allows more freedom for stops at tranquil bays, though during summer it can be busy and parking a challenge, especially at Benagil and Praia da Marinha's small and dusty car parks.

LAGOS

Endless water sports, bays backed by rock formations, trendy restaurants inside old town walls and a laid-back energy that turns hedonistic by night – Lagos doesn't do anything by halves. It's no longer just surfers and sea-cave seekers flocking here in abundance, but also luxury property developers, serious cold-brew cafes and remote workers balancing their board meetings with bodyboarding.

It was in 1415, when a fleet set sail to conquer Ceuta in Morocco, that Lagos' story became tied to the Age of Discovery. Quickly, countless other colonising expeditions to Africa followed, and the first market selling African slaves on European shores opened here, a horrific but little-discussed part of the town's history. Between 1576 and 1756, Lagos served as the regional capital until a devastating earthquake and tsunami led to Faro taking the title.

TOP TIP

Lagos is a great base for those who appreciate their urban comforts. The protected park's furthest spots are around an hour's drive by car, or the 79 bus operated by Vamus allows weekday access to the likes of Odeceixe and Aljezur.

Sailings & Sightings

DOLPHIN SPOTTING AND CAVE VISITS

With a coastline begging to be explored, it's no wonder Lagos' harbour is lined with stands hawking boat tours, dolphin-spotting trips and sunset sailings – getting out on the water is second nature here. Dolphin-watching trips offered by **SeaLife** depart the marina and are all accompanied by a marine biologist, meaning an environmental focus and plenty of knowledge shared on board. With a reported 96% sighting rate, spotting one of the six species in the surrounding waters is highly likely. The ocean-chiselled headland of **Ponta da Piedade** is another popular destination, and witnessing it from the water provides a different perspective. To get inside the grottoes and admire the theatrical sea pillars up close, opt for the greater manoeuvrability of a small boat operator – some local fishers still offer these tours.

Out on the Water

WINDSURFING AND WATER SPORTS

When the right winds come calling on Lagos, the sky above **Meia Praia** is decorated with kites as wind-riders take to the waters. If you're tempted to try this high-adrenaline sport, there are a few kitesurfing schools around town. Meia Praia is popular with surfers for its beach breaks, while **Porto de Mós** also has a reef break. Kayak and SUP rentals are abundant, with kayak tours around **Ponta da Piedade** providing perhaps the best way to admire the headland. For underwater escapades, divers are spoilt with many nearby beach and boat sites – the nudibranchs at **Rocha Negra** are particularly revered.

BEST BEACHES IN LAGOS

Praia dos Estudantes
Small cove close to the centre with a photogenic Roman-style bridge spanning two towering rocks.

Praia do Camilo
Dramatic rock formations envelop this beach, accessed by 200-plus steps.

Meia Praia
Expanse of golden sands on the marina side of Lagos, popular for windsurfing and water sports.

Praia de Porto de Mós
Spacious cliff-flanked beach beyond Ponta da Piedade with Sagres views and (usually) fewer crowds.

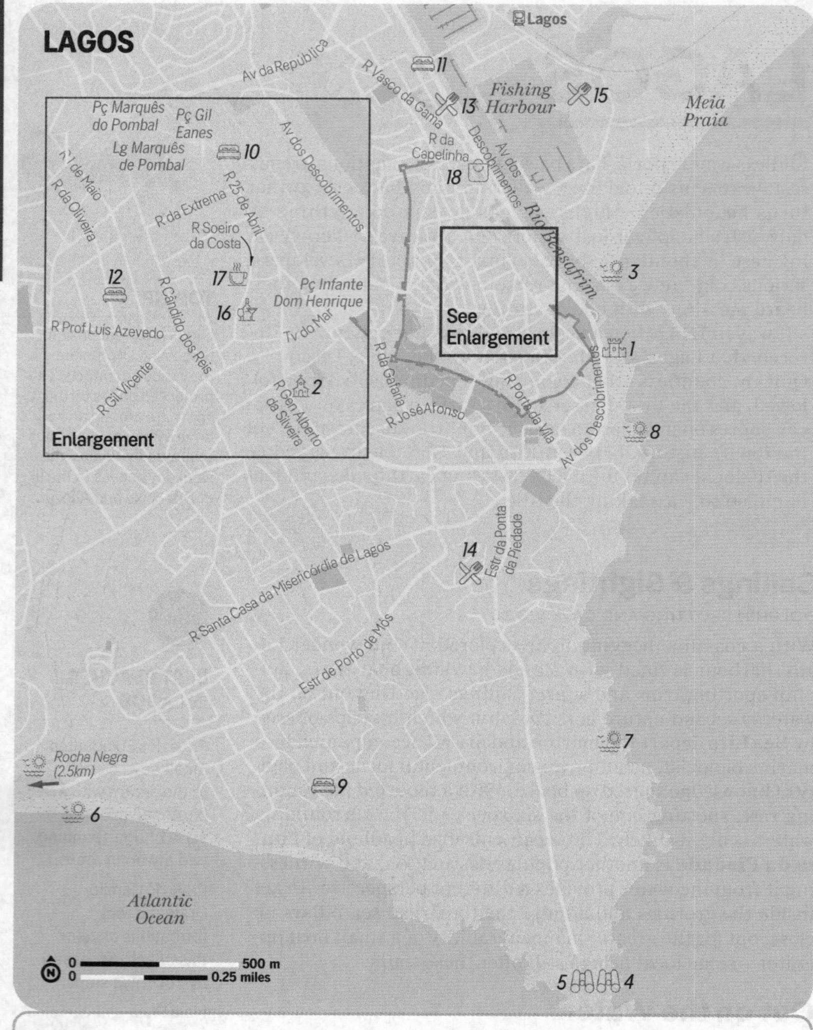

SIGHTS
1 Forte da Ponta da Bandeira
2 Igreja de Santo António
3 Meia Praia
4 Miradouro da Ponta da Piedade
5 Ponta da Piedade
6 Praia de Porto de Mós
7 Praia do Camilo
8 Praia dos Estudantes

SLEEPING
9 Cascade Wellness Resort
10 Hotel Mar Azul
11 Lagos Avenida Hotel
12 Olive Hostel

EATING
13 Adega da Marina
14 Repolho Gastrobar & Garrafeira
15 Tasca do Kiko

DRINKING & NIGHTLIFE
16 Peppers Bar
17 The Studio

SHOPPING
18 Mercado Municipal

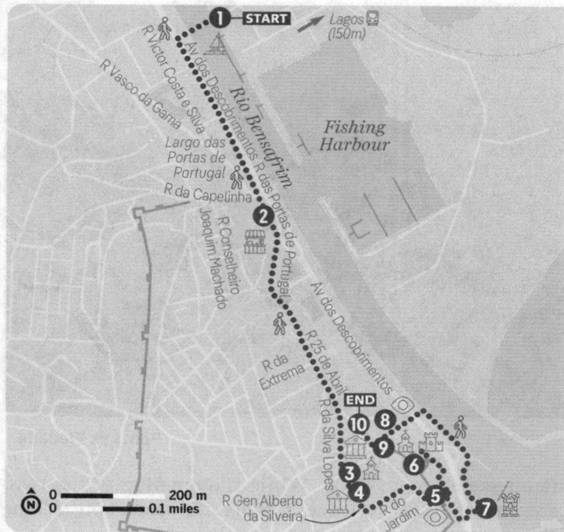

Churches, Museums & Fortifications Walking Tour

TOUR THE OLD TOWN

From the train station, walk past lively **1 Marina de Lagos**, crossing the bridge and following the palm-lined harbour to the **2 Mercado Municipal**. Turn right to enter the pedestrianised area. Stop at **3 Museu de Lagos**, a seemingly uncurated collection of finds with Roman mosaics, palm and pottery works, coins, old tools and other curious artefacts. It's also the entrance to the **4 Igreja de Santo António**, an explosion of gilded carved woodwork and detailed paintings. From here, it's a few minutes to **5 Porta de São Gonçalo**, one of the old town walls' impressive gates. On the other side, you'll see the wall joining the 17th-century **6 Governors Castle**. Cross the road to **7 Forte da Ponta da Bandeira**, a 17th-century defensive structure surrounded by a drawbridge moat.

Turning back to **8 Plaza Infante Dom Henrique**, the **9 Igreja de Santa Maria de Lagos** dominates one side of the square, while the **10 Mercado de Escravos** is opposite. Sitting on the site where Europe's first slave market opened in 1444, it's a sombre reminder of Portugal's colonial past – further darkened by the discovery of African

REMOTE WORK IN LAGOS

Jodie Dewberry, co-founder of *@thestudio.coffee* and former digital nomad, shares why Lagos is perfect for remote working.

I knew Lagos had to become 'home' when I first visited and felt its entrepreneurial energy. Everybody here has a project on the go, and it's a constant source of inspiration. My days start at CrossFit before heading to The Studio coffee shop or municipal-run CoLagos workspace. I love that I always meet someone new and see many familiar faces. I usually grab lunch there (or a Pom Pom bagel) and head to Ponta da Piedade to relax. There's always a casual meet-up, volleyball game or other free events in the evenings, especially in bars such as The Collab or Peppers Bar.

WHERE TO EAT IN LAGOS

Adega da Marina
This large, photo-decorated dining room focuses on grilled fish (the sardines are fantastic) at fair prices. €€

Tasca do Kiko
Slightly hidden beyond the train station; the creative, seafood-heavy tapas are worth hunting out. €€

Repolho Gastrobar & Garrafeira
The extensive premium *petiscos* list is best overcome by opting for the 'surprise menu' with wine pairings. €€€

BEST PLACES TO STAY IN LAGOS

Olive Hostel
Laid-back central dorms and privates with a bohemian decor and welcoming vibe – the sociable terrace is a bonus. €

Hotel Mar Azul
Good location, clean and modern rooms (some with sea views) and fair prices. €€

Lagos Avenida Hotel
This spot is city-centre chic, with a rooftop infinity pool overlooking the marina and a mouthwatering restaurant (open to non-guests) downstairs. €€€

Cascade Wellness Resort
Moments from Ponta da Piedade, this is a tranquil luxury stay thanks to the spa, sea views and gardens. €€€

NIDO HUEBL/SHUTTERSTOCK ©

Ponta da Piedade

human skeletons in 2009. While the opening of the two-storey museum acknowledges this horrific past, many feel the displays, tone and context are severely lacking.

A Craggy Coastal Headland Hike

UNFORGETTABLE ROCK FORMATIONS

Towering sandstone cliffs, craggy caverns carved by wild waves, and cliff-flanked steep beaches define the windswept area around **Ponta da Piedade**. It's a scenic setting to catch an Algarve sunset, or explore on an afternoon adventure. Around 3km out of town, the headland can be reached on foot in 40 minutes by following the main road, though the cliff trails and beach detours make it an unforgettable full-day outing.

To reach it from the 17th-century **Forte da Ponta da Bandeira**, set off along the coastal road, keeping an eye out for the Roman-style bridge above **Praia dos Estudantes**. Turning off by the convent ruins, detour in front of the hotels, with the golden shores of **Praia de Dona Ana** to your left. Clamber onto the clifftop if it's accessible (always keep erosion and safe distances in mind) or follow the road again. At **Praia do Camilo**, the steep stairs leading to this busy beach are quite the picture. Continuing along the clifftop trail where possible, hard-to-access bays and coves will draw your attention before the **Miradouro da Ponta da Piedade** presents an unimaginable panorama. Descend the stairs for a closer look (sometimes fishing boats offer tours) before marvelling at the rest of the headland's grottoes and rock formations from above.

GETTING AROUND

The old town is compact and easy to explore on foot, with the closest beaches just a short walk away. There is plenty of free (and some paid) parking around the city and nearby beaches. For Ponta da Piedade, Onda city buses will get you as far as Praia de Dona Ana, shaving about 20 minutes off the walking time. A tourist train provides an alternative to the headland in high season.

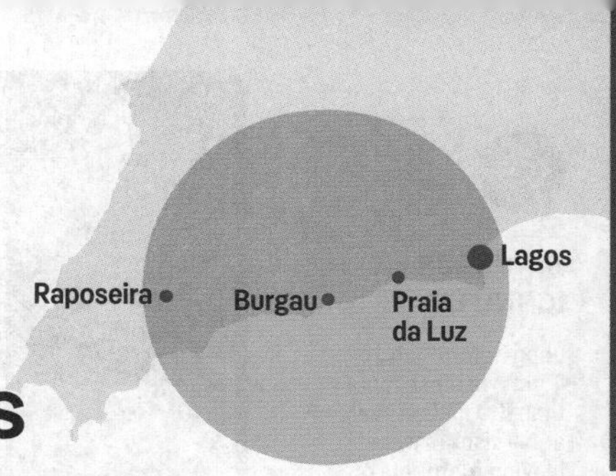

Raposeira
Burgau
Praia da Luz
Lagos

Beyond Lagos

West of Lagos, Burgau marks the start of the Parque Natural do Sudoeste Alentejano e Costa Vicentina, a hiking wonderland.

At first glance, the fishing villages turned holiday resorts between Lagos and Sagres can seem pretty underwhelming, but this storied shoreline holds fascinating history. Evidence of the Middle Cretaceous period (marine and plant fossils) are embedded in the dark volcanic cliffs, and dinosaur tracks sit beside Praia da Salema. Millions of years later, as a recent archaeological dig under the dunes has shown, the Romans had a fishing port here; divers can spot more ancient evidence underwater at Boco do Rio. There's also a shipwreck to dive – the *Océan*, which sunk off Salema's shore during the 1759 Battle of Lagos – and the slightly more sheltered beaches are a haven for snorkelling.

TOP TIP

The villages are blissfully calm in low season, so it's advisable to phone restaurants ahead to confirm they're open for lunch.

Praia do Burgau

DINOSAUR ICHNITES

Long before – and by 'long', we mean more than 100 million years ago – visitors were leaving footprints on the sand at Praia de Salema, dinosaurs were leaving theirs. You can spot these prehistoric fossils, dating back to the Early Cretaceous period, before laying out your towel if you know where to look. Head to the western end of the beach, near the staircase, and at low tide climb on the stones to access the rock shelf where the tracks are visible in a line. Alternatively, walk a little up the stairs and look back down for a clearer overhead angle.

PJ PHOTOGRAPHY/SHUTTERSTOCK ©

Praia da Luz

Coastal Trails Tracing Time

STONES WITH STORIES

The coastal trail connecting Lagos with **Praia da Luz** is the final stage of the multiday **Fishermen's Trail** (p177), which begins in the neighbouring region of Alentejo. A relatively easy hike, it can be covered in a few hours, making it a great extension if you wish to venture beyond Ponta da Piedade.

Along the route, the volcanic cliffs and sandstone layers are full of ancient stories, with fossils from marine snails to dinosaurs discovered here. The trail hugs the ocean cliffs, with vineyards and vegetation providing a verdant contrast to the ocean views, before descending to the beach. From Luz, you can take a bus back to Lagos, or if you'd rather keep walking, eventually you'll reach the village of Burgau and even Salema.

A WINDSWEPT PARK

Burgau marks the start of the Parque Natural do Sudoeste Alentejano e Costa Vicentina. Continue your hike along the Costa Vicentina (p177) for a windswept multiday adventure.

A Leap of Faith

COASTEERING AND CAVES

From the relaxed village of **Raposeira**, a 25-minute drive west of Lagos, set off on an adventure that will be anything but relaxed. Kitted out in a wetsuit and helmet on a coasteering outing, accompanied by an experienced local guide, you'll see the coastal cliffs and caves from a new perspective. Over a few hours, you can launch yourself from ridges into the refreshing Atlantic Ocean, access pristine hidden beaches, see inside sea caves and scramble up sheer rock faces. Coasteering on the cliffs between Lagos and Sagres isn't just for the experienced – it's a pretty epic backdrop for a first go at this activity.

GETTING AROUND

Onda bus 4 operates between Lagos, Luz and Burgau, and Vamus runs a service to Salema. There are small car-parking facilities near the beaches, which can quickly fill up in high season.

SAGRES & CABO DE SÃO VICENTE

Myths, legends, shipwrecks and sailors – Sagres and Cabo de São Vicente form the storied, most southwesterly point of mainland Europe. Reportedly it was here that Prince Henry the Navigator established his maritime school in 1420, the foundation for the Era dos Descobrimentos (Age of Discovery). While scholars say exploration and colonising expeditions actually set sail from Lagos, it's certainly true that this craggy headland was the last glimpse of Portugal for many voyagers.

Today the barren, ragged, windswept surrounds are a haven for surfers and birdlife. Other visitors come for the ruins of imposing forts and the edge-of-Europe feeling at the cape, which is named after the martyr São Vicente. If you believe the legends, his remains were buried here before being exhumed and laid to rest in Lisbon.

TOP TIP

Plan ahead before setting off to Cabo de São Vicente, packing a windbreaker and a picnic from Mercado Municipal 25 de Abril or a bakery in town. The lighthouse cafe's prices reflect the location, and the food trucks aren't always here outside of high season.

Experience the End of Europe

LIGHTHOUSES ON THE EDGE

Introduce yourself to the area's maritime history and defensive past on an 8km walk along the weathered sea-facing cliffs. Start at the formidable **Fortaleza de Sagres**, entering the imposing walls that divide this headland in half. Constructed in the 15th century, much of what remains is from later years. According to legend, it was here that Prince Henry the Navigator established his esteemed navigation school. What are certainly not myths are the vast 43m-wide floor-level stone compass, the 16th-century **Igreja de Nossa Senhora da Graça** and the remains of a cistern tower and former barracks. Beyond the lighthouse, contemplate the call of the sea before entering **A Voz do Mar**, a maze-like installation echoing the sound of the actual waves due to a geological fault. A new exhibition centre dedicated to the Age of Discovery has recently opened.

Leaving the fort, track the eastern clifftop road for around an hour to **Praia do Beliche** before turning left to Fortaleza do Beliche. Locked owing to erosion, its outer walls can be explored before continuing to the **Fortaleza do Cabo de São Vicente**, mainland Europe's most southwesterly point. The fort, constructed to ward off pirates, now houses a lighthouse, a cafe and the small **Museo dos Faròis**, sharing insight into Sagres' seafaring stories.

BEST FOOD SPOTS IN SAGRES

Mercado Municipal 25 de Abril
Self-caterers will find fresh fish, fruit and vegetables at this morning-only market.

Picnic
Daytime-only modern cafe with cakes, brunches, bagels and a good range of coffees.

A Tasca
Grilled seafood and *cataplanas* (seafood stew) against a backdrop of ocean and port views. Inside is equally inviting on a windy day, with terracotta ceramics and glass bottles decorating the stone walls.

SAGRES & CABO DE SÃO VICENTE

Farol do Cabo de São Vicente (3.5km)
R dos Murtórios
R do Mercado
R Mestre
R Dom Sebastião
R Comandante Matoso
R P António Faustino
R da Fortaleza
Praia da Baleeira
Porto da Baleeira
Praia do Tonel
Sítio do Tonel
Praia da Mareta
Atlantic Ocean
0 500 m
0 0.25 miles

SIGHTS
1 A Voz do Mar
2 Fortaleza de Sagres
3 Igreja de Nossa Senhora da Graça
4 Praia do Beliche
5 Praia do Martinhal

SLEEPING
6 Casa Azul
7 Lighthouse Hostel
8 Pousada de Sagres

EATING
9 A Tasca

DRINKING & NIGHTLIFE
10 Picnic

SHOPPING
11 Mercado Municipal 25 de Abril

WHERE TO STAY IN SAGRES

Lighthouse Hostel
Friendly and laid-back atmosphere with dorms, privates and a pool, a short drive from the beach. €

Casa Azul
Colourful and fully equipped apartments, just back from the beach, that are ideal for self-caterers. €€

Pousada de Sagres
Upmarket choice, with exceptional panoramas over the forts from the pool and sea-view rooms. €€€

Cabo de São Vicentre

Sample the Simple Life in Sagres

SURF AND SUNSETS

Sagres is a place in which to slow down. There aren't many attractions and surprisingly little to note of its links to maritime history, leaving days free to soak up the salt-kissed air of this seemingly end-of-the-world town. Mornings are for surfing, and whether you're a novice or experienced wave-rider, you'll find a solid choice of surf camps, schools and rental gear in town. Afternoons are for whiling away on the beach, and the soft sands of **Praia do Martinhal** are particularly inviting, thanks to the protection from the prevailing wind. Evenings are for golden-hued sunsets casting the last shadow over some of the Algarve's most dramatic scenery – especially when enjoyed, beer in hand, overlooking **Cabo de São Vicente**. Laid-back surfer bars and seafood-centric restaurants round off the day, ready for another slow-paced tomorrow.

Diving Wrecks & Canyons

UNDERWATER ADVENTURES

If you think the area's sea-sculpted cliffs are dramatic from above, wait until you see them from below. Divers will find stalactite-filled caves, canyons of crustaceans and island dive sites with shoals of fish. Unsurprisingly, given the headland's fierce waves and nautical anecdotes, shipwrecks are a common sight on the seabed. Wreck divers are in for a treat, whether exploring the barge vessel turned artificial reef in Burgau or the WWI Norwegian steam engine some 30m below Sagres' coast. Diving trips depart from Sagres.

SURFING IN SAGRES

Sara Sousa, co-founder at *@sagresnaturacamp* surf school, explains why Sagres is perfect for all surfing abilities.

Sagres is one of Europe's best surfing destinations due to having both southern and western coasts, meaning winds all the time. Conditions from June to August are great for learning, especially due to the beach breaks, and every day we can choose spots with the best conditions. September and October bring bigger waves ideal for experienced surfers, while March is a quieter time, usually with good weather. My connection to the sea stems from my father being a fisherman here, and the laid-back quality of life in Sagres is something very special to share with travellers.

GETTING AROUND

Sagres is a small town, meaning few places are more than a 20-minute stroll away. If you prefer not to walk to the headland, Vamus line 47 has a few daily services connecting Lagos, Sagres and Cabo de São Vicente; there is also a car park on the cape.

Beyond Sagres & Cabo de São Vicente

Hop between secluded bays, juniper-scented woods and rural villages – the Costa Vicentina is the Algarve's untamed coastal eden.

For many years, the Costa Vicentina was predominantly frequented by serious surfers, in-the-know travellers and biologists and botanists who came to study the unique fauna and flora, from wild orchids to ospreys – the latter thankfully returning to nest again in recent years. Further back in time, the Moors settled here, as Aljezur's 10th-century castle and the clifftop ruins of Ponta do Castelo's Islamic fishing site still testify. As part of the Parque Natural do Sudoeste Alentejano e Costa Vicentina, its lack of construction and long-distance trails far from modern life invite ramblers to slow down. Those who heed the call are rewarded with some of the Algarve's most pristine terrain and (nearly) footprint-free sands, especially in low season.

TOP TIP

For multiday hiking without baggage, companies such as Nature Transfers can collect and deliver your luggage on the Fishermen's Trail and the Historical Way.

Fishermen's Trail near Praia de Odeceixe

Costa Vicentina's Long-Distance Hiking Trails

COASTAL TRACKS AND RURAL ROUTES

The Costa Vicentina's biggest draws for ramblers are the two long-distance trails linking the Algarve and Alentejo sections of the Parque Natural do Sudoeste Alentejano e Costa Vicentina and smaller circular routes. The two long walks offer a similar get-away-from-it-all experience, the difficult choice being between coast and hinterland.

The Fishermen's Trail

Mainly hugging the ocean along coastal tracks and cliffs, the Fishermen's Trail has five sections between Sagres and Odeceixe (and three others leading to Lagos), which can be covered in their entirety or tackled as day stretches with transfers. Windswept, crashing-wave vistas, thyme- and gorse-coated hills, endemic plants, soaring birdlife and moments of shoreline sanctuary define the trail. Stories of lost settlements and archaeological sites such as the Ribat de Arrifana, an Islamic fortress, also feature.

The Historical Way

Inland, the Historical Way also has five sections between Sagres and Odeceixe, with a shift of focus from waves to rural villages, cork-tree-coated countryside and juniper-scented hinterlands. That's not to say you won't have coastal views – the natural park's narrow designation ensures that – but pine and eucalyptus forests teeming with birdlife will vie for your attention.

Shorter routes

For one-day loop trails, the paths of **Cordoama** and **Pontal da Carrapateira** are both around 10km and include coastal and scrub vistas.

The Rota Vicentina (rotavicentina.com) website has excellent in-depth information on all the park's trails.

BEST COSTA VICENTINA BEACHES

Praia do Castelejo
Secluded bay with a single beach bar – the drive here is as impressive as the beach.

Praia da Bordeira
Backed by dunes, Bordeira is a windswept wonder.

Praia da Amoreira
Otters frolic in the stream beside this immense beach, which stretches far inland.

Praia de Monte Clérigo
This scenic spot is the west coast's most accessible beach due to a boardwalk from the road to the sand.

Praia de Odeceixe
Here the Ribeira de Seixe scenically converges with the ocean, meaning Atlantic surf or calm river paddles.

Mountain Bike Adventures

RUGGED, WINDSWEPT RIDES

While most of the park's dedicated mountain-biking trails are around Odemira (p218) in the Alentejo section, you'll still find some tremendous short rides in the Algarve, utilising both

WHERE TO STAY ON THE COSTA VICENTINA

Camping Serrão
Shaded tent pitches, caravan parking and lodging, complemented by a pool and tennis near Aljezur. €

HI Arrifana Destination Hostel
Dorms, privates, ocean views and a small pool terrace, 10 minutes from the beach. €

Casa de Hóspedes Celeste
Comfy, affordable rooms and a welcoming host make this Odeceixe guesthouse a reliable choice. €€

BEST FOOD STOPS ON THE COSTA VICENTINA

Restaurante Castelejo
The secluded ocean-facing setting on Praia do Castelejo makes the fresh seafood and snack-like dishes here taste even better. €

Sítio do Forno
Clams or *cataplana* with captivating clifftop views – the highlight of this Praia do Amado spot. €€

Cervejaria Mar
Enjoy a seafood bonanza at this Aljezur hot spot. The *arroz de marisco* is delicious. €€

Altinho
This intimate spot in Odeceixe boasts an interesting *petiscos* (snack-size plates) menu paired with local wines. €€

O Sargo
Creative (mainly) seafood dishes served up with Praia de Monte Clérigo vistas. Reservations are recommended. €€€

R.NAGY/SHUTTERSTOCK ©

Moorish castle walls, Aljezur

rugged trails and roadways. Cruising the coastal roads around **Carrapateira** makes for a scenic, circular, ocean-facing route.

The most apparent trail for off-road biking is the **Historical Way**. While the coastal Fishermen's Trail is focused on hikers (p177), the inland route accommodates mountain bikers, and you can easily customise sections to suit your schedule, or complete the whole trail. From Odeceixe to Cabo de São Vicente, it's around 90km with some elevation gains – split the distance to suit your schedule and the rural accommodation offerings. However, a three-day trip with nights in Aljezur and Carrapateira is likely the best option if including sightseeing stops on the way.

WHERE TO LEARN TO SURF ON THE COSTA VICENTINA

Arrifana Surf School
Private or group lessons for all levels, paired with a spectacular beach and reliable waves.

Boa Onda Surf School
Surf and bodyboard classes, as well as rentals, mainly on Praia de Monte Clérigo.

Odeceixe Surf School
This small team has been providing lessons and courses around Odeceixe for 15 years.

Soar to a Bird's-Eye View

PARAGLIDING THE ATLANTIC WINDS

The Atlantic Ocean winds, which characterise the west coast, are a reason to celebrate for paragliders – especially when coupled with spectacular bird's-eye views of the Costa Vicentina. You can swoop above the crashing waves and dashing coves while experiencing your first foray into paragliding. The cliffs around **Praia da Cordoama** are popular jumping-off points, and Nelson Pacheco, a local expert who has competed in the Paragliding World Cup, offers introductory flights.

CROSSING THE ALGARVE BY BIKE

The sometimes demanding **Ecovia do Litoral** is a 215km multi-day ride linking Cabo de São Vicente with the Spanish border town of Vila Real de Santo António. The route is a mix of rural trails, official bike paths (although some markings have faded) and, in parts, veers inland to follow alongside the national road. Covering most of the coast's well-known landmarks, towns and villages – crossing the Parque Natural da Ria Formosa is a particular highlight – it's an active introduction to the Algarve. It's part of the long-distance EuroVelo 1, so you could even continue to Norway!

Pit Stop at the Moorish Castle

CULTURE AND COMFORTS IN ALJEZUR

Straddling a small river, **Aljezur**, a 40-minute drive north of Sagres, is divided into the old Moorish and the more modern eastern town. It's a comfortable stop for weary hikers, with a few cultural offerings. Its 10th-century **Moorish castle**, built over an Iron Age fort, has surprisingly intact walls, though wildflowers run rampant inside. There are also a few museums to visit (closed Sunday and Monday), with the church-housed **Museu de Arte Sacra** and **Museu Antoniano** focusing on religious art and materials, while the **Museu Municipal** has a collection of archaeological discoveries and Islamic ceramics. Expect sweet potatoes on menus here – they are so loved that there's a dedicated spud festival in November.

Pause Before the Alentejo

SLEEPY REGIONAL RIVER BORDER

An hour north of Sagres by car (not allowing for the near-inevitable coastal detours you'll want to take), peaceful **Odeceixe** provides a final pause before crossing the Alentejo border. The village is small, with a few decent restaurants, and the **Moinho de Odeceixe** windmill is worth a peek. However, **Praia de Odeceixe** makes this corner of the Algarve really worth visiting. Here, the **Ribeira de Seixe** completes its journey from the Serra de Monchique, curving around the sandy beach and providing a calm bathing alternative to the Atlantic Ocean. For walkers, a scenic 15km circular trail follows the river from village to coast before looping south through flower-speckled vegetation where crows and woodpeckers are often seen.

THE PARK CONTINUES

The Fishermen's Trail and Historical Way continue across the regional Alentejo border into the Parque Natural do Sudoeste Alentejano (p213).

GETTING AROUND

The wild nature of the Costa Vicentina means a car is essential to access the most remote bays if you aren't hiking the trails. Detours onto secondary coastal roads are one of the park's greatest joys, especially around the Carrapateira headland with its many viewpoints, so don't plan on heading directly from A to B. Buses are limited and mainly weekday-only services. From Sagres, an early 47 departure to Vila do Bispo allows a connection to the 22 for a short morning outing to Carrapateira or Aljezur, or stay on the bus to Lagos to connect with the 79, offering a greater choice of destinations and times. A circular route (74) from Aljezur to Arrifana operates a few times a day, excluding weekends.

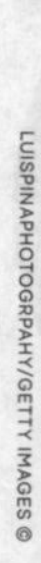

Monsaraz (p200)

THE MAIN AREAS

ÉVORA
Historic capital. p186

ALQUEVA
River beaches, wineries and stargazing. p196

THE ALENTEJO

RURAL HEARTLAND AND ANCIENT CULTURE

Welcome to Portugal's largest region, where dolmens dot the endless countryside, trails wind up in unspoiled beaches and creativity sparks from age-old workshops.

One has to admire the patience of the *alentejanos*. There's a saying here: if you plant a cork tree, you're thinking about your grandchildren. And this rings true today. It takes 25 years to grow a single *sobreiro* and another decade for it to be ready to harvest the first layer of cork. Everything takes its time here, from the handmade textiles and ceramics crafted by local artisans to the wine produced in clay amphorae following ancient Roman traditions. This is slow living at its core, and many creatives, like Ai Weiwei and Christian Louboutin, have fallen for it.

The Alentejo is also the backbone of Portugal's gastronomy: the birthplace of Delta coffee, the country's biggest wine producer, the grazing fields of the Iberian black pig, and formerly its main breadbasket.

As you head east and south from Lisbon, the change of scenery strikes you. You'll see resourceful storks nesting atop utility poles, bare red-ochre trunks from the most recent cork harvest and endless plantations of vines and olive trees. At the heart of it all is the historic capital of Évora with its Roman heritage. Up north, medieval castles and mountains await, while river dams and farmlands fill the centre and the south. And who can forget the west? Home to some of the wildest beaches in the country and an iconic coastal trail.

Find Your Way

The Alentejo covers a third of the country. We've chosen the places that capture its history, culture and natural landscape, but each is a hub to uncover your very own Alentejo.

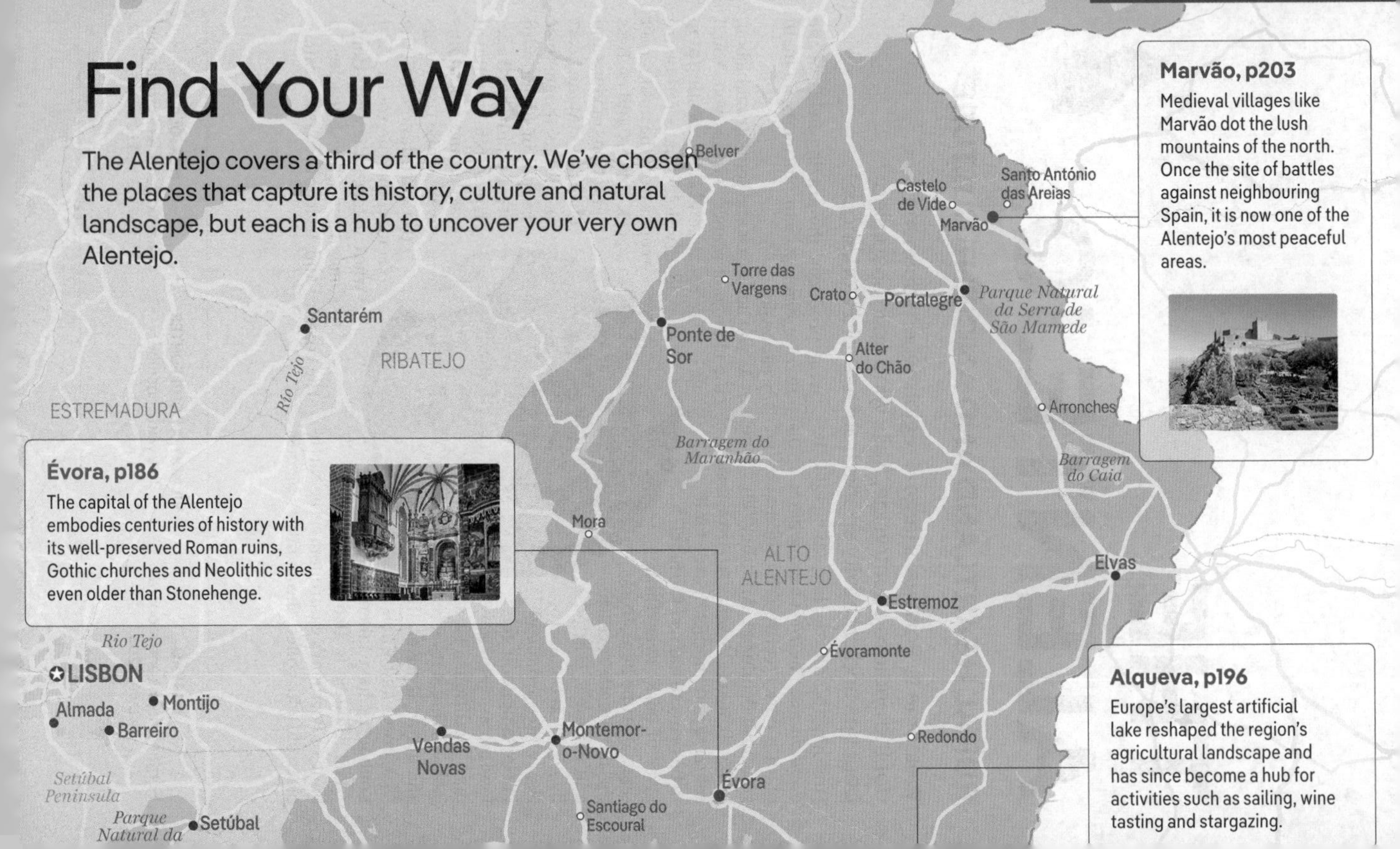

Marvão, p203

Medieval villages like Marvão dot the lush mountains of the north. Once the site of battles against neighbouring Spain, it is now one of the Alentejo's most peaceful areas.

Évora, p186

The capital of the Alentejo embodies centuries of history with its well-preserved Roman ruins, Gothic churches and Neolithic sites even older than Stonehenge.

Alqueva, p196

Europe's largest artificial lake reshaped the region's agricultural landscape and has since become a hub for activities such as sailing, wine tasting and stargazing.

Vila Nova de Milfontes, p211

The princess of the Alentejo coast is the perfect jumping-off point to explore the region's wildest beaches, follow its scenic nature trails or chase the waves.

Mértola, p220

Retrace the region's Islamic past in this whitewashed village facing the Rio Guadiana before venturing deep into the Alentejo's countryside.

CAR

Hitting the road is the best way to explore the Alentejo. You'll stumble upon its secluded beaches and castles, and easily tour the wineries scattered across the countryside.

BUS

Without a car, buses are best for reaching smaller towns, like Mértola or Marvão. Rodoviária do Alentejo covers these, while Rede Expressos and FlixBus connect the big cities and the coast, departing from Lisbon, Évora and the Algarve.

TRAIN

A train takes you from Sete Rios railway station in Lisbon to the region's main hubs: Évora and Beja. The slow-paced journey invites you to take in the rows of cork trees and olive groves along the way.

Plan Your Time

The Alentejo is a place to drift. You can wander through its wild coast, stopping for a swim in the sea, or venture inland in search of ancient sites, wineries and crafty towns.

ROSSHELEN/SHUTTERSTOCK ©

Évora (p186)

If You Only Do One Thing

● Head straight to **Évora** (p186) to delve into the Alentejo's historical roots. Treat yourself to a pastry at **Café Arcada** (p186) before setting off on a **walking tour** (p188) to take in the city's ancient monuments like the Roman temple and the Gothic cathedral.

● Spend the afternoon at the **Igreja de São Francisco** (p189) for an insight into how 17th-century Franciscan monks solved the problem of the town's overflowing graveyards. For something less chilling, you can explore the spectacular **megalithic sites** (p189) or tour the **wineries** (p189) on the outskirts of town. Then return to the city to grab dinner at **Hibrido** (p189).

Seasonal highlights

Summers in the Alentejo can be scorching hot. Luckily, you can always retreat to the nearest beach. Spring and autumn are ideal for hiking and wine tastings.

JANUARY

Winter calls for heartier meals like *ensopado de borrego* (lamb stew), often sprinkled with peppermint and served with Alentejan bread.

MARCH

The mild temperatures and blooming fields make this the perfect month for hiking the Alentejo trails.

APRIL

Viana do Alentejo celebrates the end of the Romaria a Cavalo, a four-day horse pilgrimage, with music and dance.

NATALIA MYLOVA/ SHUTTERSTOCK ©, LISANDRO LUIS TRARBACH/SHUTTERSTOCK ©, MAURICIO ABREU/ALAMY STOCK PHOTO ©

Weekend Getaway

- After exploring Évora, head south towards the **Alqueva** (p196) and settle in at one of the villages along the lake, such as **Monsaraz** (p200) or **Mourão** (p201). Join a boat tour or enjoy a swim at one of the **river beaches** (197).

- At night, find an **observatory** (p196) to gaze at the stars as this is a certified Starlight Tourism Destination. Don't leave without sampling a glass of **wine or gin** (p201) from one of the nearby producers.

Slow-Paced Adventure

- Start up north with a visit to the medieval villages of Castelo de Vide and **Marvão** (p203). Then make your way to **Elvas** (p207), a fortified city near the Spanish border. Spend a day here and then drive inland to tour the marble towns of **Vila Viçosa** (p194) and **Estremoz** (p193) and the traditional rug shops of **Arraiolos** (p193).

- Do an overnight in **Évora** (p186) and then continue south until you reach the **Alqueva** (p196). Stop by **Mértola** (p220) to admire its Islamic ruins before setting off to **Vila Nova de Milfontes** (p211) to take in the coast.

JULY
The Alentejo rolls into summer with events like the Marvão Music Festival or Festival Músicas do Mundo.

SEPTEMBER
Grape harvesting is in full swing, with many wineries inviting visitors to join the action.

OCTOBER
It's time to handpick olives in the countryside or spot flamingos migrating to the Troia Peninsula.

NOVEMBER
On the second weekend of November, Marvão comes alive with a chestnut festival, which includes samples of the season's new wine.

ÉVORA

Three rivers flow through the Alentejo: the Tejo, the Sado and the Guadiana. At the heart of their confluence is Évora. The city's strategic position made it a coveted spot for communities since prehistoric times.

During the Neolithic period, people erected menhirs and dolmens across Évora's hills. Centuries later, the Romans made Évora – or Ebora Liberalitas Julias, as they called it – part of their vast empire. We can thank them for introducing winemaking and creating the original roads to nearby villages. The maze of streets in Évora's Mouraria neighbourhood is one of the few lasting traces of the Arab occupation, while the medieval palaces remind us of a time when the city was a retreat for the Portuguese crown.

It's these historical chapters that have made Évora a Unesco World Heritage Site. But the capital of the Alentejo also has a young soul thanks to its vibrant student community, modern art galleries and creative culinary scene.

TOP TIP

In summer, Évora comes alive with several festivities. There's the Feira de São João in late June, with its lively food stalls, and the Artes à Rua, a festival that brings theatre and music performances to the city's streets and squares between July and August.

Feasting on Regional Delicacies

MUST-TRY DISHES AND RECIPES

Fresh ingredients are always within hand's reach in the Alentejo. After all, this is a region of shepherds, farmers and bakers. In Évora, history isn't just in the city's buildings, but also in the century-old recipes handed down over generations.

Pork, lamb, bread and olive oil are the top ingredients used in the Alentejo. A quintessential dish is the *açorda à Alentejana*, a bread soup topped with garlic, poached eggs and a dash of coriander or pennyroyal. Other famous soups include the *sopa de cação* (dogfish soup) and the *gaspacho alentejano*. Unlike the Spanish version, this one is often served with ice cubes and does not require blending. *Porco preto* (black pig) is another prime delicacy. You'll find it in a variety of cuts including *secretos* (behind the shoulder) and *lagartos* (rib-loin strip).

A popular side dish is *migas*, bits of bread mixed with garlic, olive oil and other ingredients such as pork fat or vegetables. Dom Joaquim serves a delicious version of these with asparagus to accompany one of their black pork dishes.

Keep an eye out for the *queijada de Évora*, a small cheese tart sold across the city's cafes, such as Café Arcada or Pastelaria Conventual Pão de Rala. Other sweet treats worth trying include *pão de rala* and *encharcada*, both made with a base of eggs, almonds and sugar.

Fancy learning the basics of Alentejan cuisine with a local chef? Sign up for a workshop at **Origens** restaurant (origensrestaurante.com) or try a weeklong course hosted by the **Portuguese Cooking School** (portuguesecookingschool.com).

BEST CAFES IN ÉVORA

Pastelaria Conventual Pão de Rala
Conventual sweets fill the counter of this traditional bakery. Try the *pão de rala* or the *queijinhos do céu*. €€

Café Arcada
Overlooking Praça do Giraldo, this is a great spot to sample the *queijadas de Évora* or some savoury empadas. €€

Do Largo
Organic and seasonal ingredients make up the menu at this brunch staple. €€

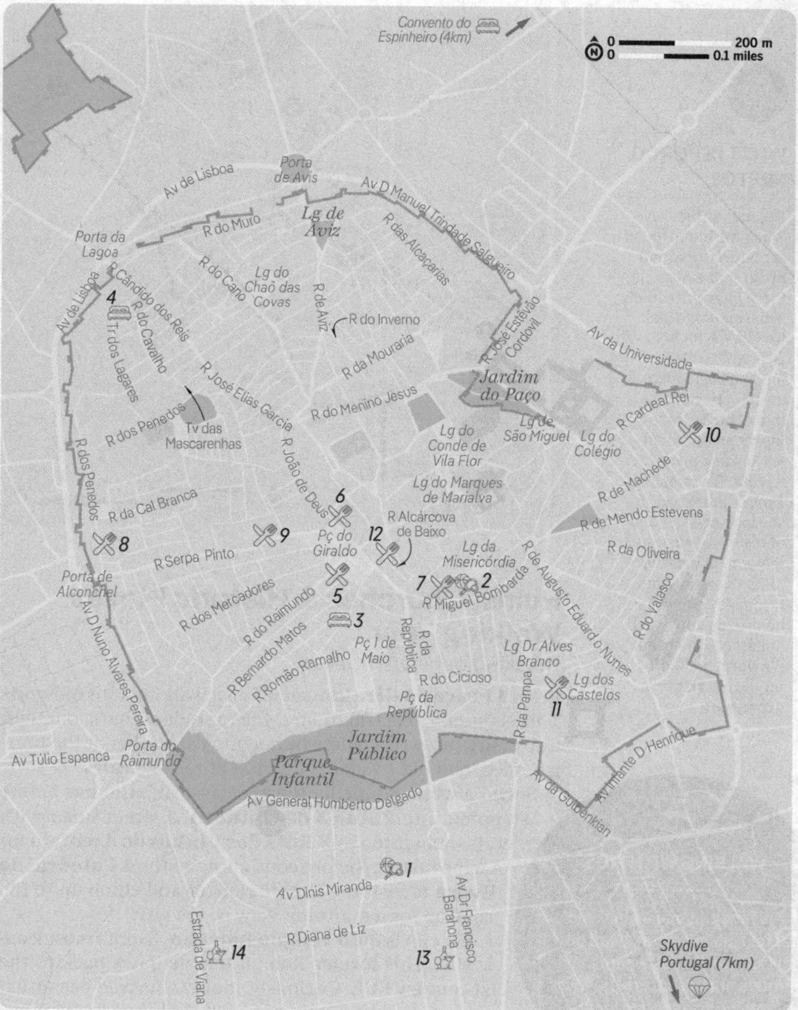

ACTIVITIES
1 Balonissimo
2 Up Alentejo

SLEEPING
3 Heaven Inn Évora Hostel
4 Hotel Albergaria do Calvário

EATING
5 Café Alentejo
6 Café Arcada
7 Do Largo
8 Dom Joaquim
9 Hibrido
10 O Combinado
11 Pastelaria Conventual Pão de Rala
12 Piparoza

DRINKING & NIGHTLIFE
13 Alkimia Wine Lounge
14 Avista Bar

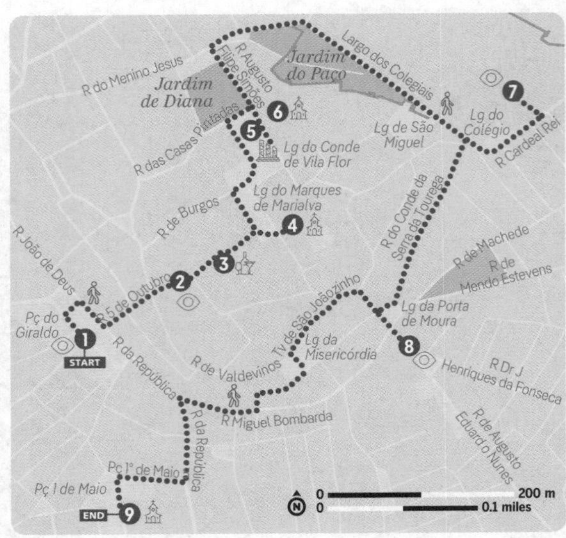

WHAT IS PORCO PRETO?

The Iberian black pig is a prime breed found across Portugal and Spain. In the Alentejo, these pigs graze freely in the *montado* (oak tree fields) for 18 to 24 months, mainly feeding on acorns. It's this special diet that contributes to the meat's marbled texture and juicy flavour. Try sampling a *porco preto* ham, a sausage or order one of the many fresh cuts featured across the region's restaurants. If you're cooking it at home, you don't need much seasoning, but it's worth grilling it for the best tasting experience.

Ruins, Churches & Historic Plazas Walking Tour

TRACKING GEMS OF THE PAST

From **1 Praça do Giraldo**, set off on a walking tour of Évora. This is the city's central square, where students burst out their university tunes, travellers bump into each other at the tourist office, and old residents unwind at terrace cafes.

Spend a while admiring the neoclassical buildings before stepping into **2 Rua 5 de Outubro**, a street lined with craft shops. Stop by **3 Rota dos Vinhos do Alentejo** for a wine tasting, before continuing to the **4 Catedral de Évora** to visit the Gothic cloister and climb up to the rooftop for a stunning view of the city.

Next up is the **5 Templo Romano**, Évora's most iconic site. This former Roman temple dates back to the 1st century BCE. Curiously, it only survived because it was a makeshift butcher in medieval times. If you feel like experiencing a Roman-style bath, head to the In Acqua Veritas spa.

Near the temple is the **6 Igreja dos Lóios**, a striking 15th-century church adorned with blue-and-white tiles, along with

WALKING WITH PIGS

If you fancy seeing a black pig or Alentejo pig in person, head down to Ourique (p225), where most farmers are based. Private tours can be arranged to local properties for a small fee.

WHERE TO STAY IN ÉVORA

Hotel Albergaria do Calvário
Occupying an old olive oil mill, the Albergaria combines a rustic interior with modern facilities. **€€**

Convento do Espinheiro
A former convent turned luxury hotel on the outskirts of Évora. **€€€**

Heaven Inn Évora Hostel
An affordable option close to Évora's main attractions offering dorms and suites. **€**

the Museu de Évora, with archaeological finds, and the Centro de Arte e Cultura featuring a patio covered in animal frescoes.

Take a walk to the University of Évora and tour the **7 Colégio do Espírito Santo**, a former Jesuit college. Then make your way to **8 Largo da Porta de Moura** and capture the Gothic-style Casa Cordovil. Finish the day with a visit to the **9 Igreja de São Francisco**, where an eerie bone chapel awaits you.

Chasing Adventure

BREATHTAKING VIEWS AND TRAILS

Évora is home to a series of walking and cycling trails that are collectively known as **Percursos Ambientais** (evora.net/percursos). These itineraries first emerged in 2005 and are still growing today. The old railway line that once connected Évora to Mora has transformed into a cycling route. Starting at Rua de Timor, the **Ecopista de Évora** stretches for around 21km, crossing the city's outskirts and ending near the medieval manor house Solar da Sempre Noiva in Arraiolos.

The **Percursos de Monfurado** take you along the west of the city, passing through megalithic sites and small villages, while the **Percurso da Água da Prata** follows a section of the aqueduct. This 8km-route passes near the Alto de São Bento (p190) and features stunning panoramic views along the way. Adventurous folks will enjoy the **Percursos do Alto de São Bento**, a trail with a steep terrain ideal for downhill mountain biking.

If you're looking for a longer hike, you can take on a section of the **Santiago pilgrimage route** (www.caminhosdesantiagoalentejoribatejo.pt). The Caminho Nascente covers part of Évora, connecting you to towns such as Viana do Alentejo (p193) and São Miguel de Machede, northeast of Évora.

Slowly glide above Évora in a hot-air balloon or put your adrenaline to the test with a skydiving experience. Several companies offer balloon rides, including **Balonissimo** and **Up Alentejo**. For tandem jumps, reach out to **Skydive Portugal**, located at the Aeródromo de Évora.

Explore Megalithic Sites

CAPTURE PREHISTORIC WONDERS

There are megalithic sites dotted all over the Alentejo, yet it's in Évora that you'll find the earliest traces of the Neolithic Age. The city was an ideal settlement for these early communities thanks to its connection to the region's main watercourses and the abundance of granite outcrops.

BEST WINERIES NEAR ÉVORA

Fitapreta Vinhos
Winemaker António Maçanita is spurring a change in the Alentejo wine world by bringing back long-lost grapes like Tamarez and Alicante-Branco.

Adega Cartuxa
This renowned winery takes its name from the nearby Cartuxa monastery. Their Pêra-Manca wine has become a classic of the region.

Casa Relvas
The vines from the Relvas family are planted across three estates. Close to Évora, the granite soils stand out, resulting in fruity, fresher wines.

WHERE TO EAT IN ÉVORA

Dom Joaquim
Local pork, wines and delicious traditional convent pastries are the highlights here. €€

O Combinado
Take advantage of the daily menu or order à la carte at this affordable restaurant. €€

Hibrido
Old Portuguese recipes have been brought to life and reinterpreted into a modern fusion of dishes. €€

WHERE TO SAMPLE WINE IN ÉVORA

António Maçanita and Alexandra Leroy are reinstating forgotten grape varieties at their Fitapreta Vinhos winery (p189). They share their favourite wine spots in Évora and beyond.

Bars
The Fitapreta wine bar with the medieval palace in the background is the ideal spot to sample our wines. We also recommend the Avista Bar, for a drink overlooking the city, and the Alkimia Wine Lounge, a promising new project.

Restaurants
Piparoza and Café Alentejo both offer good wine selections.

Wineries
Besides visiting our winery, we also recommend a tour of Monte Branco and Susana Esteban, two up-and-coming wineries, as well as old classics such as Júlio Bastos, Quinta do Mouro and Cartuxa.

JOSERPIZARRO/SHUTTERSTOCK ©

Cromeleque dos Almendres

About 4km east of the city centre is the **Alto de São Bento,** once one of the largest prehistoric villages in the area. Little remains from that era, but the hill is still a beloved spot for residents who head here to witness the sunset.

Other iconic sites can be found near Nossa Senhora de Guadalupe, a 30-minute drive from Évora. This includes the most famous monument in the city's megalithic circuit, the **Cromeleque dos Almendres**. It's roughly 2000 years older than Stonehenge, yet it receives way fewer visitors. Historians think this area might have been the gathering place of its time, much like our present plazas. The nearly one hundred stones are actually not placed in a circle, like most cromlechs, but in a horseshoe shape. While there are a few informative plaques nearby, it's best to book a guided tour for some historical background.

Ebora Megalithica provides regular tours with local archaeologists and workshops on prehistoric crafts. The meeting point is the Centro Interpretativo dos Almendres, but hotel pickups can also be arranged. The Cromeleque is the first stop, followed by the **Menir do Almendres**. This standalone menhir is said to indicate the sunrise during the summer solstice. Finally, there's the **Anta Grande do Zambujeiro**, a megalithic burial chamber uncovered only in the 1960s. Relics found here are now on display at the Museu de Évora (p189).

GETTING AROUND

You can tackle the city centre on foot, but you'll need to hire a car or book a tour to explore the nearby megalithic sites and vineyards. Taxis hang around the train station and Praça do Giraldo. It's also possible to cycle through the city's surroundings following the Ecopista de Évora (p189). Scooters and bike stations are available across the city. Évora also offers a small sightseeing bus, which covers the main attractions. If you are driving, it's best to leave your car outside the city walls as some streets can be narrow or closed to traffic. The Portas da Lagoa near the aqueduct is one of the best parking spots.

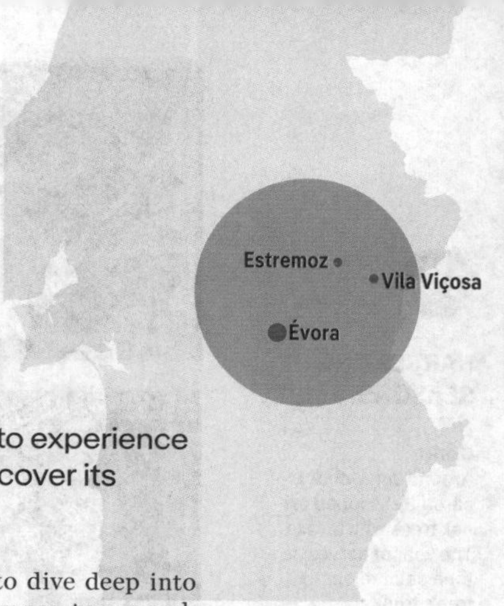

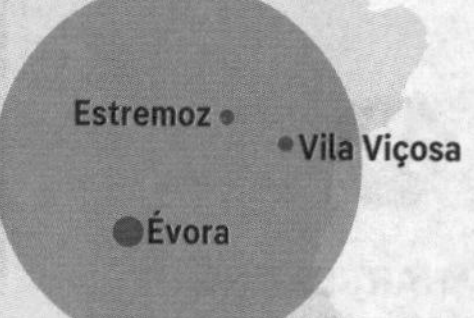

Beyond Évora

Venture beyond the walls of Évora to experience the Alentejo's rural lifestyle and discover its crafty heritage.

Évora's surroundings offer you a chance to dive deep into the region's artistic and rural traditions. You can tour a cork farm in Redondo, sample the wines at the Borba vineyards or try harvesting prickly pears near an old train station. Meanwhile, towns like Arraiolos, Estremoz and Viana do Alentejo are home to artisans crafting some of the region's most iconic ceramics and textiles. Marble is a prominent feature on the footpaths and buildings in this region, especially near Vila Viçosa, where you'll find some of Portugal's main quarries.

TOP TIP

In summer most tours run only in the morning to avoid the scorching sun.

Harvested cork bark

AH_FOTOBOX/GETTY IMAGES ©

HARVESTING SEASONS

Cork
Around June, cork is carefully stripped off oak trees with an axe. The year of harvest is then painted on the tree's trunk.

Prickly pears
August is peak season to harvest prickly pears. This is done during the evenings to avoid the heat and the spontaneous release of spikes.

Grapes
From late August to early September, the grape harvest begins. Many wineries offer harvest programs, allowing you to handpick grapes and join the traditional stomping. Alongside wine tasting, some estates may offer meals at an extra cost.

Olives
October is the ideal season to harvest the Alentejo olives. Visitors are invited to see the milling process and taste the freshly made olive oil.

ALBUM/ALAMY STOCK PHOTO ©

Ceramic figurines, Estremoz

The Rural Lifestyle

FARM TOURS AND HARVEST SEASONS

The Alentejo has long been considered Portugal's breadbasket, a nickname that gained even more significance during the Campanha de Trigo, a state-sponsored wheat campaign during the country's dictatorship era.

Those golden wheat fields are still part of the landscape, but olive groves and vineyards are plentiful. Many producers have opened their doors to visitors by offering tours of their properties. For an olive oil tasting, try **Azeite Amor é Cego** near São Bento do Mato or **Cartuxa** about 3km north from Évora's centre. This last one is also a renowned winemaker, so you can easily combine your visit with a wine tasting. Near Lavre, call ahead to tour the **Destilaria Monte da Bica**, where you can sample gin and *aguardente* (firewater) produced using artisanal methods, such as a wood-fired alembic.

Cork is another essential resource in the Alentejo and one of Portugal's biggest exports. This sustainable material is harvested from the *sobreiro* (cork oak trees) and used to produce construction materials, crafts and, of course, the traditional wine stoppers. It takes 25 years for a tree to

WHERE TO STAY FOR A RURAL EXPERIENCE

L'And Vineyards
Stay amid the vineyards of this luxury estate near Montemor-o-Novo. **€€€**

Azenhas da Seda
These no-frills tents provide access to nature trails and a private river beach 10km east of Mora. **€€**

Sleep & Nature Hotel
It's all about embracing the quiet at this retreat in an olive grove around Lavre. **€€**

produce cork, and from there, it can only be collected every eight to 10 years.

The organic farm **Pepe Aromas** explains the cork transformation process quite well during their guided tours along an oak forest. But it's their colourful 20-hectare prickly pear plantation that draws the most attention. At the end, guests are invited to visit the factory and taste the tropical cactus fruit.

Craft Towns, Festivals & Ancient Castles

DISCOVER SECRET TRAILS AND VILLAGES

Around Évora, you can explore medieval castles and come face to face with Alentejo's artistic heritage. Handmade crafts are still cherished across the region, with many towns dedicated to a single art form.

Ceramic workshops, art museums and festivities

Among Alentejo's most iconic crafts are the hand-woven rugs of **Arraiolos**. The Centro Interpretativo do Tapete de Arraiolos provides insight into this traditional craft first introduced by the Arabs. Walk down Rua Alexandre Herculano to see the series of artisanal rug shops. Avoid taking pictures of the display, as the owners don't take it kindly. On the outskirts of town is one of the few circular castles in the region and the Pousada de Arraiolos with its convent adorned with blue-and-white tiles.

In **Estremoz**, marble takes centre stage, but you'll also encounter the colourful ceramic figurines, bonecos de Estremoz. The atelier Irmãs Flores is one of the few places where you can purchase this handmade craft which has been on the Unesco Intangible Cultural Heritage list since 2017. Another must-visit is the Museu Berardo, which holds one of the largest private tile collections in Portugal.

Local potters are also at work in the small town of **Redondo** in places like the Olaria Pirraça and Olaria Xico Tarefa. The tour company Rotas Compadres organises ceramic workshops in this last pottery. Alongside this, you can visit the castle, the wine bar Enoteca and the Oficina das Ruas Floridas, a museum dedicated to the art of paper flowers, which takes over Redondo's streets every two years in summer.

In **Viana do Alentejo**, colourful plates are still shaped in the town's remaining potteries, such as Olaria Mira Agostinho. While you're here, visit the stunning Santuário de

BEST TRADITIONAL RESTAURANTS AROUND ÉVORA

Venda Azul
Waiters rush between tables with trays of Alentejo pork at this friendly restaurant in Estremoz. €

A Ribeira
The fried eel and the asparagus *migas* are a must-try at this lively tavern near Montemor-o-Novo. €

A Tasca do Gigante
For a round of regional *petiscos* and wine, head to this cosy spot in Mora. €€

Os Gémeos
It's worth taking a detour to this restaurant around Borba to sample its game dishes. €€

Restaurant Serra d'Ossa
Fuel up with a homemade meal before tackling the Passadiços da Serra d'Ossa. €€

WHERE TO SAMPLE WINE IN CENTRAL ALENTEJO

Howard's
Yorkshire-born Howard kick-started this winery in the heart of Estremoz.

Herdade do Freixo
Buried 40m underground near Redondo, Herdade do Freixo is known as much for its wine as for its iconic architecture.

Monte da Ravasqueira
Enjoy a walk through the vineyards of this 30-sq-km estate near Arraiolos.

Nossa Senhora d'Aires. This baroque sanctuary is the endpoint for the **Romaria a Cavalo**, an annual horse pilgrimage taking place in April that goes from Moita to Viana do Alentejo.

BEST POUSADAS AROUND ÉVORA

Pousada de Estremoz
Originally erected in the 13th century, the castle of Estremoz is now home to this luxury hotel. €€€

Pousada Vila Viçosa
In the centre of Vila Viçosa, this *pousada* provides easy access to the town's main attractions. €€

Pousada Arraiolos
Traditional Arraiolos rugs decorate the walls of this hotel housed in a 16th-century convent. €€

Pousada Convento de Évora
It doesn't get any more central than this hotel facing Évora's Roman temple. €€€

Prehistoric gems, castles and trails

The town of **Montemor-o-Novo** stands out with its medieval castle ruins. It was here that the plans for Vasco da Gama's trip to India were finalised in the 15th century. On your way to Montemor, you can visit the **Gruta do Escoural**, a striking prehistoric cave featuring some of the country's oldest rock art. Make sure to call ahead (☎266 857 000) to arrange a tour.

Mora has also been occupied since prehistoric times. A visit to the town's Megalithism Interactive Museum is a must if you want to learn more about the region's past civilisations.

In **Evoramonte**, you'll spot the circular turrets of another medieval castle. The village stands amid one of the highest points of the Serra d'Ossa, a mountain that crosses the heart of the Alentejo. If you're interested in exploring the natural surroundings, you can hike the **Passadiços da Serra d'Ossa**.

Other places worth exploring include the quiet village of **Brotas** with its whitewashed houses and the **Passadiços do Gameiro**, a wooden walkway that takes you along one of Portugal's most beautiful river beaches.

The Marble Route

QUARRIES, PALACES AND CHURCHES

The quarries of Central Alentejo have made a strong impact on the architecture of the surrounding towns. Start in **Vila Viçosa** and admire the marble columns of the Santuário de Nossa Senhora da Conceição within the castle walls. Then walk down to the Praça da República, stopping to capture the rows of orange trees before making your way to the Terreiro do Paço. This illustrious square is home to the **Paço Ducal**, one of the most iconic palaces in Portugal. The square leading up to the entrance is paved with white marble stones, and even the palace walls use this regional resource. To visit the building, you'll need to join a guided tour. These run every hour and are only available in Portuguese, but the guard is usually happy to translate his comments to English.

In **Estremoz**, marble has taken over every corner, including the town's bus terminal. Upon arrival, visitors are greeted with a luxurious (and cooling) waiting room made up of

WHERE TO SAMPLE WINE IN CENTRAL ALENTEJO

Quinta da Plansel
Besides producing wine, this estate around Montemor-o-Novo features an International Wine School.

MaiNova
Combine olive oil and wine tastings at this winery halfway between Évora and Estremoz.

Courelas da Torre
Sample organic wines at this sustainable estate on the outskirts of Redondo.

SOPOTNICKI/SHUTTERSTOCK ©

Paco Duçal, Vila Viçosa

QUARRY TOUR

The **Rota de Mármore** (Marble Route; rotadomarmoreae.com) offers a series of routes highlighting the region's marble heritage. Vila Viçosa is the meeting point for these organised tours. For a deep dive into the marble industry, choose the pedestrian trail, which includes a visit to a local quarry and an artisanal workshop where marble is still carved by hand.

large marble seats. An ideal tour begins in Rossio, the town's central square. If you're around on a Saturday, you might catch the local market. Walk up the hill towards the castle to admire its bright marble tower. The building is now a hotel, but visitors are welcome to explore the area. Make sure to also check out the town's ceramic workshops and tile museum (p193).

On the road between Vila Viçosa and Estremoz, you'll find **Borba**. The most iconic attractions here include the Fonte das Bicas, the Igreja do Senhor Jesus dos Aflitos and a castle. Borba is also renowned for its wine production, most of which comes from the Adega de Borba.

GETTING AROUND

There are bus connections from Évora to most towns, including Vila Viçosa, Estremoz and Montemor-o-Novo. Buses depart from the Central de Camionagem. Tickets can be bought on-site for Rodoviária do Alentejo or online for Rede Expressos buses. Many tour companies have their headquarters in town.

ALQUEVA

When the Barragem de Alqueva (Alqueva Dam) opened in 2002, it changed the Alentejo's landscape forever. Named after the village of Alqueva, where it stands, the dam that had been decades in the making had become somewhat of a myth for the *alentejanos*, but alas, it was finally here. 'Alqueva' literally means deserted land, but these days the village and its surroundings have access to a new water source, and a big one at that – the dam has created one of Europe's largest artificial lakes.

The dam had a massive impact on local agriculture, but not always for the best. What was once a land of cereal has slowly been taken over by more olive groves and orchards. Despite the controversy, many residents agree that the dam has brought a new life to their towns. Visitors call in to explore the castles, gaze at the stars or swim in the river beaches that keep popping up around its margins.

TOP TIP

The tourism website Roteiro do Alqueva (roteirodoalqueva.com) compiles a long list of activities, villages, hotels and restaurants near the reservoir. You can book many experiences directly here, including boat trips and balloon rides.

THE ALQUEVA IN NUMBERS

The 250-sq-km Alqueva reservoir covers land in both Portugal and Spain. In 1968 the two countries signed a deal to allow both the use of the river waters. Work on the dam began in 1976 and, after several interruptions, was finished in 2002. Twenty years on, the Alqueva supplies water to 200,000 residents and can irrigate more than 1000 sq km. Nearly €2.4 billion has gone into this project since its construction.

Above the Clouds

STARGAZING AND BALLOON RIDES

Hop in a hot-air balloon and soar above the Alqueva. It's only when you're up there that you can really feel the immensity of the lake. The patches of land that once surrounded a river are now islands dotted with oak trees. **Roteiro do Alqueva** and **Up Alentejo** organise balloon rides around the area, including the nearby medieval towns of **Monsaraz** and **Terena**. Flights take place at sunrise or sunset, depending on the season.

At night, your eyes will inevitably turn to the stars. The lack of light pollution has made this area one of Europe's first Starlight Tourism Destinations. There are two observatories that provide regular stargazing sessions in Portuguese and English. Near Monsaraz is the **Observatório Lago do Alqueva**. Their privileged location allows you to capture the town's hilltop castle and the stars in a single shot. It also hosts astronomy and astrophotography classes. Meanwhile, the **Dark Sky Alqueva** is hidden further inland in Cumeada, where there's literally nothing in front of you except stars. Visitors can go home with a deep-sky selfie postcard taken live on the day. Dark Sky has partnered with other local businesses, allowing you to combine your session with a glass of gin, wine tasting or a nighttime canoe ride.

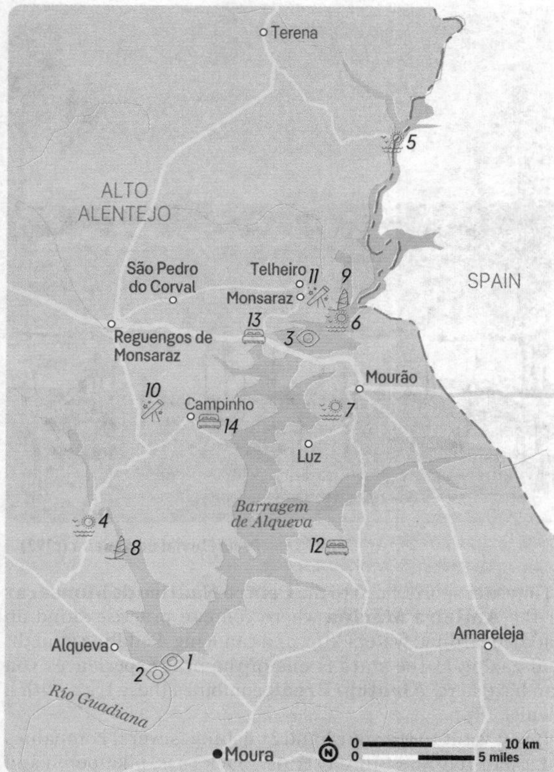

SIGHTS
1 Alentejo Break
2 Barragem de Alqueva
3 Ilha Dourada
4 Praia Fluvial da Amieira
5 Praia Fluvial de Azenhas d'El Rei
6 Praia Fluvial de Monsaraz
7 Praia Fluvial de Mourão

ACTIVITIES, COURSES & TOURS
8 Amieira Marina
9 Centro Náutico de Monsaraz
10 Dark Sky Alqueva
11 Observatório Lago do Alqueva

SLEEPING
12 Monte da Estrela
13 Montimerso Skyscape
14 Sorte Verde

Along the Margins

ADVENTURES IN THE WATER

More than a resource, the Alqueva has become a haven for water activities. Its banks have slowly been adapted into river beaches that are still somewhat of a secret. Unlike the cold waters of the Atlantic, the temperatures here can reach up to 30°C. **Praia Fluvial da Amieira**, **Praia Fluvial de Monsaraz** (accessible for people with disabilities) and **Praia Fluvial de Mourão** are some of the best beaches in the area, all offering facilities such as cafes and changing rooms. **Praia Fluvial de Azenhas d'El Rei** is the most recent addition, added in 2022.

WHERE TO STAY NEAR THE ALQUEVA

Montimerso Skyscape
Enjoy a swim amid the oak trees in this stylish countryside hotel 8km south of Monsaraz. **€€€**

Sorte Verde
Hunker down in a cosy chalet or rent a bungalow for the whole family near the village of Campinho. **€**

Monte da Estrela
Surrounded by olive groves, this hotel near Estrela village features a spa and a swimming pool. **€€**

WHAT TO DO AROUND THE ALQUEVA

Marcelo spends half his time as a national guard and the other half as a distiller at Alqueva Lake Gin (p202). He shares his favourite experiences around the Alqueva.

Ilha Dourada
The Alqueva lake is a magical place in the interior of the Alentejo. It's home to several islands, but the most well-known is the Ilha Dourada (Golden Island). It gets its name from the golden specks from degradation of the rocks. It offers a view over Monsaraz castle.

Boat trips
You can also embark on an adventure with a variety of boat trips and water sports. Sample a glass of gin on board and marvel at the wonderful landscape.

INACIO PIRES/SHUTTERSTOCK ©

Praia Fluvial da Amieira (p197)

For water sports, head to the **Centro Naútico de Monsaraz** or the **Amieira Marina** where you can practise stand-up paddleboarding, waterskiing and canoeing. Paddling at night and gazing at the stars is one of the best experiences you can have here. **Alentejo Break** combines these trips with a picnic.

If you want to try your hand at fishing, several companies offer half-day and full-day trips. Black bass, pike-perch and barbel are a few species you might catch.

Alternatively, you can book a trip on Dutch sailboat **Sem-Fim** or enjoy sunset on a small trawler with **Alqueva Tours**. You don't even have to leave the dam at the end of the day. There are houseboats available at the Amieira marina that can accommodate two to 12 people.

GETTING AROUND

A car is a must around these parts, especially if you want to travel to the beaches and observatories. There's very little illumination at night and some roads are in poor condition, so drive slowly. While there are a few signs saying 'piso em mau estado' (road in bad condition), they don't cover every section.

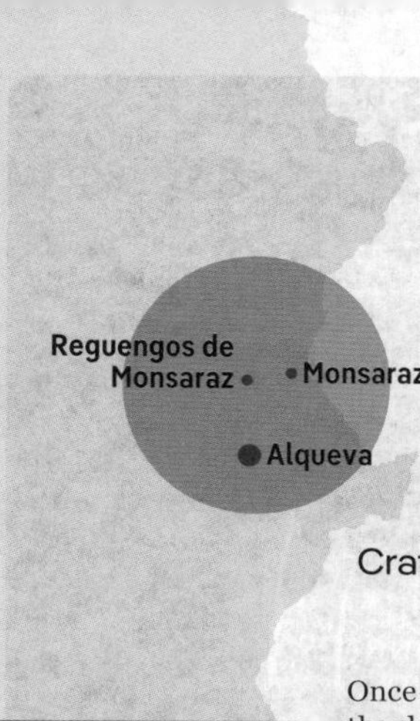

Beyond Alqueva

Crafty villages, hilltop castles and wineries await you beyond the shores of the Alqueva.

Once you've tested the waters of the reservoir and witnessed the skies from every angle, it's time to tour the surrounding villages. Wander through the medieval streets of picture-perfect Monsaraz, join a wine tasting at one of the nearby wineries or dine at a Michelin-star restaurant in Reguengos de Monsaraz. Spend a morning in São Pedro do Corval shopping for souvenirs and stop for a gin and tonic at a local distillery. You could see how many castles you can conquer in one day or take it slow; all of this is possible within just a few minutes from the Alqueva.

TOP TIP

Show off your dancing moves at Andanças (andancas.net), an international dance festival held near Reguengos de Monsaraz in late August.

Monsaraz (p200)

Honrado, Vidigueira

UNDERWATER VILLAGE

In 2002, the original village of Luz was entirely submerged by the waters of the Alqueva. Leading up to the event, houses were ripped apart and residents were reallocated to a new village nearby, built from scratch. Everything was replicated including the local church. The **Museu da Luz** tells the story of this now sunken town and its traditions, with photos comparing the old and the new.

Rural Villages & Castles

DIVE INTO THE CULTURE

The Alqueva is dotted with medieval villages and castles, and its crowning glory is **Monsaraz**. This fortified town has been considered one of Portugal's seven wonders, and you'll understand why once you step inside its walls and witness the views of the lake and the Alqueva islands. You can easily explore Monsaraz in half a day, but it's worth staying overnight to capture the clear, starry skies. Outside on Rua dos Celeiros, you'll spot the colourful blankets of Monsaraz, weaved by hand in the nearby Fabricaal factory in Reguengos. Casa Tial sells gourmet treats such as ginger liquor and

WHERE TO STAY IN MONSARAZ

Dom Nuno
In the heart of Monsaraz, this cosy guesthouse offers a terrace overlooking the Alqueva. **€**

Casa Pinto
Just opposite the parish church, this B&B features rustic stone walls and an Oriental decor. **€€**

São Lourenço do Barrocal
Rent a bike or unwind by the pool at this luxurious property nestled in the countryside. **€€€**

pastries, while the Ervideira Wine Shop offers tastings from its fantastic terrace.

Further south, you'll spot the castles of **Mourão** and **Moura** overlooking their respective towns from a hill. Then there are smaller villages like **Alqueva**, which gave name to the dam, **Terena** with its stunning medieval chapel, and the recreated version of **Luz** after the original one was deliberately submerged. **Portel** and **Alandroal** are also worth visiting, along with the **Fortaleza de Juromenha**, a medieval fortress right on the Spanish border.

The Local Brews

WINE, LIQUEURS AND GIN TASTINGS

The Alentejo's most famous wine regions are located on the edge of the Alqueva, including Reguengos de Monsaraz and Vidigueira, in the south. The **Adega José de Sousa** is one of the wineries in the centre of Reguengos. Don't expect to see many vines here. Instead, you'll find a room full of clay amphorae. This is where they age the *vinho de talha*, a wine that was introduced during the Roman age. Most vineyards are located deep in the countryside. It's on the outskirts that you'll find producers such as **Ervideira**, **Carmim** and **Esporão**.

Vidigueira has also retained the Romans' traditional winemaking methods. **Honrado**, **Gerações de Talha** and **Talha Mafia** are some of the local producers recreating this type of wine. There are also regular vineyards like **Quinta do Quetzal**, **Herdade Grande** and **Herdade do Rocim**.

The town of Alqueva houses a museum dedicated to *medronho*, a strong liqueur made from the strawberry tree. At the **Museu de Medronho**, visitors can tour a distillery and taste a glass of this boozy drink at the store. Gin has also entered the Alentejo market with big producers such as **Sharish Gin**, but also with smaller creators like **Alqueva Lake Gin** (p202).

THE STORY OF VINHO DE TALHA

The Alentejo is one of few places that still produces *vinho de talha*, a type of wine created using a process introduced by the Romans. Instead of wooden barrels, these wines age inside clay amphorae, giving them more mineral touches. There are several ways of making *vinho de talha*. The classic technique involves throwing the grapes directly onto the floor, which is tilted to allow the juice to run into an underground cistern, or *talha*. Some winemakers like to throw in the stems, while others prefer to leave these out. During the fermentation process, the must (grape juice) is stirred with a large wooden paddle at least twice a day.

The Ceramic Village

SHOPPING FOR SOUVENIRS

Arriving in **São Pedro do Corval**, you'll see a big sign announcing 'O maior centro oleiro de Portugal' (Portugal's biggest ceramics hub). It seems every door here leads to a ceramic workshop.

Before you reach into your pocket, it's worth visiting the **Casa do Barro**. Here you'll see samples from each workshop,

WHERE TO EAT AROUND THE ALQUEVA

Adega Velha
This cosy tavern makes its own *vinho de talha* and occasionally hosts sessions of Cante Alentejano (p220). **€€**

Sem Fim
Reservations are a must at this traditional restaurant housed inside an old olive oil mill. **€€**

Herdade do Esporão
Chef Carlos Teixeira leads Alentejo's only Michelin-star restaurant at this famous local winery. **€€€**

CERAMIC HERITAGE IN THE ALENTEJO

Pottery has been around the Alentejo since prehistoric times. Large clay deposits in the region contributed to the development of this craft. Men were responsible for collecting the clay and spinning the wheel, while women added the final decorations. The process may not be as physical today, but the gender roles are still very much in place. It's rare to see a woman spinning the wheel here, but new artists are moving in and changing things up.

AGEFOTOSTOCK/ALAMY STOCK PHOTO ©

Ceramics, São Pedro do Corval (p201)

giving you an overview of each artisan's style. You'll find many resemblances in the colours and patterns used to adorn the plates and vases, but there are slight differences in each. The building in the back takes you through the history of the region and its connection with clay. You can also grab a map with all the potteries here. Among the most popular ones are the **Olaria Patalim** and **Olaria Bulhão**. This last one often hosts ceramic workshops too.

Once you cover the main street, head towards the town centre where you'll find the local church. Have a break at **Bar Casa D' Avó**, a cosy cafe filled with Alentejo-style furniture. Chairs and tables here are painted in bright colours and adorned with floral motifs typical of the *pintura alentejana*, a traditional furniture painting style. Then head down the road to the tiny **Alqueva Lake Gin**, where Alentejo-born Marcelo will give you a tour and prepare you a fresh gin and tonic. The signs in town point to 'Destilaria Alqueva'. If the doors are closed, give Marcelo a ring (☎966 070 451) and he'll be on his way. Alternatively, you can call ahead of your visit.

GETTING AROUND

There are direct buses from Évora to Reguengos de Monsaraz through Rede Expressos. To reach the smaller towns you'll need to use Rodoviária do Alentejo. However, these buses only run during the week, and even then there are only one to two connections per day. Taxis are not always available here, so it's best to book a guided tour or rent a car if you want to explore these areas.

MARVÃO

Peeking through the hills of the Serra de São Mamede, the medieval stronghold of Marvão appears built into the rocks with a dramatic mountainous backdrop that continues beyond the country's borders. Portuguese writer José Saramago felt this immense landscape when he wrote: 'From Marvão, you see the whole world' in his book *Journey to Portugal*. Like many towns on the frontier, Marvão has had its share of battles and overthrows. But it wasn't always like this. Founded by Ibn Marwan, Marvão once belonged to the Taifa of Badajoz, an independent Moorish kingdom encompassing southern Spain and Portugal. Today Marvão offers a door into the Alto Alentejo, a region of medieval castles, hand-woven tapestries and endless nature trails.

TOP TIP

Every year in July, the town hosts the Festival Internacional de Música de Marvão (marvaomusic.com), a classical music festival held inside the castle walls. The idea came from the German conductor, Christoph Poppen, who hosted the festival's first edition in 2014.

JEWISH HERITAGE

Before the 14th century, Castelo de Vide was home to a Jewish community. With the rise of King Pedro I (1320–67), they were restricted to a single neighbourhood known as the Judiaria. The bridge in nearby Portagem was one of the entry points for Jews who had been expelled from Castille and Aragon in Spain. According to some accounts, 15,000 Jews crossed this toll bridge in 1492. Today there's a memorial here dedicated to these refugees.

Explore Medieval Villages

CASTLES AND JEWISH GEMS

The Porta do Rodão is one of the main entrances to the medieval town of Marvão. From here, take a wander towards the Praça do Pelourinho, where you'll spot monuments like the Câmara Velha with its clock tower and Manueline-style facade. Then head to the **Igreja de Santa Maria**, a 14th-century church housing the municipal museum. From here, it's only a few steps to the **castle**. Enjoy a walk along the 13th-century battlements, climb up to the keep and hear your voice echo in the cistern.

Back on the streets, visit the tiny ceramic atelier Olaria Maria Joaquim or shop for souvenirs at O Poial da Artesã. Afterwards, settle down with a local craft beer at **O Castelo** or try the pastel de castanha (chestnut pastries) from Marvão com Gosto. In mid-November, Marvão welcomes the **Feira da Castanha**, a two-day festival dedicated to chestnuts and the season's new wine.

Alameda dos Freixos, an avenue lined with ash trees, leads to the town of **Castelo de Vide**, 10km northwest of Marvão. Once home to a large Jewish community, there are still traces of it in the old Jewish quarter and the synagogue. Up on the hill are also the remains of a medieval castle and houses adorned with Gothic doorways. Around June, visit **Quinta das Lavandas** to see the blooming lavender fields.

SIGHTS
1 Câmara Velha
2 Castelo
3 Igreja de Santa Maria
4 Praça do Pelourinho
5 Torre do Relógio

SLEEPING
6 Pousada Marvão

EATING
7 Fago
8 O Castelo

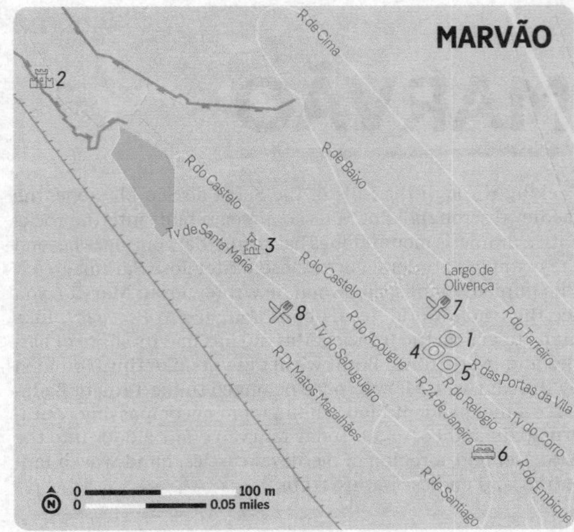

Adventures in the Mountains

RIVER BEACHES AND NATURE TRAILS

Most people think of the Alentejo as a region of dry flatlands, but there are also mountains such as the **Serra de São Mamede**, hiding waterfalls and lush nature trails. The old train tracks that once connected Marvão to Castelo de Vide have been converted into a **rail bike route** (railbikemarvao.com), allowing visitors to pedal through the middle of the valleys. **Caballos Marvão** offers horse-riding tours around the area, and there are several paths to uncover on foot too.

From Marvão, you can follow the **old medieval road** (PR1 MRV) towards Portagem. The 8km circular trail takes you through the villages of Abegoa and Fonte Souto, passing through the Convent of Nossa Senhora da Estrela and the river beach of Portagem, where

WHERE TO EAT AROUND MARVÃO & CASTELO DE VIDE

Fago
A creative seasonal menu and a glass of local *ginjinha* await you at this restaurant within Marvão's castle walls. **€€**

Mil-Homens
This family-run *tasca* (tavern) in Portagem has been serving homemade Alentejo dishes since 1967. **€€**

A Confraria
Located in Castelo de Vide, this place serves delicious pork and game dishes paired with local wines. **€€**

MAURICIO ABREU/ALAMY STOCK PHOTO ©

Chestnut trees, São Mamede

you'll find an old Roman toll bridge.

Meanwhile, the **PR3 MRV** connects Marvão to Castelo de Vide, in a 9.6km route that passes through a forest of oaks and chestnut trees.

GETTING AROUND

Driving from Lisbon, you'll reach Marvão in around 2¾ hours. You can also get a bus from the Sete Rios terminal in Lisbon to Marvão. However, the trip takes more than four hours. You're better off spending a night in Évora and then hopping on a bus to Portalegre, cutting your journey to 1½ hours. There are connections from Portalegre to Marvão (35 minutes) and Castelo de Vide (20 minutes) with both Rede Expressos and Rodoviária do Alentejo, but this last one can take longer.

BEST ALTO ALENTEJO FOOD

Diogo and Daniel run Fago, a restaurant where they share their love for the Alto Alentejo. Here are their top food spots and producers.

The organic olive oil from Azeitona Verde, the melt-in-your-mouth black pig charcuterie from Beloteiros, and the soft wines of Cabeças do Reguengo are among our favourite ingredients. Going to Mil-Homens to eat the tomato soup and roasted hen is a must when visiting Portagem in Marvão, as is the wild bull skewer from Solar do Forcado in Portalegre or the hare rice from Pompílio in Elvas. The biggest secret, however, is probably the traditional Alentejo bread and the *boleimas*, sugar-dusted cakes filled with cinnamon or apple, cooked daily in the wood-fired oven of the hidden Padaria do Porto da Espada in the village of Porto da Espada.

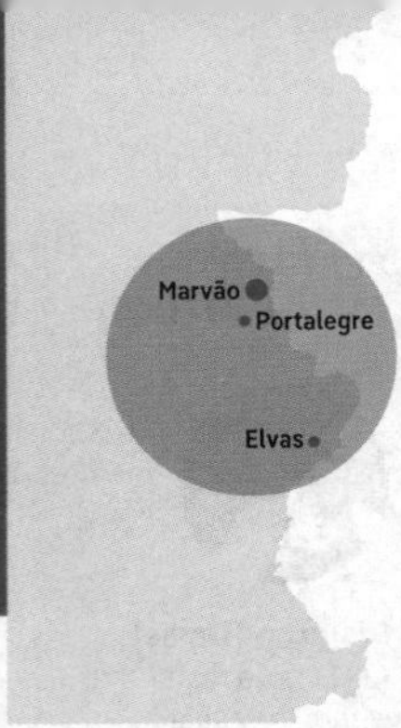

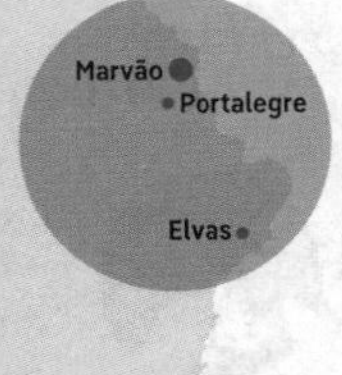

Beyond Marvão

The north of the Alentejo hides many other secrets, from riverside walks overlooking castles to iconic high-breed horses.

Past Marvão and the valleys of São Mamede lies another section of the northern Alentejo. One with riverside trails, inland castles and hidden dams. The biggest city here is Elvas, a Unesco World Heritage Site famous for its ring of fortresses that once defended Portugal against invaders. Crato stands out with its medieval monastery turned *pousada* (upmarket inn), while Alter do Chão is home to the prestige Alter horse breed. And then there's Campo Maior with its imposing castle and a traditional flower festival that happens according to the residents' will. As you travel through these highlands, you'll find yourself nearly touching the borders of Ribatejo and Spain.

TOP TIP

In August, you can catch the Festival do Crato, a lively music festival featuring acts by both local and international acts.

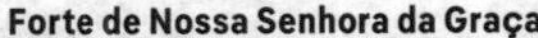

Forte de Nossa Senhora da Graça

BEARFOTOS/SHUTTERSTOCK ©

Aqueduto Amoreira

BEST RESTAURANTS IN ELVAS

Taberna do Adro
Squeeze inside this cosy tavern in Vila Fernando to sample its delicious roasted hen. €

Acontece
Prawn and codfish are the highlights at this modern restaurant with a slightly extravagant decor. €€

Adega Regional
Enjoy generous portions of classics like *migas* and tomato soup paired with regional wines. €€

The Fortress City

ICONIC BUILDINGS AND RELIGIOUS SITES

Drive 80km south of Marvão to find the fortified city of **Elvas**. You can also reach it by public transport, but you'll need to change buses in Portalegre. 'The key to the kingdom' was how people referred to Elvas in the 17th century, at the start of the Portuguese Restoration War. Back then, the city that is only 8km from the Spanish border provided the easiest access to the capital Lisbon, so it had to be protected at all costs. This resulted in the biggest concentration of bulwark fortresses in the world, a sight that helped maintain the country's independence and turned Elvas into a Unesco World Heritage Site in 2012. Among these acclaimed military structures are **Forte de Santa Luzia** and **Forte de Nossa Senhora da Graça**. At the highest point of the city is **Castelo de Elvas**. The castle has Islamic roots, but most of the current layout dates back to the 16th century. Another noteworthy site is the **Aqueduto Amoreira**, considered the largest aqueduct in the Iberian Peninsula.

Elvas is home to several religious sites. You'll spot the former cathedral, **Igreja de Nossa Senhora da Assunção**, at Praça da República. Also worth a visit is the octagonal-shaped

WHERE TO STAY IN ELVAS

Vila Galé Collection Elvas
Popular for conferences, this modern hotel features a spa, a swimming pool and two restaurants. **€€**

Hotel Santa Luzia
The rooms are decorated with traditional Alentejo folk furniture, while the restaurant serves local delicacies. **€€**

Hotel São João de Deus
An affordable option housed in a former convent. It has old-style rooms and a shady garden with a pool. **€**

JOANA TABORDA ©

Monastery of Santa Maria de Flor da Rosa, Crato

THE STORY OF THE PORTALEGRE TAPESTRY

In 1946 two friends, Guy Fino and Manuel Peixeiro, set off to revive the art of hand-knotted carpets in Portalegre. A special stitch was introduced that allowed a detailed replica of any artwork. It took a while for the tapestries to gain recognition worldwide, but when French artist Jean Lurçat saw his work recreated as tapestry, he was taken straight away, commissioning pieces from Portalegre weavers for years to come.

church, **Igreja das Domínicas**, as well as **Capela Nossa Senhora da Conceição**, a tiny chapel adorned with blue-and-white tiles.

Keep an eye out for **Porta do Templo** and **Porta da Alcáçova**, the two remaining gates from the original Islamic walls and the former mosque, a space now occupied by the **Igreja de Santa Maria de Alcáçova**. Meanwhile, the **Casa da História Judaica** showcases the city's Jewish heritage. The museum is set on what may be the site of the old synagogue.

Iconic Tapestries & Tempting Trails

DIVE INTO TRADITIONAL CRAFTS AND WATERFALLS

Portalegre may not have the cinematic feel of the surrounding mountain villages, but it does have its own charm. Just a 30-minute drive south of Marvão, it is the biggest city in the northern Alentejo, yet you can easily cover most sites in half a day.

Art museums

The city is renowned for its tapestries produced by the Manufactura de Tapeçarias de Portalegre. The **Museu das Tapeçarias de Portalegre** is the ideal place to get a real

WHERE TO EAT IN PORTALEGRE

Solar do Forcado
Wild boar skewers are the speciality at this lively restaurant. **€€**

Sal e Alho
Sample delicious local delicacies paired with an extensive wine collection. **€€**

O Cavalinho
It's all about grilled meats at this traditional *tasca* (tavern). **€€**

sense of this craft. The collection features giant handwoven versions of paintings by the likes of Picasso and Jean Lurçat, as well as Portuguese artists such as Almada Negreiros. Temporary exhibits showcase collaborations with young creators, inviting you to revisit the space. The much smaller **Museu José Régio** is the former home of the Portuguese writer. The museum features traditional furniture, ceramics and religious sculptures.

Waterfalls

Deep into the mountains of the Serra de São Mamede, you'll find idyllic waterfalls flowing in spring. Portalegre is the ideal base to explore these natural wonders. The **Cascata do Pego do Inferno** is located on the way to the town of Mosteiros, just off the M517. Other waterfalls require a bit of a hike, like **Cascata da Cabroeira** (near the Spanish border) and **Cascata de São Julião** (near Monte Sete).

Riverside Trails

BEACHES, CASTLES AND BIRDLIFE

The Rio Tejo separates the Alentejo from the neighbouring Centro region. Its margins offer the perfect setting for a hike, and there are several trails *(trilho)* worth following around here. Near **Gavião** is the **Passadiço do Alamal**. The 2km trail connects the river beach, Praia Fluvial do Alamal, to the Ponte de Belver. Standing on this bridge, you can spot the imposing Castle of Belver on the other margin. The path is mostly flat, making it accessible for families with little ones.

In **Nisa**, you'll find the **Trilhos do Conhal**. It encompases two trails, the PR4 NIS (10km) and the PR9 NIS (8.5km), which can be combined into one. The first trail is a bit more intensive and features some steep climbs. That said, it comes with many rewards, including breathtaking views of the Portas de Rodão, a rocky formation that acts like doors to the river. If you're lucky, you might even spot a griffon vulture soaring above you. While in the area, you can also check out the **Trilho da Barca d'Amieira** (PR 11 NIS). Opened in 2021, this path features a wooden walkway, a suspended bridge and a skywalk, a glass platform that looks down into the river.

Inland Castles & Dams Driving Tour

A ROAD TRIP TO THE NORTH

Leaving **1 Marvão** behind, head to **2 Crato**, where you can visit the Monastery of Santa Maria de Flor da Rosa. Part

A CRAFTY STREET

The town of Nisa is famous for its ceramics embedded with little bits of quartz in a style that resembles embroidery. So much so that the women who make it are known as the *bordadeiras* (embroidery artists). In 2021, a street in Nisa was redesigned with red and white cobblestones as a homage to this craft. Look for Rua de Santa Maria, and you'll encounter one of the prettiest streets in Portugal.

WHERE TO SAMPLE WINE IN NORTHERN ALENTEJO

Reynolds
This family-run estate near Arronches has been making wine in the Alentejo since 1850.

Adega Mayor
Award-winning architect Siza Vieira designed this winery in Campo Maior run by the owner of Delta coffee.

Herdade Papa Leite
This farm-turned-winery outside Alter do Chão produces wine and olive oil with creative labels designed by a local artist.

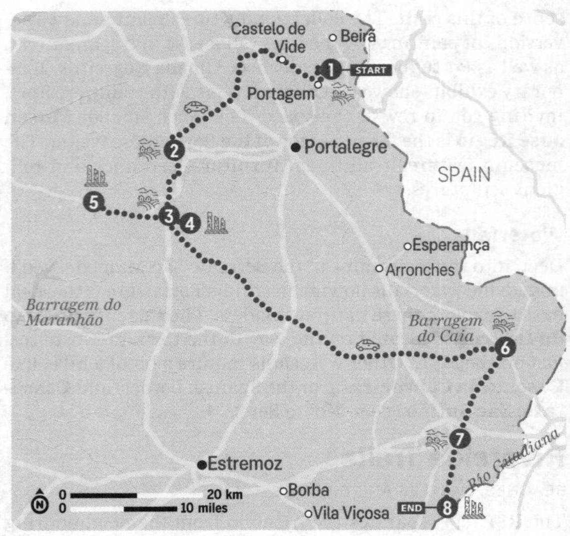

A TOWN IN BLOOM

Carefully folded paper flowers decorate the streets of Campo Maior during the flower festival, Festas do Povo. For this festival to go ahead, everyone in the village has to be on board, so there's no set date. Preparations usually begin in January with the election of the *cabeça de rua*, the person in charge of the event. Then it's off to work, with adults and children getting together to make all the tulips, roses and carnations that will hang above their houses later in the year. The last edition took place in September 2015, so there's bound to be a party underway soon.

of the building has been converted into a luxury hotel, but it's still possible to wander through the Gothic-style church. After exploring the monastery, take a trip south towards **3 Alter do Chão**. This is the birthplace of the Portuguese horse breed Alter. Established in 1748, the Coudelaria Alter (www.alterreal.pt) helps preserve this species and prepares the horses to enter the Portuguese School of Equestrian Art. They offer tours of the stable, as well as horse-riding lessons and carriage rides. Still in Alter, you can visit the town's medieval castle, which houses the municipal museum. Other attractions on the outskirts include the ruins of the **4 Castelo de Alter Pedroso** and the Roman bridge **5 Ponte de Vila Formosa**.

Continue to **6 Campo Maior**. In the centre of town is a medieval castle and the Lagar Museu do Palácio Visconde d'Olivã, a museum dedicated to olive oil production. Take a detour to the outskirts for a wine tasting at the Adega Mayor or a freshly brewed coffee at the Centro de Ciência do Café. After taking in **7 Elvas** (p207), visit the **8 Ponte da Ajuda**, the ruins of a 16th-century bridge that once connected Elvas to Olivenza in Spain.

GETTING AROUND

Rede Expressos has daily bus connections from Lisbon to Elvas, Portalegre and Campo Maior. The journey takes around three hours. For Alter do Chão and Crato, there is only one service from Lisbon per day, arriving in the evening.

With a car, you can reach Elvas in around two hours and Portalegre in 2½ hours. You'll also have much more freedom to explore the trails along the Tejo and the monuments on the outskirts of towns.

VILA NOVA DE MILFONTES

Long gone are the days when corsairs raided the port of Vila Nova de Milfontes. The constant threats made it an unattractive place to live. These days everyone wants a slice of the coast, but back in the 15th century, King João II issued a decree to convince people to move here. Milfontes started as a retreat for fugitives, and it took a while for others to find their way here. Today it is the heart of the Alentejo Litoral, a wild coast dotted with secluded beaches and fishing towns. It's also an entry to the trails of Rota Vicentina and everything that the west coast brings: surf, fresh seafood and gorgeous sunsets.

TOP TIP

Even on warm days, the Atlantic breeze hits the coastal towns in the evenings. Be sure to bring a coat if you plan on staying after sunset. Some areas are often a target for mosquitos, so come prepared with repellant, especially if you're camping.

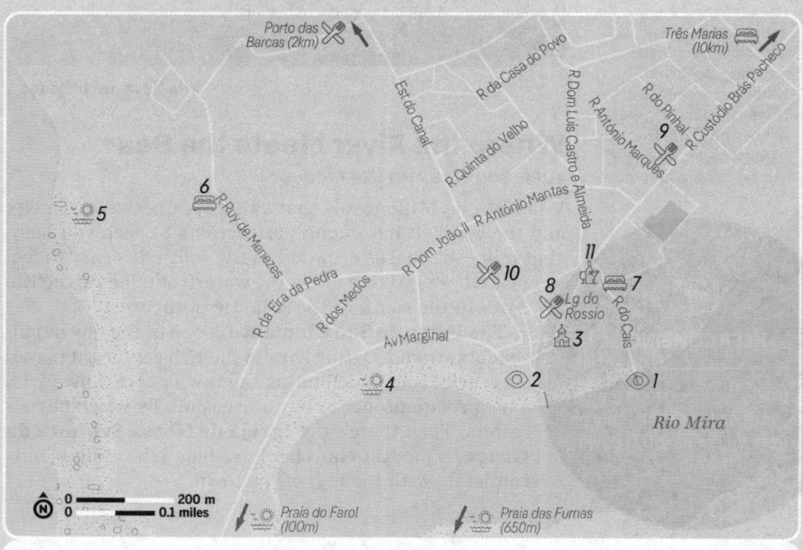

SIGHTS
1 Cais da Fateixa
2 Forte de São Clemente
3 Igreja de Nossa Senhora da Graça
4 Praia da Franquia
5 Praia do Patacho

SLEEPING
6 Duna Parque Beach Club
7 Selina Milfontes

EATING
8 18 e Piques
9 Alento
10 Tasca do Celso

DRINKING & NIGHTLIFE
11 Statera

WHY I LOVE VILA NOVA DE MILFONTES

Growing up, I spent my summers camping around Vila Nova de Milfontes. The walk to the beach was my favourite part, passing through the pine trees to reach the rocky trails of Praia do Malhão. In the evenings, we would go into town to dine at one of the local restaurants. The years have passed, and Milfontes still feels like a quiet retreat. I feel at ease here, eating freshly baked croissants from Mabi, paddling along the waters of the Mira river or watching the sunset at Praia do Farol. The hardest part is leaving.

Joana Taborda

STREETFLASH/SHUTTERSTOCK ©

Vila Nova de Milfontes

Where the River Meets the Sea

SURF, SUNSETS AND BOAT RIDES

Vila Nova de Milfontes is that sweet spot between the city and the coast. It has enough attractions to keep you busy, but it doesn't feel as crowded as the south. It's easy to feel at ease here walking along the waterfront, facing the Rio Mira in the south or the Atlantic in the west.

The **Forte de São Clemente** is one of the few monuments around. Dating back to the 17th century, it played a crucial role in defending the town against invaders. It's private property, but it occasionally welcomes exhibits. Then there's the **Igreja de Nossa Senhora da Graça**, a modest church whose blue trimming blends seamlessly with the rest of the town.

KEEP CLIMBING

If you're in the mood for a longer hike, you can follow the trails of the Rota Vicentina (p177) down to the Algarve.

WHERE TO STAY IN VILA NOVA DE MILFONTES

Duna Parque Beach Club
A family favourite offering different size apartments with equipped kitchens, ideal for a longer stay. **€€**

Selina Milfontes
Remote workers may be familiar with the Selina concept, combining accommodation and regular events. **€€**

Três Marias
A 20-minute drive from the town centre, this rural guesthouse provides a swimming pool and free bikes to explore the coast. **€€€**

Shops and bars line the streets of **Rua Barbosa Viana** and **Rua Sarmento Beires**, where you can stop for a cocktail at Statera.

Praia da Franquia is the closest beach to town, but if you're up for a hike there are many more hidden in the dunes. In the summer, boats whisk you from the Cais da Fateixa to the other side of the river where you'll find **Praia das Furnas**. It's also possible to rent stand-up paddleboards, canoes or surfboards. For sunset, stick around **Praia do Farol** or head towards **Praia do Patacho**, where you'll spot the remains of the Klemens shipwreck. Access to the beach is steep, so not advisable for people with mobility issues.

Take on the Coast

HIKING AND CYCLING TRAILS

Portugal's southwestern border is defined by the **Parque Natural do Sudoeste Alentejano e Costa Vicentina**, a natural park that stretches from Porto Covo all the way to Burgau in the Algarve (p171). There lies a wild coast of beaches, rugged cliffs and nesting spots for numerous birds, like the iconic white storks that hover above the towns. The best way to explore this side of the Alentejo is by following the trails of the **Rota Vicentina** (rotavicentina.com).

From Vila Nova de Milfontes, you can take on a section of the **Fisherman's Trail** up towards Porto Covo. The 20km stretch passes through a variety of beaches, from Praia de Vila Nova Milfontes with its towers of pebbles to the sandy shores of Praia do Malhão and the island-facing Praia da Ilha do Pessegueiro.

Another option is to head south to Almograve. You can cross the bridge over the Mira or hop on a boat towards Praia das Furnas and then hike from there. If you choose the bridge, be careful, as the path is right on the verge of the road and crosses a property with livestock. Then, it's around 15km to Almograve. If you prefer something a little shorter, you can follow the route from Praia das Furnas to the **Cascata das Furnas**, a tiny waterfall hidden amid the trees.

BEST RESTAURANTS IN VILA NOVA DE MILFONTES

Tasca do Celso
Reservations are a must at this iconic seafood restaurant in the town centre. €€€

Alento
A contemporary twist to traditional Alentejo dishes, using only seasonal ingredients. €€

Porto das Barcas
With a fishing port at its doorstep, you can expect the freshest catch to land on your plate. €€€

18 e Piques
Fuel up on breakfast here before tackling the Rota Vicentina trails. €

GETTING AROUND

Driving is the best way to conquer the whole coast and explore the most remote beaches. Rede Expressos provides direct buses to Vila Nova de Milfontes from Sete Rios in Lisbon, but it's much faster to reach it from Lagos in the Algarve. If you're up for an adventure, you can base yourself in Milfontes and tackle the Rota Vicentina on foot or by bike. Bring your own or rent one from companies such as Cycling Rentals (cycling-rentals.com). If you want to rest your back, Vicentina Transfers (vicentinatransfers.pt) can arrange luggage transfers to your next destination. Alternatively, there are many taxi services and tour companies that can drive you through the region.

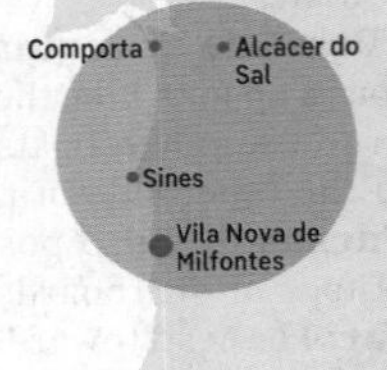

Beyond Vila Nova de Milfontes

Luxury retreats, wild beaches and marine life await you in the southwest.

There's much more to uncover on the Alentejo coast. Heading north from Vila Nova de Milfontes, you'll encounter diverse scenery, from the historic towns of Sines and Santiago do Cacém – with their hilltop castles and traditional festivals – to the natural reserve of Santo André and the rice paddies of Alcácer do Sal. You can sail to a deserted island in Porto Covo, spot dolphins and flamingos in Troia or ride a horse along the beaches of Comporta and Melides, where luxury villas have attracted many famous figures. To the south are calmer beach towns like Almograve and Zambujeira do Mar and picturesque villages like Santa Clara-a-Velha with their blue-and-white houses.

TOP TIP

The Banho de São Romão, held in August, is a festivity recreating a bathing tradition when countryfolk would go to the beach once a year. Locals ride horse carriages and dress up in traditional attire making their way to the sea.

Praia do Banho

PAULO ROCHA/SHUTTERSTOCK ©

Village of the Coast

HIDDEN COVES AND ISLAND TRIPS

Porto Covo will forever be associated with Rui Veloso's song. His 1986 hit, named after the town, describes the region's peacefulness and its legends. Before heading to the coast, take a moment to explore the town centre, passing through the **Largo de Marquês de Pombal**, a small square lined with trees and cafes. Here you'll find the **Igreja de Porto Covo**, a tiny 18th-century church that holds the image of Nossa Senhora da Soledade, the town's patron saint. Every year on the 29 August, this becomes the centre stage for the Festa Nossa Senhora da Soledade, which honours the saint with religious processions, but there are also concerts and other festivities.

Continue along the **Rua Vasco da Gama** until you reach the waterfront. To the left is the town's fishing port with its colourful boats. To the right are nothing but small coves surrounded by cliffs. Some of the best beaches on this stretch include **Praia dos Buzinhos**, **Praia do Banho** and **Praia do Espingardeiro**. End the day with a walk along the cliffs of **Praia Grande**, equipped with all the facilities. Further north, there are even more spots, including the naturist beach **Praia do Salto** and **Praia da Samoqueira**, famous for its crystal-clear waters.

WHERE TO BOOK A SURF LESSON

Surf Milfontes
With its headquarters in Vila Nova de Milfontes, this surf school offers lessons and vacation packages with accommodation.

Surf in Comporta
This family-owned school in Praia do Carvalhal, north of Sines, provides surf lessons and stand-up paddleboard tours.

Surf School ESLA
Founded in 1998, ESLA (south of Sines) was one of the first surf schools in Portugal. You can book a one-off lesson or choose a package plan.

Atlantic Port

BEACHES, SWEETS AND HISTORY

Sines has little more than 14,000 residents. The Portuguese navigator Vasco da Gama was born here and many of the town's sights are named after him. Take a wander through the city's historic streets before heading inside the **Castelo de Sines**. Climb up the castle battlements and enjoy panoramic views over the bay. Inside the walls is the **Museu Municipal**, a small museum dedicated to the history of the town, while outside is a statue of Vasco da Gama overlooking the sea. **Jardim da Alameda da Paz** houses the former train station of Sines with its well-preserved tiles. For local pastries, head to **Vela D'Ouro**. Try the *vasquinhos*, a sweet tart made with an almond, egg and fig-leaf squash filling.

The steps of **Passadiço de Penedo da Índia** connect the old town with the waterfront. If you're lucky you may be able to catch the elevator. At the **Porto da Pesca** residents still use traditional fishing methods. North of here, you can spot the lighthouse at the **Cabo de Sines** and walk along the coast following the **Passadiço da Costa Norte**, a wooden walkway amid the dunes. South of Sines you'll find the white sandy shore of **Praia de São Torpes**.

THE END OF AN ERA

The Portuguese are slowly coming to terms with their role in the Age of Exploration and slave trade. Read our essay (p412) to see how the nation is changing its views on history.

WHERE TO GO SURFING ON THE ALENTEJO COAST

Praia dos Aivados
Ideal for experienced surfers, as the currents can get strong, and there is no supervision.

L-Point
Hidden in Porto Covo, this spot is a favourite for goofy footers.

Praia de São Torpes
On the south end of this beach is the Pico Louco, a peak with consistent waves that attract surfers of all levels.

ISLAND TRIP

From June to September, you can hop on a boat to **Ilha do Pessegueiro**, a small island off the coast of Porto Covo. Boats depart from the fishing port in the morning and afternoon, but make sure to call ahead (☎965 535 683) to arrange the trip. Take a walk along the island and admire the 17th-century fortress. If you want to explore the local marine life, contact Ecoalga (ecoalga.com) for a diving session.

JUAN CARLOS MUNOZ/ALAMY STOCK PHOTO ©

Ruínas de Miróbriga

Amid the Lagoons

RUINS, GIN AND WILDLIFE

Historic town

The first car arrived in Portugal in 1895 through the young aristocrat Jorge d'Avillez. Disembarking in Lisbon, he drove to his hometown of **Santiago do Cacém**. His old garage was in **Rua Condes de Avillez**, now home to the local radio station.

From here, it's a short walk to the **castle grounds**. The walls enclose the town's cemetery, but it's possible to walk around the gardens and visit the parish church. Other attractions in Santiago do Cacém include the **Museu Municipal** and the **Moinho da Quintinha**, an old working mill providing incredible views of the city. The road leads to the **Ruínas de Miróbriga**, the remains of a former Roman village. In summer you can stop by the **Parque Urbano Rio da Figueira**, a large park with picnic areas and a swimming pool.

Safari trips and gin tastings

On the outskirts of Santiago do Cacém is the **Badoca Safari Park**, a 90-hectare property where buffalos, giraffes and

WHERE TO STAY IN ALCÁCER DO SAL

Pousada Castelo Alcácer do Sal
Sleep within the town's medieval castle, taking in the river views in the evenings. **€€**

Hotel Rural da Barrosinha
Pair your stay with a glass of wine produced in this rural estate featuring both rooms and villas. **€€**

Hotel Ordem de Santiago
This old-style hotel is a short distance from Alcácer's main attractions. **€€**

zebras roam. It's also around here that you'll find the **Black Pig distillery**, a gin-themed park featuring a bar and a botanic trail.

Swimming and birdwatching

Towards the coast is the **Reserva Natural das Lagoas de Santo André e Sancha**, a natural reserve featuring two large lagoons and sandy beaches, such as Costa de Santo André and Fonte do Cortiço. Many birds migrate to these wetlands. The Lagoa de Santo André welcomes the red-crested pochard and the Eurasian reed warbler, while the Lagoa da Sancha is a favourite spot for red herons.

A Slice of Luxury

HORSES, HIGH-END VILLAS AND SANDY BEACHES

In the 20th century, **Comporta** was nothing more than rice fields and dunes, with no luxury properties in sight. Instead, there were small sheds where the rice pickers *(ceifeiras)* would retreat after a long day's work. Over the last decade, Comporta has turned into a trendy coastal town. And it didn't take long for the famous folks to arrive, with people like Madonna and Christian Louboutin holidaying here.

The village itself is tiny, with only two or three streets lined with restaurants and beachwear shops. Every summer Comporta hosts the **Spot Market**, a pop-up event dedicated to local fashion brands.

Most people come here for the beach, though. The closest one is **Praia da Comporta**, a 20-minute walk from town. En route, you can stop at **Adega da Comporta** for a wine tasting. As the sun sets, head to **Cais Palafitico da Carrasqueira** to capture the old fishing pier balanced on wooden stilts.

Cavalos na Areia lets you gallop along the beaches of Comporta, following in the footsteps of Madonna, who rode here back when she lived in Portugal. You might even spot a dolphin in the distance. Nearby is the **Comporta Yoga Shala**, which hosts regular yoga retreats in summer.

Further south, in **Melides**, there is also the opportunity for a horse-riding lesson on the sand with **Passeios a Cavalo Melides**.

BEST RESTAURANTS IN ALCÁCER DO SAL

Porto Santana
This cosy restaurant makes some mean pork cheeks and crispy dory fillets. €€

Quintal da Liga
With a terrace overlooking the Rio Sado, this is a great spot for a quick bite and sangria. €

Tasca do Barrocas
Grouper soup and clam rice are among the specialities at this traditional *tasca* (tavern). €€

LUCKY SIGHTINGS

Comporta provides easy access to the Península de Tróia (p127), a departing point for dolphin-watching tours and a migratory stop for flamingos.

WHERE TO EAT NEAR COMPORTA

Dona Bia
Just off the EN261, this spot is famous for its rice dishes combined with a mix of seafood or monkfish. **€€€**

A Cavalariça
Housed inside a former horse stable, this contemporary restaurant has become a classic in Comporta. **€€€**

Comida Independente
After its success in Lisbon, this speciality store has set up shop near Comporta, selling wines and fresh produce. **€€**

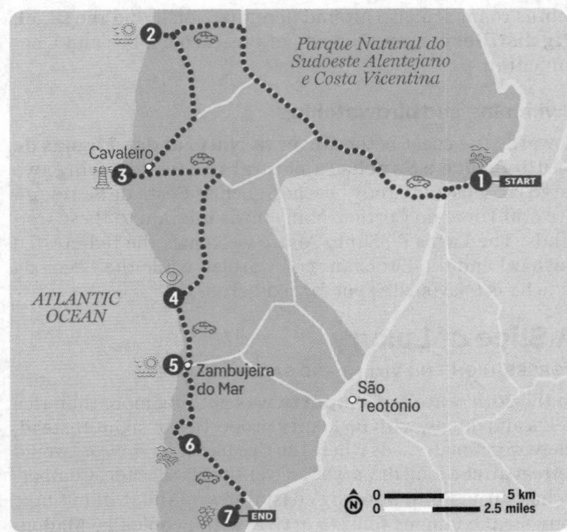

A PERFECT DAY IN SANTO ANDRÉ

Former nurses **Inês and Zé** traded their jobs in the UK for a quieter life on the Alentejo coast at their rural house *@slowliving.alentejo.* Here's how they spend a perfect day in Santo André.

The Lagoa de Santo André is a mandatory stop for those looking to connect with nature and feel the calmness of the Alentejo. Our ideal day starts with a hike along the different pedestrian trails of the lagoon. The Percurso do Salgueiral is our favourite because it has a wooden walkway crossing the forest and an observatory ideal for spotting the local flora and fauna. To finish the day, there is nothing like drinking a gin at the Black Pig distillery (p217).

The Southwest Border Driving Tour

BEACH TOWNS AND INLAND TRAILS

Like Vila Nova de Milfontes (p211), **1 Odemira** is located on the margins of the Rio Mira. Start with a walk around town by getting off at Praça da República where you can spot the town council, then follow Rua Serpa Pinto, home to the 14th-century church Igreja de São Salvador. Finally, head to the Parque Ribeirinho do Mira for a stroll along the river. From here you can start the Historic Way of the Rota Vicentina. If you want something a bit shorter, you can follow the Percurso Ribeirinho, a 650m route.

After exploring Odemira on foot, drive west towards **2 Praia do Almograve**, a wide beach with two distinct stretches, one with rocks and the other with soft white sand backed by dunes. Then go south to **3 Farol Cabo Sardão**, a 20th-century lighthouse on a cliff overlooking the sea. Head to **4 Porto das Barcas** early in the morning to see local fishermen selling their fresh catch, then on to **5 Praia da Zambujeira do Mar** for a swim. Finish off in **6 Carvalhal**, the last stretch of the Alentejo coast, stopping for a wine tasting at **7 Vicentino**.

WHERE TO STAY IN ODEMIRA

Herdade do Touril
Near Zambujeira do Mar is this relaxing estate with a pool and a famous seafood restaurant. €€

Almograve Beach Hostel
Featuring dorms and private rooms, this is a cheap option for travellers following the Rota Vicentina. €

Portugal Nature Lodge
Sleep in a luxury tent and relax at the natural pool at this glamping site. €€

The Land of Salt

RIVERSIDE TRIPS, CASTLES AND VILLAGES

Alcácer do Sal was once one of the biggest centres of salt production in Portugal. Big galleons *(galeão do sal)* would sail through the Rio Sado carrying salt up and down the country. Few of them remain today, but if you're lucky, you may catch one of the annual trips of the **galeão do sal**. Alternatively, you can contact **Sunrice Tours** (sunrice.pt), which hosts regular trips on its solar boat.

For a riverside walk, start at **Largo Luís de Camões** and follow the road towards the bridge, passing a tight cluster of houses along the way. The best views are on the other side of the river near the **Parque do Sado**, where you can capture the village framed by the rice paddies.

Rising on the hill is the **medieval castle**. The building was converted into a *pousada* (p216), but it's still possible to walk around the battlements. Nearby you'll find the **Cripta Arqueológica do Castelo**, an archaeological site featuring traces of Alcácer's diverse communities, from the Iron Age to the Roman and Arab occupation. There's also the humble 13th-century church **Igreja de Santa Maria**. Beyond the city, it's worth visiting the small whitewashed villages of **Santa Susana** and **Torrão**, both of which overlook a dam.

A Quiet River Dam

BOAT RIDES, FISHING AND PICTURESQUE VILLAGES

Moving away from the coast leads to a different sight, with valleys dotted with olive groves and cork trees. But there is water here too, in the **Barragem de Santa Clara**. You can't always trust the GPS to reach this dam. Instead, be sure to follow the signposts to 'Barragem de Santa Clara'. Many roads around here are in poor condition, so drive slowly. In summer, you can enjoy a swim at the **Praia Fluvial de Santa Clara**. This river beach has limited facilities, so pack a bag with water and food supplies. You can also go on a boat trip or kayak along the reservoir. **Bass Catch in Santa Clara** organises these activities, as well as fishing trips. Bass and carp are the most common species of fish found here.

Around the dam, you can set out on a journey to find the **Ponte Dona Maria**, an 18th-century bridge that once connected the Alentejo to the Algarve. Alternatively, you can drive to **Santa-Clara-a-Velha**, a picturesque village with whitewashed houses trimmed in blue.

ARTISANAL FISHING

Fishing has always been a part of the culture in Odemira. Local fishers still head out to sea (mainly in summer) from tiny ports like Lapa de Pombas in Almograve and Entrada da Barca in Zambujeira do Mar. It is a craft that uses only small-scale boats and traditional fishing techniques with rods or cast nets.

GETTING AROUND

Departing from Lisbon or Lagos, you can take a direct bus to most coastal towns, including Porto Covo, Sines and Zambujeira do Mar. To reach Alcácer do Sal from the capital, you need to change buses in Setúbal. While there is a train station in Santa Clara-a-Velha, it's quite far from the town and the dam. Driving will save you a lot of time if you plan on covering several towns in one day.

MÉRTOLA

Traces of Arab occupation have been erased in most of Portugal, but in Mértola you can still see remains of their presence. It's in the archways of the parish church, the decorative motifs of the hand-woven blankets and the items displayed in the town's Islamic museum. But Mértola's historical legacy goes way beyond that. Its privileged location along the Rio Guadiana made it an important trading post for centuries. The Romans, the Arabs and the Christians all saw its potential and fought over it, leaving their stamp on it.

Step inside Mértola's walls today and you'll uncover layers of history, from a Roman house to a Paleo-Christian basilica and a medieval castle, earning Mértola the nickname of 'museum village'. From here, you can set out on the trails of the Guadiana, reaching waterfalls and old mining complexes that once employed the town's residents.

TOP TIP

Every two years around May, the town celebrates its Islamic roots with the Festival Islâmico. A large souk takes over the streets, and you'll also hear music performances ranging from Arab-Andalusian influences to flamenco and even Cante Alentejano.

THE ALENTEJO SONG

In the south of Alentejo, choral groups sing the Cante Alentejano: slow-paced, a capella singing with distinct lyrics and themes associated with love, rural life or contemporary issues. Perhaps the most well-known song is 'Grândola, Vila Morena', the anthem of the Revolution of the Carnations written by José Afonso. In 2014, the Cante Alentejano was added to the Unesco Intangible Cultural Heritage list. You still hear it occasionally in local taverns and associations, but mostly during special festivities.

A Day in the Museum Village

WHERE RELIGIONS INTERSECT

The best way to enter Mértola's historic centre is from Rua da Igreja. Here you'll spot the **tourist office**, where you can request a map of the village which includes the Museu de Mértola, a network of museums spread across town. Back outside, you'll hear the sound of looms working at the **Cooperativa Oficina de Tecelagem**, a weaving workshop where women still craft the traditional Mértola blankets. From here, it's only a few steps to the **Igreja Matriz**. The interior reveals the church's past use as a mosque with its well-preserved mihrab and horseshoe arches.

Continue towards the **Castelo de Mértola**. While there's evidence of fortifications here since the Arabs, the castle you see today dates back to the 13th century, when the Order of Santiago took over. It showcases a small collection of items, but it's the views of the Rio Guadiana and the village that make it worth the trek.

Near the castle is the **Alcáçova**, where archaeologists discovered traces of an Islamic neighbourhood. South of here, inside the town hall is the **Casa Romana**, the remains of a Roman house uncovered in the 1980s. A small exhibit showcases items like coins, amphorae and sculptures. Nearby **Museu de Arte Islâmica** and **Museu de Arte Sacra** are two museums featuring exhibits on Islamic art and Sacred

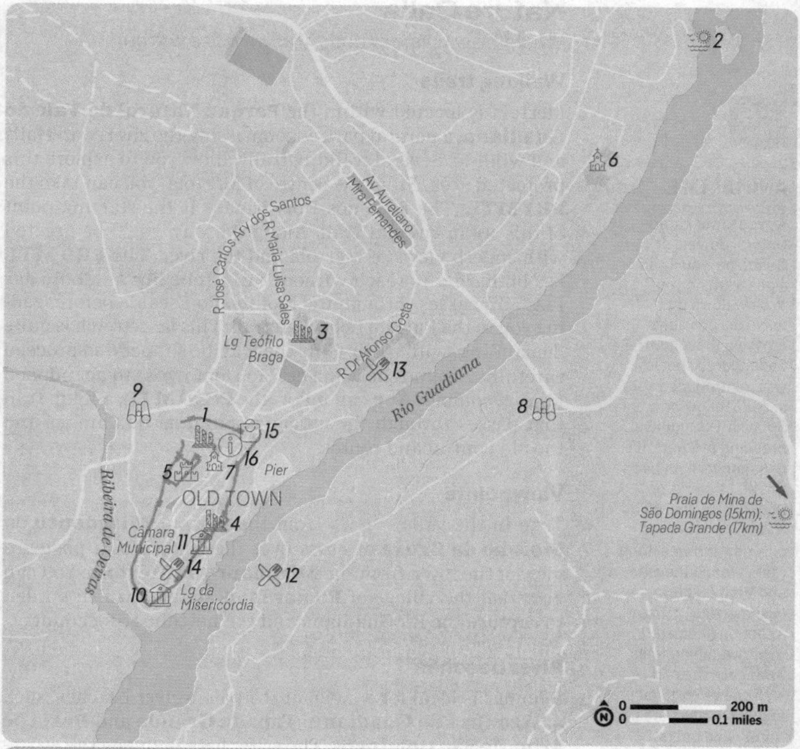

SIGHTS
1 Alcáçova
2 Azenhas do Guadiana
3 Basílica Paleocristã
4 Casa Romana
5 Castelo
6 Chapel and Necropolis of São Sebastião
7 Igreja Matriz
8 Miradouro do Moinho da Bruxa
9 Miradouro de Mértola
10 Museu de Arte Sacra
11 Museu de Arte Islâmica

EATING
12 Casa Amarela
13 Tamuje
14 Vila Velha

SHOPPING
15 Cooperativa Oficina de Tecelagem

INFORMATION
16 Turismo

art, respectively. These reveal the different faiths that Mértola has welcomed through the ages. Finally, head east to see the **Basílica Paleocristã**, an old funerary basilica, and the **Chapel and Necropolis of São Sebastião**.

WHERE TO EAT IN MÉRTOLA

Tamuje
Order the grilled cheese, before sampling the array of game dishes like deer and wild boar. **€€**

Casa Amarela
For a dinner overlooking Mértola, head to this restaurant on the other side of the river. **€€**

Vila Velha
Locally sourced ingredients are the priority at this innovative restaurant combining Portuguese and Arab flavours. **€€**

Nature Calls

RIVERSIDE WALKS, BEACHES AND WILDLIFE WATCHING

Walking trails

Mértola is located within the **Parque Natural do Vale do Guadiana**, a natural park encompassing the river, waterfalls and wildlife. Several walking trails allow you to explore this protected area. From the centre of Mértola, you can take the **PR1 MTL**. The Poço dos Dois Irmãos is the starting point of this 10km circular trail. Along the way, you'll be greeted with superb views of Mértola and the river. **The PR9 MTL** is a bit harder to reach without a car. It begins at Monte das Pias and passes through the Moinho do Escalda before leading you to the Pulo do Lobo waterfall. This last stretch is quite demanding, with rocky cliffs that can be slippery, so proceed carefully. Around the Mina de São Domingos, an abandoned mining complex, you can follow the **PR10 MTL**, a 16km trail that passes through the village of Santana de Cambas and the old contraband routes.

Viewpoints

Take in the valley views from the lookout **Miradouro do Moinho da Bruxa** or cross over the bridge for a postcard view of the town from the **Miradouro de Mértola**. You can also visit the village of **Pomarão**, near the Spanish border, to capture the RioGuadiana and the neighbouring country.

River beaches

Summer is ideal for a swim at the park's river beaches, such as **Azenhas do Guadiana**, **Tapada Grande** and **Praia de Mina de São Domingos**. The water here is among the warmest in the country, often reaching 30°C.

ANIMAL LIFE

As you enter Parque Natural do Vale do Guadiana, you'll see signs warning you to slow down due to lynxes possibly crossing the road. The endangered species was reintroduced here in 2015, following a Spanish-Portuguese breeding program. It's common to sight birds like black storks or Bonelli's eagles. **Birds & Nature** organises one-day and weeklong tours around the area, and **Visit Mértola** (visitmertola.pt) has a section dedicated to birdwatching trails. Strangely, the park is also one of Portugal's biggest hunting areas. Hares, wild boars, partridges and deer are among the animals hunted here. Fishing is also allowed. Contact **Wild Fishing Portugal** (wildfishingportugal.co.uk) for a guided tour.

GETTING AROUND

Rodoviária do Alentejo provides a direct bus from Beja to Mértola which runs four times a day. However, these do not run on weekends. Alternatively, Rede Expressos offers a daily bus from Vila Real de Santo António in the Algarve. In most cases, you'll have to stay overnight or cut your visit short to make it back in time for the last bus. The best way to explore this region at your own pace is to rent a car. It's best to park outside the walls and explore the historic centre on foot to avoid getting stuck in the narrow streets.

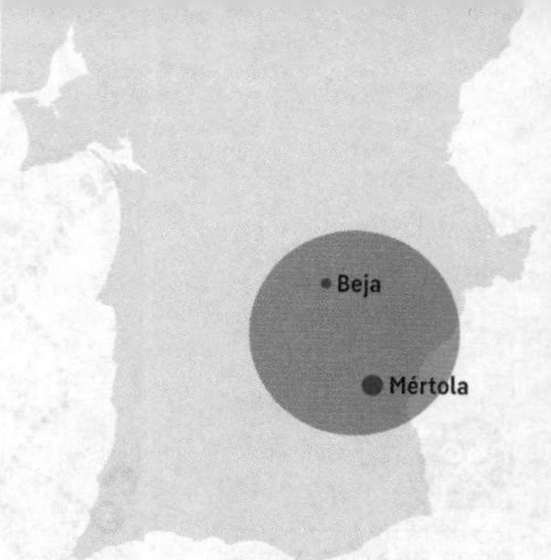

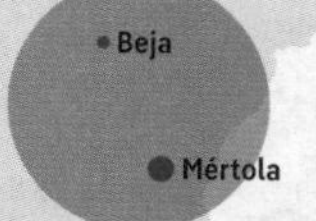

Beyond Mértola

Listen to traditional songs and visit the farms that produce the region's top ingredients.

Mértola is the key to the Baixo Alentejo. The Alentejo's southern section is the heart of the countryside, where vines grow alongside cork trees and farmers tend to the sheep and the black pigs that make the delicious cheeses and meats that epitomise the Alentejo's gastronomy. It's also the birthplace of the Cante Alentejano (p220), the traditional song that was heard in the fields and occasionally still echoes in the region's taverns. Here, you'll find Beja, the second-biggest city in the region, the wineries of Vidigueira and picturesque towns such as Serpa and Castro Verde.

TOP TIP

Witness the Abertura das Talhas in November when locals open the taps of Roman-style amphorae to taste the season's wine.

Castelo de Beja (p224)

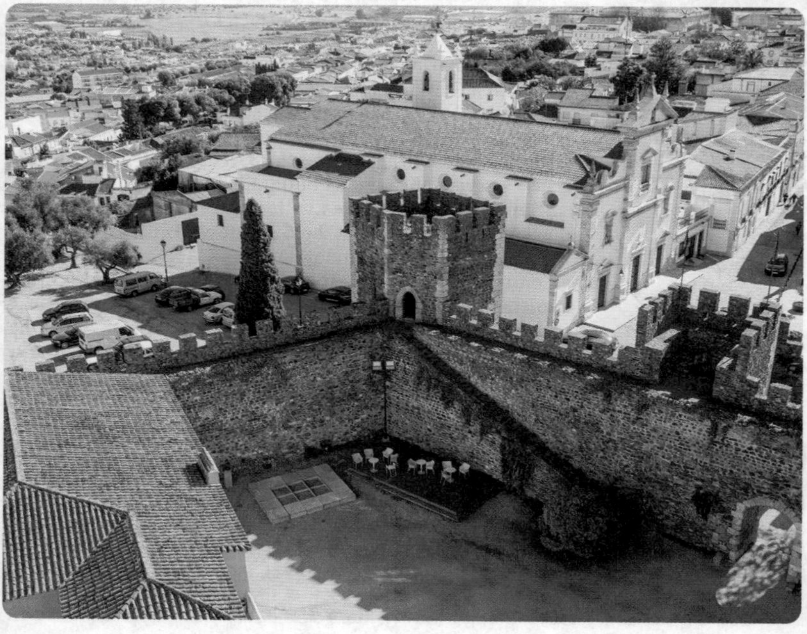

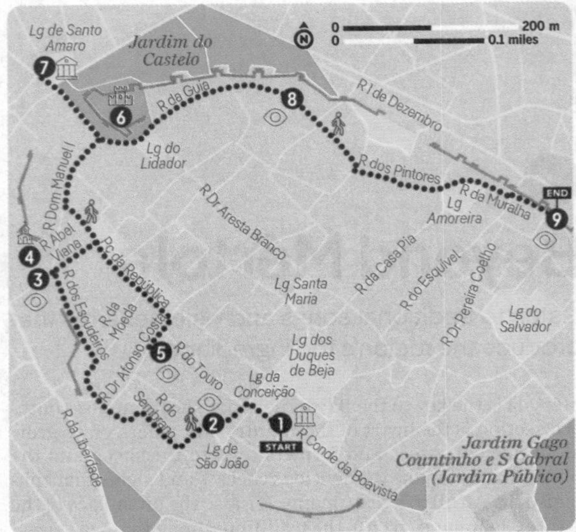

BEST PLACES TO EAT IN BEJA

Luiz da Rocha
Sample traditional pastries like the pig-shaped cake *porquinhos doces* at this local bakery. €

Pinguinhas
With its wooden panels and converted barrel tables, this is an inviting spot for a round of *petiscos* and wine. €€

Dom Dinis
Grilled meats are the speciality at this traditional restaurant near Beja's castle. €€

Sabores do Campo
Delicious vegetarian dishes are sold by weight here, a rare find in meat-eating Alentejo. €€

The Capital of the South Walking Tour

ROMANCE, ART AND HISTORY

There is a sense of calm in Beja. Perhaps that's why the Romans called it Pax Julia ('pax' meaning 'peace', and Julia after emperor Julius Caesar). Unlike Évora, where buildings were preserved, Beja lost much of its heritage over the years.

Its few Roman remains are in the **1 Museu Regional de Beja**, set in a 15th-century convent. During your visit, you'll hear about Mariana Alcoforado, a Portuguese nun who fell in love with a French soldier.

Recently, the city has become a stage for **2 urban art** with works like the giant trash-made cockerel by Bordalo II on Largo de São João. Crossing under the **3 Arco dos Prazeres**, you'll reach a series of religious buildings like the **4 Igreja Nossa Senhora dos Prazeres** with its stunning gilded altar. A quick detour from here is the **5 Januela Manuelina**, a well-preserved Manueline window.

Continue to the **6 Castelo de Beja**. Walk around the castle's gardens and climb up to the keep for the best city views. Nearby is the **7 Núcleo Visigótico** featuring a collection of Visigothic items. Finish your walk with a wander through the **8 Judiaria** (around Rua da Guia) and **9 Mouraria** (around Rua da Muralha), the old Jewish and Moorish neighbourhoods.

WHERE TO STAY NEAR BEJA

Pousada Convento de Beja
Set within an old convent, this *pousada* features an outdoor pool and a tennis court. €€

Herdade dos Grous
Combine your stay with a wine tasting at this luxury vineyard estate 20km south of Beja. €€€

Burrico D'Orada
Between Vidigueira and the Alqueva lake, this estate offers packages with wine tastings and boat rides. €€

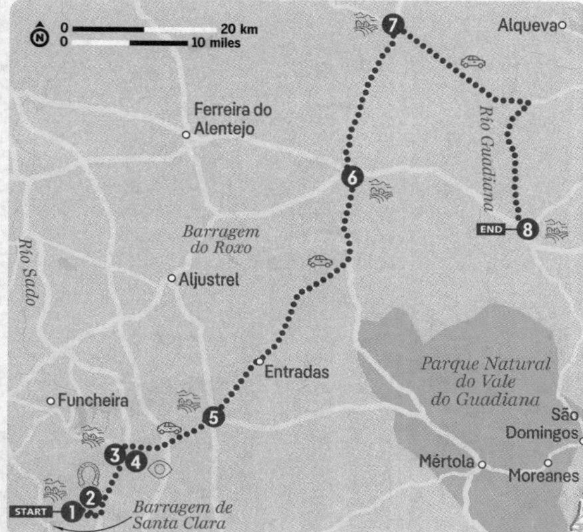

Deep in the Countryside Driving Tour

BLACK PIG, ROMAN WINE AND CHEESE TASTINGS

Start at **1 Castro da Cola**, an archaeological site featuring an Iron Age residence and fortifications added during the Arab occupation. Close by, **2 Equus Ourique** provides horse-riding lessons and feeding sessions.

Then head to **3 Ourique**, the capital of the porco Alentejano (Alentejo pork). To tour a local farm, contact **4 ACPA** (porcoalentejano.com), an association of Alentejo pig farmers. A guide will take you around a nearby property, giving you exclusive access to the pigs in different stages.

Continue to **5 Castro Verde**. Wander down to the Basilica Real de Nossa Senhora da Conceição or visit the Museu da Lucerna. Nearby, the Centro de Educação Ambiental Vale Gonçalinho is the meeting point for birdwatchers.

Drive through **6 Beja** and stop in the town of **7 Vidigueira** for a wine tasting. Housed inside a century-old winery is the Honrado Vineyards, which produces traditional *vinho de talha* (p201). Also in Vidigueira, the Quinta do Quetzal has a creative art centre and contemporary restaurant overlooking the vineyards. Heading south, stop in the beautiful village of **8 Serpa**.

BEST BAIXO ALENTEJO EXPERIENCES

Rita Valadas owns the country lodging Burrico D'Orada in the heart of Baixo Alentejo. Here are her favourite experiences in the south.

Wine tastings
Tour the wine estates and sample the *talha* wines (produced in clay amphorae).

Slow food
We have a unique gastronomy based on natural ingredients. From top-quality extra-virgin olive oils to DOP sheep cheese and black-pig cured meats.

Slow living
Our picturesque whitewashed villages and cities have an ancient history that deserves discovering – Moura, Serpa, Vidigueira, Vila de Frades, Beja, Mértola.

These things can be experienced all year long, in a stunning, off-the-beaten-track region with sun nearly every day, where time does go slowly, or as we say here: *Com vagar.*

GETTING AROUND

It's easy to reach Beja via Lisbon or the Algarve. From the Sete Rios station in Lisbon, you can catch a train or a bus to the centre of Beja. The journey takes around 2½ hours. You'll need to change trains at Casa Branca, which is slightly inconvenient. Buses from the Algarve depart from Faro and Albufeira. Rede Expressos stops in small towns like Ourique, Vidigueira and Castro Verde, but you'll need a car to reach hotels and vineyards in the countryside.

Convento de Cristo (p249), Tomar

ESTREMADURA & RIBATEJO

MEDIEVAL HISTORY, NATURE AND RELIGION

Embark on a journey where castles appear on the hilltops and the sea lurks down the street.

Nestled between the ocean and the Rio Tejo, the regions of Estremadura and Ribatejo hold traditions and stories that mirror what Portugal was and still is today. Here part of the population has turned to the sea, while the other part lives side by side with memories left by the past. After all, due to its geographical position, these regions were the stage of remarkable events in Portugal's history, which left their mark on the villages and cities. The same ones that today thrive on protecting this historical heritage.

The characteristics of Estremadura and Ribatejo stand out from the other Portuguese territories in the country's centre. From the whitewashed houses trimmed in blue and yellow to the monumental architecture classified as Unesco World Heritage Sites, from the places worthy of miracles and the natural beauty brought by the mountains, beaches and lagoons. Even the dinosaurs wanted to leave their mark here. Not to mention the dishes that arrive at the table, either with the countryside warmth or full of the Atlantic freshness.

The richness of its past and present, combined with the proximity to Lisbon, makes Estremadura and Ribatejo some of the country's most exciting areas to visit.

BILL PERRY/SHUTTERSTOCK ©

THE MAIN AREAS

ÓBIDOS	NAZARÉ	TOMAR
Medieval village. p232	Giant waves and fishing traditions. p241	Land of the Knights Templar. p249

Find Your Way

The region of Estremadura and Ribatejo borders the sub-regions of Beira Baixa, Pinhal Litoral and Alto Alentejo and is bathed by the Atlantic Ocean and the rivers Tejo and Zêzere.

Nazaré, p241

The giant waves have brought it fame, but the fishers of Nazaré have long faced the sea that inspires the streets of this town.

Tomar, p249

It is the land of the Templars, and this is very present in the Convento de Cristo, a Unesco World Heritage Site, and in the streets of the historic centre.

Pombal
Sertã
Dornes
São Pedro de Moel
Marinha Grande
Leiria
ATLANTIC OCEAN
Fátima (Cova da Iria)
Ourém
Batalha
São Jorge Cruz
Nazaré
Tomar
Porto de Mós
Bairro
Alcobaça
Barragem de Castelo de Bode
São Martinho do Porto
Minde
Serra dos Candeeiros
Parque Natural das Serras de Aire e Candeeiros
Serra de Aire
Constância
Entroncamento
Abrantes
Almourol
Foz do Arelho
Caldas da Rainha
Baleal
Peniche
Óbidos
Rio Maior
Rio Tejo

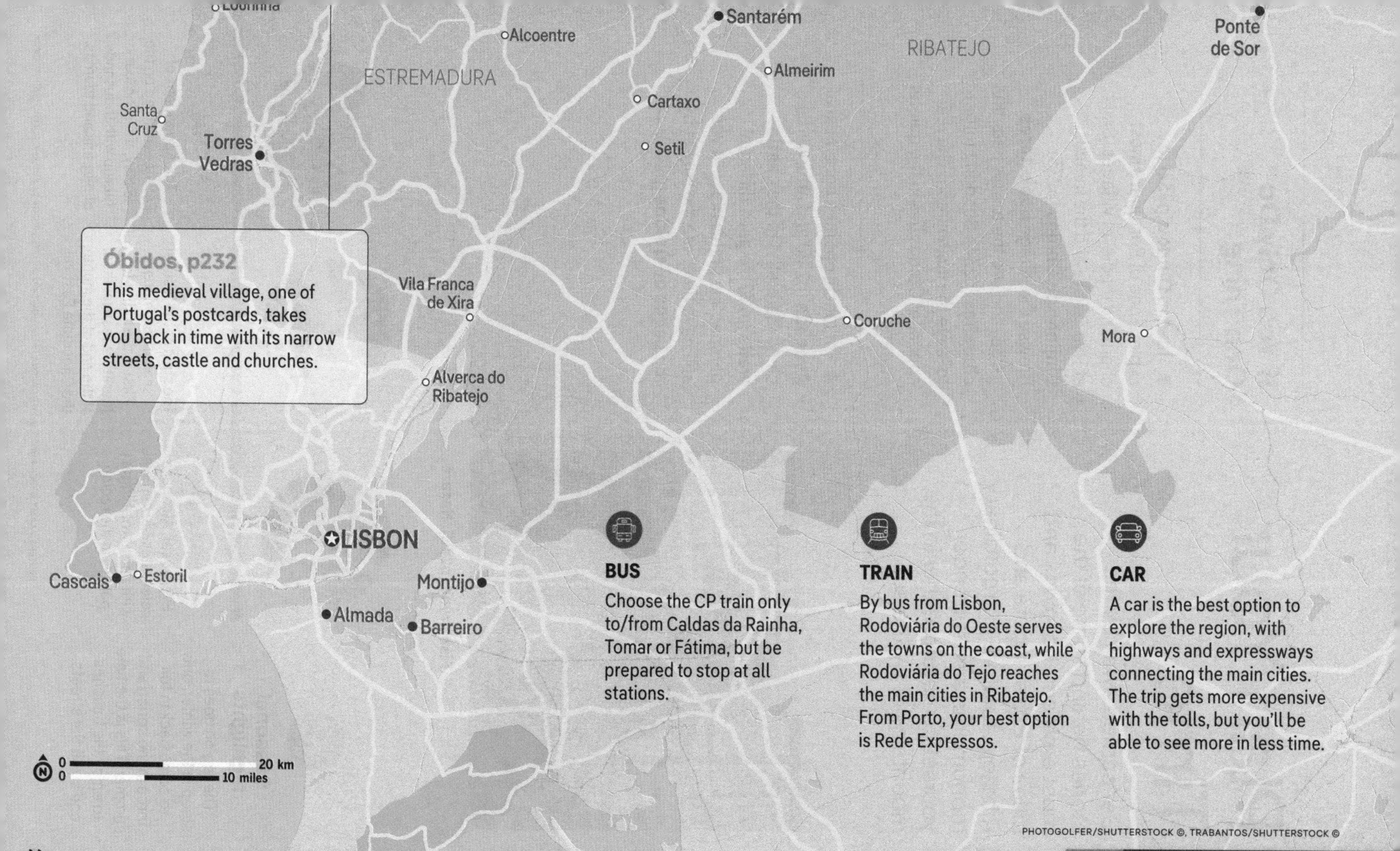

Óbidos, p232

This medieval village, one of Portugal's postcards, takes you back in time with its narrow streets, castle and churches.

BUS

Choose the CP train only to/from Caldas da Rainha, Tomar or Fátima, but be prepared to stop at all stations.

TRAIN

By bus from Lisbon, Rodoviária do Oeste serves the towns on the coast, while Rodoviária do Tejo reaches the main cities in Ribatejo. From Porto, your best option is Rede Expressos.

CAR

A car is the best option to explore the region, with highways and expressways connecting the main cities. The trip gets more expensive with the tolls, but you'll be able to see more in less time.

Plan Your Time

Get carried away by the stories behind some of the most emblematic towns and cities of Estremadura and Ribatejo. Explore extraordinary monuments and surrender yourself to nature, either in the mountains or by the sea.

ELENA BUSLAEVA/SHUTTERSTOCK ©

Fish dryng (p243), Nazaré

If You Only Do One Thing

- Head to **Óbidos** (p232) to explore one of Portugal's most charming medieval villages. Start at Rua Direita and the famous **Ginjinha de Óbidos** (p235). Browse the village **bookstores** (p236) and see the town's beautiful **churches** (p234). But don't forget to leave the main circuit. The real appeal of Óbidos lies in the quieter streets.

- For lunch, opt for a light meal at **Avocado** (p235) and afterwards climb (carefully) to the **castle walls** (p232) to get a different perspective of this place. If you still have time, see the sunset by the **Lagoa de Óbidos** (p240).

Seasonal highlights

The region goes to sleep in the winter, only to come back in full force in the spring and summer. This is the time to enjoy the beaches and stroll the streets.

FEBRUARY

Every year, Alcobaça celebrates the carnival with one of the biggest parties in the region.

APRIL

The start of the festival season in Óbidos. First is the Latitudes literature festival then, at the end of the month, the Chocolate Festival.

MAY

The Apparitions of Fátima is marked on the 13 May; the sanctuary fills up with thousands of pilgrims and tourists.

REUTERS/ALAMY STOCK PHOTO ©, MAGDALENA PALUCHOWSKA/SHUTTERSTOCK ©, JHC_PHOTO/SHUTTERSTOCK ©

Three Days to Travel Around

- After a day spent in Óbidos, head north along the coast to **Nazaré** (p241), the land of the world's biggest waves and excellent fresh fish, which you can taste at **Rosa dos Ventos** (p245). Be sure to go to the beach to see the traditional **fish drying** (p243).

- Next, explore **Serras de Aire e Candeeiros** (p247), with the incredible Grutas de Mira de Aire and the place where the dinosaurs left their footprints. Still in the natural park, make one more stop to see the **Castelo de Porto de Mós** (p248), with its captivating green towers.

If You Have More Time

- Start in **Tomar** (p249) and the **Convento de Cristo** (p249), a Unesco World Heritage Site. This is just the starting point for spending two days in this city. Wander around the old **Jewish quarter** (p250), trek through the **Mata Nacional dos Sete Montes** (p253) or indulge in some reading at **Insensato** (p249), one of Tomar's newest cafes.

- Drive to **Dornes** (p256) to visit another stunning Portuguese village and take a walk along the Rio Zêzere. After spending a half-day here, move on to another emblematic medieval town: **Ourém** (p256). Finally, add an extra day or two to explore the **Parque Natural das Serras de Aire e Candeeiros** (p247).

JUNE
The good weather invites you to go to the beaches in the west. This is also the month of the *ginja* harvest.

JULY
Every four years, the Feast of the Trays draws thousands to Tomar with its colourful procession.

AUGUST
It's harvest time for the most important fruits of the region: Pera Rocha do Oeste (pear) and Maçã de Alcobaça (apple).

NOVEMBER
The season of big waves begins in Nazaré. Surfers and fans of the sport start looking at the sea forecasts.

ÓBIDOS

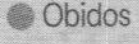

The historic centre of Óbidos stopped in time – and it's just as well. Today it's one of the best preserved medieval villages in Portugal, attracting visitors from all over with its imposing castle and beautiful churches. The labyrinth of cobblestone streets and white houses invites you to take a picture at every corner as well as at every nook and cranny full of flowers. The real discovery of Óbidos is in the inner streets, the quiet ones, where you want to get lost.

On the other hand, Rua Direita is used to the daily bustle that passes through it because it has always been the town's main artery. Stores appear from door to door, selling the famous *ginjinha* (sour cherry liqueur) and souvenirs that don't let you forget the nature of this place. After all, those who visit Óbidos want to take home a memory of this journey to the medieval past.

TOP TIP

Óbidos is one of the most touristic destinations in the west of Portugal, so be prepared for hordes of visitors, even more so in the summer or on weekends. If you want some quieter moments, go very early or stay until the last hours of light.

Castle & Ramparts

WHERE IT ALL BEGAN

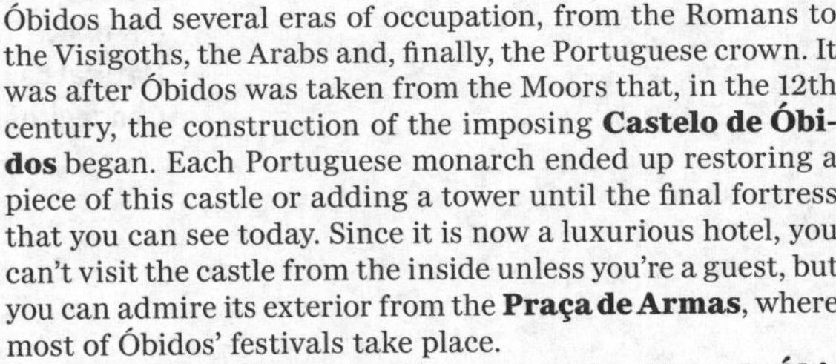

Óbidos had several eras of occupation, from the Romans to the Visigoths, the Arabs and, finally, the Portuguese crown. It was after Óbidos was taken from the Moors that, in the 12th century, the construction of the imposing **Castelo de Óbidos** began. Each Portuguese monarch ended up restoring a piece of this castle or adding a tower until the final fortress that you can see today. Since it is now a luxurious hotel, you can't visit the castle from the inside unless you're a guest, but you can admire its exterior from the **Praça de Armas**, where most of Óbidos' festivals take place.

Another approach to the castle is walking the **Muro de Óbidos** (Moorish wall) for about 1.5km around the whole town and enjoying the surrounding landscape. You can climb up using the accesses near Porta da Vila or the castle. However, this is not advisable for people with reduced mobility or who suffer from vertigo since it is several metres high (13m in some spots), the floor is quite worn and there are no guardrails. If you feel up to it, wear appropriate footwear, watch your step and be careful when crossing paths with other visitors. Take special care with children.

ÓBIDOS TILES

Despite not being of Portuguese origin, tile art has gained deep roots in the country. Óbidos does not ignore this, presenting several examples of tiles dating back to the beginning of the 16th century. You can see them on the **Porta da Vila** oratory when you enter the town's walls. Also, inside the Igreja de Santa Maria or on the Igreja da Misericórdia's interior.

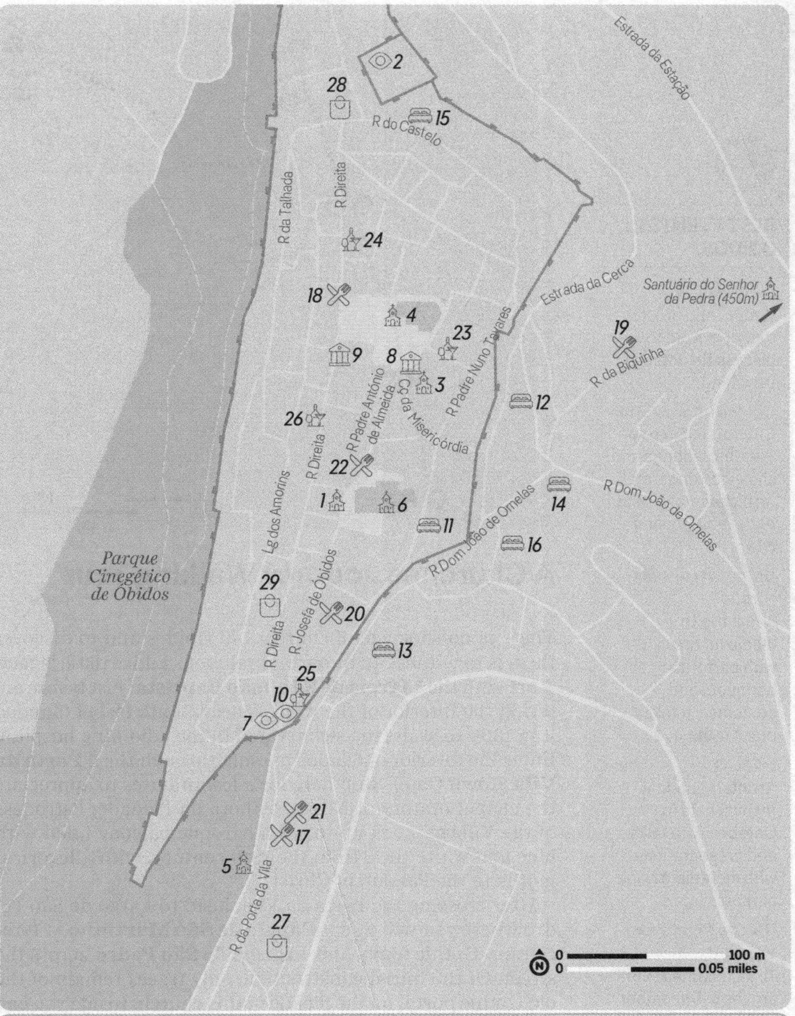

SIGHTS
1 Capela de São Martinho
2 Castelo de Óbidos
3 Igreja da Misericórdia
4 Igreja de Santa Maria
5 Igreja de São João Baptista
6 Igreja de São Pedro
7 Muro de Óbidos
8 Museu Abílio de Mattos e Silva
9 Museu Municipal
10 Porta da Vila

SLEEPING
11 Casa das Senhoras Rainhas
12 Casa do Relógio
13 Hotel Josefa d'Óbidos
14 Hotel Real d'Óbidos
15 Pousada do Castelo de Óbidos
16 The Literary Man

EATING
17 Avocado
18 Capinha d'Óbidos
19 Já!mon Já!mon
20 Lounge
21 Macaron d'Óbidos
22 Real Casa do Petisco

DRINKING & NIGHTLIFE
23 Arco da Cadeia
24 Bar Ibn Errik Rex
25 Cafeteria da Moura
26 Mariquinhas

SHOPPING
27 Livraria Artes e Letras
28 Livraria de Santiago
29 Livraria do Mercado

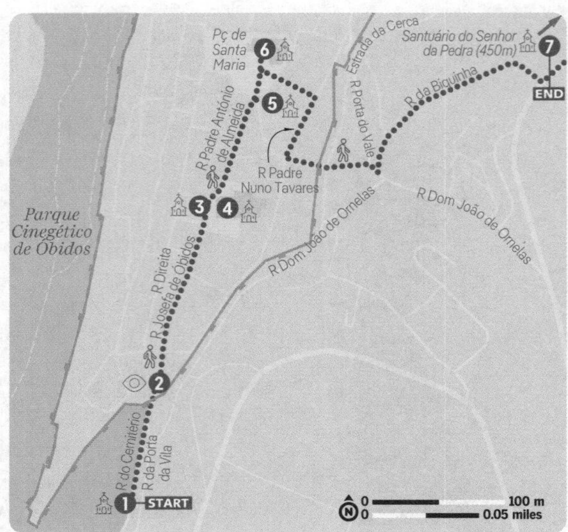

BEST EVENTS IN ÓBIDOS

Latitudes
Writers and artists gather in April to discuss the topic of travelling.

Óbidos International Chocolate Festival
Statues, tastings and show cookings, all with chocolate; held between April and May.

Óbidos Medieval Market
A real trip to medieval times, with performances, banquets and costumes. It takes place in June.

F(O)LIO
An internactional festival held in October, with talks and presentations with incredible book authors.

Óbidos Christmas Village
The Christmas spirit arrives in December with shows and entertainment for the kids.

A Churches Journey Walking Tour

ART AND FAITH, HAND IN HAND

There is no shortage of churches in Óbidos and to discover them is to witness an important religious and artistic legacy. Start with the 1 **Igreja de São João Baptista**, just before entering the interior of the walls. Queen Santa Isabel founded it in 1309 to assist the sick treated in the adjoining hospital. Enter the interior of Óbidos passing through the 2 **Porta da Vila** (Town Gate). Stop here for a few minutes to appreciate the chapel-oratory of Nossa Senhora da Piedade, Patroness of the Village. Look up to see a baroque balcony filled with blue and white tiles, from the 18th century, with allegorical motifs to the Passion of Christ.

After crossing the Porta da Vila, head to Largo de São Pedro where you will find 3 **Capela de São Martinho**, a 14th-century Gothic tomb, and 4 **Igreja de São Pedro** across the street. Of the initial construction, only traces remain of the old Gothic portal on the facade of this church. Inside you can admire the altar with a baroque altarpiece in gilded wood. From here, take Rua Padre António de Almeida, pass the 5 **Igreja da Misericórdia**, founded by Queen Leonor in the 16th century, and reach the Praça de Santa Maria. 6 **Igreja**

WHERE TO STAY IN ÓBIDOS

Hotel Josefa d'Óbidos
Next to the castle walls, this accommodation offers comfortable rooms and warm service. €€

Pousada do Castelo de Óbidos
An opportunity to sleep inside the Óbidos Castle with all the perks of a five-star hotel. €€€

Casa das Senhoras Rainhas
Small boutique hotel with rooms dedicated to the Portuguese queens overlooking the castle walls. €€€

de Santa Maria is the ex-libris of Óbidos religious buildings. Built over an ancient Visigoth temple, this church has paintings by Josefa de Óbidos, 17th-century tiles, and its ceiling is an inspiration to local handicrafts.

To visit the last church on this route, you must leave the medieval town and go to the 7 **Santuário do Senhor da Pedra**. Its baroque-style construction is one of the most interesting in the country. Look for the stone image of the crucified Christ on the high altar.

Museums & Paintings

THE STROKE OF ÓBIDOS' ARTISTS

Enter the town and follow Rua Direita to find the **Museu Municipal of Óbidos**. Located in an 18th-century manor house, this museum has a significant collection of sacred and religious art. Here you can find works by André Reinoso, the first Portuguese baroque painter, and Josefa de Óbidos, a 17th-century painter known for her religious themes, still lifes and metal engravings, who lived most of her life in Óbidos.

Then, continue along Rua Direita until Largo de Santa Maria and enter **Igreja de Santa Maria**, almost a museum itself, since it keeps paintings by Baltazar Gomes Figueira and his daughter, Josefa de Óbidos. For work by the latter, look for the altarpiece of Santa Catarina de Alexandria, dated 1611. The chapel's central retable is from painter João da Costa.

Next to the church is the **Museu Abílio de Mattos e Silva**. In this building that served as the town hall, court and prison is a collection of the works done by Abílio de Mattos e Silva, a great Portuguese painter, scenographer and costume designer of the 20th century, a native of Óbidos. Walk through the three floors to see the town's streets portrayed on paper and canvas.

In total, allow about 1½ hours to visit these three places, and be aware that the museums are closed on Monday.

Taste the Óbidos Sour Cherry

SAMPLE THE TOWN'S FAMOUS LIQUEUR

Anyone arriving in Óbidos is immediately greeted with a cup (preferably made of chocolate) of one of the country's most famous liqueurs. Although many shops have Ginjinha de Óbidos with their name on it, three brands are the oldest to produce and bottle this drink.

Just 4km from the medieval town, **Oppidum** has its small factory on Rua da Escola, in Sobral da Lagoa, the

BEST RESTAURANTS IN ÓBIDOS

Avocado
If you're looking for vegetarian or healthy food, this is the place to go. €

Real Casa do Petisco
Follow the chef's suggestions and try the crunchy piglet belly or the salmon tacos. €€

Já!mon Já!mon
This *tasca* (tavern) offers excellent tapas and Portuguese dishes. Sit on the terrace when the weather's nice. €€

Lounge
Delicious Portuguese food served in a restaurant owned by a culinary teacher. €€

LOOK UP

The ceiling of Igreja de Santa Maria is the source of inspiration for the embroidery done in Óbidos (p232). Try to match the colours you see here with the ones on the pieces sold by local artisans.

Hotel Real d'Óbidos
Set in a 14th-century building with classic decor and medieval details and has a great summer pool. **€€€**

The Literary Man
In a former convent, this hotel combines contemporary with traditional and more than 60,000 books. **€€**

Casa do Relógio
An 18th-century house in a great location turned into a guesthouse with a beautiful terrace. **€**

birthplace of sour cherry production in this region. The company passed from grandfather to father and now to daughter, keeping the business alive, even beyond borders. The family opens the factory's doors to anyone who wants to know how this sour cherry liqueur is made.

Also international is **Vila das Rainhas**, which has decades of history and know-how in producing the famous Óbidos sour cherry liqueur. With its facilities next to the Nacional 114 road in Amoreira, it is possible to visit the store and learn more about this product.

You can taste Oppidum and Vila das Rainhas in various stores and cafes around the medieval village, whereas **Mariquinhas** went further and opened its dedicated store on Rua Direita. Go here to learn about the history of this third-generation business. The Mariquinhas Experience, as the name suggests, is a place of experiences around the products made from sour cherries. Try the sour cherry liqueur aged in French oak barrels, accompanied by chocolate truffles, or choose something different, like the sour cherry sangria.

THE QUEEN'S VILLAGE

During its history, Óbidos passed from one Portuguese queen to another. It began in 1287, when King Dom Dinis gave Óbidos to Dona Isabel as a wedding gift, starting a tradition that would last until the 19th century. The work of these Portuguese queens is still notorious today. Dona Isabel ordered the construction of the Capela de São Vicente (today Igreja de São João Baptista), while Dona Leonor enriched the artistic heritage in Igreja de Santa Maria and started the Misericórdia of Óbidos. Dona Catarina de Áustria ordered the Usseira Aqueduct, and Dona Maria I reformulated the plumbing of Rua Direita and introduced the public fountain.

Book, Books & More Books

A WALK THROUGH THE LITERARY VILLAGE

Member of Unesco's Creative Cities Network since 2015, when it held the first edition of its International Literature Festival, Óbidos is a literary village for its connection with books and culture. Various bookstores and spaces of literary inspiration were born in the last decade and are waiting for you to discover them.

In Rua da Porta da Vila, just before the castle walls and entering into a patio, the **Livraria Artes e Letras** occupies an old wine cellar with antique and collector's books displayed on shelves made from wooden crates. This place is open only in the afternoon (closed on Sunday and Monday) and has a small bar with regional wines.

Inside the walls and halfway down Rua Direita is **Livraria do Mercado** (Market Bookstore), where you can find books next to organic groceries. This bookstore, in the old firefighters' barracks, is a place of secondhand books displayed in fruit boxes as a tribute to local agriculture.

Next walk down to the end of Rua Direita to find the **Livraria de Santiago**. Here, in one of the oldest churches in the village, the religious service has given way to the exhibition and sale of books. Order a coffee and spend some time browsing a book or finding your next literary obsession.

WHERE TO HAVE A DRINK IN ÓBIDOS

Cafeteria da Moura
At the village entrance, this is the perfect place to have a glass of wine at the end of the day.

Arco da Cadeia
Take a trip back in time in this bar with medieval decoration inside the old jailhouse.

Bar Ibn Errik Rex
Some say that this is the best *ginjinha* in Óbidos – try it for yourself.

Dried flower crown stall

The Stitch of Tradition

DISCOVERING ÓBIDOS' EMBROIDERY

In a small store near the pharmacy, local artisans work on one of the oldest traditions in town, unique embroideries and tapestries. The shop (open on the weekends, and daily during July and August), to which you have to climb down a staircase, has its door flanked by dried flower crowns, another souvenir that goes back to medieval times. On summer days, artisans are often outside, showing their art to passers-by, but go inside to appreciate the beauty of the work.

The embroidery of Óbidos is known for taking its designs and colours from the Igreja de Santa Maria ceiling and working with only two embroidery stitches (Pé de Flor and Pé de Galo) on a linen or silk base. This is a genuine product that dates back to the 1950s, when Maria Adelaide Ribeirete, a native of Óbidos, began teaching her art to the locals. She did this until she was 90 years old. Those who learned from her are today exhibiting and selling their work in this place and doing workshops.

BEST PASTRIES IN ÓBIDOS

Capinha d'Óbidos
For freshly baked bread or typical pastries, go to this small cafe where recipes have been shared from generation to generation since 1883. Ask for a *ferradura* (horseshoe), the house specialty.

Macaron d'Óbidos
The rustic exterior of the building contrasts with the elegance of the macarons sold here. Try it with one of the regional fillings, such as sour cherry liqueur, Pêra Rocha (pear) or Maçã de Alcobaça (apple).

ANOTHER SWEET?

Pair a *ginjinha* (sour cherry liqueur; p235) with a *ferradura* (horseshoe), a typical cake sold at Capinha d'Óbidos on Rua Direita. Tradition says it was offered by brides on their wedding day.

GETTING AROUND

Óbidos is best visited on foot since vehicles are not allowed inside the walls. But to get there, you should go by car. There are several parking lots available nearby. You can also book a tour leaving from the Portuguese capital or take a bus from Rodoviária do Oeste, in Campo Grande, Lisbon. Wear comfortable shoes with some grip, as the streets of Óbidos are all made of cobblestone, with some parts even quite slippery.

Beyond Óbidos

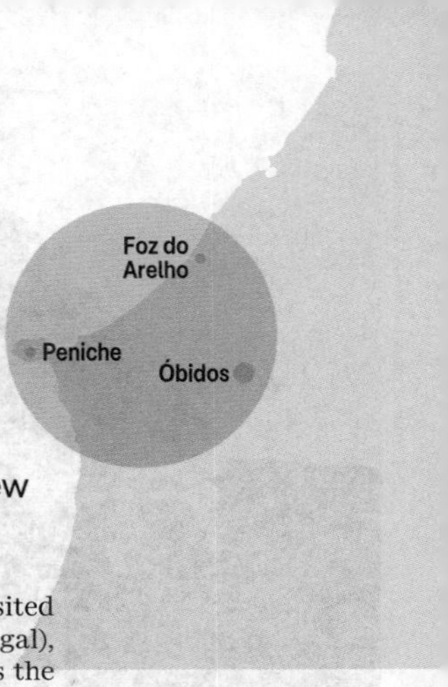

Leave history aside and venture beyond the walls. Around Óbidos, nature invites you to new discoveries.

Foz do Arelho
Peniche
Óbidos

History dictated that Óbidos is today one of the most visited places in the region of Estremadura (and even in Portugal), just an hour from the Portuguese capital. However, it is the nature around it that arouses the curiosity of those who find themselves in the area.

Over the centuries, local people have realised that opportunity lies in the water. Whether it was gathering shellfish in the lagoon that once reached the castle gates or in the islands off the coast, which are today World Biosphere Heritage, or the thermal waters where the Queen bathed in the 15th century. More recently, the waves have attracted thousands of surfers to this part of the Portuguese coast.

TOP TIP

This region is known for its more unstable weather and cool temperatures. Always have a jacket with you in case you need one.

Praia dos Supertubos

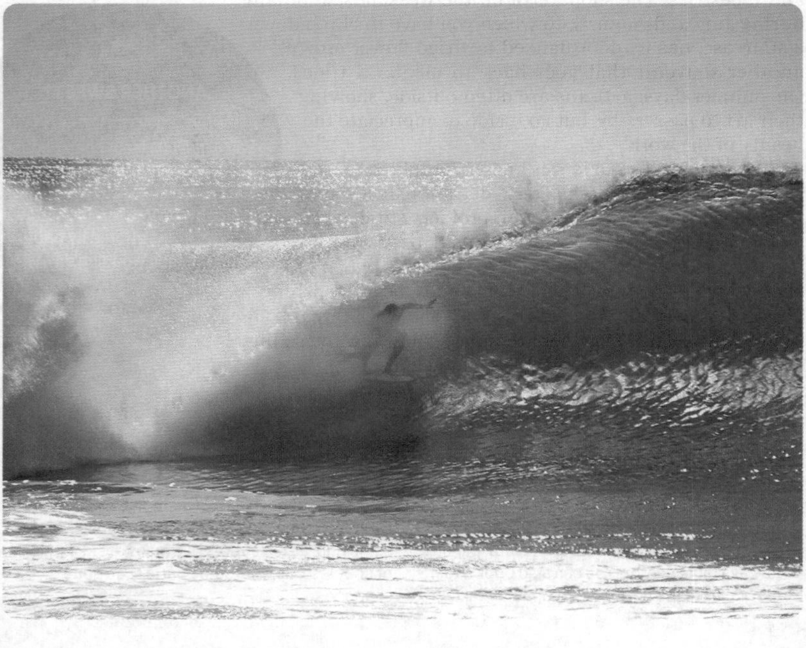

An Old Thermal Hospital Town

THERMAL BATHS AND CERAMICS

Founded in 1485 by Queen Dona Leonor, **Caldas da Rainha** has the oldest thermal hospital in the world. But this town, 15 minutes by car from Óbidos, also stands out for its art and ceramics. Pieces by José Malhoa and Rafael Bordallo Pinheiro, two well-known Portuguese artists, are exhibited in the city's museums and spread throughout the main streets. When you're here, be sure to visit the fruit market in **Praça da República**, appreciate the Art Nouveau of the buildings nearby, visit the **Fábrica de Faianças Artísticas Bordallo Pinheiro** to buy the famous ceramics and wander through **Mata Rainha Dona Leonor**.

Waves & Surfers

THE WAVE CAPITAL OF PORTUGAL

Since it joined the world surfing tour in 2009, **Peniche**, 30km from Óbidos, has become the Portuguese surfing capital. This peninsula and its fine-sand beaches offer ideal conditions for this sport, regardless of the level of the surfer.

The **Baleal** area is the place to start if you want to try surfing for the first time. Here you will find several surf schools and can rent equipment. Begin at **Praia do Lagide** or, on the opposite side, in front of Bar do Bruno. It all depends on the swell's direction. If you have some experience, try **Praia dos Belgas**, further north, or **Meio da Baía**, to the south.

Continuing south, you will reach **Praia dos Supertubos** (Supertubes), the same beach where the World Surfing Championship takes place. As the name implies, tubular waves are common here, and even if you don't feel like entering the water, it's worth watching if the sea is big and the wind is offshore.

Even if surfing is not your thing, be sure to visit the city centre. Enter the **Fortaleza de Peniche**, the fort that once served as a prison for political dissidents during the dictatorship period in Portugal. Right next to it, at the fishing port, take the boat to **Berlenga Grande** and walk around this extraordinary island.

BEAUTIFUL BERLENGAS

The **Berlengas archipelago** is one of the great natural treasures of the coastal area of Estremadura. Located just off Peniche, the natural richness and conservation state of this group of islands and reefs is so important that Unesco classified it as a World Biosphere Reserve in 2011.
Of all of them, Berlenga Grande is the largest and most visited island. Besides presenting an incredible ecosystem of endemic plants and several species of seabirds, the Farol do Duque de Bragança and the Forte São João Baptista are two iconic structures that make up the picture postcard of this island. This is also one of the best places to go diving in Portugal.

WHERE TO STAY IN FOZ DO ARELHO

Rio do Prado
Combines luxury with nature. All suites have a fireplace, and the master suite has its own spa. **€€€**

Quinta da Foz
A 16th-century farmhouse with classic rooms, century-old furniture and friendly service. **€€**

Água d'Alma
Associated with the Bikotel network, this contemporary three-star hotel welcomes travellers on two wheels. **€€**

BEST RESTAURANTS AROUND ÓBIDOS

Solar dos Amigos (Guisado)
Typical Portuguese cuisine abounds in this restaurant. Expect extremely generous portions (a half portion serves two) and leave room at the end for the dessert tray that arrives at the table.
€€

Tasca do Joel (Peniche)
Fish and seafood dominate the menu of this modern restaurant that was once a fishermen's tavern. The wine list is also an ex-libris of the house, so take your time. Book ahead.
€€€

MIGUEL ALMEIDA/SHUTTERSTOCK ©

Lagoa de Óbidos

Hiking, Kayaking & Glasswort

THE SECRETS OF THE LAGOON

Lagoa de Óbidos is the most extensive lagoon system on the Portuguese coast and is only 15km from the village of Óbidos. But it wasn't always like this – records show that this stretch of water was once even more vast, reaching the gates of the medieval castle. Today Lagoa de Óbidos is a place full of activities. Whether it's the shellfish gatherers who continue to extract the best clams in the region from this lake, the beachgoers who enjoy themselves in the waters closer to the mouth of the lake, right next to the town of **Foz do Arelho**, or the windsurfers and kitesurfers who fill the air with the colours of their sails on windy days. You can better understand the richness of the lagoon by taking a route that follows the shore. For this, be prepared with good hiking boots, a hat, sunscreen and plenty of water because you will cover between 14km to 17km.

A different way to get to know this ecosystem is to enter the water with a kayak and meet the local shellfish gatherers, discover glasswort or even taste edible seaweed. **Intertidal** (intertidal.pt), a local outdoor experience company, does both of these activities, and because they are trained in marine biology, they instil a more scientific approach to the tour. Find them on the beach near the Foz do Arelho pier and the motorhome park.

GETTING AROUND

Car is the best way to travel around Óbidos. The A8, called the Atlantic Highway, leads to the main coastal cities. But count on there being tolls on most of the route. On the other hand, Rodoviária do Oeste, departing daily from Campo Grande in Lisbon, also serves these locations and makes for a more relaxed trip.

Nazaré
Lisbon

NAZARÉ

Among several Portuguese coastal towns, Nazaré stands out for its history, legends and traditions, which are still very much alive today. The village, divided between Sítio, high up on the cliffs, and the Praia (Beach) area, which stretches for miles below, has grown over time. But it wasn't always like this. Centuries ago, Sítio used to be scrubland and later was given a sanctuary because of a miracle that took place there. Down below, it was all sea. A sea that reached as far as Pederneira, the birthplace of Nazaré.

But over time, the ocean receded and gave way to houses, shops, museums and narrow streets, so narrow in some places that only one person can fit through. The Nazarenes say nobody gets lost in Nazaré because all paths lead to the sea. After all, the ocean was and still is the protagonist of the story of this Portuguese town.

TOP TIP

It's best to explore Nazaré on foot. Arrive by car and park in the Sítio area. Go early to get a spot. Then walk down the Ladeira do Sítio to the centre to discover the traditional streets and walk along the beachfront. To return to Sítio, use the elevator and avoid the climb.

Viewpoint & Sanctuary

EXPLORE THE TOWN'S MOST VISITED AREA

Arriving in Nazaré by car, follow the signs indicating **Sítio**, and you will reach a wide square with a beautiful shrine and a **viewpoint** with one of the best views over the town centre. **Santuário da Nossa Senhora da Nazaré** immediately catches your eye and invites you to enter. Inside this church, built in 1377, you will find the main altar of gilded woodcarving with the primitive image of the Virgin of Nazaré. To see the statue up close, go to the entrance on the left of the altar to access the sacristy. There is a small fee to pay to climb up to the image.

Outside, after passing the yellow bandstand, enter the **Ermida da Memória** (Memory Chapel). This little chapel, built by Dom Fuas Roupinho in gratitude to Our Lady of Nazaré for the miracle that saved his life, has the interior covered with tiles from the 17th and 18th centuries.

A visit to Sítio can take about 1½ hours, but don't leave without tasting some dried fruit sold in small stalls by Nazarenas wearing the traditional seven skirts (p244). Also, take a peek at **Bico da Memória**, next to the chapel. Look to the left-hand side of the wall and find what is said to be the hoof print of Dom Fuas' horse. Be careful when descending from this viewpoint since the ground is uneven and even slippery.

NOSSA SENHORA DA NAZARÉ

Nossa Senhora da Nazaré (Our Lady of Nazareth) is at the heart of Nazaré's history. Legend has it that a nobleman from Porto de Mós, Dom Fuas Roupinho, was hunting on a foggy morning in September 1182 when, while chasing a deer, he found himself on the edge of a cliff. Realising the danger he was in, the knight evoked the Virgin. She appeared to him, and the horse backed away as if by miracle, thus saving his life.

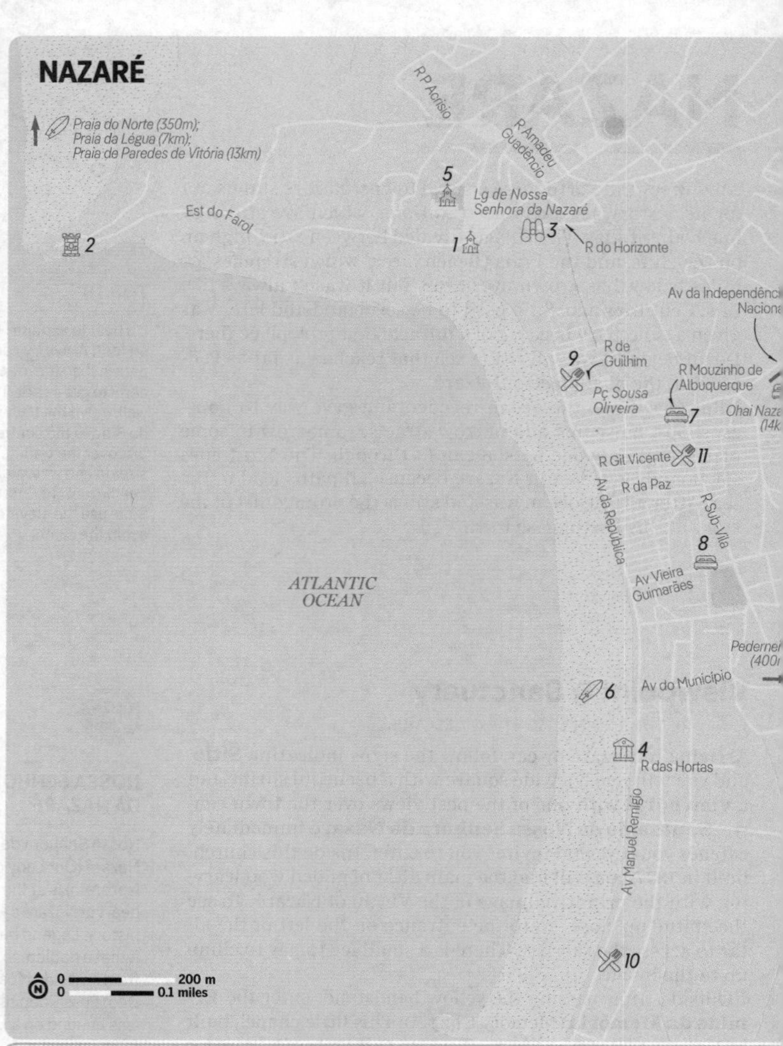

SIGHTS
1 Ermida da Memória
2 Forte de São Miguel Arcanjo
3 Miradouro do Sítio
4 Museu do Peixe Seco
5 Santuário da Nossa Senhora da Nazaré

ACTIVITIES
6 Praia da Vila da Nazaré

SLEEPING
7 Hotel Magic
8 Hotel Praia

EATING
9 Maria do Mar
10 Pangeia By the Sea
11 Rosa dos Ventos

Sun-Dried Fish & Fishing Boats

RELIVING THE VILLAGE'S PAST

Praia da Vila da Nazaré stretches for over 1km, and at its southernmost part, you can find the first (living) area of the **Museu do Peixe Seco**.

Right in front of Nazaré's cultural centre, set on the sand, are racks filled with fish drying in the sun. This secular technique has long been used around here to preserve excess fish and to be able to sell it to other markets. Today you can walk through these racks and see horse mackerel, sardines and even octopus drying in the sun for a few hours (locally called *peixe enjoado*) or two to three days before they end up in the fishmonger's stands along the boardwalk. Let your curiosity get the better of you and buy something. You can try it as it is, cured in the sun, but the taste may not be to everyone's liking. Next to the stalls, there's a set of traditional boats that once served the fishers of Nazaré.

The visit to the sun-dried fish racks and the fishing boats can be done in half an hour, but leave some more time for the remaining museum area, inside the cultural centre. In this old fish auction building, you can learn about the ancient process of sun-drying and its importance to Nazaré and see a series of old images that will make you travel back in time.

BEST SURF SPOTS IN NAZARÉ

Praia da Vila da Nazaré
The main beach of Nazaré is ideal for surfing in the mid-season, due to the size of the waves.

Praia da Légua
Surrounded by a green hillside, this beach offers an extensive stretch of sand often shared with local fishers. If you are a beginner, aim for the summer months.

Praia de Paredes de Vitória
An 18-minute drive from Nazaré and with multiple peaks, this beach offers conditions for all levels of surfers.

Giant Waves & Brave Surfers

TACKLING THE NAZARÉ CANYON

In 2011 Hawaiian surfer Garrett McNamara broke the world record for the largest wave ever surfed. He did it at **Praia do Norte** in Nazaré. From that year on, this small fishing village was on the world map as a big wave surfing destination.

In the **Forte de São Miguel Arcanjo**, you can learn about the oceanographic phenomenon responsible for the big waves in this place: the Nazaré Canyon. As the road here is closed to cars, the way to this lighthouse is done on foot from the Sítio, passing a gateway that welcomes you to 'the biggest waves in the world'. On the path, visitors are welcomed by the **Veado** (Deer), a statue of a half-surfer, half-deer, representing two essential elements for Nazaré: big wave surfing and the local legend.

As for the 1570 fort, it holds the **Centro Interpretativo do Canhão da Nazaré** and the **Surfer Wall**, an exhibition with the surfboards used to challenge the waves of Nazaré. Climb to the top for an incredible view over the village and Praia do Norte.

LORD OF THE CASTLE

Dom Fuas Roupinho was Lord Mayor of one of the most beautiful castles in the region, Castelo de Porto de Mós (p248), which stands out with its two towers covered in green ceramic tiles.

WHERE TO STAY IN NAZARÉ

Ohai Nazaré
In the largest pine forest reserve on the Iberian Peninsula, this eco-camping is perfect for families. €€€

Hotel Praia
The proximity to the beach and the rooftop pool set this four-star hotel apart. €€

Hotel Magic
A designer boutique hotel that offers thematic rooms combining art and regional culture. €€

THE SEVEN SKIRTS

Several stories surround the seven skirts worn by the women of Nazaré.
One revolves around the mythology of the number 7. As the local community say, there are 7 colours of the rainbow, 7 waves of the sea, 7 days of the week, 7 musical notes...and 7 skirts of the Nazarene women.
The other is about the connection of these women to the sea. They were fishermen's wives and, at night, on the beach, they waited for the boats to return to help their husbands. As the nights are very cold on the beach, they used half of the skirts for sitting and the rest for covering themselves and keep warm.

LIFECOLLECTIONPHOTOGRAPHY/SHUTTERSTOCK ©

Praia do Norte

If you want to witness the swells that make this place famous, go between October and February, when they are usually the biggest. Despite the allure of the waves here, don't venture out if you are not a big wave surfer or have in-water support. The town beach, Praia da Vila da Nazaré, further south, is a safer option.

Old Town Hall, Churches & a Viewpoint

THE ORIGINAL NAZARÉ NEIGHBOURHOOD

Located on a hilltop east of Nazaré's main beach, **Pederneira** was until the beginning of the 20th century the municipality's centre and where the Nazarenes lived. But well before that, life began to move downwards, following the retreat of the sea and leaving behind what is today a quiet neighbourhood and a viewpoint with the most spectacular views over Nazaré.

The 1855 Town Hall at **Largo Bastião Fernandes** is a testimony to what Pederneira represented. In front of it is the **Pillory**, a fossilised log almost 150 million years old that is also one of the oldest natural monuments in Portugal. About 20m to the right, you will find the **Igreja de Nossa Senhora**

WHERE TO EAT SEAFOOD IN NAZARÉ

A Tasquinha
A friendly family affair serving high-quality seafood in a pair of snug but prettily tiled dining rooms. €€

Casa Pires
Many locals think that this is the only place in Nazaré to eat grilled sardines. Enough said. €€

Conchinha da Nazaré
This simple place on a backstreet square serves good-value seafood, including wood-grilled fish and *açorda de marisco*. €

das Areias, built in the late 16th century, and, near the viewpoint, the **Igreja da Misericórdia**.

Paintings & Tiles

THE VILLAGE THROUGH ITS MURALS

Start by going down the **Ladeira do Sítio** to see the 300-sq-metre mural by the Brazilian surfer and artist Erick Wilson, reproducing the Nazaré Lighthouse with a giant wave. Once you reach the end of the Ladeira, you arrive at the **Meia Laranja** mural by Filipe Ferreira, inspired by old photographs of Nazaré. The next mural is in the **fishermen's quarter**, following the side street on the left of the Mercado Municipal. Authored by Topa Topera, this one approaches the woman in the Nazarene society. Finally, go back to Sítio, but this time using the **elevator**. In both stations, appreciate the ceramic and tile panels by artist Mário Reis, which portray various elements of the local culture.

Wild & Urban Beaches

TO RELAX IN THE SUN

There are two very different realities when we talk about beaches in Nazaré, and from the top of the Forte de São Miguel Arcanjo you will get a good notion of that.

Praia do Norte is the wildest, in and out of the water. Big wave surfers risk their lives challenging the larger swells on this beach. Therefore, even when there are no waves – and this rarely happens – it's not advisable to go swimming since there are currents and no lifeguards. On the other hand, the sand is wide, beautiful and incredible for spending moments away from everything. To get there, take the Pinhal Road from Sítio by car and, when you reach a roundabout, turn onto the Rua da Praia do Norte. Before you reach the beach, you will pass through a fence where you should be able to see some beautiful deers.

The complete opposite is **Praia da Vila da Nazaré**, near the town centre. With more than a kilometre of sand, this area comes alive in the summer months, with dozens of cloth huts that you can rent to protect yourself from the sun. In addition, the sea around here is quite different from Praia do Norte, with lifeguards between June and September, so you can go for a swim.

BEST PLACES TO EAT IN NAZARÉ

Rosa dos Ventos
This cosy restaurant, decorated with the owner's family photos, offers amazing fresh fish and seafood. €€

Pangeia By the Sea
Perfect for a meal by the beach. Octopus is Pangeia's star ingredient and a must-try. €€€

Maria do Mar
A friendly family restaurant known for its *caldeirada* (fish stew) and occasional fado sessions. €€

GETTING AROUND

The best way to get to Nazaré is by car. But, once there, it's not always easy to find parking, especially in the summer or when the big winter swells come to Praia do Norte. Go early in the morning. Walking is the magic formula for discovering this fishing village. It is the only way to appreciate all its details, get to the Forte de São Miguel Arcanjo or wander through the centre's narrow streets. Be prepared to do a good few kilometres, with comfortable shoes, water and a hat for the hottest days. The Sítio, higher up, and the town centre, below, are connected by a public elevator. Buy a round-trip ticket to save time at the ticket office.

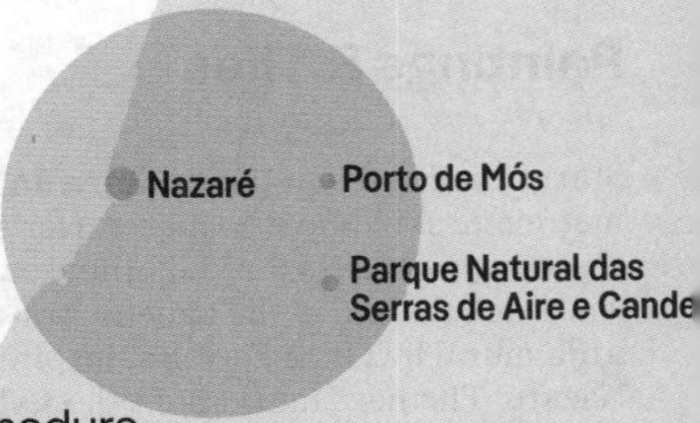

Nazaré
Porto de Mós
Parque Natural das Serras de Aire e Cande

Beyond Nazaré

The mountain calls. This is where Estremadura and Ribatejo come together in natural landscapes and ancient stories told in stone, caves and monuments.

From the tale that became a legend in Nazaré comes Fuas Roupinho, former mayor of Porto de Mós. The path traced between these two locations, once travelled by this Portuguese nobleman, is full of stories and places that appeal to the imagination. From the forbidden love that lasts for eternity to the giant dinosaurs that passed through here and left their marks.

The Serras de Aire and Candeeiros are one of the main natural attractions in the area and form a bridge between Estremadura and Ribatejo. In its interior are extended landscapes and paths that invite exploration, both on the surface and below the earth – through villages often asleep and people who welcome you with a smile, but also with the calmness of the mountains.

TOP TIP

A car is the best option to discover Nazaré's surroundings. Also, comfortable shoes are mandatory to tour the monuments and explore the mountain trails.

Mosteiro de Santa Maria de Alcobaça

SAIKO3P/SHUTTERSTOCK ©

A Stop for Lovers

FORBIDDEN LOVE IN ALCOBAÇA

Anyone who stops in front of the **Mosteiro de Santa Maria de Alcobaça** in Alcobaça may not know that it hides one of Portugal's greatest love stories. The tombs of Dom Pedro and Dona Inês de Castro, a symbol of forbidden love, occupy the church where many young couples marry today, hoping their romance will also last for eternity. But this is just one of the must-visit places inside this magnificent 12th-century monastery, a Unesco World Heritage Site.

Most visitors to Alcobaça see this unique building and leave soon after. However, the town has other attractions, such as the **Museu do Vinho de Alcobaça** and the award-winning convent sweets sold in the Alcoa pastry shop right in front of the monastery.

Going Over & Under

TRAILS, DINOSAURS AND CAVES

Of the various natural parks that make up Portugal, **Parque Natural das Serras de Aire e Candeeiros** may well be one that goes a bit under the radar. But, 40km from Nazaré, it counts on millennia of Earth's transformations, starting with the **Grutas de Mira de Aire**. Located in Mira de Aire, this vast network of underground caves, discovered in 1947, stretches for more than 11km. Of these, only 600m are visitable, and you will go down 683 steps to see them. The majesty of the galleries of this natural monument will make you feel small. After all, it is considered one of the most significant finds of Portuguese speleology.

Just 15km away, in Bairro, on the edge of the natural park, history is made differently, with engravings on stone left thousands of years ago. The **Monumento Natural das Pegadas dos Dinossáurios** lets the imagination run wild and takes you on a journey back to the time of the sauropods and their passage through this territory. There are about 20 trails, some of the longest in the world, where you can observe the marks left on the limestone surface by those herbivorous giants.

The Parque Natural das Serras de Aire e Candeeiros should be visited in at least two days, making the most of the trails, caves and viewpoints. Make sure to stop at the **Praia Fluvial dos Olhos de Água** (river beach) to take a break from the heat or go along the **Ecovia de Porto de Mós**, a trail that starts in a town called Bezerra, near its soccer field, and follows the old train track used for mining.

BEST RESTAURANTS IN THE NATURAL PARK

Cantinho da Serra
Close to Rio Maior, this rustic restaurant welcomes you with some of the best dishes from Ribatejo. Multiple starters arrive at the table but leave room for the *galo avinhado* (rooster stew). In summer, check if it's open before you go. €€

Dom Lambuças
Homemade food full of flavour is what you can expect from this *petiscaria* in the village of Alcaria. The dishes change daily, but you can count on some regional delicacies on the menu. The place is small, so get there early. €

WHERE TO STAY IN AIRE & CANDEEIROS

The Nest by Cooking and Nature
Nature is always present in this Alvados hotel that wants to be a true nest for those who visit. €€

5.ª Vigia
This boutique hotel in Porto de Mós was built next to the city park, occupying an old watermill. €€

Noz Por Cá
For a village experience, this rural accommodation in Alcaria combines tradition and comfort in spaces full of details. €€

MIRADOURO DE CHÃO DAS PIAS

Inaugurated at the end of 2021, the Miradouro de Chão de Pias is the new balcony over the city of Porto de Mós and the Lena valley. This viewpoint, at 425m high, can be found on the road that connects Serro Ventoso to São Bento and invites you to stop for long minutes and contemplate one of the most beautiful landscapes of the Parque Natural das Serras de Aire e Candeeiros. Nearby is a dry stone wall with an urban artwork by the artist Rui Basílico, a tribute to the stone walls that can be seen scattered throughout these mountains.

Castelo de Porto de Mós

The Green Tower Castle

MILITARY ARCHITECTURE FROM THE 15TH CENTURY

Dated from the 13th century, the **Castelo de Porto de Mós**, a 30-minute drive from Nazaré, could have been taken from a fairy tale, with its two towers covered in green tiles standing out in the landscape. The original military fortress gave way, in the 15th century, to a palatial building with Gothic and Renaissance influences. It was the residence of Dom Fuas Roupinho, which reconquered the fortress from the Moors and became the first Lord Mayor of Porto de Mós, but with the passage of time and several earthquakes, it was abandoned to the point that only parts of the structure remained.

The castle reconstruction took place between the 1930s and 1960s, and it was only in the 1990s that visitors began to go inside and discover its story. So, take your time in this castle, go into its various rooms, notice the details and climb the stone walls to see the valley and mountains surrounding it.

GETTING AROUND

The car is the only transportation that gives you the freedom to get to know the Parque Natural das Serras de Aire e Candeeiros. But you can use the bus if you want to go from Nazaré to Alcobaça or Porto de Mós. One leaves every day of the week from Rede de Expressos and Rodoviária do Tejo to these destinations.

TOMAR

Tomar is a vibrant city. Yet, you might presume it would be different considering all the historical weight it carries. This town, north of Ribatejo, was one of the most important in the history of the Order of the Temple in Portugal. It was also here that Prince Henry the Navigator, governor of the Order of Christ, began planning the Portuguese Discoveries.

The stories that took place in Tomar are told today in various parts of town, in monuments that have become Unesco World Heritage Sites, in old structures that have been transformed into museums, and on the face of many buildings that make up the historic centre. The city embraces this past and, at the same time, begins to open its doors to modernism and new cultural activities. Here the journey is made by the interconnected streets, the bridges crossing Rio Nabão and the desire to know more with every step you take.

TOP TIP

Getting to know Tomar's historic centre is all about walking. Take comfortable shoes and remember that temperatures can get really high in the summertime, so be prepared with a hat, sunblock and plenty of water.

Castle & Convent

DISCOVERING THE TEMPLAR ORIGINS

In the town's upper part, the **Castelo de Tomar** and the **Convento de Cristo** constitute an impressive architectural complex dating back to the 12th century. It was the headquarters of the Knights Templar in Portugal and is today a Unesco World Heritage Site. This makes it one of the most visited landmarks in the region, so try to go right at opening hours to avoid crowds.

Arriving at the Convento de Cristo, start by seeing the cloisters and stop by the **New Sacristy** to contemplate the ceiling, with iconography from the Philippine era, the cross of the Order of Christ, the armillary sphere and the royal coat of arms. Then take some time to appreciate all the details of the **Charola**, the Templars' primitive Romanesque temple. In the **Great Dormitory**, find the cell whose window overlooks the famous **Janela Manuelina** (Chapterhouse Window), an icon of Portuguese heritage.

After discovering all the convent areas, make your way to the Templar castle. Take the detour on the right to climb the **castle walls** and walk around the old medieval structure while appreciating the 40 hectares of vegetation belonging to the old convent. Unfortunately, the ground is uneven and unsuitable for visitors with reduced mobility or inappropriate footwear. Be careful.

BEST CAFES IN TOMAR

Café Paraíso
Over 100 years old, this cafe preserves the old decoration and has been used by illustrious figures, such as Umberto Eco, and as the backdrop for movies.

Estrelas de Tomar
Welcome to the birthplace of famous local sweets, such as *beija-me depressa* (kiss me quickly) or *fatias de Tomar* (Tomar slices).

Insensato
Carefully decorated Insensato combines light meals and books in a cafe full of soul.

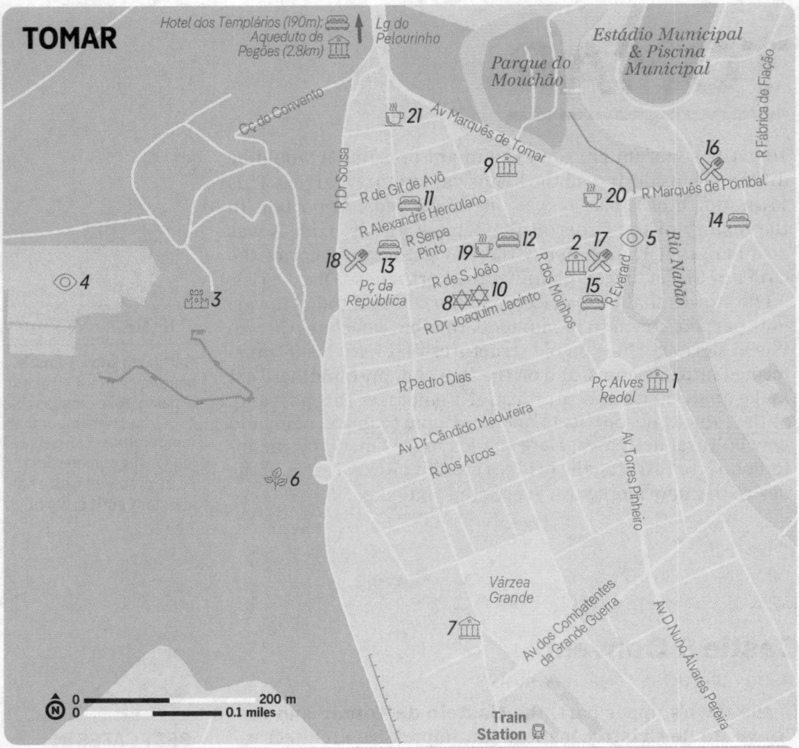

TOMAR

SIGHTS
1 Casa dos Cubos
2 Casa Memória Lopes-Graça
3 Castelo de Tomar
4 Convento de Cristo
5 Levada de Tomar
6 Mata Nacional dos Sete Montes
7 Museu dos Fósforos
8 Museu Luso-Hebraico Abraham Zacuto
9 Núcleo de Arte Contemporânea
10 Sinagoga de Tomar

SLEEPING
11 Casa dos Ofícios
12 Hostel 2300 Thomar
13 Hotel República
14 Thomar Boutique Hotel
15 Thomar Story

EATING
16 A Bela Vista
17 Casa das Ratas
18 Taverna Antiqua

DRINKING & NIGHTLIFE
19 Café Paraíso
20 Estrelas de Tomar
21 Insensato

WHERE TO STAY IN TOMAR

Thomar Boutique Hotel
These hotel rooms invite you on a journey through various city eras, including the Roman or Templar. **€€**

Hotel República
In Praça da República, the heart of the city, this five-star offers comfortable rooms and exquisite common areas. **€€€**

Casa dos Ofícios
Some of the original architectural elements of this historic 18th-century building are proudly preserved here. **€€**

RNDMS/SHUTTERSTOCK ©

Sinagoga de Tomar

The Ancient Synagogue

LEARNING ABOUT THE JEWISH PAST

In the centre of the old Jewish quarter, at Rua Dr Joaquim Jacinto, you will find the **Sinagoga de Tomar**. This is the only Gothic-style Jewish temple in the country and visiting it helps you understand the Jewish community's role in Portugal and its passage through this city. Start by visiting the **interpretive centre** (next door) to learn more about the history of Judaism in Tomar, the foundation of the synagogue in the 15th century, and life in town. You can watch a short video and scroll through an interactive screen. The Jewish community emerged in Tomar in the early 14th century. Merchants and artisans for the most part, they were in the service of the Order of the Templar and, later on, of the Order of Christ. For their contribution to the Portuguese maritime expansion, they enjoyed the protection of Infante Dom Henrique, who ordered the construction of the synagogue.

Silence takes over when you enter the temple. The small square room with a vaulted ceiling supported by columns serves today only as the **Museu Luso-Hebraico Abraham Zacuto**, with no religious service. The reason is that currently in Tomar there are only two Jewish families with six men,

THE KNIGHTS TEMPLAR

Portugal was the first kingdom of the Iberian Peninsula to establish the Order of the Temple, with King Afonso Henriques becoming a member in 1128. Thirty years later, the monarch donated Tomar to the Templars, and Master Dom Gualdim Pais ordered the construction of the castle and the Charola. Tomar was the headquarters of the Knights Templar until they were extinguished by Pope Clement V in 1314. At that time, the assets and some men passed to the recently formed Order of Christ. Today the Order of Christ maintains an honorific role and the title of Grand Master is given to the President of the Portuguese Republic.

Hotel dos Templários
Next to Rio Nabão and surrounded by greenery, this four-star hotel offers spacious rooms and pools. **€€€**

Hostel 2300 Thomar
Just minutes from the main town square, everything at this hostel is inspired by popular Portuguese culture. **€**

Thomar Story
This guesthouse, located in a 19th-century building, brings together pieces of the city's history in its decoration. **€**

LIANEM/SHUTTERSTOCK ©

Aqueduto dos Pegões Altos

THE FEAST OF THE TRAYS

It happens every four years and attracts visitors from all over the country to Tomar. Being a celebration of the Holy Spirit, the Festa dos Tabuleiros (Feast of the Trays) starts on Easter Sunday, with the Exit of the Crowns and Pendants from all the county parishes. But the most awaited moment is the procession that takes place in early July. Dozens of women dressed in white carry on their heads the 'trays', multistorey structures decorated with loaves of bread, colourful flowers and ears of wheat. At the top is a crown with the Cross of Christ or the dove of the Holy Spirit. Closing the procession are carts of bread, meat and wine that will be distributed to the community.

preventing ceremonies from taking place.

The visit to the interpretive centre and the synagogue will take less than an hour, but while you're in the old Jewish quarter, take a few more minutes to appreciate the beauty of this street, with its well-arranged houses and the flowers flanking the doors. Always with the castle peeking at the top.

From Electricity to the Foundry

WATER-POWERED INDUSTRY

In a land crossed by the Rio Nabão, it's not surprising that local industry has developed with this river's water. Buildings and hydraulic infrastructures were created early on and took on different productive and industrial activities over time.

At **Levada de Tomar**, the name this cultural complex takes on today, you can visit, in about an hour, two of the last facilities that were active here.

First stop: the **Power Station**, from 1901, with the old machines that made Tomar one of the first cities in Portugal to have public lighting. Take the opportunity to read the large panels that tell the story of this place and let yourself be involved with the sound of electricity that invades the museum as if the machines were still in operation.

Next, a few metres away, is the **Fundição Tomarense**. The history of this old foundry, also created in 1901, is told (in Portuguese) on video by former workers or their children.

Their voices accompany the tour through old workshops, passing by the furnaces, tables and instruments used until it closed, in 2005.

The Perfect Match

A TRIP AROUND THE WORLD IN MATCHBOXES

The **Convento de São Francisco** houses a unique museum: the **Museu dos Fósforos** (Matchbox Museum). This place shows a collection of 80,000 boxes and matchbooks donated by Aquiles da Mota Lima to the city in 1980. The collection started with a simple exchange of matchboxes between Mota Lima and another passenger when they crossed to London by boat to attend the coronation of Queen Elisabeth II. Today the various displays show matches from 127 countries, with the oldest dating back to 1827. Such a quantity of matchboxes can be overwhelming but go in search of those from your own country for a real journey back in time.

It's just a quick visit to this free museum, but while you're in the convent, cross the courtyard to enter the **pottery and tile workshop** and see local artisans at work.

From the Springs to the Convent

KNOWING THE AQUEDUCT

Leave Tomar's city centre via Avenida Marquês de Tomar, passing Largo do Pelourinho. At the end of Rua de Leiria, turn left and follow the arrows indicating the **Aqueduto dos Pegões Altos** to reach one of the most imposing aqueducts in the country. Built similarly to the aqueducts of Elvas and Évora, its construction began in 1597 to bring the water from four springs near the city to the Convento de Cristo (p249). Climb one of the towers to get a glimpse of the size and grandeur of the aqueduct, which extends for 6km, and the Pegões valley that stretches around it.

Ancestral Trees & Historic Wheel

STROLLING THROUGH THE GREEN

Some call it the 'lung' of the city. The **Mata Nacional dos Sete Montes**, dating from the 16th century, occupies 39 hectares of gardens and forest between the Convento de Cristo and the city centre. It was formerly known as Lugar dos Sete Montes (Place of the Seven Hills), precisely because it is part of a group of seven hills, on one of which the Templar castle stands out.

Enter in front of the statue of Infante Dom Henrique, near the tourist office, into the **Formal Garden**, an area of geometric flowerbeds that's almost 100 years old. From here, you can follow two trails: the **Charolinha** and the **Cadeira D'El Rei**. The first goes along Alameda dos Freixos and its ancient ash trees, leading to the Charolinha, a small imitation of the Charola inside the convent. The second passes by a viewpoint with a swing, the old mill and the Countess' Tower. On the way you come across many different species of trees, including cypress, pine, oak and olive, among others.

BEST PLACES TO SEE ART

Núcleo de Arte Contemporânea
This museum holds a collection of paintings, sculptures, drawings and photography, from 1932 until now.

Casa Memória Lopes-Graça
Fernando Lopes-Graça was born in Tomar and distinguished himself as a musician and composer in the 20th century. The house where he was born has information about his life and work.

Casa dos Cubos
Once used as a warehouse, this building takes on a contemporary role in the city and has earned architecture awards.

BEST RESTAURANTS IN TOMAR

A Bela Vista
Have your meal on the terrace facing the river and ask for one of the regional dishes. €€

Casa das Ratas
A Tomar classic. Try the starters or pick one of the daily specials. Vegetarian options are available. €€

Taverna Antiqua
Travel back in time, with imaginative dishes, mead and staff dressed in medieval clothing. €€

TAKASHI IMAGES/SHUTTERSTOCK ©

Mata Nacional dos Sete Montes (p253)

Get ready to spend a good few hours if you want to see the entire park. Hiking boots are preferable and take lots of water and head protection if you go during the summer months.

But this is not the only green place in town. With its entrance on Avenida Marquês de Tomar, the **Parque do Mouchão** presents itself as an island in the middle of Rio Nabão. Here you can find the Mouchão Wheel, a reconstitution of the old hydraulic wheels that occupied this riverside area. Rest on a park bench or cross the bridge for ice cream at the cafe overlooking the historic centre.

GETTING AROUND

Buses from Rede Expressos and CP trains connect Tomar to the country's main cities, but a car will be the best option if you want to travel faster and further. But when you arrive, park the car and don't touch it again – Tomar is meant to be visited on foot. There are several parking areas, but the most useful is at the Mercado Municipal or the one next to the Convento de São Francisco, where you can even charge electric vehicles.

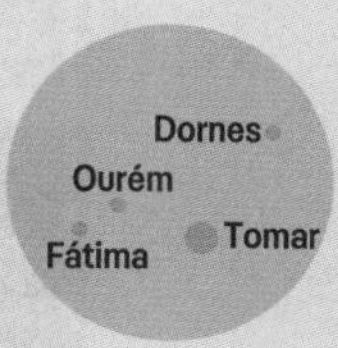

Dornes
Ourém
Fátima
Tomar

Beyond Tomar

Within a 30-minute drive from Tomar, medieval meets religion in small towns full of history.

Tomar is considered the cradle of the Knights Templar in Portugal, but the presence of the members of this religious military order was not confined to this town in Ribatejo. Just draw a radius of about 50km to keep finding traces of these knights.

From Dornes to Almourol, the Templars didn't let distance hinder their work and the battles they had to fight, so they fortified the whole Rio Tejo line.

Christian religion played an important role in Portugal in the 12th century and it is still extremely relevant in this region today. Churches and chapels are spread everywhere, as in the case of the historic medieval village of Ourém. But, above all, it is in Fátima that travellers and pilgrims can find one of the main centres of Christian spirituality in the world.

TOP TIP

Ourém and Fátima fill up during major religious celebrations – expect fewer accommodation optionss available and prices to rise at such times.

Castelo de Almourol (p257)

STOCKPHOTOSART/SHUTTERSTOCK ©

Dornes

APPARITIONS AT FÁTIMA

On 13 May 1917, three children – Lucia dos Santos, aged 10, Francisco Marto, aged 9, and Jacinta Marto, aged 7 – were tending to their family's flock when a woman 'brighter than the sun' appeared before them. She asked the three little shepherds to pray every day as a way to save sinners and to return to that exact spot in the upcoming months, always on the 13th at that same hour. The children did so in the following months, and on 13 October, about 70,000 people accompanied them at the last apparition. Identifying herself as the Lady of the Rosary, she asked that a chapel be built in her honour in that very place.

Wander Around a Medieval Village

A CASTLE, COBBLED STREETS AND SOUR CHERRY LIQUEUR

The medieval elements found throughout Tomar quickly gain even more meaning in **Ourém**. This medieval village, with a 12th-century castle at its centre, calls for walks through narrow cobbled streets, with white houses and coats of arms carved into their walls. Visit **Largo do Pelourinho**, the beautiful **Escadinhas da Sociedade Filarmónica** and enjoy the views from **Jardim de Santa Teresa**.

With some similarities to Óbidos (p232), *ginjinha* is also here to stay and invites you to a long chat at an outdoor cafe while appreciating the architecture of the **Igreja Matriz**, which houses the tomb of Dom Afonso, the fourth Count of Ourém.

The Enchanted Peninsula

EXPLORING THE VILLAGE IN THE ZÊZERE

Located about 30km from Tomar, **Dornes** appears on a strip of land that juts out into the Rio Zêzere. It's considered one of the most beautiful villages in Portugal, and its privileged position led the Knights Templar to build a tower as part of their

WHERE TO EAT IN OURÉM & FÁTIMA

Taverna da Matilde
Go for some *petiscos* in this friendly restaurant in the heart of the medieval village of Ourém. €

O Curral
The warm service and the fish of the day are more than enough reasons to visit. €€

Casa Plátano
Try the house codfish in this contemporary restaurant, a short distance from the Santuário de Fátima. €€

defensive system against the Moors. The pentagonal shape makes it unique and the most prominent symbol of this town.

Between the **Templar tower** and the **Igreja de Nossa Senhora do Pranto**, a visit to Dornes will not take much time since it's relatively small. But let yourself stay a little longer to enjoy the calmness around here, go down to the boat dock or into the local restaurant to taste the fish caught in the river.

Sanctuary & the Little Shepherds

FOLLOWING IN THE FOOTSTEPS OF FAITH

No matter what your beliefs are, **Fátima** continues to impress those who visit. Located 36km from Tomar, the **Santuário de Fátima** is one of the largest Christian shrines in the world and welcomes millions of people each year. Many Christians seek out this place to find peace of mind and renew their faith. Apart from the celebrations on 13 May and 13 October, you can visit this complex in relative tranquility, especially during the winter.

The **Capela das Aparições** (Chapel of the Apparitions) is one of the most important sites since it was built where the Virgin appeared in 1917. Other important buildings are the **Basílica de Nossa Senhora do Rosário de Fátima**, with the tombs of the three little shepherds, and, at the other end of the sanctuary, the **Basílica da Santíssima Trindade**.

The Castle on the River

FOLLOWING THE KNIGHTS TEMPLAR

Go to **Vila Nova da Barquinha**, located 23km south of Tomar, to learn about the history of the Knights Templar of Almourol. This interpretation centre, inside Centro Cultural de Vila Nova da Barquinha, introduces the knights and their representation in Portugal, highlighting details ranging from their robes to their insignias and weapons.

After learning more about the Knights Templar, head towards the **Castelo de Almourol**, a 10-minute drive east along the river. The entrance ticket to the interpretation centre gives you access to the castle and the boat that takes you there. This castle is in the middle of the Rio Tejo, and although it almost seems you could make the crossing on foot at low tide, you always have to take the boat to access it.

BEST RIVER BEACHES NEAR TOMAR

Praia Fluvial do Agroal
Relax on this beach that lies next to the largest spring of Rio Nabão. The water is usually quite cold, but it is said to have therapeutic properties.

Lago Azul
In Castanheira, this beach makes the best use of the Rio Zêzere. In summer, you can count on the floating pool to go bathing safely.

Praia Fluvial Aldeia do Mato
This beach, near the Castelo de Bode dam, has a floating pool and is perfect for water sports.

GETTING AROUND

To better explore the surroundings of Tomar, you need a car, but be prepared because parking can be a challenge when visiting historic or religious areas. Leave the car outside the medieval village of Ourém, as it is easy to scratch it on the town's narrow streets. Also, go early to Fátima to get parking, especially on days of celebration. And stop at the gates of Dornes, as the walk is not long and is worth doing on foot.

ALBERTO LOYO/SHUTTERSTOCK ©

Moliceiros in Aveiro (p275)

THE BEIRAS

COAST, COUNTRYSIDE, CITIES AND SUMMITS

From the sprawling shores of the Silver Coast to mainland Portugal's highest peak, with cultured cities and hidden villages etched with traditions.

The Beiras, stretching from the Atlantic Ocean to the Spanish border, are defined by three historic provinces and the four elements.

Characterised by water, Beira Litoral clutches the coast. Crashing waves and swathes of golden sand entice surfers and beachgoers, while the springs of Alcabideque lured the Romans to construct Conímbriga, a vast, ruined settlement that can still be visited. Nearby, the Rio Mondego, the longest river entirely within Portugal, flows through the provincial capital of Coimbra, home to the country's oldest university.

Moving to the upper peaks, Beira Alta is shaped by the mountain air – scorching in summer and bringing snow by winter. Long-lost glaciers have crafted magnificent, hike-friendly valleys in the Serra da Estrela, while stone villages cling to hilltops, embracing the winds. Around Viseu, Dão's wine country is shielded from the Atlantic draft, protecting some of the country's oldest vines.

Continuing southeast, Beira Baixa is defined by arid hinterlands and hills dotted with cork and olive trees. Near-abandoned settlements still keep their eye on borderlands, or lay low deep in the forest, finally accessible by road and still linked by rambling trails.

While these three provinces were lost from maps following the 1976 constitution, their stories live on, allowing travellers glimpses of traditions among the spellbinding landscapes.

THE MAIN AREAS

Aveiro, p275

Art Nouveau architecture and a sprinkling of canals are bundled together in the compact centre, a short hop from a colourful, dune-backed coastline.

Viseu, p283

Legends, leafy gardens, elegant architecture and a vast collection of Vasco Fernandes' artwork make Viseu a cultured city, with vineyards on its peripherals.

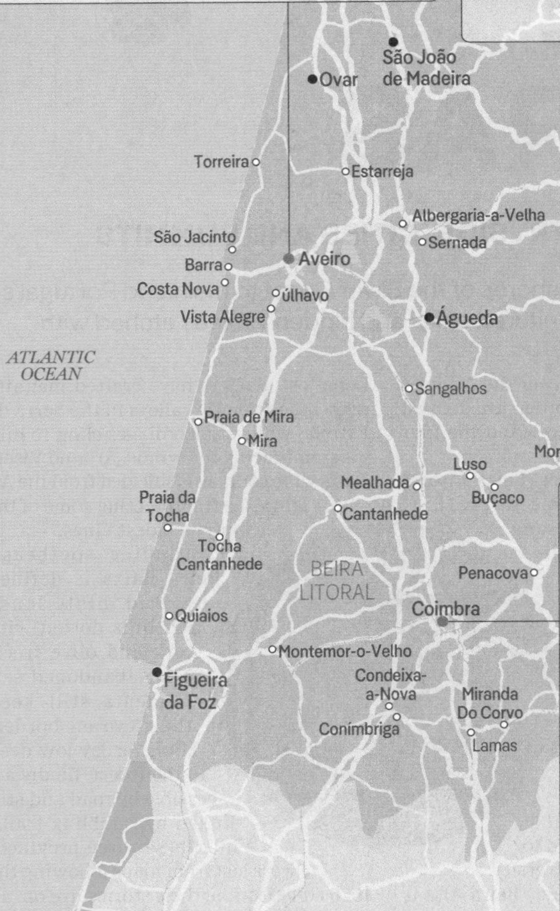

São João de Madeira
Ovar
Torreira
Estarreja
São Pedro do Sul
Albergaria-a-Velha
São Jacinto
Sernada
Barra
Aveiro
Viseu
Costa Nova
Ílhavo
Vista Alegre
Águeda
Caramulo
Santar
Nelas
ATLANTIC OCEAN
Tondela
Tonda
Sangalhos
Carregal do Sal
Praia de Mira
Mira
Mortágua
Santa Comba Dão
Luso
Mealhada
Buçaco
Praia da Tocha
Cantanhede
Tocha Cantanhede
BEIRA LITORAL
Penacova
Quiaios
Coimbra
Montemor-o-Velho
Figueira da Foz
Condeixa-a-Nova
Miranda Do Corvo
Conímbriga
Lamas
Proença-a-Nova

Coimbra, p264

Students (serenading and celebrating) still shape the atmosphere of Portugal's oldest university city, with Roman ruins and riverside adventures nearby.

Find Your Way

Covering nearly a third of the country, the Beiras can be challenging to traverse. Major cities have regular fast trains, while forgotten villages may see one bus weekly – studying timetables is a pre-trip planning essential.

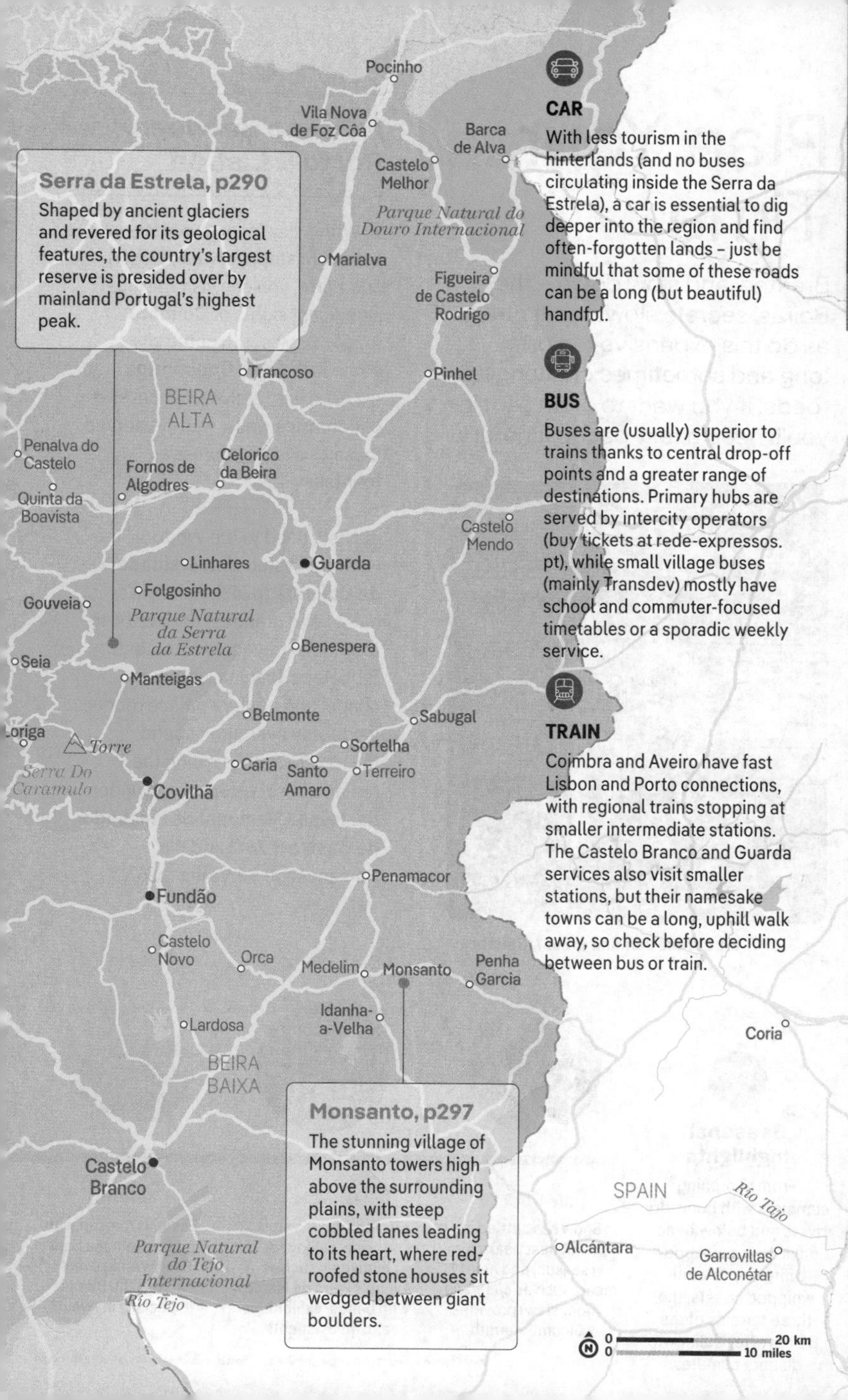

Serra da Estrela, p290

Shaped by ancient glaciers and revered for its geological features, the country's largest reserve is presided over by mainland Portugal's highest peak.

Monsanto, p297

The stunning village of Monsanto towers high above the surrounding plains, with steep cobbled lanes leading to its heart, where red-roofed stone houses sit wedged between giant boulders.

CAR

With less tourism in the hinterlands (and no buses circulating inside the Serra da Estrela), a car is essential to dig deeper into the region and find often-forgotten lands – just be mindful that some of these roads can be a long (but beautiful) handful.

BUS

Buses are (usually) superior to trains thanks to central drop-off points and a greater range of destinations. Primary hubs are served by intercity operators (buy tickets at rede-expressos.pt), while small village buses (mainly Transdev) mostly have school and commuter-focused timetables or a sporadic weekly service.

TRAIN

Coimbra and Aveiro have fast Lisbon and Porto connections, with regional trains stopping at smaller intermediate stations. The Castelo Branco and Guarda services also visit smaller stations, but their namesake towns can be a long, uphill walk away, so check before deciding between bus or train.

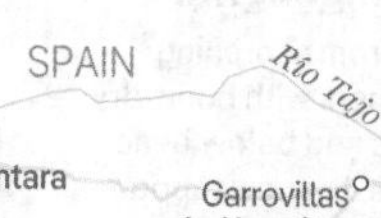

Plan Your Time

Breathe, and slow down – the Beiras' secrets slowly spill out, as do this expansive region's long and sometimes challenging roads. If you want to cram a lot in, you'll need a fast-paced itinerary.

SOPOTNICKI/SHUTTERSTOCK ©

Biblioteca Joanina (p267), Coimbra

A Pause Between Porto & Lisbon

- With a day (or even better, an overnight stop) between Lisbon and Porto, you can visit the most significant sights of **Coimbra** (p264). Start south of the city at the **Ruínas de Conímbriga** (p270), a vast archaeological site of defensive walls, well-preserved mosaics and an impressive fountain villa.

- Next, head to the World Heritage-listed **Universidade de Coimbra** (p267), Portugal's oldest and grandest university, to tour the extravagant 18th-century Biblioteca Joanina, baroque chapel and opulent palace rooms. If you stay overnight, spend the next morning visiting the remarkable cryptoporticus under the **Museu Nacional de Machado de Castro** (p264) and the Romanesque **Sé Velha** (p267).

Seasonal highlights

From scorching summers with bone-dry rivers and balmy beach days, to snowcapped winters with wind-whipped coasts, the three terrains of the Beiras offer their own distinct climates.

JANUARY

Snow has settled in the highest peaks for ski season, and hearty meals such as *chanfana* (goat stew) provide welcome warmth.

MARCH

Temperatures start to rise, calling for festivities such as Aveiro's Feira de Marco, with bands, exhibitions and amusements.

APRIL

Easter is marked with sombre Semana Santa (Holy Week) events across the Beiras, especially in Aveiro.

NATALIA MYLOVA/SHUTTERSTOCK ©, ZNM/GETTY IMAGES ©, ANAMARQUES/SHUTTERSTOCK ©

Seven Days from Coast to Peaks

- Following two days in Coimbra (see left, but slower paced), track the shore north, visiting **Praia de Mira** (p280) and the colourful houses of **Costa Nova** (p280). Overnight on the coast or in **Aveiro** (p275), where you can wander the compact canal-lined centre spotting Art Nouveau architecture.

- Heading inland to **Viseu** (p283), stay for a couple of nights to visit the city's museums and enjoy side trips to the vineyards of the **Dão wine region** (p287) and medieval **Trancoso** (p288). End your whirlwind tour in the mountainous **Serra da Estrela** (p290), visiting mainland Portugal's highest peak, **Torre** (p290).

Two Weeks Traversing the Beiras

- Spend your second week traversing forests and near-forgotten villages. Continuing from Torre (see left), hike through the glacial valley of **Zêzere** (p290) to overnight in the verdant village of **Manteigas** (p293. From here, drive southeast, pausing en route at historical villages such as **Belmonte** (p295) before spending a night or two in hilltop **Monsanto** (p297), where boulder-wedged homes rule supreme.

- Next, visit the museum-rich city of **Castelo Branco** (p301) before finishing in the schist villages of the **Serra da Lousã** (p271) or extremely remote **Piódão** (p296) for some final days on slow-paced trails.

MAY
Join Coimbra's students to celebrate Queima das Fitas, or enjoy hikes in the Serra da Estrela before temperatures soar.

JUNE
Official beach season arrives (with lifeguards), alongside Coimbra's Medieval Fair and Trancoso's Festa da História.

AUGUST
Beach days are followed by festival nights, such as Viseu's Feira de São Mateus and Aveiro's Festa da Ria.

SEPTEMBER
The Dão Harvest Festival is one of the most exciting and interactive times to tour the vines around Viseu.

PAULO M. F. PIRES/SHUTTERSTOCK ©, SERGIO AZENHA/ALAMY STOCK PHOTO ©, RUBENREBELOPHOTO/SHUTTERSTOCK ©, BARMALINI/SHUTTERSTOCK ©

COIMBRA

Coimbra is a city shaped by students, both historically and in the present day. The World Heritage–listed university, the oldest in the country, astonishes travellers with its elegant palace rooms and baroque library, where some of the nation's most renowned poets, politicians and artists – and the dictator Salazar – studied. Today's scholars contribute equally to the city's atmosphere and culture, from the traditional black-cloaked and caped *tunas* (musical groups) that serenade on the streets, to the crowded *repúblicas* (student housing) garnished with political statements. Visit outside of term time and you'll experience an almost different city.

Long before it was an esteemed education centre, the Romans founded Aeminium, as it was known then, which grew and prospered under a century of Muslim rule. Following the Christian conquest, Coimbra became Portugal's medieval capital until 1255. With a history as steeped as its hills, the city's traditions are as entrenched as they are enchanting.

TOP TIP

Visits to the university's Biblioteca Joanina are time-scheduled, so book tickets online in advance to plan your day around the allocated slot. You can take self-guided tours of the rest of the accessible areas of the university, with tiered pricing depending on which areas you wish to see – allow at least half a day.

BEST PLACES TO DRINK IN COIMBRA

Praça da República
Head to this party-heavy, student-laden square and follow your ear.

Praxis
Coimbra's spacious main brewery offers beer-flight tastings with a decent menu.

Passaporte
Premium cocktails in a renovated heritage building, best enjoyed at sunset on the terrace.

Café Santa Cruz
Come for a coffee and *crúzios*, the cafe's renowned almond-egg cake, in a retired chapel.

A Timeless Museum

ARCHAEOLOGY, ART AND CRYPTOPORTICUS

Coimbra's **Museu Nacional de Machado de Castro** (closed Monday) can sometimes be overlooked in the rush to tour the university. However, it's worth spending at least a couple of hours exploring the myriad treasures here. Entering through the 16th-century loggia, you'll step further back in time as you explore the fascinating cryptoporticus (underground covered passageways) underneath, which supported the city's old Roman Forum. The rest of the museum houses numerous collections, including sculptures spanning centuries, prized Renaissance art, Muslim and Christian ceramics and a reconstructed chapel.

Celebrate Alongside Students

QUEIMA DAS FITAS

Just after the clock chimes midnight on a May night, the sound of a guitar, followed by soulful singing, takes over the stairs and square in front of Sé Velha. A crowd of black-cloaked students stare in silence, listening to the 'Serenata Monumental'. This marks the start of **Queima das Fitas**, translated as Burning of the Ribbons, as that is precisely what students do (in a cauldron, no less) to mark the end of the academic year. Over the next eight days, celebrations take over the city, from cultural concerts and upscale balls to sports events and some seriously hardcore, beer-indulging partying. There's also a grand procession *(cortejo)*, with floats decorated to represent their faculty colours, accompanied by a slice of satire.

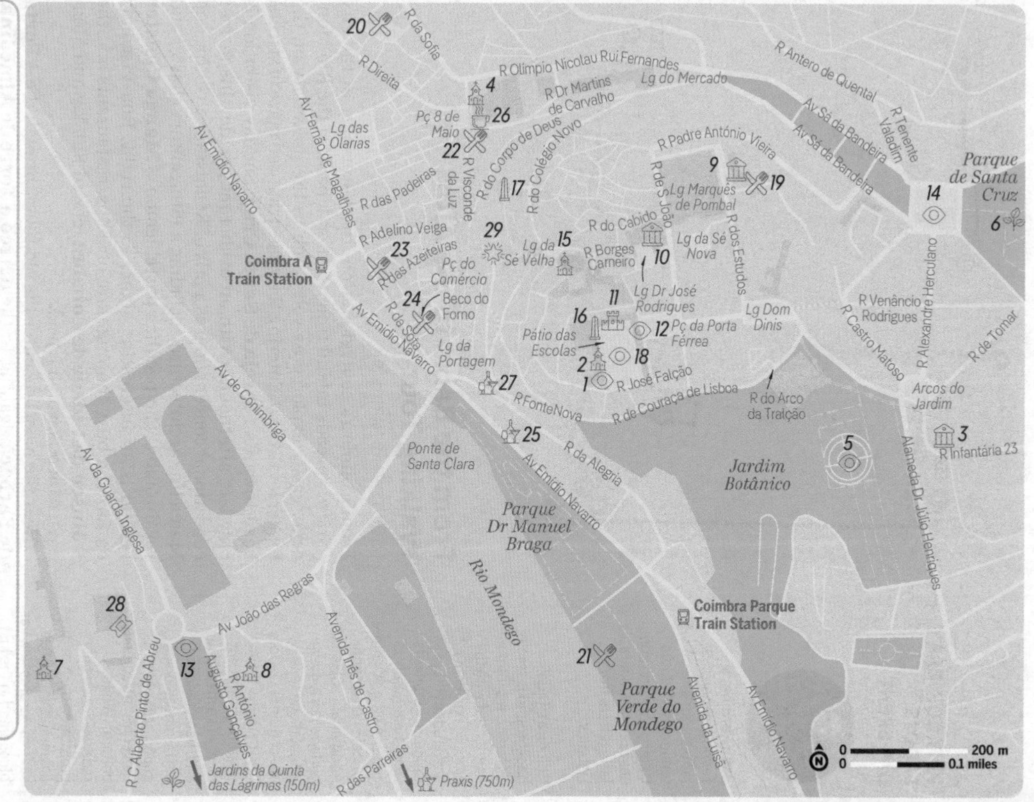

SIGHTS
1 Biblioteca Joanina
2 Capela de São Miguel
3 Casa Museu Bissaya Barreto
4 Igreja de Santa Cruz
5 Jardim Botânico
6 Jardim da Sereia
7 Mosteiro de Santa Clara-a-Nova
8 Mosteiro de Santa Clara-a-Velha
9 Museu da Ciência
10 Museu Nacional de Machado de Castro
11 Paço das Escolas
12 Porta Férrea
13 Portugal dos Pequenitos
14 Praça da República
15 Sé Velha
16 Torre da Universidade
17 Torre de Anto
18 Universidade de Coimbra

EATING
19 Cafetaria do Museu da Ciência
20 Cantinho do Reis
21 Itália
22 Sete Restaurante
23 Solar do Bacalhau
24 Zé Manel dos Ossos

DRINKING & NIGHTLIFE
25 Bixos
26 Café Santa Cruz
27 Passaporte

ENTERTAINMENT
28 Convento São Francisco
29 Fado ao Centro

WHY COIMBRA'S FADO IS DIFFERENT

João Farinha, a second-generation fado singer and co-founder of Fado Ao Centro concert room, shares why Coimbra's fado differs from Lisbon's.

Coimbra's fado background is totally different; it's intimately connected with the city, the university and student life. As Coimbra's students were, historically, a cultural elite, it's more lyrical and romantic. Additionally, Coimbra's *guitarra portuguesa* is tuned one tone lower than in Lisbon, the rhythm is mainly quaternary and not binary like in Lisbon, and, here, fado is performed in black capes, part of the university's traditional uniform. While fado was once only preformed by men (the university was single-sex), the profession has blossomed in the last 20 years.

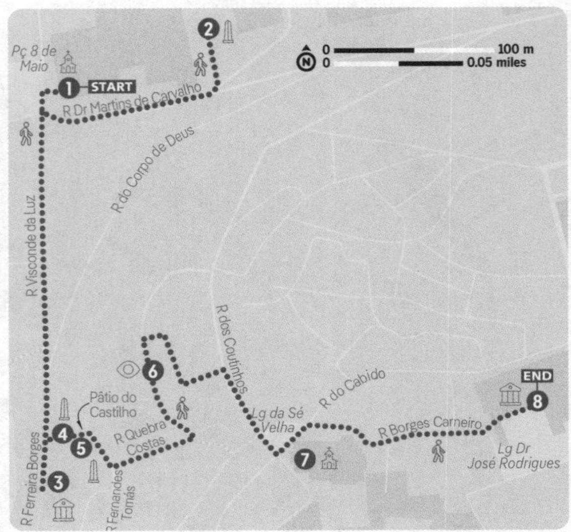

From the Baixa to the Alta Walking Tour

TOUR THE HISTORIC CENTRE

From Coimbra's central station, the lower part of the city *(baixa)* spreads inland from the north bank of the Rio Mondego, easily explored as you climb to the university on the higher level *(alta)*. Entering the pedestrianised maze of streets, head towards **1 Igreja de Santa Cruz** (Sunday visitation is only late afternoon). With an exuberant facade, this former educational convent houses a mix of Renaissance, Gothic and Manueline architecture, including a 16th-century cloister and royal tombs. The peculiar pastel-lemon **2 Manga Cloister** behind is an interesting sight. To the right, Rua Visconde da Luz is a busy thoroughfare of shops, restaurants and the **3 Museu da Cidade de Coimbra** (closed Sunday and Monday), which is worth a peek.

Near the museum, enter the old town through the **4 Porta de Barbacã**, leading to the **5 Arco e Torre de Almedina**, part of the medieval wall rebuilt in the 11th century during Muslim rule. Inside the tower, a small museum (closed Sunday and Monday) covers the wall's history. Starting the climb

WHERE TO EAT IN COIMBRA

Cafetaria do Museu da Ciência
Excellent-value fixed-price lunch near the university, with soup, main, wine, coffee and dessert included. €

Cantinho do Reis
Big terrace, big portions, great prices and regional dishes such as *chanfana* (pork stew). €

Zé Manel dos Ossos
Small, intimate dining room coated in handwritten notes, with delicious traditional dishes. €

on the steep stairs, take a detour left on 6 **Rua Sobre Ribas** for towers and architectural finds before looping back to 7 **Sé Velha**. The grand 12th-century fortified cathedral is a fine example of surviving Romanesque architecture, with Gothic tombs inside and, breaking from traditional *azulejos* (hand-painted tiles), detailed Hispano-Moresque tiles. Climb a little further to reach the *alta* and 8 **Museu Nacional Machado de Castro** (p264).

Classrooms, Curiosities & the Grand Library

HISTORIC WORLD-HERITAGE UNIVERSITY

Walking through the grand 17th-century **Porta Férrea**, you'll be flanked by the esteemed World Heritage–listed **Universidade de Coimbra**. A statue of King João III, the man responsible for the conversion of the former palace into the university in 1537, stands in the courtyard's centre.

Before entering the 18th-century **Biblioteca Joanina**, you'll wait a short time in the medieval jail, which later served as the academic prison for misbehaving students. Once you climb the stairs, prepare to be in awe of the ornate, three-roomed baroque interior. Elaborate gilded wooden shelves house 60,000 ancient volumes and manuscripts, guiding your eyes to the frescoed ceiling. Next, wander the rooms of **Paço das Escolas** (Royal Palace), where ancient traditions and student presentations still take place in dark-panelled halls adorned with portraits of Portuguese royalty. Afterwards, head into the baroque **Capela de São Miguel** for a look at the colourful ceiling and climb the **Torre da Universidade** (separate ticket) for sweeping views.

Away from the central courtyard, the **Museu da Ciência** is fun for kids, though the Cabinet of Curiosities' taxidermy isn't everyone's cup of tea. Meanwhile, the **Jardim Botânico** is a serene space of fountains, flora and a small bamboo forest.

Across the Mondego Walking Tour

GARDENS, CONVENTS AND CULTURE

Across and along the Rio Mondego, a Coimbra of green spaces, stories and convents provides a contrast to the student-heavy upper city. From 1 **Largo da Portogem**, follow the riverside path through tree-shaded 2 **Parque da Cidade Manuel Braga** and 3 **Parque Verde do Mondego**, where a handful of

SERENADES ON THE STREET

Often when dining in Coimbra, a group of students in their official *traje* uniforms (dark-cloaked and capped) will appear, instruments in hand, and an impromptu concert will start. These groups, called Tunas Académicas, are formed by musically talented students (usually from the same faculty or with another connection) who have decided to perform together. While these performances can include Coimbra's fado, they aren't limited to it, and other serenades and songs the group enjoys – and often their own compilations – are also performed. Likely originating from a Spanish tradition of sopistas – students who would sing for their lunch – the Tunas of Portugal took form in the 19th century.

Sete Restaurante
Portuguese flavours are turned into creative and well-presented plates, paired with regional wines. €€

Itália
Reliable pizza and pasta at one of the few terrace restaurants actually on the river. €€

Solar do Bacalhau
This vast, multi-roomed cod house offers the chance to try *bacalhau* in countless variations. €€

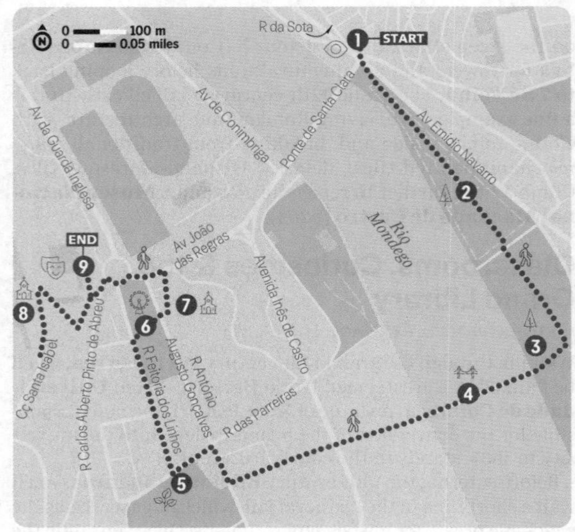

MORE SIGHTS IN COIMBRA

Casa Museu Bissaya Barreto
The ornate home and private collection of Bissaya Barreto, including sculptures, ceramics and paintings.

Torre de Anto
One of the medieval towers of the old walls now hosts a small museum dedicated to fado.

Jardim da Sereia
This city-centre park has bronze monuments, tiles and statues, serving as a leafy garden gallery.

water-view restaurants and cafes reside. The **4 Ponte Pedonal Pedro e Inês**, a multicolour-panelled bridge named after the protagonists of a forbidden love story, provides the river crossing. Behind the bridge, the gorgeous **5 Jardins da Quinta das Lágrimas** (closed Monday and during January) are worth a stroll to see the Fountain of Tears, supposedly marking the spot where Inês' fate was sealed. Close by, **6 Portugal dos Pequenitos** highlights the nation's monuments in miniature and a few grand religious buildings are worth a visit. The older Gothic **7 Mosteiro de Santa Clara-a-Velha** (closed Monday) displays archaeological finds, while the more elevated 17th-century **8 Mosteiro de Santa Clara-a-Nova**, constructed due to regular flooding in the old convent, is dedicated to Queen Isabel's memory. Between the two, the **9 Convento São Francisco** has been reborn as a cultural venue, with a varied performance programme.

GETTING AROUND

Coimbra has two train stations: Coimbra-B, a little outside the city, where most long-distance trains pass through, and Coimbra, near the centre, on the local line. Exploring is best done on foot, but the old town is steep in parts, so comfy shoes are a must. SMTUC operates a reliable municipal bus system and car parks, allowing for park and ride.

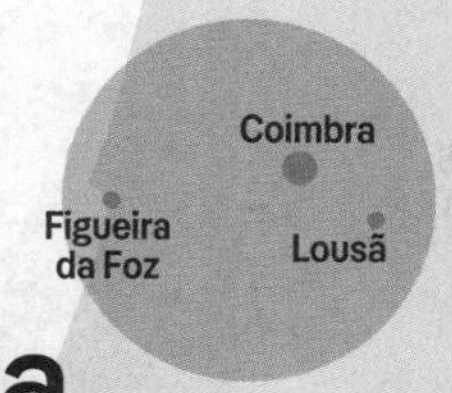

Coimbra
Figueira da Foz
Lousã

Beyond Coimbra

Ruined Roman settlements, schist village trails, verdant royal retreats and a coastal casino city – Coimbra's surrounds have it all.

Conímbriga, with its ruined Roman villas and well-preserved mosaics, might be the crown jewel of Coimbra's surrounding area, but plenty more gems spill out from Beira Litoral's capital city. Inland, shaded trails lead north through the hermitage-dotted Buçaco Forest or southeast to the schist villages of the Serra da Lousã. Flowing from the interior to the coast, the Rio Mondego passes rice fields and Montemor-o-Velho's castle, one of the country's best preserved, with the river making for a serene kayak adventure. At the ocean, the river meets the casino resort town of Figueira da Foz, which has been pulling in beachgoers, gamblers and wave-riders since the 19th century. Oh, and there are *espumante* (sparkling wine) vineyards, too.

TOP TIP

Booking in advance for kayaking experiences and the Aliança Underground Museum tours is advisable, especially in summer.

Casa dos Repuxos (p270), Ruínas de Conímbriga

BEST SIGHTS NEAR COIMBRA

Portugal Roman Museum in Sicó
Interactive museum focusing on the Roman presence in the Sicó lands and general Roman culture – great for kids.

Castellum de Alcabideque
The source of Conímbriga's water, with a tower and tank used to collect the water before it passed through the aqueduct.

Museu da Villa Romana do Rabaçal
Further south, this second Roman villa site is not as grand, but the museum is informative; a guide will take you to the ruins.

MIGUEL ALMEIDA/SHUTTERSTOCK ©

Castelo de Montemor o Velho

A Grand Roman Affair

RUINS, VILLAS AND MOSAICS

To Coimbra's south, the expansive **Ruínas de Conímbriga** were the original Roman settlement before relocation to Aeminium (Coimbra). Founded in the 1st century BCE – although human life had been here since Celtic times – it's the country's most extensive and best preserved Roman site. Start your visit at the museum, where mosaics, archaeological finds and a panel showing Conímbriga's timeline gives a decent introduction.

In the open-air site, signs indicate the different houses and baths that the low walls define, though your eyes will be drawn to the much higher **defensive wall**. Constructed in the 3rd century when facing invasion, it essentially cut the settlement in half. Sadly for the Romans, the significant barrier didn't prevent the Suebians from seizing the city, but it did stop all the mosaic work from being lost. The most impressive are found in the covered **Casa dos Repuxos** (House of Fountains), a 1st-century water villa where the floor tiles depict vivid illustrations of the four seasons. The mosaics at **Casa da Cruz**

CENTRAL COAST

For a shore-hugging road trip along the Beira Litoral, continue to laid-back Praia de Mira (p280) and then the colourful striped houses of Costa Nova (p280).

WHERE TO EAT & DRINK IN FIGUEIRA DA FOZ

Burgus
Great stacked burgers and sunset rooftop cocktails, served in an old defensive fort. €€

Cervejaria Marisqueira Sagres
Fair-priced seafood platters in a no-frills restaurant just back from the beach. €€

Restaurante Caçarola Dois
Well-regarded seafood restaurant with platters and catch of the day near the old casino. €€€

Suástica (House of the Swastika) – the swastika being a symbol of good luck in Roman times – are also well preserved.

Excavations continue slowly in the surrounding area, with the archaeological work sometimes visible in pits. With a small team and budget (which may also explain the growing weed problem in the complex), it will be many years, if ever, before all of Conímbriga's story is revealed.

A Picture-Perfect Castle

MONDEGO MEDIEVAL FORTRESS

One of the most impressive medieval fortifications in the country, **Castelo de Montemor o Velho**, only a 30-minute drive west of Coimbra, sits pretty as a postcard atop a hill. Overlooking the vividly green rice fields of the Rio Mondego, this fine fortress location has seen plenty of action. Once occupied by the Romans, it became a Muslim stronghold in the 8th century. Later, when King Alfonso VI captured the location, a similar structure and church layout that we see today was designed, although extensive reconstruction has followed. Once serving as a royal residence, the luxury has long gone, but walking inside and on the walls of such an important historic site is more than reason enough to visit.

Escape to the Coast

WILD VAST SANDS

Coimbra's closest beach destination, **Figueira da Foz**, is a one-hour train ride west. A highly popular sun-and-sand resort for over a century, it can get crowded in summer. Luckily, there's an extensive coastline, and serenity-seekers can head to **Praia de Buarcos** at the beach's northern end, while **Praia de Cabedelo** is the go-to for surfers. In the city, a modern casino sits next to the grand older gaming house, and a few museums act as side attractions – it's worth leaving the sands for the fairy-tale-like **Castelo Engenheiro Silva** (closed Tuesday), displaying contemporary art, and **Casa do Paço** (closed Sunday and Monday), housing thousands of Dutch Delft tiles.

Schist Village Trails

HIKING BETWEEN FORESTS AND STONE

Spreading across the Lousã and Açor mountain ranges, 27 schist villages (with buildings mainly constructed from schist rock), perfect for an escape from the city, hide among dense forests. From Coimbra, **Lousã**, an hour by bus, serves as the easiest access point to the **Serra da Lousã**. A 40-minute walk

PASTEL DE TENTÚGAL PIT STOP

In the 16th century, Carmelite nuns in Tentúgal began baking sweet egg-filled pastry delicacies called Pastel de Tentúgal from behind the walls of Convento Nossa Senhora do Carmo. Around a 25-minute drive from Coimbra, en route to Montemor-o-Velho, the village's *pastelarias* (O Afonso is great) offer a chance for you to pause and sample the pastries in their birthplace. Still crafted with the original recipe, using a simple flour-and-water dough, it's the incredibly fragile and thin, almost translucent pasty sheets, paired with the sweetened egg-yolk cream filling, that make the beloved sweet so impressive and delicious.

WHERE TO HAVE LUNCH IN LOUSÃ

Salty Lousã
Interesting tapas, tasting plates and snacks with quick, friendly service on Praceta Sá Carneiro. €

O Burgo
By Lousã's river beach, with upscale regional flavours such as deer and boar. Reservations essential. €€

Villa Lausana
Well-seasoned traditional dishes (and vegetarian options) with modern flair in a stylish setting. €€

from town, **Castelo da Lousã**, a river beach and 15th-century sanctuary sculptures provide a cultural introduction to the locale. From here, you can hike (or drive) through oaks and pines on a network of trails linking nearby villages.

Pretty **Talasnal**, although perched high, is easily accessible by road, meaning tour groups often visit. For a rural walk, make a loop from the castle to **Candal** and then **Cerdeira**. Climbing Candal's narrow, photogenic streets, you'll enjoy panoramas across the valley before joining the forested trail that winds its way to hidden and well-restored Cerdeira, where a cafe (which can call a taxi) awaits.

LIFE IN THE SCHIST VILLAGES

Catarina Serra, manager of *@cerdeirahomefor creativity*, shares why the Serra da Lousã is the perfect retreat.

There are no distractions here, and you stop hearing the noise of your day-to-day life, which inspires creativity. Beauty is everywhere; all the different colours and materials in the schist stone, deer watching, listening to the sound of the birds, and at night you always hear the spring water. It's a place where the elements are in control, and you can connect with nature or the people around you over wine and deep conversation. I'm a river girl, so I love going to Cabril do Ceira, a wild river beach with an amazing waterfall between the cracks of the mountains.

A Creative Forested Retreat

ARTISTIC REVITALISED VILLAGE

Once ruined and almost lost, the village of **Cerdeira** has been reborn as a creative retreat, thanks to two artistic and passionate families. Renovated schist houses now serve as a hostel and holiday homes, each with bespoke work from local artists. The serene and distraction-free setting lends itself perfectly to the offered workshops, ranging from half-day classes working with schist, to longer retreat-style courses led by national and international creative tutors. There's also a residency programme for creatives wishing to work on longer personal projects.

Meander Down the Mondego

SERENE RIVER KAYAKING

From a dusty riverside car park in Penacova, guides from **O Pioneiro Do Mondego** will get you kitted out and briefed, ready for a kayak adventure along the **Rio Mondego**. The longest of Portugal's rivers to flow entirely within the country, it once served as the divide between the Muslim and Christian kingdoms. Nowadays, this serene, forest-straddled waterway, with the occasional small hamlet, is ripe for gentle adventures and bird spotting, especially in winter when herons and stilts usually arrive in abundance. From Penacova, you can opt to paddle and float downstream to Torres do Mondego (18km) or continue to Coimbra (25km).

On the way, there are a few river beaches, such as **Praia Fluvial de Palheiros e Zorro** with a bar and restaurant, where you can pause and soak in the sun in the warmer months. The rest of the time, it's just you and natural serenity, with the occasional mild rapid. While the route takes between three and five hours, depending on the distance chosen, it's best

WHERE TO DINE IN BUÇACO & LUSO

Rosa Biscoito Luso
Teas, craft beers and tasty small plates next to the Luso thermal springs. €

Lourenços
Decent portions of traditional dishes and *prato do dia* (dish of the day) in a large, popular dining room. €€

Bussaco Palace Hotel Restaurant
Steep set menus allow non-guests the chance to enter and dine in the grand palace. €€€

JOALACERDA/SHUTTERSTOCK ©

Talasnal

to go slow and enjoy stops on the way, especially as there is a re-grouping for lunch before the final stretch. Tours operate year-round, and transfers are available from Coimbra.

A Regal, Verdant Sanctuary

BOTANIC FOREST AND THERMAL SPRINGS

For a tranquil afternoon strolling between water features and religious monuments, head to the walled woods of **Mata Nacional do Buçaco**, 35 minutes by car from Coimbra. Benedictine monks resided in the area first, followed by the Carmelites, who built the many fountains and hermitages, which you can explore on marked trails. They also contributed to the vast and varied collection of native and imported flora, including cypress trees from Mexico and spring-blossoming camellias. In the middle of the park, the fairy-tale-like **Bussaco Palace** dominates. Constructed to be an opulent royal retreat, it's now a luxury hotel (p274), technically closed to non-guests. Still, the views of the Neo-Manueline building and gardens are sublime, and you can enter the **Convento de Santa Cruz do Buçaco** next door. Post walk, head to the town of Luso below to be pampered in the thermal spring spa.

BAIRRADA WINES

Although not well known internationally, the Bairrada DOC produces interesting wines. Influenced by the Atlantic – thus generally quite acidic – baga is the region's primary grape, and there's extensive production of *espumante*, Portugal's sparkling wine. Start your journey at **Bairrada Wine Museum** (closed Monday) in Anadia before taking a cellar tour. At the curious **Aliança Underground Museum** (tour booking required), the wine caves have an array of art among the barrels, ranging from Portuguese ceramics to Niger artefacts (it's questionable as to whether some items should be here), with tours rounded off with a tasting. For a more traditional tour and sampling, head to **Caves of São Domingos** (closed weekends).

WHERE TO COOL DOWN AROUND COIMBRA

Praia Fluvial do Rebolim
The closest river beach to Coimbra provides cooling dips on a sliver of sand.

Choupal National Forest
A shaded and spacious forest with some bamboo, just outside of Coimbra.

Canyoning in Ribeira da Pena
Epic Land offers adrenaline-fuelled rappels and routes exploring rocky waterways in Góis.

DARK SKY HUNTING

Stargazers and astrophotographers will find the limited light pollution in Coimbra's surrounding forests and mountains hard to resist. The **Dark Sky Aldeias do Xisto** project is so celebrated for its night skies that in 2021 it was recognised as a 'Starlight Tourist Destination', joining Alqueva (in the Alentejo) as the second Portuguese destination to be accredited. Leading the way is the municipality of **Pampilhosa da Serra**, at the heart of the region's 27 schist villages. Renowned for their remote landscapes, clean air and nocturnal near-silences, these get-away-from-it-all abandoned homes turned rural accommodation offerings are ideal for long nights lost in the constellations.

MIKEHOWARD/ALAMY STOCK PHOTO ©

Bussaco Palace Hotel

Sleep in a Palace

A GRAND OVERNIGHT RETREAT

Be seduced to sleep in a royal residence at the **Bussaco Palace Hotel**, which provides a surprisingly fair-priced opportunity – a reflection of the hotel's slightly dated rooms and lack of luxury features. Regardless, once inside, you'll feel like royalty as you climb the central staircase, adorned with *azulejos* depicting battle scenes, admire the Neo-Manueline archways in the dining room, and sip sparkling wine behind the gargoyle-adorned terrace pillars. The restaurant's menu is upscale, with an extensive list of the palace's own aged wines.

GETTING AROUND

The Ruínas de Conímbriga can be accessed by Transdev bus, with morning departures going directly to the museum and the last return around 1pm – later departures only go as far as Condeixa. For Lousã, regular services are operated by Metro Mondego, with the departure point and ticket sales at Coimbra station; if you're getting on at subsequent stops, you can purchase tickets onboard. Buçaco (the station is closer to Luso), Figueira da Foz and Montemor-o-Velho are on the regional train line.

AVEIRO

Aveiro is often dubbed the Venice of Portugal, though it's hard to believe anyone who has been to Italy's canal-lined masterpiece would make such a comparison. Sure, there are similarities, such as the high-prowed boats and canals backed by colourful buildings, but beyond that the two cities are considerably different. Aveiro's youthful university energy, Art Nouveau architecture, dune-backed beaches and birdlife-filled *salinas* (salt pans) mean the city can stand proud without drawing any parallels.

The city was a thriving seaport in the 16th century, until a storm shuttered the Rio Vouga's mouth in 1575, essentially ending ocean trade. In the following centuries, residents relocated until the Barra Canal opened in 1808, re-linking the city and sea. Quickly, as salt headed to Newfoundland for the booming *bacalhau* industry, wealth returned, illustrated by Aveiro's Art Nouveau buildings. Nowadays, *moliceiro* boats ferry visitors rather than collect algae, and seafood restaurants line the canals. Times may have changed, but the sea still defines Aveiro.

TOP TIP

The municipality offers a free bike-rental service (with an ID deposit) from the BUGA kiosk. Restaurant bookings are advisable around the canals and Costa Nova, especially in summer, when tourist numbers swell.

Museums, Churches & Monuments

BEYOND THE WATERWAYS

Set out on foot from **Museu da Cidade** (closed Monday), allowing at least 30 minutes inside to learn about the city's history, lagoons and culture. Cross the bridge in front of the **Assembleia Municipal**, one of the best spots for photographing *moliceiros* framed by a grand building. Walking away from the river, pass the blue-tiled **Misericórdia de Aveiro** and **Casa de Santa Zita** on the pedestrianised route, soon arriving at the **Museu de Aveiro** (closed Monday). Inside the 15th-century convent, admire classical paintings and extravagant rooms, from the outlandishly detailed gilded chapel to the baroque marble tomb chamber, the final resting place of Princess Santa Joana – her life portrayed by painted tiles on the lower walls. Across the street, the **Sé** pales in comparison. Walking towards Ponte Laços de Irene, you'll return to the canal.

Cruise the Canals

TRADITIONAL BOAT RIDES

Aveiro's bright and colourful, high-prowed *moliceiro* boats have seen a rebirth taking travellers on a journey along the canals. Initially used to collect algae in the early 19th century, the vessels are decorated with religious (or often highly inappropriate) paintings. Most trips last around 45 minutes, usually with a guide. As the tours rarely make it out of the city-limit channels, a kayak rental is a solid alternative if you wish to explore the lagoons and *salinas*.

SALT THERAPY

The bright-white **Flor de Sal of Aveiro** is a celebrated seasoning, yet it's also superb for treatments. At **Cale do Oiro**, a natural spa with huts stilted above the salt pans, massage therapies are provided, harnessing the power of the pure salt, paired with natural oils, for a full-body scrub. The peaceful experience, often with a soundtrack of just birds, water and wind, is rather special. **Marinha da Noeirinha** offers an outside salt spa, where you can lounge in the healing waters before moving to the lagoon pool, where a high concentration of salt gives you the potential to float.

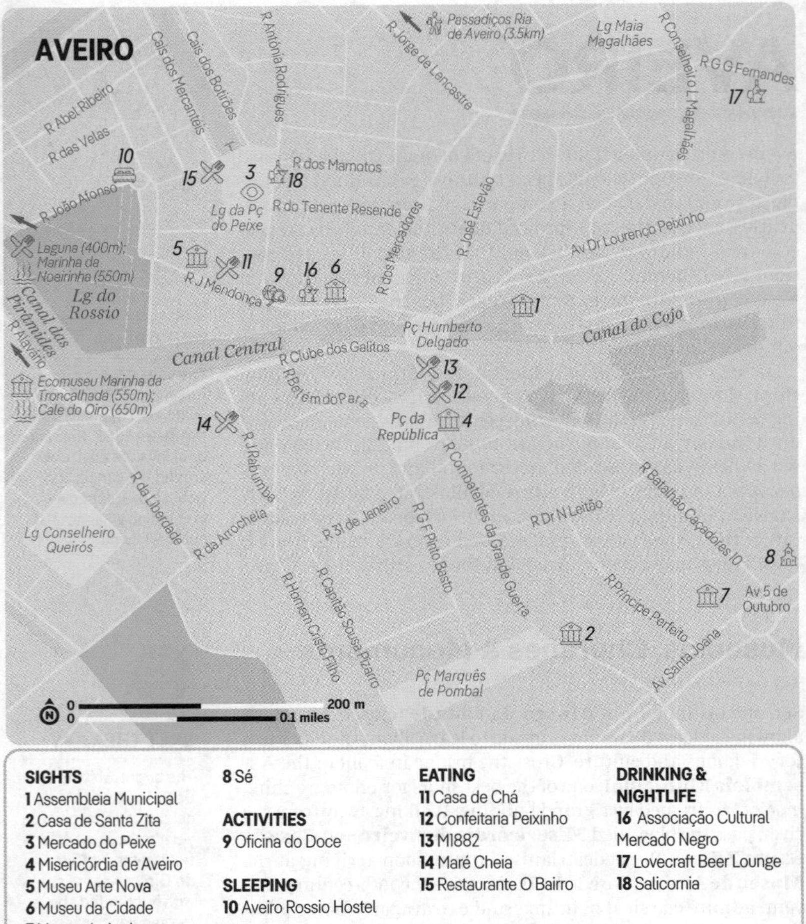

AVEIRO

R Abel Ribeiro
R das Velas
Cais dos Mercantéis
Cais dos Botirões
R Antónia Rodrigues
R Jorge de Lencastre
Passadiços Ria de Aveiro (3.5km)
Lg Maia Magalhães
R Conselheiro L Magalhães
R G G Fernandes
R dos Marnotos
R João Afonso
Lg da Pç do Peixe
R do Tenente Resende
R José Estevão
R dos Mercadores
Av Dr Lourenço Peixinho
Laguna (400m); Marinha da Noeirinha (550m)
R J Mendonça
Lg do Rossio
Canal das Pirâmides
R Alavário
Canal Central
Pç Humberto Delgado
Canal do Cojo
R Clube dos Galitos
R Belém do Pará
Ecomuseu Marinha da Troncalhada (550m); Cale do Oiro (650m)
Pç da República
R J Rabumba
R Combatentes da Grande Guerra
R Batalhão Caçadores 10
R da Liberdade
Lg Conselheiro Queirós
R da Arrochela
R 31 de Janeiro
R G F Pinto Basto
R Dr N Leitão
R Príncipe Perfeito
Av 5 de Outubro
R Homem Cristo Filho
R Capitão Sousa Pizarro
Av Santa Joana
Pç Marquês de Pombal
0 200 m
0 0.1 miles

SIGHTS
1 Assembleia Municipal
2 Casa de Santa Zita
3 Mercado do Peixe
4 Misericórdia de Aveiro
5 Museu Arte Nova
6 Museu da Cidade
7 Museu de Aveiro
8 Sé

ACTIVITIES
9 Oficina do Doce

SLEEPING
10 Aveiro Rossio Hostel

EATING
11 Casa de Chá
12 Confeitaria Peixinho
13 M1882
14 Maré Cheia
15 Restaurante O Bairro

DRINKING & NIGHTLIFE
16 Associação Cultural Mercado Negro
17 Lovecraft Beer Lounge
18 Salicornia

An Art Nouveau Walking Tour

CANALS AND COLOURFUL ARCHITECTURE

For an introduction to Aveiro's web of canals and finest Art Nouveau buildings, take yourself on a walking tour, starting from the train station. Just next door, the original terminal, **1 Antiga Estação**, adorned with incredible *azulejos* (hand-painted tiles)

WHERE TO TASTE OVOS MOLES IN AVEIRO

Confeitaria Peixinho
Since 1856 this shop has been using the original recipe; it now has a chic, pastel-hued interior.

M1882
Tucked away on a side street, the celebrated treats from here are worth hunting out.

Oficina do Doce
Play chef for an hour to make *ovos moles* and learn about their history.

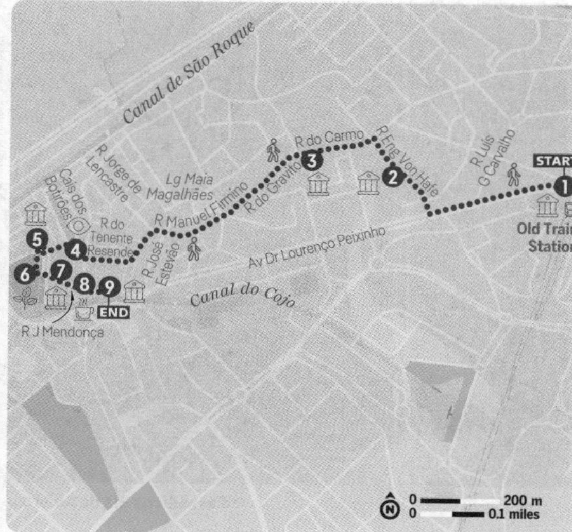

depicting regional scenes, is quite the sight. Following the main avenue, turn right towards 2 **Hotel As Américas**, where the stone-carved windows shine, before continuing on to 3 **Casa da Silva Rocha**, a mustard-hued family home with flower-decorated tiles. Continuing towards the modern, glass-fronted 4 **Mercado do Peixe**, you'll catch your first glimpse of canals and *moliceiros* – it's an ideal spot to pause for a coffee along the waterways.

Slightly back from the canal, the pastel-blue 5 **Aveiro Rossio House** is a modest Art Nouveau building, now operating as a hostel. From here, stroll alongside a larger canal and the city's main garden, 6 **Jardim do Rossio** (closed for landscaping at the time of research), before arriving at a cluster of highly ornate buildings leading towards the bridge. The most impressive, Major Pessoa House, with sculpted arched windows and gold-embellished iron balconies, houses the 7 **Museu Arte Nova** (closed Monday). Inside, a small museum on the city's Art Nouveau movement and a pretty courtyard cafe awaits. A few doors down, the facades of 8 **Café a Barrica**, 9 **Museu da Cidade** and the salmon-coloured and flower-tiled house next door are particularly camera-friendly.

BEST PLACES TO EAT IN AVEIRO

Casa de Chá
In the courtyard of Aveiro's prettiest Art Nouveau building, enjoy tea, coffee, drinks and light dishes. €

Restaurante O Bairro
Decent-size portions with inventive takes on Portuguese staples close to the canals – bookings essential. €€

Maré Cheia
The *arroz de marisco* (seafood rice) is reason enough to visit, with plenty more delicious dishes on the seafood-focused menu. €€

Laguna
Fancy dining on a floating barge, with a mainly seafood-inspired menu – book a table waterside for *moliceiro* boat views. €€€

WHERE TO DRINK IN AVEIRO

Salicornia
Friendly small bar and terrace with good brews – try its local seaweed-infused beer.

Associação Cultural Mercado Negro
Multiple laid-back rooms of an Art Nouveau building, sometimes with live music.

Lovecraft Beer Lounge
Dimly lit yet welcoming bar with a vast choice of local and international craft beers.

AVEIRO'S OVOS MOLES

Hailing from Aveiro's 17th-century convent, *ovos moles* are so revered in the city that they have a dedicated monument in Cais da Fonte Nova. Combining sugar syrup and egg yolks, which were in abundance when the nuns used the egg whites in housekeeping chores, the secret sweet recipe has since earned Protected Geographical Indication. The signature shell shape takes inspiration from the nearby ocean and lagoon. For a better understanding of *ovos moles'* history, and the chance to play chef for an hour, book an experience at **Oficina do Doce** to create your own sweet egg-yolk treats.

Passadiços Ria de Aveiro

Salina Strolls & Bike Rides

BIRDLIFE AND BOARDWALKS

The **Ria de Aveiro** expands far beyond the city's *salinas* (salt pans), encompassing a vast estuarine area that provides a haven for birdlife, especially during the winter migration. Storks, herons, flamingos, sea ducks and raptors are some of the winged residents (permanent and temporary) you may spot here. It's a tranquil setting, easily explored on foot, though a bicycle rental – the city has a free hire scheme – will allow you to cover more ground.

Start by delving into Aveiro's famed salt production by heading to **Ecomuseu Marinha da Troncalhada**. In this open-air museum, you can walk through the salt pans, often meet the workers of the *salinas*, and learn about the methods of capturing and harvesting from information boards.

Continue to the **Passadiços Ria de Aveiro**, which stretches far from the centre, for more birdlife sightings. Starting from Cais de São Roque, near the Ecomuseu, a 7.5km route hugs the lagoon. Once you've made the short bike ride to Cais da Ribeira de Esgueira, the wooden walkway (and magic) begins. The flat route meanders along and over the marshes to the **Vouga River**, with scenic views across the salt pans, mudflats and pine forests. Along the way, signs highlight the fauna and flora you may encounter, and enthusiastic cyclists can continue beyond the walkways, far into the more untouched lagoon system.

GETTING AROUND

Aveiro's centre is compact, flat and easily explored on foot. The *salinas* are also close enough to walk, although a bike rental will maximise your time.

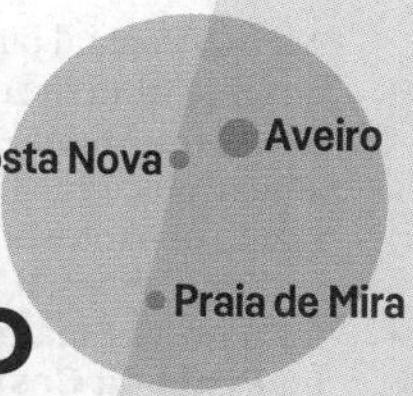

Beyond Aveiro

Head to the coast for multicoloured houses and dune-backed beaches, or inland for an epic suspension bridge and wooden walkways.

Whether you're topping up your tan at the colourful surf town of Costa Nova, exploring the crustacean-laden lagoons beyond the city, or heading inland to cross Arouca's suspension bridge, you're exploring lands shaped by waters.

Millions of years ago, Arouca Geopark, now better known for its river-hugging walkway, was under the ocean, as evidenced by the trilobites seen in the park. Aveiro's lagoons were formed in the 1570s following a ferocious storm that blocked the port, with the retreating shoreline leaving salt pans behind. Meanwhile, the Atlantic waves and wind, which ensure the region's famed surf, helped shape the coast's signature dunes.

TOP TIP

Book your Paiva Walkways and (especially) Arouca Bridge tickets online (passadicosdopaiva.pt) in advance to guarantee a time slot.

Costa Nova (p280)

JULIA LAV/SHUTTERSTOCK ©

Surf, Sand & Striped Houses

COLOURFUL COASTAL ESCAPE

Aveiro's coastal playground starts at **Costa Nova**, a 20-minute bus ride from the city. Having recently found (Instagram) fame for its traditional *palheiros* – striped colourful cottages – it's a busy place in summer, with waits for restaurant tables and plenty of photoshoots going on. Still, even with the crowds and souvenir shops, it retains something of a fishing-village charm for now. The main reason to venture here is to top up your tan on **Praia da Costa Nova** or **Praia da Barra**, beautiful low-dune-backed beaches with sublime sunsets, swells and upbeat beach bars. Surfers are also well catered for, with a handful of surf schools on the northern end of the beach offering one-off classes and courses for beginners, plus rentals for more experienced board riders. Riactiva, on the lagoon side, offers kitesurfing lessons and rents out kayaks and SUPs in the estuary, where the waters are calmer than on the Atlantic side.

VISTA ALEGRE PORCELAIN

Since 1824, Vista Alegre has been a high-end name in Portuguese porcelain. Founded on a farm in Ílhavo, a 10-minute drive south of Aveiro, it grew into what is now the Vista Alegre Factory after being granted a Royal Licence by King João VI, leading it to become a Royal Factory. In 1964, it opened a museum, highlighting a vast collection of pieces you can admire, as well as witness first-hand the intricate painting of the ceramics. The old theatre, chapel and housing estate can also be toured, and workshops (weekdays only) are offered in pottery and painting.

Seafaring History

MARITIME MUSEUM

Heading towards Costa Nova, the **Museu Marítimo de Ílhavo** (closed Monday) is a short bus ride from Aveiro. An impressive and modern museum, it dives into Portugal's maritime history, with a particular focus on cod fishing. Displays and exhibits include a collection of Portuguese boats (smaller models and full-sized), which aids the mainly local-language information. The **Navio Museu Santo André** (a 15-minute drive from Aveiro), an old cod fishing trawler, can also be toured.

Laid-Back Beach Day

GOLDEN SANDS AWAY FROM CROWDS

A 40-minute drive south of Aveiro, **Praia de Mira** is very much a sun, sea and surf destination. Slightly more laid-back than the main beaches close to the city, its fine sands stretch in either direction as far as the eye can see. Just back from the beach, the Barrinha Lagoon is ideal for wave-free water sports, with family-friendly pedalos also available to rent.

Forested Island Trails

DUNE-BACKED NATURE RESERVE

If you'd prefer your dune-backed beach day with a spot of tree-shaded birdwatching, make a beeline to the **Reserva Natural das Dunas de São Jacinto**. To the north of Costa

WHERE TO EAT IN COSTA NOVA

Atlântida
Casual cafe close to the colourful houses with coffee, cakes and affordable snacks. €

Bronze Seafood & Lounge Bar
Sea views, good tunes and quality dishes – expect a queue in summer. €€

Peixe na Costa
Great service and premium seafood dishes away from the water. €€€

CHRISS73/SHUTTERSTOCK ©

Sand dunes near Costa Nova

Nova, behind Praia de São Jacinto, this peaceful, protected park with a 7km loop trail and bird-spotting huts is best accessed by ferry. From the pier, it's around a 15-minute walk to the **interpretation centre**, which has a small exhibit room covering the park's wildlife. You should register here before embarking on the trail, although recently reduced opening hours can make this challenging. Opt for the smaller loop, or entire route, which passes by ponds and is mainly shaded by pines, though some segments are more exposed, making it an intense stroll on a summer day. To protect the delicate dunes, walking over them is prohibited, meaning access to the beach needs to be via an official route, not from the trail, extending the return walk.

Along & Over the Rio Paiva

SUSPENSION BRIDGE BOARDWALKS

The **Passadiços do Paiva**, around an 80-minute drive from Aveiro, is one of the region's most impressive linear trails. Hugging the **Rio Paiva**, the nearly 9km-long route follows wooden walkways, steep staircases and flat gravel paths, all accompanied by river rapids and a soundtrack of birdsong.

CHURCHES WORTH A DETOUR

To the north of Aveiro, two churches stand out for their *azulejos* (hand-painted tiles) and can be visited together on a short side trip. The most captivating, **Igreja Matriz de Santa Maria de Válega** (hours vary), a 30-minute drive, breaks away from the traditional blue-and-white tile work and is adorned with a multicoloured facade. While the church was constructed in the 18th century, the tiles depicting biblical themes came in the mid-20th century. Inside, vibrant tiled artworks adorn the walls, complemented by impressive stained-glass windows. **Igreja de Santa Marinha de Cortegaça**, 20 minutes further north, has more traditional blue-and-white tile work.

WHERE TO STAY AROUND AROUCA

Casa do Centro
Cosy and inexpensive central rooms with shared facilities, perfect for resting between trails. €

Quinta de Alvarenga
Close to the 516 Arouca bridge, a rustic yet modern guesthouse with pool. €€

Hotel Sao Pedro
Quality contemporary Arouca hotel – the balcony mountain-view rooms are worth the extra. €€

AROUCA GEOPARK

Covering an area of 328 sq km, this vast open-air geological museum might have found recent fame due to the engineering marvel of the 516 Arouca bridge, but there's plenty more to discover in the park. Over 500 million years ago, this area was under the sea, accounting for some of the 40-plus major geological attractions, ranging from trace fossils and volcanic rocks to giant trilobites (extinct arthropods). The **Centro de Interpretação Geológica de Canelas** (closed Monday) is a good starting point for getting acquainted with the marine zooarchaeology. The park also offers dramatic waterfalls, river rafting adventures, canyoning and rock climbing, and 14 theme-focused walking trails for a more adventurous tour.

ANDRE97ALMEIDA/SHUTTERSTOCK ©

Passadiços do Paiva (p281)

The trail can be walked in either direction, although starting at the Areinho trailhead means you can tackle the steepest stairs before easing into the walk (Espiunca would then be the end point).

There are cafes and toilets at both trailheads, and the river beach, **Praia Fluvial do Vau**, provides a shady halfway picnic spot and refreshing dips. Along the trail, the undisturbed natural setting invites you to pause and spot birdlife, such as eagles, blackbirds and crows, and information boards highlight geosites, waterfalls and wildlife. The **516 Arouca** bridge, the world's longest pedestrian suspension bridge when it opened in 2021, is another side adventure. The 516m marvel stretches high above the Rio Paiva.

At the end of the trail, you can either walk back in reverse to your car or, usually, you can share a taxi with other people back to the car park. The trails do require a ticket (bookable online), which can either be just for the walkways or also include the 516 Arouca.

GETTING AROUND

Reaching Costa Nova by bus is simple from Aveiro, and likewise for Praia de Mira – though services can reduce outside of summer. To reach the Dunas de São Jacinto, a combined bus and ferry ticket is offered by aveirobus line 13. Driving to Arouca allows for the best access to the park, though it's not impossible by bus – but plan on an overnight stay. Taxis are a pricier option to the walkways, or you can stay overnight and then take the twice-daily, weekday-only bus to either Espiunca or Vilarinho stops, which are the closest to the trailheads.

VISEU

Viseu's compact medieval old town, fetching leafy gardens, renowned ancient vines and vibrant paintings by Portugal's most prominent Renaissance artist make the former Beira Alta capital one of the region's most attractive cities.

Like most great settlements, Viseu's story starts from a heroic legend. Viriato, chief of the Lusitani tribe, defending the land from Roman invasion, supposedly called this place home just before his assassination. You'll see his statue alongside the equally curious Cava de Viriato, the largest monument on the peninsula. While this extensive raised octagonal mound has its own myths, it's believed to have been constructed in the 10th century by Ramiro I to relocate the city before being abandoned. What is certain is that the Romans had a fortified camp (Vissaium) close by, followed by the Visigoths, before Viseu was crowned a royal town leading the conquest mission of surrounding Moorish strongholds.

TOP TIP

Before arrival, download the Walk Viseu app (and the guides inside) to your phone. It offers a tourist route around the city, alongside text and audio guides to some of the museums, all in various languages, allowing any information written only in Portuguese in the museums to be easily understood.

Viseu's Verdant Retreats

GARDENS AND PARKS

Viseu's self-adopted title as 'The Garden City' might have been a marketing gimmick of the early 20th century, but it doesn't make it any less factual today. Parks, gardens and green spaces enclose the city; some are particularly inviting for a peaceful stroll. Central **Parque Aquilino Ribeiro**, behind the Igreja dos Terceiros de São Francisco, has a tranquil cafe alongside a lake, perfect for a peaceful lunch. **Mata do Fontelo** is best for lazy strolls, with student-crafted artwork dotting the trails and the occasional peacock sighting. At **Quinta da Cruz**, on the city's outer limits, grand gardens are blended with contemporary artwork, with statues sitting alongside plants and the mansion now hosting exhibitions. The **Cava de Viriato**, an octagonal raised fortress base shrouded in mystery, is believed to have been constructed by the Lusitanians (although others will argue it's the work of Romans or the Moors) and is a bizarre monument with more questions than answers.

Summer Celebrations

A CENTURIES-OLD FAIR

Dating to 1392, the **Feira de São Mateus** has become integral to Viseu's history. While it has changed a lot since its inception, the colourful event, which takes place across most of August and September, keeps some traditions alive, such as handicrafts and traditional market stalls. Expect amusement rides, music concerts and plenty of food stalls – eel and *farturas* (Portuguese churros) are fair staples.

BEST RESTAURANTS IN VISEU

Prema
Take a break from the meaty regional cuisine with Prema's varied vegan menu, including adapted local dishes. €

Porta 64
Above-and-beyond service paired with excellent Portuguese and international dishes – the terrace is great; the basement not so much. €€

+55 Brasil de Norte a Sul
Sample some of Brazil's best dishes on the terrace of this restaurant in the old town. €€

VISEU

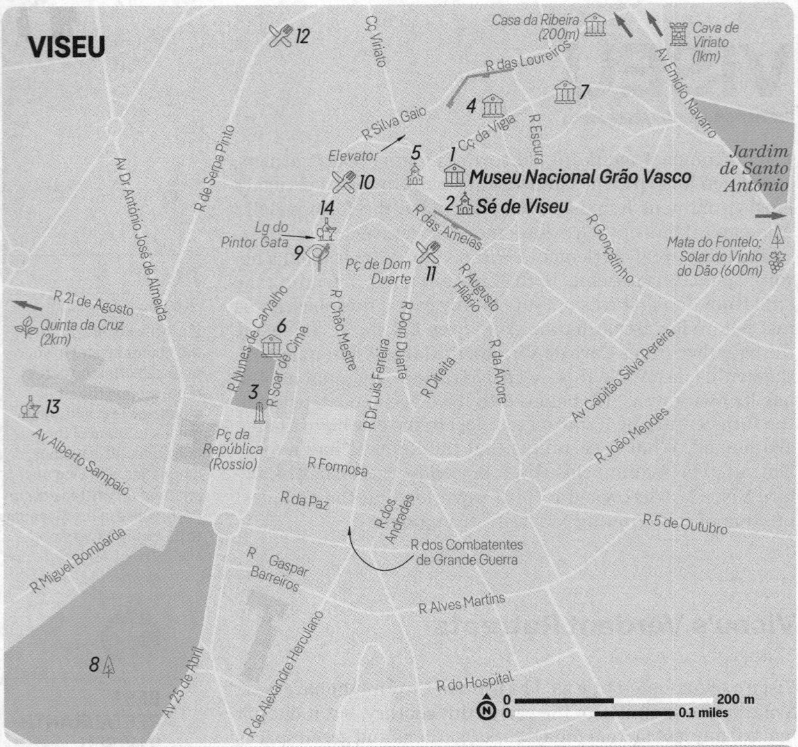

HIGHLIGHTS
1 Museu Nacional Grão Vasco
2 Sé de Viseu

SIGHTS
3 Azulejos
4 Casa do Miradouro
5 Igreja da Misericórdia
6 Museu Almeida Moreira
7 Museu Keil Amaral
8 Parque Aquilino Ribeiro
9 Porta do Soar

EATING
10 +55 Brasil de Norte a Sul
11 Porta 64
12 Prema

DRINKING & NIGHTLIFE
13 Pinguinhas
14 The Irish Bar

Myths, Museums, Artwork & Churches Walking Tour

A CULTURED CITY STROLL

Introduce yourself to Viseu's past and prominent figures on a walking tour starting at leafy **1 Praça da República**, where Joaquim Lopes' hand-painted tiles, **2 Painel de Azulejos**, depict typical regional life. Going up, enter the old town through **3 Porta do Soar**, a 17th-century gate, and you'll soon arrive at Praça da Sé, where the **4 Igreja**

WHERE TO DRINK IN VISEU

Pinguinhas
Fado restaurant with a laid-back, tree-shaded bar terrace out back.

The Irish Bar
Not so local, but with quality beer and an old-town terrace, it's a winner.

Solar do Vinho do Dão
Pop into this palace-turned-wine-office during the day to taste regional Dão wines.

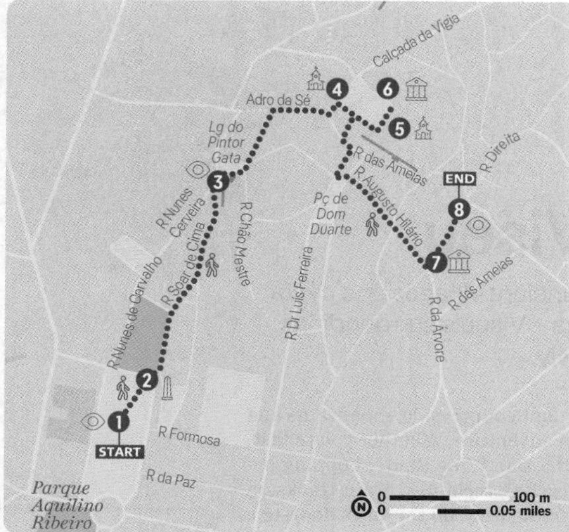

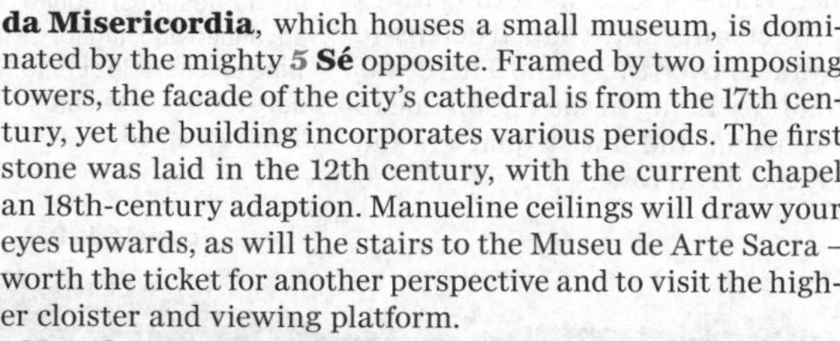

da Misericordia, which houses a small museum, is dominated by the mighty **5 Sé** opposite. Framed by two imposing towers, the facade of the city's cathedral is from the 17th century, yet the building incorporates various periods. The first stone was laid in the 12th century, with the current chapel an 18th-century adaption. Manueline ceilings will draw your eyes upwards, as will the stairs to the Museu de Arte Sacra – worth the ticket for another perspective and to visit the higher cloister and viewing platform.

Next door, the old bishop's palace houses the **6 Museu Nacional Grão Vasco** (closed Monday), a testament to the talents of celebrated Viseu-born artist Vasco Fernandes. His works are a primary focus, with the grand altarpiece he produced for the cathedral on show alongside majestic Renaissance canvases. Continue on, wandering down Rua Augusto Hilário, the former Jewish quarter, to the **7 Museu de História da Cidade** (closed Monday). Allow 45 minutes for an introduction to the city's myths, legends and history, from the Lusitanians and Romans through to the modern day. You're then on **8 Rua Direita**, Viseu's historic thoroughfare.

MORE MUSEUMS IN VISEU

Museu Almeida Moreira
A private collection in a 19th-century house displays paintings and sculptures from artists including Bordallo Pinheiro and José Malhoa.

Museu Keil Amaral
Dedicated to the life of the creative Keil Amaral family, one of whom – Alfredo Keil – wrote the national anthem.

Casa do Miradouro
A small archaeological museum dedicated to the work of local history teacher and researcher José Coelho.

Casa da Ribeira
Quaint riverside museum with temporary exhibitions mainly focused on local handicrafts.
All museums are closed Monday.

GETTING AROUND

Viseu's centre is compact and easily walkable, though it's a bit steep heading to the old town. An accessible (and currently free) funicular service runs from near the Estacionamento Cava do Viriato car park to behind the Praça de Sé. MUV operates the city bus routes.

Beyond Viseu

Tour aged vines, visit ancient villages and cycle abandoned train tracks – Viseu's surroundings are best explored slowly.

Spilling out from Viseu, verdant countryside, mountains and thermal springs promise an adventure. Whether you're tasting from ancient vines on the Dão Wine Route, hopping between historic villages, or cycling reclaimed train tracks on the Ecopista do Dão, you'll find nature on the city's doorstep.

Long before train tracks came and went, myriad people had traversed these lands, evidenced by Neolithic dolmens dotting the countryside. Walled villages, such as 13th-century Trancoso, and Almeida, a 17th-century star-shaped defensive town, tell the stories of invaders over the years. There was also a sizeable Jewish community living in the region due to the 15th-century Spanish expulsion, and Jewish quarters and symbols are visible in many medieval towns.

TOP TIP

Some vineyards and *quintas* (estates) require advanced booking for wine tastings. Be sure to have cash in case cards aren't accepted.

Ecopista do Dão

Discover Dão's Ancient Wines

TOURING THE VINES

Designated in 1908, the Dão Demarcated Region takes its name from the river and is best explored on one of five themed wine routes. Start your journey at Viseu's **Solar do Vinho do Dão** (closed Sunday, and also Monday in summer), where the wine certification takes place in a converted 16th-century palace. Although not a museum, it has a tasting room and detailed guides to the **Dão Wine Route**, which includes around 50 of the region's 160 producers. Modern vintners and ancient vines are both represented across a collection of vineyards, some with tasting rooms and restaurants, others with accommodation, and some which require pre-booking to visit.

Chão de São Francisco is one of the closest vineyards to Viseu, offering tours and tastings with reservations, while a few vineyards such as **Lusovini** (a 30-minute drive) open their tasting room daily for drop-ins. Expect a mix of reds, whites, sparkling and rosés from eight main grapes. Of the reds, dark Touriga Nacional, with an intense, complex flavour, and delicate Jaen, with hints of raspberries, stand out. From the whites, well-balanced and elegant Encruzado, and citrus-hued, floral Malvasia Fina, are flavoursome. September is one of the best times to visit as some vineyards – such as **Taboadella** or **Caminhos Cruzados** – allow you to join the harvest, perhaps even rolling up your trousers to crush the wines by foot in the most traditional vineyards.

Cycling Old Train Tracks

FROM CITY TO COUNTRYSIDE

When the Linha do Dão train line closed in 1988, tracks lay abandoned and stations fell into disrepair. Some 20 years later, a project to reconnect this old route, albeit by bike, was initiated, and the **Ecopista do Dão** was born. Railways have been concreted over and stations reinvented as cafes, creating a 47km trail traversing rivers, vineyards and villages between Viseu and Santa Comba Dão. Often promoted as a one-day ride, we recommend spreading it over two days, if time allows. Not only does this remove the pressure of completing the path by a specific time if using a transfer service, but you can slow down with detours to vineyards and villages. **Ninho D'Arara** in Tondela provides accommodation on the route, as do nearby towns.

Starting in Viseu means you'll (for the most part) have a gradual descent. Once you're outside the city limits, the route

AN INTRODUCTION TO DÃO WINE

Isabel Duarte, a Dão wine expert from the Solar do Vinho do Dão, shares how to introduce yourself to the region's wines.

The Dão's landscapes are unforgettable, with mesmerising mountains, vigorous rivers and imposing forests, but the most cherished memories come from visiting the *quintas* (estates). I remember being welcomed into homes and learning about the region while tasting wines by the fireplace and petting the house cat – to me, that experience characterises the people of the Dão. In Viseu, our welcome centre at the Solar do Vinho do Dão highlights various producers with tastings, information and wines at vineyard rates.

WHERE TO SLEEP IN A VINEYARD

Quinta da Fata
Just outside Nelas, this small, family-run vineyard has characterful antique-dotted rooms. **€€**

Quinta do Medronheiro
Just 15 minutes from Viseu is this delightful vine-shrouded stone accommodation with a pool and restaurant. **€€€**

Casa da Ínsua
An opulent baroque manor in Penalva do Castelo delivering a luxury five-star vineyard stay. **€€€**

BEST PASSADIÇOS NEAR VISEU

Passadiços (wooden walkway routes) provide picturesque strolls in the Portuguese countryside, with stairs on the steeper parts.

Passadiços do Távora
This relaxing 1.5km boardwalk tracks the river, with swimming stops at Praia Fluvial de Vila da Ponte.

Passadiços da Reserva Botânica do Cambarinho
Around 2km in length, this circular trail passes through the Cambarinho Botanical Reserve. In May and June, the rhododendron-ponticum blooms.

Passadiços do Pereiro Rio Seia
Less than an hour from Viseu, this 8.5km pedestrian and cycle trail links mills, bridges and viewpoints. Parts were damaged by the summer 2022 fires, with repair works planned.

RIBEIROANTONIO/SHUTTERSTOCK ©

Trancoso

has forest and mountain views, with eucalypts, olive trees and ferns decorating the trail – just don't expect much shade. The most beautiful parts are around **Tondela's vineyards**, followed by impressive rock formations and the Rio Dão's unofficial **river beaches**. Schedule a little time for **Santa Comba Dão**, a pretty town where three rivers converge, at the end of the ride. For food and rest stops, there are three cafes and restaurants spread over the first 30km.

Inside Medieval Walls

STORIED STONES AND STREETS

Medieval **Trancoso**, an hour by bus from Viseu, will transport you back through history, especially if you visit during June's **Feira Medieval**. Entering the walls, which are considerably intact, through the imposing Portas d'el Rei, a web of narrow cobbled streets, many framed by flowers, spills out before you. The well-preserved (and renovated) **Castelo** guards the far side of the town, and the **tower** (surviving since Moorish rule) promises far-reaching panoramas.

Home to a prominent Jewish community before the 1497 Portuguese expulsion, the old **Jewish Quarter** covers around a

WHERE TO EAT IN HISTORIC VILLAGES

Granitus
This no-fuss restaurant serves up hearty portions of traditional Portuguese dishes just outside Almeida's walls. €

Páteo do Castelo
Daytime-only terrace in Castelo Rodrigo for coffee and cakes with village and hinterland views. €

Dois Valles Wine & Bar
Wine shop with flavourful small plates on a quaint, quiet pedestrian street in Trancoso. €€

third of the town. Seek out **Casa do Gato Preto**, decorated with symbolic Jewish carvings, and visit the modern **Centro de Interpretação da Cultura Judaica**, dedicated to the 17th-century physician Isaac Cardoso, who was born here, practised in Spain and later took refuge in Verona. The space houses a recreated wooden synagogue, exhibits dedicated to the community's history, and a memorial to the town's 500-plus prisoners and victims of the Inquisition. Another of the city's legendary residents was Bandarra, a 16th-century shoemaker and fortune teller. While it's highly debated whether he descended from Jews, in 1541 he was tried by the Inquisition regardless. At **Casa do Bandarra**, a subtitled video shares more about his story.

If you visit during August, the **Feira de São Bartolomeu** (dating back to 1274) will be in full swing. The **Visigothic tombs** outside the walls are also worth visiting.

NEOLITHIC MEGALITHS

Evidence of life around Viseu stretches back thousands of years. For those with time and patience, there is an opportunity to visit some incredibly well-preserved megalithic tombs. **Dólmen de Antelas** (access arranged through the Câmara Municipal de Oliveira de Frades) is one of the most impressive on the peninsula, as the burial chamber remains intact. Inside, the pillars still display ancient black and red paintings. The **Anta do Repilau**, **Dolmen Cunha Baixa** and **Anta do Penedo** are not as well preserved, nor do they have internal illustrations. However, they have the bonus of not requiring pre-arranged access, and the ancient burial stones are mainly part of walking routes.

Hopping Between Historic Villages

CASTLE AND COUNTRYSIDE ROAD TRIP

Beyond Trancoso, six notable villages dot the *planalto* (plateau) between the Douro and the Spanish border. Best combined into a road trip, it would be a long rushed day to visit them all, taking around four hours total if looped from Trancoso. For a more in-depth exploration and to slow down, just as these sleepy settlements have, pick an overnight base halfway.

Start by travelling to **Pinhel**, among Portugal's oldest towns. It was a 13th-century stronghold, and is today sprinkled with Manueline architecture and an impressive castle. Next, continue to **Almeida**, one of the country's most important fortified towns, its star-shaped defensive walls having seen numerous battles over the centuries. The ruined medieval **Castelo Rodrigo** has a cistern and turreted walls to explore; the site is most enchanting when illuminated at night.

En route to **Marialva**, pause at the **Miradouro da Faia**, which extends over the Rio Côa, before exploring the tiny but hauntingly beautiful historic village. Mounted on a massif, this location has been inhabited since Lusitanian times, and the remains of the old fortress and the clifftop castle are impressive. In **Penedono**, the medieval crenellated castle is most camera-friendly, as are the picturesque stone streets and houses below. Lastly, **Sernancelhe**, surrounded by chestnut trees, boasts the only free-standing Romanesque statues in the country, which are housed inside the 12th-century church.

GETTING AROUND

A car (and designated driver) is the best way to explore the wine route, or book a tour to visit a certain number of vineyards. Trancoso is connected with Viseu by regular intercity buses booked through Rede Expressos, while visiting the other historical villages in a day is complicated on public transport. From Santa Comba Dão, at the end of the cycle route, there is only one early morning bus service (connecting at Vouzela) back to Viseu, which complicates the return from the ride. A taxi back (if you can find one with space for bikes) cost €33 at the time of research.

SERRA DA ESTRELA

Portugal's first and largest (891 sq km) protected park, the Parque Natural da Serra da Estrela, is a rugged land of oak and pine forests, boulder-littered plateaus and rivers flowing from their sources. Designated as a Unesco Global Geopark, thanks to the glaciers that shaped the landscape millions of years ago, its icy lagoons and imposing rock formations create a dramatic setting for hikers. Trails pass traditional shepherds' huts, flocks of sheep and river mills that once used to weave wool. Foxes, genets, eagles and falcons are found here, alongside bellflowers, junipers and endangered flora. Reaching mainland Portugal's highest peak, Torre (1993m), you'll find spellbinding panoramas year-round and a small set of winter ski runs.

Tragically, wildfires tore through 25% of the park in August 2022, and the damage assessment is ongoing. In September 2022, we witnessed top-canopy charring and extensive fire damage, but the main valley hikes and villages were as lush and impressive as before.

TOP TIP

The weather in the Serra da Estrela can be extreme. In winter, snow and ice can cause dangerous conditions on roads, while summer can bring occasional wildfires, so check warnings before hiking, which is best during spring and autumn. Download the GUIA – Estrela Geopark app for GPS location tracked trails.

MOUNTAIN GRUB

Amid the Serra da Estrela's cold winters, hearty, warming dishes are essential. *Feijoca* features Mantegias's highly regarded white beans, which are slow cooked in a flavoursome broth and topped with cuts of meat. *Cozido à Portuguesa* is a popular meat-heavy dish hailing from the Beiras, with blood sausage, bacon, beef, cabbage and potatoes overflowing from the plate. Cheese is also a big deal, and Queijo Serra da Estrela, a rich and intense sheep's-milk wheel, is among the country's most celebrated.

From the Top to the Valley

SUMMITS AND LONG-GONE GLACIERS

If you only have one day in the Serra da Estrela, the 17km **PR6 MTG** trail from the highest peak into a glacier-shaped valley delivers a good overview. Starting from **Torre** (via taxi or rideshare), mainland Portugal's highest peak – artificially boosted by a small turret – the trail begins with far-reaching panoramas. Following the sparsely coated, rocky land downwards, and soon you'll spot a couple of lakes sparkling in the distance before arriving at **Nossa Senhora da Boa Estrela**, a small sanctuary carved into the mountainside. Continuing, you'll reach a vast meadow, the **Nave de Santo António**, which leads into an area of shady trees. Beyond this wood, you'll join the road leading towards the towering **Cântaro Magro** rock formation. Pause at the **Covão d'Ametade** for a shaded picnic (don't rely on the tiny bar being open), poorly maintained toilets and the source of the Rio Zêzere, often dry in summer.

Further along the road, the descent into the **Zêzere Glacial Valley**, carved millions of years ago, begins. The route between the forested slopes mostly stays near the river, passing shepherds' huts and granite features – but don't expect much shade. A couple of kilometres before reaching Manteigas, there is a **thermal spa**, worth booking in advance for a rewarding treatment. An alternative is to start in Manteigas and just loop into the valley and back. Tourism offices provide maps for the countless other trails.

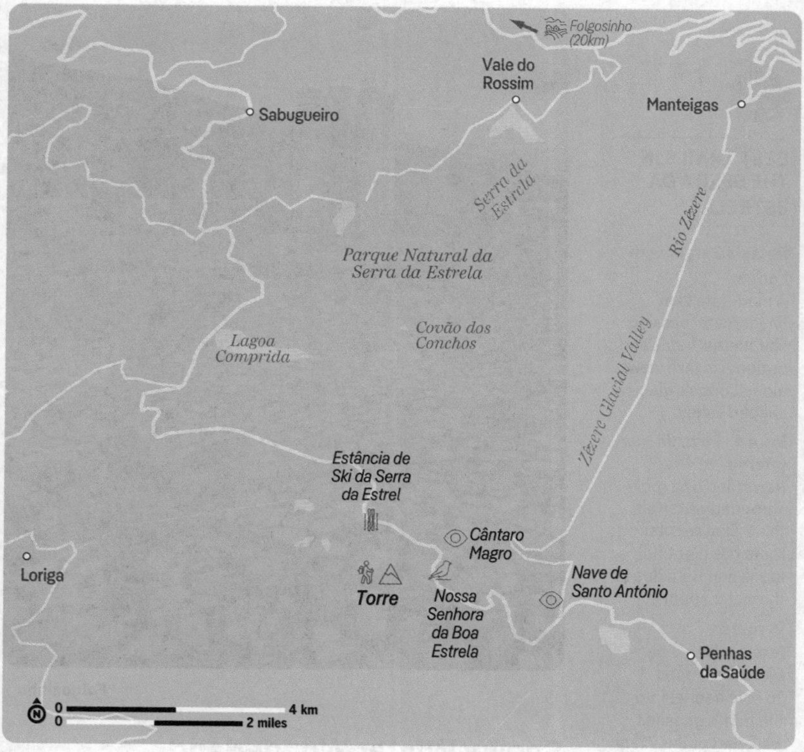

Folgosinho (20km)
Vale do Rossim
Sabugueiro
Manteigas
Serra da Estrela
Rio Zêzere
Parque Natural da Serra da Estrela
Covão dos Conchos
Lagoa Comprida
Zêzere Glacial Valley
Estância de Ski da Serra da Estrel
Cântaro Magro
Loriga
Torre
Nossa Senhora da Boa Estrela
Nave de Santo António
Penhas da Saúde
0 4 km
0 2 miles

Waterfalls, Lakes & River Beaches

COOLING DOWN

The Serra da Estrela can be a relentless place in summer when temperatures soar. But lakes and river beaches provide the chance to cool down. In , you can get out on the lake courtesy of Let's SUP, which offers rentals and tours, including wheelchair-adapted boards. For something more active, EntreSocalcos' canyoning trips from Loriga venture to scenic waterfall surrounds, with some abseiling. To relax by the water, head to the tiny natural pool of **Poço do Funil** or the circular spillway of **Covão dos Conchos**.

BEFORE YOU HIKE

In Seia (p296), the Serra da Estrela Interpretation Center (closed Monday) presents an interesting video overview alongside a geological exhibition.

WHERE TO STAY IN MANTEIGAS

Hotel da Vila
Modern, white, central hotel with a rooftop seating area and frosted glass bathrooms in the rooms. €

Casa do Comendador
Old, grand and creaky – this manor has a pool looking back on the village. €€

Casa das Obras
This luxury 18th-century home keeps true to its past with elegance and old-fashioned touches. €€

BEST TRAILS IN THE SERRA DA ESTRELA

Rota da Garganta de Loriga
A moderate 9km linear route, passing shepherds' herds and outlandish lake views along Loriga's glacier-shaped valley.

Rota do Poço do Inferno
Rewarded by a rock-shrouded waterfall, this 2.5km circular route has plentiful fauna and flora due to the water supply.

Percurso Interpretativo da Geodiversidade
To dive deeper into the park's geosites, walk part of this 72km interpretative trail, which tracks the geographical history that earned the Serra da Estrela its Unesco classification.

ALEXILENA/SHUTTERSTOCK ©

Folgosinho

Snowy Winter Wonderland

SLOPES AND SKIING

While the glaciers are long gone, snow still makes an annual appearance on the lofty Serra da Estrela peaks – it's usually reliable enough for skiing between January and March. The small **Estância de Ski da Serra da Estrela**, around Torre, has three lifts and mainly easy pistes. Concerns have been raised about the environmental consequences of skiing on these fragile lands, although studies are hard to find.

Portugal's Highest Village

CHEESE, WOOL AND PUPPIES

Sabugueiro, born from shepherds' huts, is just a short drive from Seia. If you want only a taster of the park's mountains

WHERE TO EAT IN THE SERRA DA ESTRELA

Central
Affordable *pratos do dia* (dishes of the day) and regional recipes with friendly service in Manteigas. €

Restaurante A Torre
This spacious ski-resort-style restaurant at the top of Portugal offers buffet lunches and snacks. €€

Varanda da Estrela
Rustic Penhas da Saúde dining room with local dishes such as wild boar with chestnuts. €€

and landscapes, the country's highest village, at 1050m, is a good pick. There's not much here, but the brief drive is scenic. The village is best known for its quality cheese, shops selling fleece and wool products and, sadly, the native Estrela mountain dogs peering from roadside cages – though thankfully, the cages are vacated on hotter days.

Village Road Trip

HIDDEN HAMLETS

In the north of the Serra da Estrela, you can combine two tiny tucked-away villages, 30 minutes apart, into a rural road trip. Medieval **Linhares da Beira** is one of the region's designated historic villages, and the imposing castle with panoramic vistas is the main draw. Near the stream, you can also see some of the stones from the old Roman road leading to Mérida. In **Folgosinho**, a tiny, circular turreted castle looks down on the village's cluster of orange-roofed houses from a rocky outcrop. There isn't much to do in either village, other than taking far too many photos, but that's very much the charm.

An Aerial Perspective

CLIMBING AND PARAGLIDING

There's no need to be jealous of the eagles and falcons flying above the Serra da Estrela, as a bird's-eye view of the park is possible. For some adrenaline, venture to medieval Linhares da Beira, regarded as one of the best paragliding sites in the country. It even hosts an annual competition. Clube Vertical, based slightly south in Sameiro, offers tandem flights and courses for those wishing to make the leap. For a less lofty perspective, companies such as Centro Montanha can get you kitted out with a helmet, rope and local guide for a rock climbing adventure inside the park.

BEST BASES IN THE SERRA DA ESTRELA

Manteigas
Well-developed town with the best choice of hotels and restaurants; it's reachable by public transport, with the Zêzere Glacial Valley nearby.

Penhas da Saúde
This wind-battered cluster of homes with a few hotels is ideal for lofty hikes, access to Torre, and the winter ski resort.

Loriga
Best known for its river beach, Loriga is a decent base for exploring the park's south, with a choice of accommodation and access to the Vale Glaciar de Loriga.

Sabugueiro
Portugal's highest village is just inside the park, with limited bus access from Seia. A small choice of hotels and restaurants.

GETTING AROUND

A car is essential to explore the park fully, even if some of the roads can be a bit challenging, especially in winter. Inside the park proper, there is no public transport. The municipal websites list taxi numbers, and Manteigas has a taxi stand that may have a vehicle waiting. A taxi from Manteigas to the top of Torre will cost around €25 one way – good if you plan to hike back to the village. Dedicated mountain-biking routes allow for two-wheeled exploration, and electric mountain bikes can be hired in Manteigas. To get into the park, Transdev runs a twice-daily weekday bus service from Guarda to Manteigas, and Auto Transportes de Fundao operates a route from Seia to Sabugueiro (schedule under revision at research time).

Beyond the Serra da Estrela

Serra da Estrela
Guarda
Seia
Belmonte

Hugging the edges of the Serra da Estrela, scenic soaring cities and towns keep a watchful eye on the lowlands.

Surrounding the Serra da Estrela, centuries-old settlements cling to the ridges and cascade down the edges of the mountains. From Guarda, a medieval stronghold and mainland Portugal's highest city, to Belmonte, a hilltop town home to the only Jewish community to survive the Inquisition years, stories line the cobbled streets. Popular as a less-rural base from which to explore the park, these outlying communities are filled with museums, galleries and cultural events, as well as traditions. The vastly different seasons will dictate your type of trip, with sweltering summers, and winters often delivering a layer of snow. This weather also creates the unique flavours of the Beira Interior's wines.

TOP TIP

The main cities and towns on the Serra's mountain edges all have regular public transport, unlike inside the park.

Sé, Guarda

City at the Top

UP TO THE MEDIEVAL CATHEDRAL IN GUARDA

Hitting a lofty 1056m, **Guarda**, a short drive northeast of the Serra, is Portugal's highest city. The fetching medieval **old town**, easily explored on foot, is a cultured side trip from the park. Crowning the city is the **Sé**, built between 1390 and the Manueline period. It's a hulking, mainly Gothic structure, and the exterior outshines the more modest interior. Surrounding the cathedral, historic and striking buildings flank **Praça Luís de Camões**, such as the 16th-century former town hall and an 18th-century manor house. Heading slightly down, walk around the **Old Jewish Quarter**, before continuing to the impressive 13th-century **defensive walls**. Request a QR code at the tourism office to access the **Torre dos Ferreiros** for some fine photo-vantage points.

Medieval Hilltop Town

SYNAGOGUE AND CASTLE

Casting an eye over fertile farmlands below, the medieval castle at **Belmonte** sits just above a small web of old town streets. The town, however, is mostly known for its Jewish community and resilient history. Under the Muslim rule of Portugal, estimates suggest that 10% of the population was Jewish. There was also a growing Jewish community following the Spanish expulsion of 1492. However, Portuguese royalty soon decreed forced Christian conversion or expulsion. This led to Belmonte becoming a secret refuge for a small group of Sephardic Jews, who orally passed on their traditions from the 15th century through until today. In town, you can visit a small **Jewish museum** and occasionally, on request, the **synagogue**.

Murals on the Mountains

CITY ROUTES OLD AND NEW

Clinging steeply to the Serra's eastern side, **Covilhã** is the place to head to learn about the region's 18th-century textile industry, with museums dedicated to wool making. The fully accessible **Museu da Covilhã** is also fantastic, tracking the region's history over multiple floors with sensory exhibits of artefacts, interactive displays and embossed-edge photos (translations are by QR code).

On the streets, an **Urban Art Trail** crosses the city, bringing together vibrant murals alongside aged buildings. They are produced mainly thanks to **WOOL**, the city's urban art festival. Ask the tourism office for the route that links the

BEST BASES AROUND THE SERRA DA ESTRELA

Guarda
Reasonable accommodation and quick access to the park, though there's not too much going on for the most significant nearby city.

Seia
Seia is only a short drive into the park via Sabugueiro, and has plenty of restaurants, accommodation and some informative museums.

Covilhã
Clinging to the park's eastern slopes, Covilhã has fascinating museums and well-developed tourism infrastructure.

Linhares de Beira
This historic village on the northern slopes has a few options for a rural stay on the park's outskirts; a reliable choice if you don't want a city.

WHERE TO HAVE LUNCH IN SEIA

Pastry Zé Manel
Quick service, decent coffee, snacks and cakes in a quaint tiled room or roadside. €

Mercado Municipal
Modern food hall with a few restaurants and a craft-beer bar. €

Museu do Pão
Enjoy the fantastic views from the city's bread museum with a filling Portuguese buffet. €€

25-plus pieces together. Daniela Guerreiro's student-depicting mural, Bordalo II's upcycled 3D owl installation, and the juxtaposition between the blue street art and blue-tiled Igreja de Santa Maria Maior are particularly noteworthy.

Seia: A Municipality of Museums

POWER, PLAYTHINGS AND PÃO

Set on the western edges of the Serra da Estrela, Seia's small aged centre is great for wandering, but the main reason to visit this municipality is the museums (all closed Monday). At the modern and interactive **Museu do Pão**, learn about Portugal's social and political history through bread. Similarly, the **Museu do Brinquedo** traces Portuguese toys through the ages, providing societal insight. For more context on the mountains, the short film at the **Serra da Estrela Interpretation Centre** will fill you in, while the **Natural Museum of Electricity**, a brief drive away, offers insight into one of the country's oldest hydroelectric power stations, inaugurated in 1909.

JEWRY ROUTE

Belmonte Jewish Museum (closed Monday) is a good starting point for learning about the region's Jewish history and collecting maps to follow the **Jewry Route**, which traces Portugal's Jewish communities around the Beiras. In **Covilhã**, symbols of the past can be spotted on doors, such as Porta do Sol. In **Guarda** the old Jewish quarter, close to Porta d'El-Rei, was once one of the country's most important – a small plaque highlights the Judiaria's location. Signs of 15th-century Jewry can still be seen in **Penamacor** around Rua de São Pedro, and in **Linhares da Beira** you can see a Manueline house that was once the synagogue.

Hiking to the Hidden Village

SCHIST FOREST BOLTHOLE

Tucked away in the **Serra do Açor**, an hour's cinematic drive from Torre, **Piódão** is a true bolthole. Isolated and without a formal road until the 1970s, this schist-and-slate village remains relatively unchanged today. It's a long, winding, narrow drive to get here, urging you to slow down and relish the forested scenery before the village, cascading down the terraced valley, comes into view. Being so remote, historical Piódão has avoided a starring role in the country's history, although it's believed to have been a favourite hideaway for fugitives. Amongst the dark-stone houses, the whitewashed and blue-detailed cylindrical buttresses of **Igreja de Nossa Senhora da Conceição** stand out.

The village is the star, but the surrounding verdant trails make for a flawless sequel, and a 10km up-and-down circular route (PR2 AGN) takes you on a journey through time. In **Foz d'Égua**, a rival to Piódão's charm, stone arches cross the river, and a suspension bridge hangs over the gorge, while at **Chãs d'Égua**, prehistoric rock art is the main draw. To fully immerse yourself on the trails, plan for a full day's outing, which is best avoided on the hottest days. If you stay the night in Piódão (there's a hotel and some of the stone houses are rentable), the dimly lit village under a starry sky becomes even more bewitching.

GETTING AROUND

All the main cities around the Serra da Estrela receive intercity buses booked through the Rede Expresso website (rede-expressos.pt) and supported by Transdev local routes. There are also a few local operators with seasonal timetables, so it's worth asking at the bus station if there are additional routes or times for your specific journey. Belmonte train station is a long walk from town, so opt for a bus, and Guarda's train station requires a sharp uphill climb, making the bus station more appealing.

MONSANTO

In 1938 Monsanto won the title of 'most Portuguese village' – yet it's anything but ordinary. Towering above the surrounding golden-hued plains, the historic hilltop settlement has finally rested its weary eyes after centuries of watching over the Spanish border for invasion, though the spellbinding panoramas remain just as timeless.

Defined by granite outcrops and mammoth boulders, the terrain was the architect of the village's design. Homes are wedged between, under and atop giant rocks, seemingly ready to crush the dwellings at any second. Steep cobbled streets squeeze through crevices climbing to long-abandoned castle ruins, where the Romans, Moors and, later, King Dom Sancho I left their fortified marks. Legend has it that when they were under siege from Romans, the villagers hurled their last calf over the walls, pretending they had an abundance of food, a tradition marked each 3 May by a festival and the tossing of baskets of flowers.

TOP TIP

Public transport to and around Monsanto is minimal, so a car is advisable if you plan to use the village as a base from which to explore Beira Baixa. Book accommodation in advance, as options are somewhat limited, and many are private home rentals without walk-up receptions.

Portugal's Most Unusual Village

CLIMBING TO THE RUINS

Monsanto's compact yet steep nature lends itself to slow rambling, with the seemingly precariously balanced granite boulders calling for countless photography stops en route. Starting at **Igreja Matriz de São Salvador**, where you'll enter the village proper, take yourself on a walking tour. Head towards **Torre de Lucano**, a clock tower topped with a replica of the 'most Portuguese village' award (a silver rooster), before looping around to **Portas de Santo António**, once part of the fortified walls. From here, walk back into the village via the tangle of cobbled streets, which gradually get narrower towards the **Gruta**, an old animal cave shelter you can enter. Across the street, the **Miradouro do Forno** has an excellent vista, including a red restaurant door framed by giant boulders below and the alarmingly placed Penedo do Pé Calvo rock above.

Starting the ascent up **Rua do Castelo**, you'll spot a house entirely covered by rock formations to one side, before the trail turns into a slight clamber to the **Castelo**, with incredible views accompanying you on the way. On reaching the open-air stone fortress, where wildflowers and winds have taken charge, the Portuguese and Spanish plains stretch before you, calling out for a camera. Walk around the castle to the Romanesque **Ruínas da Igreja de São Miguel** and nearby rock-carved tombs, before ambling down to the village from the other side.

ALDEIAS HISTÓRICAS

The Aldeias Históricas de Portugal (Historic Villages of Portugal) highlights 12 villages. Ranging from ruined castles on hilltops to schist villages hidden in forests, a 600km circular route (GR22) connects all their stories, from mountains to hinterlands, alongside the villages. By mountain bike, the 13 sectors make for an intense but rewarding two-week trip. On foot, the hikes between the villages are a gift to those seeking a car-free holiday, allowing the chance to visit harder-to-reach hamlets, although the trail provides little respite in the height of summer.

SIGHTS
1 Castelo
2 Gruta
3 Igreja Matriz de São Salvador
4 Miradouro do Forno
5 Portas de Santo António
6 Ruínas da Igreja de São Miguel
7 Torre de Lucano

EATING
8 Adega Típica O Cruzeiro
9 Petiscos & Granitos

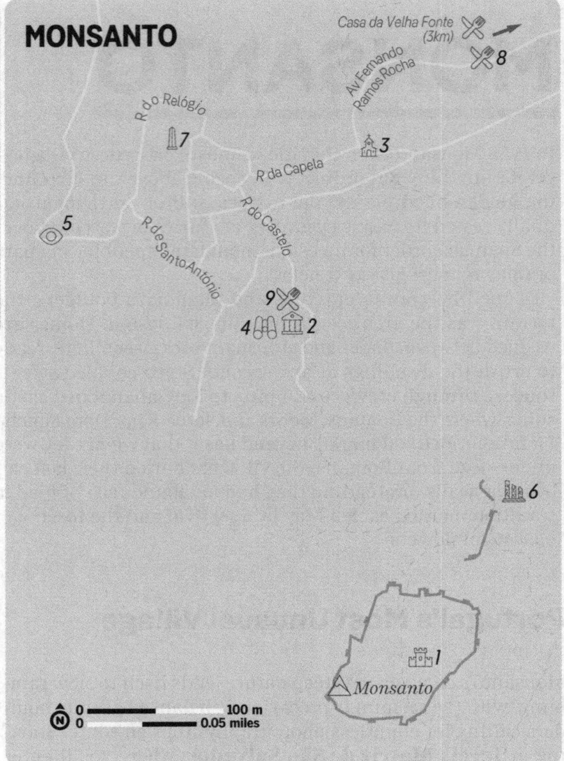

Ramble to Roman Reminders

A NEAR-ABANDONED WALLED VILLAGE

Sitting in the shadow of Monsanto, **Idanha-a-Velha** has a history is no less impressive. It's around a 9km downhill trek (but in the summer heat, a car is advisable) to this tiny walled village with under 100 residents. Founded as a Roman settlement in the 1st century BCE and later named Civitas Igaeditanorum, reminders of its origins remain, including a bridge and parts of thermal baths. The **cathedral** (originally 5th century) later served as a mosque before falling into ruins and being renovated in the 16th century by the Templars. Inside, you'll find remains of marble, frescoes and repurposed Roman columns.

WHERE TO EAT IN MONSANTO

Adega Típica O Cruzeiro
Landscape views paired with well-cooked Portuguese dishes compensate for the slightly bland decor. **€€**

Casa da Velha Fonte
Top-quality presentation and flavours in Idanha-a-Velha, often with local specialities such as rabbit. **€€**

Petiscos e Granitos
Sunset views from the giant boulder terrace and traditional meals. **€€**

Monsanto

The old mill turned **tourism office** (closed Monday, as is the cathedral) houses Latin-inscribed stones alongside a grand olive-oil press crafted from a giant tree trunk.

Artificial Lake Escapes

CALM WATERS WITH A FESTIVAL 'SECRET'

In these arid hinterlands, the **Barragem Marechal Carmona** is something of a surprising find. The artificial river lake, a dam of the Rio Ponsul, is an especially welcome sight in summer. With river beaches and shaded spots under the trees, it's perfect for cooling off, especially if you have your own kayak or SUP to enjoy the calm waters. Don't expect comfy roads or many facilities, but do expect a remote retreat – except for one week every other July, when **Boom Festival**, a celebration of psychedelic trance music, welcomes some 30,000 people to these shores.

WHY I LOVE MONSANTO

On my first visit, my guesthouse host had no change, offering that we share a beer (well, a couple) together instead. Much more valuable, both in monetary and memory terms, we got lost in conversation about village life. Around us, the sun glinted off granite rocks – glowing like they'd turned to lava – and I abandoned my sunset castle-hike plan as quickly as I extended my stay. Monsanto, to me, is about getting lost in time. The timelessness of the steep streets, the evening silence when day-trippers leave, the magic of finding little lanes wedged between boulders, and the joy of knowing this massif-mounted village can't really expand, thus remaining just as timeless whenever I return.

Daniel James Clarke

GETTING AROUND

Public transport to/from Monsanto is limited but not impossible on weekdays – although a day trip from Castelo Branco would require a return taxi. Idanha municipality (idanha.pt) buses travel between Castelo Branco and Idanha-a-Nova a few times each weekday. From there, you can connect to Monsanto on the once-daily (weekdays only) Transdev afternoon service – sadly, the Transdev return from Monsanto leaves early morning, making a day trip impossible without a taxi, but staying overnight allows for a magical sunset before a morning return. With just a few taxis in the area, it's advisable to call and book in advance, especially to avoid the strenuous return hike from Idanha-a-Velha. If you arrive by car, there is a small car park at Miradouro de Monsanto and further parking on the road (check signs).

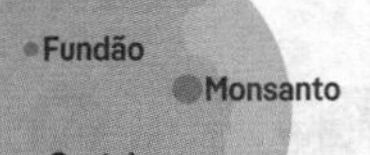

Beyond Monsanto

Hinterlands spill out from Monsanto towards historic stone villages, the museum-rich provincial capital and forested borderland parks.

Beira Baixa has seen its fair share of Portugal's history, with the marks of the past still visible. Trilobites (fossils) imprinted in rocks tell the area's ancient undersea story, while the ruins of a Templar castle nod to the Christian Reconquista. High on hilltops, defensive villages remind us of centuries of Spanish aggression, a far cry from today's calm farmlands and parched plains. Trails for hikers and cyclists provide an intimate exploration, leading through oak and olive trees toward forests and protected parks. Sweltering in summer, it's a region best toured in spring, when the land is less arid and small waterfalls, nesting birdlife, wider rivers and cherry blossoms brighten the landscape.

TOP TIP

Castelo Branco may be a more suitable base than Monsanto (especially if using public transport) to explore the surroundings.

Jardim do Paço Episcopal, Castelo Branco

Museums, Gardens & Castle Ruins

TOUR THE PROVINCIAL CAPITAL

Castelo Branco, the provincial capital of Beira Baixa, is a museum-filled city with a constantly growing cultural scene. Its artistic nature is discreetly entwined in the street's *calçadas* (traditional-style pavements) and not so discreetly in the bulky and modern **Centro de Cultura Contemporânea**. There are also significant cultural highlights, all sharing a part of the city's story.

Start at **Museu Francisco Tavares Proença Junior** (closed Monday) to gain an overview of local history through archaeological finds and the city's *colchas* – magnificently detailed, hand-embroidered bedclothes. Next door, the **Jardim do Paço Episcopal** provides a serene escape. Fountains and statues feature heavily in this perfectly manicured baroque garden, with the statues lining the stairs dedicated to kings and religious figures particularly intriguing. For more modern art, visit the **Museu Cargaleiro** (closed Monday), a two-building affair mainly focused on Portuguese-born Manuel Cargaleiro's finest ceramic and paintings.

At **Casa da Memória da Presença Judaica** (closed Monday), you'll learn the legacy of the Jewish community, which briefly grew substantially following the 15th-century Spanish expulsion. You can also follow a route to trace symbols of Sephardic Jews who called this city home. The **Castelo** is a reminder of the Templars' presence here, though if the city's name had you expecting a white castle, you'll be disappointed – it's not white or even much of a castle anymore, but the remains of the walls and turrets provide decent panoramas.

BEST RESTAURANTS IN CASTELO BRANCO

Piso Risco
A proper Portuguese restaurant with stews, soups and sardines. Expect generous portions and great prices. **€**

Restaurant Mãos de Horta
There's no menu at this trendy-but-historic restaurant with a courtyard; instead, a delicious daily vegetarian loaded plate is offered. **€€**

Palitão
A modern, stylish restaurant with traditional Portuguese dishes. The menu is varied, but the steaks are especially good quality. **€€**

Pessoa Wine Spot
Wine's the focus in this blue-hued space that spills out onto the street, but the cheeseboards and tapas are also decent. **€€**

Follow the Fossils

TRACKING THE PAST

The quaint village of **Penha Garcia**, 15 minutes east by car from Monsanto, is the starting point for the 3km circular **Rota dos Fósseis** trail. Setting off from the church, the route descends towards the river gorge with a small beach, cascade and a cluster of old mills, used as recently as the 1960s. Most interesting are the trilobites (extinct arthropods) that give the trail its name, and many of the finds are housed inside one of the schist buildings, where a guide will show you around if present. Regardless, you can spot ancient traces of marine life (this valley was once under the sea) on the quartzite rocks. Without a car, the GR-12 path (around three hours one way)

WHERE TO HAVE LUNCH IN FUNDÃO

Tasca da Estação
This busy cafe opposite the train station is renowned for its battered codfish sandwiches. **€**

Tertílias
In the shade of Parque das Tilias, this kiosk cafe serves coffee, cakes and snacks. **€**

Divino
Simple food cooked well, with burgers, pasta and local plates such as *bitoque* (steak). **€**

CHERRIES OF FUNDÃO

Fundão, a delightful small town worth a lunch stop, is the nucleus for the surrounding cherry farms – the municipality's most celebrated product. For around two weeks in spring (usually March or April), the surrounding orchards come alive with the pastel pinks of the cherry blossom, and the whole community comes out to celebrate. Hot-air balloon rides promise panoramic views above the trees, sweet cherries are devoured, and there is plenty of cherry liqueur to go around. In June, the **Festa da Cereja** continues the party with entertainment and tastings. Year-round, the **Casa da Cereja** in Alcongosta, housed in a converted primary school, provides insight into the region's beloved fruit.

JORGE ANASTACIO/SHUTTERSTOCK ©

Sortelha

connects Monsanto with Penha Garcia and continues to the thermal-spa town of Monfortinho.

Two-Wheel Tracks

VILLAGES AND VISTAS

Set in the **Serra da Gardunha**, a relatively small mountain range peaking at 1227m, the **Cyclin'Portugal Centre** is a hub for two-wheeled adventures around the park. Access to the routes is via the centre, which has high-pressure washing facilities, a tyre-inflation machine, GPS trails and a water source. From here, 250km of signposted trails of varying

WHERE TO COOL DOWN BEYOND MONSANTO

Piscinas Idanha A Nova
Municipal swimming pool (inside and outside) with toilet and changing facilities.

Fonte do Pego
Small natural pool with a waterfall (possibly dry in summer) and a wooden walkway.

Praia Fluvial de Quadrazais
You'll fine this summertime lake swimming spot on the edge of the Serra da Malcata.

difficulty spread outwards, including dedicated mountain-bike tracks inside the **Parque Do Convento**. The routes link together tiny villages (some schist, especially along the Rio Zêzere section), open plains, forest groves and lakes, with the chance to spot amphibians and small reptiles.

Trails along the Tejo

CROSS-BORDER RIVER PARK

To the east and south of Monsanto, the **Parque Natural do Tejo Internacional** straddles the border with Spain. Unnumbered roads cross what is one of Portugal's wildest lands, surrounding a 50km stretch of the Tagus, establishing the frontier. Rare birds such as black storks, royal eagles and Egyptian vultures are among the 150-plus species that call this area home, while dramatic canyons and slopes add to the scenery. Of the marked trails, the 11.5km **Rota dos Abutres** (Route of the Vultures), starting from the church in Salvaterra do Extremo, is the easiest to access. The route includes a bird observatory with views over neighbouring Spanish Extremadura, and passes the old watermills of the Rio Erjas. For more remote adventures, a guided off-road tour (or canoeing trip) is the best way to explore the park.

Historic Village-Hopping

MORE STORIED STORIES

In Monsanto's proximity, you'll find four more Aldeias Históricas de Portugal (Historic Villages of Portugal): Penha Garcia and Idanha-a-Velha, covered on Monsanto's trails; and Castelo Novo and Sortelha, which can be combined into a village-hopping road trip. Start in **Castelo Novo** (one-hour drive), which has medieval and Knights Templar roots, and is dotted with Manueline and baroque architectural remains. You can tour the castle's ruins. The **Museu do Queijo** (closed Monday) is an interesting pit stop before arriving at the medieval border town of **Sortelha**. The 13th-century rock castle and walls (parts of which were rebuilt later) make it one of the most photogenic historic villages. From Sortelha, **Castelo do Sabugal** is a short, worthwhile detour.

THE IBERIAN LYNX

Inside the **Reserva Natural da Serra da Malcata**, a less-visited border park, important conservation work has been quietly under way for the Iberian lynx, a wild and highly endangered big cat (usually slightly larger than a fox) endemic to Spain and Portugal. Tragically, it seemed extinction was inevitable for this species, and indeed the risk remains. However, due to a concentrated breeding and reintroduction programme, the wild population is very slowly increasing in the Serra da Malcata. Spotting one is highly unlikely, but the reserve near to Penamacor is a verdant land of vegetation and streams, and even without a sighting, the trails make for some peaceful rambling.

GETTING AROUND

With limited public transport, a car is essential to explore the natural parks around Monsanto. If you use Castelo Branco (which has good intercity train and bus connections) as a base, you will have more options. However, the bus network focuses on the towns inland from Castelo Branco, not the border regions. Fundão is served by trains and intercity buses, while Piódão currently only has a Transdev bus every Thursday, which requires a prior connection in Arganil – it's one of those places best visited by car, on a tour, or on a long hike.

BARMALINI/SHUTTERSTOCK ©

Vines in the Douro Valley (p323)

PORTO, THE DOURO & TRÁS-OS-MONTES

HISTORY AND WINE CULTURE

This complex region crosses the entire northern part of Portugal, blending tradition and innovation among vibrant urban centres, stunning farmland, remote villages and pristine wilderness.

For millennia, the mighty RioDouro invited the crossing and settlement of numerous communities along its snaking path, defining distinct regions with diverse and fascinating cultures.

Porto, the country's second-largest city, sits on the banks of the Douro's estuary. A liberal, progressive and ferociously independent city, ever proud of its roots, accent and culture. While its ancient old town is a centuries-old architectural paradise, its downtown is dotted with traditional commerce and an endless parade of restaurants.

Towards the east, the rugged Douro region shows us the meaning of hard work. Labour of hardship and dedication, breaking the bedrock and shaping the hills into astonishing sequences of terraces that define this wine region. Tending the vines under the sweltering heat of summer and the freezing winters to produce the nectar known as Port wine. The people of the Douro know that sacrifice and excellence live together in the astonishingly beautiful landscape they created.

Further northeast and cornered by Spain, Trás-os-Montes peeks behind the mountains. For centuries, the population lived isolated in a harsh wilderness and unforgiving climate. A different culture emerged, as did a singular personality. Independent and strong-minded, the *transmontanos* go about their lives with an innate respect for tradition, which they seek to preserve. These customs are distinct, deep-rooted and fascinating, nested in local celebrations, gastronomy and crafts.

THE MAIN AREAS

Find Your Way

This vast region spans five districts, making a 150km beeline through the north. The selected hubs will allow you to set up a base for building your vision of this incredibly diverse territory.

Porto, p310

The capital of the north is a historic spectacle, but exudes youthfulness with its artistic spirit, vibrant architecture and some of the country's best food.

Vila Real, p318

With open doors to the Douro wine region, you'll discover a hearty gastronomy, lush natural parks, curious villages and relaxing thermal springs.

Lamego, p326

On the southern bank of the Douro, Lamego attracts visitors with its historic centre, local gastronomic specialities, exceptional wineries and ancient wine villages.

CAR

Driving is the easiest way to get to know this region, including its many remote villages and parks, and to hop around the wineries scattered around the Douro Valley.

BUS

Buses are the best alternative to a car. The coverage here is comprehensive and will allow you to visit all the main hubs and smaller towns. Rede Expressos provides the most extensive network and connections, while FlixBus has buses to select primary and secondary towns.

TRAIN

Train is a convenient way to reach Porto from any main coastal city, including Lisbon. There's a slower line with stops along the Douro Valley in Régua, Tua and Pocinho. The MiraDouro train (p341) is one of the country's most scenic train rides.

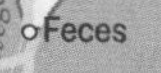

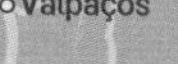

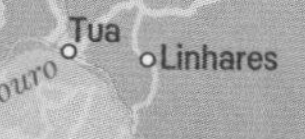

Bragança, p334

In the heart of Trás-os-Montes, you'll uncover ancient folk traditions, isolated community villages and the wilderness of Parque Natural de Montesinho.

Vila Nova de Foz Côa, p340

This archaeological paradise withholds the world's most extensive open-air prehistoric art gallery, along with scattered Roman ruins and some of the Douro's best vineyards.

Plan Your Time

To make the most of this region, start with a discovery of the historical urban hub of Porto and then venture inland, exploring the vineyards, the gorgeous towns and isolated villages, as well as the magnificent wilderness.

MATYAS REHAK/SHUTTERSTOCK ©

Mercado do Bolhao (p313), Porto

Pressed for Time

- Arrive in **Porto** (p310) and start by exploring the narrow medieval streets of the Ribeira and Sé neighbourhoods. Visit the vibrant **Mercado do Bolhão** (p313) and then grab lunch at **Cervejaria Gazela** (p313). During the afternoon, explore the monuments and streets around Clérigos and pop into a few of the fun stores dotted around downtown. If you have time, fit in a **museum** (p310).

- The next day explore **Vila Nova de Gaia** (p316) and its **port wine lodges** (p316). Return to Porto to cycle the waterfront and head out to **Matosinhos** (p317) to watch the sunset and enjoy a seafood dinner at **O Valentim** (p317).

Seasonal highlights

Douro and Trás-os-Montes are very hot during the summer, so spring is ideal for outdoor activities and autumn for wine programs. Porto is wonderful during spring, early summer and autumn.

JANUARY

The cold of winter is ideal for making smoked meats *(fumeiro)*, which is celebrated in several specialised fairs in Trás-os-Montes.

FEBRUARY

Spring brings ancient fertility rituals like the Carnaval de Podence and Carnaval de Lazarim.

MARCH

The spectacle of the almond trees in bloom besieges Portugal's biggest almond producer, Vila Nova de Foz Côa.

RUIBENTO/SHUTTERSTOCK ©, CARLOS GONZALEZ XIMENEZ/SHUTTERSTOCK ©, BRUNO ISMAEL SILVA ALVES/SHUTTERSTOCK ©

Five Days to Travel Around

- After two days in Porto, head east to **Vila Real** (p318) and visit the majestic **Casa de Mateus** (p318) before you grab lunch at **Casa de Pasto Chaxoila** (p320).

- Next is a quick stop in **Peso da Régua** (p323) and then a drive along the cinematic **EN222** (p331) road to Pinhão, stopping to admire the beautiful valley **viewpoints** (p331). Enjoy a **boat ride** (p323) on the Rio Douro to take in the spectacular scenery, or visit one of the area's **wineries** (p323).

- The following day drive to **Vila Nova de Foz Côa** (p340) and admire the rock art.

If You Have More Time

- Add another two days to travel to **Bragança** (p334) and explore the **historic centre** (p335) and the surrounding area. For lunch, head over to **Mirandela** (p339) and delight yourself with the artisanal smokehouse. Once satiated, it's time to explore the **Parque Natural de Montesinho** (p339) and its dozens of small villages.

- The next day drive to **Miranda do Douro** (p338) to experience the Mirandese culture and cuisine. Take advantage of the proximity to **Parque Natural do Douro Internacional** (p344) to marvel at the rocky escarpments.

JUNE
Porto commemorates the Festas de São João, a midsummer celebration filled with music, food, fireworks and plastic hammers.

SEPTEMBER
Wineries enter grape harvesting mode, often opening their doors for visitors to participate in the vintage.

OCTOBER
The village of Vilar de Perdizes hosts the annual Halloween party, the country's spookiest celebration.

NOVEMBER
The olives are ripe and ready to produce Trás-os-Montes olive oil, so join the manual harvest at a local farm.

PORTO

Porto is the city that gave Portugal its name and so much more. Its proximity to the river and the ocean made it an attractive place for various peoples to settle, including Celts, Iberians, Romans and Moors. The city grew from the ancient Morro da Sé hilltop neighbourhood to the riverfront neighbourhood of Ribeira and expanded in multiple waves.

The city's independent spirit acted as the country's ideological compass; it served as an incubator and stronghold for liberalism in the 1830s, ultimately defeating absolutism in the last civil war. For almost 900 years, it has maintained its status (and nickname) as the 'undefeated city', Invicta.

Today Porto is a remarkably dynamic city with its own artistic expression and architecture. Locals are known for their distinct accent and hospitality and for not mincing their words. The University of Porto, the largest in the country, contributes to perpetually renewing the city's youthful and rebellious spirit.

TOP TIP

Although hilly, Porto is preferably explored on foot. It is pretty rainy in the autumn and winter months, so the best time to enjoy the outdoors to the full is in spring and summer. Watch out for July and August when there will be a large concentration of tourists in the historic areas.

FESTAS DE SÃO JOÃO

The longest night in town on 23 June involves a lot of grilling, music and slamming heads with squeaky plastic hammers. The Festas de São João were once a pagan celebration of the summer solstice but were later rebranded as a religious festivity. Traditional events occur before and after, but the timeline for the night is simple. Grab a grilled sardine and a *caldo verde* (kale soup) and look for a place to watch the firework show by the river. For some, the night ends here; for others, it's just the beginning because the dancing, drinking and eating only end at sunrise.

On the Museum Trail

EXPLORING ART AND HISTORY

Visiting Porto's many museums is a great way to absorb the culture. The great masters of Renaissance and baroque painting can be seen at the impressive **Museu da Misericórdia do Porto** (MMIPO). For contemporary art, head to the groundbreaking **Serralves Museum** and allow timefor the beautiful gardens. For Portuguese arts and crafts, head to **Museu Nacional Soares dos Reis**, the country's first public museum, with unique pieces of jewellery, furniture and ceramics. Brush up on Porto's history at the 14th-century **Casa do Infante**, believed to be the birthplace of Henry the Navigator.

Porto of the Arts

SEEKING OUT CREATIVE HUBS

One of the city's most renowned artistic contributions is the Porto School, a contemporary architecture movement. Get to know the work of the movement's key architects, Souto Moura and Siza Vieira, by admiring their works at **Faculdade de Arquitectura**, **Casa das Artes** and the **Serralves Museum**. For a perfect cocktail of music, architecture and design, head up to **Casa da Música**. Architect Rem Koolhaas' diamond-shaped obsession has a spectacular acoustic performance and is the city's main concert hall. Porto was also home to some of the nation's greatest poets and novelists, like Sophia de Mello Breyner, Agustina Bessa Luís and Júlio Dinis.

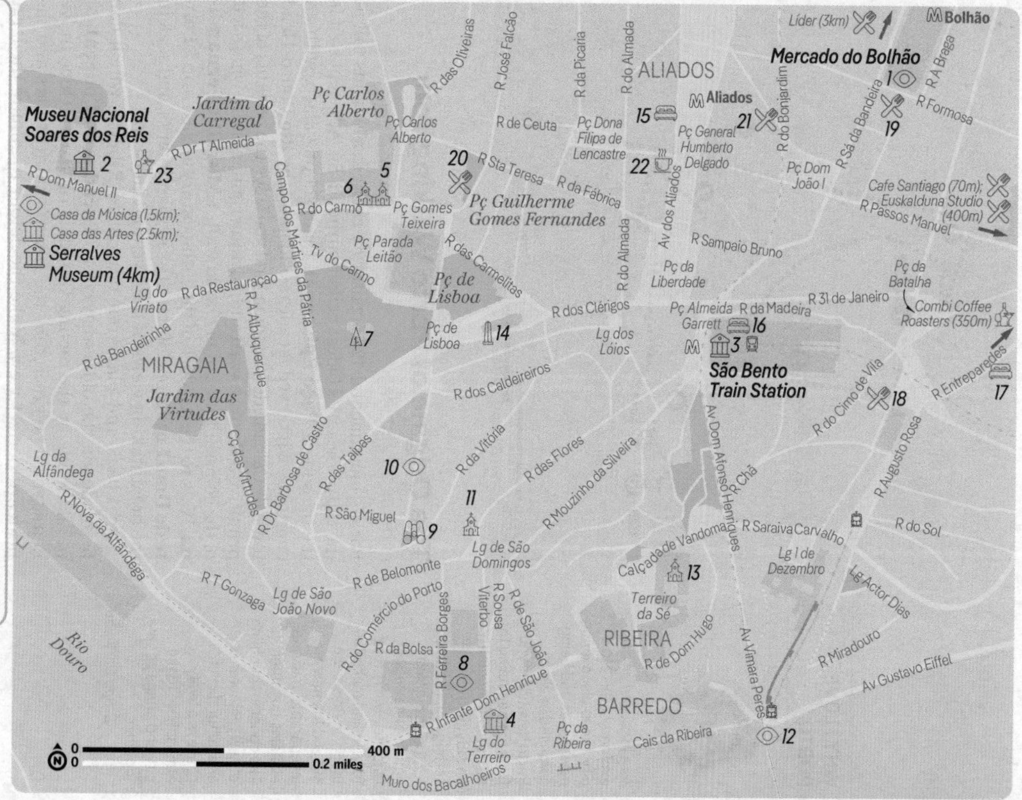

HIGHLIGHTS
1 Mercado do Bolhão
2 Museu Nacional Soares dos Reis
3 São Bento Train Station

SIGHTS
4 Casa do Infante
5 Igreja das Carmelitas
6 Igreja do Carmo
7 Jardim da Cordoaria
8 Jardim do Infante Dom Henrique
9 Miradouro da Vitória
10 Mosteiro de São Bento da Vitória
11 Museu da Misericórdia do Porto
12 Ponte de Dom Luís I
13 Sé do Porto
14 Torre dos Clérigos

SLEEPING
15 Le Monumental Palace
16 The Passenger Hostel
17 Torel Palace

EATING
18 Cervejaria Gazela
19 Confeitaria do Bolhão
20 Padaria Ribeiro
21 Pastelaria Moura

DRINKING & NIGHTLIFE
22 Café Guarany
23 Época

WHY I LOVE PORTO

As a local and an avid explorer of this old city, I keep discovering new places and being surprised by them. Porto bewitches you from the beginning for all its monumentality and idyllic riverside setting. But likewise for the easygoing nature of its people, who are always ready to help and make you laugh. In Porto, the old and the new are inseparable, and one explains the other. The constant bubbling of new restaurants and cultural events conveys a lively atmosphere to the city and brings people together.

Bruno Carvalho

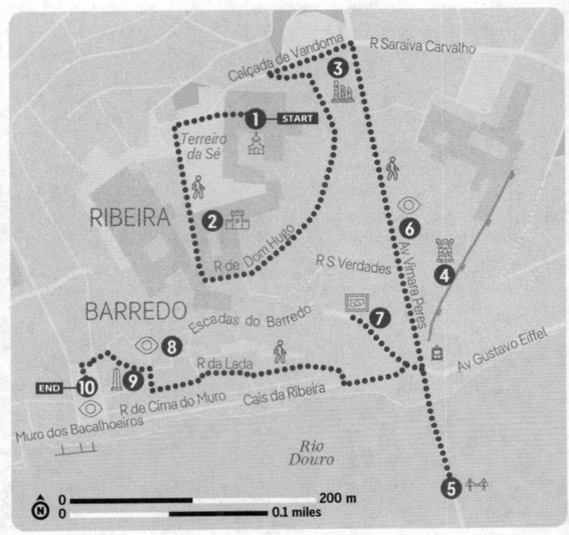

The Origins of Porto Walking Tour

FROM SÉ TO RIBEIRA

Porto's monumental 12th-century 1 **cathedral** stands tall at the top of the city's oldest neighbourhood, Sé. Adjacent to it is the baroque 2 **Paço Episcopal**, the bishop's palace, with an enormous windowed facade overlooking the Rio Douro. Head towards Calçada de Vandoma, and you'll see the remains of the primitive 3 **Roman wall** and, turning right, admire what's left of the colossal 10m-tall medieval wall, 4 **Muralha Fernandina**. Walk to the top deck of the 19th-century arched iron 5 **Ponte de Dom Luís I**, one of the city's key landmarks, and soak in the breathtaking views of the river and cityscape.

Turn back and plan your descent to Ribeira, which can be made via the old stairway of 6 **Escadas do Codeçal**, or in fast mode by the reeling Guindais funicular. Once in Ribeira, you'll be greeted by the Douro's shiny waters and the postcard-perfect view. Make the detour to admire the large 7 **Ribeira Negra tile mural** by Portuguese artist Júlio Resende, representing Ribeira's historically hard but beautiful life. In the backstreets, you'll find the fascinating medieval area and the old 8 **Barredo** neighbourhood. Get lost in the

WHERE TO STAY IN PORTO

Le Monumental Palace
A luxury five-star hotel with a splendid atmosphere, central location and a spa. **€€€**

Torel Palace
Literature-themed luxury boutique hotel in a 19th-century palace with stupendous ceilings. **€€€**

The Passenger Hostel
Sleep inside the magnificent São Bento train station, in comfortable and modern rooms or dorms. **€**

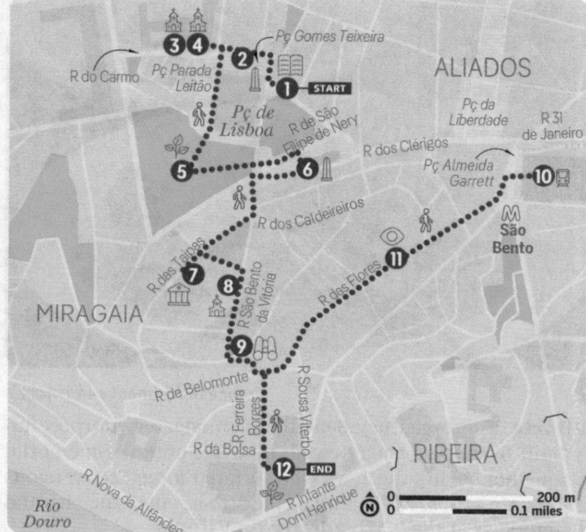

maze of narrow, shady streets, noticing the markings representing former floods and one of the city's oldest houses, the 13th-century **9 Torre do Barredo**. Find your way to the cheerful **10 Praça da Ribeira**, and then continue your discovery into the little alleyways.

Steps of History Walking Tour

MONUMENTAL SIGHTS

Start at the beautiful neo-Gothic **1 Livraria Lello bookstore**. Then head to the iconic **2 Lions' Fountain**, in front of the University of Porto's rectory. Your gaze will be captivated by the blue-tile facade on the flank of the rococo **3 Igreja do Carmo**, which shares walls with another church, the less impressive **4 Igreja dos Carmelitas Descalços**.

Continue to the **5 Jardim da Cordoaria**, known for its pathway of deformed plane trees, which are overlooked by the 76m-high **6 Torre dos Clérigos**, a baroque spectacle and national landmark. Crossing the street, admire the 17th-century former **7 Cadeia da Relação**, where famous writer Camilo Castelo Branco was once imprisoned. To the left, a narrow side street will lead to **8 Mosteiro de São Bento da**

BEST PLACES TO EAT IN PORTO

Euskalduna Studio
The ultimate avant-garde food experience showcasing Portuguese ingredients with a medley of techniques and influences. €€€

Cervejaria Gazela
A mandatory stop to try an irresistible local snack: the crispy, smoky and spicy *cachorrinho*. €

Café Santiago
The place to try *francesinha*, a sandwich on steroids that's love at first sight for meat lovers. €

Líder
Adventurous eaters can show their worth by tasting the local staple *tripas à moda do Porto*, a tripe and bean stew. €€

Mercado do Bolhão
No food journey would be complete without a visit to this spectacular, gigantic and lively market. €

WHERE TO HAVE A COFFEE IN PORTO

Cafe Guarany
A beautiful historical cafe established in 1933, famous for its coffee and *rabanada* with egg cream. **€**

Época
A small cafe obsessed with the quality of their products, also serving healthy vegetarian meals. **€**

Combi Coffee Roasters
This cafe slash coffee roaster ticks all the right boxes for coffee connoisseurs. **€**

FAITH & PAPERWORK

Every August since 1942, Foz do Douro has celebrated the remarkable **Cortejo de Traje de Papel**. This colourful festivity in honour of São Bartolomeu involves people of all walks of life, with several generations united by community spirit. The parade starts in the Sobreiras garden, crosses the main streets, and reaches its hiatus at Ourigo beach. At first, this looks like a simple march with music and people in costume representing scenes of Portuguese history and traditions. All is exposed when the euphoric paraders run into the ocean to receive their blessing. Their intricate outfits are revealed to be made of paper and dissolve into the tide; these crêpe paper costumes are carefully sewn together by local seamstresses and take months to prepare.

BONCHAN/SHUTTERSTOCK ©

***Francesinha* (meat sandwich)**

Vitória, a 16th-century Benedictine monastery purposefully built over the former Jewish quarter; note the memorial plaque honouring the Jews who suffered forced conversions in the late 1400s. At the end of the street, enjoy the city and water views at the **9 Miradouro da Vitória**.

Turn back and walk down Rua dos Clérigos to admire the 20,000 hand-painted tiles in the **10 São Bento train station**. Cross the street and walk along the busy pedestrianised **11 Rua das Flores** with its centuries-old manor homes until you reach the landscaped **12 Jardim do Infante Dom Henrique**.

The Delicious Side of Porto

FOOD EUPHORIA AND MARKET MADNESS

Porto is a gastronomical city by nature. The menus usually combine foods from different centuries, from heavy stews to finger-licking snacks. You can't ignore the city's most ancient and prized dish, *tripas à moda do Porto* (tripe stew), which gave the locals the nickname of *tripeiros* (tripe eaters). But there are other, more recent and easygoing dishes like the meat-monster sandwich, *francesinha*; the spicy hot-dog rendition dubbed *cachorrinho;* and the local codfish dishes like *bacalhau à Zé do Pipo* or *bacalhau à Gomes de Sá*. The best approach is to tackle a few *petiscos* (tapas) at a tavern, trying small portions of traditional dishes to determine your favourites. Then head out to the city's many restaurants and enjoy a full-size meal. Dessert time will come naturally, as it has become a local sport. Local pastries are everywhere, but the best sweets can be tried at select pastry shops.

GETTING AROUND

Walking is the best way to get around Porto's centre, although there are several steep hills. When it rains, be careful with the slippery *calçada portuguesa* (traditional pavements). The city centre is not bike-friendly due to traffic and hills, although the waterfront is flat. Also, avoid driving in the historical area at all costs. To reach other parts of Porto, use the metro system or STCP buses.

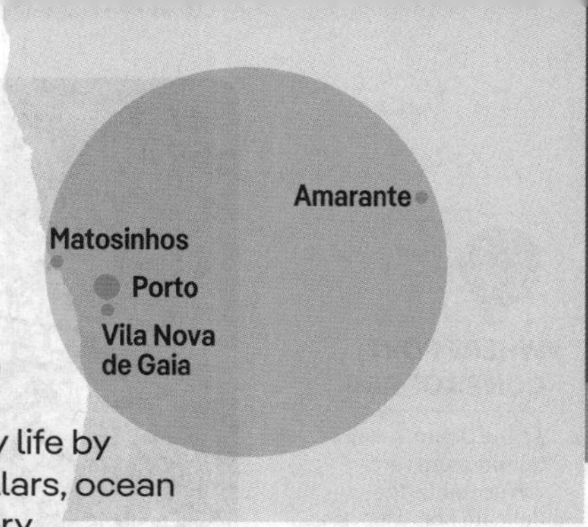

Amarante
Matosinhos
Porto
Vila Nova de Gaia

Beyond Porto

Take a break from Porto's busy city life by exploring towns featuring wine cellars, ocean views, delicious seafood and history.

While Porto is the epicentre of social, cultural and commercial life, its surroundings show a historical past rooted in specialised industries. The closest cities, Vila Nova de Gaia and Matosinhos, share a Roman past. The former has for centuries been shaped by the industrious port wine industry, which settled its wine cellars along the bank of the Douro. The latter is a historically seafaring city that once had a thriving canning industry but now is a bustling fishing and port city. Further along the coast, Vila do Conde was once home to the region's best shipbuilders and a large fishing community. Inland, toward the Douro, the city of Amarante was shaped by its religious importance and pilgrimages.

TOP TIP

All destinations can quickly be reached by bus or metro, except Amarante, which requires a long bus ride or drive.

Amarante (p317)

WHERE PORT COMES OF AGE

As the Douro Valley's temperatures are too unstable, the delicate port wine has for centuries been aged in the cellars of Vila Nova de Gaia, where it can lay quiet for just a couple of years or several decades, depending on the wine's style. The southern margin of the Douro is speckled with more than a dozen port wine cellars, all adorned with large signs you can easily read from Porto. Historically, producers settled in Gaia due to its cooler climate, better storage conditions, and exemption from paying taxes to the Bishop of Porto. Although the cellars' business is ageing wines, most of them are open to visits and tastings. **Poças**, one of the few Portuguese family-owned brands, provides an intimate visit.

HERACLES KRITIKOS/SHUTTERSTOCK ©

Vila Nova de Gaia

Vila Nova de Gaia

SPECTACULAR VIEWS AND LONG WALKS

A five-minute walk along the top deck of the Ponte de Dom Luís I will take you to Vila Nova de Gaia on the southern bank of the Douro. One of the highest points on the waterfront is the massive 16th-century monastery, **Mosteiro da Serra do Pilar**, with its elegant round church. Across from it, you'll find **Jardim do Morro**, a popular spot for exceptional sunset views and the entrance to the **cable car** that descends to the Cais de Gaia docks below. Take a deep breath and try to assimilate the colossal views over Porto. Alternatively, go down via the hilly Calçada da Serra and all the **port wine lodges** will parade in front of you.

If long walks are your thing, you can take the 6km trail west, where you'll pass the marina, the fishing town of **Afurada**, the **Cabedelo natural reserve** and the successive beaches of Gaia.

WHERE TO EAT IN VILA NOVA DE GAIA

Mario Luso
The short menu at this rustic restaurant includes simple dishes like roasted codfish, octopus and grilled meats. **€€**

Stramuntana
Trás-os-Montes' cuisine is reflected in this restaurant's cured meats, main dishes and desserts. **€€**

The Yeatman
This Michelin-starred restaurant creates exceptional Portuguese cuisine with a contemporary twist. **€€€**

The Seafaring City of Matosinhos

SURFING, CANNING AND SEAFOOD

Once a land of navigators and sea trade, the Atlantic-bathed city of Matosinhos, a 28-minute metro ride from Porto, is now a fishing and port-oriented city and a booming neighbourhood. The vast sandy shore of **Praia de Matosinhos** is ideal for those who love water sports or want to learn surfing and bodyboarding, always with sight of the gorgeous ribbon-shaped **Terminal de Cruzeiros de Leixões**. Nearby, alongside the fish auction market, you'll find one of the busiest restaurant areas in Porto. This is where Porto locals flock to eat fish and all sorts of seafood, and for good reason.

While there, don't skip a visit to the authentic and seafood-rich market, **Mercado Municipal de Matosinhos**. Also, revisit Matosinhos' 20th-century industrial past, once marked by the fishy aroma of dozens of fish canning factories, by making a tour of the 1920s artisanal cannery, **Conservas Pinhais**.

BEST PLACES TO EAT SEAFOOD IN MATOSINHOS

Esplanada Marisqueira A Antiga
A Matosinhos classic that features one of the most impressive arrays of fresh and seasonal shellfish. €€€

O Gaveto
An elegant yet family-style seafood restaurant with traditional seafood dishes and quality shellfish. €€

O Valentim
The day's catch is grilled on-site over flaming charcoal, steps away from the fish auction market. €€

The Sweets & Prayers of São Gonçalo

BETWEEN THE SACRED AND THE PROFANE

The small city of **Amarante** is a 50-minute drive east from Porto and is often the first oasis during a road trip to Douro. There's enough to entertain you in the beautiful historical centre for a few hours, but if you want to take things slower and explore beyond, you'll need half a day.

As you start walking around, your eyes will be held by the facade of the 16th-century **Igreja de São Gonçalo**. Inside, the wear on the saint's tomb results from his fame as a matchmaker and the hands who touch it wish for divine intervention. Proof of that is all the vendors outside the church selling an oddly phallic pastry. The former convent, adjacent to the church, is now the **Museu Amadeo de Souza-Cardoso**, dedicated to the modernist paintings of local artist Amadeo de Souza-Cardoso (1887–1918).

On the other side of the 18th-century **Ponte de São Gonçalo**, over the Rio Tâmega, you can't miss the local conventual pastries at **Confeitaria Lailai** or **Confeitaria da Ponte**.

PHALLIC PASTRIES?

Read about how Amarante's cheeky traditional sweets, *doces fálicos*, deemed too risqué by the Estado Novo regime, became a symbol of defiance (p490). Vila Real has a similar sweets tradition.

GETTING AROUND

Porto's metro system is the easiest way to get to Vila Nova de Gaia and Matosinhos. Matosinhos can also be reached by taking the slower STCP 500 bus, but the double-decker is worth taking for the views of the waterfront. Rodonorte and Rede Expressos have direct buses to Amarante several times a day, which take around 35 to 50 minutes.

VILA REAL

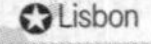

Vila Real lies on top of the cliffs of the Rio Corgo, surrounded by nature and overlooking the mountains. Moors, Celts, Barbarians and Romans all passed through these lands, but the area was sparsely populated until the 12th century. By then, the kings had made efforts to reorganise the city and settle the population.

The medieval walls didn't last until today, nor did Vila Real erect majestic sanctuaries as its neighbours did. Still, the city preserves a series of monuments and ruins from its foundation, as well as one of the most spectacular baroque buildings in the country.

The city also lies within the sphere of influence and innovation of the University of Douro and Trás-os-Montes. The university brings youth, progress and innovation to the local wine industry, a pivotal matter for the region, considering the pressing challenges of the future, such as the effects of climate change on winemaking.

TOP TIP

Vila Real's centre is small and relatively flat, making it easy to walk around. You can take the Corgo walkway for a semi-wild walk, and the botanical garden is just across the river. Be prepared for low temperatures and occasional snowfall if you visit during the winter.

BEST PLACES TO SNACK IN VILA REAL

Casa Lapão
An unmissable pastry shop to try an assortment of expertly made regional and conventual sweets.

Pastelaria Gomes
Order the local speciality, *covilhete*, a delicate and flaky meat pie, best eaten when warm.

Casa das Cristas
This pastry shop is celebrated for the rooster crest-shaped conventual sweet, *crista de galo*.

Iconic Casa de Mateus

BAROQUE APOTHEOSIS

This dazzling spectacle of baroque architecture seems almost too perfect to be true: 18th-century **Casa de Mateus** is the opus magnum of this style in Northern Portugal. It is believed to have been designed by the Italian architect Nicolau Nasoni.

Once inside the palace, you'll probably feel slightly crushed by the dramatic ceiling in the lobby, as intended by design. Moving on, you'll sense the careful preservation and selection of furniture that makes this palace feel lived in. When outside, take a relaxed stroll through the delightful gardens, walking along the camellia garden, the cedar tunnel, the boxwood hedges and the ponds.

Contrary to popular belief, it isn't here that the globally famous Mateus rosé wine is produced, even though it uses the manor's image. Casa de Mateus does, however, make its own wines, which are available for tasting. During the summer, evenings are often dedicated to classical music concerts. The palace is only a short bus or car ride away from Vila Real.

Meaty Meals in Vila Real

COMFORT FOOD AND CHEEKY SWEETS

The gastronomy of Vila Real is generous, comforting and straightforward. You can first focus on the city's renowned *covilhetes* (crispy meat pies), which are hard to find elsewhere.

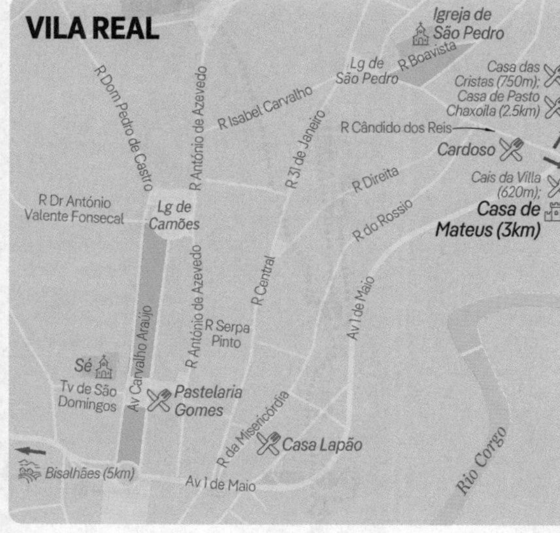

But soon, your appetite will be calling for more, and you'll have to turn to the heavy artillery.

The *transmontanos* have a saying that explains why meat is usually the protein of choice: 'fish don't pull wagons'. Local restaurants deliver succulent *cabrito assado* (roast goatling), *tripas aos molhos* (stewed and stuffed rolled tripe) or the well-known *posta à Barrosã*, an absolute must for all steak lovers. Remember to side your meal with an elegant Douro wine, or discover the Trás-os-Montes wine region, known for smooth, floral white wines and slightly astringent and fruity red wines.

Vila Real also has peculiar and delicious examples of conventual pastry, such as the *cristas do galo, pastéis de Santa Clara* and *tigelinhas de laranja* or the mischievous and seasonal *ganchas* and *pitos de Santa Luzi*a. All can be found in speciality pastry shops in the city centre.

Be sure to investigate the **Tabernas do Alto Tâmega** project, which unveils the taverns scattered through the city and the surrounding regions. This project aims to reveal the intimate relationship between the food and the people behind it, leading you on a curious journey, as sometimes the taverns are inside local family homes.

THE CITY'S EDEN

A quick 12-minute walk from the centre of Vila Real will take you to the **Jardim Botânico da Universidade de Trás-os-Montes e Alto Douro**, one of the biggest of its kind in Europe. On the 80 hectares of land of this living museum, you can find over 1000 species from all over the world as well as common and rare species that are endemic to Portugal.

WHERE TO STAY IN VILA REAL

Casa Agrícola da Levada
This self-proclaimed eco-village provides comfortable and sustainable stays within nature. **€€**

Borralha Hotel
Fully relax at the hotel's spa and pool, and enjoy a delicious meal at the restaurant. **€€**

Douro Village Hostel
A practical and friendly hostel conveniently located in an old townhouse in the city centre. **€**

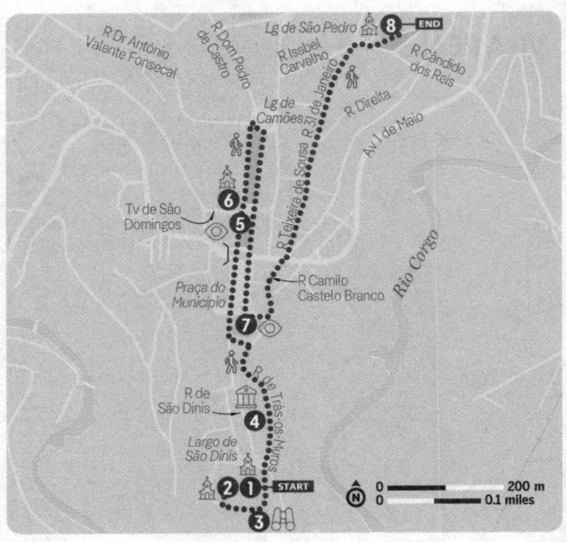

THE BLACK POTTERY OF BISALHÃES

The little village of Bisalhães, 40 minutes southwest from Vila Real by bus, is on the map of Portuguese crafts for its mastery of the art of making black pottery, primarily for decoration and cookware. The singularity of *olaria de Bisalhães* led to its classification as Intangible Heritage by Unesco, a title that has helped keep this craft alive. This labour-intensive pottery takes several steps, starting with making the clay, the piece's moulding and embellishment, and, finally, the baking process. The clay baking takes place in large open pits, where carqueja, broom and pine needles are burned and then smothered in soil. The smoke gives the clay its characteristic black tone and shine.

Foundations & Celebrations of Vila Real Walking Tour

RUINS AND RISKY DANCING

Squeezed between the Rio Cabril and the high escarpment of the Rio Corgo stands Vila Real, founded in the late 13th century by King Dinis.

Start your journey at the city's small foundational nucleus formed by the Romanesque church **1 Igreja de São Dinis** and the medieval funerary chapel, **2 Capela de São Brás**, surrounded by a cemetery. The **3 Miradouro da Vila Velha** will reward you with views of the area's surrounding mountains. The archaeological findings of the modern museum **4 Museu da Vila Velha** are just a few steps away.

Head towards **5 Avenida do Carvalho Araújo**, a central point that will lead to the newer part of town. Right at its start, you'll face the **6 City Hall**, which incorporates pieces from the former 16th-century Convento de São Francisco. A few steps up, to your left, you'll find **7 Casa de Diogo Cão**, a 14th-century stone house where the navigator Diogo Cão is believed to have been born. Further along, the avenue is home

WHERE TO EAT IN VILA REAL

Casa de Pasto Chaxoila
A local classic preparing delicious regional dishes, including the famed stewed rolled tripe with herbs. €€

Cais da Villa
This old railway warehouse hides an innovative restaurant based on regional ingredients and recipes. €€€

Cardoso
This local institution is famous for its *francesinha* and has other snacks and daily specials. €

Igreja de São Pedro

to one of the area's oldest monuments, the 15th-century granite **8 Sé**, but beware, for it is not fully visible from the street.

Take a detour to observe **9 Capela Nova**, a baroque church attributed to Nicolau Nasoni. Continue up Rua 31 de Janeiro until you find the austere facade of **10 Igreja de São Pedro**, which doesn't anticipate the incredible ceiling and altar. Continue to the **11 Mercado Municipal de Vila Real** to stock up on local specialities. Return to the main avenue for a well-deserved rest and a crispy *covilhete* (meat pie) at **12 Pastelaria Gomes** (p318).

ANCIENT COURTSHIP TRADITIONS

The history of Portuguese sweet-making has some unexpected twists. This includes an array of sexually inspired sweets associated with age-old traditions. On 13 December every year, the girls of Vila Real engage in an ancient courtship ritual. They will offer their boyfriend a *pito de Santa Luzia* (the name is suspiciously cheeky), a sweet pumpkin filled-pastry. This sweet can be enjoyed all year, despite the ceremony. On 3 February, the boys will get even. They give their girlfriends a *gancha*, a phallic caramel candy cane representing the staff of St Brás that, as expected, also withholds a sexual connotation. These canes are made for the event by Casa Lapão (p318) and also families around the old chapel of São João Esquecido.

GETTING AROUND

Vila Real's historic centre is small and easy to get around on foot. There are some hills, but you won't need to catch your breath. You can use Urbanos Vila Real buses to cover distances.

A 13-minute bus ride using Rodonorte will take you to Casa de Mateus. If you're driving, remember that most parking in the centre is metered.

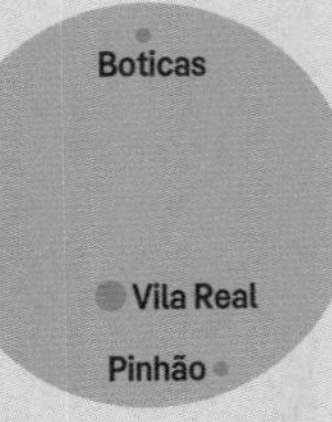

Beyond Vila Real

Take a tour through the diverse customs and landscapes of the Douro's winegrowing region and the distinct villages of Trás-os-Montes.

The mountains drawn along the horizon of Vila Real city have contributed dramatically to the region's climate, wild nature and traditions that stretch north from the Rio Douro to the isolated border with Spain. The whole territory is prolific in human-made and natural attractions. At its northernmost end, the area is dominated by wild nature and hot-water springs that have lured those seeking wellness since the Roman era. Behind the mountains, pots are stirred over the fire with delicious Barrosã recipes, and meats hang out to cure in smoke. Everything changes on the southern border, where the now placid Douro and the vineyard terraces take over the landscape, softening the centuries of challenging past.

TOP TIP

This region is plentiful with things to do and see, although early autumn brings the bonus of wine harvest activities.

Douro wine region

BARMALINI/SHUTTERSTOCK ©

Doorway to the Douro Wine Region

RIVERSIDE WINERIES, MUSEUMS AND VIEWPOINTS

Drive 45 minutes to **Mesão Frio** village and you'll find the doorway to the Douro wine region, the demarcated area for the production of port wine and DOC Douro wines. The village's highest point, the 145m-high **Miradouro do Imaginário**, was built in honour of the parish's *rabelo* boat builders and crews. Since the village and its well-kept manor houses are off the fastest route from Porto, it's less crowded than other sites. Following the river on the left bank for 25 minutes will bring the sight of three bridges, signalling the city of **Peso da Régua**. The excellent **Museu do Douro** showcases the region's history surrounding wine, from archaeological findings to the present day. For some river intimacy, hop on a cruise.

A further 30-minute drive leads to **Pinhão**. Those who arrive by train are greeted by a tile panorama, a warm-up for what's to come. Some of the most remarkable *quintas* (estates)are within walking distance from the station. Cross the Gustave Eiffel–designed bridge to **São João da Pesqueira** (p345) and pause at the 550m-high viewpoint at **Quinta das Carvalhas** for a hypnotic view.

SAIL THE RIO DOURO

From Pinhão, Peso da Régua or Tua, you can take a boat trip along the Rio Douro, slowly navigating the twists and turns for a whole new perspective. Among the steep escarpments and the sloping hills, you will find solitary *quintas* (estates) scattered throughout a geometric labyrinth of vines. Boat rides can range from 20 minutes to three hours (round trip). Choose a smaller boat company for a more intimate experience and to gain a deeper understanding of the valley's flora and fauna, or for a more comprehensive experience of the Douro, it is worth sailing farther away.

Winemaker for a Day

JOIN THE PURPLE FEET CLUB

The harvest, which usually happens between September and October, is the culmination of an entire year's work. It's the busiest time of the year in the vineyards, with all hands on deck, running against time to ensure the grapes don't stay too long in the heat. The work starts right after sunrise, with the pickers filling their buckets and taking advantage of the morning's cold. The grapes are eventually taken to the *adega* (winery) to initiate the maceration, a process now fully automated at most wineries. Some *quintas*, however, still have traditional foot treading, which comes with folk music and dancing. You can often participate in the different stages of the harvest, from picking the grapes to the famous *mata bicho* (snack break) and traditional lunch, but reservations are essential.

Portugal's Smallest Natural Park

OAK FORESTS, VILLAGES AND WATERFALLS

A 15-minute drive north of Vila Real is the 72-sq-km **Parque Natural do Alvão**. Excellent hiking opportunities are possible along the park's many trails, passing by shady native

WHERE TO EAT IN PINHÃO

Bomfim 1896
Local comfort food created by a Michelin-starred chef in the charming Quinta do Bomfim. **€€€**

Veladouro
Excellent quality grilled fish and meat dishes and a good wine selection, right by the waterfront. **€€**

Cozinha da Clara
Modern renditions of regional cuisine on a beautiful terrace overlooking the river. **€€€**

INTRODUCING THE MOSCATEL DO DOURO

The sweet and unctuous Moscatel wines are made in several European countries, always using muscat grapes. In Portugal, Moscatel is a popular fortified wine that is traditionally produced in the Peninsula of Setúbal and the Douro. Here most production is based in the towns of Favaios and Alijó. The Moscatel do Douro DOP is exclusively made using the fragrant Moscatel Galego Branco grape variety, producing complex wines that must age for at least 18 months in wood. Some producers will let it age 10 or 20 years in wood, producing exceptional wines. The wine has sweet, citrusy and nutty flavours with a floral aroma.

LUIS CARLOS CARVALHO/GETTY IMAGES ©

Fisgas de Ermelo

oak forests and discovering the historic villages of Ermelo, Barreiro and Lamas de Ôl. The park is also home to the Iberian wolf, Eurasian eagle owl, otters and wild goats, who share their habitat with the local Maronesa cows. The park's main attraction, however, is the 300m jaw-dropping waterfall **Fisgas de Ermelo**, where the pristine mountain water forms small lagoons. Try the 13.3km Barragens–Barreiro–Lamas de Ôl loop or the challenging but rewarding 12.4km trail leading to the waterfall.

The Villages of Wine & Bread

QUIET CHARM, MOSCATEL AND BREAD

On the northern side of the Douro Valley lie two wine villages that are part of the Aldeias Vinhateiras do Douro, a group of six historical wine villages.

A 30-minute drive will take you to **Provesende** in Sabrosa. This rural wine village was once the most prominent in the region, reaching its viticultural heyday in the 18th century. In the late 1800s, Provesende was home to the first grafter school to fight the phylloxera plague that was annihilating the

WHERE TO EAT IN BOTICAS

Taberna Ti João
Carefully prepared regional recipes that follow the seasons, with a highlight the freshly fished trout. €€

Casa de Vilar
Excellent home-cooked meals with mastery of the grill. Try the seasonal wild mushrooms, when available. €

Restaurante Martinho
A humble restaurant focused on *pregos*, simple but delicious buns with grilled Barrosã steak. €

Douro's vineyards. Stroll the charming village's quiet, well-preserved streets, filled with opulent manor houses.

A further 30-minute drive from Provesende leads to the wine village of **Favaios**. Famous for more than just port wine, the **Adega Cooperativa de Favaios** also produces the popular Moscatel wine. Book a visit to its cellars and have a proper Moscatel tasting. If you're feeling peckish, stop at **Padaria da Manuela Barriguda**, where the artisanal bread is baked in huge wood-fired ovens. For more on the local history of these foodstuffs, visit the **Museu do Pão e Vinho**.

THE WINE OF THE DEAD

Although the name may sound intimidating, *vinho dos mortos* (wine of the dead) is one of Boticas' most cherished products. The origin of this wine is believed to have occurred during the second French invasion in 1808. Upon the attack, the people of Boticas hurried to hide their belongings in unlikely places. The wine bottles were buried in the ground of the wine cellars, and there they remained until their rightful owners returned. Afraid that it would be spoiled, they hurried to taste it, only to find that it had become lighter in colour, low in alcohol and slightly fizzy. The locals enjoyed the accidental result so much that the tradition of burying wine in Boticas lives to this day.

The Fertile Lands of Barroso

FOOD, FARMING AND TROUT FISHING

The unforgiving climate and rugged terrain of the Barroso, encompassing Boticas and Montalegre, are harnessed by the resourceful inhabitants, who make the most of the land's spoils. A 50-minute drive will lead you to the little town of **Boticas**, known for flavourful *fumeiro* (smoked meats) and traditional Barrosã recipes prepared with local ingredients. When travelling north, this is a great gastronomical detour. In town, remember to visit **Casa das Artes Nadir Afonso**, home to many works of the imaginative modernist painter.

The agriculture of the Barroso region is classified as a Globally Important Agricultural Heritage System by FAO. Special focus goes to the village of **Vilarinho Seco**, where the entire community works together to complete agricultural tasks. Teams are formed for chores such as ploughing the land, tending to the Barrosã cattle or collecting grains. There are also several communal spaces like the bread oven or the granary.

A Thermal Escape

HOT WATER AND WELLNESS

The healing thermal waters of the city of **Chaves**, 50 minute' drive from Vila Real, were no mystery to the Romans, who founded the city of Aquae Flaviae here. Today you can pop in for a soothing session at **Termas de Chaves**, where the thermal water rises to the surface at a steamy 76 degrees C. It's believed that these mineralised, carbonated and sodium-bicarbonate-rich waters have many health benefits.

The well-kept historic centre is also worth a look, including the medieval Chaves Castle and the baroque Igreja da Misericórdia with its blue-tile interior. Before you leave, try a *pastel de Chaves*, a flaky pastry filled with veal, at **Pastelaria Maria**.

GETTING AROUND

A car is your best bet in this area, especially for Boticas. However, daily Rodonorte buses depart Vila Rea for Chaves (two hours) and Ovnitur services head to Peso da Régua (25 minutes) several times daily. Reaching Pinhão by bus will require a stopover and may take 1½ hours.

LAMEGO

Lamego is an ancient city, known to have been inhabited by the Ligures and Turdli tribes. The Romans settled in the 1st century CE, and the city was later occupied by the Celts, Visigoths and Suebi. Centuries before Portugal's existence, Lamego was persistently on the battlefield, alternating hands between Moors and Christians. In the early 12th century, Afonso Henriques' grandfather reconquered it permanently for the latter. Decades later, Afonso Henriques was proclaimed the first king of Portugal in the Cortes of Lamego.

Religion had a dominant and central role in the city, as it was one of the country's first dioceses. This is evident when observing the extraordinary religious buildings built over the centuries.

Lamego is also known nationwide for its gastronomy and the incredible and singular wine regions within its boundaries, Douro and Távora-Varosa. The Rio Douro, surrounded by immense terraced vineyards, is one of the region's most distinctive landscapes.

TOP TIP

Late August will be the time to participate in local religious and musical celebrations.

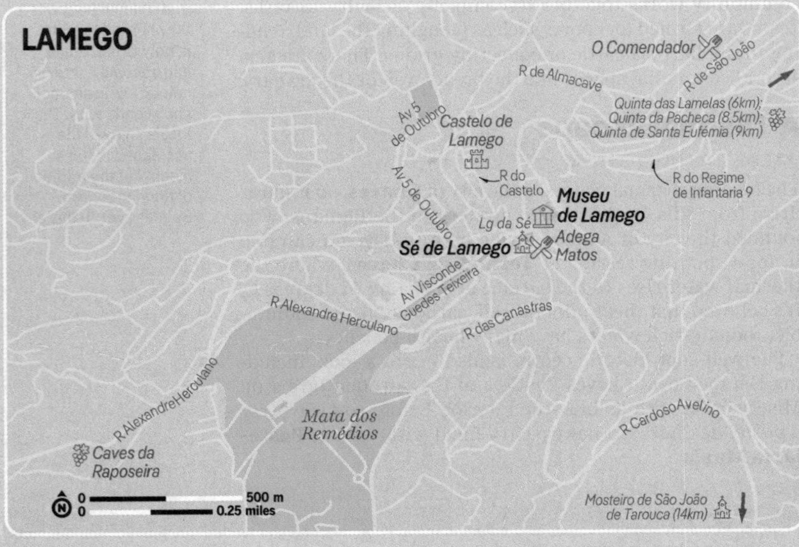

Sé de Lamego

SERGIO AZENHA/ALAMY STOCK PHOTO ©

Lamego's Historic Centre

EXPLORING CASTLES AND DIVINE STAIRWAYS

The city of Lamego constantly tests your stamina, as the reward of fully exploring the main points of interest usually comes after defeating a few elevations. But if you focus on the flat area first, you'll get a glimpse of the castle's tower guarding the city atop a hill. Walk through the Gothic entrance of the **Sé de Lamego** to discover the fresco paintings on the ceiling and the exuberant gilded woodwork that will make you feel small.

The main avenue, **Avenida Dr Alfredo Sousa**, is positioned in a way that will make you stare bottom to top at the majestic 686-step baroque stairway, richly ornate with blue tilework statues, fountains and chapels, as if inviting you to keep going. At the top rises the monumental facade of the

BEST RESTAURANTS IN LAMEGO

O Comendador
This elegant hotel restaurant offers a lovely view over the river and vineyards. The small menu changes in favour of the season and includes carefully prepared regional dishes as well as vegetarian options. €€

Adega Matos
You'll want stretchy pants for this one. Located right in the city's centre, this super-casual restaurant serves local products with pride. The menu has broader options for meat dishes, such as roast goatling and *salpicão* rice. Seasonal dishes, like river fish, occasionally appear on the menu. €

WHERE TO STAY IN LAMEGO

Six Senses Douro Valley
A luxurious spa in a historic building focused on natural elements, food and wine. **€€€**

Quinta da Pacheca
A charming hotel surrounded by vineyards; stay in the barrel rooms for some extra fun. **€€€**

Casa de Santo António de Britiande
A refined manor house, with food, wine and nature activities available upon request. **€€**

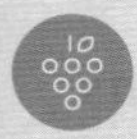

TÁVORA-VAROSA WINE REGION

This wine region, surrounded by the rivers Távora and Varosa, was the first in Portugal to be designated for sparkling wine production. The granite and schistous soils provide the perfect terroir for producing wines with ideal acidity. Besides the favourable environmental conditions, the settlement of the Cistercian monks in the region brought new grape varieties and techniques, greatly impacting this wine's production. A testimonial of the Cistercian occupation can be seen in the massive 12th-century **Mosteiro de São João de Tarouca**, 15km southeast of Lamego. The cellars of some producers gained a monumental status by housing thousands of bottles in dank, cold tunnels dug along the underground rock, the ideal conditions for bubbling.

ALBERTO NOVO/SHUTTERSTOCK ©

Santuário Nossa Senhora dos Remédios

Santuário Nossa Senhora dos Remédios with magnificently carved granite details. Inside, the colourful stained glass and the gold and blue combination create a special atmosphere.

More hiking awaits as you explore the complex of the **Castelo de Lamego**, with its 13th-century defensive wall and the barrage of narrow streets that converge to the last resort of defence, the 20m-tall **Torre de Menagem**, built in the 12th century. Make your way to the picturesque castle entrance, **Porta dos Figos**, which also withholds an archaeological museum. You can also visit the 13th-century water deposit, the Cisterna, historically essential for the town's survival.

Snacking in Wine Paradise

CURED MEATS, REGIONAL SPECIALITIES AND WINERIES

Lamego offers an array of fine meats, wines, and desserts. The region's cured meats are revered nationwide, in particular the distinctly smoky *presunto de Lamego* (ham) and other sausages like *moiras* (blood sausage) and *salpicões* (cured chuck). These meats can be incorporated into another revered delicacy, the thin and moist pie dubbed *bôla de Lamego*. This

WHERE TO SNACK IN LAMEGO

Dalila Bôlas de Lamego
Try the local savoury speciality, *bôla de Lamego*, a thin meat or fish pastry. €

Pastelaria da Sé
This pastry shop specialises in *bôla de Lamego* and sinful conventual pastries. €

A Presunteca de Lamego
Indulge in a board of local cured meats and cheeses on-site or as takeout. €

savoury pastry originated from local convents and can also be prepared with codfish, sardines or marinated pork.

The local main dish staples are *porco em vinha d'alhos* (marinated pork in wine and garlic), roast goatling or trout. The desserts of the old Convento de Chagas can now be tasted in some specialty pastry shops; keep an eye out for *peixinhos de chila* and *barquinhos de Santa Clara*.

Lamego lies within the Baixo Corgo, the Douro's rainiest and most humid sub-region. Local wine estates such as **Quinta da Pacheca**, **Quinta das Lamelas** and **Quinta Santa Eufémia** are responsible for producing some of the region's best port and Douro wines. For a more in-depth approach, you should pre-book a visit to the vineyards and cellars and taste the different styles of wine. To leave no stone unturned, book a visit to the tunnel cellars of **Caves da Raposeira**, 2km from the centre, and check out their sparkling wines.

WHAT IS PORT WINE?

Viticulture has existed in the Douro region since Roman times. However, what we know as port wine was only developed centuries later by unknown inventors. During the production process, the fermentation is stopped early by adding wine spirits, retaining much of the natural sweetness. Port is thus a fortified wine and comes in a spectrum of styles. The key difference between the two main types, ruby and tawny, is the contact with oxygen. Tawnies age in oxygen-exposed wooden barrels, gaining caramel and nutty flavours that pair well with desserts. Rubies age briefly in barrels and, in the case of vintages, can age and develop beautifully for even longer in oxygen-free environments (like bottles), earning fruitier, berry-like flavours.

Treasures of the Lamego Museum

SCULPTURE, PAINTINGS AND DECORATIVE ARTS

The **Museu de Lamego** is located in a magnificent 18th-century building that once served as the Lamego bishop's residence. It was converted into a museum in 1917, and its collections are considered among the country's most valuable.

Inside, you will be faced with what, at first glance, may appear to be just giant carpets. They are, in fact, unique pieces of a 16th-century Flemish tapestry depicting the story of Oedipus from Greek mythology. Commissioned by the bishop of Lamego, they have undergone a thorough restoration to restore their former beauty. It is still unclear why a bishop would commission an incestuous representation. Other treasures include the various chapels with exuberant gilded woodwork and the magnificent ceiling of the former Palácio Episcopal's private chapel.

Art & Music in the Streets

A FREE SUMMERTIME FESTIVAL IN LAMEGO

The streets of Lamego are invaded every August by the four-day **Zigurfest**. This music and art festival involves over two dozen national bands playing music all over town, on stages set in historical and cultural spaces. The fine arts are also part of the event, represented in several exhibitions, performances, screenings and workshops. The icing on the cake is that the festival is entirely free, as is camping on the festival's dedicated camping site.

GETTING AROUND

The centre of Lamego is walkable and parts of it are relatively flat, but you should prepare for some tiring hills in the castle area. Getting up to the sanctuary is also no easy task. The touristic road train will take you to the top of the hill and around Lamego's landmarks. If you're driving, note that most parking in the centre is metered. Having your own wheels will make it easier to visit the wine estates.

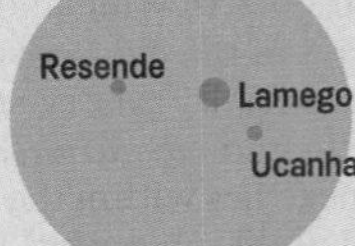

Beyond Lamego

Take a step back and discover the true roots of port wine and forgotten villages that keep their culture alive.

In the surroundings of Lamego, you'll find a world of living traditions and villages preserved in time. The settlement of the Cistercian monks in the 12th century in the Varosa valley led to the creation of two monasteries that significantly impacted the region's future. The white monks were heavily invested in agriculture and viticulture and built infrastructures that led to the settlement of the population. Their legacy lives on in the picturesque villages, winemaking traditions and architecture they left behind. Meanwhile, in other towns, the rurality awakes ancient carnival traditions where people dance and play the devil. The winding back roads connecting these places make the journeys longer and more memorable.

TOP TIP

A car will let you experience the magnificent EN222 road trip and take you to Resende and the wine villages.

Carnaval de Lazarim

CARLOS GONZALEZ XIMENEZ/SHUTTERSTOCK ©

PIXEL TO THE PEOPLE/SHUTTERSTOCK ©

Road near Peso da Régua

In Search of the Perfect Road

NARROW CURVES AND WIDE VIEWS

The **EN222** is a road designed to take drivers through the heart of the Douro wine region. The route begins in **Vila Nova de Gaia** (p316), home to the port wine lodges, and continues upstream towards the vineyards. Unwittingly, you'll follow the wine's journey upside down, from its ageing to its inception.

Three Unesco World Heritage Sites grace the path's 226km serpentine curves, and the landscape is permanently changing as the seasons pass by. For this purpose, focus on the 27km section of road that parallels the river opposite **Peso da Régua** (p323) and **Pinhão** (p323), a mere 13-minute drive from Lamego. This stretch of road is considered the best freeway in the world. Despite the complicated formula used to identify this road's perfect mathematics, you won't think about numbers as you slide along the asphalt.

Careto-Spotting at Carnaval de Lazarim

DANCING WITH THE DEVIL

Every carnival, the streets of the tiny village of Lazarim are taken by storm by a devilish and cheeky troupe of *caretos*. They are adorned with masks carved in alder wood by local artisans, portraying zoomorphic and devil-like features, and

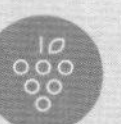

TREKKING THROUGH VINEYARDS

A 2.4km detour from the EN222 in Penajóia will take you to the village of **Samodães**. Here starts what is likely the most beautiful hike of the Douro Valley, the **PR2 – Lamego**, or Trilho do Vinho do Porto. This moderate 7.8km circular trail starts at the church of Samodães and then follows the shepherd's path through narrow cobblestone streets. The trail then turns to a dirt road, and the vineyards and panoramic views of the valley start popping up around you. You'll eventually cross the EN222, enter the vineyards around Six Senses Douro Valley hotel, and descend to the banks of the Douro. Then you'll need to walk back up to Samodães, which will be the most challenging part of the hike.

WHERE TO FIND VIEWPOINTS ALONG THE EN222

Foz do Tedo
A slight detour leads to the spectacular view of the Rio Tedo snaking into the Douro.

Miradouro da Quinta das Carvalhas
This vineyard view delivers a panorama of Pinhão's hypnotising terraced hills.

Miradouro da Quinta do Seixo
Tour the beautiful estate and enjoy a glass of port overlooking the valley views.

PAULOMACHADO_9/SHUTTERSTOCK ©

Medieval bridge, Ucanha

WRITERS OF THE DOURO

It may be difficult for some to find the right words to express the vastness and stillness of the Douro. But it wasn't an issue for the writers living in the region or visiting for inspiration. The Sabrosa-born Miguel Torga frequently mentioned the overwhelming natural beauty of the Douro Valley in his poems. The cosmopolitan Eça de Queirós wrote one of his most acclaimed books, *A Cidade e as Serras*, inspired by a house and family in Tormes. This region also fascinated many other celebrated writers, including Agustina Bessa Luís, Aquilino Ribeiro and Camilo Castelo Branco.

bodies covered with improvised costumes made from straw, leaves or rags. These devilish figures run around, parading across the streets, often carrying noisy cowbells. This ancient tradition has several stages and usually ends in an R-rated public roast of the village youngsters, followed by an outdoor feast around an open fire.

Wine Villages on the South Bank

REALM OF THE WHITE MONKS

The soils in this region have been growing vines for millennia, but it was the Cistercian monks who developed the region following the nation's genesis in the 12th century. As part of their contribution, they shaped the human-made landscape we know today.

A significant part of this heritage is preserved in the small village of **Ucanha**, near the Rio Varosa, a 30-minute drive from Lamego. You'll enter the town through the **fortified medieval bridge** that disappears below a toll tower; both infrastructures were built by the early settlers. In the village surrounds, you can still see elderberry plantations, once common for counterfeiting port wine (and now a source of fine elderberry liqueur).

WHERE TO VISIT VINEYARDS IN TABUACO

Quinta do Pôpa
Besides excellent visits and tastings, you can enjoy a picnic or participate in the grape harvest.

Quinta do Seixo
Visit the cellars and taste the ports of this hilltop *quinta*, but remember to book ahead.

Quinta do Monte Travesso
This small family estate was established in 1896 and provides intimate tours and tastings.

Surprisingly, Ucanha's most celebrated wine isn't port. This is also the wine region of Távora-Varosa (p328), where top-quality sparkling wines are produced and aged. Make time to visit the 1km long tunnels of **Caves da Murganheira** dug in the blue granite rock, where the wines are kept at a constant temperature the whole year.

A six-minute drive from Ucanha leads to the sister village of **Salzedas**, where the same principles were applied. You can't miss the phenomenal **Mosteiro de Santa Maria de Salzedas**, which dates from 1168 and is one of the Cistercian's most influential monasteries.

Both these villages are part of a cluster of six historical wine villages in the Douro, dubbed Aldeias Vinhateiras do Douro (p324).

Cherries, Cake & Black Clay

ABUNDANT SWEETNESS AND RARE CRAFTS

It takes just over half an hour to drive to the little town of **Resende** from Lamengo. Springtime here means stretches of cherry trees blooming like a white cloud hovering above. If you're not here at this time, the 6km cherry flower route has other less perennial highlights like the 16th-century manor **Solar de Porto Rei** and the refreshing **Porto de Rei** beach. The charming fruit and wine estate **Quinta da Massôra** is worth an extended visit.

You won't have trouble finding the sticky sweet sponge cake *cavacas de Resende* to feast upon when back in town. Before you leave, don't forget to admire the local craft, *barro negro*. Cooking the clay on top of charcoal and burying everything together results in a striking black colour; the production of a batch usually involves a firepit party, the *soenga*.

The Escherian Stairs of Varosa

AN INSANE CONCRETE STAIRWAY

A 15-minute drive east will lead you to the **Barragem do Varosa**. This 76m-high hydroelectric dam collects water from the Rio Varosa and is surrounded by captivating natural scenery. But perhaps the most impressive part of this site is the insane maintenance access staircase on the dam's side. The uber-steep, chaotic staircase is assembled on a succession of dozens of concrete terraces that follow the rugged nature of the rock outcrops surrounding it. Unfortunately, the stairway is not accessible to the public, though few would dare to climb it.

THE DOURO DEMARCATED REGION

In the mid-17th century, the serving prime minister, the Marquês de Pombal, created a supervisory organisation to regulate and ensure the quality of port wine production. As international demand for port wine increased, counterfeit wines emerged, which prompted the government to take action. Besides defining the rules for the manufacture and sale of wines, the operation involved the distribution of marked stone pillars that defined the legal borders for production, thus creating the world's first demarcated and regulated wine region, established in 1756. Since then, the demarcated area has increased manifold. It is now up to the Instituto dos Vinhos do Douro e Porto to oversee the production of Douro and port wines.

GETTING AROUND

Having your own wheels is the easiest way of moving around the region. Taking the A24 motorway from Lamego will connect you to the famous EN222. Bus services to the small villages are unavailable, and even Resende is hard to reach by public transportation.

BRAGANÇA

Bragança's role as a boundary between two kingdoms led to the medieval development and fortification we can still see today. Often a battlefield for fierce conflicts, it managed to keep the patina of the centuries in its streets and traditions.

The city also became a refuge for the Jews who fled from Spain in the late 1400s. The Jewish traditions and activities profoundly influenced local culture, and they persisted, even when the Jews were forced to convert to Christianism and secretly practised crypto-Judaism. This is a land where the popular imaginary takes various forms, travelling through Judaism, Christianism and paganism.

The region is marked by geographical isolation, and the landscape does not conceal its harshness and scarcity of resources. Even though Bragança is one of the country's largest districts, it nevertheless suffers from the evils of desertification, making the mission of spreading its local culture and history even more important.

TOP TIP

The best time to visit Bragança depends on your interests, but be aware that winters are icy and long, and the summers are short and hot. If you plan to go beyond the city and do some hiking, then late spring and early autumn are excellent choices.

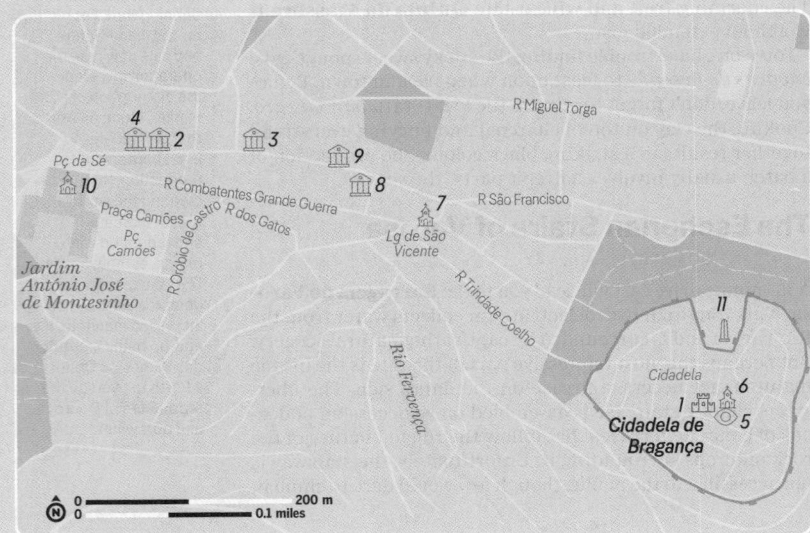

HIGHLIGHTS
1 Cidadela de Bragança

SIGHTS
2 Centro de Arte Contemporânea Graça Morais
3 Centro de Fotografia Georges Dussaud
4 Centro de Interpretação da Cultura Sefardita do Nordeste Transmontano
5 Domus Municipalis
6 Igreja de Santa Maria
7 Igreja de São Vicente
8 Memorial e Centro de Documentação – Bragança Sefardita
9 Museu do Abade de Baçal
10 Sé
11 Torre de Menagem

The Citadel & Beyond

AN IMPENETRABLE CASTLE

Bragança's **Cidadela** takes you back to medieval times. Strategically located to deter any curious Spaniard, it acquired the design you see today to withstand the battles with the Kingdom of Castile. Inside the castle's second defensive wall is an imposing Gothic **Torre de Menagem**. Next to it is the Romanesque **Igreja de Santa Maria**, featuring baroque elements on its facade and an uncommon exposed brick arch structure. Only a few steps away is the **Domus Municipalis**, a rare Romanesque building with a social room and a water storage system.

Outside the walls, you'll be immersed in the post-medieval expansion, dotted with grandiose 16th-century manor homes. Behind its minimal facade, the Mannerist and baroque **Igreja de São Vicente** hides a spectacular golden woodwork chancel. It's also worth looking at the 16th-century **Sé Velha de Bragança**, a former Jesuit school now converted into a cultural centre.

The Flavours of Bragança

ODD SAUSAGES, COUSCOUS AND FORAGING

Bragança is known for its comfort food, made to keep the body warm during the harsh winters. A panoply of different colours, shapes and flavours of all cured meats is produced here. The very best Bísaro pork meats are smoked in a traditional *fumeiro*, a wood-fired smokehouse.

One of the most interesting sausages is the chunky *butelo*, a bone sausage. It is typically sided with boiled *casulas* (dried green beans) and is considered the epitome of local gastronomy, a symbol of a flavourful cuisine with humble origins. It is popular during carnival and can be tasted at the annual **Festival do Butelo e Casulas**.

Another curious and improbable food is *cuscos* (couscous), made from Barbela wheat, a legacy of Arab gastronomy. You must also taste the cheeses from native sheep and goats, like the *Terrincho de cabra transmontana* and the regional bread, such as *folar* and *bôla sovada*, all DOP or IGP products from the area. Chestnut products are also a local staple.

STREET ART

Bordalo II
This renowned street artist builds his works from trash, expressing a climatic and anti-consumerist message. Check out the spectacular textural murals representing a chameleon, boar and genet.

Frederico Draw
The artist has several works spread around the city; one of the most noteworthy is the representation of a craftsman sculpting a carnival mask (*O Artesão)* and the visually stunning man holding a rooster.

Daniel Eime
The artist's minimalist and realistic graphics portray powerful emotional facial expressions, as seen in the work *Estanco*.

MORE CURED MEATS?

Take a culinary journey to Vinhais or Mirandela (p339), where the art of sausage smoking is a yearly tradition that provides meat for the rest of the year.

WHERE TO STAY IN BRAGANÇA

Pousada de Bragança
This comfortable *pousada* in the city's heart provides excellent views over the castle and a great restaurant. €€

Quinta da Rica-Fé
You can experience rural Bragança's tranquillity on this 120-hectare farm from the 14th century. €€

Candeias do Souto
A charming rustic property with mountain views invites you to cycle through the countryside. €€

BEST PLACES TO EAT IN BRAGANÇA

Solar Bragançano
One of Bragança's classic restaurants, with spectacular game dishes and excellent service. €€

O Geadas
A welcoming restaurant preparing remarkable regional cuisine. Try the game meat and river fish. €€

G Pousada
Michelin-starred cuisine with Portuguese heart, using products from small and local producers. €€€

O Javali
Old-school restaurant specialises in boar recipes as well as other regional delicacies. €€

Tasca do Zé Tuga
Unusual but delectable interpretations of local cuisine make this *tasca* (tavern) an essential stop. €€

O Copinhos
This unpretentious little tavern serves delicious homemade traditional *petiscos* (little portions). €

SERGIO FORMOSO/SHUTTERSTOCK ©

Citadela (p335)

Museum-Hopping in Bragança

ART, COSTUMES, JEWISH HERITAGE AND MORE

Bragança is a highly cultural city, with plenty of activities and sites to visit. It's easy to go on a museum run and get lost in centuries of human creativity and ingenuity; along **Rua Abílio Bessa**, known by locals as the 'museum street', there are several museums in just 500m.

Among Bragança's museums, the highlight must go to **Museu do Abade de Baçal**, a vast archaeological, ethnographic, religious, numismatic and artistic collection compiled by an adventurous abbot. The **Centro de Interpretação da Cultura Sefardita do Nordeste Transmontano** (CICS) and **Memorial e Centro de Documentação – Bragança Sefardita** are essential to learn more about the rich Jewish traditions and culture in Trás-os-Montes.

On the artistic spectrum, it's well worth a visit to the **Centro de Arte Contemporânea Graça Morais**, designed by Pritzker-awarded architect Eduardo Souto Moura in honour of the native neo-expressionist painter Graça Morais. Another crucial photographic memoir of Trás-os-Montes can be admired at the **Centro de Fotografia Georges Dussaud**.

GETTING AROUND

You can tackle the relatively small historic centre on foot and leave the car to explore the surroundings. The city also has a 6km bike lane crossing most sites and an e-bike sharing system called Xispas. Three STUB urban bus lines cover the city, but the frequency is at best twice an hour, with big gaps in the morning and afternoon.

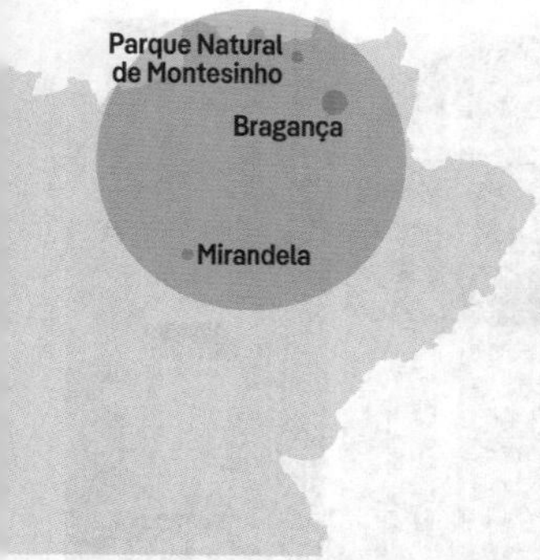

Parque Natural de Montesinho
Bragança
Mirandela

Beyond Bragança

Explore Bragança's surroundings, built upon wilderness and isolation, creating distinctive cultures and communities.

TOP TIP

To explore the area thoroughly, get yourself a car. Buses are an option for several locations if you plan ahead.

Behold a vast region where the punishing climate provides long, freezing winters – time in which the locals make the best of the situation by producing some of the country's best and most peculiar smoked meats.

The region preserves extensive wild areas well defined by two fauna- and flora-rich natural parks. Regional agriculture is present throughout, with extensive crops adapted to the rigorous climate, such as olive trees, chestnut trees and grazing sheep and goats for cheese production.

The obvious geographical constraints contributed to the historical isolation of the region's villages, which created their own language and a communal way of life that ensured their survival. These populations are resilient, and hold on dearly to their culture.

Parque Natural de Montesinho (p339)

ANDERS BLOMQVIST/GETTY IMAGES ©

RICHARD SEMIK/SHUTTERSTOCK ©

Cathedral, Miranda do Douro

CARNAVAL DE PODENCE

The Carnaval de Podence, one of the country's most amazing carnivals, takes place between Shrove Sunday and Shrove Tuesday in the village of Podence, just 30 minutes from Bragança. The *caretos* take to the streets, dressed in full-body costumes filled with colourful wool fringes and devilish zinc masks. In packs, they parade through the streets to the tune of the cowbells they wear around their waists. These ghoulish and chaotic characters seek to fulfil an ancient and profane fertility ritual, by shaking their cowbell belts on women. The uniqueness of this celebration has been recognised by Unesco as an Intangible Cultural Heritage of Humanity.

The Singular Culture of Miranda

STICK DANCERS, TEXTILES AND MIRANDESE

Miranda do Douro, an hour's drive from Bragança, is one of the unmissable towns of Trás-os-Montes. Sitting on a gorge over the Rio Douro and overlooking Spain, this heavily fortified frontier town played a critical role in Portugal's early days. The sheer isolation and Leonese influence over the region led to the development of a singular language, Mirandês, Portugal's second official language, which you can spot on road signs.

Inside the walls are the well-preserved streets of the old town. Admire the 14th-century Manueline buildings along **Rua da Costanilha**, then head toward the imposing 16th-century two-towered **cathedral**. Inside, look at the curious Menino Jesus da Cartolinha, a figure of infant Jesus in a top hat to which the Mirandese attribute miracles and protection. Back outside, walk toward the **Miradouro da Sé** and take in the dramatic views. Feast on *posta à Mirandesa* (a hefty steak dish) before leaving.

WHERE TO HIKE IN PARQUE NATURAL DE MONTESINHO

PR3 – BCG Porto Furado
This iconic trail weaves its way through breathtaking nature and archaeological treasures.

PR12 – Guardamil
Red and fallow deer are often spotted on this circular trail from the village of Guardamil.

PR11 – BCG
The trail begins in Rio de Onor and explores the surrounding natural landscape and village infrastructures.

Parque Natural de Montesinho

EXPLORING THE SNOWY MOUNTAINS

The splendour of the **Parque Natural de Montesinho** is less than 15 minutes from Bragança's centre. Covering more than 740 sq km of verdant land, the relatively gentle terrain is crowned by mounds and crossed by multiple rivers and streams. At the heart of Terra Fria, the park is often covered in snow in winter. The park's many different habitats are home to numerous flora and fauna, including the elusive Iberian wolves, wild cats and otters. The human presence is seen in the dozens of little villages – divided Rio de Ono, picturesque Gimonde and wonderfully preserved Montesinho – dotted around the park, most of which maintain their traditional agricultural and shepherding practices.

THE ROUTES OF TERRA FRIA

The territory of Terra Fria ('Cold Land'), encompasses Bragança, Vinhais, Mogadouro, Miranda do Douro and Vimioso. It's not necessarily colder than its counterpart, Terra Quente ('Hot Land'), as both suffer from very hot and cold temperatures, to Portuguese standards. Officially, the Rota da Terra Fria Transmontana has 455km in extension and encompasses six different municipalities. It overlaps Parque Natural do Douro Internacional (p344) and part of the Parque Natural de Montesinho. The Rota da Terra Fria is divided into eleven sections, which can most easily be accomplished by car, although it is also possible to cycle. There are also 28 hiking and cycling trails to explore specific geographical areas and even a thematic path that treads upon the former contraband routes.

Vinhais & Mirandela

SMOKEY FLAVOURS AND REGIONAL DELICACIES

A 40-minute drive from Bragança, **Vinhais**, in the heart of Terra Fria, is well-known for its masterful cooking. Smoked meat production is the primary fuel for the local economy, holding the native Bísaro pig as a flagship; the annual **Feira do Fumeiro de Vinhais** brings travellers from far and near to taste and buy the local pork charcuterie. The chestnut, aka 'oil of Trás-os-Montes', trails slightly behind. The latter are incorporated into several regional sweets like the *económico de castanha* (chestnut cake). Try local dishes such as the *alheira de Vinhais* (bread and meat sausage), *posta à Mirandesa* (steak from a regional breed) and the local lamb at restaurant **Vasco da Gama**.

An hour south, deep inside the Terra Quente, lies the town of **Mirandela**. A *fumeiro* (smokehouse) powerhouse in its own right, it is believed to be the birthplace of the *alheira*. Some theorise that the Jewish converts created this bread and smoked sausage (without pork) to deceive the Inquisition during the many centuries of persecution. Most contemporary recipes include pork, and the *alheira de Mirandela* is an IGP product. Many premium DOP here, including the delicious, slap-in-the-face-strong goat's cheese *(queijo de cabra transmontano)*, Terra Quente honey, Trás-os-Montes olive oil and the local goatling *(cabrito transmontano)*.

GETTING AROUND

Hopping into a rental car is a time-saving way of visiting the surroundings of Bragança and getting serious about exploring the Parque Natural de Montesinho and the more remote community villages. However, it is possible to use buses to reach many destinations. There is a daily Rodonorte bus to Miranda do Douro, which takes around two hours. STUB's R5 line will take you to Rio de Onor in an hour, and buses usually run twice daily. Getting to Mirandela is relatively easy and fast, as several FlixBus and Rodonorte buses make the one-hour trip daily. There are also Rodonorte buses headed to Vinhais a few times a day.

VILA NOVA DE FOZ CÔA

Vila Nova de Foz Côa
Lisbon

The wild lands of Vila Nova de Foz Côa were a haven to the palaeolithic people, who drew their experiences in stone across the Côa valley. Later, the Romans, Suebi, Visigoths and Moors left their mark here. The creation of Portugal led to an interest in organising and further occupying the area. Still, the population only grew substantially after the railroad arrived in the 1800s, bringing progress and people. For centuries, the area's main activities have remained the same: wine and olive oil production and almond culture, which employ part of the population of roughly 3100 people. The exceptional wine and almonds compensate for the otherwise unforgiving conditions of extreme heat; after all, it's in the Terra Quente ('hot land').

The small historical centre isn't a widely visited tourist area, but it's worth a couple of hours of exploration. The area's most attractive sites are primarily out in the open.

TOP TIP

You should get a rental car to make the most of your trip here. The best months to visit are probably late February and March, when the almond trees bloom, or in the grape harvest season (September and October), when the temperatures are more mellow and the colours are beautiful.

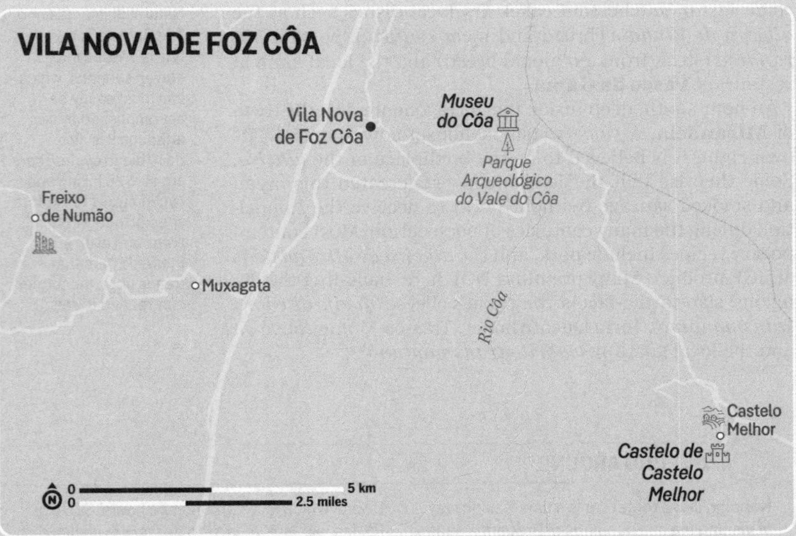

Paleolithic rock art, Côa Valley

The Côa Valley Art Gallery

PREHISTORIC ROCK ART

The banks of the Rio Côa are bordered by hard schist outcrops, with tall slabs of slate protruding from the ground. The prehistoric populations of the Côa valley made use of this natural canvas to engrave what is the world's most extensive outdoor collection of prehistoric art. There are engravings of aurochs, horses, goats and humans spanning 22,000 years of history. The 200 sq km of rock art led Unesco to classify the site as a World Heritage Site in 1998.

To view the engravings, you must prearrange the visit with the **Museu do Côa**. This architecturally stunning building sits on an elevation over the valley. Inside, you can admire the highly visual and interactive exhibition that explains the context and history. From here, you'll ride on the museum's all-terrain cars and head out to the **Parque Arqueológico do Vale do Côa**.

The museum and park are around 2.8km from the village of Vila Nova de Foz Côa and can be reached by car or on foot.

THE MIRADOURO TRAIN

This classic MiraDouro train ride connecting Porto to Pocinho follows the natural curves of the Rio Douro. The train's vintage 1940s carriages have large windows that deliver a panoramic view and can be lowered for a better look at the riverside landscape. Throughout this scenic journey, you'll feel like you're gliding along the landscape, occasionally passing through dark tunnels, and sometimes you might swear that the train will plunge into the river. Whichever way you ride, you'll be astonished by the contrast between the wilderness of Vila Nova de Foz Côa, the subsequent laborious labyrinth of vineyards through the valley and the beautiful urbanity of Porto. The trip lasts three hours and 40 minutes.

WHERE TO EAT IN VILA NOVA DE FOZ CÔA

Aldeia Douro
This small and contemporary restaurant slash wine bar features regional *petiscos* with a modern twist. €€

Taberna do Barriga Verde
Traditional *petiscos*, fine regional wines and hearty main courses await in this modern tavern. €€

Restaurante Côa Museu
The restaurant at the Côa museum offers spectacular views and tasty food. €€

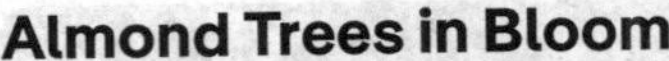

Almond Trees in Bloom

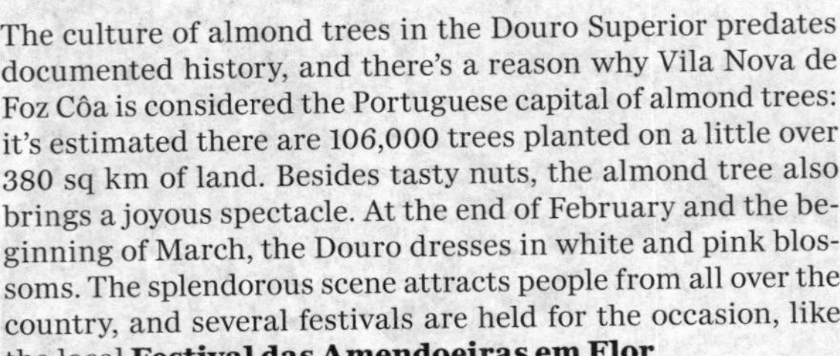

DOURO DRESSED IN FLOWERS

The culture of almond trees in the Douro Superior predates documented history, and there's a reason why Vila Nova de Foz Côa is considered the Portuguese capital of almond trees: it's estimated there are 106,000 trees planted on a little over 380 sq km of land. Besides tasty nuts, the almond tree also brings a joyous spectacle. At the end of February and the beginning of March, the Douro dresses in white and pink blossoms. The splendorous scene attracts people from all over the country, and several festivals are held for the occasion, like the local **Festival das Amendoeiras em Flor**.

Medieval Castelo Melhor

PRESERVED BY ABANDON

At the top of an olive-laden hill in the village of Castelo Melhor lie the ruins of the medieval **Castelo de Castelo Melhor**. The circular castle was fortified during the heyday of the reconquest of the Iberian Peninsula from the Moors. However, it is believed to have been built upon the ruins of a pre-Roman hillfort. The castle's military significance decreased after the 17th century and it was eventually abandoned. Ironically, the lack of investment in its reconstruction allowed the castle to retain its original features, although battered by the action of time. The hike from the village to the castle is short but steep.

The Ruins of Freixo de Numão

AN ARCHAEOLOGICAL WONDERLAND

A 15-minute drive east will bring you to **Freixo de Numão**, a history-rich region filled with archaeological treasures. Head out to the magnificent baroque manor home that is today the **Museu da Casa Grande** and which hosts two different exhibitions. The ethnographic exhibition displays local wine, olive and almond production tools. The archaeological collection is diverse, but Roman and medieval ruins are out in the backyard.

Take an additional 12-minute drive to **Estação Arqueológica do Prazo**, the scenic well-preserved ruins of a Roman town and medieval community dating back to the 1st century. It's also worth taking a detour to **Castelo Velho**, a Bronze Age hillfort, another magnificent viewpoint over the valley.

THE PHENOMENAL D ANTÓNIA FERREIRA

D Antónia Ferreira (or Ferreirinha) was an extraordinary woman. Born in 1811 and widowed at a young age, Ferreirinha took the helm of her family's wine estate (Casa Ferreira) and became the most prominent entrepreneur of her time. She bought, expanded and modernised dozens of farms, including the crown jewel, Quinta do Vesúvio (p345). She made great efforts to restore the Douro to its former glory after the vineyards were devastated by a phylloxera plague in the 1860s. Her innovative spirit brought prosperity and renovated glory to port wine while also helping the small farmers and estates survive the many crises of the century. Known to be generous and selfless, Ferreirinha's numerous contributions to the local populations gained her the title of 'mother of the poor'.

GETTING AROUND

A car is essential to conveniently reach all points of interest, including the wine estates and the Museu do Côa. The latter can be reached on foot with a 40-minute walk, but it should be avoided during the hot season.

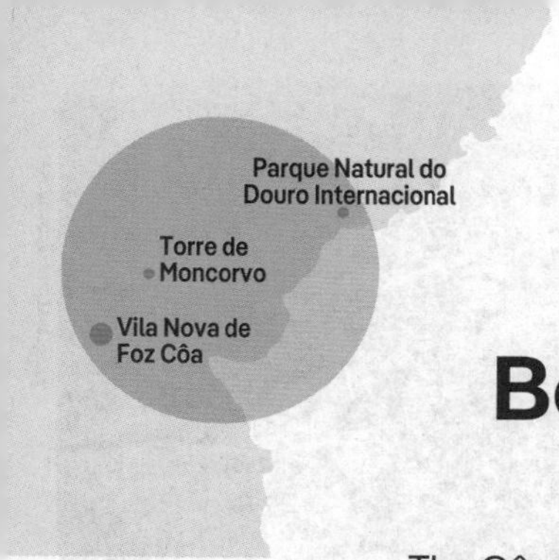

Parque Natural do Douro Internacional

Torre de Moncorvo

Vila Nova de Foz Côa

Beyond Vila Nova de Foz Côa

The Côa valley is a harsh but beautiful landscape of sheer wilderness, only partly tamed by tenacious human resilience.

Vila Nova de Foz Côa is surrounded by the Côa valley. As well as ancient rock art, there are persistent archaeological finds here from a plethora of eras that indicate how significant this sliver of northeastern Portugal has been throughout the millennia. In this countryside of climatic extremes, humankind has, for centuries, been stubbornly taming the topography to sow the land and reap its spoils. It has generously repaid with elegant wines, olive oil and almonds. And so, the people built villages and communities in its realm. But this land is still wild and very much untamed. The landscape humbles the eye and teaches us that nature is still the master of this wild east.

TOP TIP

This part of the Douro requires a rental car; you can reach all sites within a 50-minutes or less drive.

Torre de Moncorvo (p345)

ROGER DAY/ALAMY STOCK PHOTO ©

MIGUEL ALMEIDA/SHUTTERSTOCK ©

Parque Natural do Douro Internacional

THE HORSE OF MAZOUCO

A prehistoric masterpiece lies hidden in the tiny village of Mazouco, Freixo de Espada à Cinta. An unsuspecting schist outcrop overlooking the mirrorlike waters of the Albargueira stream and the Rio Douro contains a precious 62cm engraving of a horse. The equine is believed to have been carved in stone over 10,000 years ago and was the first piece of rock art to be discovered outdoors in Europe. For decades, it remained a secret among locals, who talked about the 'ram' concealed in the bushes, later revealed by scientists to represent a (possibly pregnant) mare. It was the first significant piece of rock art found in the Douro region, predating the discovery of the Côa engravings by almost 10 years.

Parque Natural do Douro Internacional

CLIFFS, VIEWPOINTS AND BIRDWATCHING

A 40-minute drive from Vila Nova de Foz Côa will take you to **Parque Natural do Douro Internacional**, which follows the 122km where the Rio Douro serves as a natural border between Portugal and Spain. This protected area follows the deep canyon dug by the river, forming spectacular cliffs that can be witnessed in the park's many viewpoints.

One of the most dazzling is the **Miradouro da Fraga do Puio**, close to Miranda do Douro, where a glass platform allows you to walk above the horizon and gaze into the mesmerising and rugged cliffs over the Douro. Alternatively, the harder-to-access **Miradouro do Carrascalinho** and the **Miradouro do Penedo Durão** offer breathtaking views but are also ideal birdwatching sites. This park is also a habitat for several large and endangered birds, and if you look up, you'll likely see a hovering griffon and, if you're lucky, a migrating Egyptian vulture.

WHERE TO EAT IN TORRE DE MONCORVO

Taberna do Carró
A humble tavern with well-executed regional and seasonal dishes, including its classic asparagus omelette. **€€**

O Lagar
A decades-old classic serving delicious regional slow food recipes and a great selection of local wines. **€€**

Pastelaria Bom Gosto
This tiny bakery is home to the most authentic regional pastries covered with almonds. **€**

Medieval Streets with Jewish Heritage

ALMONDS, MONUMENTS AND VIEWS

With a quick 20-minute drive, you'll come upon **Torre de Moncorvo**. Explore the narrow medieval streets and discover the austere yet monumental Mannerist **Basílica de Torre de Moncorvo**, Trás-os-Montes' largest church. Discover the ruins of the **Moncorvo Castle**, and the simple **Igreja da Misericórdia** Renaissance church and its museum. During Easter, you may hear *cobrideiras* rattling their thimbles on copper pans, candying the almonds known as *amêndoa coberta de Moncorvo.* The recipe is thought to be of Jewish heritage, since the town was once the head Jewish community in Trás-os-Montes. Touring the **Rota dos Judeus** will let you learn more.

A 50-minute drive east of Foz Côa will lead you to the ancient town of **São João da Pesqueira**, the biggest Douro table wine producer. Here you can explore the medieval streets and monuments around the Praça da República, as well as the narrow Rua dos Gatos, said to be the site of the Jewish quarter, established in the 1400s. The surroundings are known for great viewpoints, particularly the sensational **Miradouro de São Salvador do Mundo**, with panoramic views over the Valeira dam.

The Wineries of Douro Superior

VISIT EXTRAORDINARY ESTATES

Vila Nova de Foz Côa lies in the heart of the Douro Superior, the largest of the Douro's three regions. Its boundary starts in Cachão da Valeira and extends to the border with Spain. The climate is arid and relentless, with scorching summers and little rain, which makes for outstanding wines. Unsurprisingly, some of Douro's most legendary wineries can be found here.

Built in 1827 by the heroic entrepreneur D Antónia Ferreira (p342), **Quinta do Vesúvio** is undoubtedly the region's most iconic *quinta* (estate). On private visits to this massive 326-hectare estate you'll travel the vineyards by 4WD, tour the *adega* (winery) and its enormous granite *lagares* (winepress), taste the wines and have lunch on the veranda.

Established in 1877, also by D Antónia Ferreira, **Quinta de Vale Meão** is the birthplace of the legendary Barca Velha wine. Book ahead to explore the 100 hectares of vineyards and taste the estate's ports and table wines in the *adega*.

Founded in the late 1800s, **Quinta de Ervamoira** is located inside the Côa valley archaeological park. It is the first and only estate to have all its vines planted vertically. Visits to the *quinta* must be pre-booked and include a visit to the **Sítio de Ervamoira Museum**.

BEST WINERIES IN SÃO JOÃO DA PESQUEIRA

Quinta de Ventozelo
A 500-year-old *quinta* in perfect communion with nature, where the vineyard develops beautifully down the long sloping terraces. Book a wine tasting, hike the vineyard's trails or stay at the hotel and experience the restaurant Cantina do Ventozelo.

Quinta das Carvalhas
A colossal 18th-century estate with one of the Douro's most complete collections of indigenous grape varieties. The vineyard mainly comprises *vinhas velhas* (old vines), which makes for complex wines. It's an essential estate that illustrates much of the Douro's identity. Book tastings in advance.

GETTING AROUND

Driving the national roads and the IP2 is undoubtedly the most effective way of getting around in the area. It's often the only option other than taking a taxi. Public transportation is limited to one or two bus lines headed toward Torre de Moncorvo once a day.

BENNY MARTY/SHUTTERSTOCK ©

Arco da Porta Nova (p355), Braga

THE MINHO

VERDANT LANDSCAPES AND DEEP TRADITIONS

Welcome to the soulful Minho, a lush green countryside surrounded by an endless sandy coastline, a region infused with thriving traditions and a youthful spirit.

The Minho area was once home to Celts, Romans, Suebi and Moors, and was one of the first regions to integrate the new kingdom of Portugal in the 12th century. Centuries later, the northern border with Spain was strengthened with impressive fortifications, which are now regularly invaded by the Spaniards for leisure and shopping.

Minho's geography is composed of the districts of Viana do Castelo and Braga. To the north, the region is bordered by the Rio Minho, the natural frontier with Spain. It faces the Atlantic to the west, Porto to the south and Vila Real to the east. As a result of a persistent maritime influence and rainfall, Minho is recognised for its lush green scenery. This phenomenon inspired the naming of one of its prodigal children, the *vinho verde* ('green' wine).

The capital of Minho, the city Braga, is set inland and is packed with ruins from its 2000 years of history. The omnipresence of religious buildings gained it the nickname 'Portuguese Rome'. Viana do Castelo, on the other hand, is a coastal city with a long seafaring tradition and an entire culture built around the ocean, river and farmland. The Minho also represents a culture in which geographical limits are fluid. The prolific culture of the costumes, crafts, processions, folk dancing and gastronomy transpire throughout the territory and can't be contained.

THE MAIN AREAS

BRAGA
The historic capital. **p352**

VIANA DO CASTELO
Beaches, folklore and local gastronomy. **p360**

GUIMARÃES
Monuments and museums. **p369**

PARQUE NACIONAL DA PENEDA-GERÊS
Hiking, waterfalls and mountain views. **p377**

Viana do Castelo, p360

This seafaring city sits on the verdant coastline of Costa Verde, alluring beachgoers, windsurfers and hikers. Count on fresh seafood from the Atlantic and crisp wines.

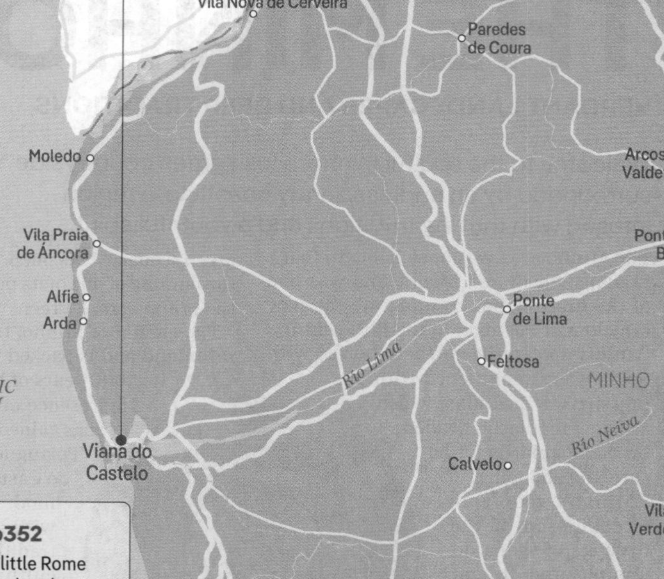

Braga, p352

Portugal's little Rome teems with churches and ruins spanning over 2000 years of history while simultaneously enjoying a cosmopolitan vibe and booming cultural scene.

NAURIS VASILEVSKIS/SHUTTERSTOCK ©, LUISCOSTINHAA/SHUTTERSTOCK ©, GLEN BERLIN/SHUTTERSTOCK ©

Find Your Way

The Minho is Portugal's oldest region but represents only 5% of the country's area. Each of our chosen destinations provides insight into Minho's cultural, historical and natural heritage and can serve as a springboard to further exploration.

Parque Nacional da Peneda-Gerês, p377

Wander through the wild landscape of this national park to emerald-green lagoons, camouflaged waterfalls and secluded stone villages.

Guimarães, p369

The nation's birthplace is home to a pristinely preserved historic centre, a flurry of monuments, delicious food and excellent museums.

CAR

Driving maximises your exploration of the Minho in terms of time and coverage. This is especially true for the smaller towns, remote villages and the natural scenery of Parque Nacional da Peneda-Gerês.

BUS

Buses are a safe bet for reaching smaller towns, but you should program your schedule well. Transdev has multiple lines running through south and north Minho, while AV Minho covers most coastal destinations. Rede Expressos and FlixBus also offer connections from Lisbon and Porto.

TRAIN

The train is one of the best options for visiting hubs like Viana do Castelo, Braga and Guimarães. The slow but scenic regional train of Linha do Minho covers all the coastal towns up to Valença.

Plan Your Time

Spend your time exploring the Minho's scattered historic towns and taking detours within the omnipresent green milieu that invites you to refresh at idyllic river beaches, lagoons and waterfalls.

Pressed for Time

- Head toward **Braga** (p352) and hit the streets of the ancient **historic centre** (p354), where you can admire the many monuments, baroque architecture and **museums** (p355). Stop for a traditional lunch at **Tasquinha Dom Ferreira** (p355) and then a coffee at **Café Vianna** (p355).

- In the afternoon, gather your strength to climb the steps of the spectacular **Santuário do Bom Jesus do Monte** (p352), or take the hydraulic funicular instead. If there's still time, enjoy a relaxing stroll at the **Mosteiro de São Martinho de Tibães** (p359) or, alternatively, take a short drive to **Barcelos** (p358) and dive into the rich pottery culture.

TOMASZ WARSZEWSKI/SHUTTERSTOCK ©

Santuário do Bom Jesus do Monte (p352), Braga

Seasonal highlights

Spring is ideal for hiking and other nature-related activities, while the warm summers on the coast are best spent at the beach. Reserve autumn for wine programs and visiting historic towns.

JANUARY

The cold of winter begs comfort food, bringing in hearty recipes like *papas de sarrabulho*, a meat and blood-based porridge.

FEBRUARY

Lamprey season begins, and Minho restaurants are dishing out the delicious but weird-looking cyclostome until mid-May.

APRIL

Braga celebrates the solemn Semana Santa the week before Easter with impressive processions and biblical reenactments.

RICHARD SEMIK/SHUTTERSTOCK ©, GRANDPA/SHUTTERSTOCK ©, BRUNO ISMAEL SILVA ALVES/SHUTTERSTOCK ©

Three Days to Travel Around

- After a day in Braga, head out to **Guimarães** (p369). Explore the **historic centre** (p369) and the monuments of **Monte Latito** (p371) before lunch at **Florêncio** (p371). After lunch, visit the hillfort of **Citânia de Briteiros** (p375) and enjoy a tasting at a *vinho verde* **winery** (p373).

- The next day, travel north to discover the historic centre of **Viana do Castelo** (p360), then climb to the **Santuário do Monte de Santa Luzia** (p360) to enjoy the panoramic views. In the afternoon, either hit the **beaches** (p362) or hike through the wilderness of **Serra d'Arga** (p367). Return to have dinner at **Tasquinha da Linda** (p363).

If You Have More Time

- If you have more time, spend three extra days exploring the **Parque Nacional da Peneda-Gerês** (p377). On the first day, discover the villages and forests of the **northern section** (p377). The following day, head to the **central section** (p378) for adventure sports, trail hiking and swimming in the lagoons. On the last day, take the morning to explore the mystical village and sanctuary of **Pitões das Júnias** (p379). In the afternoon, drive to the terraced hillside village of **Sistelo** (p381) and take in the amazing scenery.

MAY
Water still abounds in the lagoons and waterfalls, and the mild weather makes it an ideal time for hiking.

JULY
Summer calls everyone to Minho's coastal and river beaches. It's also a great time to engage in water sports.

AUGUST
Time for the massive religious festivity of Festas da Senhora da Agonia and music festivals like Festival Paredes de Coura.

SEPTEMBER
The grapes are ripe for picking, and the wine estates in the *vinho verde* region get busy harvesting.

BRAGA

The Roman city of Bracara Augusta was founded in 16 BCE, making it the country's oldest city. It was once the capital of the kingdom of Galicia, where multiple Roman roads converged. Today Braga rules as the heart of Minho.

Braga is also regarded as the country's religious epicentre, hosting Portugal's oldest cathedral (which precedes the nation), deep-rooted Catholic celebrations and the most significant religious studies centres. The characteristic unison chime of dozens of church bells is a familiar soundscape when walking around the city.

The monument-rich historic centre has been through two millennia of changes, and the passage of time is visible in every corner. Nonetheless, this city of 144,000 inhabitants hasn't frozen in time. The University of Minho and its institutes bring in thousands of students and professionals, contributing to a youthful, cosmopolitan and multicultural city. This adds to the multi-layered nature of this avant-garde but traditional, historic but innovative city.

TOP TIP

Braga's centre is easily explored on foot, and the city is relatively flat. TUB buses are a good option to cover bigger distances within the city, in particular, to reach Bom Jesus or Sameiro.

VIOLA BRAGUESA

The slender, short-necked, 10-stringed *viola braguesa* is inspired by the 15th-century guitar, but it appeared two centuries later. It has a smaller and narrower body than a classical guitar, and the sound hole is either round or shaped like a *boca de raia* (stingray's mouth). It is traditionally used in Minho's folk music. It can be heard in contemporary music, including Portuguese rock and pop. The *bracarense* luthier Domingos Machado is one of the most famed artisans and has several specimens in his museum, **Museu dos Cordofones**, dedicated to Portuguese string instruments in Tebosa, Braga.

A Stroll Around Praça da República

SPECKLED WITH HISTORY

The pretty central square of **Praça da República** and the gardens of Avenida Central invite you to wander. Behind the scenic gallery of **Arcada**, you'll uncover the remains of Braga's demolished castle, the sturdy 30m **Torre de Menagem**, from the 14th century. A few metres away lies the iconic **Casa dos Crivos**, a Renaissance shop and house with an intriguing wood-lattice facade. Head toward Avenida da Liberdade to admire the pink facade of **Theatro Circo**, one of the country's finest theatres, and continue to **Fonte do Ídolo**, a 1st-century Roman shrine to the cult of water.

Sacred Steps to an Endless View

A DEMANDING STAIRWAY TO HEAVEN

The sacred hill where **Santuário do Bom Jesus do Monte** is built has been a site for religious pilgrimage since ancient times. The complex is considered by many to be Europe's most majestic calvary hill. Arriving at the bottom, you will see the sanctuary's endless **stairway**. Jesus' suffering leading up to the crucifixion is depicted throughout the 573 steps of this baroque and rococo staircase. This stairway is the most complex of its kind due to its size and elaborate ornamentation, including statues and fountains. You will hear flowing water as you pass fountains themed around the five senses and the three virtues.

For a knee-friendly climb, board the world's oldest **hydraulic funicular**. At the top, the late 18th-century neoclassical basil-

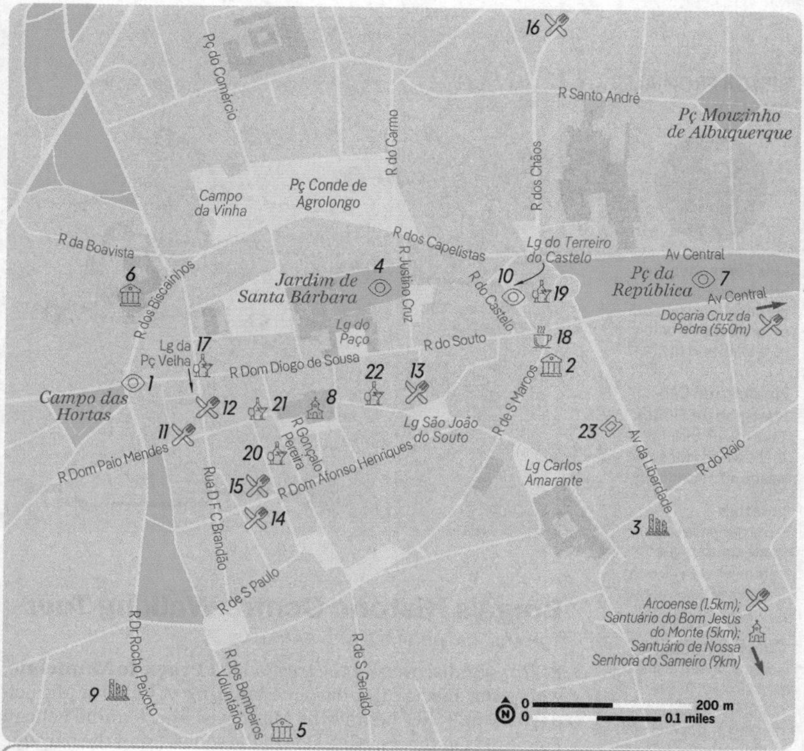

SIGHTS
1 Arco da Porta Nova
2 Casa dos Crivos
3 Fonte do Ídolo
4 Jardim de Santa Bárbara
5 Museu de Arqueologia D Diogo de Sousa
6 Museu dos Biscainhos
7 Praça da República
8 Sé
9 Termas Romanas do Alto da Cividade
10 Torre de Menagem

EATING
11 Adega Malhoa
12 Cozinha da Sé
13 Frigideiras do Cantinho
14 Kartilho
15 O Filho da Mãe
16 Tasquinha Dom Ferreira

DRINKING & NIGHTLIFE
17 APE Coffee
18 Café A Brasileira
19 Café Vianna
20 Letraria – Craft Beer Library
21 Mal Amado
22 Setra

ENTERTAINMENT
23 Theatro Circo

ica marks the finish line. Look around and see as far as **Pitões das Júnias** (p379). The extensive park surrounding the sanctuary has a fascinating grotto and other architectural highlights for exploration. A seven-minute drive from here leads to another sanctuary, the 19th-century **Santuário de Nossa Senhora do Sameiro**, with a 256-step stairway. The staircase does not match the previous one, but it will transport you to the highest point in Braga, where you can explore the basilica and green spaces.

WHERE TO STAY IN BRAGA

Melia Braga Hotel & Spa
Enjoy the good life in Braga's most luxurious hotel, which includes a spacious spa. **€€**

Braga Heritage Lofts
Sleek and comfortable lofts in a tastefully renovated building in front of Jardim de Santa Bárbara. **€**

Vila Galé Collection Braga
Sleep inside this former 15th-century hospital turned hotel with a spectacular baroque facade. **€€€**

BRAGA FROM ALL ANGLES

Luís Fernandes, the artistic director of gnration *(gnration.pt)*, recommends a balance of the old and the new.

Mosteiro de São Martinho de Tibães
Take a walk through these woods for some peace and tranquillity.

gnration
A must-visit is this contemporary arts centre where you can find exhibitions, shows and workshops.

Centésima Página
Located in the historic Casa Rolão, this is a mandatory stop for reading and socialising in the garden.

FROM THE SANCTUARY TO THE MONASTERY

For a more personal and intimate insight into the religious way of life, visit the Mosteiro de São Martinho de Tibães (p359).

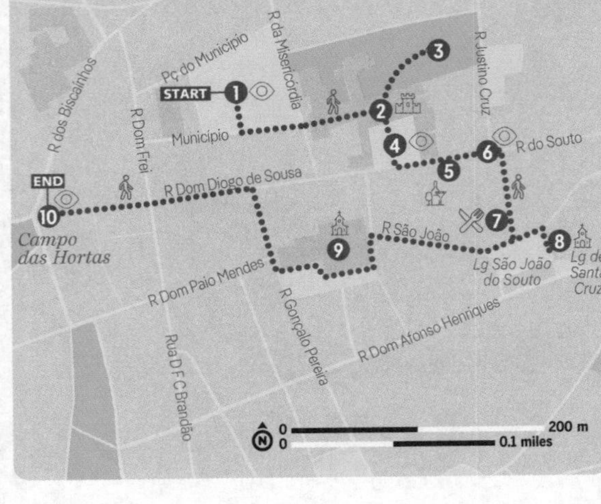

Braga's Historic Centre Walking Tour

ROMANS, CATHEDRALS AND BANANAS

Begin your discovery at the tree-laden **1 Praça do Município**, where the spectacular baroque building of Câmara Municipal (city hall) lies behind the Mannerist and Joanine Pelican Fountain. On the opposite side of the square, spot the baroque palace that hosts the Municipal Library. Continue towards the back of the building, and you'll see that it flows into the medieval **2 Paço Episcopal**, wrapped by the flower-filled gardens of **3 Jardim de Santa Bárbara**. Make your way to **4 Largo do Paço**, and you'll see a continuation of these buildings and the home of the rectory of the University of Minho.

Across the street, pop into **5 Casa das Bananas** for a shot of Moscatel wine and a banana – a local Christmas tradition. Continue through the pedestrian **6 Rua do Souto** and browse the shops of Braga's main commercial street.

Nearby, at Largo São João de Souto, snack on veal pies at **7 Frigideiras do Cantinho**; don't miss the Roman ruins inside. Heading out, take a moment to observe the interesting Manueline **8 Capela dos Coimbras**. Continue toward the **9 Sé de Braga**, the country's oldest cathedral, built in the

WHERE TO HAVE A DRINK IN BRAGA

Mal Amado
A relaxed and intimate bar next to the cathedral, with a wide selection of craft beers.

Setra
A cocktail-focused bar with an irreverent atmosphere; also serves other drinks and snacks.

Letraria – Craft Beer Library
A welcoming pub serving a variety of its brand's craft beers, plus snacks and meals.

11th century. Regard its Romanesque naves, the cloister and the tombs of the parents of the country's founding father. Finally, visit the elaborate baroque and neoclassical arch, **10 Arco da Porta Nova**, one of Braga's renowned landmarks, which used to be part of the medieval wall.

The Indoor Museums of Braga

FROM PREHISTORY TO NOBLE PALACES

While Braga is something of an open-air museum, there are many things to discover behind closed doors. The **Museu dos Biscainhos** is housed in a 17th-century palace and demonstrates the way of life of nobility and serfs. It also preserves several original collections of jewellery, furniture, paintings and musical instruments and is surrounded by beautiful gardens. A few blocks away, the **Museu de Arqueologia D Diogo de Sousa** exhibits archaeological finds from the Palaeolithic to the Middle Ages. Roman artefacts are also highlighted, as Braga played a significant role in the Roman Empire. It's also worth visiting the Roman and Suebi ruins at the **Domus Escola Velha da Sé** (by appointment), or the more distant **Núcleo Museológico de Dume**.

Codfish Sanctuary & Dessert Wonderland

OPULENT PORTIONS AND STRONG FLAVOURS

Much like other parts of the Minho, Braga's food is characterised by abundance and bold flavours. The city has a thing for codfish dishes, particularly the widespread *bacalhau à Narcisa*, which is served with onions and chips fried in olive oil. Family-run **Augusta**, northeast of the centre, is a great choice for trying this local speciality.

As a popular and widely used meat, pork is often paired with its innards, as seen in *rojões à Minhota* and *papas de sarrabulho*, which can be tasted at the rustic **Adega Malhoa**. The easy-to-like *arroz de pato à moda de Braga* (duck rice) should also be added to your to-eat list.

If you feel like snacking, you can indulge in a *frigideira*, a flaky meat pie, at the 18th-century **Frigideiras do Cantinho**.

A variety of rich, egg-filled desserts can be found in Braga. The *leite creme* (custard) with burnt sugar or the classic *pudim do Abade de Priscos* (an egg-yolk, port wine and lard flan) will make your taste buds tingle; besides restaurants, the latter can be tried at **Doçaria Cruz da Pedra**.

BEST RESTAURANTS IN BRAGA

Cozinha da Sé
This blue-toned chalet house presents carefully crafted Portuguese delicacies, focusing on seafood. **€€**

O Filho da Mãe
A delicious fusion of Portuguese and South American flavours is served at this modern, casual eatery. **€€**

Kartilho
A meat-heavy restaurant focused on premium cuts that are aged in-house; also a great wine selection. **€€€**

Tasquinha Dom Ferreira
A cosy and rustic *tasca* (tavern) with delicious duck rice and *bacalhau à moda de Braga*. **€€**

WHERE TO DRINK COFFEE IN BRAGA

Café A Brasileira
Opened in 1907, this elegant cafe is the local's favourite spot for a cup and a chat.

Café Vianna
This historic cafe, opened in 1858, was once a stomping ground for famous writers and revolutionaries.

APE Coffee
A two-storey speciality coffee shop focused on house-toasted beans and special blends.

BRAGA'S HOLY CELEBRATIONS

Semana Santa is a weeklong celebration open to everyone, where Jesus' birth, life, death and resurrection are embodied in multiple processions with figurines dressed in period costumes. One of the most anticipated moments of the week is the **Ecce Homo Procession**, where groups of *farricocos* storm the night silence on the Thursday before Easter. They walk barefoot, face covered, wearing black robes while tilting live flames over their heads and shaking noisy *matracas* (ratchets). Meanwhile, the biggest celebration in town, **São João**, is entirely opposite: it's all about dancing, singing and drinking. Grab your plastic hammer and join the cheerful crowd expecting the bright firework show.

TRABANTOS/SHUTTERSTOCK ©

Termas romanas do Alto da Cividade

Ruins of Roman Wellness

BRAGA'S ROMAN BATHS

The Roman city of Bracara Augusta lies beneath your feet – but now and then, its memory reappears from the underground. The public baths known as **Termas Romanas do Alto da Cividade** are protected under a massive rust-coloured roof, a few minutes southwest of the historic centre. The baths are believed to have been built in the 1st century, during the Flavian dynasty, and comprised a massive infrastructure that occupied much more than the currently exposed 850 sq metres. In fact, an enormous Roman theatre is still being carefully excavated beside it.

GETTING AROUND

The centre of Braga is walkable and relatively flat. Driving in the centre isn't necessary, and parking can be a challenge, as well as the many one-way streets. The city is well served by TUB buses that can take you longer distances.

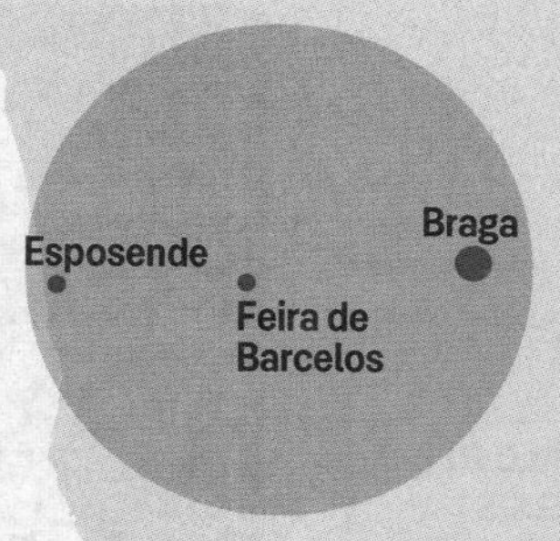

Beyond Braga

Braga's surroundings are blessed by the Cávado valley's beauty and interesting towns filled with crafts and great food.

A key city in the region surrounding Braga is Barcelos, a municipality founded by the nation's first king in the mid-12th century. A few centuries later, it became a commercial hot spot due to its exceptional weekly market. Even today, thousands of visitors are attracted to the market by the abounding local pottery and crafts. At the mouth of the Rio Cávado, you'll find the town of Esposende, which separated from Barcelos in 1572 and was historically dedicated to fishing, naval construction and maritime commerce. This culture generated a seafood-rich cuisine, attracting many visitors who also hit the beaches during the summer.

TOP TIP

The pottery haven of Barcelos is just a quick drive from Braga and makes for a great shopping escapade.

Feira de Barcelos (p358)

Ceramic roosters, Barcelos

The Pottery Paradise of Barcelos

EXPLORE THE COUNTRY'S OLDEST MARKET

A 20-minute drive from Braga will take you to the city of Barcelos. On Thursday, Barcelos attracts people from far and wide with its iconic **Feira de Barcelos**, one of the country's oldest and largest outdoor markets. If you love handicrafts, you'll be spoiled for choice as dozens of vendors sell ceramics, pottery, basketry and woodwork from all over the region. The fair is also rich in produce, artisanal food and everyday items, and you'll need a few hours to go through it.

The picturesque historic centre is worth a leisurely stroll. Other interesting sites include the derelict palace of **Paço dos Condes**, now an open-air archaeology museum. Here you can find the crucifix associated with the legend of the Barcelos rooster, a local and national icon. Seek out the 15th-century **Torre da Porta Nova**, the only surviving tower from the city's former walls. Close by is the baroque octagonal church, **Templo do Senhor Bom Jesus da Cruz**, home of the renowned celebrations of **Festas da Cruz**, held in May. You'll also want to visit the **Museu da Olaria**, which is dedicated to the region's most renowned craft, pottery. Moreover, fol-

THE GALO DE BARCELOS

The rooster of Barcelos is a familiar icon of Portugal. Legend has it that a Galician pilgrim of Santiago de Compostela was wrongly condemned to death and was on his way to the gallows. His desperate father summoned the roasted rooster the judge was eating to sing if his son was innocent, and his son was saved. Nonetheless, the rooster only truly became a national icon through Estado Novo's propaganda in the 1930s. They sourced the typical clay statues of roosters made by the potters of Barcelos and used them as a symbol of Portuguese popular art in international exhibitions. Today creating and hand-painting these black dotted roosters is still a tradition in Barcelos.

WHERE TO EAT IN BARCELOS

Pedra Furada
Famous for its Barcelos-style stuffed roast rooster, this little restaurant over-delivers with outstanding regional dishes. €€

Casa dos Arcos
This rustic restaurant cooks up hearty portions of traditional recipes and showcases a sinful dessert table. €€

Turismo
With privileged views of the Rio Cávado, this restaurant brings a contemporary twist to local classics. €€€

low the pottery route, **Rota da Olaria**, focused on the northeast part of the municipality. You can visit the many potters that produce the clay cookware and dinnerware known as *louça de Barcelos*.

Tibães Monastery

AN AGRICULTURAL POWERHOUSE

A 30-minute bus ride northwest of Braga will take you to the **Mosteiro de São Martinho de Tibães**. This massive 11th-century monastery is surrounded by 40 hectares of gardens, agricultural land and pastures. Formerly the motherhouse of the Benedictine monks in Portugal and Brazil, this community was a wealthy agricultural powerhouse. With time, they also invested in the arts and became an influential school for architects, sculptors, gilders and engravers. The church's nave is a jaw-dropping spectacle of rococo gilded woodwork, contrasting with the dignified but austere dwellings inhabited by the Black Monks. A visit to the entire space, including the cloisters, barns and other living, working and prayer spaces, is worth your while and should take a good part of a morning or afternoon.

A Trip to the Coast

BEACHES, WINDMILLS AND SEAFOOD

The coastal county of Esposende is worth a 30-minute drive if you're missing the ocean. In **Apúlia**, you can explore the scenic windmills and relish fabulous seafood in its restaurants, while in **Fão**, you can devour sweet *clarinhas de Fão*. The golden beaches of **Esposende** are great for basking in the sun or adventuring in water sports. Try Praia de Ofir, a wide sandy beach surrounded by dunes, pretty Praia da Apúlia for sunbathing and sport fishing, or long, golden Praia da Ramalha Sul, well known for being one of the north's few pet-friendly beaches.

The River Beach of Adaúfe

TIME TO COOL DOWN

If the heat of Braga is getting under your skin, drive 20 minutes to **Praia Fluvial de Adaúfe**. This peaceful beach on the Rio Cávado is a perfect family getaway, complete with all necessary infrastructures, sports equipment and lifeguards.

BEST RESTAURANTS IN ESPOSENDE

A Cabana
An informal, family-style restaurant where the sea dominates the atmosphere and the menu. The seafood and grill have made this place famous, and the *mariscada à Cabana*, an assortment of freshly caught local seafood, is a must-try. **€€**

Sra Peliteiro
This restaurant presents a careful cuisine with a Portuguese soul and a focus on codfish and octopus, while the meats have a more international approach. Enjoy your meal in the panoramic dining room or on the terrace overlooking the golf course and the Rio Cávado. **€€**

GETTING AROUND

Direct Transdev or Rede Expressos buses will take you from Braga to Barcelos in 40 minutes. Taking the train is roughly the same but requires an interchange. Other than driving, buses are your only option to reach Esposende, Tibães and Praia Fluvial de Adaúfe.

VIANA DO CASTELO

Gallant and distinctive, Viana do Castelo stands on the banks of the Rio Lima as Alto Minho's capital. The area has been inhabited since the Neolithic era, but Viana was only officially founded by Afonso III in 1258. It quickly became a maritime trade epicentre and was heavily guarded against pirates. In the 20th century, Viana led Portugal's massive codfish fishing fleet and became a significant shipbuilding centre. The interaction between the river and the sea is a pivotal part of its identity and industry; it's still a land of fishers, sailors, *sargaceiros* (sargasso harvesters) and shipyard workers.

More than anything, though, Viana is known for its passion. The *vianenses* are warm, amusing and cheerful. They adamantly hold on to their culture in their pilgrimages, crafts, gastronomy, music and folk traditions, which they gladly share with visitors. Add to that the vibrant markets, nature and fine beaches, which explains Viana's popularity as a holiday hot spot.

TOP TIP

It's easy to walk around the centre of Viana do Castelo. However, take the train to explore the beaches unless you prefer to ride a bike. The Ecovia Litoral Norte can be cycled from Viana do Castelo to Caminha and passes by all the beaches.

WHY I LOVE VIANA

This city has always had a special place in my heart. Growing up, many summers were spent in and around Viana do Castelo, enjoying the warm nights dining outdoors in the city's wonderful restaurants and then strolling around the medieval quarter. To me, Viana harbours history and creativity to feast the eyes, brilliant gastronomy to feed the stomach, and peaceful nature and beaches to soothe the soul. And you can always count on the delightful *vianenses* to reply with a smile and kind hospitality, so very typical of Minho.

Maria Sena

Holy 360-Degree Views

A SANCTUARY IN THE SKIES

Santuário do Monte de Santa Luzia, a sanctuary that sits on top of Monte Santa Luzia (228m), is easily the region's most well-known landmark. Built between 1904 and 1959, the church has an eclectic mix of architectural features, with an apparent Byzantine influence. The massive Gothic-influenced rose windows add gentle, colourful lighting to the interior. Climb up to the church's dome to enjoy the even more spectacular view of the city of Viana do Castelo and Lima's estuary. The site can be reached by car or the little **funicular** that climbs the steep hill.

Atop Monte Santa Luzia also lie the ruins of an Iron Age settlement, **Citânia de Santa Luzia**. Believed to be reduced to only a third of its original size, this Romanised settlement displays a cautious defensive structure, lined by three defensive walls with towers and moats. Inside, you can observe the foundations of over three dozen houses, most of which display typical circular architecture and the odd bread oven. The incredible views are no coincidence: its strategic location allowed the population to control all entries into the Lima estuary and surrounding land.

Codfish, Costumes & Ceramics

MUSEUMS OF VIANA DO CASTELO

Several interesting museums provide an insight into the local culture. The **Museu do Traje** displays incredible costumes,

SIGHTS
1 Antigos Paços do Concelho
2 Chafariz da Praça da Rainha
3 Igreja de Misericórdia
4 Museu de Artes Decorativas
5 Museu do Traje
6 Navio-Hospital Gil Eannes
7 Praça da República

EATING
8 Casa de Pasto Maria de Perre
9 Confeitaria Manuel Natário
10 O Laranjeira
11 O Manel
12 Taberna do Valentim
13 Tasquinha da Linda

DRINKING & NIGHTLIFE
14 Confeitaria A Brasileira
15 Zé Natário

TRANSPORT
16 Elevador de Santa Luzia

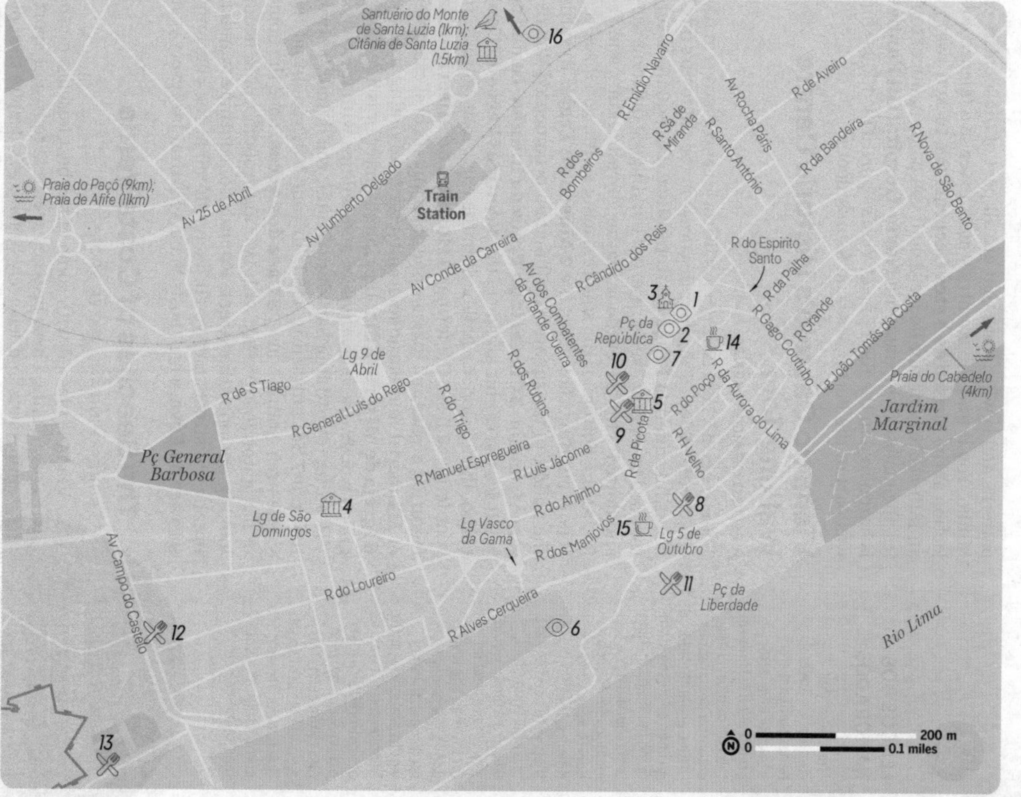

LENÇOS DOS NAMORADOS

The *lenços dos namorados* (lovers' handkerchiefs) are a form of love letter popularised in Minho in the 19th century. These colourful declarations of love are embroidered on linen or cotton cloth, using multiple stitching techniques. They include motifs such as hearts, keys, doves and flowers. Traditionally, they were used as part of a courtship ritual, where a woman would sew a handkerchief for the man she loved. If the affection was reciprocal, the man would proudly wear the handkerchief. It was also offered as a token of love when the man had to travel far. The text was often misspelt due to poor literacy, and current reproductions maintain these errors.

patterns and sewing work that are all part of the identity of Minho. You'll find the country's most extensive faience collection at the **Museu de Artes Decorativas**, tucked away in an 18th-century manor house. And if you enjoy nautical topics, the majestic ship museum **Navio-Hospital Gil Eannes** is harboured in the Rio Lima at Viana's port. This 1950s ship was part of the Portuguese cod fishing fleet.

Viana do Castelo's Historic Centre Walking Tour

A FLOOD OF MONUMENTS

The streets of Viana do Castelo's historic centre have a markedly medieval feel. Start your discovery in the old town's most beautiful square, **1 Praça da República**. The square is surrounded by elegant, well-preserved buildings of different ages and dotted with the outdoor seating of restaurants and cafes. At the bottom of the square, facing south, you'll see the yellow building that hosts the **2 Museu do Traje**. Towards the middle of the square, you'll find an ornamented Renaissance fountain, **3 Chafariz da Praça da Rainha**. Behind it, you'll see the Gothic arcade of the **4 Antigos Paços do Concelho**, the former city hall built in the early 16th century. To your left, you'll see the former **5 Hospital da Misericórdia** featuring arches and loggias, one of Portugal's best examples of Mannerist and baroque architecture. Adjoining it is the **6 Igreja de Misericórdia**; the church's interior is filled with gilded woodwork, blue *azulejos* and ceilings with frescoes.

Heading toward Rua Sacadura Cabral, you'll find the two-towered **7 Sé**, finished in 1483. To your left, you'll find the single-arch Gothic house, **8 Casa dos Arcos**, once the home of navigator João Velho, with two anthropomorphic heads looking out onto the street. From here, continue wandering the old streets and you'll likely end up at the charming **9 Praça da Erva**, which hosts Viana's Festival Jazz every year.

MORE BEACHES?

The Praia de Moledo (p366) in Caminha is the north's most famous beach, and in the summer, it attracts politicians, musicians and other celebrities.

The Beaches of Costa Verde

SUNBATHING AND WATER SPORTS

Viana is blessed with some of the best beaches on the Costa Verde. These beaches are great for water sports enthusiasts and leisurely beachgoers despite the cold water. The vast sandy shore of **Praia de Afife** is protected by green dunes and has a small lagoon formed by the Rio Afife. The charming **Praia do Paçô** is overlooked by the 17th-century fortification of **Forte do Paçô** and is

WHERE TO HAVE COFFEE IN VIANA DO CASTELO

Confeitaria Manuel Natário
This historic pastry shop is known nationwide for its famous *bolas de Berlim*. €

Confeitaria A Brasileira
Open since 1902, this historic cafe is the right place for an espresso and a *sidónio* (bean tart). €

Zé Natário
Enjoy a coffee and a sweet at the pleasant outside seating on the main avenue. €

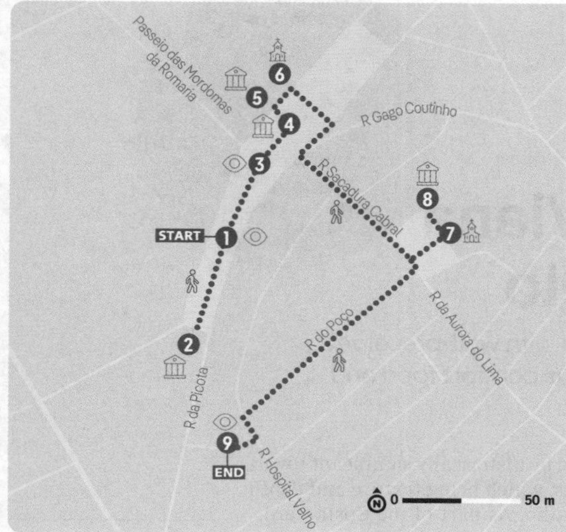

sheltered from the sometimes rough north winds. However, the often windy **Praia do Cabedelo** is particularly good for water sports like surfing, kitesurfing and windsurfing, hosting several competitions every year.

The Gastronomy of Viana do Castelo

AN ODE TO SEAFOOD

Viana is bordered by the ocean and river, so most tables take fish for granted. Its strong ties to cod fishing are present in dishes like the roasted codfish dish, *bacalhau à Viana*. Other notable marine recipes include *polvo à Lagareiro* (confit octopus), *pescada à Vianense* (roast hake) and colourful *caldeiradas* (fish stews). Seasonal fish like lampreys (p366), shads and trout are also popular.

The meat repertoire is no less impressive and includes the velvety *arroz pica no chão* (chicken and blood rice) and the hearty pork-fest *rojões à moda do Minho.*

Wrap it all up with some *arroz doce* (rice pudding) or head out to Manuel Natário to try a conventual dessert like *meias luas* (a little half-moon pie), or their famous *bolas de Berlim* (a doughnut-like sweet stuffed with a delicious eggy custard).

BEST RESTAURANTS IN VIANA DO CASTELO

O Laranjeira
Family-owned restaurant serving carefully presented traditional recipes and excellent homemade desserts. €€

Camelo
A long-standing bastion east of the centre that serves traditional seafood dishes, praised for its seasonal *lampreia* recipes. €€

Casa de Pasto Maria de Perre
A rustic old-school restaurant that serves authentic regional food, revered for its *bacalhau* and pork dishes. €€

Tasquinha da Linda
A popular seafood-only restaurant inside Viana's fishing dock, with superb fish recipes. €€€

Taberna do Valentim
Freshly caught grilled fish with a fresh Alvarinho wine is the go-to combination of this Viana classic. €€

GETTING AROUND

Viana do Castelo's centre is very walkable, and two electric buses circle the historic centre during the day. There are some slight hills, but the waterfront is flat and good for cycling. If you are driving into the city, there are convenient underground parking lots on the main avenue.

Valença do Minho
Viana do Castelo
Ponte de Lima

Beyond Viana do Castelo

The Alto Minho is filled with well-preserved historic towns, delicious comfort food and delicate white wines.

Viana do Castelo is encircled by historically significant towns filled with unique traditions, which bring texture and depth to the character of Alto Minho. As part of the Costa Verde, the surroundings also present exceptional beaches and natural escapes. However, not everything develops around the coast, so be prepared to travel inland to visit certain areas. That's the case with Ponte de Lima and Valença do Minho, which deliver rich historic centres and excellent markets if your trip coincides with those days. Moreso, the verdant wine country of Monção and Melgaço deserves its own exploration. Ideally, plan at least two or three days to dig what lies beyond the city of Viana do Castelo.

TOP TIP

Taking the train or bus will get you far, but driving is convenient for Melgaço and essential for Serra d'Arga.

Ponte Romanae e Medieval, Ponte de Lima

Riverside Escapade in Ponte de Lima

HORSES, MARKETS AND CANOES

A 40-minute drive will take you to the bucolic town of **Ponte de Lima**, which sprawls along the banks of the Rio Lima and offers a delightful half-day escapade. Its pedestrianised historic centre is small, well preserved and brimming with opulent manor homes and palaces. Explore the city's cobblestone streets and the medieval **Igreja Matriz**, and unleash your inner child at the Portuguese toy museum, **Museu do Brinquedo Português**. Rest at the pleasant cafes of **Largo de Camões**, adorned with a Renaissance fountain, before heading out for lunch in the backstreets' several restaurants.

Cross the town's prominent landmark bridge, the **Ponte Romana e Medieval**, with sections belonging to the Roman and medieval periods. Ponte de Lima is also known for its excellence in water sports like canoeing and kayaking, so head out to **Clube Náutico de Ponte de Lima** and navigate the nature-filled riverbed of the Rio Lima. You can also rent a bike and hit the idyllic riverside trails of **Ecovia do Rio Lima**.

The bimonthly **Feira de Ponte de Lima** is one of Minho's best – and one of the country's oldest – markets, attracting droves of locals and newcomers. Annual events such as the **Feira do Cavalo** (horse fair) in July and the high-spirited *romaria* (pilgrimage) of **Feiras Novas** in September bring thousands to this otherwise peaceful town.

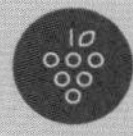

BEST WINERIES IN PONTE DE LIMA

Quinta do Ameal
This 18th-century farm is in close contact with the Rio Lima and the vineyards are surrounded by a dense forest. Book ahead to enjoy wine tastings, river activities and trekking, or even spend the night.

Aphros Wine
These pioneers in biodynamic winemaking are creating a new generation of wines made with local varietals. Upon reservation, visitors can tour the 17th-century estate's modern cellar, equipped with state-of-the-art technology and the medieval cellar, devoid of any technology for producing amphora wines.

The Stronghold of Valença do Minho

FORTS, HISTORY AND BUYING FRENZY

A 40-minute train ride from Viana do Castelo will take you to the fortified town of **Valença do Minho**, protected by a network of bulwarks, ravelins and moats, and staring directly at Spain. Separated by the Rio Minho, these neighbours have made amends after centuries of conflict. Every weekend, the cobblestone streets are invaded by Spaniards on a shopping stampede, feasting upon the dozens of stores selling linens, toiletries, baskets and other crafts. On Wednesday, a colossal market attracts people from far and wide and is worth the trip from Viana do Castelo.

Besides the complex fortification, interesting sights include the Romanesque **Igreja de Santa Maria dos Anjos**, the Manueline manor house **Casa do Eirado** and the 1st-century **Roman milestone** of the old road from Braga to Astorga.

WHERE TO EAT IN PONTE DE LIMA

A Carvalheira
A local favourite serving seasonal delights like the eerie lamprey, focusing on regional cuisine and superb desserts. €€

A Tulha
This rustic eatery serves delicious meaty *rojões* and *arroz de sarrabulho*, and tasty fish dishes. €€

Taverna Vaca das Cordas
Excellent meat dishes and codfish with mashed potatoes are the highlights in this old-school tavern. €€

THE LAMPREY ODYSSEY

One of Portugal's most exotic foods is lamprey, a jawless fish swathed in myths. This parasitic cyclostome preys on other fish's blood with its terrifying sucking disk filled with sharp teeth and eel-shaped body. Indeed, this seasonal delicacy is granted a love-or-hate status. Lampreys migrate into the Portuguese rivers every year between February and May. Along the Rio Minho, a popular lamprey fishing site, there are around 900 *pesqueiras ancestrais*, ancient stone constructions for trapping river fish. After being captured, these creatures are kept alive in restaurant aquariums until ordered. Popular recipes include *lampreia à Bordalesa* (lamprey stewed in its own blood, red wine and vinegar).

ENRIQUE ROJAS/SHUTTERSTOCK ©

Iberian wolves

Caminha & Vila Nova de Cerveira

GET-TOGETHERS, BEACHES AND ART

A 22-minute train ride from Viana do Castelo takes you to the medieval town of **Caminha**, which overlooks Spain, a short ferry ride over the Rio Minho. It's a popular holiday resort, and its central square overflows with lively get-togethers during the summer months. The charming historic centre hosts delightful seafood restaurants and interesting historic buildings. **Praia de Moledo**, the region's most renowned beach, is definitely worth a visit.

An 18-minute train ride from Caminha will take you to **Vila Nova de Cerveira**, the region's cultural capital. Every two years, it hosts the **Bienal de Cerveira**, an influential art festival. The town's streets are populated with artwork by notable Portuguese artists, which can be discovered by following the self-guided tour **Roteiro das Artes**.

The Lands of Alvarinho

WINE, THERMAL SPRINGS AND CASTLES

Two towns of great historical and winemaking importance lie on the northernmost tip of Portuguese territory. While Monção and Melgaço share a common history as military strongholds, they also share a particular Atlantic micro-

WHERE TO EAT IN MELGAÇO

Adega Sabino
This unassuming restaurant attracts clans keen on roasted goatling and stewed lamprey, when in season. €€

Tasquinha da Portela
This regional restaurant serves local cuisine in epic portions, always paired with *vinho verde*. €€

Tasquinha de Melgaço
A small restaurant showcasing signature dishes, including the exceptional codfish with stone crab. €€

climate, tempered with a continental influence. The climate shaped this corner of the *vinho verde* region, giving birth to one of the nation's most famous white grape varieties: Alvarinho. It's here that Alvarinho wines reach their peak of perfection, and visits to the wine estates of **Palácio da Brejoeira** and **Quinta do Soalheiro** are unmissable.

An 80-minute drive from Viana leads you to the old town of **Melgaço**, where you can explore the medieval **Castle of Melgaço** and the Romanesque **Igreja Matriz**. Check out the **Solar do Alvarinho**, dedicated to promoting Alvarinho wines, complete with tasting rooms and a shop. The delicious *fumeiro de Melgaço* (smoked meats) will keep your stomach full if you're feeling hungry. Further west from town, treat yourself to the thermal water treatments of **Termas de Melgaço**.

In the peaceful old town of **Monção**, an hour's drive from Viana, walk through the walls of the medieval **Monção Castle**, then explore the Gothic **Igreja Matriz**. Then head out to the pleasant **Praça Deu-la-Deu**, where you can see the 17th-century **Igreja da Misericórdia**. The thermal springs of **Termas de Monção** are also worth a dip.

BEST SUMMER MUSIC FESTIVALS

Festival Vilar de Mouros
The oldest Iberian music festival happens in late August. The stage is set near the banks of the Rio Coura, inviting attendees to take a dip.

Festival Paredes de Coura
This alternative music festival in August takes place surrounded by nature. A backdrop of lush greenery, the Rio Coura and a charming forest camping site.

Neopop Festival
August delivers four days of electronic music to Viana do Castelo, bringing in thousands of techno aficionados from all over the world.

Return to Nature in Serra d'Arga

WILDERNESS OF THE GRANITE MOUNTAINS

A 50-minute drive from Viana do Castelo will take you to the mountain range of **Serra d'Arga**, where almost 45 sq km of wilderness is populated by tiny villages. These scenic granite mountains are dotted with cows, goats and wild Garrano horses, who can easily be spotted grazing through the brush or lazily walking the dirt roads.

Serra d'Arga is also a refuge for many sensitive species, including badgers, otters, Lusitanian salamanders, Iberian frogs, Eurasian eagle-owls, griffon vultures and Iberian wolves, as well as delicate flora like carnivorous and aromatic plants. You can see these species in the Serra's wide variety of habitats, such as plains, marshlands, oak forests, granite upwellings and lagoons.

Although the mountaintop (at 825m) can be more easily reached by car, the area is a hiker's paradise, with six official hiking trails to choose from. You can also explore by mountain bike, with set trails and even bike stations for any necessary maintenance. Both hiking and bike trails will take you through some of the area's most interesting points, including its villages, viewpoints, waterfalls and lagoons.

WHERE TO FIND LAGOONS IN SERRA D'ARGA

Cascata do Pincho
This picturesque waterfall is famous for its crystal clear waters, fanning beautifully among the rocks.

Cascata e Lagoa Janela do Céu
Surrounded by forest, this lagoon emulates an infinity pool before dropping into a waterfall.

Lagoa da Esturranha
There's plenty of room to roll out your towel next to the turquoise waters of this lagoon.

WILD MOUNTAIN PONIES

An ancient indigenous horse breed, the Garrano is native to all of Northern Portugal. This short, stocky brown pony can be seen roaming freely in the mountains of Serra d'Arga, Peneda-Gerês, Soajo and Cabreira. It is, in fact, a semi-wild horse, which also explains its remarkable adaptation to its environment. Even so, it is considered an endangered horse, primarily because of a lack of interest in the breed and not due to its natural predator, the Iberian wolf (also endangered). In the past, the Garrano played an essential role as an agricultural workhorse and pack horse. Today it's gained importance as a vital tool against wildfires, and is also becoming a tourist attraction.

DAVID WIECZOREK/SHUTTERSTOCK ©

Garrano horse

Every year, on 29 August, the procession known as **Romaria de São João d'Arga** takes pilgrims up the mountain on foot until they reach the little monastery of São João d'Arga. The night is filled with music, dancing and food, including plenty of *aguardente* (spirits) with local honey (known as *chiripiti*).

GETTING AROUND

You can catch either the Regional or InterRegional train in Viana do Castelo to get to Valença, Vila Nova da Cerveira and Caminha. Ponte de Lima is a 40-minute or less bus ride away using Ovnitur or Rede Expressos buses.

FlixBus, Rede Expressos and AV Minho have several buses to Monção, but there are less options for Melgaço. Renting a car to visit both may be more convenient, and also for exploring remote areas like Serra d'Arga.

GUIMARÃES

Formerly known as Vimaranes, the city of Guimarães has deep roots as the nation's birthplace. Not only was the country's first king, Afonso Henriques, born here, but it is also where, as a young man, he fought and won the first battle for the country's independence in the 12th century. Indeed, it was in the Middle Ages that Guimarães saw its biggest boom as the kingdom's first capital, a title it eventually lost to Coimbra.

Its pristinely preserved historic centre is an architectural showcase and a Unesco World Heritage Site. But Guimarães did not stop in time. Today Guimarães has a population of just over 54,000 and stands as one of Portugal's most industrialised regions, producing some of the finest textiles and cutleries. The demographic is kept lively with the many students that attend the University of Minho and also on account of the city's rich cultural events.

TOP TIP

The centre of Guimarães is a pleasure to walk around, but beware of the long hill you must trek to the castle. Due to being inland, the city can be sweltering in the peak of summer, so plan your walks to avoid the hottest hours.

The Historic Centre of Guimarães

A UNESCO WORLD HERITAGE HIGHLIGHT

An architectural spectacle lies within the narrow pedestrianised streets of Guimarães' old town. Visiting the meticulously preserved historic centre will transport you back in time. The pride of the *vimaranenses* in their heritage is palpable, and it is the sole reason why history seems to be so alive here.

Make your way through **Rua de Santa Maria**, one of the town's oldest streets. Keep your eyes open for the Gothic noble homes, and don't forget to admire the baroque **Convento de Santa Clara**, once one of the city's richest convents. Inevitably, you'll walk under the granite arch of **Casa do Arco**, and moments later you'll face the imposing **Igreja de Nossa Senhora da Oliveira**. Built in the 14th century by order of King João I in honour of the victory in the battle of Aljubarrota, the church's name takes after 'Our Lady of the Olive Tree', hence the olive tree planted in the middle of the charming **Largo de Oliveira**. Stop and appreciate the **Padrão do Salado**, a remarkable Gothic canopy shrine built in the 14th century. Try to spot the two-faced statue on top of the **Antigos Paços do Concelho**, the former city hall, and then walk under the arches to discover another medieval square, **Praça de São Tiago**, enclosed by quaint houses. Hereon, what better than to get lost in the small alleyways and explore.

COLLECTIVE CELEBRATION

The **Festas Gualterianas** began in 1906 as a cattle fair in honour of St Gualter. Over the years, the fair has become the city's most beloved celebration and part of the identity of *vimaranense*. On the first weekend of August, locals and visitors can still enjoy the inaugural cattle exhibition, followed by many musical events, a carnival, religious procession, chariot parade and fireworks. Last but not least is the bubbly and fun Gualterian parade, complete with thematic floats and figurines.

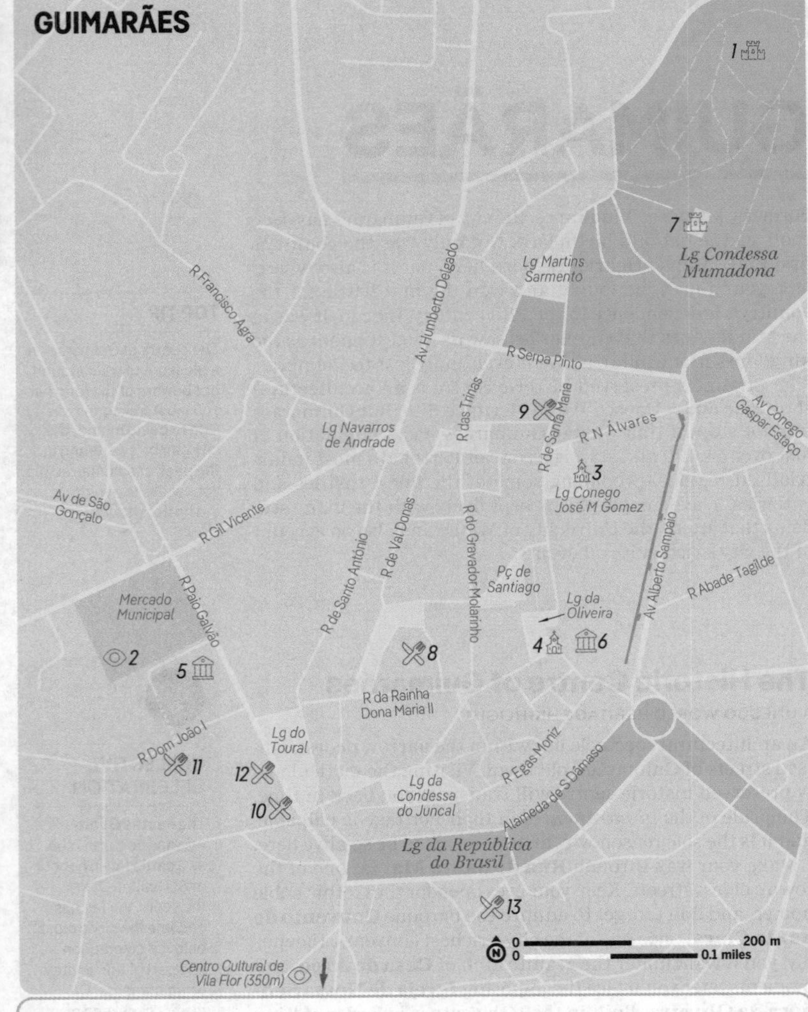

SIGHTS
1 Castelo de Guimarães
2 Centro Internacional das Artes José de Guimarães
3 Convento de Santa Clara
4 Igreja de Nossa Senhora da Oliveira
5 Museu Arqueológio Martins Sarmento
6 Museu de Alberto Sampaio
7 Paço dos Duques de Bragança

EATING
8 A Cozinha
9 Casa Costinha
10 Clarinha
11 Le Babachris
12 Pastelaria Nova Camir
13 Taberna Trovador

The Medieval Medley of Monte Latito

BETWEEN CASTLES AND PALACES

Uphill from the historic centre is the **Monte Latito**, a hill home to the city's most important monuments. The **Castelo de Guimarães** was initially built in the 10th century by the mighty Countess Mumadona Dias to fend off the Vikings. Today this medieval castle is not only a symbol of Guimarães but also of the nation itself. This eight-towered granite stronghold, which has been remodelled several times during its existence, is believed to have been the birthplace of Portugal's first king, Afonso Henriques, who fought within its walls several times.

Nearby is the monumental **Paço dos Duques de Bragança**. Construction of this elegant palace, which tower over the city of Guimarães, began in 1420 by D Afonso. It's the largest and most well-preserved medieval palace in Portugal. Its distinctive brick chimneys would have kept the inhabitants warm, and the palace even had running water, uncommon for the time. After centuries of neglect, the palace was restored as a presidential residence in the mid-20th century. Despite debate among specialists, the restoration has proven to be more faithful to the original project than initially thought.

BORDADOS DE GUIMARÃES

Elaborate Guimarães embroidery can only be made in a single colour, most frequently bright red. Nonetheless, there are six official colours of cotton thread (red, blue, beige, white, black and grey) that may be threaded into the white linen base. This certified technique includes 20 different needlepoint stitches, which require years of practice and skill to achieve. The motifs are highly sophisticated and often display plants, flowers, monograms, hearts and other geometric figures. The history of this technique is poorly documented and the first written evidence only shows up in the 19th century. Today it's used mostly in decorative home items, but also wedding dresses.

From the Heights of Penha

NATURE, LEISURE AND DEVOTION

The mountain of **Penha** has an altitude of 617m and is draped in over 60 hectares of green landscape and large boulders. It's a popular weekend relaxation spot for many *vimaranenses*. The topmost of the mountain is home to several religious sites, including the **Santuário da Penha**, to which many pilgrims roam. The building is dull, but the view over the valley is mesmerising. Several walking and biking trails along the mountain will allow you to enjoy the quiet woodland, often interrupted by giant granite boulders, many of which are fuzzy with verdant moss. The 10-minute **cable car** ride from Guimarães to the mountaintop provides unbeatable views.

Uncovering Art & Archaeology

THE MUSEUMS OF GUIMARÃES

The meticulously preserved historical backdrop of Guimarães led to its election as the European Capital of Culture in 2012, pivoting the city into a hub of museums, galleries and cultural events.

WHERE TO EAT PASTRIES IN GUIMARÃES

Pastelaria Clarinha
Guimarães' sweetheart, famous for its tortas de Guimarães, beijinhos and toucinho-do-céu. €

Pastelaria Nova Camir
A gem for regional pastry and seasonal delights like pão-de-ló or bolo-rei. €

Casa Costinha
Tucked in a medieval street, this centenary shop bakes mouthwatering toucinho-do-céu and tortas de Guimarães. €

The **Museu de Alberto Sampaio** has a rich collection of religious art, including textiles, jewellery and gilded woodwork. It includes the golden chalice that belonged to Sancho I and the tunic worn by João I in the Battle of Aljubarrota. Meanwhile, the **Museu Arqueológico Martins Sarmento** is one of Europe's leading museums on the ancient *cultura castreja* (hillfort culture; p375). Inside the Gothic cloister of São Domingos, the museum holds a valuable compendium of pre- and protohistoric pieces and other collections.

Contemporary art exhibitions can be admired at the **Centro Internacional das Artes José de Guimarães**, a striking building with gleaming golden walls. The **Centro Cultural de Vila Flor** hosts temporary art exhibitions, concerts and plays, and Guimarães' biannual illustration and textile exhibits.

BEST RESTAURANTS IN GUIMARÃES

A Cozinha
Michelin-starred modern Portuguese cuisine with a special focus on sustainability and local ingredients. **€€€**

Florêncio
Traditional Minho comfort food with notable rabbit, pork and *bacalhau* dishes and regional desserts. **€€**

Le Babachris
A tiny restaurant with an ever-changing tasting menu of delicate dishes inspired by market ingredients. **€€€**

Traditional Fare in Guimaraes

AMONG PETISCOS AND VINHO VERDE

Guimarães follows Minho's tradition of hearty food and tempting desserts. Start your meal with some *petiscos* (tapas) like *punheta de bacalhau* (raw codfish salad), *polvo em molho verde* (octopus salad) or *sopa de nabos* (turnip soup). The casual contemporary **Taberna Trovador** is a great spot for sampling an array of *petiscos*.

Follow with main dishes like *bacalhau com broa* (codfish with cornbread) and *cabrito assado* (roast goatling), or the more challenging but delicious *arroz pica no chão* (chicken and blood rice), *bucho recheado* (stuffed pig's stomach) or *rojões com papas de sarrabulho* (fried pork with blood porridge). Traditional restaurants like the old-school Florêncio are bastions of this delectable, slow-cooked cuisine. The ideal companion to every meal is the local white *vinho verde*, a crisp, citrusy, and slightly sparkling regional wine.

Last but not least, head out to local-favourite **Pastelaria Clarinha** to sample traditional sweets such as *toucinho-do-céu, tortas de Guimarães* or *douradinhas*, all of which are composed of eggs, almonds and marrow.

CASTLE AFICIONADOS

If you love exploring castles, then the Castelo de Lanhoso (p375) should be your next stop. This castle is perched on a dizzying rocky mass and deliberately inaccessible.

The Leather Tanning Quarter

MEMORIES OF AN INDUSTRY

A slight detour from the historic centre will take you to an industrial archaeological site. The **Zona de Couros** is a homage to one of the most essential trades in Guimarães since the medieval era: leather tanning, an industry

WHERE TO STAY IN GUIMARÃES

Conquistador Palace
A former palace house in the historic centre turned into a stylish guesthouse. **€€€**

Hotel da Oliveira
A cosmopolitan hotel delivering excellent meals and views over beautiful Praça da Oliveira. **€€**

Pousada Mosteiro de Guimarães
Monastery turned hotel allies luxury to antiquity, offering a five-star experience. **€€**

Rojões com papas de sarrabulho

that came to its height in the 19th century. Here you can observe the tanks used to transform the pelts into leather until the mid-20th century. On the lower end of the street, spot the discreet Couro (leather) river, which used to fill the tanks and wash away the smelly remains of the industry. On your way down, a wooden gate to the right hides the **Ilha do Sabão**, a housing unit for tannery workers.

BEST VINHO VERDE WINERIES IN GUIMARÃES

Casa de Sezim
This estate has been in the same family since 1376. Enjoy tours and tastings or participate in the harvest by making a reservation.

Quinta dos Encados
This small estate is owned by a passionate family whose efforts have produced award-winning wines. You can even roll up your sleeves during harvest season (book in advance).

Quinta da Aveleira
This centuries-old, family-owned farm produces the award-winning wine Valle dos Três Irmãos; book ahead for tours and tastings.

GETTING AROUND

The granite slab streets of the centre of Guimarães can be easily tackled on foot, but there's a long upward hike to the castle and Paço dos Duques. Local Guimabus buses are useful for getting around the city. If you're driving, the historic centre is off limits during specific schedules; the best bet is to park in the public parking lots in the vicinity.

Beyond Guimarães

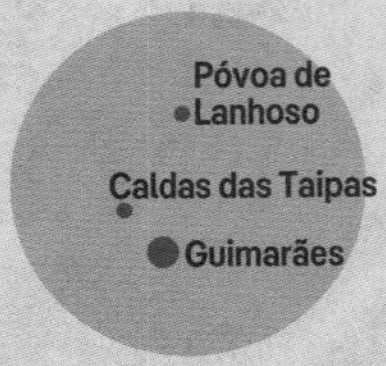

The area surrounding Guimarães is rich in history, featuring plentiful ruins and remnants of early settlers.

Póvoa de Lanhoso
Caldas das Taipas
Guimarães

Considering Guimarães' antiquity, it's unsurprising that the surrounding territories have evidence of a long path in human yore. There's much history to explore north and northeast of the city, where you can find remnants of the Iron Age, some of the country's finest archaeological sites as well as demonstrations of the profound changes that occurred after the Roman invasion. History continues in Póvoa de Lanhoso, with its 10th-century castle setting the stage for the nation's birth, together with Guimarães. However, you can also explore the vast natural landscape and mountain ranges through hikes or adventure sports. A full day should be enough to scour the most interesting sites and activities.

TOP TIP

Ramp up your energy to visit Citânia de Briteiros: the site is big, and the terrain is very uneven.

Citânia de Briteiros

The Hillfort of Citânia de Briteiros

AN ARCHAEOLOGICAL DELIGHT

A 30-minute drive from Guimarães will take you to one of the most important landmarks of the Iberian protohistory. Partially hidden by the woodland, the **hillfort of Briteiros** overlooks the Rio Ave. Within the lichen- and moss-laden defensive walls and cobblestone streets, you can see remnants of life in the Iron Age, around the 10th century BCE. Evidence shows that the site was occupied during the Roman invasion, as many artefacts were found in the excavations. As you walk through the streets of this little town, pay attention to the bathhouse and its engraved monolith stone, the typical round houses, reconstructed in the 19th century, and the wide circle that composes the council house, used as a local senate.

Roman Baths of Caldas das Taipas

THERMAL CULTURE THROUGH THE AGES

The small town of **Caldas das Taipas** is a 20-minute drive from Guimarães and is the central hub of the Portuguese cutlery industry. The region's mineral-rich thermal waters led the Romans to build thermal bathhuses in the **Banhos Velhos**, now a cultural centre. Other evidence of Roman occupation can be found in different points of the town, like the **Ara de Trajano**, an engraved monolith in honour of the emperor Trajan, or the low Roman bridge that crosses the Rio Ave. But Caldas das Taipas' main attraction continues to be the wonderful therapeutic and thermal spa experiences at **Taipas Termal**.

Castles, Hillforts & Adventures

EXPLORING THE LANDS OF LANHOSO

Reachable with a 35-minute drive, **Póvoa de Lanhoso** is worth a half-day trip from Guimarães, particularly for sightseeing and for those who love adventure sports like rafting and canyoning.

Once you arrive, you'll understand why few castles in Portugal are as impenetrable as the **Castelo de Lanhoso**. Strategically built on top of the magnificent rocky mass of **Monte do Pilar**, likely around the 10th century, the only access to the castle used to be an uneven stairway carved through the treacherously steep granite slopes. The view from the top provides a sensational 360-degree view over the entire region, including the Serra da Cabreira. A few

THE CULTURA CASTREJA

The *cultura castreja* (hillfort culture) was prevalent in northern Portugal and Galicia between the Bronze Age and the 1st century CE. The *castro* is a fortified settlement, protected by granite walls and moats and filled with round houses. Usually they were located on hills with good visibility and plenty of natural resources. Thousands of castros have been identified in the Minho and Trás-os-Montes regions. Due to constant invasions, the northern Iberian populations were forced to live in isolation and in a permanent defensive state. When the Romans conquered the Iberian Peninsula, they changed the organisation of the *castros*, creating defined neighbourhoods and several public infrastructures. Still, with time, they ceased to exist.

WHERE TO EAT IN PÓVOA DE LANHOSO

O Victor
A gastronomical staple known far and wide for the most delicious grilled codfish with smashed potatoes. **€€**

Restaurante Velho Minho
Located in the heart of town, this traditional restaurant highlights codfish dishes and roast goatling. **€€**

Pastelaria Maria da Fonte
A pastry shop filled with delicious traditional pastries, including the popular speciality *rochas do pilar*. **€**

THE FILIGREE OF PÓVOA DE LANHOSO

The ancient technique of using gold or silver threads to create intricate jewellery is called *filigrana* (filigree) and has been employed in Póvoa de Lanhoso since pre-Roman times. Manual filigree production involves high-level craft skills and meticulous handwork. Dozens of these small segments, sometimes as thin as 0.8mm, are assembled into one piece. However, not all *filigrana* is artisanal, so handmade pieces are entitled to certification. The most traditional pieces include the earrings and necklaces. The latter, a heart-shaped piece that seems to be made out of a thousand grains, represents the epitome of *filigrana*. Together with traditional costumes, these intricate jewels are proudly displayed by women during Minho's *romarias* (festivals).

STOCKPHOTOSART/SHUTTERSTOCK ©

Santuário de Nossa Senhora do Pilar

steps down is the 16th-century **Santuário de Nossa Senhora do Pilar**, a sanctuary built with stone removed from parts of the castle's ruins. On your way downhill, you can also explore the **Castro de Lanhoso**, a pre-Roman hillfort.

The region is an adventure sports hub, hosting one of the biggest adventure parks in Europe, **Diverlanhoso**. You can participate in the park's multiple activities such as rafting, canyoning, rock climbing and horse riding. There are also several walking trails throughout Póvoa de Lanhoso, including the **Via Romana XVII**, part of the Roman Antonine Itinerary that connected Braga to Astorga, as well as 10 official bike trails that cross several of the region's most interesting sights.

GETTING AROUND

Reaching Citânia de Briteiros from Guimarães by public transportation is lengthy and requires switching buses; the same goes for Póvoa de Lanhoso. A rental car is more convenient for both locations. Transdev has a quick 15-minute bus to Caldas das Taipas.

PARQUE NACIONAL DA PENEDA-GERÊS

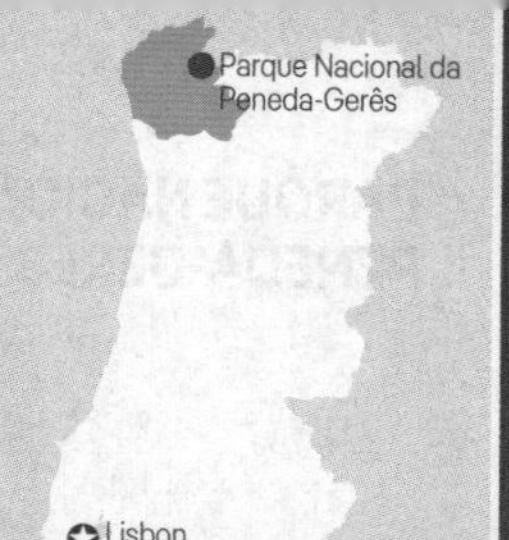

Established in 1971, this is Portugal's only national park. Almost 700 sq km of protected landscape are spread over four mountain ranges, the Serras of Peneda, Amarela, Gerês and Soajo. The valleys have dozens of small villages with history and ancient traditions. As evidenced by many megalithic structures and rock art, humans have inhabited this territory for thousands of years. The Romans crossed the land with a modern road, the Geira, paving the way for progress. Despite this, most of the region remained widely untouched. The granite-clad mountains provide numerous habitats for a great diversity of flora and fauna. You'll come across unspoiled oak forests, peat bogs, riparian forests, dry scrub, beautiful lagoons and waterfalls. The effort to protect the area is not only to guarantee that future generations will enjoy this natural reserve but also to safeguard these mountain populations' threatened way of life.

TOP TIP

Despite the park's popularity and vigilance, it's easy to get into trouble. The park is massive, and people do get lost. Avoid hiking late in the day, and always take supplies and adequate clothing. Be aware that you will often lose your phone signal. Always be extra careful when exploring waterfalls. Stay safe and follow the rules.

Explore the Park's Northern Section

VILLAGES, GRANARIES AND CASTLES

The entrance to the park's northern section is at the **Gate of Lamas de Mouro**. Driving 7km east, you'll find the isolated village of **Castro Laboreiro**, a shepherding community assisted by the land's eponymous dog.

A long 38km drive south will take you to **Soajo**. This small village is enmeshed with granite houses in narrow streets, culminating in an elevation topped with mighty granite *espigueiros* (granaries). These communal structures are supported by mushroom stones to protect the drying corn from vermin. In the same spirit, a short 10km drive will take you to the village of **Lindoso**, where next to the medieval castle, you'll find a bewitching agglomeration of 50 granaries built between the 1600s and the 1700s. You can make a brief detour through Spain to get to **Cascata da Portela do Homem**. This picturesque waterfall fills a lagoon with gorgeous emerald-coloured water and is just begging for a dip. Be warned: the water is cold.

Head out to the close-by **Mata da Albergaria**, one of the park's most important forests. This secular oak forest is filled with protected species and is crossed by the **old Roman road** (Geira). Don't miss the gorgeous **Cascata das Lagoas**. Vehicle access to the park is limited during the summer. From here, you're only 46km from the central town of Caldas do Gerês, which is an excellent base for exploring the park.

BEST PARK HIKES

PR9 – Trilho dos Poços Verdes
This moderate 12km loop trail crosses lagoons, waterfalls and viewpoints.

Trilho Pertinho do Céu
This beautiful 6km loop trail wanders through the foothills of the Peneda mountains..

PR7 – Caminhos do Pão e Caminhos da Fé
An easy 5.4km loop trail snakes around the village of Soajo.

Castro Laboreiro Loop
A short hike to the ruins of the medieval castle delivers stunning panoramic views.

PARQUE NACIONAL DA PENEDA-GERÊS

SIGHTS
1 Caldas do Gerês
2 Cascata da Portela do Homem
3 Cascata de Pincães
4 Cascata do Arado
5 Cascata Fecha de Barjas
6 Mata da Albergaria
7 Miradouro de Fafião
8 Miradouro Novo da Pedra Bela

Central Section of the Park

MAGICAL WATERFALLS AND VIEWPOINTS

Starting at the thermal town of **Caldas do Gerês**, you can easily explore the central part of the park. Make a pit stop 6km south to observe the overwhelming views over Gerês from the **Miradouro Novo da Pedra Bela**; it's probably the entire park's best viewpoint.

Take a short 3km drive to Miradouro das Rocas and park there. Go on foot up the bumpy dirt road leading to the Rio Arado bridge. Here you'll spot the **Cascata do Arado**,

WHERE TO EAT REGIONAL CUISINE

Lurdes Capela
A renowned family-run restaurant in Vila do Gerês serving superb regional dishes and seasonal game meat. €€

Adega Ramalho
Rustic tavern famous for its mouthwatering *costeletas de vitela* (veal chops) and chocolate mousse. €€

Tasquina Ti'Mélia
Enjoy the delicious Cachena steak with bean rice or an assortment of regional *petiscos*. €€

one of Gerês' most photogenic waterfalls (when there's water).

Five kilometres southeast, you'll pass the community village of Ermida and head toward **Cascata Fecha de Barjas**, also known as Cascata do Tahiti. Park by the bridge over the Rio Arado and head downhill towards the tropical-looking waterfall. Be aware that this is a popular spot during the summer.

You can continue your route 5km east to reach the **Miradouro de Fafião**. Set on top of two gigantic granite boulders connected by a suspended bridge, this viewpoint delivers a panoramic and vertigo-inducing view over the valley. You can also see **Fojo do Lobo**, a stone structure used in bygone times as a wolf trap.

If you're feeling hot, head 4km east to Pincães and park in the village. Follow the 1km trail to **Cascata de Pincães**, where you can have a long-deserved swim in the lagoon's splendid emerald waters.

Pitões das Júnias

JOURNEY TO DIVINE ISOLATION

Perched 1200m above sea level is **Pitões das Júnias**, one of the region's most fascinating villages. The remote location was at first the site of a small hermitage, which in the 12th century became the Cistercian **Monastery of Santa Maria das Júnias**. The shepherding monks soon attracted a small population, which settled higher up at the top of the valley, with a background of dramatic granite peaks. This extraordinary landscape is often covered in snow during the winter and is blessed by wilderness, with wild goats, deer and wolves that can sometimes be seen prowling in the distance. Meanwhile, you will likely encounter herds of goats or Barrosã cows, guided by the local shepherds. In the village, you will be engulfed by the ancestral granite houses connected by narrow cobblestone streets. Take a peek at the communal oven, and learn about local life at the **Ecomuseu de Barroso – Corte do Boi**.

A visit to the area would never be complete without the 4km hiking trail that starts at the village's cemetery and descends to the valley that hides the isolated monastery. Take your time to explore the beautiful and mystical ruins of the sanctuary, and then continue your descent to the viewpoint of the **Cascata de Pitões das Júnias**. Take a breath before you hike your way back up to the village.

BEST ACTIVITIES IN THE PARK

Canyoning
The many rivers and streams of Peneda-Gerês are ripe for exploring, delivering an outstanding canyoning experience.

Canoeing
Peacefully navigate your canoe on the still waters of the Caniçada dam or venture into the rapids with experienced guides.

Horse rides
Enjoy the serene landscape while following the trails on horseback; several one- to two-hour horse treks are available in the region.

Rafting
If you're travelling in a bigger group, rafting the park's roughest waters is a great way to get an adrenaline rush.

GETTING AROUND

It is possible to reach certain parts of Peneda-Gerês by bus, but these are limited and infrequent. To thoroughly explore the park, you need to get your hands on a rental car. Be aware that the roads are frequently curvy and driving distances often take longer than anticipated.

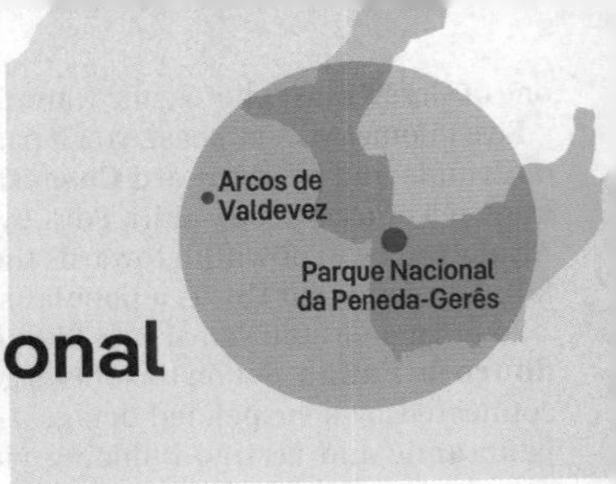

Arcos de Valdevez
Parque Nacional da Peneda-Gerês

Beyond Parque Nacional da Peneda-Gerês

The eastern section of Lima valley is dotted with important historic towns that live in communion with nature.

The park's northwestern border is intimate with the Lima valley and its tributaries. The Rio Vez originates in Serra do Soajo, near the hillside village of Sistelo. Once a medieval settlement, it expanded in the 19th century, maintaining the terraces that allowed it to increase the arable land. The picturesque town of Arcos de Valdevez lies a few kilometres downstream. Inhabited since prehistoric times, it saw growth in the medieval era, with the fixation of monasteries and the development of shepherding and agriculture. The Vez eventually merges into the Lima, close to Ponte da Barca. Birthplace of Magellan, this ancient town gained commercial and travel importance by building its superb medieval bridge.

TOP TIP

If you're already driving around the park, then stick to it. If not, buses are available to reach the various towns.

Ponte da Barca

MARC VENEMA/SHUTTERSTOCK ©

SERGIO AZENHA/ALAMY STOCK PHOTO ©

Igreja Matriz, Arcos de Valdevez

Three Towns along the Vez

BEYOND THE LITTLE TIBET

A 25-minute drive from Soajo, in the northern section, will take you to the town of **Ponte da Barca**, named after an ancient barge bridge. Even before the bridge existed, pilgrims passed here on their way to Santiago de Compostela. Explore the narrow streets lined with noble manor houses and, if the weather allows, cool off on the small river beach that follows the bridge.

About 1km north, you will find an **Ecovia do Vez** walkway entrance next to the Ponte de Santar bridge. It will take you on a 50-minute nature walk along the river to the town of **Arcos de Valdevez**. Wander through the narrow streets which preserve the local architecture, despite being often deserted. The town has several churches and chapels with various artistic expressions. The highlight goes to the gilded wooden altar of the **Igreja Matriz**, the adjacent rococo chapel, **Capela do Calvário**, and the outstanding Gothic and Romanesque palace, **Paço da Giela**, across the river. Several groves of trees flank the Rio Vez, adding to the feeling that nature is always present. During the summer, the peaceful river beach, **Praia da Valeta**, attracts droves of people.

The Ecovia do Vez continues upstream and invites you to cycle 19km to the village of **Sistelo**, sometimes called the little Portuguese Tibet. The result of generations exploiting these soils can be seen in the verdant terraces, a fertile breeding ground for indigenous cattle breeds.

BEST RESTAURANTS IN ARCOS DE VALDEVEZ

Costa do Vez
The menu at this hotel-restaurant features several recipes using Cachena beef (reared in the Minho), roast goatling and the plentiful Arcos-style *cozido* (stew), among other treats. Finish off with a triad of house desserts. **€€**

Saber ao Borralho
This rustic restaurant has a cosy, firelit atmosphere during the winter. Try the grilled or roasted regional Cachena beef sided with rich, brothy vegetable rice. The codfish dishes are also highly tempting. **€€**

GETTING AROUND

AVIC, Renex and FlixBus make the connection between Ponte da Barca and Arcos de Valdevez in 10 minutes. AVIC has two daily buses connecting Arcos de Valdevez and Sistelo in 35 minutes. You can cycle the Ecovia do Vez from Ponte da Barca to Sistelo – but it's not for beginners. Otherwise, driving is the best solution to visit all locations.

GRATIA PLENA

TOOLKIT

The chapters in this section cover the most important topics you'll need to know about in Portugal. They're full of nuts-and-bolts information and valuable insights to help you understand and navigate Portugal and get the most out of your trip.

Igreja do Carmo (p313), Porto

Arriving

Lisbon is the primary point of entry for most travellers visiting Portugal. The airport is about 6km from the city centre. All flights, domestic and international, arrive at Terminal 1. Terminal 2 is used by low-cost carriers for departing flights. It's also possible to fly directly to Porto in the north or Faro down south, but there are fewer connections outside Europe.

Visas

EU nationals don't need a visa for any length of stay. Those from the UK, Canada, the US, Australia and New Zealand can stay for up to 90 days in any six months without a visa.

Withdrawing cash

ATMs available in the arrivals area past baggage reclaim. Avoid Euronet as it often charge extras for withdrawals. Look for signs saying Multibanco or featuring the MB initials.

Border crossing

Foreign nationals arriving in Portugal via an EU member state not subject to border control, such as Spain, must submit a Declaration of Entry within three days of arrival. Get this form at sef.pt.

Wi-fi

Free wi-fi is available at both terminals but it's usually slow and unreliable. Elsewhere in Portugal, wi-fi access is widespread.

Public transport from airport to city centre

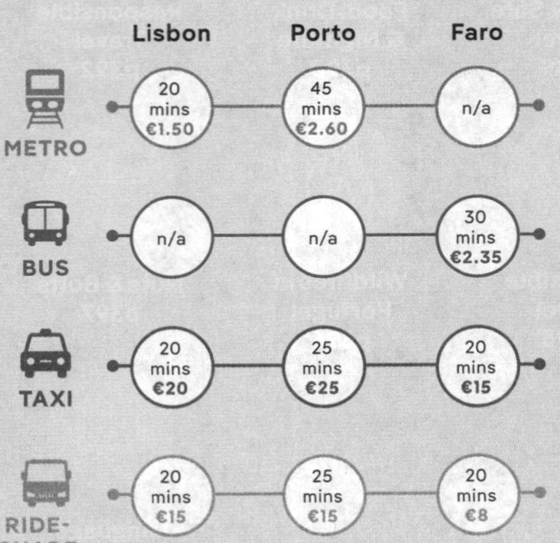

	Lisbon	Porto	Faro
METRO	20 mins €1.50	45 mins €2.60	n/a
BUS	n/a	n/a	30 mins €2.35
TAXI	20 mins €20	25 mins €25	20 mins €15
RIDE-SHARE	20 mins €15	25 mins €15	20 mins €8

LISBON AIRPORT

In 2022 Lisbon's airport was considered one of the worst airports in Europe by AirHelp due to its recurrent delays. To avoid any issues, plan to arrive early, especially if you have bags to check in. Note that the metro only stops at Terminal 1. To access Terminal 2, you'll need to catch the free shuttle bus, departing every 10 to 20 minutes. The metro stops running between 1am and 6.30am. If you have a flight to catch between those times, schedule a taxi in advance to ensure you make it. Taxis can stop at any terminal. Also, keep in mind that passport control comes after the duty-free shops.

Getting Around

Buses and trains can take you on a slow journey around the country, but renting a car is ideal if you want to set off on your own pace.

TRAVEL COSTS

Rental
From €50/day

Petrol
Approx €1.70/ litre

EV charging
€8–10/hour

Train ticket Lisbon to Porto/Faro
From €23

Hiring a car

Car-rental companies charge per 24 hours, not per calendar day. Most cars in Portugal are manual; automatic transmission cars are typically more expensive. Rentals are available at all airports, but Lisbon offers a wider choice.

Road conditions

Paid-toll *autoestradas* (motorways) and high-traffic secondary roads (IPs and ICs) are generally in good condition. Smaller, toll-free roads (N or EN) are usually narrow and curvy in mountainous areas, and poorly lit at night.

TIP

Choose the Zapping top-up card available at Lisbon's ticket machines to save money on the city's transport network.

QUEUES AND STRIKES

In Portugal, people generally respect queues for buses, often giving priority to the elderly. However, when it comes to metros and trains, locals tend to rush in and out, often without waiting. This happens especially in big cities like Lisbon and Porto. If you would like to hop off and there's someone in your way, you can say *'com licença'* to pass through. Transport strikes are common in Lisbon throughout the year, which may affect travelling.

DRIVING ESSENTIALS

Drive on the right.

Speed limit is 50km/h in urban areas, 90km/h on secondary roads and 120km/h on motorways.

.05

The blood alcohol limit is 0.5g/L.

Bus & Train

Along the coast, most places are well served by a reliable network of trains and long-distance buses. Popular destinations inland are easy to reach by bus, but rail has lacked investment in recent years, and most stations are closed. Bus services are limited in more remote areas, often requiring time-consuming transfers.

Metro

Metro is available in big cities such as Porto and Lisbon. Most are served by stairs, which makes it hard to navigate if you're carrying loads of luggage or have mobility issues. Escalators and elevators exist, but they can often be out of order.

Air

TAP operates regular domestic flights from Lisbon to Porto (one hour) and Faro (45 minutes). Tickets are not cheap – nor is the carbon footprint – so unless you need to get somewhere fast, weigh the pros and cons of travelling by air and consider opting for a comfortable, hassle-free train trip with a lower impact.

Money

CURRENCY: **EURO (€)**

Credit cards

Most hotels and smarter restaurants accept credit cards; smaller guesthouses and some *tascas* (taverns) might not. Restaurants usually display a sign with the cards they accept. When in doubt, ask staff before going in.

Digital payment

The facility to pay through mobile phones or smart watches isn't yet common, but it's growing. Tap and pay is ubiquitous, though some places may only accept Portuguese cards. Most large retailers have online payment options.

Taxes and refunds

Prices in Portugal almost always include 23% VAT. Non-EU passport holders can claim back the VAT on goods from participating retailers – be sure to ask for the tax-back forms and get them stamped by customs. Refunds are processed at the airport or via post.

Tipping

Hotels €1 per bag is standard; gratuity for cleaning staff is at your discretion.

Restaurants In touristy areas, 10% is fine; few Portuguese ever leave more than a round-up to the nearest euro.

Taxis Not expected, but it's polite to round up to the nearest euro.

HOW MUCH FOR A...

Museum entry
€5–10

Discount card for attractions
From €6 (Porto)/ €21 (Lisbon)

Boat Lisbon to Cacilhas
€1.28 with a precharged ticket

Train Lisbon to Sintra
€1.90 with a precharged ticket

HOW TO... SAVE SOME EUROS

Students and people aged over 65 (with proof of age) will get reduced admission to many sights. If you plan to do a lot of sightseeing in the main cities, the Lisboa Card and Porto Card are for you; sold at tourist offices, these offer discounts or free admission to many attractions and free travel on public transport.

LOCAL TIP

Always carry a bit of cash and loose change with you. You might need it for that coffee and *pastel de nata* later on.

BUDGET TRAVEL

Portugal is one of the cheapest destinations in Western Europe. You don't have to spend a penny to lay on its beaches or hike its trails, and even a quality glass of wine costs less than a fiver here. The tourism boom has pushed up the prices in the capital and bigger cities like Porto, but it's still possible to find good deals, especially if you avoid the high season and eat at local restaurants.

Accommodation

Sleep like royalty

Pousadas de Portugal (pousadas.pt) is a network of old monasteries, convents, forts, castles and palaces transformed into luxury hotels by the Pestana Group, a member of Historic Hotels of Europe. Despite the modern facilities, each hotel respects the history and architectural traits of the former monuments. Prices vary according to location, but rates start at around €100 per night.

Find a local guesthouse

Alojamento Local (AL) is an umbrella term used to designate guesthouses, as well as short-term rentals available on major booking platforms. At this type of accommodation, breakfast is usually not provided or comes at an extra cost, private bathrooms might be optional, there is no 24/7 front-desk service, and in-room amenities are limited.

Go rural

Privately owned country houses come in all shapes and sizes: country hotels (HR – Hotéis Rurais), old manors and palaces (TH – Turismo de Habitação), small country houses (CC – Casas de Campo) and farmhouses and wine estates (AG – Agro-turismo). A large breakfast of local products is usually included. Other meals may be provided upon request.

HOW MUCH FOR A NIGHT IN...

a pousada
€100–120

a hostel dorm
€20

a guesthouse
€50

Camp out

Camping options range from simple sites with modest facilities to large complexes of permanent campervans, often by a beach and crowded in the summer. Prices start at around €10 per person and per tent or campervan. Nearly all campgrounds have hot showers, electrical hookups and a cafe. Glamping is also increasing, with luxury tents and bungalows allowing you to stay amid nature without giving up comfort.

Budget sleeps

Portugal has scores of hostels, particularly in Lisbon and Porto. If you're thinking bare-bones, smelly backpacker lodging, think again: Lisbon's hostels are among the best in Europe, with stylish designs, often in heritage buildings, and excellent amenities. High-season dorm beds typically cost around €20. Many hostels also offer simple doubles with shared bathroom, and some have small apartments.

THE IMPACT OF TOURISM

Around 9.6 million people visited Portugal in 2021. That is still lower than the 24.6 million that came in 2019, pre-COVID. A high intake of tourists throughout the country, especially in larger cities, has direct consequences for its permanent residents. Locals have seen a high rise in both rental and purchasing costs for housing, resulting from the conversion of homes into short-term rentals, in the worst cases forcing some to relocate. Prices of goods and services have gone up, and locals experience crowded streets and public transport. Consider staying in a small guesthouse or hotel. If that is not viable, opt for a short-term rental in a less crowded area.

Family Travel

The great thing about Portugal for children is its manageable size and the range of sights and activities on offer. There's a small but well-run train network that connects key sites, great food on offer, and a wide selection of appealing accommodations. Locals tend to be caring towards families, and children are welcome in most restaurants and cafes, where they're often free to roam.

See the sights

Child concessions (and family rates) often apply to tours, admission fees, accommodation and transport, with some discounts as high as 50% off the adult rate. However, the definition of 'child' varies between under five, 12 or 18 years, so always check. Even those attractions that don't offer a discounted fee, usually have a day, or time of the day, when entry is free for everyone.

Baby facilities

- Nappy-changing facilities *(fraldário)* available at airports but harder to find in restaurants.
- Most hotels (but rarely budget places) have cots, although most only have a few, so reserve one when booking. If requesting a *berço* (cot), ask for a larger room.
- Bring a light pram that easily folds with thicker wheels to deal with cobblestones and pack a baby carrier.

KID-FRIENDLY PICKS

Oceanário de Lisboa **(p82)**

Marvel at the marine life and explore an underwater world with the whole family.

Quinta da Regaleira **(p106)**

Journey down the mystical well and feed the children's imagination with a tour of the gardens.

Serras de Aire e Candeeiros **(p247)**

Kids will enjoy following the dinosaur footprint trail and be dazzled by the caves.

Getting around

Discounts are available for children (usually under 12) on public transport. Those under four generally ride free. If you're hiring a car, ideally bring your own child safety seat rather than pay hire fees, which typically are about €10 per day.

Eating out

A specific menu *infantil* (children's menu) isn't always available, but you'll often find options like soup or *bitoque* (steak and fries). You can't rely on restaurants having *cadeiras de bebé* (highchairs), although some do. Those that do rarely have more than one.

CHILDREN'S FILMS

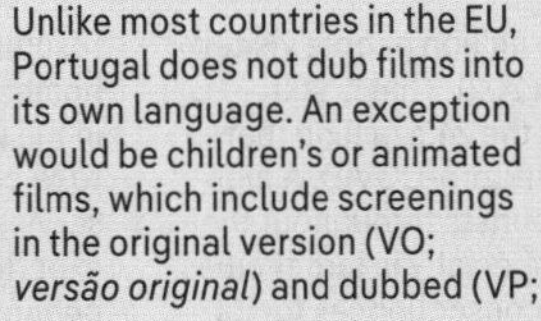

Unlike most countries in the EU, Portugal does not dub films into its own language. An exception would be children's or animated films, which include screenings in the original version (VO; *versão original*) and dubbed (VP; *versão portuguesa*), making it a viable option for an afternoon of entertainment for the whole family. This cultural stance might contribute to the high English literacy rate in the country.

Health & Safe Travel

INSURANCE

Insurance is not mandatory to travel to Portugal, but it's good to have. Consider one that covers flight cancellation and medical care. Alternatively, or additionally, EU travellers can apply for the European Health Insurance Card that covers emergency medical treatment free of charge.

Earthquakes

Portugal is in an active earthquake zone and experiences regular tremors. According to historical records, most earthquakes affecting mainland Portugal have an epicentre southwest of the Iberian Peninsula or in the Lower Tagus Valley. The most vulnerable areas are around Lisbon and the south of the Algarve. The last major earthquake in continental Portugal occurred in 1969.

Jellyfish and sea urchins

In general, jellyfish aren't a major problem in Portuguese waters, though there can be sightings along the south coast. Lifeguards are trained to deal with these issues. Watch for sea urchins around rocky beaches. If needles become embedded in skin, immerse the limb in hot water to relieve the pain. To avoid infection, visit a doctor and have the needles removed.

SCAMS

Scams in larger cities include raising funds on the street for charities that don't exist in exchange for a fixed-fee photo, and selling 'drugs' (bay leaves and flour), particularly in touristy, pedestrian-only streets.

SWIM SAFELY

Green flag
Safe to swim

Yellow flag
You may remain at the water's edge, but no swimming

Red flag
Danger, no swimming

Checkered flag
Beach is temporarily unmanned

Blue and purple flags
Dangerous marine life has been spotted

Cannabis

Although Portugal decriminalised the use and possession of all drugs, regarding addiction as a disease not a crime, not everything goes. While being caught with a small amount of cannabis for personal use (up to 25 grams) is not a crime, you don't see people smoking it freely on the streets.

THEFT

While streets in Portugal are relatively safe, there is still a risk of theft, with pickpocketing and vehicle break-ins most common. Be mindful of your possessions when walking through crowded areas, and avoid leaving items visible in your car. Report stolen items directly to the police. They will hand you a certificate which you can use to make an insurance claim back home.

Food, Drink & Nightlif

When to eat

Pequeno-almoço (breakfast, 8am to 10am) is generally a simple affair with coffee and toast or a pastry.

Almoço (lunch, noon to 3pm) can be a two-course fixed-price special, or something more casual, depending on the spot.

Jantar (dinner, 7pm to 10pm) generally features more elaborate (and slightly pricier) dishes, though some places specialise in *petiscos* (sharing plates).

MENU DECODER

Couvert The bread, olives and other nibbles brought to your table; note that these are not free

Prato do dia Daily special or dish of the day

Ementa turística Tourist menu

Menu de degustação Degustation menu

Petiscos Small dishes to share; similar to tapas

Dose Portion, generally big enough for two people

Meia dose Half portion, big enough for one person

Sobremesa Dessert

Serviço Service charge

Marisco Seafood

Peixe Fish

Bacalhau Codfish

Vaca/Vitela Beef

Porco Pork

Peru Turkey

Frango Chicken

Queijo e fiambre Cheese and ham

Ovos Eggs

Vegetariano Vegetarian

Vinho Wine

Vinho branco White wine

Vinho tinto Red wine

Vinho verde Green wine

Vinho rosé Rosé wine

Jarro de vinho Wine jar

Garrafa de vinho Wine bottle

Cerveja Beer

Imperial/Fino Small beer in Lisbon/Porto

Caneca Pint of beer

Where to eat

Tasca (tavern) Old-fashioned place with daily specials, fair prices and a local crowd.

Churrasqueira or churrascaria (grill house) Specialising in chargrilled meats, specifically *frango no churrasco* (barbecue chicken).

Marisqueira (seafood restaurant) Serves up fish and crustaceans, often priced by the kilo.

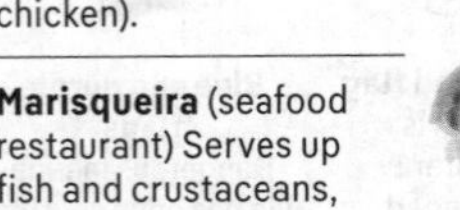

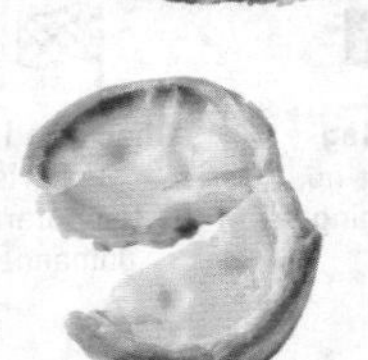

Cervejaria (beer house) Either a brewery serving local beer or a traditional place similar to a *marisqueira* serving seafood dishes.

Adega (wine tavern) Usually decorated with wine casks and boasting a rustic, cosy ambience; expect hearty, inexpensive meals.

HOW TO... (politely) decline couvert

So you've sat down at a restaurant, and the waiter drops an assortment of cheeses, bread and sometimes even shrimp at your table. As enticing as it looks, before you dig in, you should know that these 'offerings' aren't free. This is part of the *couvert*, or starters menu, and you'll be charged for each item you eat at the end of the meal. To avoid any surprises when you're about to pay, you can politely refuse the *couvert*, by saying one of the following things:

Before the waiter puts it on the table: *Obrigado(a), mas não quero o couvert.* (Thank you, but I don't want the couvert.)

If it's already on the table: *Pode levar o couvert.* (You can take the couvert.)

If you only want one item, you can say: *Pode deixar isto* (You can leave this) and point to the plate you want them to leave on the table.

HOW MUCH FOR A...

Pastel de nata
€1.10

Tosta mista (ham and cheese toast)
€2.50

Espresso (Bica)
€1

Galão
€1.50

Lunch at a *tasca*
€8–10

Dinner at a Michelin-star restaurant
€200

Beer
€1.50/3 small/large

Glass of wine
€3–5

HOW TO... order a coffee

The Portuguese weren't always a fan of the bitter taste of coffee. As the story goes, coffee sellers created a slogan to encourage customers to buy this new delicacy. Posters were hung saying 'Beba isto com açúcar' (Drink this with sugar) across the country, but some say it was the Lisbon cafe A Brasileira (p67) that pioneered the idea. The advertising stunt worked, and the initials BICA became synonymous with ordering an espresso, particularly in the capital. The word is still in use today, but now there are a dozen more ways of ordering coffee in Portugal.

Coffee count

Coffee beans are mostly imported from South America or Africa and roasted in Portugal. There is only one place that grows coffee in Portugal, and that's the island of São Jorge in the Azores.

Café or bica The regular espresso. You can order it in a smaller version (*café curto* or *bica curta*) or the full cup (*café cheio* or *bica cheia)*.
Café duplo Double espresso.
Descafeinado Decaf espresso.
Café com cheirinho Coffee with a drop of *aguardente* (firewater)
Carioca Weak espresso.
Italiano A very short espresso, similar to the Italian *ristretto*.
Pingado Espresso with a drop of milk.
Garoto Milk with a drop of espresso.
Abatanado Large dark coffee similar to an Americano.
Meia de leite Half coffee and half milk served in a large cup.
Galão 1/4 coffee, 3/4 milk in a tall glass cup. You can order it with more milk *(galão claro)* or less *(galão escuro)*.

GOING OUT

A night out in Portugal often starts with watching the sunset at the nearest viewpoint. Friends pick up a bottle of wine or beer from the grocers and cheer as the sun goes down. In case you were wondering, yes, you can drink outside here. After that, it's off to a restaurant for a bite to eat, before initiating the bar crawl. In Lisbon, that means hopping between the bars of Bairro Alto, while Porto residents head to the Galerias de Paris.

The best time to hit the clubs is around midnight to 1am. Any earlier, and you might find yourself dancing on your own. Most clubs are quite casual when it comes to the dress code, but others can be slightly strict. When in doubt, check the club pictures before you head out. Once inside, you can stay as long as the music plays (often as late as 6am).

If you see a group of people dressed in black capes, you might have stumbled upon a student community. Every year, first-year university students go through a series of initiations known as *praxes*, which often involve drinking in cheap bars across the city. This is particularly common in student cities like Lisbon, Coimbra and Porto.

Responsible Travel

Climate change and travel

It's impossible to ignore the impact we have when travelling, and the importance of making changes where we can. Lonely Planet urges all travellers to engage with their travel carbon footprint. There are many carbon calculators online that allow travellers to estimate the carbon emissions generated by their journey; try resurgence.org/resources/carbon-calculator.html. Many airlines and booking sites offer travellers the option of offsetting the impact of greenhouse gas emissions by contributing to climate-friendly initiatives around the world. We continue to offset the carbon footprint of all Lonely Planet staff travel, while recognising this is a mitigation more than a solution.

Cork

Cork oak forests are among the most bio-diverse environments on the planet, with endangered species like the Iberian imperial eagle and Iberian lynx being dependent on these ecosystems. Portugal is one of the world's largest cork producers, and while most of it ends up sealing wine bottles, locals have found other creative purposes for this sustainable material, using it to make anything from coasters to shoes and umbrellas. Find some at Cork & Company (corkandcompany.pt) in Lisbon.

Sample Syrian cuisine at **Mezze**, a restaurant run by Pão a Pão (paoapao.pt), an association that promotes the integration of refugees in Portugal.

Grab a coffee at **Café Joyeux** (cafejoyeux.com) which employs people with cognitive disabilities.

Stay longer and support local initiatives with **Portugal Voluntário** (portugalvoluntario.pt). Seasonal programmes can also be found on international volunteering websites such as **World Packers** (worldpackers.com) and **WWOOF** (wwoof.net).

OLGAGI/SHUTTERSTOCK ©, VELIAVIK/SHUTTERSTOCK ©
OPPOSITE PAGE: AJCESPEDES/SHUTTERSTOCK ©

Try fresh, local ingredients at farmers markets like Mercado Biológico do Príncipe Real in Lisbon or meet the producers at the weekly food market hosted by Comida de Independente (comidaindependente.pt).

Save food

Download the app Too Good To Go (toogoodtogo.pt) to get discount deals from local cafes (yes, pastries included) and restaurants, while also preventing food waste.

Stargazing

Stargaze at the Dark Sky Alqueva, which covers approximately 10,000 sq km around Alentejo's Alqueva lake. The area has been developed under a strategy of integrated sustainable development and emphasises local development and environmental preservation. See p196 for more.

Walk the trails of Portuguese forests and plant trees along the way. See plantarumaarvore.org for more.

Take a farm-to-table cooking class or pick fruit with Portugal Farm Experiences (portugalfarm experience.com).

16

The Global Sustainability Index ranks Portugal in 16th place worldwide. The country has produced a roadmap to achieve carbon neutrality by 2050, which includes targets to reduce greenhouse emissions and a shift to renewable energies.

Arts and crafts

Buy local artwork at Portugal Manual (portugalmanual.com), a network of contemporary Portuguese artists with branches inside the Centro Cultural de Belém and Depozito in Lisbon.

RESOURCES

impactrip.com Volunteering opportunities with social enterprises.

natural.pt Information on the best of Portugal's protected areas.

quercus.pt Information about environmental issues.

Ditch the hire car and take the scenic route by bike or on foot along coastal and countryside trails. See portuguesetrails.com for details.

LGBTIQ+ Travellers

In 2021, Portugal came second as one of the world's best LGBTIQ+ friendly countries in the Spartacus Gay Travel Index. For a country that has spent decades under a dictatorship, liberal ideals are something of a novelty. Same-sex marriages were only allowed in 2010, and while adoption got approved in 2016, some negative attitudes still linger.

The big shindigs

If you're up for a rave, schedule your trip around Pride. Lisbon throws the biggest party in June. The **Arraial Lisboa Pride** (lisboapride.ilga-portugal.pt) had its first edition in 1997 and hasn't stopped since. Another noteworthy event is the film festival **Queer Lisboa** (queerlisboa.pt). Held in late September, it brings in a series of screenings and events dedicated to queer folks. Meanwhile, Porto's **Marcha do Orgulho** (parade), which takes place in July, sadly started as a response to a brutal murder of a trans woman in 2006.

VOLUNTEERING & SAFE NETWORKS

ILGA (ilga-portugal.pt) is the main LGBTIQ+ association in Portugal. It runs the Centro LGBTI in Lisbon, which often hosts events and provides helpful resources for the queer community. You can also reach out to them online to learn more about volunteering opportunities.

OLDER MINDSETS

Generally speaking, Portugal is welcoming to everyone, and that goes for the LGBTIQ+ communities, too. However, older generations might share different ideals and make the occasional rude remark. Cities can also feel more progressive than smaller rural towns.

Gay-friendly districts

Lisbon has an area full of gay-friendly bars and clubs (lisbongaycircuit.com). Seek out Príncipe Real, home to the country's infamous gay club, Trumps, or Bairro Alto (p56), where bars cater to the whole queer family. Further north, in Porto, the action spreads through several neighbourhoods. The Porto Gay Circuit (portogaycircuit.com) is a good starting point to find your favourite hangout in town.

TOURISM RESOURCES

Variações (variacoes.pt) is a Portuguese LGBTI Chamber of Commerce and Tourism. Members include the **Lisbon Beach** (lisbonbeach.com), which organises gay-centric tours, and **The Late Birds** (thelatebirdslisbon.com), one of the city's all-male gay hotels. **Proudly Portugal** (proudlyportugal.pt) is also an ideal resource for travel tips in Portugal, and **Time Out Lisbon** (timeout.pt/lisboa/pt/gay) has a gay section with news updates.

All Things Drag

Drag queens take over the stage at Lisbon's **Finalmente** (finalmenteclub.com), one of the oldest gay clubs in the country, open since 1976.

Accessible Travel

Portugal has accessibility challenges, but efforts are being made to promote inclusive tourism. Changes are slowly taking place across the country to accommodate all visitors, improving accommodation infrastructures, transport access and adapting museum exhibits.

Accessible beaches

The Accessible Beach award honours beaches and other swimming areas for their wheelchair-friendly facilities. As of now, more than 200 places are certified. **Scan this QR code for the list**

At the airport

Portuguese airports offer a MyWay assistance service for passengers with reduced mobility. Request the service from your airline 48 hours before departure.

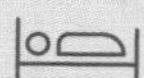

Accommodation

Newer and larger hotels tend to have some adapted rooms, though the facilities may not be up to scratch; ask at the local *posto de turismo* (tourist office). Most campgrounds and some hostels have accessible facilities.

COBBLES

With its cobbled streets and hills, Lisbon may be difficult for wheelchair users or people who are visually impaired, but it's not impossible. The Baixa's flat grid and Belém are fine, and all the sights at Parque das Nações are accessible.

Metro and train stations

A list of accessible stations in Lisbon's metro network is available online at metrolisboa.pt/viajar/mapas-e-diagramas. Porto's metro is better-equipped, as every platform is at a low level or provides a ramp. The Portuguese railway offers discounts for customers with special needs and their companions.

Visually impaired

The Shrine of Fatima MyEyes app helps visually impaired people navigate the shrine site through audio descriptions. Blind people can also interact with exhibits at the Museu da Covilhã.

FESTIVALS

In 2019 the government launched the Festivais + Acessíveis project to distinguish events that present accessibility conditions for people with specific needs, including pregnant women, seniors, wheelchair users and those who are visually impaired.

RESOURCES

Accessible Portugal *(accessibleportugal.com)* promotes accessible tourism and is the brains behind the TUR4all website and app (iOS only), a database of accessible tourist resources and services.

Tourism for All *(tourism-for-all.com)* provides self-guided itineraries around Portugal along with personalised tour packages, transport rental, wheelchairs and personal assistance staff.

Portugal 4All Senses *(portugal4allsenses.pt)* provides tailor-made tours that include sensory experiences tested by individuals with visual impairments.

Portugal was bestowed with the Accessible Tourist Destination 2019 award by the World Tourism Organization in partnership with ONCE Foundation. It was the first country to be granted the title, recognising its efforts to promote tourism accessibility.

Wildfires in Portugal

Heatwaves, lack of rain and neglected rural lands have all contributed to the rise of wildfires in Portugal. In 2022 the country had one of the highest percentages of burned land in Europe, with 1% of its territory consumed by flames. Things get especially precarious in summer, with drylands acting as a fuel. Travellers on the road can easily be caught off-guard by these events, especially if they're not keeping track of the local news. The following covers a short background on Portuguese wildfires, what to do in case of emergency and how to help out when the dust settles.

Tragic memories

Sixty-six people died in the large fire that broke out in the region of Pedrogão Grande in June 2017. Many of these casualties were attempting to escape the flames by car. More recently, a series of fires hit the Serra da Estrela. The highest mountain in continental Portugal saw 200 sq km of its territory burn in the summer of 2022. The fire raged for 11 days causing lasting effects on the habitat of local fauna and flora. If you're travelling through fire-prone areas in peak summer, such as forests and rural sites, always speak to locals about weather conditions and follow the directions of local emergency services if you do happen to get caught near a wildfire.

Helping out

As Portugal struggles with the effects of the fires, it is crucial to rehabilitate the land. Initiatives like Plantar Uma Árvore (plantarumaarvore.org) help to clear out invasive species associated with fire risk and replanting native trees.

Stay tuned

Fire-prone areas are found across the country, but higher-risk regions include Vila Real (in the north), Castelo Branco (in the centre) and the Algarve down south.

IMPA (ipma.pt/en/riscoincendio/rcm.pt) Latest reports on wildfire risk.

Fogos.pt Provides a map with all the current fires, using a red marker to represent the ones that are still active.

European Forest Fire Information System (effis.jrc.ec.europa.eu) For wildfire data across Europe.

THE CAUSES & FIGHTERS

Many people regard the eucalyptus as Portugal's biggest fire hazard, but there's a lot more at stake. The long periods of drought and the strong Atlantic winds can also contribute to the matter. With people leaving for the city, often chasing better work opportunities, many rural properties are left unattended, and it only takes one spark to start a flame. Nearly 90% of firefighters are volunteers *(bombeiros voluntários)* as opposed to professional firefighters *(bombeiros sapadores)*. These are people from various backgrounds who use their spare time to help their local fire department.

SAFETY & EMERGENCY

If you're planning to host a barbecue in a park, make sure to check the fire risk for your area first. When driving, don't throw your cigarette butts out the window. 112 is the general emergency number in Portugal. It connects you to the fire service, as well as medical services. If you're calling in English, try and speak slowly. Avoid making any rush calls and always follow the directions provided.

Nuts & Bolts

OPENING HOURS

Opening hours vary throughout the year. We provide high-season opening hours; hours will generally decrease in the shoulder and low seasons.

Banks 8.30am–3pm Monday to Friday

Bars 7pm–2am

Cafes 9am–7pm

Clubs 11pm–4am Thursday to Saturday

Restaurants noon–3pm and 7–10pm

Shopping malls 10am–10pm

Shops 9.30am–noon and 2–7pm Monday to Friday, 10am–1pm Saturday

Smoking

Smoking, including e-cigarettes, is not allowed in public spaces, except within designated areas. Most restaurants and cafes don't have a smoking section.

GOOD TO KNOW

Time Zone
GMT/UTC in winter, GMT/UTC plus one hour in summer

Country Code
351

Emergency number
112

Population
10.34 million

Weights & Measures

Portugal uses the metric system. Decimals are indicated by commas, thousands by points.

Water

Tap water is safe to drink and of good quality throughout Portugal.

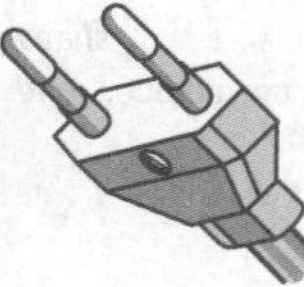

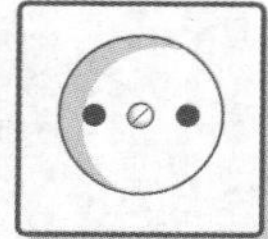

Type F
230V/50Hz

PUBLIC HOLIDAYS

Portugal has 13 national public holidays. Some businesses and non-essential services may be closed. Regional holidays include patron saint celebrations in summer.

New Year's Day 1 January

Carnaval Tuesday February/March – the day before Ash Wednesday

Good Friday March/April

Liberty Day 25 April

Labour Day 1 May

Corpus Christi May/June – ninth Thursday after Easter

Portugal Day 10 June – also known as Camões and Communities Day

Feast of the Assumption 15 August

Republic Day 5 October

All Saints' Day 1 November

Independence Day 1 December

Feast of the Immaculate Conception 8 December

Christmas Day 25 December

Language

Portuguese comes from the Romance language family and is closely related to Spanish, French and Italian. It's descended from the colloquial Latin spoken by Roman soldiers.

Basics

Hello. Olá. *o·laa*
Goodbye. Adeus. *a·de·oosh*
Yes. Sim. *seeng*
No. Não. *nowng*
Please. Por favor. *poor fa·vor*
Thank you. Obrigado/a (m/f). *o·bree·gaa·doo/a*
Excuse me. Faz favor! *faash fa·vor*
Sorry. Desculpe. *desh·kool·pe*
What's your name? Qual é o seu nome? *kwaal e oo se·oo no·me*
My name is ... O meu nome é ... *oo me·oo no·me e ...*
Do you speak English? Fala inglês? *faa·la eeng·glesh*
I (don't) understand. (Não) Entendo. *(nowng) eng·teng·doo*

Directions

Where's the ...? Onde é ...? *ong·de e ...*
Could you please write it down? Podia escrever isso, por favor? *poo·dee·ashkre·ver ee·soo poor fa·vor*
Can you show me (on the map)? Pode-me mostrar (no mapa)? *po·de·me moosh·traar (noo maa·pa)*

Signs

Entrada/Saída Entrance/Exit
Aberto/Fechado Open/Closed
Há Vaga Rooms Available
Não Há Vaga No Vacancies
Informação Information
Esquadra da Polícia Police Station
Proibido Prohibited
Casa de Banho Toilets
Homens Men
Mulheres Women
Quente/Frio Hot/Cold

Time

What time is it? Que horas são? *kee o·rash sowng*
It's (10) o'clock. São (dez) horas. *sowng (desh) o·rash*
Half past (10). (Dez) e meia. *(desh) e may·a*
in the morning. da manhã. *da ma·nyang*
in the afternoon. da tarde. *da taar·de*
in the evening. da noite. *da noy·te*
yesterday. ontem. *ong·teng*
tomorrow. amanhã. *aa·ma·nyang*

Emergencies

Help! Socorro! *soo·ko·rroo*
Go away! Vá-se embora! *vaa·se eng·bo·ra*
Call ...! Chame ...! *shaa·me ...*
a doctor. um médico. *oong me·dee·koo*
the police. a polícia. *a poo·lee·sya*

NUMBERS

1 **um** *oong*
2 **dois** *doysh*
3 **três** *tresh*
4 **quatro** *kwaa·troo*
5 **cinco** *seeng·koo*
6 **seis** *saysh*
7 **sete** *se·te*
8 **oito** *oy too*
9 **nove** *no ve*
10 **dez** *desh*

DONATIONS TO ENGLISH

Numerous – you may recognise **albino, brocade, dodo, molasses, commando**

DISTINCTIVE SOUNDS

Throaty 'r' (similar to French) and nasal vowels (pronounced as if you're trying to force the sound through the nose).

False Friends

Warning: many Portuguese words look like English words but have a different meaning altogether, eg salsa *saal·sa* is 'parsley', not 'sauce' (which is molho *mo·lyoo* in Portuguese).

Must-Know Grammar

Portuguese has both a formal and an informal word for 'you' (*você* and *tu* respectively). Verbs have a different ending for each person – like the English 'I do' vs 'he/she does'.

Street Talk

Slang in a foreign language is tricky, but listen out for these words and phrases and even have a go at using them.

tudo bem? – more of an end-all phrase than an actual expression of concern from the person asking how you are

então – a flexible word that changes meaning at each inflection. It can be a short form of a concerned question or a replacement for 'hello' *(então?)*, a polite 'watch it' *(então!)*, or a pause someone makes before starting a lengthy explanation *(então...)*

t'fona-me – a super-contracted short form for *telefoname* (call me), mainly used in the Greater Lisbon area

pá – translates as bread, however, is usually used as an interjection meaning 'man!' or 'dude!'. Depending on context, *pá* is also used in the place of 'uhh...' when you are thinking.

tipo – used in the same context as how many English speakers use 'like', however, it literally translates as 'type'

WHO SPEAKS PORTUGUESE?

The global distribution of the Portuguese language began during the period know as *Os Descobrimentos* (the Discoveries), the golden era of Portugal's colonial expansion into Africa, Asia and South America. In the 15th and 16th centuries, the peninsular nation had enormous economic, cultural and political influence. The empire's reach can be seen today in the number of countries besides Portugal where Portuguese still has the status of an official language – Brazil, Madeira and the Azores in the Atlantic Ocean off Europe, Cape Verde, São Tomé and Príncipe, Guinea-Bissau, Angola and Mozambique (all in Africa), and Macau and East Timor in Asia.

STORYBOOK

Our writers delve deep into different aspects of Portuguese life

Monument of Discoveries, Lisbon

A HISTORY OF PORTUGAL IN 15 PLACES

Portugal's is a story of comings and goings: the civilisations and invaders who came and left; the explorers who left and returned with new ideas and riches; and the rulers who left their mark and the rulers who were displaced. This is not an itinerary – it's a journey through time from prehistory to modernity.

LOCAL LEGEND HAS it that Odysseus, on his journey back home, was the first to port on these coastal shores. Having found unwalled Lisbon, he set out to sea again, driven by homesickness. What he left is the story of what would become the future capital and a feeling that the Portuguese would identify as *'saudade'*.

Rooted in the hearts of the Portuguese, *saudade* is a sense of deep longing and nostalgia for a person, place or period of time. It is in the poems written about sailors gone to sea during the Age of Exploration, in the myths of a dead king that will return on a foggy day to save Portugal from its foreign invaders, and in the tales of grandparents who lived through a dictatorship.

To this day, Portugal lives in a constant limbo, attached to its past, yet wanting to embrace the future. We've been taught to look at our history with rose-tinted glasses, taking pride in the conquests of our ancestors and ignoring the inherent consequences. But it seems that we're finally pushing these boundaries, with institutions and artists coming together to portray a more accurate view of the country's background and redefining its future as a modern, creative and welcoming nation.

1. Parque Arqueológico do Vale do Côa

SAVED FROM THE FLOOD

Côa has been called the largest open-air collection of Paleolithic rock art in the world. And for such an ancient site – some of the carvings go back 22,000 years – it's had quite an impact on modern Portuguese culture and politics too. Over 1200 carvings, mainly of animals, such as horses and cattle, have been uncovered. The first discovery was in the early 1990s, as Portugal's biggest energy company was excavating the area, close to the northeastern border with Spain.

A landmark moment for archaeologists, the discovery proved to be a disaster for the dam builders and their political sponsors. The prospect of flooding the valley and losing access to the carvings forever enraged the public and many international supporters. In 1995, a new government was elected and lost no time in cancelling the dam project. The Battle of Côa, as it became known, was a rare victory of heritage and culture against the developers.

For more on Côa, see page 341

2. Conímbriga

A HISTORY OF LUXURY

The luxury villa is nothing new in Portugal. During the reign of the emperor Vespasian (69 to 79 AD), this small town in Lusitania (ancient Portugal) became fabulously wealthy, providing homes to 10,000 people at its height. That is until the barbarians invaded it three centuries later. There are plenty of swish villas in Portugal today, from the Algarve to Estoril, but maybe none match the size and opulence of the House of Cantaber. This 1st-century Conímbriga residence was one of the largest in the western Roman world and featured its own private thermal baths, while the Casa dos Repuxos (House of Fountains) had 569 sq metres of mosaic floor.

For more on Conímbriga, see page 270

3. Mértola

RESTORED ISLAMIC LEGACY

Portugal was part of the Islamic Umayyad Empire for five centuries, from the Muslims' arrival in 711 to the start of the Christian reconquest in 1139. Today just 0.5% of the population is Muslim, and for generations, Portuguese education and literature painted the 'Moors' as an existential enemy. A more balanced view has emerged in recent years as scholars reveal the legacy of this period. One estimated that 19,000 words in modern Portuguese have their origins in Arabic. (Many start with 'Al-', such as 'Alfama' or 'algodão' (cotton).) Material remnants are harder to trace, but since 1978, archaeologists working in the Alentejo town of Mértola unearthed rich evidence of daily life at a time when the majority of Portuguese were Muslim. In 2001 a new biennual festival emerged to celebrate the town's, and by extension, Portugal's Islamic roots.

For more on Mértola, see page 220

PIGPROX/SHUTTERSTOCK ©

4. Castelo de Guimarães

A STATEMENT IN STONE

These rectangular Gothic towers announce the arrival of the medieval period – and Portugal as a nation. The country's first capital was located here, southeast of Braga: it was purportedly the residence of Count Henry and the birthplace of his son Dom Afonso Henriques, who would become the first king of Portugal. The fact that the fortress was built to defend the land from Norman invaders from the north, as well as Moors from the south, tells you much about the world the new nation emerged into.

For more on Guimarães, see page 369

5. Convento de Cristo

A PLACE OF QUESTS

A Unesco World Heritage Site since 1983, the Templar Castle and the Convent of the Knights of Christ in Tomar is a vast site in Central Portugal that captures seven centuries of the country's history – and looks even further back in time. This was originally a Roman place of worship. The convent's impressive Gothic architecture prompted director Terry Gilliam to shoot his 2018 *Don Quixote* movie here. The filming crew was later accused of damaging the building and gardens. But it looks like this faux pas has already been overlooked, with the convent opening its doors again to stage Netflix's *Damsel* in 2022.

For more on the convent and Tomar, see page 249

6. Universidade de Coimbra

LEARNING AND LATE NIGHTS

The institution has been around since 1290, making it one of Europe's oldest universities. In 1537, the university made a permanent move north from Lisbon to its current site. Coimbra remains very much a medieval and a university town in the vein of Heidelberg or Cambridge, though with a more humble vibe. As well as the raucous nightlife you get with a student population – especially during the Queima das Fitas celebrations – there is also a political edge here – witness the graffiti statements outside the *repúblicas* (communal student dwellings) addressing current political issues.

For more on Coimbra, see page 264

7. Mercado de Escravos

AN ARRIVAL POINT

For millions of tourists every year, Faro Airport is the entry point for a relaxing, sun-drenched Algarve holiday. An hour west, in Lagos, there is another arrivals point: it is here that the first African slaves arrived on European soil in the 15th century. In 2016 the *mercado* became a museum documenting the slave trade. The new curators first had to fight the army, which had been using the place as a recruitment centre and were reluctant to leave. For some, the exhibit still falls short of delivering the full extent of the country's connection with this dark period.

For more on Lagos, see page 167

8. Mosteiro dos Jerónimos

WEALTH AND A NEW STYLE

If you want to see the moment of Portugal's peak global power and wealth, seek out the style of architecture unique to the country, known as Manueline. You are looking at a combination of Late Gothic and Mudejar elements, where maritime ornaments and representations of the Age of Exploration are prevalent. The style emerged as the profits from the spice trade began to flow in the 16th century. It was given its name by Brazilian Francisco Varnhagen, a 19th-century author, following his visit to Jerónimos. He named it after King Manuel I, as his reign (1495–1521) coincided with the development of the monastery.

For more on Mosteiro dos Jerónimos, see page 76

9. Terreiro do Paço

A HISTORY OF PORTUGAL IN ONE PLACE

This huge, three-sided square, also known as the Praça do Comércio, is a microcosm of modern Portuguese history – and its contradictions. The plaza – with one side open to the sea – was the centrepiece of Lisbon's rebirth after the earthquake of 1755. It was designated as a centre of commerce, but became the headquarters for the most important government departments. It is dominated by a statue of King José I. Yet this is also the site where the monarchy effectively ended, when Carlos I and his eldest son were assassinated in 1908. That was designed as a blow for freedom – in a place where Lisbon's first consignments of slaves arrived.

For more on Praça do Comércio, see page 66

10. Martinho da Arcada

WHERE IDEAS BREW

It's not just about grand squares and official monuments – history has also been made in corner cafes such as this one. It was here that writer Fernando Pessoa had his last *bica* (espresso) in 1935, three days before his death. Since its opening in 1782, Martinho da Arcada became a meeting point for politicians, artists and writers, Pessoa included. He was a regular, writing many of his poems here. Indeed, one of Pessoa's famous portraits depicts him sitting at the cafe, painted by his friend Almada Negreiros, who met him on that last visit.

For more on Pessoa's favourite hangouts, see page 67

11. Largo do Carmo

DESTRUCTION AND REBIRTH

Another symbolic spot that ties together the 18th and 20th centuries. This square in Lisbon is home to the Convento do Carmo, which was all but destroyed in the 1755 earthquake and has remained in ruins to remind people of this tragic event.

It is also the spot where modern Portugal was born. It was here that the last leader

of the totalitarian New State surrendered in 1974 at the culmination of the Carnation Revolution, which may also be the first revolution to be started by a Eurovision Song Contest entry. Portugal's 1974 song was used as a signal for the military to act.

For more on Convento do Carmo, see page 67

12. Fátima

A VISION IN THE VILLAGE

On 13 May 1917, and in each subsequent month until October that year, three young peasant children, Lucia dos Santos and her cousins Francisco and Jacinta Marto, reportedly saw a woman who identified herself as the Lady of the Rosary. On 13 October, a crowd (generally estimated at 70,000) gathered at Fátima and witnessed a 'miraculous solar phenomenon' immediately after the lady had appeared to the children.

Pope John Paul II travelled here several times and announced the beatification of the children. Pope Francisco joined the centenary of the apparitions in 2017.

For more on Fátima and its festivals, see page 257

13. Ponte 25 de Abril

BREAKING THE BORDERS

The first bridge to connect Lisbon to the other side of the Rio Tejo, making the fantastic beaches of the Costa da Caparica a lot more accessible to *lisboetas*. But bridges, like many places in this list, are symbolic as much as functional. Originally, those Lisbon-dwellers crossed a bridge named after the dictator Salazar (it was opened in 1966, four years before his death). Its new name commemorates the date of the revolution that overthrew the dictatorship he founded.

For more on the bridge and its surrounds, see page 93

14. Parque das Nações

WATER, DESIGN AND FIBRE OPTICS

The 1998 Lisbon World Exposition (universally known as the 'Expo') was a big moment in the creation of modern Portugal. This is the legacy: a redeveloped waterfront area that featured a new wave of architecture for a hitherto conservative city. The World Expo also plays a role in Lisbon's 21st-century story as a hub for digital nomads, hosting the annual Web Summit, and it's home to one of the country's largest concert venues, regularly welcoming big international acts.

For more on Parque das Nações, see page 80

15. MAAT

A CREATIVE SPARK

Portugal's latest landmark is the Museum of Art, Architecture & Technology, created from the shell of a former power station in 2016. Designed by British architect Amanda Levete, it blends seamlessly with Lisbon's waterfront landscape with a wave-shaped rooftop that has since become a favourite sunset hangout. Its exhibits provide a dialogue between politics, technology and the art world, where national and international creativity thrive, a bond that represents Portugal today.

For more on MAAT, see page 76

MEET THE PORTUGUESE

Do expect a friendly welcome. But don't be offended if people are late for dinner or say the odd rude word. JOANA TABORDA introduces her people.

PORTUGAL MAY BE a small country, but it has its regional differences like any other. There's a saying in Portuguese that goes: 'Braga prays, Porto works, Coimbra studies and Lisbon has fun.' And the facts sometimes back up the stereotypes.

Braga still holds on to its religious beliefs, but elsewhere in the country this is starting to fizzle out. In the 2011 census, 88% of the population identified as Catholic, but the number has been going down since the '90s.

Porto is still a hardworking city, but it also knows how to party, some say better than the capital. You'll often hear northerners swear. It's a part of the daily vocabulary – naughty words just flow out when they feel at ease with someone.

The *alentejanos*, like rural folk the world over, get teased for taking life at a pretty slow pace.

Everyone agrees that people in Lisbon can be a bit rude – except the *lisboetas*. We like to think they don't have an accent, but beyond the capital, everyone catches how we eat our vowels – *'brigad'* instead of *'obrigado'* (thanks). Maybe we are just in too much of a hurry to annunciate.

Differences aside, there are also plenty of similarities. The Portuguese are usually the last people to arrive at a party. Being late can be a pet peeve for many outsiders who are not used to this carefree attitude, but live here long enough and you may surrender to it.

Many of us also share the same name: I must know 14 other 'Joanas'. So you get categorised: João from football, João from work, João from the cafe down the road – and Joana the writer. Portuguese parents are only allowed to choose from a handful of names to give at birth, and let's just say the list isn't long. On the bright side, you don't have much time to mull over it as a parent.

The birthrate is on a downturn in Portugal: the country has one of the lowest in the EU. There is a huge elderly population. Many young people choose to move abroad for work. In 2019, 80,000 of us left, and more than a quarter went to the UK.

But there is one thing that all Portuguese seem to have in common and that is how welcoming they are. This outward-facing land has certainly adopted the world language: Portugal is ranked the 7th best country in the world for English proficiency. Pretty much everywhere you go, you'll find someone who speaks English. Even if they don't, they'll often go out of their way to help you pick a restaurant, choose a dish or simply give you directions to the nearest cafe, where you might bump into João.

WHO & HOW MANY

Portugal has a population of just over 10 million. The majority (95%) are of Portuguese descent. The remaining 5% are composed of groups of Brazilians, Han Chinese and people from Portugal's former colonies in Africa and Asia.

Clockwise from top left: Rural goatherd; Fado band, Lisbon; Tavern, Alentejo; Carnaval, Sesimbra

I'M PORTUGUESE. BUT IT'S COMPLICATED...

I was born in Lisbon, but, like many other Portuguese, I have roots all over. My maternal grandparents originally came from Goa, and spent most of their lives in Mozambique, before moving to Portugal in the 1970s following the fall of the dictatorship. My parents met in Brazil, but they too decided to return to Portugal to raise my brother and me. Many others have similar journeys: António Costa, Portugal's current prime minister, also has a Goan heritage.

Lisbon wouldn't be the same without its diverse communities. Some, like my grandparents, arrived shortly after decolonisation. Others came here more recently, seeking refuge from war or to start a new life abroad. In 2020, 183,875 Brazilians migrated to Portugal, making it one of the largest diasporas in the country. At the same time, the number of British in Portugal has more than tripled in the last decade from 14,096 to 46,238, fuelled in some part by Brexit. This increasing diversity has contributed to the country's economic growth, with an influx of capital and new talents. But it has also highlighted faults in the system, especially regarding issues like affordable housing.

PUN INTENDED

Listen close enough, and you'll make out songs littered with cheeky innuendos. Look closer, and you'll notice boats adorned with suggestive characters. Maybe you'll 'accidentally' end up choosing something rude from the sweet counter. For a country with a deep conservative background, the Portuguese sure are playful with their double entendres. By Joana Taborda

NO MATTER HOW hard you try, there are some jokes that are inevitably lost in translation. That's what it feels like when you attempt to deconstruct a *pimba* song to a foreign friend. You can dance to this traditional upbeat music without understanding a word of it, but you wouldn't be in on the joke, and sometimes that's for the best.

Take 'Garagem da Vizinha' by Quim Barreiros, one of the most popular singers of this Portuguese music genre. While on the surface, this song is about parking the car in your neighbour's garage, it doesn't take the most imaginative of minds to undress this shallow metaphor.

But what is it about *pimba* music that makes it so incredibly popular? Is it the fast tempo of the accordion, the awfully catchy melody, or perhaps those eyebrow-raising lyrics? These songs are enjoyed by everyone, after all. Danced to by old and young as they blare out at local festivities such as St Anthony's day in Lisbon, the graduation ceremonies of Coimbra, during carnival and at weddings across the country. They are fun and frivolous throwaway songs, and it doesn't seem to matter whether you are in on the joke or not. But it certainly helps to give it context.

It's a genre that sprung from the fall of the dictatorship, a regime that strove to control and censor people in any way it could. Using the *'lápis azul'*, meaning 'blue pencil', the government would cross out text and images deemed unfit for public consumption. Song lyrics were reviewed in detail, of course, as were other less obvious art forms. The constant surveillance gave rise to a traditional practice of sneaking in subliminal messages.

On a casual stroll along Aveiro's waterfront, you might stop to admire the *moliceiros*, the city's Venician gondolas. But on closer inspection, you'll notice that the colourful bows and sterns are adorned with something a little more (out of the) blue. Docked alongside more 'acceptably' decorated boats, depicting famous figures, such as fado singer Amália or the poet Camões, and religious iconography, there will surely be one painting that would make a saint blush. Think phrases like: 'Oh Alberto, is your chorizo good?', or 'What a beautiful fig' scrolled across the boat. Some pan-

Left: Moliceiros, Aveiro (p275); Right: Parque Eduardo VII (p89), Lisbon

els have become more explicit in recent decades, featuring scantily dressed women. But in the 20th century, wordplay was key to evading the eagle-eyed government.

In Amarante, the manufacturing of a particular sweet (p317) was almost completely eradicated by the Estado Novo regime, too. The reason? Its not-so-subtle phallic-shaped pastries *(doces fálicos).* However delicious, they were considered just a little too risqué for the conservative folks in power. The tradition was kept alive, though, thanks to the townsfolk who baked these sugary penises in secret, prohibition style. Once the dictatorship fell, Amarante embraced its naughty creation wholeheartedly.

Visit this northern town during its summer festivities, and you'll see the streets decorated with phallic-shaped bunting waggling in the wind and women selling equally bawdy sweets of all shapes and sizes. The tradition returns in January when locals offer these treats to friends and family to help usher in a fertile and favourable new year. No one really knows the origins of this cheeky sweet. Some say it's related to pagan rituals of the past, while others attribute it to the matchmaking skills of São Gonçalo, the town's patron saint. It's become such a popular symbol that bakers are now offering these suggestively shaped sweets year-round.

In Caldas da Rainha, alongside more traditional ceramics, like the cabbage-shaped bowls of Bordalo Pinheiro, which the town is synonymous with, one might find a smattering of 2ft penis bottles. This cultural heritage dates back to King Luis I (1838–89), who was so taken with these phalli that he took them back to entertain his court. Today there are only a few artists who dedicate themselves to crafting the so-called Falos de Caldas. The large penises have since had offshoots: smaller versions with bright designs, and some with funny – even scary – little faces are now popping up, continuing the long tradition.

And so it was, as a fitting farewell to the dictatorship and its control of freedom of expression, that a statue was commissioned to commemorate the Carnation Revolution 23 years later. In Parque Eduardo VII, atop a hill, looking down onto the capital, stands a marble obelisk some 6m tall called Monumento ao 25 de Abril. Stepping back, you might question what you are actually looking at. While artist João Cutileiro (1937–2021) often denied the apparent phallic connotation of his work, you can't help but wonder if this erected statue serves as a middle finger, if nothing else, to the fallen dictatorship.

Portugal has always been, and still is, by and large a conservative country. Religion still plays a major role here, so these symbols may come as a surprise to an outsider. Indeed, they're often looked down upon by people in the bigger cities who prefer to shy away from this crude side of Portuguese culture which has its roots in rural areas. Eating phallic sweets after mass, dancing to *pimba* after a procession: it's a contradiction that is undoubtedly hard to grasp. It's tongue-in-cheek humour that might be conceived as puerile and dated to the outsider gaze. Yet it gets dusted off and brought out every single year to kick off the country's biggest festivities. It still has its place.

Maybe the reason why we still take simple pleasure in this provocative form of entertainment is that we were silenced for so long. The freedom to express yourself was suppressed by the overbearing reach of the Estado Novo, a regime that cast a shadow over the people. Upon throwing off the shackles of censorship, the Portuguese people chose to dance and make merry, rejoicing and sticking their tongues out at those that once forbade them from doing so.

Today we still enjoy a good *trocadilho* (pun), and we don't take ourselves too seriously. So the next time you're at a party celebrating a patron saint in Portugal and you see people laughing and dancing, join them. Perhaps even ask them what that song is about.

A SOUL MADE OF SEA

The sea has always had a powerful presence in the life of the Portuguese. It impelled them to travel the world aboard ships during the Age of Discovery or to face the waves on a surfboard. By Marlene Marques

THE PORTUGUESE WRITER Fernando Pessoa once wrote, in one of his best-known poems, that the salt in the sea comes from the tears of the Portuguese. With this, one of Portugal's most famous writers wanted to demonstrate the country's connection to the sea. It is one of tears and effort, but also of hope and conquest.

With more than 900km of territory bathed by the ocean and the third-largest stretch of beach in the world, between Troia and Sines, it is not surprising that Portugal and the Portuguese have always had their attention turned to the sea.

The curiosity about what was beyond the waves gave birth to the Age of Portuguese Discoveries, led by Prince Henry the Navigator. Between the 15th and 17th centuries, generations of men set out to discover new lands, even though this thirst for conquest brought heavy consequences to the lands they passed through. They

Waves off Nazaré (p241)

sailed ahead in the Atlantic and stumbled upon Brazil. They sailed down the coast of Africa and crossed the Cape of Good Hope, facing tales of monsters and terror, to reach India. Later, to China and Japan.

The Portuguese have always been adventurers, often beyond the sanity of fear, leaving behind their families and going in search of their dreams. The same has always happened closer to home, with generations of fishers facing the sea to bring food to the table. There is no shortage of fishing villages and stories that tell the hard life on board the boats, the days when fishers came home almost empty-handed, with clothes stuck to their bodies and fingers crooked from the cold. But there are also the tales of those days when there was no room for more fish on board or the sea was so clear and flat you could see thousands of fish to catch.

THE SOUL OF PORTUGAL AND THE PORTUGUESE IS THE SIZE OF THE SEA.

In the Algarve, fishing has always been done in warmer waters, brought by the proximity to Morocco. But as you go up the map, the reality is more cold and harsh. Sesimbra, Ericeira, Nazaré, Costa Nova and Afurada are all places where fishing still marks the life of the village, and the traditions are still very present. The importance of the sea can also be seen in Portuguese cuisine, with fish being a regular feature on all menus. Boiled, baked, grilled or in recipes that pass from generation to generation.

But fishing is no longer the only activity at sea in Portuguese coastal areas. Instead, the boats give more and more place to surfboards, and you can see thousands of Portuguese scattered along the coast, experiencing the pleasure of gliding over the waves. The first evidence of the origin of surfing in Portugal dates back to the 1920s. Then, in the 1970s, it began to appear more frequently on Portuguese beaches, brought by foreign surfers who early on recognised the potential of the waves in this country.

The curiosity for the sport has been gaining more and more fans, in such a way that, decades later, it is now a source of income for many Portuguese, who make surfing tourism or teaching the sport a prosperous and growing business. And the Portuguese love surfing. You can see them heading on pilgrimage to Praia dos Supertubos in Peniche to watch the World Surfing Tour events or gathering by the hundreds near the Forte de São Miguel Arcanjo in Nazaré when the big wave alert is issued.

Fernando Pessoa once reminded us that the size of the soul makes everything worthwhile. And the soul of Portugal and the Portuguese is the size of the sea.

Grilled sardines

LEFT: JOAKIM LLOYD RABOFF/SHUTTERSTOCK © RIGHT: HLPHOTO/SHUTTERSTOCK ©

COLONIALISM: ADDRESSING A DARK PAST

Portugal's national identity stands on the shoulders of the navigators who braved the seven seas in search of faraway riches. They'd become 'discoverers', heroes, the forefathers of the vast Portuguese Empire. Now is the time to address those feats in a new light, but is Portugal ready to do it? By Sandra Henriques

IN MANY WAYS, Portugal has yet to address its colonial past, its role in the traffic of enslaved African people between Brazil and North America, and its issues with structural racism. Why hasn't it yet? Because the country's national identity has been built over five centuries on the feats of the Portuguese navigators or, as they are still called, the Discoverers. After all, as the poet Camões wrote, they gave 'new worlds to the world'. Today, addressing that dark part of the country's history is still perceived as an attack on the country's collective ego.

Indeed, if you follow any discussion in the media regarding the impact of colonialism on racism and inequality in Portugal today, most of the comments urge people to 'let it go' because that was then and this is now, ignoring the connection between the past and the present. But small steps towards change have begun.

The birth of the Portuguese Empire

Portugal's expansion over four centuries to become one of the world's largest empires is an intricate web of war and politics, often sugar-coated and glorified. The symbols on the country's flag still praise that past. Case in point: the yellow armillary sphere in the centre stands for the world 'discovered' by the Portuguese and the people with whom they 'traded' knowledge and products (take this official statement with a pinch of salt), and the seven castles represent the strongholds established by Dom Afonso Henriques (the first King of Portugal) after taking the land from the North African Muslims (known then as Moors) who had settled in the Iberian Peninsula four centuries before.

Officially, the Portuguese maritime explorations began in 1415 when troops under the command of King João I conquered Ceuta. In the following decades, as new expeditions set sail (allegedly) to discover and map new land – strongly motivated by mercantile reasons disguised as a religious mission – the Portuguese continued to take over more land, establishing military strongholds in strategic coastal towns. Despite what most official chroniclers wrote at the time (their orders were to document events but also paint the ruling monarch in the best light), the motivation was purely business oriented.

By 1543, after most of the surveying expeditions had been completed, Portugal controlled the major sea trade routes between Europe and South America, Asia and Africa. The Portuguese exploited the local resources for products that were in high demand in Europe: gold, spices (mainly pepper), ivory, sugar and cotton. They also were the first to transport enslaved African people for forced labour in the sugar-cane plantations, first in Cape Verde and Madeira and later in Brazil.

Marquês de Pombal (the Prime Minister to king Dom José I and the man responsible for overseeing the reconstruction of Lisbon after the 1755 Great Earthquake) banned slavery in 1761. The Portuguese (sometimes even political figures during their speeches on equality) will often take this undisputed fact as a banner for Portugal being the first country in the world to stop the slave trade. In reality, though, the ban was only for importing enslaved Africans to the Portuguese mainland and India; the business continued between Africa and Brazil. The transatlantic slave trade was only officially outlawed in Portugal in 1836.

The Portuguese Empire spread across three continents, establishing strategic colonies in Brazil (until 1825), Goa, Daman and Diu in India (until 1961), Guinea-Bissau (until 1973), São Tomé and Príncipe, Cape Verde, Mozambique and Angola (until 1975), and Macau (until 1999).

Dictatorship, Colonial War & decolonisation

Portugal's so-called First Republic (1910–26) was chaotic and ended with a coup d'état that paved the way for the conservative dictatorship known as Estado Novo (1933–74). An event that aligned with the growth of similar post-WWI nationalist regimes in Italy and Germany at the time.

'God (Deus), Homeland (Pátria) and Family (Família)' was Estado Novo's motto, a reflection of the personal beliefs of the country's traditionalist president, António Salazar, and what he considered to be indisputable foundational values. Homeland was a broad concept, depicted as a vast territory that included Portugal (mainland, and the archipelagos of the Azores and Madeira) and what were then called Overseas Provinces (instead of colonies).

After WWII ended, independence movements began to shake the bases of the fascist regime in the territories where Portugal still had colonies – first in India (following the country's independence in 1947) and later in Africa (starting in the 1960s). Clinging to the idea that the Portuguese Empire was to be maintained at all costs, Portugal refused to withdraw from Africa, unlike how other European countries had done in the 1950s and the 1960s. An expensive 13-year-long war followed.

The Colonial War (known as the War of Liberation in the former African colonies) left marks on both sides of the trenches, which have never been properly addressed. The wounds are still fresh and, for many, especially for some white Portuguese ex-soldiers, the colonised are still 'the enemy', the inferiors, the unwanted.

The coup that overthrew the dictatorship on 25 April 1974 (the Carnation Revolution), led by the Armed Forces Movement, marked Portugal's transition into a democracy and the start of the decolonisation in Africa. For the African-Portuguese (those who had settled in the former colonies and those, Black and white, who had been born in the Overseas Provinces, therefore legally a Portuguese territory), the process was abrupt, with government officials and the military abandoning the countries and those communities practically overnight. They were called *retornados* (returned) even though most of them had never set foot in Portugal; that label is still a stigma.

Deconstructing the colonial past

References to colonialism and enslaved people remain scarce in Lisbon tourist sites. Tour guides also regularly omit historical facts about colonialism and enslaved Africans in an attempt to save travellers from gruesome, uncomfortable details. To use a personal anecdote, I recall being on a walking tour in Lisbon with a couple from the US. My fellow tour-goers had many questions regarding Salazar, the dictatorship and the Colonial War. However, our guide kept changing the subject, which, understandably, left them flustered. At the end of the tour, as we were drinking a complimentary shot of *ginjinha*, the guide confessed that they weren't comfortable addressing those topics.

However, several sites attempt to acknowledge or unpack Portugal's colonial past – although, understandably, for many, it still feels insufficient. The final interactive room at Quake, a Belém attraction that simulates the 1755 Great Earthquake, depicts the 18th-century Portuguese capital with archetypes of different citizens (based on historical sources) and their role in rebuilding the city after the earthquake. One of them is an enslaved African woman sold in Lisbon through an ad in the local newspaper. In Lagos, the Mercado de Escravos (Slave Market Museum) attempts to address this southern city's role in the trade of enslaved people at the location of the first market that opened in 1444. At the same time, the Museu do Aljube in Lisbon tries to address colonialism as part of the bigger picture of the fight for democracy in Portugal.

SEVERAL SITES ATTEMPT TO ACKNOWLEDGE OR UNPACK PORTUGAL'S COLONIAL PAST – ALTHOUGH, UNDERSTANDABLY, FOR MANY, IT STILL FEELS INSUFFICIENT

Towards a more truthful telling

Over the last several years a number of projects around Portugal's history have been driven by local organisations, communities and to some extent government, sparking both discussion and awareness.

In 2017, then-mayor Fernando Medina was running for re-election for Lisbon's City Council. One of his electoral promises was to build a Museum of the Discoveries, which would focus on the 'most and least positive aspects of the Age of Discoveries', including exhibits dedicated to slavery. Seen by many as a proposal full of good intentions, it was welcomed with open criticism by local and international academics and Black activists. If this was going to be done right, then the name of the museum needed to reflect the change, not insist on the misleading notion of 'discovery'.

A year later, in 2018, *lisboetas* voted for their favourite city project, and Kiluanji Kia Henda's PLANTAÇÃO (plantation) was the winner. The art installation and memorial to the enslaved people has yet to take its designated place at Campo das Cebolas, in Alfama, due to delays caused by the COVID-19 pandemic. When it does happen, a field of 400 black aluminium sugar canes will rise up – one sugar cane for each year of slavery.

In 2020, Goethe-Institut Portugal launched the project ReMapping Memories Lisbon–Hamburg (re-mapping.eu) to tell the history of both cities from the point of view of the colonised, not the coloniser (thus shifting the ongoing perspective). The project included a website mapping locations that played a role in colonialism (often hidden or ignored), conferences, events and art exhibitions. After the planned two-year duration (ending in 2022), the website will remain online to inform and inspire future projects.

Many Portuguese born after or in the last years of the Estado Novo dictatorship (mid- to late 1970s) grew up with a misleading and glorified representation of the so-called Age of Discoveries – and generations to follow weren't taught much differently. Finally, however, it feels like that might be slowly changing.

P413: Monument to the Discoveries, Lisbon; Above: Mercado de Esravos (p169), Lagos

INDEX

Map Pages **000**

Map Pages **000**

"Rising from a thickly wooded peak and often enshrouded in swirling mist, Palácio da Pena (p104) is Sintra's crown jewel."

"Towering sandstone cliffs, craggy caverns carved by wild waves, and cliff-flanked steep beaches define the windswept area around Ponta da Piedade (p170)."

THIS BOOK

Design development
Marc Backwell

Content development
Mark Jones, Sandie Kestell, Anne Mason, Joana Taborda

Cartography development
Katerina Pavkova

Production development
Sandie Kestell, Fergal Condon

Series development leadership
Darren O'Connell, Piers Pickard, Chris Zeiher

Commissioning editor
Amy Lynch

LEFT: TAIGA/SHUTTERSTOCK ©
RIGHT: TRAVELLER70/SHUTTERSTOCK ©

Paper in this book is certified against the Forest Stewardship Council™ standards. FSC™ promotes environmentally responsible, socially beneficial and economically viable management of the world's forests.

nited
CRN 554153
13th edition - May 2023
ISBN 978 1 83869 406 7

10 9 8 7 6 5 4 3 2 1
Printed in China